ALSO BY BENJAMIN M. FRIEDMAN

The Moral Consequences of Economic Growth

Day of Reckoning: The Consequences of American Economic Policy
Under Reagan and After

Religion and the Rise of Capitalism

Religion and the Rise of Capitalism

Benjamin M. Friedman

 ALFRED A. KNOPF | NEW YORK | 2021

THIS IS A BORZOI BOOK
PUBLISHED BY ALFRED A. KNOPF

www.aaknopf.com

Library of Congress Cataloging-in-Publication Data
Names: Friedman, Benjamin M., author.
Title: Religion and the rise of capitalism / Benjamin M. Friedman.
Description: New York: Alfred A. Knopf, 2021. | Includes bibliographical references and index.
Identifiers: LCCN 2020010391 (print) | LCCN 2020010392 (ebook) |
ISBN 9780593317983 (hardcover) | ISBN 9780593317990 (ebook)
Subjects: LCSH: Economics—Religious aspects. | Religious thought—History. |
Capitalism—Religious aspects.
Classification: LCC HB72 .F745 221 (print) | LCC HB72 (ebook) | DDC 330.12/2—dc23
LC record available at https://lccn.loc.gov/2020010391
LC ebook record available at https://lccn.loc.gov/20200

Jacket image: *High Street, Edinburgh,* (detail) by Joseph Mallord William Turner.
Yale Center for British Art, Paul Mellon Collection.
Jacket design by Tyler Comrie

Manufactured in the United States of America
First Edition

Again for B.A.C.

Love, always

Contents

Adam Smith (1723–1790)

Introduction

Where do our ideas about how the economy works, and our views on economic policy, come from? Most people in the Western world, and especially in America, simply take for granted that we organize one of the most essential aspects of human activity—the economic sphere—primarily around private initiative channeled through markets. But where did that presumption come from? And why do so many people, again especially Americans, often see any challenge to our market-centered conduct of economic affairs as a fundamental threat to our way of life?

The economist John Maynard Keynes famously suggested that the thinking of even the most practically minded people, who believe they are exempt from any influence from the world of ideas, is nonetheless the product of what economists and other academic thinkers said some time before.[1] This may be true, but if so it merely raises a further question: where did the economists' ideas come from? The European historian Fritz Stern once reflected that why historians think as they do may be just as important as what they think.[2] Why economists think as they do matters as well.

The central argument of this book is that our ideas about economics and economic policy have long-standing roots in *religious* thinking. Most of us are unaware of how religious ideas shape our economic thinking, and when such links are occasionally suggested they are mostly misunderstood. But religion—not just the daily or annual cycle of ritual observances, but the inner belief structure that forms an essential part of people's view of the world in which they live—has shaped human thinking since before there were written words to record it.[3] In this book I argue that the influence of religious beliefs on modern Western economics has been profound, and that it remains important today. Critics of today's economics sometimes complain that belief in free markets, among economists and many ordinary citizens too, is itself a form of religion. It turns out that there is something to the idea: not in the way the critics mean, but in a deeper, more historically grounded sense.

But the point is more than just a matter of the history of ideas. The influence of religious thinking also bears on how Americans today, along with citizens of other Western countries, think about many of the most highly contested economic policy issues of our time. This connection between people's economic views and religious beliefs— often including religious beliefs that they do not personally hold— stems from before the creation of the American republic, and it runs to the core of how economics came to be the line of thinking we know today. It also helps explain what we often view as the puzzling behavior of many of our fellow citizens whose attitudes toward questions of economic policy seem sharply at odds with what would be to their own economic benefit.

The foundational transition in thinking about what we now call economics—the transition that we rightly associate with Adam Smith and his contemporaries in the eighteenth century—was importantly shaped by what were then new and vigorously contended lines of religious thought within the English-speaking Protestant world. The resulting influence of religious thinking on modern economic thinking, right from its origins, established resonances that then persisted, albeit in evolving form as the economic context changed, the questions economists asked shifted, and the analytical tools at their disposal expanded, right through the twentieth century. Although for the most part we are not consciously aware of them—this is why their consequences seem puzzling whenever we stumble across them—especially in America these lasting resonances with religious thinking continue to shape our current-day discussion of economic issues and our public debate over questions of economic policy.

I am well aware that the idea of a central influence of religion on Adam Smith's thinking, or on that of many of his contemporaries, will initially strike many knowledgeable readers as implausible on its face. Smith's great friend David Hume, who also played a key role in the creation of modern economics, was an avowed skeptic and an outspoken opponent of organized religion; Hume notoriously referred to Church of England bishops as "Retainers to Superstition." Smith, as far as we can tell, was at best a deist of the kind Americans identify with Thomas Jefferson. There is little evidence of Smith's active religious participation, much less religious enthusiasm. My argument is most certainly *not* that these were religiously dedicated men who self-consciously brought their theological commitments to bear on their economic thinking.

Rather, the creators of modern economics lived at a time when religion was both more pervasive and more central than anything we know in today's Western world. And, crucially, intellectual life was more integrated then. Not only were the sciences and humanities (to use today's vocabulary) normally discussed in the same circles, and mostly by the same individuals, but theology too was part of the ongoing discussion. Part of what Smith taught, as a professor of moral philosophy at the University of Glasgow, was natural theology. He and his colleagues and friends were continually exposed to what were then fresh debates about new lines of theological thinking. I argue that what they heard and read and discussed influenced the economics they produced, just as the ideas of today's economists are visibly shaped by what we learn from physics, or biology, or demography.

This idea importantly changes our view of the historical process by which the Western world arrived at today's economics. The conventional account is that the line of thinking we know today as economics was a product of the Enlightenment: more specifically, that the Smithian revolution and the subsequent development of economics as an intellectual discipline were part of the process of secular modernization in the sense of a historic turn from thinking in terms of a God-centered universe toward what we now broadly call humanism. Nicholas Phillipson, in his prize-winning biography of Adam Smith, referred to one statement of Smith's as a reminder that not just *The Wealth of Nations* but Smith's entire project for a modern science of man was "built on the foundations of the Enlightenment's quintessential assault on religion."[4] Phillipson was merely stating the commonly accepted view. As a matter of what Smith and his contemporaries consciously intended, it is accurate enough. But explanations of important developments that rely simply on the conscious intentions of the actors involved are necessarily limited. As the American historian Gordon Wood put it, people are often not so much the manipulators but the victims of their ideas.[5] Even cultural influences that seem obvious from the perspective of decades or, better yet, centuries later were often invisible to those whose ideas they crucially shaped.

Realizing that the Smithian revolution partly grew out of new ideas in theology, and that the religious debates of that day shaped it—not because that is what Smith and the other creators of modern economics intended, but because the theological debates of their time fundamentally altered how they thought about human nature and the underpinnings of everyday human interaction—puts a different gloss on the matter. So does understanding the ways in which the evolution of economic thinking during the two-plus centuries since has continued to reflect this initial religious influence. So too does recognizing the consequences of this deep intellectual connection for our current-day policy debate.

Taking account of this from-the-bottom-up connection between economic thinking and key strands of religious thinking—the theological questions under so much dispute during Smith's time—helps explain a wide variety of puzzling phenomena, now and in the past: Why do so many Americans who have only the remotest prospect of ever making their way into the top income tax bracket nonetheless favor keeping the tax rate on top-bracket incomes low? More startling yet, why do so many Americans who have no chance whatever of inheriting money from a taxable estate passionately advocate abolishing "death taxes"? And is it merely a coincidence that these antitax crusaders, along with opponents of government regulation of business, and the countless lower-income supporters of benefits for corporations for which they do not work (and whose stock they do not own), disproportionately belong to the nation's increasingly influential evangelical churches? Nor is the present-day relevance of this historical influence of religious thinking on economic thinking limited to the United States: Why is there, today, an "Anglo-Saxon model" of how to organize an economy and run a country's economic policy? And why do so many people, in countries otherwise very similar to ours, reject it?

Nearly a hundred years ago the English historian R. H. Tawney published a book with the same title as this one.[6] Both the setting and the argument were different. Tawney's book was a response, in part a rebuttal, to Max Weber's classic work, *The Protestant Ethic and the Spirit of Capitalism*. Weber had claimed that Calvinist religion—specifically, the belief that whether or not individual men and women are saved is a matter determined before they are even born, and over which they have no control—was historically a spur to forms of personal behavior that gave rise to modern capitalism. Moreover, Weber argued, this influence of belief in predestination persisted long after most people had ceased to hold it: indeed, long enough for most people to forget that such a belief had ever influenced their parents' or grandparents' behavior in the first place.

My argument in this book shares some strands of that long-ago controversy—the powerful influence of religion, and the continuing force of this influence even after the driving religious beliefs have faded—but in substance it is more nearly Weber upside down. The primary focus here is not on economic behavior, but *thinking* about economics. Even more different, the creators of modern economics lived not during the time Weber emphasized (whether his view of the matter was right or wrong), but a century and more later when belief in predestination was in retreat among English-speaking Protestants. I argue that what opened the way for the early economists' insight into the beneficial consequences of individually motivated initiative carried out in competitive markets was the expanded vision of the human character and its possibilities that the movement *away from* predestinarian Calvinism fostered. Further, this benign sense of our human potential, enabled by the historic transition in religious thinking that first preceded and then accompanied it, has continued to influence the trajectory of modern Western economic thinking ever since.

Just as Max Weber looked to America as the prime example illustrating his idea about the influence of religion on economic development, here too, in charting the historical influence of religion on economic *thinking*, after Adam Smith's death (in 1790) the focus shifts to the United States. The reason is certainly not that I regard the American economists of the nineteenth century as the new discipline's leading thinkers of their time. That distinction goes mostly to the great English economists, including David Ricardo, John Stuart Mill, Stanley Jevons, and Alfred Marshall. But a key part of my purpose here is also to illuminate the bearing of this religious influence on our public conversation about economics and our ongoing debate over economic policy questions today, and nowhere is that influence more powerfully at work, yet more perplexing without understanding its origins, than in the United States.

Understanding the historical connection between religious thinking and the economic thinking that is ours, and that shapes the world in which we live today, helps to explain not only how economics came to be what it is but also aspects of our current economic policy debate that are otherwise difficult to fathom, including especially questions that revolve around the efficacy and appropriate role of markets and, in parallel, the appropriate role of government in our society. We may not be aware of the religious influences that mold our economic views—part of my point is precisely that we are not—but they are at work nonetheless, and our future economic trajectory depends on them. As the work of another great American historian, Bernard Bailyn, demonstrated, not only do ideas matter for events; often ideas operate over the heads of the participants, guiding both their thinking and their choices in ways they cannot foresee and that we cannot otherwise explain.[7]

The influence on economics of certain strands of religious thinking—the affinity to some ideas, the instinctive dislike of others, at the broadest level simply our way of looking at the world of which markets and incentives and economic behavior are an essential part—turns out to be quite understandable in historical perspective. Our confidence in the outcome of individual striving for self-improvement, played out primarily in the economic sphere; the respect we attach to economic self-improvement as an expression of political liberty; the commitment to economic development on the national and even world scale, both on material grounds and because we assume economic progress leads to moral progress as well; above all, the belief in the efficacy of the market mechanism as a way to harness our individual economic energies for our own good and that of others too—all are reflections of an influence of religious thinking that is both historical and ongoing. This influence of religious thinking pervades the way in which ordinary citizens today think about economic questions. And because over time it has become particularly American, it also affects how the rest of the world sees our country and sees us.

Economics as we know it is still a young science. The influence of religious thinking was present at its creation.

Benjamin M. Friedman
Cambridge, Massachusetts
July 2020

Religion and the Rise of Capitalism

1

Economics, Politics, and Religion

Scientific thought is a development of pre-scientific thought.
—ALBERT EINSTEIN

Economic ideas are always and intimately a product of their own time and place.
—JOHN KENNETH GALBRAITH

Seventeen seventy-six was a year of momentous events, not just in retrospect but in the eyes of those who lived through them. To Americans, the date speaks for itself: in January, Thomas Paine's stirring call to arms, *Common Sense,* followed at the end of the year by *The American Crisis* ("These are the times that try men's souls. . . .");[1] in March, the British driven out of Boston by Washington's army of raw recruits; and, to immortal effect, the new nation's Declaration of Independence on July 4. Nor were the year's significant events limited to the Revolution, or even to the thirteen small colonies hugging the continent's eastern shore. Three thousand miles away, in what is now California, a new structure arose on a bay of the Pacific Ocean. It became San Francisco's Presidio.

Across the Atlantic, in Britain's lively world of ideas and letters, 1776 likewise saw a series of memorable events. In February, Edward Gibbon, a Member of Parliament, published the first volume of his monumental *The Decline and Fall of the Roman Empire.* The work eventually ran to six volumes, and it remains today one of the most familiar histories in the English language—a saucy account of ancient

Rome's descent into decadence and corruption that many of Gibbon's readers took to be a commentary on Britain in their own day. In August, following a long illness, David Hume died at home in Edinburgh. Hume's contemporaries regarded him as the most stellar figure of the Scottish Enlightenment. Their judgment has endured. In the meanwhile, in March, Hume's closest friend and intellectual protégé, another Scot, had published a book of his own. Adam Smith was never as prolific as his friend and mentor. At age fifty-two, he had produced only his second book. But *The Wealth of Nations* would prove one of the most influential works of all time, shaping Western ideas as well as the conduct of everyday life ever since. Its importance was evident almost immediately. By the time Smith died, fourteen years later, it had already gone through five editions in English plus translations into German, French, Danish, and Italian. Within another dozen years editions in Dutch, Spanish (delayed until then by opposition from the Inquisition), Swedish, and Russian had followed.[2]

The Wealth of Nations marked a fundamental ground shift in thinking about what underlies economic behavior, what consequences follow from it, and how governments might therefore act to foster the prosperity of their peoples and the vitality of their nations. Like a very few before him, Smith understood that private initiative, undertaken for no reason other than to advance a person's own economic interest, can nonetheless end up making other people better off too. His crucial insight was that the setting in which such beneficial consequences would follow was the market economy, and that the mechanism that delivered this outcome was competition. In time, following the publication of Smith's pivotal contribution, centuries of top-down direction of economic activity gave way to more individually propelled, competitive enterprise. Where it did not—the Soviet Union, for example, or Maoist China—those in power either altered course or were swept away. The few remaining holdouts, like Cuba and North Korea, stand as symbols of human tragedies that did not have to be.

But where did Smith's ideas, and those of his immediate predecessors on which he drew, come from? Why did this all-important transition in thinking about such a central aspect of human activity take place mostly over the course of the eighteenth century, rather than a hundred years before or after? What change in the intellectual soil, or in the broader currents shaping the creative air that they breathed and through which they talked to one another, prompted Hume and Smith and many of their contemporaries to think in this new, so powerfully influential direction?

One element of the story, widely understood and well documented, was Newtonian science with its emphasis on systematic laws of physical behavior and the mechanisms that stand behind them.[3] A large part of David Hume's agenda, and Adam Smith's as well, was to construct a science of man comparable to what Copernicus, Galileo, Kepler, Newton, and other great scientists not so long before had achieved for the physical world. By Hume's and Smith's time Isaac Newton's *Principia Mathematica*, first published in 1687, had become part of the common intellectual property of educated men in both England and Scotland. Its influence was pervasive. By contrast, in his *Treatise of Human Nature*, written when Smith was still an undergraduate, Hume observed that studies of human behavior remained in the same condition as astronomy found itself before the time of Copernicus.[4]

A second powerful influence—much less understood, and mostly overlooked—was religious thinking. There were actually *two* transitions in thinking that culminated in the latter half of the eighteenth century. One, which we rightly associate with Adam Smith, was in economic thinking. The other was in the religious thinking of the English-speaking Protestant world. The movement away from the orthodox Calvinist doctrines that had dominated both English and Scottish religious life since the Reformation brought new ideas about human nature, about the purpose of men and women's lives on earth, and about their destiny after their mortal lives end. At the heart of this new thinking was a more expansive concept of human agency than under strict Calvinist precepts, implying a more optimistic view of the possibilities for the choices made and the actions taken by everyday people. At the same time, long-standing debates about the ultimate fate not just of individual men and women but the world as a whole also took new forms. By the time Smith and Hume reached adulthood, both theologians and ordinary clergymen preaching from their pulpits thought differently about these questions than they had a century before. Moreover, the fact that these new lines of religious thinking were inevitably controversial, and highly contended, made them all the more salient to thoughtful contemporaries not in the clergy.

The coincidence in timing was not mere happenstance. The influence of the change in religious thinking on the Western world's crucial break in economic thinking was profound, and it has proved lasting. Not just the Smithian revolution of the eighteenth century, but the course of Western economic ideas ever since has reflected the continuing influence of the fundamental changes in religious thinking that were still in progress during Hume's and Smith's time. Especially in the United States, this influence is readily visible today in the country's ongoing public debate over economic policy.

But why, and how, could changes in religious thinking have altered the trajectory of ideas in a realm as seemingly removed as economics?

The creators of modern economics were not religiously dedicated men, nor did they seek to bring their personal theological orientation to bear on their secular thinking. Hume was an outspoken agnostic— many thought him an atheist—openly scornful of all forms of organized religion.[5] His friend William Robertson, a prominent Scottish churchman, referred to him as "that virtuous Heathen."[6] Smith kept his beliefs about religious matters to himself; but there is no evidence, in his writings or his known behavior, of any genuinely deep commitment. The answers must lie elsewhere.

Albert Einstein, writing in 1918—three years before he won the Nobel Prize, but after he had published his theory of general relativity—set down his thoughts on how research scientists come up with their ideas. Einstein chose not to limit himself to scientists, however, because in this regard he saw them as no different from creative, thinking human beings more generally. The greatest need, he thought, was some way to see through complexity. To do so requires a simplifying mechanism, a ready reference framework that skips over distracting details to highlight what is important. "Man seeks to form for himself," Einstein wrote, "in whatever manner is suitable for him, a simplified and easy-to-survey image of the world and so to overcome the world of experience by striving to replace it to some extent by this image. This is what the painter does, and the poet, the speculative philosopher, the natural scientist, each in his own way."[7]

Einstein's notion of an image of the world—another translation from Einstein's German would be a "worldview"—that shapes an individual's thinking, especially at the frontier at which creativity confronts reality, has appealed to others as well.[8] Erik Erikson, the psychologist who probed the depths of human motivation in his biographies of Gandhi and Martin Luther, referred to a person's "all-inclusive conception" of the world, or of life, or reality, in whatever respect matters most for the challenges to be faced.[9] Gerald Holton, a historian of science and himself the leading late-twentieth-century authority on Einstein's thought, called it a "thematic presupposition."[10]

Importantly, the image of the world that shapes a person's creative thinking is often not that person's alone. Holton interpreted it as, more likely, a commonly shared aspect of the era in which someone lives. What matters is the thinker's cultural roots, the "milieu in which he and his fellow scientists grew up," the "internal architecture of a person *or a period*."[11] Something about a particular time, or a place, or even a period of time in a particular place, pervasively influences the thinking of many people who inhabit it. In the same vein, Robert Merton, the historian of science who famously explored the intellectual atmosphere in which the English in the mid-seventeenth century founded the Royal Society, the world's oldest scientific institution in existence today and still one of the most distinguished, referred to the "cultural soil" that encourages new ideas to emerge, and then either flourish or not.[12] Closer to the social sciences, the political theorist Eric Nelson described what matters for powerful new thinking as the "organizing assumptions" through which a person interprets the world. The consequence of these background beliefs is that a person acquires "habits of mind," a whole unseen mental world of meanings and associations.[13]

The idea of a shared worldview, common to a time and a place, is not particular to the sciences. Anticipating Einstein by three-quarters of a century, but emphasizing the origins of such a worldview outside one's self, Ralph Waldo Emerson noted that any writer "needs a basis which he cannot supply: a tough chaos-deep soil," which the popular mind of the day supplies. The ideas of the time are "in the air," Emerson believed; they "infect all who breathe it." We absorb them "almost through the pores of our skin." They constitute the "spirit of the hour."[14] Closer to Einstein's time, the British economist Alfred Marshall referred to "mysteries"—he had in mind industrial skills, but the idea applies much more broadly—that "become no mysteries; but are as it were in the air, and children learn many of them unconsciously."[15] In the same vein, the early-twentieth-century philosopher Alfred North

Whitehead spoke of assumptions that become so obvious that "people do not know what they are assuming because no other way of putting things has ever occurred to them."[16]

Why might someone's worldview in this sense matter for the development of scientific ideas? Returning to the subject more than a decade later, Einstein was straightforward: scientific thinking does not emerge on its own. Thinking about scientific questions and thinking about other aspects of life, or the world around us, are intimately connected. In another of Gerald Holton's illuminating metaphors, "subterranean connections" provide a bridge connecting the humanistic parts of culture—what the inhabitants of a particular place at a particular time have in common—and the scientific parts. The result is a "coherence" of different elements of the person's, or the age's, worldview.[17] Moreover, as Einstein saw the relationship, *the worldview comes first* and scientific ideas follow from it: "Scientific thought is a development of pre-scientific thought."[18]

Coming from Einstein, with echoes by these twentieth-century historians of science, the idea of a central role for some worldview behind creative thinking conjures images of physicists contemplating the fundamental nature of matter and energy, or chemists or biologists at work in their research labs. As Holton summarized the argument, a scientist's theory is just one part of his or her more general world image.[19] But in pointing also to painters and poets and philosophers, Einstein made clear that in his view *any* line of creative thinking necessarily follows from, and is therefore coherent with, the worldview that underlies it. Emerson thought the same principle applied to writers, and Whitehead believed it applied to philosophers. There is no reason economics should be different.

No doubt the idea will offend some economists. Economics, in many current-day practitioners' view, straightforwardly traces out the implications of theoretical assumptions and observed evidence, in whatever combination is apt for the question at hand. The cultural soil in which the economist has grown up, or his or her internal mental architecture, has nothing to do with the analysis put forward. Even less would Emerson's spirit of the hour. Anyone confronting the same evidence or making the same assumptions should think to carry out the same analysis, and therefore would arrive at the same conclusions.

Most economists today understand that this idealized description is inaccurate. Individual researchers choose to work on one, or at most a few, among an astonishing variety of questions presented by the full range and diversity of modern economic life. More to the point, each chooses to frame whatever is the chosen question in a particular way. A researcher investigating any specific question picks one set of beginning assumptions, or another, or perhaps another (each consistent with some more basic underlying presumptions, like purposeful human behavior). What evidence to bring to bear, among all of the potentially relevant aspects of observable economic activity, is likewise a matter of choice.[20] In short, economic analysis is a highly individualistic endeavor. There is no reason Einstein's insight should apply to economists any less than to physicists—or poets or painters. Paul Samuelson, one of the great economists of the twentieth century, certainly thought it did. "It is good advice," Samuelson wrote, "to always study the preconceptions of a science."[21] He had in mind his own subject.

Joseph Schumpeter, a twentieth-century economist who briefly served as finance minister of his native Austria following World War I and later taught for nearly two decades at Harvard, thought the relevance to economics was self-evident. Schumpeter took it as obvious that in order even to consider any question in a field like economics, we "first have to visualize a distinct set of coherent phenomena as a worth-while object of our analytic efforts." Whatever analysis we do, therefore, "is *of necessity* preceded by a preanalytic cognitive act that supplies the raw material for the analytic effort."[22] Schumpeter's term for this preanalytic cognitive act was Vision (with a capital V). He meant by it what Einstein meant by a worldview.

Adam Smith presumably had such a worldview. And because he and David Hume and the other thinkers of the Scottish Enlightenment who turned their keen minds to what became the field of economics mostly lived in the same place at the same time, the worldview animating what they thought and wrote—their Vision, as Schumpeter put it—was one they shared. It was the spirit of *their* hour, and the new intellectual discipline that they created reflected it. John Kenneth Galbraith, an economist whose long career at Harvard briefly overlapped with Schumpeter's, thought this kind of link was pervasive: "Economic ideas are always and intimately a product of their own time and place. They cannot be seen apart from the world they interpret."[23]

Moreover, Smith's and Hume's new line of thinking reflected the prevailing worldview of their time all the more, precisely because the intellectual discipline they were creating was new. Neither of them ever thought of himself as an economist; in their day there was not yet a field of inquiry identifiable as economics. Samuel Johnson's *Dictionary*, published in 1755, gave five definitions of "economy"—none carrying today's meaning. Smith was a professor of moral philosophy, not economics. Only over the course of the hundred years following publication of *The Wealth of Nations* did the new discipline that Smith's contribution did so much to create coalesce—at first under the label "political economy," and not as "economics" until near the end of the nineteenth century.

Thomas Kuhn, the philosopher and intellectual historian best known for his work on what he called the structure of scientific revolutions, followed Einstein in recognizing the importance of nonintellectual aspects of culture, specifically the role of "institutional and socioeconomic" factors in scientific development. But Kuhn, who took as his examples not just long-established fields like physics but also newer ones like heredity and evolutionary biology, observed that the influence of these institutional and socioeconomic underpinnings is greatest when an area of inquiry is in its infancy. Early in the development of a new field, he argued, "social needs and values" are a major force determining what problems its practitioners take up. So is "contemporary common sense." By contrast, as a field matures, its practitioners may continue to import techniques from other disciplines, and new information from previously unexploited sources presumably remains welcome, but the fundamental concepts on which the field rests typically become "insulated" from such external influences.[24] It is always possible that some major shock may undermine a mature field's standard assumptions; Schumpeter gave as an example the Great Depression of the 1930s, which led John Maynard Keynes and his followers to see that a market economy does not automatically restore itself to full employment without protracted distress. But otherwise the plasticity of a field's basic concepts and assumptions, its openness to influence at that fundamental level, gradually erodes as the field reaches maturity.

The initial influence of whatever worldview its early creators bring to bear therefore remains long after they have personally disappeared from the scene. Hume and Smith applied their thinking to economics at the field's inception; indeed, the inception occurred largely because of what they thought and wrote. The economics that they created was therefore particularly subject to influence from the culture of the society in which they lived.

What, then, formed the worldview of Adam Smith and his contemporaries?

The revolution in economic thinking that culminated with the insights of *The Wealth of Nations* was a product of the Scottish Enlightenment.[25] In parallel to the Enlightenment in France associated with such classic thinkers as Montesquieu, Voltaire, and Rousseau, and following on the earlier achievements of Englishmen like Hobbes, Locke, and Shaftesbury, in the middle decades of the eighteenth century a spectacular intellectual efflorescence emerged in the interaction among a colorful and fascinating group of (mostly) men living in Edinburgh and Glasgow. (One prominent exception was the writer and literary hostess Alison Cockburn, one year younger than Hume.[26]) Their impact on Western thinking, especially thinking about economics and government, remains enormous more than two hundred years later.[27]

These were men of extraordinary talent, to be sure, and extraordinary intellectual energy too. But they were also thinkers of great intellectual range, knowledgeable about fields of inquiry well beyond their best known areas of individual expertise. Smith, for example, wrote interestingly on topics ranging from astronomy and physics to music, dance, and poetry. At the time of his death, he was working on what he intended as a major work encompassing all of the "imitative arts." Hume, whose insights likewise continue to figure prominently in today's economics, especially on topics like international trade and the relationship between money and prices, also wrote on government, classical history, and moral philosophy, not to mention such specific subjects as love and marriage (an odd topic for a lifelong bachelor), the immortality of the human soul (he was dubious), and how to write an essay. In his own lifetime Hume was best known for his six-volume *The History of England*, published between 1754 and 1761.

Like Hume even more so than Smith, many of the major figures in the Scottish Enlightenment were prolific writers—their term for themselves was "literati"—voluminously producing both books and essays. They took what one another wrote seriously, and they found time to read it and discuss it: through correspondence, in personal visits with each other, via public lectures (Smith gave a set in Edinburgh, sponsored by the Philosophical Society), and at meetings of the numerous clubs and societies that they formed to regularize their ongoing conversation. Glasgow, where Smith taught at the university for nearly a decade and a half, is only forty-odd miles from Edinburgh, where Hume usually lived. The two friends were on sufficiently familiar terms that Hume kept a room in his lodgings for Smith to use on his overnight stays. Even under eighteenth-century travel conditions, Smith could leave Glasgow on the morning coach, arrive in Edinburgh in time to dine with one of the clubs to which he and Hume belonged ("dinner" being the meal that normally began at two in the afternoon[28]), and return to Glasgow early the next day. Kirkcaldy, Smith's boyhood home where he later wrote much of *The Wealth of Nations,* was even closer, although the need to cross the Firth of Forth by ferry (there was no bridge until 1890) made that journey less reliable.

The Enlightenment era in Scotland also seems, by today's standards, an extraordinarily social time. Above all, the literati enjoyed dining in like-minded groups. Glasgow had its Literary Society and a Political Economy Club. In addition to the Philosophical Society that sponsored Smith's lectures, Edinburgh had the Select Society, the Oyster Club, the Poker Club (so named to connote stirring up fires, not gambling at cards), and even the ponderous-sounding Edinburgh Society for Encouraging Arts, Sciences, Manufactures, and Agriculture in Scotland. Numerous other groups sprang up too, to bring together the educated elites of Edinburgh and Glasgow. Like Smith and Hume, most of the key Enlightenment figures belonged to most of the intellectually distinguished clubs; they apparently dined out a lot.

Nor did the key figures whose ideas we recall today separate into different clubs to take up different interests. Both Smith and Hume were among the original members of Edinburgh's most intellectually distinguished dining club, the Select Society, established in 1754. The thirty-one founding members were a professionally diverse group. The largest contingent, fifteen, were lawyers—not surprising in light of the role of lawyers in society and government, then even more so than now, and the fact that the 1707 Act of Union between England and Scotland had specifically preserved the independence of the Scottish legal system. During much of its existence, the Select Society's dinners were held in the public rooms beneath the Advocates' Library, a law library of which Hume was the keeper, or head librarian, located in the building that had once served as Scotland's parliament but after 1707 became the law courts. (It remains today the seat of Scotland's High Court.) But the Select Society's original membership also included five Church of Scotland ministers, four university professors (including Smith), three medical doctors, and two military officers, as well as one merchant, one independent man of letters (Hume), and one painter.[29]

Scotland in the middle two quarters of the eighteenth century did not lack for pressing economic and political issues—and, as is often true, the two were deeply intertwined. In 1707, just four years before Hume's birth and barely a decade and a half before Smith's, the Scots had, in effect, voted their country out of existence. By accepting the Act of Union with England, which already incorporated Wales, Scotland abolished its independent parliament (not to be reconstituted until 1998). It also further downgraded the status of its royal court, already diminished by the union of the English and Scottish crowns a century earlier. The motivation for this unique political act was mostly economic. Scotland at the turn of the eighteenth century remained desperately poor, dependent on a still largely feudal form of agriculture and mostly barred from overseas commerce by England's restrictive trade and navigation laws. Union would bring access to the highly profitable international trade that the English enjoyed through their overseas empire and with the support of the Royal Navy. It would also open the English market to cattle raised on Scotland's ample grasslands.

Although the combined country created in 1707 had acquired the status of an established fact by the time Hume and especially Smith reached their adulthood, the issues behind its creation remained central, especially in Scotland. The union had always been a top-down initiative, generally unpopular among ordinary Scots. Opposition persisted, not just to Scotland's place in the now unified Kingdom of Great Britain but, more acutely, to its Protestant and Hanoverian monarchy. In 1745—Hume was in his mid-thirties, Smith in his early twenties—anti-Union and anti-Hanover forces took up arms against the British government. The Jacobite Rebellion, though it ended in failure, became a lasting part Scotland's lore and legend. At the time, it resulted in widespread death and destruction. No one in Scotland could fail to take notice. Smith's description of the event, written more than a decade later, suggests his state of alarm at the time: "In the year 1745, four or 5 thousand naked unarmed Highlanders took possession of the unimproved parts of this country without any opposition from the unwarlike inhabitants. They penetrated into England, and alarmed the whole nation, and had they not been opposed by a standing army, they would have seized the throne with little difficulty."[30]

The economic issues underlying Scotland's exchanging independence for union remained as well. Joining England's overseas trade was not an abstract objective. The principal goal of union had been to increase Scotland's prosperity, but at mid-century that was largely yet to happen. Despite a better-educated population, Scottish incomes and living standards still fell far short of what the English enjoyed. Adam Smith, writing in *The Wealth of Nations,* lamented a rate of child mortality that was shockingly high even for that time, with up to half the children of laboring families dying by age four in some areas.[31] The book, with its carefully spelled out argument for competitive markets in place of the long familiar web of monopolies and government interventions, was in part a how-to guide for a country—now a region of a larger country—that sought to achieve greater economic success. By that time Scottish merchants were handling much of Britain's trade with America in tobacco (the largest was Alexander Houston in Glasgow), but there was more trade to be had, and more to be earned at home as well. Smith addressed his book to both.

Moreover, just as Smith was in the midst of writing *The Wealth of Nations,* Scotland's more immediate economic problems became acute. In 1772 a London bank, in which the well-known stock speculator Alexander Fordyce was a partner, failed, triggering a cascade of failures in Britain and even on the continent. In Scotland the result was the worst banking crisis in two generations. On top of his concern for the depressing effect on Scotland's economy, Smith took a particular interest because his great patron, the Duke of Buccleuch—for whom he had served as tutor and traveling companion for two years in the 1760s, and whom he continued to advise in financial matters—was the leading outside shareholder of Douglas, Heron & Company, a bank in Ayr whose failure was at the center of the crisis in Scotland.[32] But the more general economic damage mattered as well. Writing to Smith at the height of the crisis, Hume recounted the latest bank closures, industrial bankruptcies, spreading unemployment, and even growing

"Suspicion" regarding the soundness of the Bank of England. Knowing that Smith was working on a new book that would address economic issues, Hume asked his friend, "Do these Events any-wise affect your Theory?"[33] They did: in *The Wealth of Nations* Smith had a good deal to say about banking reform, along with other practical questions raised by the crisis. But the subject was in the air more generally, a topic of discussion when and wherever concerned Scots met.

Developments in America were in the air too. The American independence movement, building for some years, turned into armed conflict just as Smith was nearing the end of his writing. The slavery debate was of longer standing; the abolition movement in Britain began earlier than in America (and, in the nineteenth century, it came to fruition earlier too). As was true throughout Britain, in Scotland these were hotly argued questions. Smith foresaw that in time whatever political entity emerged on the North American continent would far outstrip Britain both in population and economically, so that retaining it as a colony would eventually become untenable.[34] He therefore favored American independence, urging Britain simply to strike the best deal it could get. (For this reason Smith was unwelcome in British policy-making circles until Lord North's government fell in 1782, following the American victory at Yorktown the year before. He was welcomed as a celebrated policy advisor beginning the next year once William Pitt, who had favored negotiations with the colonists' Continental Congress almost from the start of the conflict, became prime minister.) Smith also opposed slavery, not just on the moral grounds put forward by other British abolitionists but because he believed slaves to be economically less efficient than free labor. *The Wealth of Nations* addressed both issues.

Beyond these specifically British and American matter, political questions of a more conceptual nature were a staple of conversation and debate throughout much of the Western world in the late seventeenth and eighteenth centuries. Thinkers in Britain, in France, in the Netherlands and elsewhere argued over the relative merits of monarchy versus a republic, the viability of democracy, and the value of personal liberty versus the need for limits to restrain it. By the middle of the eighteenth century, the ideas of Thomas Hobbes and John Locke in England, and Montesquieu and Rousseau in France, were part of the common knowledge of educated men and women. The American Revolution, and the creation of the new republic under the Constitution of 1787, were outgrowths of that extended political discussion. So, less successfully, was the French Revolution. The thinkers of the Scottish Enlightenment were active participants in this ongoing conversation.

Religion was a central element of their worldview too: not because the most important thinkers at that time and in that place were religious men—to repeat, they were not—but because religion then played a more central, more pervasive, and more integrated role in society than anything comparable in the Western world today. Indeed, the very distinction between the religious and the secular is a modern concept, unknown throughout most of human history.[35]

Religious thinking held a significant place in the ongoing social and intellectual interaction around which the Scottish Enlightenment revolved. Among the original members of the Select Society, for example, the five Church of Scotland ministers outnumbered any other professional group except the lawyers. Over the years that the club was in existence, just over a hundred men were elected; fourteen were clergymen. To understand why people of a time and place different from our own thought as they did, we must know something of the world in which they lived and the assumptions that their world embraced. As one eminent historian of the field of economics observed, to probe the origins and significance of economic ideas "we must imagine ourselves eavesdropping upon a bygone conversation . . . with the language and literature, religion and politics, tastes and morals, of those we are observing."[36] When Smith and Hume dined out, professional divines regularly took part in the conversation.

The same regular interaction with the clergy marked university life as well. In the eighteenth century, universities in both England and Scotland (America too) were still largely ecclesiastical institutions, established in the first instance to train clergymen, and both religion and the clergy played central roles in them. Of the five ministers among the Select Society's founding members, the most prominent was William Robertson. Two years older than Smith, Robertson frequently served as moderator of the Church of Scotland Assembly. But he was also a historian who wrote multivolume works on Europe, on Scotland, and on America, as well as the principal—in today's American vocabulary, president—of the University of Edinburgh. (Thomas Jefferson owned Robertson's history of Scotland, along with Hume's history of England.[37]) Adam Ferguson, Smith's exact contemporary, was a philosopher, an early economic thinker, and a prominent figure in the Scottish Enlightenment. He was professor of natural philosophy, and then professor of moral philosophy, at Edinburgh. (He put his name forward to be principal of the university, but the post went to Robertson instead.) Ferguson was also a licensed Church of Scotland preacher, and earlier on he had served as chaplain to the renowned Black Watch regiment.

Unlike at most universities today, in Adam Smith's time no one had yet thought to segregate the theologians into separate "divinity schools," much less locate them on the periphery, at some physical distance from the rest of what happens at the universities to which they are attached. (Today the Harvard Divinity School is a separate faculty and student body, housed in its own buildings half a mile from Harvard Yard; the Yale Divinity School is splendidly situated "on the hill," more than a mile away from Yale's campus center.) Most university faculties were then too small, and the curriculum too integrated, to make such a separation sensible anyway. The University of Glasgow's faculty numbered only fourteen professors when Smith taught there. Alongside subjects like mathematics and logic and moral philosophy (Smith's chair), all of which are standard in university arts and sciences faculties today, there was also a professor of church history as well as a professor of divinity.

Moreover, religious thinking was integrated into the curriculum in ways that went well beyond merely having on the faculty professors of subjects like divinity and church history. Not surprisingly, the standard undergraduate sequence included both physics and moral philosophy. But both were taught as aspects of natural theology: the attempt to learn about aspects of the divine by studying the world God had created. Newton's *Principia Mathematica* was of course assigned, but it too was taught as part of studies in natural theology—just as Newton himself conceived it.

In this era before Darwin, scientists mostly saw no contradiction between their findings and the precepts of Christianity. (True, more than a century before, the Inquisition had tried and convicted Galileo for his claims supporting Copernicus's theory that the earth and other planets revolved around the sun, but by the eighteenth century heliocentrism was accepted knowledge.) To the contrary, many of the greatest contributors—Newton in particular—were deeply religious men. They understood the physical sciences to be supportive, not subversive, of religion as they knew it. The physical laws and mechanisms that they uncovered were part of the beauty of God's creation. The university curriculum therefore readily formed a functional commonality of interest among professors responsible for areas of thought that today we would regard as distinct, and that we would normally identify as either religious or secular, respectively. The intellectually integrated curriculum required ongoing collaboration in arranging the university's teaching as well.

Appointments to teach at Scottish universities (as at Oxford and Cambridge) were also contingent on religious approval, and instructors were subject to subsequent discipline on religious grounds. The teacher whom Adam Smith admired most during his undergraduate years at the University of Glasgow was Francis Hutcheson, the professor of moral philosophy. Smith later succeeded him in that chair. In 1738, when Smith was a student, the Glasgow Presbytery brought formal charges against Hutcheson for teaching that contradicted Church of Scotland doctrine. A public controversy ensued, with one of Hutcheson's former students attacking his teaching—on the same grounds—in print, while a group of his fellow faculty members defended him. (Another Glasgow faculty member had faced similar charges a decade earlier, but Smith was a young boy then and probably took little notice.)

Significantly for the subsequent evolution of economic thinking—not just Smith's but in the nineteenth century as well—Hutcheson's alleged heresy included his belief that whether some action promoted human happiness was the standard by which to judge its moral goodness. The charges against him led to a formal trial, at the end of which Hutcheson was vindicated. But the public attack on his favorite professor no doubt left a significant impression on the young Smith. In order to take up his own professorship at the university, thirteen years later, he had to appear before the city's Presbytery and sign the Westminster Confession of Faith, the Calvinist creed promulgated a century earlier by England's Puritan Parliament. Smith's thoughts on the matter went unrecorded, but he registered no public objection.[38] (He did request permission to skip the mandatory prayer at the beginning of each lecture; the request was denied.)

By contrast, Smith's friend and mentor David Hume despite his titanic intellectual accomplishments never managed to secure a university appointment. In 1744 the chair of ethics and pneumatical philosophy (roughly equivalent to moral philosophy, but also with a concern for the relationship between humans and the Holy Spirit) fell vacant at the University of Edinburgh, and a group of Hume's friends lobbied for his candidacy. Not everyone shared their tolerant attitude toward installing a notorious skeptic to teach the subject to Scotland's youth. Moreover, the university senate had also charged the holder of this chair with the duty to reconcile moral philosophy with divinity, and in particular to teach on "the Truth of the Christian religion." The principal of the university at the time, William Wishart, opposed Hume's appointment, as did twelve of Edinburgh's fifteen active ministers. So too did Francis Hutcheson in Glasgow. After several rounds of increasingly bitter politicking, including formal charges by Wishart against Hume's views, and a written defense from Hume,[39] the position finally went to an otherwise undistinguished Edinburgh merchant who had taken over the previous incumbent's classes during his extended absence prior to his official resignation. But for Hume, the story did not end there. In the words of his biographer, "Astonishingly, Hume was willing to stand in 1751 for the Logic Chair at Glasgow University, but happily for his peace of mind, with the same result."[40]

Even more important for men like Hume and Smith, in the eighteenth century religion was inseparable from politics. What today we regard as purely theological disputes—about the nature of God, about the relationship of God to man, above all about which men and women will achieve spiritual salvation, and how, and what will be the ultimate fate of those who do not—were then questions over which nations fought and men died. Sometimes the fighting and the dying were within a single country, as had happened not so long before in both England and Scotland. But even when the battles were not between armies in the field, they were still the stuff of political combat between parties and among factions. The ideas they were fighting over could not help but shape Hume's and Smith's worldview.

By the time of the Scottish Enlightenment, religion and politics throughout most of Europe had been thoroughly intertwined for well over two centuries. After more than a thousand years of unity under the Roman Catholic Church—to be sure, marked along the way by factional disputes within the church and even occasional schisms— the Reformation set in motion by Martin Luther in 1517 had opened a lengthy era of struggle to determine who would remain Catholic and who would become Protestant. In the abstract, this struggle could have played out at the level of individual churches, or even individual families. But against the background of so many centuries of near-uniformity in formal religious attachment under Catholicism, most of western Europe soon adopted the principle of *cuius regio, eius religio*: in plain language, your religion is that of your ruler (or as expanded by one historian, "where you come from decides your religion, and within that region no other can be tolerated"[41]).

The consequence was an interweaving of religion and politics, most immediately in the form of a struggle for religious allegiance at the level of the political unit. Sometimes this meant a single city, like Zurich or Geneva, sometimes a region like one of the German principalities or Dutch provinces, and sometimes a large nation-state like Poland-Lithuania or, more to the point, England and Scotland. Part of what *cuius regio, eius religio* meant was that, at least nominally, the ruler of each political entity, or its ruling body in the case of a republic, chose which religion it would follow; but a choice that cut too deeply across the grain of local preference, especially among the politically influential elites, could jeopardize the ruler's hold on power. The struggle between Catholicism and Protestantism, and among competing forms of Protestantism once the new movement fragmented, therefore inevitably took place in part at the political level.

The series of conflicts that ensued was not just high politics; it was destructive and deadly. And it was still ongoing in Hume's and Smith's lifetime. The 1745 Jacobite Rebellion in Scotland had been partly about nationalism, including continuing resistance to the submergence within the new united country of what had been an independent nation, but even more so it was about competing visions for Great Britain itself, including rival dynastic and religious loyalties. Both the Highlanders who rebelled and their allies in England were fighting for the restoration of Britain's exiled Stuart monarchy, in opposition to the Hanoverians who had reigned since 1714. The man they wanted as their king was the "Old Pretender," James Francis Edward Stuart, the still surviving son of King James II, who had been deposed a quarter-century before that. (When James II died, in exile in France, Louis XIV immediately recognized his son as the rightful king of England, Scotland, and Ireland.) The rebels' charismatic young leader, Bonnie Prince Charlie, the "Young Pretender," was James II's grandson.

But the main reason James II had been driven from the throne was his religion. He was a Catholic, his wife was a Catholic, and she had just borne a son (the future Old Pretender) whom they planned to raise as a Catholic. The English, committed since the reign of Elizabeth I to having a Protestant monarch and a Protestant church, responded with the Glorious Revolution of 1688. James II fled the country, and the monarchy, and the Church of England and Church of Scotland too, have been Protestant ever since. The Glorious Revolution still stands out, along with such milestones as the Magna Carta and the Great Reform Act of 1832, as among the signal steps of English constitutional development. It took place within the lifetime of both Adam Smith's and David Hume's fathers.

This blending of politics and religion, often with deadly consequences, was not just a Scottish affair. A century before, the English Civil War had lasted much longer than the Jacobite Rebellion would, and it inflicted far more casualties. It too was partly a religious conflict, in that case between rival views of Protestantism. In 1633 King Charles I had named the energetically anti-Puritan William Laud to lead the Church of England as Archbishop of Canterbury. Predictably, Laud soon began persecuting the Puritans, reviving the infamous Star Chamber trials, and instituting other vehicles of oppression.[42] The parliamentary faction that formed to oppose the king, together with the military force it assembled and in time put under the leadership of Oliver Cromwell, consisted mostly of Puritans. The fighting between parliamentary and royalist forces lasted, off and on, for nine years, with an estimated 200,000 deaths—somewhat greater, as a percentage of England's population at the time, than what took place in World War I nearly three centuries later.[43] Looking back from the 1720s, Jonathan Swift had the King of Brobdingnag in *Gulliver's Travels* refer to the period as "a Heap of Conspiracies, Rebellions, Murders, Massacres, Revolutions, Banishments."[44]

Once the parliamentary side gained dominance, its supporters brought the king to trial on charges of high treason. After achieving a conviction, they executed (loyalists would have said murdered) the king—Laud had already been executed several years before—and abolished the English monarchy that by then had been in place for nearly eight centuries. The Puritan Commonwealth that they established in its place, soon followed by a Protectorate under Cromwell and then Cromwell's son, lasted only eleven years. As we shall see, that brief period marked the high tide, in Britain, of the Puritans' religious movement and of the orthodox Calvinist theology that it embraced. By the middle of the eighteenth century these Calvinist ideas were well in retreat, but they nonetheless remained widespread in Scotland and in parts of America, and in Adam Smith's time the English Civil War was still a fresh memory. Many people's grandfathers had fought in it, and many of those had died. During the political agitation that led to the American Revolution, handbills distributed by the rebellious patriots were sometimes signed "OC"—for Oliver Cromwell.

Continental Europe by then had an even more deadly history of religious conflict. In the sixteenth century Catholic France had fought eight civil wars against the country's Protestant Huguenots. More than three thousand Huguenots died in the Saint Bartholomew's Day Massacre in Paris, in 1572. (The word "massacre" was first used, in both French and English, to refer to the atrocity, and the word "refugee" was first used to refer to Huguenots fleeing France.) The Thirty Years' War was likewise mostly a Catholic versus Protestant conflict, although an additional complication was that large parts of western Europe were then under at least the nominal rule of either the Spanish or the Holy Roman Empire (both of which were Catholic), and either the rulers or the populace of some parts of these empires aspired to free themselves from their imperial ties for reasons having little to do with their preference for one religion over the other. The fighting that began in 1618 spread over much of central and northern Europe, and the destruction was vast. Standard estimates indicate some eight million deaths including those due to disease spread by the various armies—as a percentage of Europe's population, twice the death rate in the First World War and comparable to that in the Second.[45]

Much of European thought during the next hundred years, also including that of Englishmen like Hobbes and Locke, was motivated by the aspiration to avoid such human tragedies in the future. Memorable events of the Thirty Years' War had included the Defenestration of Prague, in which Protestant delegates to the Bohemian Estates reenacted the bold defiance of their ancestors two centuries earlier by throwing two of the Catholic Habsburg emperor's representatives from a palace window; the siege and then sack of Heidelberg by troops of the Catholic League (in addition to the death and destruction, the entire Palatine Library was taken off to the Vatican); the Battle of the White Mountain, which permanently ended Protestantism in much of central Europe;[46] and the sack of the Imperial Free City of Magdeburg, in which some twenty thousand inhabitants, mostly Protestants, were either killed outright or burned alive in the fire that consumed the town. All became part of the standard lore of European history, taught to every schoolchild. A century and a half later they too were still fresh memories. The demarcation between Protestant Europe (mostly in the north) and Catholic Europe (mostly in the south) remained then, as it remains today, where the Thirty Years' War left it.

By then both the independent Church of Scotland and its Protestant, and Presbyterian, character were firmly secured. Religion was such a sensitive subject that the Act of Union uniting Scotland with England avoided the subject altogether. Instead, a separate Act for Securing the Protestant Religion and Presbyterian Church Government achieved just what the name declared. By Adam Smith's and David Hume's day the lines of conflict within the Scottish Church were strictly factional: between the Moderates, who mostly favored a more liberal stance on matters of doctrine and observance, and the more conservative evangelicals. ("Moderates" was what the more liberal group called themselves; "evangelicals" is a later label for their more conservative opponents.) Both groups were Protestant, and both identified themselves as followers of the French-Swiss reformer John Calvin, who two centuries before had led what amounted to a second Protestant Reformation in the wake of Martin Luther's in Germany. The issues on which the Moderates and evangelicals disagreed were real, however, and their antagonism was fierce.[47] Against the background of the past century and a half of religious conflict, everyone understood that the stakes were potentially far-reaching. To ignore religious dispute was therefore to refuse participation in important dimensions of politics— something neither Hume nor Smith would have considered doing.

The Moderates were the dominant faction in the Church of Scotland during Smith's adult lifetime, and although certainly not churchmen, he and Hume were very much part of the "Moderate literati" circle. The clergymen with whom they dined at the Select Society were all Moderates. The group's de facto leader within the Church's Assembly was their friend William Robertson, the Assembly's frequent moderator and also principal of Edinburgh's university. Until his death in 1746 Francis Hutcheson, Smith's teacher at Glasgow, had been the Moderates' chief philosophical mentor. Smith openly expressed his admiration for men such as these in *The Wealth of Nations:* "There is scarce perhaps to be found anywhere in Europe a more learned, decent, independent and respectable set of men than the greater part of the Presbyterian clergy of Holland, Geneva, Switzerland and Scotland."[48]

The Moderates' worldview was therefore part of his, and after years of friendship and dining with these men he could not have avoided an awareness of the theological ideas that they advanced in their debates with the evangelicals. Precisely because these ideas were under such fierce debate, people talked about them and wrote about them. And, like all the literati of the Scottish Enlightenment, the Church of Scotland Moderates were extraordinarily articulate talkers and writers. Simply from being a part of the society and culture in which they participated, at the time and in the place in which they lived, Smith and Hume and other intellectuals outside the clergy were continually exposed to their clerical friends' notions of divine benevolence and their benign view of human character. As we shall see, the content of Smith's economic thinking as set forth in *The Wealth of Nations*—specifically, his insights concerning the beneficial consequences of behavior motivated by individual self-interest, and the role of market competition in bringing those consequences about—was strikingly congruent with the Moderates' theology.

Both in university settings and through the rich array of independent social and intellectual activities that characterized the Scottish Enlightenment, therefore, Smith and his contemporaries were regularly exposed to ongoing debates, tensions, and new ideas in religious thinking, in the same way that most people engaged in one intellectual discipline or another today—including economists—continually encounter ideas in other areas of inquiry. Cross-fertilization among intellectual disciplines is a familiar enough phenomenon, and when ideas in one line of thought are sufficiently large in scope, and important enough, to arrest attention more broadly, they often influence thinking in other areas too, sometimes including areas far from their origin.

Ever since Newton, for example, concepts of mechanism and systematic "laws" have powerfully shaped Western thinking across a wide range of subject areas well removed from what we normally associate with physics. In effect, these concepts serve as organizing principles that define the standard for what it means to explain any observed phenomenon. Similarly, following the explosive introduction of Charles Darwin's controversial hypothesis in the middle of the nineteenth century (*On the Origin of Species* was published in 1859), the concepts of evolution and adaptation became metaphors for structuring thinking about many other subjects too, such as political institutions and social organizations. Also during the nineteenth century, as new advances in chemistry attracted the public's attention, the idea of reactions, and of reactions triggered by catalysts, took on a similar role as structural metaphors for thought across a range of disciplines. The same kind of influence occurred in the twentieth century, when the public's fascination with exciting breakthroughs in atomic and then nuclear physics led the already familiar idea of dividing units of any kind into subunits, and those into yet smaller component parts, to take on a heightened role in many areas of thought. Still later on, with the development of rockets capable of reaching beyond the pull of the earth's gravity, the concept of escape velocity likewise became a standard metaphor in a broad range of unrelated applications.

Economic thinking in the modern era has certainly drawn its share of ideas from other scientific disciplines. One immediately evident example concerns international trade. Ranked by the dollar volume of exports that the United States sends to each country, America's top trading partners are Canada, Mexico, China, and Japan. This list immediately suggests two influences that foster trade between countries: physical proximity (Canada and Mexico are the only two countries that share borders with the U.S.), and size (China and Japan, in that order, are the world's largest economies after the U.S.). A standard framework that economists today use to explain how much trade countries have with one another posits that, all else equal, the volume of trade between any two countries is proportional to the size of each one's economy, and inversely proportional to some function of the distance between them. (Other potential influences, such as the two countries' political relations, or whether either or both are located on a seacoast, or what transportation facilities are available, are of course at work as well; they are part of the "all else" that the simplified theory holds equal.) But such a relationship—with the strength of some connection between two entities being proportional to the size of each and inversely proportional to a function of the distance separating them— closely mimics Newton's universal law of gravitation.[49] The resemblance is not coincidental. Economists regularly refer to this theory as the "gravity model" of international trade, acknowledging its inspiration in the physical analog.[50]

Another example, rendered all too familiar by the worldwide events of 2007–2009, concerns the development and spread of financial crises. Because of interrelationships among banks created by patterns of cross-deposit holding and cross-lending, as well as both deposit and credit relationships between banks and the nonfinancial firms that are their largest customers, the failure of one institution can threaten the viability of another. What sometimes turns one bank's idiosyncratic mistakes or one firm's unique business misfortune into a more general crisis is just this dependence of any one bank on many others: every troubled borrower's liabilities are someone else's assets. And when banks in large numbers encounter difficulties, their inability to lend (in case of failure, even to honor their liabilities) often triggers an economy-wide contraction of output and employment. Drawing on biology, and more specifically on medical fields like epidemiology and immunology, economists seeking to understand this kind of financial interdependency turn to models of "contagion," and refer to one failing bank as "infecting" others. In the wake of the 2007–2009 financial crisis, both economists and policymakers have made reducing such financial contagion a primary objective of public policy.[51]

Yet another example, again from international economics and business relations, concerns the pace and pattern by which technological advances developed in a country like the United States or Germany, at the frontier of existing technology, come into use in lower-income countries further from the technological frontier: How long does it take for an innovation developed in the West—a new crop like hybrid corn, or a new way of making steel or semiconductors, or a new telecommunications technology—to be put into practice in Africa? And just how do African farmers, or manufacturers, or telecom companies, gain access to the new technology? Drawing on both chemistry and biology, economists often represent cross-border technology transfer as a process in which the new technology "penetrates" the less advanced economy in ways analogous to what those sciences have shown about how particles penetrate living membranes.[52]

Still another familiar example is the way in which, over time, an economy's labor force shifts from one sector or one industry to another. The movement of labor out of agriculture into higher-productivity employment in newly established manufacturing industries is a typical aspect of the early and middle stages of economic development, experienced in England in the first half of the nineteenth century and in the United States in the nineteenth and early twentieth, and widely seen in countries like China and India and Brazil today. But even in advanced economies that are already deeply industrialized, international competition or emerging technology frequently results in significant and ongoing reallocation of labor. The United States today has far fewer workers making shoes, or televisions, than it did fifty years ago, while there are far more doing software design and network operations. Economists often look to the field of demography for systematic ways of thinking about such "migrations"—in this case migrations not from one place to another (although that too can be involved) but from one form of employment to another.[53]

Each of these influences on economics originated in one or another of the natural sciences: physics, biology, chemistry, or demography. Each is the result of economists' deliberately borrowing from these other disciplines. But there is nothing that naturally limits the process of intellectual cross-fertilization to ideas originating in the sciences; this pattern simply reflects modern economists' exposure to other disciplines that are also central to university life as it is structured today. Nor is the process limited to borrowings that economists, or other thinkers, consciously seek out.

In Adam Smith's era, and for well over a century after, the scholars whom we today regard as economists were commonly exposed to ideas from a different range of disciplines, importantly including religious thinking. And in many cases, certainly including Smith's, they were exposed to these religious ideas not out of any deliberate exploration on their part but merely through the ordinary intellectual intercourse that formed the core of their everyday lives. These ideas were simply part of their "cultural soil," the "spirit" of their time. And because the ideas that were new in the religious thinking of the English-speaking Protestant world during this period were highly controversial, and hotly contended, they were all the more salient for the thinking—whether conscious or not—of contemporaries who were neither clerics nor theologians.

The new theological ideas to which Smith and his contemporaries were continually exposed, especially those concerning the nature of man, the ultimate destiny that this nature implied for individual men and women, and the possibilities for human agency while they were living, shaped their fundamental sense of the world and how it works. These ideas formed part of the mindset that they brought to their own thinking and writing. In Einstein's phrase, these ideas were part of their worldview; in Schumpeter's, their preanalytic Vision. It is not surprising that the economics that Smith and those who followed him created bore a deep affinity to the religious ideas amidst which they lived.

It still does, and the connection continues to matter. Economics not only has cultural roots, appreciation of which helps to understand economics itself and where it came from. Today the field has a far broader significance and influence within the world in which we live. Understanding the roots of economic thinking, and what those roots signify, informs our understanding of our society and our politics as well.

The Road to Adam Smith

Although there is nothing so opposed to Charity, which relates all to God, as Self-love, which relates all to itself, yet there is nothing so resembling the effects of Charity as those of Self-love.

—PIERRE NICOLE

The worst of all the Multitude Did something for the Common Good.

—BERNARD MANDEVILLE

The central insight underlying modern Western economics—the idea that we know today as the invisible hand, even though Adam Smith's use of the phrase was neither original nor so specific—is that behavior motivated merely by individuals' self-interest can, and under the right conditions *will,* lead to beneficial outcomes not merely for those individuals but for others as well. A few other thinkers had offered the same suggestion before, but none had provided so complete an explanation and the idea had gained little currency. Smith's explanation, centered on competitive markets, was substantive and it proved powerful. In the Western world, and especially in the English-speaking countries and most of all in America, it has marked the central channel of economic thinking and economic policy for the past two hundred years. Today most Americans simply take it for granted.

As recently as the beginning of the eighteenth century, however, most people who thought about such matters at all had a very different conception. The few serious thinkers on the subject sometimes did and sometimes didn't ascribe to everyday individuals the ability to know what was in their own economic interest. More importantly, there was no presumption that people's pursuing their self-interest, even if they perceived it correctly, would have any more broadly beneficial consequences. Quite the contrary—so much so that acting purely on one's individual self-interest was taken to be a vice, and the standard adjective applied to such behavior was "vicious." Before then, the mercantilists of the seventeenth century had likewise been skeptical that individually motivated behavior could make a nation's economy better off; their approach was to run economic affairs from the top down. Earlier still, the medieval scholastics, rooted in the traditions of the Roman Catholic Church, had taken a dim view of individually motivated economic activity and the role of markets more generally, preferring to theorize about what constitutes a "just price" for anything bought or sold.

It was Smith's *The Wealth of Nations*, published in 1776, that first offered a coherent, fully developed explanation for the private-interest-leads-to-public-good idea as it has come down to us: Individuals do correctly perceive their self-interest. (At least they do when they work at their jobs or run their businesses; Smith, ever the insightful moral philosopher, remained highly skeptical of consumers' choices, especially among the rich.) The desire to pursue our self-interest is an inherent aspect of human nature, no more to be deemed morally opprobrious than the fact that we eat or breathe. Pursuing our self-interest, under the right economic conditions—namely, markets—leads to outcomes that are beneficial for others as well as ourselves, indeed optimal. And the mechanism that delivers these more broadly optimal outcomes under market conditions is competition. Not surprisingly, with Smith's contribution the vocabulary of vice and vicious was finally gone.

The Wealth of Nations was an immediate success. Adam Smith became a sought-after political advisor at home and an international celebrity as well. By the end of the century, Smith's idea of the invisible hand of competition in a market setting, and the benefits that followed from it, was well known and broadly accepted. It has formed the basis of Western thinking about economics and economic policy ever since.

Where did this fundamentally new way of looking at such an important matter come from? And why did it emerge when it did, and with what seems, in historical perspective, such suddenness?

.   .   .

What to think about self-interested behavior and what to do about the trouble it sometimes creates—the moral challenge as well as the practical problem—have been central to human thinking since mankind first began to commit thought to writing (and probably long before). Both the Hebrew Bible and the New Testament display a deep awareness of the temptations, and the dangers, associated with people's looking out for themselves without regard for anyone else. In a different way, so did other early Middle Eastern texts both religious and secular, and classical philosophers both stoic and epicurean. The question likewise underlies much of post-biblical Jewish and Christian moralizing and, starting from the seventh century, Islamic thinking too. The tradition of Renaissance humanism, hailing the republican virtues that people of the time associated with ancient Greece and pre-empire Rome, likewise addressed the need to put the polity before one's self.

What was much newer in Adam Smith's day was thinking about *economic* welfare. Until roughly the time of Smith and his contemporaries, there was little consensus that aggregate economic welfare in today's sense of a society's standard of living was a subject to think much about at all. There was even less consensus that anyone could do much about it. In biblical times people understood that economic conditions could be good or bad, but they mostly attributed the difference to two influences: plentiful versus meager harvests, and war versus peace. In a mostly agrarian economy the harvest was naturally of paramount importance; but there was little room for economic initiative to affect it. The Bible's view of the matter was that good harvest conditions were a reward for proper moral and religious behavior. ("And it shall come to pass, if you shall hearken diligently unto my commandments which I command you this day, to love the Lord your God, and to serve him with all your heart and all your soul, that I will give you the rain of your land in his due season, the first rain and the latter rain, that thou mayest gather in thy corn and thy wine and thy oil. And I will send grass in thy fields for thy cattle, that thou mayest eat and be full."[1]) And, though surely not for this reason only, hopes for peace were a biblical centerpiece. ("Blessed are the peacemakers: for they shall be called the children of God."[2])

Both the early Christian fathers and the scholastics of the Middle Ages likewise took little interest in what might enhance a society's material living standard. In Christianity, far more than Judaism, the focus was not on this life but the life to come. ("Lay not up for your-selves treasures upon earth."[3]) Economic behavior mattered, to be sure, but mostly because the individual acts that comprised it could poten-tially be sinful, and therefore might impede an individual soul's salva-tion. ("They that will be rich fall into temptation and a snare, and into many foolish and hurtful lusts, which drown men in destruction and perdition."[4]) From the viewpoint of the society as a whole what mat-tered was not the standard of living, which presumably no one could influence anyway, but whether people's economic interactions were channeled according to religious principles. Buying and selling were accepted, as long as the price was just. So was individual borrowing and lending, but only if no interest was charged.[5]

Further, in the eyes of the church, improving the general standard of living was not necessarily desirable even if it were somehow possi-ble. Augustine had regarded an undue desire for material possessions as one of man's three principal sins, along with sexual lust and desire for power. Riches were a danger, no matter how acquired. ("Verily I say unto you, that a rich man shall hardly enter into the kingdom of heaven."[6]) Early Christian thinking instead glorified an ascetic life, proliferating hermits and even stylites. In the Middle Ages monks and many in the laity too committed themselves to a life of poverty, with mendicant orders like the Franciscans and Dominicans eschewing sources of material support other than private charity.

The Renaissance took a different direction, idealizing the aristocratic pursuit of honor and glory. What the thinkers of the day considered glorious, however, was not anything to do with mass living stan-dards but instead sumptuous display by princes and their hangers-on, together with the public monuments—palaces, churches, fountains, gardens—that they built. Honor and glory for princes also came from military adventures. A society's productive capacity mattered because it potentially enabled construction of monuments and the manufacture of weapons, not on account of any direct benefit to the general popu-lation. At the same time, having a larger population became desirable too. Smaller states lived under constant threat of conquest by larger ones. (Preference for a larger population, on military grounds, did not disappear after the Renaissance; Britain following World War I and Germany under Hitler both pursued pronatalist policies. Mao's famous dictum was *Ren Duo Li Liang Da*: with many people strength is great.[7])

In Europe the resulting subordination of economic activity to "reasons of state," and in parallel a preference for larger population, reached new heights in seventeenth-century France under the Sun King, Louis XIV. But while Louis ruled for more than seven decades, over the time horizons that mattered for most rulers there was little way to increase a country's military-age population. The alternative was to hire foreign mercenaries to augment domestic armies. Mercenaries, however—even more so, the foreign rulers who supplied them—had to be paid. Along with the need to buy arms, the potential need for mercenary troops led to regarding the state's holdings of monetary metals, primarily gold and silver, as the relevant measure of its wealth.

The standard mercantilist economic program therefore promoted domestic manufacturing, especially of products likely to appeal to export markets, and in parallel discouraged imports—all in order to accumulate and retain gold and silver bullion. To this end, Louis XIV's longtime finance minister Jean-Baptiste Colbert founded the Gobelin tapestry works, as well as enterprises making a variety of other products. After founding a French glassworks, Colbert likewise prohibited imports of Venetian glass. Such ideas were hardly limited to France. One of the era's best-selling English works on political economy, published in London in 1664, was titled *England's Treasure by Forraign Trade, or, The Ballance of our Forraign Trade Is The Rule of our Treasure.* According to the author, Thomas Mun, the purpose of the national economy was to build up the "sinews of war."[8] In the 1670s England prohibited imports of French goods such as wine, linen, and brandy.[9] In the next century, the British Navigation Laws partly served the same purpose.

Not by accident, such mercantilist policies were far from neutral in whom they favored. A monopoly over some good's production, or its sale, protected the interest of whoever received the royal license and blocked anyone else who might seek to enter that line of business. The sale of monopolies also provided a much needed source of revenue for the king. Over time, therefore, the "reasons of state" behind such policies became conflated with the interest of producers; after all, they made the goods that either generated payments in gold and silver when exported or conserved metal specie when bought domestically in place of imports. By contrast, the public's consumption at best absorbed goods that might be sold abroad, and sometimes required imported goods. A further element of the mercantilist program, therefore, was to keep wages, and hence the population's standard of living, low. More generally, mercantilist policies required top-down implementation, involving a profusion of state-granted monopolies and state-imposed restrictions on trade.

It was not until the eighteenth century, primarily in England and even more so in Scotland, that thinking about economic questions began to focus on improving a nation's overall standard of living. The Scots' desire to gain access to England's colonial trade, and thereby achieve a level of economic development comparable to what the English already enjoyed, was, as we have seen, the principal motivation for entering into the Act of Union with England in 1707. Abolishing their country's parliament, and for most practical purposes its royal court as well, was bound to be controversial. Andrew Fletcher, a prominent Scottish politician and economic thinker who led the opposition, likewise sought to accelerate Scotland's development; instead of union with England he favored a plan for Scotland to build its own overseas trading empire, beginning with a colony in what is now Panama.[10] But Fletcher's scheme collapsed in 1700, following three disastrous expeditions that together lost some two thousand lives and more than half of the company's subscribed capital. Its failure, along with a run of poor harvests in Scotland (on some contemporary estimates, a third of the population died of starvation[11]), gave a final boost to the movement for union, which went forward just a few years later.

It is not surprising, therefore, that it was in Scotland, and in the decades following the Act of Union, that the concept of a nation's standard of living and the objective of improving it entered economic thinking in more or less the form we know today. David Hume, writing at mid-century, constructed the most penetrating rejection of mercantilist ideas on international trade, especially the obsession with accumulating gold and silver. Hume explained that increases in a country's holdings of specie would raise the prices of its goods, thereby undoing much of what the mercantilists hoped to achieve through a positive trade balance. He also showed how, once thinking moved past the viewpoint of military rivalry, prosperity among a country's foreign competitors was beneficial not just to those other countries but at home too: greater wealth abroad meant greater foreign demand for home-produced goods. "Not only as a man, but as a British subject," he wrote, "I pray for the flourishing commerce of Germany, Spain, Italy, and even France itself. . . . Great Britain, and all those nations, would flourish more, did their sovereigns and ministers adopt such enlarged and benevolent sentiments toward each other."[12]

The understanding that the route to wealth was to trade with other nations—rather than to conquer them, and then plunder their riches and enslave their populations—was only just dawning on Europeans' thinking, and Hume's theory of international trade reflected it.[13] His account of the benefits of international trade, as well as of the mechanics of the connection between money and prices, remain accepted parts of Western economic thinking today.

Adam Smith further elaborated the idea of trade as the avenue to prosperity and made even more explicit the objective of improving a country's general standard of living. The title of Smith's great work referred to living standards, not holdings of gold and silver. *The Wealth of Nations* was, in effect, a guidebook for policymakers seeking to take a country from a low state of economic development like Scotland's to a more prosperous level like England's. Throughout, Smith was clear about the primary goal. "No society can surely be flourishing and happy," he declared, "of which the far greater part of the members are poor and miserable." What mostly mattered was "the condition of the labouring poor, of the great body of the people."[14] The question he took on was how to improve it.

The time was ripe too for new thinking about self-interest. Traditional approaches to this most human of problems had centered on two ways to restrain potentially harmful individual behavior: external restraint imposed by the state or by smaller communities right down to the family, and internal restraint created by religion. Each was valuable to the purpose, but even the two together were plainly inadequate. Despite millennia of utopian dreaming, no society had ever found a way to abolish crime, much less the entire range of noxious behavior that falls short of that mark.

The subject was a particular focus of public concern in Britain during the century or so leading up to Adam Smith's time. Questions of civic virtue versus corruption—often with an explicit link drawn between corruption and market-based commerce—were a staple of debate throughout England's Puritan revolution and then, after the parliamentary side's victory in the English Civil War, under the republican Commonwealth.[15] The subsequent restoration of the monarchy under Charles II, complete with the usual ostentatious luxury characteristic of European royal courts of the day, brought a moral backlash against extravagant consumption together with heightened concerns over the nation's moral character.[16] Perceived effeminacy, associated with luxury since classical times, was a particular concern. Thomas Mun's book on trade, published just four years after the Restoration (though written much earlier), lamented "the general leprosie of our Piping, Potting, Feasting, Fashions, and the mis-spending of our time in Idleness and Pleasure." Such indulgences, Mun thought, had "made us effeminate in our bodies, weak in our knowledg, poor in our Treasure, declined in our Valour, unfortunate in our Enterprises, and contemned by our Enemies."[17] By contrast, as the politician and political theorist Algernon Sidney proclaimed, the mother and nurse of virtue is poverty.[18]

The issue did not go away with Charles's death. After assuming the throne in the Glorious Revolution of 1688, William and Mary issued repeated proclamations against "vice, immorality and corruption." In 1699 the Church of England established a Society for Promoting Christian Knowledge, with much the same purpose in mind. In addition to its missionary work abroad, at home in England the society instituted charity schools to educate children in the usual subjects of the day including religion and morality. Queen Anne, who ascended to the throne on William's death in 1702 (Mary had predeceased him), in turn issued a Proclamation for the Encouragement of Piety and Virtue and for the Preventing and Punishing of Vice, Profaneness and Immorality.

But concern over public morality was more than a matter of frustrated authority at the top. Starting in the 1690s, private Societies for the Reformation of Manners emerged, in London and other towns, to enforce moral discipline by informing on their neighbors' misdeeds: sexual misbehavior, drunkenness, gambling, profanity, even merely failing to observe the Sabbath. These voluntary groups had limited success, however, and within a few decades the effort collapsed.[19] In the meanwhile, popular essayists like Joseph Addison, writing in *The Spectator*, repeatedly emphasized the same theme.[20] James Whiston, a merchant engaged in buying and selling commodities, complained of

"Idleness, Luxury, Debauchery," along with "Decay of Religion, Vertue and common Justice."[21] The marvelously energetic title character of Daniel Defoe's *Moll Flanders* (1722) exemplifies the contemporary view of loose individual morality. Referring to a time only slightly later, historian Bernard Bailyn wrote of "the self-indulgence, effeminizing luxury, and gluttonous pursuit of gain of a generation sunk in new and unaccustomed wealth."[22]

The economic dimension of such vice and immorality took on particular visibility after 1720, with the bursting of the South Sea Bubble, one of financial history's classic episodes of speculation followed by collapse, comparable to the Dutch tulip mania a century before and to numerous classic shakeouts of market excess since. The British government had created the South Sea Company nearly a decade earlier along conventional mercantilist lines, granting the privately held firm a monopoly over Britain's trade with the Spanish colonies in South America. The government also looked to the new company as a vehicle for consolidating Britain's national debt. In 1719 the company issued shares to the public, and in the ensuing speculation the share price soon increased tenfold. When the company collapsed a year later, many individual investors, including people of substantial prominence, were ruined. While the better-known investors who lost money in the collapse were from the peerage and the propertied gentry—with King George I himself as the company's honorary governor, owning shares appealed to an elite clientele—many small investors lost their stakes too.

Worse, the South Sea fiasco also became an emblem of corruption on a grand scale. The astonishing run-up in the company's share price turned out to have involved what today seems the usual chicanery. Abuses that have since become thoroughly familiar, but in the early eighteenth century struck the public as novel—stock manipulation, inside dealing, fanciful touting of the company's earnings prospects, lending to investors on the security of current holdings to finance purchases of still more shares—all played a role in the debacle. It also emerged that key members of Parliament had taken bribes in return for promoting the venture at the outset. Even at the time, however, the South Sea Company was hardly unique; other unscrupulous promoters were carrying out similar schemes, engaging in many of the same forms of manipulation but on a smaller scale. In 1734 Parliament passed an act condemning the "wicked, pernicious and destructive Practice of Stock-jobbing."[23]

The South Sea episode turned into a public spectacle, attracting both scorn and ridicule. Jonathan Swift's poem *The Bubble*, published the year after the collapse, captured the public's derision:

> *Ye wise Philosophers explain*
> *What Magick makes our Money rise,*
> *When dropt into the Southern Main;*
> *Or do these Juglers cheat our Eyes?*
> *Put in your Money fairly told;*
> *Presto be gone—'Tis here agen;*
> *Ladies, and Gentlemen, behold,*
> *Here's ev'ry piece as big as Ten.*[24]

William Hogarth's highly symbolic engraving *The South Sea Scheme*, also from 1721, shows an imaginary London scene centered on a carnival ride representing the financial wheel of fortune, ridden by the kinds of ordinary people who had bet and lost on South Sea shares: a gentleman, a clergyman, a prostitute, and other familiar characters. Elsewhere in the scene a pickpocket robs another gentleman; Catholic, Jewish, and Nonconformist Protestant clergymen (each easily identifiable by his dress) gamble at dice, posed like the soldiers playing for Christ's mantle in many familiar pictures of the Crucifixion; honest Fortune, wearing a blindfold to indicate her lack of bias, is tortured by a devil as the crowd applauds; another devil whips Honor with a lash; and the base of a giant column, styled after Christopher Wren's commemorating the great London fire of 1666, reads "This monument was erected in memory of the destruction of this city by the South Sea in 1720." The engraving attracted enough of a popular audience to launch Hogarth's career.[25]

Well after the immediacy of the South Sea Bubble had faded from public attention, playwrights, novelists, and artists continued to parody the vice and sin, and the outright foolishness both often entailed, that popular opinion then saw as characteristic of British life especially in London and the larger towns. John Gay's *The Beggar's Opera*, written in 1728, features a whole cast of characters committed to greed and vice, headed by the immortal Polly Peachum (who was partly a satirical

William Hogarth, *The South Sea Scheme* (1721).
Hogarth was just twenty-four when he parodied the financial and moral
debacle that the collapse of the South Sea Bubble revealed.

representation of Robert Walpole, then prime minister). George Lillo's
The London Merchant (1731), Samuel Richardson's *Clarissa* (1748), and
Henry Fielding's *Tom Jones* (1749) all include characters personifying
greed and immorality.

In the same vein, a series of six engravings done by Hogarth in 1732,
titled *The Harlot's Progress,* portrays the London career of a young
country girl, from innocent new arrival to elegant gentlemen's mis-
tress to street prostitute to prison inmate to an early death from vene-
real disease. Hogarth's *Strolling Actresses Dressing in a Barn,* from 1738,
likewise highlights the tawdry side of contemporary theater life, with
numerous allusions to the presumed easy morals of women who performed on stage for typically affluent audiences. His 1751 masterpiece,
Gin Lane, is a riot of perversion, destruction, and death, all attributed to
drunkenness among more ordinary citizens (gin was mostly the drink
of the poor), and pictured with horrifying realism in contrast to the
mostly amusing South Sea allegory from thirty years before. All of these

William Hogarth, *Gin Lane* (1751).
Many of the images in Hogarth's portrayal of squalor and depravity referred to widely known events of recent years that had shocked London's population.

engravings drew a large popular audience, as did similar works by other, less known artists of the time. Concern for the nation's moral fiber was not confined to a narrow elite.

The subject was a principal focus of intellectual discourse as well. Spurred by the trauma of the Reformation and then the Civil War—and on the continent the Thirty Years' War, the Spanish-Dutch Wars, and numerous other hostilities—much of British discussion of issues of vice and virtue at the end of the seventeenth century and the beginning of the eighteenth reflected memories of the cruelty and death that these conflicts had brought, and the intolerance, fanaticism, and persecution that stood behind them. The discussion centered on the question of man's "sociability," or lack of it, and the implications that followed for how human societies could govern themselves.[26] The ever increasing complexity and anonymity of the market society in which people now lived further compounded this challenge.

The opposite ends of the debate were the contrasting views of Thomas Hobbes and Anthony Ashley Cooper, the Earl of Shaftesbury. Like many of his time, in due course including both David Hume and Adam Smith, Hobbes sought to place the study of man on a sounder scientific footing. His thinking also reflected a post-Renaissance realism (many, then and now, would call it cynicism) about human nature. What classical times and the Renaissance had construed as heroic virtues, Hobbes thought were merely forms of struggling for survival—the most basic self-interest of all. Life in what he called a state of nature was "solitary, poore, nasty, brutish, and short." Living in "continuall feare, and danger of violent death," humans had resorted to a social contract to save themselves from perishing in the "war of all against all" that would otherwise have engulfed them.[27] The need had not lessened with time. Even after thousands of years of civilization, looking to inborn virtue to restrain people's often conflicting self-interest was fanciful. As the philosopher and theologian John Norris put it at the end of the seventeenth century, "Charity not only *begins* at home, but for the most part *ends* there too."[28]

Shaftesbury took a more benign view of human nature, more in line with the soon-to-blossom Enlightenment. He posited that men and women are born with not just the five familiar physical senses but a sixth as well: a moral sense, in effect a set of "sentiments about sentiments"[29] that enable us to understand the difference between happiness and unhappiness, right and wrong, virtue and vice, without needing to be instructed by religion or constrained by the state. Further, this inborn moral sense leads us to *prefer* moral acts over immoral ones. Just as the Greek and Roman stoics had argued long before, the path to human happiness was therefore to lead a virtuous life. As long as men acknowledged that happiness was possible *and* understood its proper basis, there was no conflict between virtue, either public or private, and a person's self-interest—which, after all, was to be happy. Virtue and self-interest coincided.

Hobbes's fatalistic pessimism and Shaftesbury's stoic (some would say utopian) optimism marked the poles of late-seventeenth-century English thinking on fundamental questions of human nature and the ensuing prospects for a people to live together peaceably and govern themselves. But where did economic activity fit into this scheme? The connection seemed readily apparent. Even leaving aside Hobbes's identification of self-interest with basic survival, including the need for food and shelter and clothing, the economic sphere was perhaps the most obvious arena in which everyday behavior by ordinary men and women revolved around self-interest.

The question only grew in importance as Britain's economy, still mostly agricultural, evolved toward an ever greater role for commercial markets. Subsistence farming had long since ceased to be the norm (if it ever was). Most farmers now looked to markets, and increasingly so, for their economic existence. Even tenants who farmed on lords' estates relied on shopkeepers and goods purveyors of all kinds to supply their daily necessities. Tradesmen and townspeople were in most cases entirely dependent on market interactions, acting both as sellers of whatever they produced and buyers of whatever they needed. By the end of the seventeenth century, the challenge confronting thinkers like Hobbes and Shaftesbury importantly included seeking to understand the social basis underlying what was becoming an ever more commercialized economy.

Just as man's self-interested desire to protect himself and his family from others, and even to dominate them if possible, threatened a Hobbesian war of all against all in which everyone might perish and many surely would, in the new market economy the unfettered pursuit of self-interest likewise seemed to threaten disaster. But no economic equivalent of Hobbes's metaphorical once-for-all-time resort to a social contract was readily apparent. Nor did it seem safe simply to assume that most people would conduct themselves virtuously in their market dealings out of some stoic sense that doing so is what would ultimately enable them to be happy.

Especially in the arena of economic life, overcoming the dangers posed by self-interest therefore seemed an insurmountable challenge. The advance of commercial society and corresponding retreat of traditional agriculture prompted particular concern in a nation long used to identifying landed property with dignity and virtue, and commerce— including speculative finance—with corruption. The Roman Catholic

Church, which in many countries owned huge tracts of agricultural land, had typically regarded rural life more favorably than urban. This prejudice persisted in many Protestant countries after the Reformation. The movement now of ever larger elements of the population from the countryside into cities and towns therefore only exacerbated the threat of moral decline in many people's eyes (as the same movement did, in the nineteenth and on into the twentieth century, in America).[30]

Long before the South Sea Bubble, the establishment of the East India Company (1600), and more recently the Bank of England (1694), had given an official blessing to the rise of commerce and finance, but the association with corruption and moral decay, and with it effeminacy, persisted in the public mind. Writing in 1706, Daniel Defoe described Lady Credit as a prostitute, "a coy Lass" who "will court those most, that have no occasion for her." By contrast, "If you court her, you lose her, or must buy her at unreasonable Rates."[31] The courtesan whom Defoe made the title character of his 1724 novel *Roxana* was Lady Credit's personification. The development of financial markets, now supported by the Bank, also facilitated the growth of government debt, then as now perceived by many as a particular temptation to public corruption and decline (and part of the origin of the South Sea episode).

Moreover, everyone also understood that self-interest potentially threatened the society's ability to govern itself peaceably. Again in contrast to the comfortable traditions surrounding landed wealth handed down within families or held by the monarch, the corrupting influence of the quest for financial riches seemed to many to threaten personal liberty, political stability, and even the capacity of the nation to defend itself. In his first major work, published in 1739, David Hume highlighted the widespread fear that economic self-interest provoked. All other human passions, Hume wrote, "are either easily restrain'd, or are not of such pernicious consequence, when indulg'd. . . . This avidity alone, of acquiring goods and possessions for ourselves and our nearest friends, is insatiable, perpetual, universal, and directly destructive of society."[32]

A more optimistic way of thinking about the practical consequences of self-interest, especially in the economic sphere, first emerged late in the seventeenth century, in France. Oddly, the fount from which this optimism developed was a group within the Roman Catholic Church that took a harshly negative view of the human character. The Jansenists—followers of the Dutch-Belgian bishop Cornelius Jansen, who had been active in Paris as well—were Augustinians, committed to St. Augustine's view of the centrality of sin in human existence. But Augustine also held that the behavior spurred by sin is, in some degree, the remedy for sin. Man's socially destructive impulses are partly held in check, he thought, by other human desires that are also the consequence of his sinful nature. As a result, men have some ability, albeit limited, to live together peaceably. (Augustine similarly saw human institutions such as marriage, slavery, private property, and the state as partial remedies for pervasive sinfulness.)

The route to the insight that bore on economics stemmed from a further key Augustinian belief also shared by Jansen and his followers: that because of this sinful nature only some men and women will achieve spiritual salvation—and, crucially, that it is impossible to know who will be saved and who will not.[33] This view acquired renewed salience in the sixteenth and early seventeenth century with the rapid spread of Calvinism in many parts of northern Europe, partly in reaction to the perceived smugness of many Calvinists who seemed assured of their own salvation. (If Augustine was right, how could they know?) It also presented a conundrum for Catholics, however, because in so many familiar settings people can readily observe one another's actions: Some people devote their lives to charity. Others selfishly pursue their own interests. Catholics believed (and still believe) that a person's earthly "works" play an important role in determining his or her eventual salvation. Why, then, is it impossible to judge whether a person is likely to be saved or not?

Jansen had been careful not to publish his views on the subject within his lifetime, while the Thirty Years' War was still being fought and religious heterodoxy was dangerous. His principal work, titled *Augustinus*, appeared only in 1640, two years after he died. In it he acknowledged the importance of righteous acts—"charity"—for salvation, but nonetheless embraced enough elements of Protestant thinking, questioning the efficacy of works for this purpose, that Pope Urban VIII promptly condemned the book. At the request of Louis XIV, who saw Jansen's ideas as not just theologically unsound but a threat to the French state as well, Urban's successor Innocent X condemned *Augustinus* again a dozen years later. Jansen's attempt to bridge the gap between Catholic and Protestant thinking nonetheless still held substantial appeal, especially in France. The Jansenist movement, headquartered at the Port-Royal, just outside Paris, continued to flourish until its final rejection by the church, reinforced by excommunications, in 1718. Even afterward, however, Jansenist thinking and influence persisted in many French institutions of learning.[34]

During the later decades of the seventeenth century, when the movement was at its height, a series of French Jansenist thinkers took up penetrating inquiries into moral questions that also led them to insights into aspects of what in time became the field of economics.[35] The two who gained the greatest prominence were Pierre Nicole, a Catholic priest and theologian who lived and taught at the Jansenist school in the Port-Royal, and Jean Domat, a lawyer and legal scholar also closely associated with the Port-Royal community. Both were born in 1625, so that they had been fifteen when Bishop Jansen's *Augustinus* appeared. Although the two men's writings on the subject were similar in many respects, it was Nicole who offered the most direct argument for the compatibility of self-interest with the welfare of either society as a whole or individuals within it.

Nicole was a prolific writer, with a wide audience in English as well as French. In 1662 he and his fellow Jansenist Antoine Arnauld published *The Art of Thinking*. More than seventy years later, when Adam Smith was an undergraduate in Glasgow, the university was still using the book as a text for teaching logic. Nicole's better known work, however, was his *Moral Essays*, written in French in the 1670s and quickly published in English translation.[36] The English-language audience took the essays seriously. (John Locke translated three of them himself, only to discover that an English translation already existed, and he never published what he had done.[37])

The essay in which Nicole most directly addressed the puzzle presented by Jansen's implicit rebuke of Calvinist confidence in salvation was titled "Of Charity and Self-Love."[38] At first looking inward, Nicole explained that because human motives are complex it is impossible for people to determine, even from careful introspection, why they do what they do. In any given instance, are we acting out of pure benevolence? Or for some self-serving purpose? Or perhaps a combination of the two? Nicole concluded that no matter how intently we scrutinize our own motives, we simply cannot tell. Only God can truly inspect the human heart.

Moving to external appearances, he argued that the same inability to determine motives applies in judging other people as well—despite our ability to observe what they do. But this proposition in turn led him to the crucial insight: actions motivated in part or even in whole by self-interest must therefore sometimes lead to *consequences* that are indistinguishable from those of actions motivated by charity. If they did not, it would be easy to tell whether someone was acting out of charity or self-interest merely by observing what the person did. "Although there is nothing so opposite to Charity, which relates all to God, as Self-love, which relates all to itself," Nicole acknowledged, "yet there is nothing so resembling the effects of Charity, as those of Self-love."[39]

Nicole's explanation was that even though we may be driven entirely by self-interest—"what a monster we harbour in our bosoms"—we nonetheless understand that acting with *apparent* charity toward others is often *in our own interest*. Our self-interest leads us to seek to please other people, and therefore to conceal the very self-interest that motivates us. Self-interest "knows so well how to trim it self up with the appearances of Charity, that it is almost impossible to know exquisitely what distinguishes it from Charity." It "imitates perfectly Charity . . . it makes us the same answer that charity does, and engages us in the same ways." In the end, charity and self-interest result in the same outward conduct. What appears as virtue may simply be a mask hiding vice. Once again, only God, inspecting the human heart, can know.[40]

One implication of Nicole's insight, fully in line with Jansenist Augustinian thinking, was that self-interest itself provides the answer to Hobbes's concern over humans' ability to live together with one another. Although each person's interest opposes the interests of others, "Self-love which is the cause of this war, will easily tell the way how to make them live in peace." Social order is possible, not despite but because of our corrupt nature. With self-interest guiding our behavior in this way, even "in Estates where Charity hath no admittance, because true Religion is banished from thence, men do not cease to live with as much peace, safety, and commmodiousness, as if they were in a Republick of Saints." Society maintains itself not just in the presence of its members' sinful self-love but by its effects—presumably because

God "providentially" designed the world in such a way that this could happen.[41] It is God's way of enabling his corrupt creature to survive.

Nicole also saw that the same principle applies to ordinary *economic* activity. Further, not only does our self-interest make us act in ways that resemble the actions to which charitable motives would lead us, for purposes of providing our material wants it may be even better. "This is the source and foundation of all Commerce practiced amongst men," he concluded.[42] In another of his essays, Nicole illustrated the point with the example of travelers' ability to find lodging in cities where they have no friends: "Going in the Country we meet almost every-where People that are ready to serve those that pass on the Road and who have Houses furnisht to entertain them." Innkeepers, he explained, provide these services not from charity but from their own self-interest. "What a piece of Charity would it be, to build for another an intire House, furnish it with all necessary Household-stuff; and after that deliver him up the Key?" But motivated by economic self-interest, the innkeeper does so cheerfully. In just the same way, "by the means and help of this Commerce, all necessaries for this life are in some sort supplied without intermixing Charity with it."[43]

Do these essential human outcomes—allowing men and women to live together in peace, providing for their material needs—therefore make self-interest morally good? Nicole, faithful to his religious principles, did not take this further step. In his argument self-interest turns out to have useful practical consequences, but it is still an aspect of humans' corrupt nature. Indeed, it is useful precisely because of their inherent moral shortcomings. Each man "loves himself without limits, and without measure; loves only himself, and refers all to himself."[44] But he nonetheless acts with the appearance of charity, because he knows that doing so is advantageous *to himself*. We cannot escape our inborn imperfection, but according to Nicole we should not applaud it, much less attach moral or religious value to it. Because God turns our evil actions to good ends, self-interest turns out to be beneficial in the secular world, but it is still spiritually fatal. Charity and self-love may achieve a practical symbiosis, but they remain morally opposed.

But whether morally acceptable or not, the fact that self-interested behavior had the consequences that Nicole (and Domat too) attributed to it bore significant implications for economics. Yet another Jansenist thinker, the administrative official and judge Pierre de Boisguilbert, pressed this insight further to develop an almost modern conception of economics.[45] A generation younger than Nicole and Domat, Boisguilbert was educated at the Port-Royal at a time when the shortcomings of Colbert's mercantilism were becoming increasingly evident. The attempt to run the French economy as a business—as if it were merely the Sun King's personal estate—simply was not working. Boisguilbert's contribution was to recognize that it was also unnecessary.

Boisguilbert's *Detail of France,* published in 1695 and pointedly subtitled *A Treatise on the Cause for the Reduction of Its Wealth and Means to Remediate It,* was the first serious attack on the French mercantilism of the day from an economic point of view.[46] His 1704 *Treatise on the Nature, Cultivation, Trade and Interest of Grains* (an important subject in a primarily agricultural economy) carried the analysis yet further.[47] The French authorities took notice. Ironically—in that Boisguilbert himself worked as a censor of the press—both books were banned when he republished them a few years later as part of his collected works. He was even exiled from the country for some months.

Boisguilbert argued that the conditions required for a country like France to achieve economic "opulence" were achievable without intervention by the state. The key was free trade, not top-down directives encouraging exports and prohibiting imports. By extending Nicole's reasoning to the economy as a whole, he argued that when individuals followed their own self-interest (even though it naturally conflicted with everyone else's) the actions they took collectively propelled the society to prosperity. Boisguilbert exploited this basic insight to make significant progress in thinking about the role and functioning of markets, including their unintended but potentially positive consequences— "reciprocal utility," as he thought of it.[48] Despite its early date, his analysis was highly sophisticated, showing an understanding of the role of prices that anticipated Adam Smith's contribution in *The Wealth of Nations* three-quarters of a century later. The *Treatise on Grains* even showed an understanding of the importance of competition in this process. "It is in the interest of all buyers that there be a number of merchants and many commodities," Boisguilbert wrote. "It is only the merchant's certainty that his neighbor, whose shop is filled with similar items, will be more reasonable, that makes him reasonable."[49]

Boisguilbert's writings had limited direct impact outside France and beyond his lifetime. (Remarkably, they have still not been translated.) But they shaped the thinking of the French-Irish banker and merchant Richard Cantillon, a generation younger. Cantillon's *Essay on the Nature of Trade* incorporated and further elaborated what Boisguilbert had done.[50] Apparently written in the early 1730s, the book did not appear in print until 1755, more than twenty years after Cantillon's death. It was freshly under discussion during Adam Smith's stay in France in the 1760s.[51] Smith owned a copy, and he referred to Cantillon's views on workers' wages in *The Wealth of Nations*.[52]

In the meanwhile, a similarly optimistic way of thinking about the long-standing problem of self-interest—but, importantly, without the Augustinian/Jansenist moralism of Nicole and even Boisguilbert—had burst forth in England, just after the turn of the eighteenth century, with Bernard Mandeville's sensational *The Fable of the Bees*. Mandeville too was a continental European—in his case a Dutch medical doctor, born in Rotterdam and educated in Leiden—but he had emigrated to London in the 1690s and he wrote in English.[53] He initially presented his argument in 1705 in the form of a satirical poem titled *The Grumbling Hive*, a snide reference to citizens of countries like England and his native Holland who enjoyed their elevated living standards but fretted about what they saw as luxury and corruption. In 1714 he expanded the poem into a book, including prose explanations of what the verses meant. He then further enlarged the book in 1723, in the wake of the South Sea Bubble collapse. It was this enlarged edition that attracted so much attention (and created a major scandal).

Mandeville's choice of a hive of bees to represent human society, including the economy, would have been thoroughly familiar to contemporary readers. Classical writers such as Plato and Aristotle and Virgil had drawn analogies between the well-ordered beehive and either the Greek *polis* or the Roman *civitas*. Medieval writers as well as artists had focused on bees' efficiency and selfless labor, often drawing a parallel to life in a monastery; many pictorial images of bees carried the text *non nobis* (not for ourselves). The association of bees with good order was familiar in the Renaissance as well. In Shakespeare's *Henry V*, the Archbishop of Canterbury meaningfully tells the young king, "for so work the honey bees, creatures that by a rule in nature teach the act of order to a peopled kingdom."[54] Many political theo-

Anonymous English print (circa 1692).
The Latin caption on the left, paraphrased from a line attributed
to Virgil, translates as "Thus we bees make honey, not for ourselves."
The caption on the right states that "All things are in books."

rists of the time, alluding to the role of the queen bee, also took the well-ordered beehive to represent the supposed advantages of government under an absolute monarchy.[55] In the sixteenth and seventeenth centuries the beehive was also a familiar religious symbol—sometimes even used for humor; *The Beehive of the Holy Roman Church*, a satirical tract first published in 1569, was reprinted numerous times over the next two hundred years. The English Puritans had likewise seen bees as symbols of the unity and obedience of Christian society.[56] (The same usage is familiar in America as well; the nineteenth-century Mormons christened Utah the Beehive State.)

The first question Mandeville needed to settle for purposes of his *Fable* was how to assess men's actions from a moral point of view. Perhaps sincerely, but more likely as a foil for the central thrust of his argument, he followed Nicole and Domat, whose thinking he knew well from his education in Holland, and behind them the "morality of intention" that had been a staple of religious teaching since the twelfth century:[57] what matters *for moral purposes* is people's intent, not whatever consequences follow from what they do. "Men are not to be judg'd by the Consequences that may succeed their Actions," he asserted, as if replying to Nicole, "but the Facts themselves, and the Motives which it shall appear they acted from."[58] Further, Mandeville adopted a rigorous notion of virtue that excluded any element of self-interest whatever; from a moral perspective, mixed motives were no better than mere self-interest.

In the landscape of contemporary English debate, therefore, Mandeville assumed the posture of the anti-Shaftesbury: virtue, properly defined, is largely beyond human nature; almost all of the actions we take are motivated, at least in part, by self-interest; most human behavior is therefore vice. His intended target was, in the first instance, what he saw as the hypocrisy of widely respected religious leaders who preached charity but all the while enjoyed the wealth and public esteem that their offices brought them. His broader purpose was to unsettle his comfortable readers more generally, forcing laymen too to question their benign image of themselves. Any supposed connection between wealth and virtue was unfounded.

Mandeville's real point, however, was the same as Nicole's. Vice, for him meaning no more than behavior motivated by individual self-interest, could nonetheless be useful to society. The subtitle he chose for his book—*Private Vices, Publick Benefits*—aptly summarized his central message. Taking aim at what he saw as the smug self-righteousness of the church, as well as the pious platitudes repeatedly proclaimed by supporters of private charities, he archly observed that "Pride and Vanity have built more Hospitals than all the Virtues together."[59]

In his enthusiasm for the *practical* implications of human behavior, therefore, Mandeville out-Shaftesburyed Shaftesbury. Further, just as Nicole had claimed (and as Boisguilbert later elaborated), he sought to show that this principle was especially likely to hold in matters of economic behavior. Indeed, in the economic sphere, vice in this sense is not just useful but *necessary*. Precisely because of what it was commonplace to consider vice, "the laziest and most unactive, the profligate and most mischievous are all forc'd to do something for the common good." Moreover, the benefits that other people reap from our so-called vicious actions are nothing that we either foresee or intend. Ordinary people, the "short-sighted Vulgar," can see no further than one link ahead in the chain of events that their actions set in motion. The law of unintended consequences, in time a mainstay of Enlightenment thinking, applied in force in the economic realm.[60]

The heart of Mandeville's argument was that economic self-interest leads each person (in his *Fable,* each bee) to seek out ways to be useful to everyone else, even if being useful merely means helping to satisfy others' foolish wants. The economy (the hive) therefore consists of "Millions endeavoring to supply Each other's Lust and Vanity." The result is not only full employment—"more Work than Labourers"—but a well-functioning society that enjoys public order while meeting the needs and desires of the individuals who comprise it. "Every Part was full of Vice," Mandeville acknowledged, "yet the whole Mass a Paradise." Led by no more than self-interest, even "the worst of all the Multitude Did something for the Common Good."[61]

Mandeville was explicit that what leads to this astounding prosperity and public order is each person's (each bee's) striving to enable other people to satisfy desires that, taken on their own, might seem contemptible. "Luxury [which to the seventeenth- or early-eighteenth-century ear conveyed an aura of immoral excess] Employ'd a Million of the Poor, and odious Pride a Million more. Envy it self and Vanity Were Ministers of Industry." Even the specific human foibles to which Mandeville pointed, which resonate with the lament of anti-consumerists both then and since, turned out to have the same beneficial effect: "Fickleness in Diet, Furniture and Dress . . . was made The very Wheel that turn'd the Trade."[62]

And there was to be no doubt that the sum of all this industrious activity, spurred by these individual vices, delivers a higher standard of living for everyone: "Thus Vice nurs'd Ingenuity, Which join'd with Time and Industry, Had carry'd Life's Conveniences, Its real Pleasures, Comforts, Ease, To such a Height, the very Poor Liv'd better than the Rich before."[63] In time, the theme of living standards so improved that today's poor live better than yesterday's rich became a staple of Western thinking about progress. Before the century was out, Adam Smith echoed the same observation. By the middle of the nineteenth century, the historian Thomas Babington Macaulay was scornful of those who looked back with nostalgia on "times when noblemen were destitute of comforts the want of which would be intolerable to a modern footman, when farmers and shop-keepers breakfasted on loaves the very sight of which would raise a riot in a modern workhouse," and "when men died faster in the purest country air than they now die in the most pestilential lanes of our towns."[64] The sentiment was Mandeville's long before.

While Mandeville was serious in his argument, he spiced his *Fable*—and no doubt greatly increased his readership—with a humorous tone combined with a wealth of satirical examples spoofing familiar figures in the society of his day: lawyers who stretched out litigation in order to increase their fees, doctors who prescribed needless medications, lazy and ignorant priests, dishonest government ministers, as well as everyday "Thieves and House-breakers . . . Pilferers and Robbers." Many of his examples were deliberately outrageous: "Sharpers, Parasites, Pimps, Players [meaning gamblers], Pick-pockets, Coiners [counterfeiters], Quacks, Soothsayers."[65] Likewise (in a separate essay that was part of the expanded book), the Fickle Strumpet, the haughty Dutchess, the profuse Rake, even the "Covetous and perjur'd Villain that squeez'd an immense Treasure from the Tears of Widows and Orphans."[66] All, he claimed, somehow make others better off even as they act out of nothing more than their own perverted self-interest. Other writers in English, such as John Houghton and Nicholas Barbon, had made similar arguments before (Houghton had even used the same image of consumers' driving the wheel of industry[67]). But it was Mandeville, with his gleeful embrace of everything self-righteous moralists deplored, who attracted intense public reaction.

In the same mocking tone, Mandeville also exploited the beehive image to make the further point that in the economic sphere such vice is not just beneficial, but necessary. At the end of the poem, the bees, lamenting their moral shortcomings, appeal to the gods to be rid of vice and filled with "Honesty" instead—and their wish is granted. But this newfound virtue squelches all industry. Without the fickle pursuit of fashion and luxury, there is no work to be done, economic activity collapses, and the hive's prosperity disappears. So many bees then flee, in the face of unemployment and enforced idleness, that those who remain can no longer defend the hive against its enemies.[68] Even the old mercantilist requisite of a population sufficient to provide for military security is impossible to maintain without vice driving the economy.

But of course vice here meant no more than acting on one's self-interest, and so Mandeville's point, like Nicole's before him, was also the irrelevance of intent for the practical consequences of a person's actions. The dichotomy between intent and consequences presumably held particular attraction for Mandeville as a practicing physician.[69]

Given the level of medical knowledge at the time, and the absence of regularized certification of the kind that even the most advanced countries did not institute for nearly another two centuries, it was difficult for Londoners of the time to distinguish good doctors from quacks. Both were treating their patients primarily from the same motive: to earn a living. But their intent, even their personal character more broadly, was irrelevant for this purpose. What mattered—at least what Mandeville hoped would matter to patients choosing between him and some other doctor—was the consequence of the treatment received. The fact that the physician's treatment ultimately sprang from the "vice" of his wanting to support himself and his family may have represented a moral failing on his part, an absence of sufficient Christian charity; but it was irrelevant to the medical result. For purposes of practical outcomes, Mandeville's repeated emphasis on the importance of intent to the morality of human behavior was at best a distraction. Rhetorically, it was a highly effective foil.

In the end, not only do private vices lead to public benefits, as Mandeville's subtitle proclaimed. More than that, "where the People would be great," vice—self-interest—is "necessary to the State." Seeking to eliminate vice, of this kind, is misguided, even dangerous. "Fools only strive To make a Great an Honest Hive."[70]

Why isn't this Adam Smith's invisible hand? And why, therefore, don't today's economists look to Mandeville, or perhaps Nicole, rather than Smith, as the father of their discipline?[71]

The eighteenth century was, intellectually, the Age of Newton; and the great scientist had taught inquiring people of that era to see the world in terms of system and mechanism. During a career that spanned forty years, Isaac Newton had revolutionized human understanding of the physical laws of the universe, including those governing motion and gravity, optics, astronomy, and many other natural phenomena besides. He had likewise created physical tools for scientific investigation, like the reflecting telescope, as well as conceptual tools like modern calculus. But overarching these specific contributions, Newton created a scientific worldview: observable phenomena—apples falling to the ground, the movement of the tides, planets orbiting the sun, a beam of light separating into a rainbow of colors—were reflections of a universal system that governed not just these visible manifestations but the entire physical world. And underlying this universal system was a set of laws and mechanisms that men were capable of understanding and applying. While the natural order may be unimaginably vast and complex, it is nonetheless possible to understand some of its elements and the laws that govern them.[72]

Newton's scientific eminence and his impact on the thinking of his contemporaries and the generations that followed are difficult to overestimate. He had arrived at Trinity College, Cambridge, in 1661, as a nineteen-year-old student. He stayed until 1701, when he accepted a political appointment—a kind of government pension, although he took the job very seriously for the remaining twenty-six years of his life—as master of the Royal Mint in London. In 1703 he was elected president of the Royal Society. He was reelected president annually, as long as he lived. In 1705 he became the first British scientist to be knighted.

Newton published his *Philosophiae Naturalis Principia Mathematica* in 1687. Even in Latin, the book's impact was enormous. The title notwithstanding—it translates as Mathematical Principles of Natural Philosophy—the *Principia* (as it is usually called) is primarily a work of what we would today consider physics. Among other subjects, it lays out Newton's laws of motion, the principle of universal gravitation, the laws governing planets' orbits, and the rest of what has since become known as Newtonian mechanics. Newton put the book through two further Latin editions within his lifetime, but not until 1729, two years after his death, was it finally translated into English.[73] Colin Maclaurin, a protégé of Newton's who then became a mathematics professor at the University of Edinburgh, further expanded the book's range of influence by producing a textbook presentation, published in 1748 (shortly after Maclaurin's own death). But well before then, the *Principia* had become part of the standard curriculum at Cambridge, Glasgow, and other universities, guiding young Englishmen and Scots to see the world in terms of system and mechanism.

To the eye of intellectuals educated along Newtonian lines, neither Nicole's essay nor Mandeville's *Fable* measured up as a substantive theory. Neither offered any system to its argument, nor any mechanism underlying what each clearly held out as a cause-and-effect relationship. Nicole perceived that people see it to be in their self-interest to act as if they have charitable motives, but he did not say why that was so. He merely offered an insightful observation. Mandeville repeatedly made the point that individuals' self-interest leads them to act in ways that enable others to meet their needs and satisfy their desires, but he did so by presenting a series of clever examples with no real explanation behind them. Both men, especially Mandeville, emphasized the economic sphere as the aspect of human life in which this insight was most applicable. But neither had anything to say about the conditions under which the beneficial effect of self-interest would or wouldn't obtain, or the mechanism that made it work. Even when Mandeville connected the aggregate effect of this individual self-interest to overall prosperity and the smooth running of society, he offered no explanation for why this was so.

Evidently pressed on the point, in the enlarged edition of the *Fable* Mandeville merely pointed to "the dexterous Management of a skillful Politician"—a notion consistent with the earlier Jansenist thinking but hardly a systematic mechanism that would have satisfied readers accustomed to think in Newtonian terms, and certainly not a viable basis for the line of thinking that went on to become economics.[74] More specifically, to anticipate the core of Smith's contribution three-fourths of a century later, neither Nicole nor Mandeville showed any awareness of the role of markets, or of the mechanism of competition, in bringing about the favorable outcomes they claimed for self-interested behavior (although Boisguilbert did). Despite their having put the basic insight forward long before Smith, therefore, there is really no puzzle over why today's business leaders and politicians who tout the merits of the market economy point to Smith, and not Nicole or Mandeville, as the fount of their ideas, nor over why we take *The Wealth of Nations,* rather than Nicole's essay or Mandeville's *Fable,* as the starting point of modern economics.

Nicole's essay generated relatively little discussion in the English-speaking world, and Boisguilbert's books never found an English translator. By contrast, Mandeville's *Fable* triggered an intense debate. Like Hobbes's work before, what Mandeville had written stirred widespread concern on grounds that it would undermine people's attachment to religion. But the response reflected secular interests too, both in popular literature and in the intellectual world. Henry Fielding, for example, repeatedly expressed dismay over Mandeville's ideas in his novels *Tom Jones* and *Joseph Andrews*. (Fielding meaningfully shortened the name to Mandevil; some other writers rendered it more obviously as Man-devil.[75]) At the same time, much of what the leading figures of the English and Scottish Enlightenment wrote about these questions during the middle two quarters of the eighteenth century—including Adam Smith in his early years, but before him, Francis Hutcheson, as well as David Hume—was in reaction to Mandeville.[76] At the time of his death, eighty-five years after Mandeville's poem first appeared, Smith was still working on revisions to what he had written about it in his own book on *The Theory of Moral Sentiments*.[77]

Part of this reaction was provoked, as Mandeville had presumably intended, by his satirical tone and the deliberately offensive examples (sharpers, parasites, pimps) that he chose to illustrate how Private Vices lead to Publick Benefits.[78] *The Fable of the Bees* appeared as the epitome of immoralism.[79] It gained further notoriety, soon after the enlarged edition's publication in 1723, when a grand jury in London brought charges against it as a "public nuisance"; in the end, the book got the added publicity without being censored. Beyond its mocking tone and the moral paradox of its core argument, the *Fable* also struck, again deliberately, on several highly sensitive issues under debate in early-eighteenth-century England and Scotland. In contrast to the pious intentions of the Societies for the Reformation of Manners, or the more concrete program of the Church of England's charity schools (an undertaking he publicly opposed), in seeking to instill virtue in Britain's youth, Mandeville's book amounted to an argument for skipping the moral edification and letting "vice" do its productive work. His casual attitude toward "vicious" behavior also at least appeared to condone the increasingly visible corruption of the administration of Robert Walpole, since 1721 Britain's de facto prime minister (the office did not yet formally exist).[80]

But the interested thinkers of the day were also intrigued by the substance of Mandeville's fundamental argument. While he had shown no understanding of how the private-vices-public-benefits result came about, he was clearly onto something of importance. Joseph Butler, a Church of England clergyman who some years later achieved eminence as Bishop of Bristol and Dean of St. Paul's, was quick to denounce the blatant amorality displayed in the *Fable's* 1723 edition. (Butler was also a proponent of the charity schools that Mandeville had scorned.) Along with the grand jury indictment, several widely discussed sermons that Butler preached in London in 1725 and 1726 added enormously to the public notoriety of the book and its author.

But despite his denunciation of the *Fable* on moral grounds, Butler, whose thinking frequently ranged beyond religion to engage with the broader philosophical debates of the time, ended up accepting the core of Mandeville's insight. Not only is self-love a duty commanded by Christ, he acknowledged ("love thy neighbor as thyself"); it is a "chief Security of our right Behaviour towards Society." Indeed, "in the common Course of Life, there is seldom any Inconsistency between our Duty and what is *called* Interest." Butler's explanation for this fortuitous coincidence was a view of the harmonious relationship between God and man, and of the benevolence of God in endowing man with rational and sociable instincts—"Reason and cool Reflection"— grounded in a Christian rendering of classical stoic philosophy.[81] Men were instruments in the hand of Providence, likely to do public good as well as private. As the stoics had maintained, the true path to virtue lay in achieving a proper balance among our disparate and often conflicting desires.[82] By improperly construing self-love as vice (and then cynically applauding it as such), he maintained, Mandeville had falsely given an unholy interpretation to behavior that was actually both morally and religiously acceptable. Bishop Butler's thinking carried significant weight in the subsequent development of thinking about the role of markets and commerce, and both Hutcheson and Hume acknowledged his influence.[83]

Francis Hutcheson, writing in 1725, likewise accepted elements of the argument offered by both Nicole and Mandeville. Like Nicole, he recognized the difficulty in attempting to sort out even our own motives, much less those of others. "As all Men have Self-Love, as well as Benevolence," he wrote, "these two Principles may jointly excite a Man to the same Action." As a result, "In most Cases it is impossible for Men to know how far their Fellows are influenc'd by the one or other of the Principles."[84] And following Mandeville, Hutcheson agreed that no matter how generous or public-spirited we might aspire for people to be, at least some element of self-interest is needed to induce them to do the work that any society needs done. Even "the most extensive affections could scarce engage a wise man to industry," if he derived no personal gain from it.[85] The thought was hardly Hutcheson's alone. At about the same time Charles Rollin, rector of the University of Paris and yet another Jansenist, asked, "If men were all at ease, all rich & opulent, who would bother to plow the land, dig mines, and sail across the high seas?"[86]

But Hutcheson nonetheless clung to a more benign interpretation of underlying human nature, along the lines suggested earlier by Shaftesbury: we are born with the five familiar physical senses plus a moral sense that underlies our instinctive approval of virtue, and disapproval of vice. (Going Shaftesbury one better, Hutcheson also thought we have a seventh sense, an inborn sense of beauty that enables us to make aesthetic judgments.) This inborn moral sense gives us a natural disposition to benevolence toward our fellow creatures, and hence a desire not only to be happy ourselves but to see others happy too. As a result, *we* derive satisfaction from whatever we do to help other people achieve what *they* want. And doing so is therefore in *our* self-interest. For Hutcheson, as for Shaftesbury, virtue and self-interest coincide. This idea too had substantial popular appeal. Alexander Pope's *Essay on Man,* in 1734, declared "That *Reason, Passion,* answer *one great Aim/ That true Self-love* and *Social* are the *same.*"[87]

Like Butler's Christian stoicism, Hutcheson's moral-sense interpretation offered an alternative explanation for the prosperity that Mandeville's beehive enjoyed—if, that is, one had sufficient confidence in the benevolence that this supposed moral sense fostered. But both Butler's response and Hutcheson's failed to meet Mandeville's challenge on its own terms. For Mandeville, or at least from the perspective of the ideas that he (sincerely or not) set forth in the *Fable,* acting out of self-interest is still a vice even if the self-interest motivating our actions is merely to enjoy the sight of other people's happiness; it is, in the end, doing what makes *us* happy. Moreover, Mandeville would hardly have accepted such an expansive notion of self-interest to begin with.

David Hume also wrote in reaction to Mandeville. "Men of libertine principles," he wrote in 1752—with the *Fable* still prominently under discussion, there could be no mistaking whom he had in mind—"bestow praises even on vicious luxury, and represent it as highly advantageous to society." Yet, "on the other hand, men of severe morals blame even the most innocent luxury." From a famously outspoken critic of organized religion and the clergy, here too Hume's readers knew whom he meant.[88] But concern over the moral corruption of material comforts was hardly limited to the church. The various definitions of "luxurious" given in Samuel Johnson's *Dictionary* included "lustful," "libidinous," and "enslaved to pleasure."[89]

What, then, should a reasonable person conclude? Following the movement in some elements of English thinking to strip away the moral baggage associated with the concept of luxury,[90] but also with his broader goal in mind to reconstruct the study of man along the lines of what Newton had achieved for our understanding of the physical world, Hume pushed the argument away from its origins in distinguishing virtuous actions from vicious ones. Was the desire for material luxury, even including Mandeville's fickleness in diet, furniture, and dress, truly a vice? Did it necessarily lead to effeminacy and loss of "martial spirit"? Hume demurred. "Luxury is a word of very uncertain signification," he maintained, and so "the bounds between the virtue and the vice cannot here be fixed exactly." Hence no gratification, however sensual, could of itself be deemed vicious. One reason was that what one age sees as a luxury in time comes to be viewed as a necessity. More important, however, rather than coupling poverty and virtue as medieval religious thinkers as well as more recent philosophers like Algernon Sidney had done, Hume emphasized the *moral improvement* that followed from living in what he called "the more luxurious ages." More than two thousand years before, Aristotle had suggested that higher living standards foster democracy.[91] Hume now argued that a higher material standard of living promotes "industry, knowledge and humanity," and ultimately liberty.[92] Higher living standards brought the spread of science, improved prospects for self-government, more benevolent behavior, and more polite manners. The theme of material progress leading to moral improvement ran throughout his later *History of England,* and in time it became a centerpiece of Enlightenment thinking.

Josiah Tucker, who had been Bishop Butler's chaplain in Bristol, followed his mentor (and Hutcheson too) in finding a religious basis for accepting that self-love leads people to seek ways of gain that, while serving themselves, also promote the public good—all the while explicitly rejecting the "selfish hypothesis" of Mandeville as well as the larger cynicism and skepticism that he associated with both Mandeville and

Hobbes. Writing in 1750, nearly a quarter-century after Butler first denounced the book, he exclaimed, "What an Absurdity, therefore, was it in the Author of *The Fable of the Bees,* to say, *That Private Vices are Publick Benefits!*" To the contrary, "It is *Virtue* alone, which can make a Nation *flourish*."[93]

More so than his mentor Butler, Tucker went on to write explicitly about economic issues including the damage done by Britain's mercantile system. By the middle of the century, Tucker was offering influential ideas on the economic relations between advanced and poor countries, and between the rich and the poor within any one country, as well as calling for free trade to replace mercantilism and monopoly. Anticipating Adam Smith in *The Wealth of Nations,* more than two decades later, Tucker also had a good understanding of the importance of specialization in production—what Smith called "division of labour."[94] But the lesson drawn from the debate over Mandeville's *Fable* remained a centerpiece. Self-love was "the great Mover of created Beings." It was the principle that "all Arts and Sciences, and the very Being of Government and Commerce, depend upon."[95] The task was "to make Self-interest and Social coincide."[96] Adam Smith owned several of Tucker's published writings,[97] and in all likelihood knew him personally via their mutual friend Hume.

As of the middle of the eighteenth century, therefore, the stage was set for a new breakthrough: a way of accounting for Nicole's and Mandeville's paradox that would satisfy the Newtonian standard of systematic explanation based on a clearly understandable causal mechanism. The way forward presented at least three forks in the intellectual path.

First, should the explanation focus narrowly on the economic sphere of human activity, as Mandeville had done, or seek to identify and explain beneficial effects of self-interested behavior more broadly—as, for example, Hutcheson's moral-sense theory had attempted to do?

Second, what should the explanation assume about the intent, and expectations, of those who acted in this way? Should it follow Mandeville in viewing people as the shortsighted vulgar who are incapable of seeing more than one link ahead in any causally driven chain of events, or, like Shaftesbury before him and Hutcheson after, instead assume that even though people are behaving out of self-interest they nonetheless foresee the consequences of what they are about to do, including the likelihood that others will benefit?

And third, should this line of thought continue in the long-standing tradition that framed such questions in the context of human virtue versus vice, as Nicole, Domat, Mandeville, Shaftesbury, and Hutcheson had all done? Or would it be better, taking Hume's lead, to drop the moral language of vice and virtue and instead simply focus on whether, and if so how and under what conditions, behavior motivated by self-interest has practically beneficial consequences?

Adam Smith tried both paths on each of the three.

3

Philosophical Underpinnings

It is chiefly from this regard to the sentiments of mankind that we
pursue riches and avoid poverty.

—ADAM SMITH

Adam Smith was a product of the Scottish Enlightenment, and he
lived to become one of the period's most outstanding figures. Born
in 1723 to an educated though hardly prosperous family in the village
of Kirkcaldy, across the Firth of Forth from Edinburgh, he attended the
local parish school and at fourteen entered the university at Glasgow.[1]
The standard curriculum taught there in the 1730s clearly shaped
his future thinking: instruction in the Greek classics, importantly
including the stoic philosophers (Smith's particular favorites, then and
later, were Epictetus and Marcus Aurelius); in logic, using the text coauthored by the French Jansenists Pierre Nicole and Antoine Arnauld,
as well as John Locke's *Essay Concerning Human Understanding*; in
mathematics; and in physics, including astronomy and Newtonian
mechanics.

Especially significant for the development of Smith's thinking, the
curriculum also included instruction in natural theology: the study of
God based not on authoritative revelation, as recounted in the Bible,
but instead on logical principles and on observation of the human and
physical world in which we live, which God presumably created.[2] But

the field of natural theology, as taught at the time, was not limited to subjects narrowly identified with religion as such. It incorporated moral philosophy, as well as natural jurisprudence—meaning, in parallel, the study of legal principles based on logic and observation as opposed to learning the specific laws enacted by a country's political authority. In time, Smith's work encompassed both of these inquiries. The instructor at Glasgow who most influenced his thinking was Francis Hutcheson, the professor of moral philosophy. More than forty years later, Smith affectionately wrote of him as "the never to be forgotten Dr Hutcheson."[3]

In an era when science and religion were still mostly seen as allies rather than in conflict, natural theology also included the physical sciences. As the Puritan minister Richard Baxter had summarized the connection nearly a century earlier, physics is the knowledge of the knowable works of God.[4] The same idea is also apparent from the title of a widely heralded late-seventeenth-century book by the Cambridge naturalist (and also a clergyman) John Ray: *The Wisdom of God Manifested in the Works of the Creation.*[5] One of the texts used for instruction in natural theology during Smith's time at Glasgow was Newton's *Principia*—just as Newton had intended. As the great scientist explained, some years after the book's publication, "When I wrote my Treatise about our System, I had an Eye upon such Principles as might work with considering Men, for the Belief of a Deity, and nothing can rejoice me more than to find it useful for that Purpose."[6]

Studying Newton had a major influence on Smith's thinking.[7] In his essay on the history of astronomy, which he apparently began as a young man but did not allow to be published until after he died—it was the only as-yet-unpublished work that he did not ask his friend Hume to destroy on his death—Smith lavishly expressed his admiration of Newton as not just a scientist in today's sense, but a philosopher. (The essay's full title was "The Principles which lead and direct Philosophical Enquiries; illustrated by the History of Astronomy.") The superior genius and sagacity of Sir Isaac Newton, he wrote, constituted "the greatest and most admirable improvement that was ever made in philosophy." Newton's ideas had a "firmness and solidity that we should in vain look for in any other system." They amounted to no less than the greatest discovery that ever was made by man.[8]

A large part of what Smith so admired in Newton's thinking was its unity and coherence: "the discovery of an immense chain of the most important and sublime truths, all closely connected together, by one capital fact, of the reality of which we have daily experience."[9] In the public lectures that first brought him to the attention of Edinburgh's intellectual elite, he distinguished Newton's system, with its ability to explain many different phenomena from just a few fundamental principles, from that of Aristotle, which offered a different principle for each phenomenon to be explained. Newton's system, he told his audience, was greatly superior to Aristotle's.[10] In this regard as well, it was clear that Smith thought the import of what Newton had achieved, indeed of the physical sciences as a whole, was broader than just science in today's narrower sense. At the time of his death, he owned copies of not only the *Principia* but four other books by Newton as well.[11]

At age seventeen Smith took up a scholarship at Balliol College, Oxford, where he remained for six years. No doubt he used the time to read extensively, and to think about what he read. But he produced no serious writings of his own during these years, and he left little record of what he read or what he thought. He apparently found scant intellectual stimulation from either the dons or his fellow students during these years. "In the university of Oxford," he later recalled, "the greater part of the publick professors have, for these many years, given up altogether even the pretence of teaching."[12] He returned home in the late summer of 1746.

Back in Kirkcaldy, superbly educated but at twenty-three lacking paid employment, Smith soon came to the attention of Edinburgh's intellectual elite. Edinburgh, indeed Scotland as a whole, was struggling to recover from the Jacobite Rebellion that had ended only that April with the defeat of the Stuart forces at the battle of Culloden. But the post-Rebellion period also marked the outset of what proved the height of the Enlightenment era in Scotland. Through the patronage of Henry Home, Lord Kames, a wealthy Scottish lawyer and also a prominent thinker about government and politics (and very distantly related to David Hume[13]), Smith received a commission to deliver two sets of public lectures: one on rhetoric, the other on jurisprudence.

The lectures, which he presented in Edinburgh between 1748 and 1751, provided an opportunity to begin work on the project, inspired by Hume, of building a systematic scientific study of human behavior comparable to what Newton had achieved for the physical world. The objective of this program, as Hume had articulated it in his *Treatise of Human Nature* a decade before (written before he reached his twenty-fifth birthday), was to construct "a compleat system of the sciences, built on a foundation almost entirely new."[14] Smith enthusiastically joined the effort. Although he did not publish what he wrote at the time, aspects of his later thinking, including parts of *The Wealth of Nations* as well as a course of lectures that he taught at Glasgow (not published until long after his death), seem to have taken their initial shape from these early public lectures in Edinburgh.

More immediately, the Edinburgh lectures enhanced Smith's reputation and visibility in Scottish intellectual circles—enough so that when the professorship of logic and metaphysics at Glasgow fell vacant, in late 1750, Smith was elected. He returned to the university in time to start teaching when the new academic year began the next October. A month later, however, the professorship of moral philosophy became vacant, and the following spring Smith was elected to that position instead. At age twenty-nine, he now occupied what had been his teacher Francis Hutcheson's chair.

The chief product of Smith's years of teaching at Glasgow was *The Theory of Moral Sentiments*, published in 1759. Following Hume, but also before him classical philosophers such as Lucretius, Smith took the distinguishing characteristic of our species to be the human imagination, and he built his theory around it.[15] For both men, the activity of the imagination was in part a search for order in the universe. Confronted with the vast and seemingly chaotic complexity of the world in which we live, we feel an instinctive need to impose some sense of order on our perceptions, and it is our imagination that enables us to do so.[16] (In this respect Einstein's view of the origin of a person's worldview—*Weltbild* in the original German—followed closely what Hume especially had thought nearly two centuries before.)

This desire for order is particularly urgent in our dealing with other people. Smith argued that our mental ability to put ourselves in others' shoes—to see matters as others saw them, while of course remaining nothing other than ourselves—was the key to our ability to engage in social interaction. (He would probably have been fascinated with today's study of autism as in part the *in*ability to imagine others' impressions.) "As we have no immediate experience of what other men feel," he wrote, "it is by the imagination only that we can form any conception of what are his sensations. . . . By the imagination we place ourselves in his situation."[17]

To be sure, this putting ourselves in another person's situation, as Smith called it, was merely an "illusion of the imagination."[18] But the illusion was sufficient for his purposes and it laid the basis for his thinking about economic behavior that still lay years ahead. Although he did not pursue the point in this first book, the social interactions that such an illusion makes possible naturally include our economic dealings. Commerce, centered on different people's producing different goods and then exchanging them among one another, does not emerge out of nothing. In *The Wealth of Nations,* Smith simply assumed that we are able to supply other people with the goods or services they want, once they give us adequate incentive to do so. (Mandeville implicitly made the same assumption in his *Fable.*) But that ability in turn presumes the prior capacity to know what it is that other people want. He had no need to explain this prior awareness because part of what he had established in *The Theory of Moral Sentiments* was that our imagination enables us to make at least a reasonable guess of what other people think, and therefore what they are likely to want.

The imagination was the foremost of the human attributes on which Smith based his argument in *The Theory of Moral Sentiments,* but others mattered too. Proceeding in the mode of Newton, Smith grounded his analysis on a set of first principles—in this case a set of characteristics of the human species—that he simply took as observed fact. Our having imagination was merely one of them. A second was man's intrinsically sociable nature, deriving pleasure from interaction with other people while also caring about their well-being. Smith made no effort to explain where these inborn social preferences came from either (other than to acknowledge that without the imagination our caring about others' well-being would be meaningless); they were just part of our makeup. "Nature, when she formed man for society," he asserted, "endowed him with an original desire to please, and an original aversion to offend his brethren."[19]

This idea clearly echoed his teacher Hutcheson's claim of an inborn moral sense, as well as Hutcheson's views of man's inherent benevolence—so that our moral sense not only enables us to distinguish right from wrong but also makes us *prefer* to see right done to our fellow human beings. Instead of positing some kind of sixth sense, however, Smith simply asserted as an observed fact that an interest in the well-being of other people, including a desire to please them and a reluctance to offend, is part of human nature. And beneath it, our imagination is what gives us the ability to anticipate whether the other people about whom we care in this way will be pleased or offended by whatever action we might think of taking.

A further essential assumption enabled Smith to link this highly optimistic theory of human sociability with implications for government, always the ultimate objective of Enlightenment social theorizing. Smith took human happiness to be an unquestioned goal. Why? Because, as he put it in a later revision of the book, "that great, benevolent and all-wise Being who directs all the movements of nature . . . is determined . . . to maintain in it, at all times, the greatest possible quantity of happiness." Who, or what, was this all-wise Being? Perhaps God? In *The Theory of Moral Sentiments* Smith used other such locutions as well (and likewise with initial capitals[20]): the great Director of the universe, the great Conductor of the universe, even "that divine Being whose benevolence and wisdom have from all eternity contrived and conducted the immense machine of the universe." Elsewhere in the book Smith was more explicit, explaining that the administration of the great system of the universe is "the business of God and not of man." And so the answer is presumably yes, Smith was attributing these features of our world to divine origin.[21] But regardless of whether such formulations were a genuine appeal to divine intent or merely a personification of nature couched in the conventional vocabulary of the time, the implication—which again echoed Hutcheson and Hume, but marked a significant departure from seventeenth-century thinking— was that the purpose of human institutions, including government, was to promote human happiness.

And what makes people happy? Here Smith turned to his training in the stoics—but with a twist that reflected the emphasis of Hume, indeed of the Enlightenment as a whole, on man's role as a social being. The essence of happiness is tranquility and enjoyment, Smith stated, just as Epictetus or Marcus Aurelius would have claimed, and in a similar vein he went on to praise the familiar stoic virtues "of self-denial, of self-government, of that command of the passions which subjects all the movements of our nature to what our own dignity and honor, and the propriety of our own conduct require." But the stock caricature of the stoic as a self-controlled and self-contained man of honor and virtue, relishing calm tranquility in austere isolation, is not what Smith had in mind. True, leading a tranquil life was the key to happiness; but instead of social isolation, "society and conversation . . . are the most powerful remedies for restoring the mind to its tranquility."[22] What interested Smith was not man as a singular organism, but the possibilities and challenges to which our inherently sociable nature gives rise. Smith began as a moral philosopher and he became an economist; he was not a biologist.

The principal upshot of these interrelated assumptions—our capacity for imagination, our inherently social nature, our desire for happiness together with the essentially social origins of happiness itself—is what Smith famously labeled, in the title he gave to his book's opening chapter, Sympathy. In this respect too, he was following his mentor. Twenty years earlier, Hume had written, "No quality of human nature is more remarkable, both in itself and in its consequences, than that propensity we have to sympathize with others."[23] Sympathy, which followed from the human imagination, became the centerpiece of Smith's theory of what he called our moral sentiments.[24]

Regardless of how selfish man may sometimes seem, Smith assumed, "there are evidently some principles in his nature, which interest him in the fortune of others and render their happiness necessary to him." But interest in other people's happiness—this Sympathy—makes sense only because our imagination enables us to infer whether they are happy or not. It is the "imaginary change of situation upon which his sympathy is founded," he explained. Imagination, however, for this purpose is more than mere dreaming. In our minds we change places with someone else, as we might in a dream; but all the while we are aware that we are doing so. As a result, this "changing places in fancy" is also "the source of our fellow-feeling." And with our intrinsically social nature, we look for this sense to be mutual, not just having such feelings for others but being the object of others' feelings for us as well: "nothing pleases us more than to observe in other men a fellow-feeling."[25] One readily observable consequence is that we gladly do in the presence of others what we would regard as a waste of time if we were alone (for example, reading aloud from a book we have already read). The *shared* aspect of the experience is what matters.

Importantly for Smith's line of argument, however—though not for the economic implications he was later to draw from it—the sympathy that gives rise both to this capacity for fellow-feeling on our part and to our desire for fellow-feeling from others is merely a reflexive consequence of human nature. It is not motivated by any conscious self-interest (at least not as Smith saw it), and so his argument (he believed) did not fall into the trap laid by Mandeville's specifying that anything we do even partly in our own self-interest constitutes a vice. Instead, human sympathy—our capacity for fellow-feeling and our desire for it—is simply a Newtonian first principle, assumed on the basis of observation and introspection rather than derived from some more primitive underlying proposition. Rather than stemming from our self-interest, in which case it would have been suspect on Mandeville's grounds, what Smith intended by sympathy was simply part of our inborn nature. But it serves as a crucial counterforce that prevents our yielding to self-interest to an extent that might threaten the everyday social fabric.

Smith was well aware of the problems posed by self-interest, and part of what he found attractive in stoic philosophy was the aspiration to overcome them. In his early thinking as reflected in *The Theory of Moral Sentiments*—before his insight into the role of markets, indeed before he turned his attention to specifically economic behavior at all—our natural sympathy is what served this purpose. "To feel much for others and little for ourselves," he wrote, "to restrain our selfish, and to indulge our benevolent affections, constitutes the perfection of human nature."[26] Smith understood that mankind would never attain perfection, but knowing in what direction perfection lay could be a valuable guide to what was practically achievable.

How, then, do we judge our actions? According to Smith even our moral judgments are socially based. "Since our sentiments concerning beauty of every kind, are so much influenced by custom and fashion," he explained, "it cannot be expected, that those concerning the beauty of conduct should be entirely exempted from the dominion of those principles."[27] The specific social mechanism that he suggested for this influence followed from our desire for fellow-feeling with other people, together with our ability (again, in imagination) to know what other people are thinking. Endowed with those attributes, we assess our actions not purely internally but as we think others will see them.

Smith's mental construct for this purpose was an "impartial spectator" whom we imagine as seeing our actions as "every indifferent person" would—in other words, as anyone would who has no personal stake in the matter.[28] (His fellow Scot Robert Burns, who expressed admiration for Smith's *Theory of Moral Sentiments,* later captured the idea in his famous line "O wad some Pow'r the giftie gie us/*To see oursels as others see us.*"[29]) Further, Smith appealed to this concept of the impartial spectator to make clear that what he meant by sympathy was different from the more familiar concept of pity, or admiration, in how we regard other people. The sympathy that we feel for someone subjected to injustice and abuse, for example, is not "the rage which they are apt to excite in the breast of the sufferer." It is "the indignation which they naturally call forth in that of the impartial spectator."[30]

The parallel between Smith's impartial spectator and the standard notion of the individual conscience—and more than that, the resonance of the impartial spectator with the introspection and self-evaluation called for by many religious traditions—is obvious, and Smith did not shy away from it. "It is the great precept of nature," he wrote, "to love ourselves only as we love our neighbor, or what comes to the same thing, as our neighbor is capable of loving us."[31] And how do we know whether our conduct is such that our neighbor can love us? Only because we are creatures with imagination. In short, the imagination, guided by our sense of the impartial spectator, has *ethical* force as well.[32] But in Smith's rendering, this ethical force grows out of nothing more than inborn human nature, without the familiar appeal to either religion or some extra sense. Moreover, because the impartial spectator is merely an "indifferent" onlooker, and those whose love we value are no more than our neighbors, this ethical force is rooted in the social conventions of the circumstances in which we find ourselves. It is through society that we catch sight of ourselves. Smith did not pretend to lay out a universal morality.[33]

The idea that our imagination enables us to see ourselves as an impartial spectator would see us also led Smith to a further distinction that, in time, more directly informed his economic thinking: between praise and what he called "praise-worthiness," between being respected and being respectable. To be sure, we desire both. Nature endows us with not only a desire that others approve of us but, further, a desire to be what others *ought* to approve of. Moreover, Smith was unambiguous that, of the two, praise-worthiness—to be "the natural and proper object of praise"—matters to us more. (Correspondingly, we have a "horror of blame-worthiness.")[34]

What if we receive praise without being praise-worthy—for example, if someone gains public recognition, or wins a medal or a prize, for something that was actually done by another person? Smith dismissed such undeserved accolades as ignorant, and any pleasure we might take in them as unworthy. Only the weakest and most superficial people, he wrote, take satisfaction from such unmerited praise. Conversely, if we fail to receive the recognition that is properly our due, we should take comfort in reflecting that although no praise has actually been bestowed on us, our conduct has been such as to deserve it. Here too, our natural desire to be what *ought* to be approved of has ethical force. It restrains our self-interested behavior through our own natural inclinations, without having to rely on either religion or the state.[35] It also serves a crucial economic function, underpinning the trust in other human beings, including strangers, that allows the ordinary transactions that are the stuff of everyday commercial interactions to take place.

In addition to laying these foundations for understanding what motivates individual behavior, in this first major work Smith also anticipated a key part of the line of analysis that he developed with such force (and to such acclaim) nearly two decades later in *The Wealth of Nations*. Indeed, the analysis in which he appealed to the image of the "invisible hand" in *The Theory of Moral Sentiments*—he used the phrase only once in each book—comes closer to our commonly accepted understanding of what this now standard metaphor conveys than the context in which he did so in his later book. In both cases, the idea Smith was seeking to illustrate was the familiar Enlightenment principle of unintended consequences. The profound implications of this idea for economic arrangements, in particular competitive markets, was the subject of Smith's second book. But even in *The Theory of Moral Sentiments*, the setting he used to illustrate it was an economic one.

The specific issue to which Smith applied the invisible hand image in his first book was the extreme concentration of land ownership. Landholding in Scotland in the eighteenth century was even more highly concentrated than in England, and it remains so today. Vast estates owned by the descendants of feudal fief holders accounted

for great tracts of arable land and pasturage, while much of the agricultural workforce consisted of landless tenants and paid laborers.
And, as always, urban workers produced no basic foodstuffs. A natural concern, therefore, might be that most of the country's citizens
would have too little to eat. But that outcome is not what Smith and
his contemporaries thought they observed. Instead, "in ease of body
and peace of mind, all the different ranks of life are nearly upon
a level."[36]

How could this be so? The answer, Smith explained—the force
underlying this nearly equal distribution of food despite the extreme
inequality of land ownership—was nothing other than self-interested
behavior, channeled through the law of unintended consequences.
"The proud and unfeeling landlord," he supposed, "views his extensive
fields and, without a thought for the wants of his brethren, in imagination consumes himself the whole harvest that grows upon them."
But the landlord's thinking in this way is of no consequence because
"the capacity of his stomach . . . will receive no more than that of the
meanest peasant." Meanwhile, the landlord derives pleasure from items
other than food, including goods not yielded up in any direct way by
the fields he owns. Either to reflect his contempt for rich landowners, or perhaps merely to heighten the force of the argument, Smith
pictured these goods as "baubles and trinkets" of no essential value;
their appeal is merely to the landlord's vanity.[37] But like the fickleness
and vanity of Mandeville's bees, that vanity provides employment, and
therefore ultimately food, for the townspeople.

While Smith did not explicitly examine the market mechanism
here—that came only later, in *The Wealth of Nations*—the role of economic exchange was central to his explanation nonetheless: in order
to acquire whatever other items he desires, the landlord is "obliged" to
give up most of the food his lands produce to the workmen and merchants who provide him with the various baubles and trinkets he wants.
Whether through direct barter or by monetary transactions (goods
for cash and then cash for goods), the landlord trades the agricultural
produce that is his for the silver shoe buckles and fancy buttons that
he seeks to satisfy his vanity. As a result, he, and the townspeople on
the other side of this exchange, "are led by an invisible hand to make
nearly the same distribution of the necessaries of life which would have
been made, had the earth been divided into equal portions among all
its inhabitants."[38] The argument was a powerful one, and Smith's con-

temporaries took note of it. Edward Gibbon, very near the beginning of his *Decline and Fall,* offered a version of it to characterize the early Roman Empire.[39]

By choosing an example centered on basic human necessity to illustrate the principle at work—nothing is more essential than having enough to eat—even in his first book Smith was already embracing the idea, by then familiar from such thinkers as Nicole and Mandeville, and most recently Josiah Tucker, that behavior motivated merely by one's own self-interest can make others better off as well.[40] In the end, the townspeople have plenty of food. Moreover, Smith's description of how this result comes about was emphatic: the landlord acts "without a thought for the wants of his brethren." Although he ends up providing for the sustenance of the population as a whole, he does so "without intending it, without knowing it."[41]

Was this seemingly Providential outcome the result of some kind of divine intervention? Many of Smith's readers over the years have thought so.[42] After all, there was a long-standing tradition, going back at least to Plato, of masking the role of God behind an imagined invisible hand.[43] Elsewhere in *The Theory of Moral Sentiments* Smith observed that "When by natural principles we are led to advance those ends, which a refined and enlightened reason would recommend to us," the ultimate cause of our actions "in reality is the wisdom of God."[44] But just as he avoided saying who or what the great Director of the universe was, in his discussion of how everyone had enough to eat despite the highly skewed ownership of land Smith simply invoked the invisible hand and left it at that.

At this point in the evolution of his ideas, he had not yet arrived at the fully developed principle that economists today, following *The Wealth of Nations,* think of as *the* invisible hand. While the exchange of food for trinkets is central to Smith's example, whether this exchange takes place in a market, and if so whether the participants on either side of the market are competing with one another, are not yet part of the story. But the principle of unintended and unforeseen consequences is plain enough, and the chief consequence here is that the actions the landlord undertakes, even though intended solely in his own interest, also "advance the interest of the society."[45]

.   .   .

The setting for Smith's invoking the invisible hand metaphor in *The Theory of Moral Sentiments* also reveals an attitude toward consumers' behavior that partly undercuts what has subsequently become the conventional interpretation of his core economic argument—a reminder that Smith's thinking was far richer than the simplified (and politically sanitized) characterization, sometimes bordering on caricature, that often pervades appeals to his imprimatur today. In contrast to the reverence that much of current economic thinking attaches to whatever choices individual consumers bring to their purchases, Smith had little respect for consumer preferences, especially among the rich.[46] To the contrary, in this regard his thinking echoed what Mandeville had written about the vanity and fickleness and folly of his *Fable*'s bees. What motivates the landlord in Smith's example is merely to accumulate baubles and trinkets. Elsewhere in *The Theory of Moral Sentiments* Smith dismissed such objects as "toys . . . baubles . . . of which the whole utility is certainly not worth the fatigue of bearing the burden." Further, the desire for such objects is not just foolish but in many instances harmful. "How many people ruin themselves," he asked, by "laying out money on trinkets of frivolous utility?"[47]

Smith likewise thought most people attach exaggerated value not just to individual objects but to wealth and power more generally—and that this misperception too often proves morally harmful. "This disposition to admire, and almost to worship, the rich and the powerful," he wrote, is "the great and most universal cause of the corruption of our moral sentiments." Repeating the dismissive language he used in denigrating people's desire for individual consumer items, he argued that even "wealth and greatness are mere trinkets of frivolous utility." What really matters is moral character, and "there are hypocrites of wealth and greatness, as well as of religion and virtue."[48]

Like Mandeville, however, Smith saw an economic usefulness to these misguided preferences—in his example, they enabled town dwellers to obtain food and other necessities—and he therefore refrained from any injunction that people should reform their ways. Mandeville had defended such foibles as "the very Wheel that turn'd the Trade."[49] Smith too, despite his scorn for people's desire to satisfy what he labeled frivolous desires, often centered on trifling or even contemptible objects, nonetheless concluded "it is well that nature imposes upon us in this manner." His explanation was almost a paraphrase of Mandeville's: "It is this deception which rouses and keeps in continual motion the industry of mankind."[50]

Wholly apart from the danger to our moral character, Smith offered a sophisticated psychological argument for thinking that many people are misguided not just in their desire for specific objects they might buy but even in their aspiration for a higher material standard of living overall. The reason, he believed, is that they fail to anticipate that getting used to some new living standard—either higher or lower—will change the way they see matters. "The great source of both the misery and disorders of human life," he wrote, "seems to arise from overrating the difference between one permanent situation and another": between riches and poverty, as well as between obscurity and having a public reputation. To the contrary, it was a never-failing certainty that all men, sooner or later, will accommodate themselves to whatever becomes their permanent situation. Because of this human capacity to adapt to whatever life brings us, his beloved stoics had been right that "between one permanent situation and another there was, with regard to real happiness, no essential difference." In contrast to Smith's usual emphasis on the power of the human imagination, here the cause of the misery and disorders that he saw ensuing from our pointlessly seeking a higher standard of living is a *failure* of the imagination: we are so focused on putting ourselves in someone else's shoes that we neglect the new shoes we will be wearing ourselves once we become accustomed to our new living standard.[51]

The idea that human happiness is therefore mostly independent of our material standard of living, once we have surpassed some minimum level (which, alas, too many of his poor countrymen failed to reach), reflected Smith's training in stoic philosophy. But his explanation for this phenomenon, grounded in the way our opinions and preferences adapt to whatever living standard we become accustomed to having, framed the argument in a more Newtonian way by positing an explicit mechanism to underlie what the stoics had taught. To what extent this form of adaption (the modern term for it) blunts the connection between living standards and the happiness of either individuals or an entire society remains a highly contested subject of debate among economists and psychologists today.[52] So does the question of whether people might anticipate, and take into account in advance, that how they view either their overall living standard or their consumption of specific items will adapt in this way.[53] (An obvious example of people's *not* taking such future adaptation into account is choosing to engage in addictive behavior like smoking cigarettes or using heroin.) But unless these adaptive human processes are dismissed altogether, the implication is once again to undermine the mainstream modern economic thinking—ironically, often popularly identified with Smith— that attaches unquestioned priority to satisfying whatever preferences consumers happen to have.

Following Mandeville, Smith also argued in *The Theory of Moral Sentiments* that many of our consumer choices, unlike the basic need for food that he placed at the center of his example of the beneficial operation of the invisible hand, are socially driven.[54] In his satirical poem, Mandeville's bees desire the newest items of clothing and furniture simply out of vanity. But in one of the prose explanations that he provided in the expanded *Fable,* he offered a more practical explanation. When people travel to places where they are unknown, they naturally want the people they meet to think well of them. The only basis strangers have to judge them, however, is the clothes they wear. Mandeville likewise argued that the same motivation applies even at home, when people live in large towns "where obscure Men may hourly meet with fifty Strangers to one Acquaintance, and consequently have the Pleasure of being esteem'd by the vast Majority, not as what they are, but what they appear to be." Especially when traveling elsewhere, each person has an incentive "to wear Clothes above his Rank."[55]

For Smith, our demand for goods like fine clothing is likewise socially based, but with a more admirable moral basis. Like our desire to be praise-worthy, these consumer demands stem from our ability to imagine what others might think of us, together with our desire for "fellow-feeling": we seek a higher standard of living not for its own sake but for the favorable impression we believe it will make on other people. "It is chiefly from this regard to the sentiments of mankind," Smith thought, "that we pursue riches and avoid poverty." Just as we hold other people in sympathy, we want them to hold *us* in sympathy as well. But we believe people will sympathize more with our joys than our sorrows, and so "we make parade of our riches, and conceal our poverty."[56] We want people to have sympathy toward us—not pity, but sympathy in Smith's sense of fellow-feeling—and we think appearing to be rich and hiding our misfortunes will prompt them to do so.

Years later, in *The Wealth of Nations,* Smith went on to elaborate this social basis for our consumption preferences in greater detail, once again with implications that run counter to what has become the dominant tendency of modern economic thinking. His point there was that even our perception of what constitutes a necessity is a social artifact. By necessities, he specified, "I understand not only the commodities which are indispensably necessary for the support of life but whatever the custom of the country renders it indecent for creditable people, even of the lowest order, to be without."[57] To illustrate what he meant, he drew a contrast between wearing a linen shirt, which on this definition he thought was a necessity in most of Europe, and leather shoes—which in England qualified as a necessity for both men and women, but in Scotland only for men, and in France for neither.

In both books, however—*The Wealth of Nations* no less than *The Theory of Moral Sentiments*—the basis for Smith's argument about the social origin of our preferences was not just appearances for appearances' sake but our concern for the *moral* impression we make on others: "In the present times, through the greater part of Europe," he observed, "a creditable day-labourer would be ashamed to appear in publick without a linen shirt." And the reason? Not having one "would be supposed to denote that disgraceful degree of poverty which, it is presumed, no body can well fall into without extreme bad conduct."[58] We avoid appearing poor to that extent because others will think if we are so poor we must be *morally* deficient as well.

In *The Theory of Moral Sentiments* Smith even anticipated the idea of "conspicuous consumption" famously articulated more than a hundred years later by the American economist Thorstein Veblen: that our desire to attract other people's admiration through our spending affects not only *how much* we buy but *what.* [59] Writing at the end of the nineteenth century, Veblen was seeking to explain the grandiose displays put on by Gilded Age financiers and industrialists who—in his account—put up enormous houses and staged sumptuous entertainments mostly to impress their social peers as well as the public at large. Anticipating Veblen's argument, Smith pointed out that palace gardens, carriages, and other accoutrements of the rich are "objects of which the obvious conveniency strikes everybody." Tiny, more private devices like a toothpick or a fingernail cutter may be just as useful to us, but are not so obvious to everyone else. As a result, these small but useful objects "are less reasonable subjects of vanity than the magnificence of wealth and greatness; and in this consists the sole advantage" of more conspicuous (to use Veblen's adjective) expenditures.[60] As Veblen did more explicitly, here too Smith exhibited a skepticism about consumer preferences that is deeply subversive of a central tenet of modern economic thinking.

Moreover, each of these aspects of Smith's jaundiced attitude toward our preferences as consumers—whether based on the mere foolishness of our choices, or our failure to anticipate the consequences of our growing accustomed to a different living standard, or how our desire to impress other people skews what we want for ourselves— was not some early view that he left behind when he moved on, in his later work, to focus more squarely on economic activity. *The Wealth of Nations* reflects much the same set of dismissive attitudes toward the consumption choices of the rich. There too, Smith referred to the objects purchased by the well-to-do as "trinkets and baubles, fitter to be the play-things of children than the serious pursuits of men."[61]

In Smith's later thinking, this tendency of the rich to squander their incomes on satisfying childish and frivolous desires assumed importance in yet a different context. Smith's chief concern was always to improve the lot of what he called "the labouring poor . . . the great body of the people."[62] As his thinking advanced, he increasingly understood the key role of investment—not just in factories and equipment, as we mostly think of it today, but in improving agricultural productivity as well—in enabling living standards to rise. As a practical matter, however, that investment could come only from those with incomes sufficient to provide for their living requirements and have something left over: in other words, mostly the rich. Useless spending on trifles from which they ultimately derived no real pleasure therefore wasted the resources that people of means could otherwise put into investment, investment that would make their farm tenants or shop employees more productive and thereby result in an increase in working people's wages and living standards.

For purposes of Smith's great contribution to understanding the essential role of markets and competition, however, what matters is only that individuals understand what is in their interest when they act as producers and suppliers of goods and services, not when they consume goods they acquire from others. Despite his reservations concerning our mistaken notions of how material consumption will affect our happiness, he saw no point in criticizing people for merely pursuing their self-interest as they saw it. He simply accepted self-interested behavior as an element of inborn human nature (a principle that he later made still more explicit in *The Wealth of Nations*). More than that, Smith concluded that our acting in our self-interest, even in these sometimes misguided ways, was *morally* beneficial to us as individual men and women. "The habits of economy, industry, discretion, attention, and application of thought, are generally supposed to be cultivated from self-interested motives," he wrote, and all are "very praiseworthy qualities." By contrast, carelessness and lack of thrift ensue not "from a want of benevolence, but from a want of the proper attention to the objects of self-interest."[63]

As a result, pursuing our self-interest and looking out for our own private happiness and interest are laudable principles of action, capable of leading most people to a virtuous life despite their ignoble and sometimes even foolish motivations. "In the middling and inferior stations of life," Smith wrote—referring to the great bulk of the population of his day—"the road to virtue and that to fortune . . . are, happily in most cases, very nearly the same." By contrast, "in the superior stations of life the case is unhappily not always the same."[64]

And, having concluded that for most people pursuing our fortune puts us on the road to virtue, Smith firmly left behind any notion of identifying self-interested behavior with vice. The words "vice" and "vicious" do appear in *The Theory of Moral Sentiments,* and with some frequency. But they always mean something else—unsocial passions, like hatred or resentment or revenge; injustice, such as fraud or brutality or violence; even acts that run contrary to our self-interest, like intemperance—never the mere pursuit of self-interest.

There was still something missing. Smith had now shown—as had Nicole, Mandeville, Butler, and others before—that when people act in their own self-interest they can make others better off. He had given a powerful example in which this outcome occurs explicitly through economic exchange. He had even identified this example with the working of a metaphorical invisible hand. And he had done all this with an extraordinary depth of insight about the motivations underlying individual behavior. But *The Theory of Moral Sentiments* still failed to push the fundamental argument much past where *The Fable of the Bees* had left it. Smith's repeated jibes at the frivolous motives of landlords, in the explanation he gave for the nearly equal distribution of food despite highly concentrated landholding, even recalled Mandeville's vain and fickle bees. Most important, Smith had not specified the *mechanism* that made all this work. From the perspective of the ideas that subsequently developed into the core of modern economics, what was missing was the role of markets, competition, and prices. That had to wait for his second book, seventeen years later.

The advances in Smith's thinking between the two books reflected his own independent ideas, to be sure, but also his absorption of two significant themes in what others were then writing, or had written. Over the prior century many parts of Europe, Scotland and England included, had progressively become more commercial. Cities and towns were growing in both size and importance. In 1600 just 3 percent of England's population had lived in towns of forty thousand or larger; by 1750 more than 8 percent did. In another hundred years, almost 20 percent would (and by 1900 more than 50 percent).[65] This progressive urbanization was, in part, the point of the invisible hand example in *The Theory of Moral Sentiments*—the increasingly numerous townspeople needed to eat too—and Smith would go on to explore the growth of towns further in *The Wealth of Nations* (although without using the invisible hand phrase in doing so). At the same time, agriculture was also becoming more commercial, with ever more farmers producing crops for sale in markets of ever wider scope. And, primarily in London but in some of the larger towns as well, the sophistication of financial markets, including borrowing and lending, was increasing rapidly as well.

Especially in the aftermath of the South Sea Bubble, these developments had elicited widespread expressions of concern, much of it along moral grounds. But an opposing viewpoint was emerging too. According to some thinkers on the subject, the advance of market-based commerce exerted a *positive* moral influence. In his treatise on *The Spirit of the Laws,* published just a decade before Smith's *The Theory of Moral Sentiments,* the French political theorist Baron Montesquieu wrote that "it is almost a general rule that wherever the ways of man are gentle there is commerce; and wherever there is commerce, there the ways of

man are gentle." Montesquieu went on to claim that commerce "polishes and softens barbarian ways as we can see every day."[66]

The basis for Montesquieu's enthusiastic assessment was the voluntary nature of participation in commerce—an aspect that figured
prominently in Smith's thinking as well. In contrast to the traditional
fixed relationships that governed economic exchange in many rural
settings, which were both personal and highly stable over time, in the
typical town-center marketplace shoppers faced many suppliers from
whom they could buy any particular item. There was no requirement
to buy today from whichever merchant a customer had patronized
yesterday. Fishmongers or butchers who gained a reputation for cheat-
ing their customers, or even just treating them rudely, would see their
prospective trade move on to the next stall. Under commerce, Montesquieu's argument went, sellers *had* to acquire gentle manners; otherwise they would do no business. The same principle applied to market
labor as opposed to traditional tenancy or apprentice arrangements.
Surly or uncooperative workers would earn no wages. The dictates of
the marketplace had a natural affinity for civil behavior.[67]

But the benefits claimed for commerce went beyond mere personal politeness. Others among Smith's contemporaries extended the
same thought to more essential moral qualities. Bishop Butler had
seen modern forms of commerce as a moralizing, even Christianizing, force.[68] (In one 1739 sermon, Butler pointed out that commerce
among nations provided opportunities for the "Profession of Christianity," and the "Propagation of it," to peoples as yet unexposed to true
religion.[69]) His protégé Josiah Tucker asked "how are the Ends of both
Religion and Government to be answered but by the System of universal Commerce?" Commerce was the foundation not only of justice but
benevolence, charity, and compassion too.[70] Joseph Priestley, likewise
a Church of England priest but also a scientist best known today for
discovering oxygen (just two years before Smith published *The Wealth
of Nations*), and like Butler and Tucker a typical Enlightenment figure
interested more generally in philosophy and human relations, wrote
that commerce "tends greatly to expand the mind, and to cure us of
many hurtful prejudices."[71] Smith in his personal library had five books
and pamphlets written by Priestley.[72]

Others, personally closer to Smith, expressed similar views. His
friend and fellow club member William Robertson, the principal of

Edinburgh University and a Church of Scotland minister as well, but also a historian, extended the idea to international relations. "Commerce tends to wear off those prejudices which maintain distinctions and animosity between nations," he wrote; and, echoing Montesquieu, "it softens and polishes the manners of men."[73] David Hume even thought the benefits of commerce extended to stimulating learning.[74]

Belief in the civilizing effect of commerce was not limited to France and England. In America Benjamin Rush, the Philadelphia physician and reformist politician, wrote that he considered the effects of commerce "as next to those of religion in humanizing mankind."[75] Benjamin Franklin and Thomas Jefferson, sent by Congress after the Revolutionary War to negotiate treaties with the European nations, wrote of hoping to achieve "an object so valuable to mankind as the total emancipation of commerce and the bringing together all nations for a free intercommunication of happiness."[76] Even Thomas Paine, author of the fiery tract that helped rally American patriots to the Revolutionary cause in 1776, went on to write that "the invention of commerce . . . is the greatest approach towards universal civilization that has yet been made by any means not immediately flowing from moral principles."[77] With sentiments like these in the air, and with the interest in economic arrangements that Smith had already displayed, it is no surprise that commerce—in the sense of voluntary exchange in a market setting—played a central role in his further work.

A second and much older strand of thinking, one that had been available to Mandeville too although he failed to draw on it, had revolved around an idea that when applied to the economic sphere, and especially in the context of market-based commerce, suggested a particular role for competition. The familiar issue was how to restrain the pursuit of self-interest, for this purpose originally conceived as the pursuit of honor and glory by princes. The traditional notion had been to *repress* these and other "passions," a task to which both religion and the state had long aspired but with limited success. But a different idea, associated mostly with continental thinkers, was to *harness* such potentially destructive tendencies by pitting one passion against another in such a way as not only to prevent harm but perhaps even to direct the underlying energy to some worthwhile purpose.[78] Hume, in struggling to understand how Mandeville's intriguing insight might be valid despite the apparent offense he gave to accepted moral principles, had likewise speculated that "two opposite vices in a state may be more advantageous than either of them alone."[79]

Claude Helvétius, a philosopher of the French Enlightenment (with whose widow Benjamin Franklin notoriously took up during his stay in Paris during the American Revolution), put the point more sharply. The object, he suggested, was "to arm our passions against one another," on the ground that "only a passion can triumph over a passion."[80] Baron d'Holbach, a French-German philosopher who was Smith's exact contemporary (both born in 1723), took this idea to a further level by making explicit the goal of achieving a public purpose: "The passions are the true counterweights of the passions; we must not at all attempt to destroy them, but rather try to direct them; let us offset those that are harmful by those that are useful to society."[81] This extended discussion, though in some ways abstract and philosophical, nonetheless bore practical implications. Smith personally knew both Helvétius and d'Holbach, and their ideas are evident in his emphasis on markets and competition in *The Wealth of Nations*. The system of political checks and balances built into the U.S. Constitution a decade later, and elaborated by both James Madison and Alexander Hamilton in *The Federalist Papers*, clearly reflects the influence of this thinking as well.[82]

Moreover, some strands of this line of thought had explicitly suggested a special role for *economic* self-interest in the conception of countervailing passions. Avarice, though normally considered an opprobrious human trait (not to mention a cardinal sin according to Catholic doctrine), had long been perceived as involving a particular form of calculating rationality.[83] Among an individual's potentially dangerous instincts, it therefore seemed natural to look in the first instance to this more rationally oriented desire for material gain as the most plausible restraint on the others. And as both Hume and Smith believed, that desire is always operating on individuals' thoughts. Hume argued that "avarice, or the desire of gain, is an universal passion which operates at all times, in all places, and upon all persons."[84] Smith, in *The Wealth of Nations*, made the same assumption.

But if one passion can restrain another within the thought process of a single individual—and, further, if the passion most capable of effecting this restraint is economic self-interest—then it was only one more step to suppose that one person's desire for economic gain might restrain another's. Seen in this light, Hobbes's metaphorical social contract represented the reining in of each man's aggressive passions by every man's even stronger instinct for survival. In the economic context, however, no such once-for-all arrangement is apparent, even hypothetically; the desire for economic gain, and the effort to which it gives rise, are unending. As Smith's thinking continued to develop, the role of markets and competition became an *ongoing* way of setting one person's *economic* self-interest against another's. In so doing, competition would not only restrain them both, but at the same time harness the energy and initiative to which each person's self-interest gives rise, in such a way as to achieve some common purpose. Proceeding along the path indicated before him by Bishop Butler and Dean Tucker, and by Boisguilbert in France, this is precisely the further step Smith took in *The Wealth of Nations*. It provided the missing mechanism at the root of Mandeville's challenging paradox.

4

The Competitive Market Mechanism

The natural effort of every individual to better his own condition . . . is so powerful a principle, that it is alone, and without
any assistance, not only capable of carrying on the society to
wealth and prosperity, but of surmounting a hundred impertinent obstructions with which the folly of human laws too often
incumbers its operations.

—ADAM SMITH

S mith remained as professor of moral philosophy at Glasgow after
The Theory of Moral Sentiments was published, continuing to push
forward the Hume-inspired effort to construct a comprehensive and
securely founded science of man. In contrast to his first book's focus
on the inner thoughts of individuals, however, now he turned his attention to the origins and evolution of social institutions, including the
organization of economic life. Drawing in part on the thinking he had
done a decade earlier, for the public lectures he gave in Edinburgh
after his return from Oxford, in the early 1760s he lectured at Glasgow
on "justice, police [meaning what we call policy], revenue and arms."[1]
Smith never published these lectures, nor even left them in his writings. But long after his death, the extensive notes taken by two students
who heard them were compiled into a book under the title *Lectures on
Jurisprudence*.[2] He later incorporated some of the ideas that he developed in these lectures in *The Wealth of Nations*.

In 1764, at the age of forty-one, Smith resigned his university
position at Glasgow to take up an appointment as tutor and traveling
companion to a seventeen-year-old Scottish nobleman, the Duke of
Buccleuch. From February of that year until October 1766, the two

traveled together—first to Toulouse, then Geneva, and finally Paris. The duke's younger brother and another Scottish friend joined them in the fall of 1766, and it was the brother's death, in Paris, that brought the trip to an abrupt end. But Smith's close relationship with the Duke of Buccleuch continued long after the young man reached maturity, as he went on to advise what was probably the wealthiest man in Scotland on his financial affairs, as well as to enjoy his patronage. Smith's close attention to the 1772 Scottish banking crisis, for example, stemmed in part from the duke's role as the largest shareowner in the bank at the center of the debacle.[3] But the two men's relationship remained personal as well. As the duke reportedly expressed his sentiments years later, "We continued to live in friendship until the hour of his death." Smith was "a friend whom I loved and respected, not only for his great talents, but for every private virtue."[4]

Living for nearly three years in these intellectual centers on the continent gave Smith, who was already widely known as the author of *The Theory of Moral Sentiments,* an opportunity to exchange ideas at first hand with many of the leading thinkers of the French Enlightenment, including Voltaire, d'Holbach, and Helvétius. Others whom he met, such as Jacques Necker, who a decade later would become Louis XVI's finance minister, and Anne-Robert-Jacques Turgot, who later served as comptroller general of finance, had a more direct interest in questions relating to economics.[5] Smith's thinking about how human societies advance economically from a primitive to an advanced state, and what consequences ensue for their laws and government, closely paralleled what Turgot in particular had said in his lectures at the Sorbonne in 1751; but since Smith had already laid out these ideas in his own lectures at Glasgow, well before coming to Paris, whatever discussions he had with Turgot were clearly not their origin.[6]

The most influential of these new contacts for Smith's subsequent thinking was François Quesnay. A medical doctor nearly thirty years older, Quesnay had taken up studying economic questions and by the time of Smith's visit had emerged as the leading figure among a school of French thinkers known as physiocrats for their emphasis on land and agriculture as the sole source of economic wealth. (Not surprisingly, the physiocrats' policy program called for higher prices on farm products.) Smith found this narrow focus on agriculture unpersuasive, but some of the physiocrats' ideas significantly influenced his thinking.[7] The physiocrats, for example, emphasized the need for an "agricultural surplus"—in other words, production of more food than those working in the agricultural sector required—to make possible economic development beyond agriculture. The idea resonated with what Smith had already written in *The Theory of Moral Sentiments* about the exchange of food for town-made goods, but that discussion bore no direct implications for economic growth or development. In *The Wealth of Nations,* Smith returned to the subject and drew conclusions of just that kind: a surplus somewhere in the economy, though not necessarily in agriculture, was necessary for investment to occur. More generally, Smith found the physiocrats' opposition to French mercantilism highly compatible with his own thinking.

Smith was also attracted to Quesnay's systematic way of thinking about the interrelatedness of different elements of a nation's economy. Quesnay's recently published *Tableau Economique* had used an analogy to William Harvey's discovery of the circulation of blood, more than a century before, to analyze the way in which one sector's spending became another sector's income.[8] The two men became good friends during Smith's ten-month stay in Paris, and when Quesnay published his book *Physiocratie,* in 1767, he sent Smith a copy.[9] Despite Smith's reservations about the emphasis placed on agriculture—and despite the physiocrats' omission of any understanding of either the price system or the significance of the division of labor, two centrally important elements of his own ideas—in *The Wealth of Nations* he praised Quesnay's approach as "perhaps, the nearest approximation to the truth that has yet been published upon the subject of political oeconomy," well worth the attention of anyone interested in the subject.[10] He later said that if Quesnay had lived to see the publication of *The Wealth of Nations* (he died two years too soon), he would have dedicated his own book to his French friend.[11]

Beyond the direct influence of the people whom he met personally, Smith's time in France usefully exposed him to other lines of thought that he went on to develop in his own subsequent work. In *The Wealth of Nations* Smith referred to Cantillon, though not to Boisguilbert. But Cantillon's book from 1755 was itself an outgrowth of Boisguilbert's thinking from sixty years before. Although neither was still alive for Smith to meet, their ideas were already influential in French circles. Their emphasis on the positive role of markets—albeit without the close analysis of the competitive mechanism and the central role of the price system, and also without the confidence in that mechanism's robust power to improve living standards—presaged Smith's later contribution.[12] So too did their consequent opposition to mercantilist policies. It was apparently while in France that Smith first began to work on *The Wealth of Nations*. As he wrote to Hume in July 1764, "I have begun to write a book in order to pass away the time."[13]

After returning from Paris, Smith paused in London for some months and then went home to Kirkcaldy. He devoted most of the next nine years to working on what became *The Wealth of Nations,* in the meanwhile paying close attention to economic and political events including the developing crisis in the North American colonies. What he wrote partly reflected these contemporary concerns. In response to the widely damaging Scottish banking crisis of 1772, for example, *The Wealth of Nations* called for a prohibition on banks' lending at more than 5 percent interest—Smith thought only borrowers with highly risky projects to finance would be willing to pay such excessive rates— together with tight restrictions on how banks could fund themselves. (Smith favored these restrictions, he said, on the same grounds that he approved of the regulation requiring fire walls between the row houses in Edinburgh.) And he thought more about what he had absorbed during his years in France.

But the chief practical impetus to his thinking remained the challenge that had driven Scotland to give up its independence at the very beginning of the century: how to increase economic activity, and make it more productive, so as to improve everyday living standards. By the middle of the eighteenth century, it seemed that nearly everything the state tried to do in the economic sphere was at best unnecessary and more likely counterproductive. At the same time, the material progress that was occurring by this time sprang entirely from individual initiative and owed nothing to the direction of the state.[14] Mercantilism was clearly not any kind of solution. Rejecting state intervention, however, after centuries of reliance on government-granted monopolies, licenses, and other restrictions, would be a wholesale change in thinking. Making a persuasive case for such a shift would require a sound theoretical foundation.

In 1773 Smith returned to London, where he then remained, working on the book, until its publication in March 1776.[15]

As he had in *The Theory of Moral Sentiments,* in *The Wealth of Nations* Smith laid down specific assumptions from which his argument proceeded. One, reaffirming the view he had taken in the earlier book, was the universal force of people's desire to improve their material living standard. "The desire of bettering our condition," he now wrote, "comes with us from the womb, and never leaves us till we go into the grave. In the whole interval which separates those two moments, there is scarce perhaps a single instant in which any man is . . . without any wish of alteration or improvement."[16] Although in his earlier book Smith had pointed to "tranquility" as the route to human happiness, he nonetheless now recognized that constant restlessness and striving more nearly characterized human existence.[17]

And Smith was clear that the condition most people seek to better is their *economic* condition: "An augmentation of fortune is the means by which the greater part of men . . . wish to better their condition."[18] Smith might still prefer that people adopt his own stoic outlook, seeking tranquility and enjoyment from society and conversation. But he saw his work as science, not sermonizing—as both Hume and Rousseau had put it, taking men as they are—and for purposes of his second book he now simply accepted as an observed fact that most people are intent on improving their material well-being.[19] Whether their underlying motivation is socially driven as he had argued in *The Theory of Moral Sentiments,* so that a higher material living standard is merely the means of attracting sympathy and fellow-feeling, was not important to what he was trying to accomplish in the new book. Nor was whether the aspects of living standards that loom largest are therefore those that others can readily observe, rather than something else that might contribute more to people's genuine happiness. What mattered for his current purposes was "the uniform, constant, and uninterrupted effort of every man to better his condition," together with the fact that for most people the principal route to achieving that end is a higher material standard of living.[20] The focus of *The Wealth of Nations* was squarely on the world of economic activity.

Smith further assumed that this economic world was one of "commerce." In lecturing to his students at Glasgow, after *The Theory of Moral Sentiments* was published, he had speculated about how commerce historically arose and why over time it largely displaced earlier forms of economic organization like subsistence farming or nomadic pasturing of animals. But just as he was now leaving behind his earlier analysis of *why* people are so concerned with their material living standard, instead simply assuming that they are, in *The Wealth of Nations* he likewise moved beyond *how* commerce had come to dominate. For purposes of this new book, it too was a given fact.

What he had to say about each of the two key constituent elements of commerce—specialized production and voluntary exchange—made up a large part of the new book's lasting contribution. Just as *The Theory of Moral Sentiments* had begun with an assertion of the universal prevalence of human sympathy, the very first sentence of *The Wealth of Nations* trumpeted the advantages of specialization in production—division of labor, as Smith called it.[21] The opening paragraph of the second chapter then tied specialized production to voluntary exchange. Much of the rest of the book can be read as an elaboration of the role of these two crucial features of what he and his contemporaries meant by commerce.

Smith began the book by emphasizing that specializing in economic production—as opposed to everyone's trying individually to carry out as many productive activities as possible (as is typical of subsistence farming, for example)—conveyed a crucial advantage. It was, as he saw it, the primary way by which any society got more output from its available labor and material inputs, and thereby raised its standard of living. "The greatest improvement in the productive powers of labour," he asserted, "and the greater part of the skill, dexterity, and judgment with which it is anywhere directed, or applied, seem to have been the effects of the division of labour." And he quickly went on to the famous illustration of the numerous specialized tasks assigned to workers in a pin factory ("pin" being the standard eighteenth-century word for what we call a nail). Moreover, because consumption was "the sole end and purpose of all production," the fact that dividing production tasks in this way makes labor more productive meant that doing so also delivers a higher standard of living for the working population as a whole—which remained, throughout the book, Smith's primary objective. The initial focus of his thinking, therefore, was "this division of labour, from which so many advantages are derived," and he enthusiastically hailed the general prosperity to which it leads.[22]

Smith's emphasis on specialized production as the key to advancing productivity and living standards was in part a reflection of the time and place in which he wrote. He knew that everyday living standards, especially in England, were much improved from what they had been in earlier times, and there had to be a reason. His goal was to enable Scotland, and other countries like Scotland, to rise to that higher level. Larger markets allowed larger-scale production, which in turn enabled more specialization. Gaining access to English markets, especially including England's overseas trade, would allow Scotland to reap those benefits.

Although some of the major technological advances that spurred what we now call the Industrial Revolution were in use by the time of *The Wealth of Nations*—James Hargreaves's "spinning jenny," for example, and Thomas Newcomen's early steam engine (though not yet James Watt's improved version)—they were apparently too recent for Smith, or anyone else for that matter, to understand their fundamental importance. They were also still too limited geographically. As of the 1770s these new devices were in widespread use only in one county

A Hargreaves spinning jenny, late eighteenth century.
Invented in the 1760s, the spinning jenny greatly increased productivity
in cotton textile manufacturing by enabling a single worker to spin thread
onto multiple spools (in later versions, more than one hundred) at once.

in England (Lancashire) and one in Scotland (Lanark). One indication that Smith failed to grasp the technological basis of the Industrial Revolution was his choosing a pin factory, rather than textile manufacturing, as the stereotype for increased productivity; by the early nineteenth century it was clear that the center of gravity of the Industrial Revolution in England was the textile industry.[23]

Not until the 1830s, and even then not in Britain but America, did thoughtful observers begin to see ongoing technological progress as a source of ever-increasing productivity.[24] Once that realization hit, its impact was enormous, not just for economic thinking but more broadly. But writing more than a half-century earlier, Smith didn't see it. He focused instead on the increasing specialization in workmen's tasks that he witnessed in the earliest stages of industrialization, and knew to have happened still earlier in many craft trades. Ever greater division of labor was the only source he could see for the ongoing increase in productivity and therefore improvement in living standards.[25]

Perhaps for this reason, Smith was at pains to argue that most workers do not take on different specializations primarily from any inborn differences in their abilities. To the contrary, he argued, it was mostly the experience of working at their respective tasks that led to their different abilities. "The difference of natural talents in different men is, in reality, much less than we are aware of," he wrote. Instead, the different skills that distinguish people in one line of work from those in another are not the cause but rather the effect of division of labor. Invoking an example no doubt intended to be striking, but also amusing to anyone who noted that the book's title page identified its author as formerly a professor of moral philosophy, Smith went on to claim that "the difference between the most dissimilar characters, between a philosopher and a common street porter, for example, seems to arise not so much from nature, as from habit, custom, and education." Until age six or eight, he suggested, the two are mostly indistinguishable; but then they take up very different occupations, and from then on their respective talents diverge "till at last the philosopher is willing to acknowledge scarce any resemblance."[26]

The point was more than just a matter of personal modesty and indirect humor. If people's specialized roles in economic production mostly reflected differences in their inborn human talents, those biological differences would present a natural limit to how far the division of labor, and with it economic productivity and the standard of living, could advance. By contrast, if education and experience are what make different people more productive in different tasks, it should be possible to train people for ever more specialized roles. At least in principle, therefore, the division of labor could become ever greater, and living standards could go on improving without limit (as indeed they have, though not just for that reason).

At the same time, Smith also expressed profound reservations about the consequences of such increasing specialization—again on the ground that it was people's experience that shaped their abilities and not the other way around.[27] Writing at the outset of the Industrial Revolution, he was keenly sensitive to the human costs of the ever more specialized and repetitive work he saw people performing in the emerging mass-production economy. His concern was more than mere fretting that most men would not become philosophers. Taking up again the way in which he had described the division of labor in a pin factory, he wrote that as the division of labor advances, what most people do in their work "comes to be confined to a few very simple operations; frequently to one or two." The problem was that someone who repeatedly spends his entire workday in this way, with the same few operations always leading to the same results, "has no occasion to exert his understanding, or to exercise his invention in finding out expedients for removing difficulties which never occur."[28] In short, such a person has no need to think.

Smith went on to describe in stark language the effect of this kind of dull, repetitive work on a person's human capacities: "He naturally loses, therefore, the habit of such exertion, and generally becomes as stupid and ignorant as it is possible for a human creature to become. The torpor of his mind renders him, not only incapable of relishing or bearing a part in any rational conversation, but of conceiving any generous, noble, or tender sentiment." Nor was the danger limited to a few special cases. In every economically advanced society, this would be the fate of the great majority of working people "unless government takes some pains to prevent it."[29] The remedy, Smith argued, was publicly funded universal education.[30]

If these deplorable consequences followed from specialization among workmen, what led to this way of organizing economic activity in the first place? Smith argued that division of labor was not due to differences in innate ability from one person to another, and he also rejected the possibility that it was any kind of deliberately planned strategy. (His thinking left no room for Mandeville's skillful politician.) How, then, did it arise? It was a straightforward consequence, he argued, of each workman's desire to be individually more productive, together with our natural inclination to engage in exchange: as he famously put it, "a certain propensity in human nature . . . to truck, barter, and exchange one thing for another." This common propensity Smith simply accepted as yet another observed aspect of human nature, a plainly evident fact, the origin of which "it belongs not to our present subject to enquire." Instead, he took the eagerness to trade with others as one more distinguishing human characteristic. "It is common to all men," he observed, "and to be found in no other race of animals." Both in simply accepting this proclivity on our part as an observed fact, and in thinking of it as uniquely human, his treatment in *The Wealth of Nations* of the human propensity to exchange closely paralleled his treatment of human imagination and sympathy in *The Theory of Moral Sentiments*.[31]

Smith therefore explained specialized production as an outgrowth of the desire to be more productive together with our inborn desire to engage in economic exchange. But it is also evident that the desire to exchange economic goods—more than that, the *need* to do so—is in turn a consequence of specialized production: blacksmiths can't eat horseshoes, and dairy maids can't wear milk. And some people, like philosophers, produce none of what is physically necessary for survival. The need to exchange one good for another is therefore as much a *consequence* of specialized production as it is the cause along lines that Smith argued. Either way, however, the point was that the two essential features of commerce naturally go together.

Moreover, unlike specialized production, which is useful mostly for reasons having to do with physical aspects of the production process, the vital importance of economic exchange also reinforced the broader social thinking that Smith had laid out in *The Theory of Moral Sentiments*. Interpersonal communication and contact are essential to man's social nature, he argued there, and if individuals' economic needs force them to interact with other people then so much the better. Like Hume and other thinkers before him whose work Smith also knew (the seventeenth-century German philosopher Samuel Pufendorf, for example), Smith saw *economic* need as part of the origin of human sociability. "Man has almost constant occasion for the help of his brethren," he noted—indeed, "he stands at all times in need of the cooperation and assistance of great multitudes"—but "it is in vain for him to expect it from their benevolence only."[32] As he had put it in his lectures at Glasgow years before, what was needed was some means of procuring their help.[33] Our inborn propensity to barter and exchange presented a natural avenue for doing so. And our ability to anticipate what goods or services someone else might be willing to accept in exchange for whatever we can offer them was itself a consequence of the sympathy made possible by the human imagination.

What was new in *The Wealth of Nations,* however—and what made the book so important, then and now—was Smith's sophisticated understanding of competition conducted within markets as the principal organizing mechanism of economic activity carried out under commerce. His analysis centered on the dynamic role played by prices, including wages as the price of labor services. Smith did not work out mathematically the joint interaction of supply and demand; that came a hundred years later, with Alfred Marshall.[34] But he clearly understood, and carefully explained, the several functions that prices serve: as reflections of scarcity, enabling consumers to buy more of goods that are cheap and forcing them to hold back on expensive ones; as incentives to production, motivating craftsmen and manufacturers to make more of some goods and less of others; and as guides to allocation, steering scarce and therefore expensive resources toward uses in which they are more highly valued, while allowing more plentiful and therefore cheaper ones to be used in less valuable ways. Today these roles played by prices are central to even the most basic understanding of Western economics. In *The Wealth of Nations,* they were new.

Most importantly, Smith grounded the mechanism of price determination on nothing more than buyers' and sellers' pursuit of their respective self-interest. In the market for labor, for example, "What are the common wages of labour depends every where upon the contract usually made between those two parties, whose interests are by no means the same. The workmen desire to get as much, the masters to give as little, as possible."[35] That workers prefer higher wages, and employers lower, was not cause for moral concern; it was merely human nature. What led the market to the right wage—right, that is, for purposes of reflecting the scarcity of labor, and thereby motivating the right number of men and women to work and placing them in the production activities that would best use their efforts—was the way workers and employers pit their respective self-interest against one another. Each side's pursuing its own interest led to the right wage for the market as a whole.

In other markets too, what led buyers and sellers to the price that fully reflected the scarcity of the goods being produced and the cost of the labor and material inputs used to produce them, and that steered production to the right goods and the best techniques for making them, was again the way these demanders and suppliers compete among themselves, once again with no more than their respective self-interest in mind. The same principle, always grounded in market competition together with the opposing self-interest of the parties on opposite sides of each buy-sell transaction, was at work again and again, in one setting after another.

With this insight, Smith finally had the key to the paradox posed by Nicole and Mandeville beginning more than a century before: it was self-interest, *operating through the market mechanism*, that led each of Mandeville's bees to satisfy the others' desires and therefore, taken all together, to make the hive prosper. In Nicole's vocabulary, no charity was necessary. As Smith concluded, in what became one of the most frequently quoted passages in *The Wealth of Nations*, "It is not from the benevolence of the butcher, the brewer, or the baker, that we expect our dinner, but from their regard to their own interest. We address ourselves, not to their humanity but to their self-love, and never talk to them of our own necessities but of their advantages."[36] *Market competition* was the mechanism behind the benefit to others created by our pursuing our self-interest, and the price system was how market competition worked. Channeled through competition carried out in markets, and operating through the effect of that competition on prices, the effort of each individual to do no more than improve his own condition was "the principle from which publick and national, as well as private opulence is originally derived."[37]

The outcome was a striking example of the closely related Enlightenment-era principles of unintended consequences and spon-

taneous order, and Smith repeatedly emphasized that far from intending the benefits to others that resulted from their own actions, the
participants in the process did not even foresee them. True, human
beings have sympathy for one another, as he had argued at length in
The Theory of Moral Sentiments; but that sympathy is not what was at
work here. And even if people were disposed to advance others' economic well-being, Smith did not want his version of a Newtonian "system" to have to depend on their having sufficient knowledge to be able
to do so. In the labor market, for example, "though the interest of the
labourer is strictly connected with that of the society, he is incapable
either of comprehending that interest, or of understanding its connection with his own."[38] Such far-seeing insight was impossible, but it was
also unnecessary. Merely by seeking as high a wage as possible *for himself,* each worker did his part in getting wages *overall* to the right level.

Here, at last, was what both economists and the general public, ever
since, have understood as the "invisible hand" (even though Smith did
not specifically use the famous metaphor in this section of the book).[39]
The implication was that even as both parties to an economic transaction vied against one another, and even though each was pursuing his
or her own interest only, under the right conditions *both* would benefit, as would others as well. In modern terms, economic relations—
again, under the right conditions—are not zero-sum. In contrast to
Hume, who had stated that people's interest in acquiring goods and
possessions is "directly destructive of society," Smith now showed how
market competition enabled the universal effort to better one's condition via an "augmentation of fortune" to advance living standards more
broadly, and even foster human sociability.[40] Others, like Boisguilbert
and Tucker (and Nicole and Mandeville before them), had grasped that
self-interested behavior could promote the common good. But it was
Smith who explained how market competition made it so. The idea,
in Smith's form, was new and far-reaching. It rapidly proved to have
enormous appeal.[41]

Smith's confidence in the power of the principle of unintended but
nonetheless beneficial consequences, operating through markets, ran
throughout *The Wealth of Nations.* In his first book he had explained
in some detail how the exchange of agricultural produce for various
goods that the landlord (foolishly) wanted resulted in a nearly equal
distribution of food despite highly concentrated holding of land. In

that example, the craftsmen who made these objects clearly benefited from the exchange. Apart from satisfying their misguided vanity, however, the landowners did not. Smith returned to this subject in *The Wealth of Nations*, even more scornful of what the landowners individually obtained through the exchange: all they achieved, through the "trinkets and baubles" they received, was "gratification of the most childish, the meanest and the most sordid of all vanities."[42]

But the point Smith had in mind now was broader. It was only by virtue of this exchange of food for trinkets that town life was even possible. The economic interdependence of town and country was a common theme in eighteenth-century thinking, already implicit in Mandeville and appearing in the work of many writers following. The emergence of town life, Smith now argued, ended up benefiting not just the townspeople but society as a whole. Moreover, the improvement that followed from the creation of towns was a matter of liberty and governance, as always the height of Enlightenment aspirations.[43]

Smith well understood the weakness, and at the same time the tyrannical nature, of government in primitive societies. In the eighteenth century the Scottish Highlands were, for the most part, just such a place. There were few roads, no mail service, and little presence of police; there were plenty of armed bands. Clan chiefs, who held absolute power over their vassals until after the failure of the Highland rebellion, maintained retinues of armed retainers who frequently fought with their neighbors. Cattle theft was common, and clan warfare not infrequent. Religious conflict was especially intense, with opponents captured and tortured, sometimes killed (one archbishop was assassinated), and more than three thousand women and men hanged for witchcraft in the century and a half leading up to Union.[44]

In Smith's account in *The Wealth of Nations*, what the landowners ultimately gave up in enabling town life was not just the foodstuffs that grew on their land but their ability "to make war according to their own discretion" and their unfettered latitude for "interrupting the regular execution of justice" and "disturbing the peace of the country." Before the advent of towns, the countryside had been "a scene of violence, rapine, and disorder." Once towns emerged, "regular government was established in the country as well as the city." The end result was "order and good government, and with them, the liberty and security of individuals, among the inhabitants of the country, who had before lived almost in a continual state of war with their neighbors, and of servile dependency upon their superiors."[45] It was the emergence of towns that precluded Hobbes's war of all against all, and it was economic exchange that allowed it to happen.

And, crucially, this outcome was intended by no one. As a result of nothing more than self-interested market exchange, "a revolution of the greatest importance to the publick happiness, was in this manner brought about by two different orders of people, who had not the least intention to serve the publick." Neither group had either knowledge or foresight of what would follow from "the folly of the one, and the industry of the other." Smith's account of this extraordinary outcome closely resembles what he had written in illustrating the principle of unintended consequences (and invoking the invisible hand) in *The Theory of Moral Sentiments*, but it is not the same. In his earlier thoughts on town-and-country exchange, only the townspeople benefited. In *The Wealth of Nations*, society as a whole did.[46]

In keeping with Smith's objective in writing his great book, the principle of positive but unintended benefits stemming from market competition had not just descriptive power but normative force too. In the absence of perpetually ongoing technical progress, which he did not foresee, the only way Smith thought an economically advanced country could continue to improve its productivity and hence its standard of living was to keep increasing the degree of specialization—division of labor—with which it produced ordinary goods and services. But a country starting off with an insufficiently developed system of markets, or with adequate markets but a host of government-imposed monopolies and other bars to competition within them, could achieve a once-for-all productivity gain by eliminating these impediments.

Smith was sharply critical, therefore, not only of mercantilist systems like what he had observed in France but likewise of the many forms of economic restrictions then in place in England and Scotland. In *The Wealth of Nations* he set forth at length his opposition to mercantilism, beginning from the "popular notion"—which he showed to be false—"that wealth consists in money, or in gold and silver." Because of this false notion, he argued, "all the different nations of Europe have studied, though to little purpose, every possible means of accumulating gold and silver in their respective countries." He went on to explain, with copious historical detail, the failure of the policies to which this effort frequently led. More fundamentally, he argued that while "Consumption is the sole end and purpose of all production," so that the interest of the producer is worth promoting only to the extent necessary for achieving better outcomes for consumers, under mercantilism the opposite orientation dominates: "in the mercantile system, the interest of the consumer is almost constantly sacrificed to that of the producer; and it seems to consider production, and not consumption, as the ultimate end and object of all industry and commerce."[47] To Smith, such thinking was simply backward.

At a more concrete specific level—referring now to England and Scotland specifically—Smith opposed local customs taxes as well as either taxes or outright prohibitions on imports from abroad (in each case in order to allow freer flow of goods);[48] traditional guild-enforced apprenticeship regulations (freer allocation of labor); government-granted monopolies (freer choice of what to produce and who could produce it); and entails and other restrictions on property transfers (freer ownership, and therefore allocation, of land). Writing about Britain's colonies in America and the Caribbean, he opposed slavery. Smith intended his book as a practical guide for raising a country's standard of living. Allowing market competition to function naturally, as people's inborn desire for economic gain and propensity for trade propelled them, was the most effective way to achieve that end.

Smith also recognized that government is not the only source of harmful impediments to competition. On just the same grounds that he opposed state monopolies and licenses, he was outspoken in his criticism of attempts by businessmen to monopolize markets or otherwise band together to force prices higher or wages lower. In Glasgow and Edinburgh, and probably in London too during his extended stays there, he had observed merchants and employers sufficiently closely to become skeptical of their motives and their methods. "Whoever imagines . . . that masters rarely combine," he bluntly stated, "is as ignorant of the world as of the subject. Masters are always and every where in a sort of tacit, but constant and uniform combination." The popular image of Smith as an advocate of free markets is correct, but today's frequent representation of him as therefore a supporter of whatever private businesses seek to do is not. Businessmen, he wrote, constitute "an order of men . . . who have generally an interest to deceive and even to oppress the publick, and who accordingly have, upon many occasions both deceived and oppressed it."[49]

But notwithstanding the harm that he associated with impediments to competition created by either government or the collusion of businessmen, and the gains that he argued a country could reap by eliminating them both, Smith nonetheless emphasized not the fragility of the market mechanism he had identified but instead its astonishing robustness.[50] Because of this strong confidence in the positive force of markets, he was never the rigid opponent of all regulation that many political conservatives today hold him out to be. He favored tight restrictions on banking (tighter than in any Western country today) in order to prevent financial crises and consequent economic collapse like what Scotland had experienced in 1772, and he favored public education (less comprehensive than what we have today, but well beyond what England in particular had then) as a way to overcome the dulling effect on the human intellect that he feared from ever advancing division of labor.

In the same vein, he also advocated progressive income taxes, on straightforward distributional grounds ("It is not very unreasonable that the rich should contribute to the publick expence, not only in proportion to their revenue, but something more than in that proportion"); heavier highway tolls on luxury carriages, likewise on distributional grounds (so that "the indolence and vanity of the rich is made to contribute in a very easy manner to the relief of the poor"); taxes on the retail sale of liquor, and especially heavy taxes on distilleries (despite living in Scotland!); and, of course, taxes on any kind of monopoly profit ("the gains of monopolists, whenever they can be come at, [are] certainly of all subjects the most proper" for taxation).[51]

Even less was he the antigovernment ideologue that some more extreme representations mistakenly portray. Smith was well aware of the human propensity to invade and destroy one another, and so what commercial society needs in order to flourish is not just liberty but security and justice too. The twin foundations of commerce, which together delivered such benefits to mankind, were specialized production and *voluntary* exchange. Smith in opposing slavery was well aware of what economists and others today call "repugnant" transactions.[52] Even if security can be provided privately, there is no substitute for the state as the guarantor of justice. Much of what Smith wrote in *The Wealth of Nations* is, in one way or another, about the rule of law. Only the state can provide it.

Most important, in contrast to the view among many economists and political figures today that a market economy is such a delicate piece of machinery that any interference—especially one aimed at achieving more equitable outcomes—will seriously undermine it, Smith thought the power of self-interest, harnessed by market competition, was sufficient to overcome most obstacles that either government or colluding businessmen created.[53] "The natural effort of every individual to better his own condition," he wrote, "is so powerful a principle, that it is alone, and without any assistance, not only capable of carrying on the society to wealth and prosperity, but of surmounting a hundred impertinent obstructions with which the folly of human laws too often incumbers its operations." No classic republican sense of virtue, in which individuals willingly sacrifice their self-interest for the common good, is involved. All that is necessary is "the natural system of perfect liberty and justice." The force of self-interest, operating in competitive markets, is "frequently powerful enough to maintain the natural progress of things toward improvement, in spite of the extravagance of government, and of the greatest errors of administration."[54]

It is therefore ironic, in light of how the invisible hand metaphor has come to stand for Smith's insight into the working of the competitive market mechanism, that in the one place in *The Wealth of Nations* in which Smith used the now famous phrase, what underlies his argument is actually an impediment to freely functioning markets—though not one created by government or by private collusion. The question at issue was businessmen's choice of whether to invest at home versus abroad. The underlying concern, which is familiar enough today too, was that while the businessman himself might earn more from investing in some other country, the wages paid to his employees would then go to foreign rather than domestic workers. The investor's self-interest would then conflict with the interest of the society (in this case, the nation) as a whole.

As usual in *The Wealth of Nations*, Smith argued that economic actions undertaken merely out of self-interest end up economically benefiting the society more generally. In this instance, however, the reason to which he pointed was not the unrestricted flow of investment in a perfectly frictionless market but what he had observed as most businessmen's preference, *because of a market imperfection*—specifically, worries over security—to invest in their own country rather than abroad. Smith thought the typical businessman would regard investing at home as more secure than doing so in a foreign country, and he argued that this concern for security was all it took for the usual result to follow.[55] "By preferring the support of domestick to that of foreign industry," he wrote, the businessman "intends only his own security." But given this one added consideration, the force of self-interest takes over and the usual benefit to his fellow countrymen ensues. "By directing that industry in such a manner as its produce may be of the greatest value, he intends only his own gain, and he is in this, as in many other cases, led by an invisible hand to promote an end which was no part of his intention."[56] (Significantly, Smith wrote that the businessman is led "by an invisible hand"—not *as if* by an invisible hand, as he is often misquoted.[57])

And, consistent with his confidence in the pervasiveness and robustness of the principle that individual pursuit of self-interest channeled by market competition leads to unintended consequences of more general benefit, Smith went on to observe that the businessman's focus only on his own fortune probably was of more benefit—not just to himself but others too—than any conscious effort he might otherwise make on society's behalf: "By pursuing his own interest he frequently promotes that of the society more effectually than when he really intends to promote it." In yet another echo of Mandeville's jibe that pride and vanity built more hospitals than all the virtues together, Smith went on to observe, "I have never known much good done by those who affected to trade for the publick good."[58]

With this fundamental insight into the role of market competition in harnessing self-interest for the general good, in *The Wealth of Nations* Smith not only resolved the paradox presented by Nicole and Mandeville but pushed forward the broader project on which Hume's mentorship had launched him. To be sure, he had not addressed the full range of human thought and activity. But within the realm of man's *economic* engagement—an essential dimension of human existence, and one to which most adults devote the majority of their waking hours—he had delivered a "system": a cogent account that connected cause and effect via a Newton-like mechanism, all firmly grounded in observation and clearly specified assumptions. What made Smith's argument compelling was his demonstration that *under conditions of market competition* the beneficial consequences of individuals' self-interested actions were not just unintended and unforeseen, they were systematic and therefore fully explainable. He had laid out the mechanism for everyone to understand.

Even the language that Smith used in his account of the market mechanism had a strikingly Newtonian flavor. Hume, in a 1752 essay on the balance of international trade that remains the foundation for much thinking on the subject, had used an analogy to the force of gravity to explain how gold is drawn to nations that have a surplus of exports over imports.[59] In explaining how a market for any good maintains its price at the level that renders supply equal to demand, Smith now wrote that what he called the "natural price"—what today we think of as the price that prevails in a market-clearing equilibrium—is "the central price, to which the prices of all commodities are continually gravitating. Different accidents may sometimes keep them suspended a good deal above it, and sometimes force them down even somewhat below it. But whatever may be the obstacles which hinder them from settling in this center of repose and continuance, they are constantly tending towards it."[60] He could just as well have been writing about planets settling into their orbits.

What Smith had done went beyond Newton in one important respect, however. In Newton's system the earth orbits the sun, rather than falling in and becoming incinerated or flying off into space and freezing, not because it has any intent in the matter but because the physical mechanisms at work balance the in-pulling and out-pushing forces affecting it. Unlike planets, humans do act with intent, and analyzing their motivations was a large part of Smith's effort in both *The Theory of Moral Sentiments* and *The Wealth of Nations*. He assumed, on the basis of observation, that in the economic sphere their intent is just to advance their own self-interest. But through the working of the mechanism he laid out, the actions they take, merely for this reason, end up making others better off as well. The systematic cause and effect that he posited requires no intent, nor even foresight, on the part of its human actors. And because this mechanism relies on nothing other than inborn human nature, it will emerge in one setting after another, wherever it is not blocked by either government interference or private collusion.

Smith's argument in *The Wealth of Nations* held out other attractions too. It paralleled Hume's thinking in its emphasis on the positive role of *society*, in the sense of humans' natural interaction with one another. In contrast, however—and in contrast also to Smith's own emphasis in his earlier book—in *The Wealth of Nations* what primarily motivates participation in society is *economic* need. Commercial society provided the material basis, but also created the need, for human society. The central role of markets likewise presented a contrast to Hobbes's emphasis on the necessity of the state (although Smith too assumed a role for the state in providing the security and the rule of law on which market-based economic activity relies). Finally, the mechanism at the core of Smith's argument was one that worked best under conditions of human liberty, always a paramount Enlightenment value. If the key to economic success was market competition, then liberty was doubly desirable: not only for itself but also instrumentally, as a vehicle for promoting, via the market mechanism, greater productivity and higher living standards.

With *The Wealth of Nations,* Adam Smith assumed the place in the forefront of Enlightenment thinkers that he has held ever since. The book attracted immediate acclaim, both in England and Scotland and in foreign translations. But especially following the set of public lectures given in 1800–1801 by Dugald Stewart, it rose to a heightened level of prominence. Stewart, thirty years younger than Smith, was the professor of moral philosophy at the University of Edinburgh for thirty-five years, from 1785 until 1820. Just as Colin Maclaurin had helped to popularize Isaac Newton's *Principia Mathematica* a half-century before, now Stewart's lectures called *The Wealth of Nations* to the attention of a broader audience. (Because Smith wrote in English—and wrote extremely well—there was no need for Stewart to follow Maclaurin in producing a textbook translation.)

More important, with *The Wealth of Nations* the fundamental basis of what we now call "economics" was established. One historian of economic thought rightly labeled the book "the fountain-head of classical political economy."[61] It has served as the fundamental source of modern economic thinking as well. The role of market competition has remained the discipline's central conceptual apparatus. Much of the field's development since then has involved working out in greater depth and sophistication just how market competition works, and what consequences ensue when it fails to do so. In one Western country after another, much of the surrounding policy debate has likewise turned on how to enable competitive markets to do their job, and what to do when they can't.

What enabled Smith to come to these powerful insights? To be sure, he had learned from others who came before. From his time in France, he knew the market-oriented work of Boisguilbert and Cantillon. He had spent decades pondering the challenge posed by Mandeville, and he knew the responses—from Butler, Hutcheson, Hume, and many others—that Mandeville's shocking ideas had provoked. Although there is no direct evidence on the matter, he also presumably knew Nicole's essay on the outward resemblance of charity and self-love.[62] And there were contemporary economic thinkers in Britain whose work he knew as well: not just his friend and mentor Hume but also their fellow club member Adam Ferguson; Josiah Tucker, Bishop Butler's protégé, who like Smith thought of the economy as a kind of self-regulating mechanism, and therefore wrote in opposition to mercantilism and other market restrictions; Sir James Steuart, a fellow Scot who, unlike Smith, favored top-down economic systems and called for better public management of the economy; and more besides.[63]

Smith's education and experience mattered too. The presumption of a harmony in nature stemming from the inherent rationality and order of the universe, which he had absorbed from studying the stoics, was fully consistent with the belief that natural human desires and proclivities, left alone, led to beneficial outcomes that no one either anticipated or intended. Nature was fully compatible with reason, and human instincts with rational designs.[64] From this perspective, both government regulation and private monopoly represented corruption of the natural order.[65] Even the invisible hand metaphor was a familiar stoic motif, emblematic of the convergence of natural tendencies and what reason would choose.[66] Parts of Smith's analysis also reflected his close observation of the many aspects of economic activity he had encountered, from village life in Kirkcaldy to mercantile bustle in

Edinburgh, Glasgow, and London, and including what he saw when he visited France and Switzerland. These experiences often served to ground his more specific generalizations about how different economic actors behaved under various circumstances.

Yet another influence was the high value that Smith, like so many of his contemporaries, attached to personal liberty. Smith's generation grew up in the lingering glow of the Glorious Revolution, embracing not just the political stability that it had brought but also the renewed assurance of traditional liberties. The enhanced freedom of action that market exchange transactions provided, importantly including in the labor market, was surely an attraction. Any economic system that offered to provide that liberty was bound to draw support.

But even these influences hardly seem sufficient to account for the astonishing intellectual breakthrough that Smith achieved with *The Wealth of Nations*. Something else was at work as well, shaping the worldview—in Einstein's sense—that not only channeled his thinking but also made his contemporaries so willing to accept his insights once he presented them.

Predestination and Depravity

Our nature is not only destitute and empty of good, but so fertile and fruitful of every evil that it cannot be idle.

—JOHN CALVIN

By the decree of God, for the manifestation of his glory, some men and angels are predestinated unto everlasting life; and others foreordained to everlasting death.

—WESTMINSTER CONFESSION OF FAITH

The momentous change that Adam Smith and his contemporaries effected in thinking about human prospects in the economic realm was not the only intellectual groundswell under way in their society during their time. Religious thinking was undergoing a profound shift as well. The Protestant revolt against the Roman Catholic Church, which had begun in Germany two centuries before Smith was born (following an earlier, unsuccessful attempt in Bohemia a century before that), had largely reached a mature stability by his adult lifetime. The respectively Protestant and Catholic areas of Europe were by then approximately what they are today. By contrast, the struggle over what Protestants thought about the essential questions that any religion faces was still very much in progress. It was especially so within the English-speaking world.

The issues at the core of Luther's Reformation were, for the most part, *not* what English and Scottish Protestants were debating by the eighteenth century. Pre-Reformation Catholicism had revolved around the centralized institutional role of the universal church. According to established doctrine the church was the necessary intermediary between humans and the divine, personified in the office of the Catholic clergy. Lay individuals obtained salvation by grace and by their participation in the church's sacraments, administered by the clergy, and by their own good works. And when people sinned, as humans in their imperfection inevitably do, the church had authority to grant indulgence for the sins that they confessed. (An indulgence reduced the time a sinner had to spend in purgatory, suffering punishment for his sin, but it had no bearing on his ultimate salvation.)

The movement that crystallized under Martin Luther's leadership reflected deep-seated discontent among elements of both clergy and laity. Many in the clergy resisted the centralized authority of the church hierarchy, seeking instead to diffuse power to local clergymen as well as appropriately selected laymen. At the same time, many laymen yearned for a more personal form of piety, with a direct relationship to God not requiring their entering a monastery or convent, and not intermediated by a priest. Some in the clergy—for example, Thomas à Kempis in his influential *Imitatio Christi* (Imitation of Christ), at the middle of the fifteenth century—also endorsed this kind of expanded conception of the laity's place within the church. With spreading literacy, and increased private ownership of books, the desire for more direct lay participation included the ability to read and interpret the Bible on one's own. But for most laymen this required translation into a language other than the official Latin text.

The church mostly opposed translations of the Bible into contemporary languages, however—not so much from resistance to translation per se but out of concern to preserve the church's control over the Bible's meaning.[1] Many of the church's doctrines and practices (the sacrament of penance, for example) sprang from specific words in the Latin text. True, the Latin Vulgate was itself a translation from the original Hebrew or (for the New Testament) Greek, and understanding of these ancient languages had improved since the fourth century. But because of the Vulgate's "long usage of so many ages," the church nonetheless regarded it as fully authoritative, so that "no one is to dare, or presume to reject it under any pretext soever."[2] Further, some held that St. Jerome and the other translators of that time had been divinely inspired, and so if there were errors they served a divine purpose. Rendered into another language, the words might convey different theological content. Worse yet, a difference in wording that conveyed

Guido Reni, *Angel Appearing to Saint Jerome* (circa 1638).
Jerome, a fourth- and early-fifth-century theologian and one of the four great
Doctors of the Western Church, produced the Vulgate, the Latin translation
of the Bible that remained authoritative for more than a thousand years.

different theology might even be what a heretically minded translator intended. But even without any change in meaning due to translation, untrained readers might misinterpret the text. Widespread access to the Bible in everyday language, church authorities feared, would therefore lead to misunderstandings, even heresies.[3]

In time, advances in technology determined the course of events. Once Gutenberg developed movable-type printing, in 1439, enabling mass production of books at a cost many people could afford, the translation movement became unstoppable. (The famous Gutenberg Bible, published in 1454, presented no direct threat; it was the official Latin text.) By the end of the fifteenth century some 350 towns across Europe had printing presses, thirty thousand titles had been issued, and nine million books had been printed.[4] There was no way the church could prevent vernacular Bibles from being among them.[5]

The immediate catalyst for the Reformation was widespread revulsion at the perceived corruption associated with the church's sale of indulgences, often promoted via campaigns that in some ways resembled modern-day marketing efforts, along with the readily visible luxury among the church hierarchy that this practice financed. In the early years of the sixteenth century, Pope Julius II authorized several new forms of indulgences intended to fund his grand renovation of St. Peter's Basilica in Rome. After Julius died, in 1513, his successor, Leo X, followed the usual custom of revoking all indulgences proclaimed by his predecessor, but made an exception for the so-called St. Peter's Indulgence. Two years later, Leo made it a plenary indulgence, remitting punishment in purgatory for all sins committed within a person's lifetime. Moreover, those receiving it need not make confession or even be contrite in their hearts. The new indulgence was to be sold for a period of eight years, in designated regions of Germany, France, and other countries.[6]

The sales campaign prompted widespread resentment. Martin Luther, a monk living in one of the targeted areas of Germany, nailed his *Ninety-five Theses on the Power and Efficacy of Indulgences* to the church door at Wittenberg Castle on the last day of October 1517. In his *Sermon on Indulgences and Grace*, written in German, he laid out the issues as he saw them for an even wider audience. Again the technology of printing proved important. First printed in early 1518, as a twelve-page pamphlet, Luther's sermon went through more than twenty printings within two years, averaging a thousand copies each. It reached a wide readership among the educated classes. And he continued to write prolifically. By 1521, half a million copies of his various works were in circulation.[7]

At first Luther's intent was to bring about reform within the existing church—hence the name attached to his movement. But in early 1521 the pope excommunicated him, and within a few years he had not only left the priesthood but married. He and his followers increasingly understood that their reformed churches could not reunite with Roman Catholicism. Although Lutheranism became recognizable as a distinct Protestant denomination in the modern sense only after Luther's death, more than two decades later, the result of their work was to establish a new church, not to reform the old one. The Lutheran church remains today the dominant form of Protestant religion in Germany as well as throughout Scandinavia.

The principal thinker behind the Protestant movement in countries like Switzerland and the Netherlands—and soon in England and Scotland too—was John Calvin, whose work and influence amounted, in effect, to a second Reformation. Although Luther initiated what is still called "the Reformation," today and especially in English-speaking countries *Reformed* Protestantism (or the Reformed Church) means Protestantism according to Calvin.

Born in France in 1509, and therefore a generation younger than Luther, Calvin left the Roman Catholic Church while still a young man and at some point in 1534 or 1535 (the historical record is unclear) fled to Switzerland in the face of spreading violence directed against the new "Protestants." (The label stemmed from the formal statement of protest, *protestatio* in Latin, put forth by the reformers at the Diet of Speyer in 1529.) In 1536 he published the first edition of his *Institutes of the Christian Religion,* the seminal text for the Protestant theology that in time would bear his name. Calvin continued to revise and expand his great work for the remainder of his life (not to mention writing much else besides). The original edition was roughly two hundred pages. The final version published in 1559, which today is normally taken to be authoritative, runs to more than 1,500. It was first translated into English in 1561.

Also in 1536, Calvin settled in Geneva, which remained his home until his death in 1564. Under his leadership the city became a form of theocracy, with little distinction between civil authority and the newly established Reformed Church. From Geneva, Calvin inspired younger disciples, in Switzerland and elsewhere, who carried on his work after his death. Within a century the dominant religion in the Netherlands and in Britain was unmistakably Calvinist in content as well. By then the Church of England and the Church of Scotland had both become products of Calvinist thinking.

It was therefore mostly Calvin's thinking, not Luther's, that framed the intense and sometimes violent debate over religious ideas in the midst of which Adam Smith and his contemporaries lived. Importantly, that debate was not between religiously committed adherents and nonbelievers, nor between Protestants and Catholics. What was at issue was what English-speaking Protestants themselves believed.

Three fundamental questions stood at the debate's center. First, what is the moral essence of human nature? Are humans "utterly depraved," meaning that they are unable on their own to make moral choices and act in a moral way? Or did God, in creating our species, endow the human character with an inherent goodness such that any man or woman, with the right encouragement and teaching, can aspire to a morally upright life and potentially achieve it?

Second, what becomes of humans after death? And if individual men's and women's spiritual destinies differ, what determines those different paths? Is *anyone* potentially eligible for salvation, or only some? If it is only some—and maybe only a few—what determines who is saved and who isn't? In particular, do people's own choices and actions matter to this end? Or are individuals "predestined" so that some inevitably achieve salvation while others, just as inevitably, not only do not but cannot?

And third, why do humans exist in the first place? For religious believers, at a time before Darwin, the answer was of course that humans exist because God created them. But to what end? For God's own glorification? For some other purpose? Whatever the purpose, does human happiness matter for it? More than that, is human happiness a, perhaps even *the*, divine intent for our kind?

The debate over the human character, although in this instance carried out among Christians, stemmed from the creation narrative in the Hebrew Bible. Genesis describes God as placing the newly formed man and woman—the not-yet-named Adam and Eve—in a garden, assigning them "to dress it and to keep it," and giving them dominion over all animal life as well as plants. God also gave them permission to eat any plant life there (permission to eat animals came later, after the flood). But there was one exception: "of the tree of the knowledge of good and evil, thou shalt not eat of it."[8] Tempted by a talking serpent, however, Eve did eat the fruit of the forbidden tree, and then gave the fruit to Adam, who ate it as well.

God's response to this violation of his explicit instruction was a threefold curse on Adam and Eve and their descendants. (God also cursed the serpent and its descendants.) To women, painful childbearing: "I will greatly multiply thy sorrow and thy conception. In sorrow thou shalt bring forth children." To men, the need to work: "cursed is the ground for thy sake; in sorrow shalt thou eat of it all the days of thy life. . . . In the sweat of thy face shalt thou eat bread." And

Benjamin West, *The Expulsion of Adam and Eve from Paradise* (1791).
West's depiction of the tragic moment only hints at the glory of the garden
from which the man and woman (and the serpent too) have been driven,
as a dark and unwelcoming new world waits before them.

to both, mortality: the need to work would endure "till thou return
unto the ground; for out of it wast thou taken, for dust thou art,
and unto dust shalt thou return."[9] In place of the effortlessness of life in
Eden, mankind was to inhabit a world characterized by universal scarcity. To symbolize both the advent of mortality and the need to work in
order to survive, God drove the two humans from the garden, out into
the world, and placed at the gate both cherubim and a flaming sword
to bar their reentry. Human life in the lushness and comfort of the
garden gave way to the struggle to survive in a harsh and threatening
world.

But beyond the physical realities of childbearing and work and death,
what *moral* implications followed for Adam and Eve's descendants—
that is, for all subsequent humanity? Were the as yet unborn, for all
future generations, somehow implicated in their ultimate ancestors'
sin? Was the moral imperfection revealed by the disobedience of the
first man and woman evidence of a proclivity to sin inherent to the
entire species that they spawned? (With benefit of today's knowledge

of genetics and the role of DNA, it is possible to frame the question in a more mechanistic way; but the theologians of prior centuries presumably would not have chosen to do so even if they had been able.) Perhaps most troubling of all, since God had made humans in the first place—and, moreover, had made them "in his own image, in the image of God"—what would such an inborn tendency toward sin imply about either God's intention or even the nature of the divine itself?[10]

Augustine, the late-fourth- and early-fifth-century bishop perhaps best known today for his searing autobiographical *Confessions,* charted what became for centuries the dominant Christian view. God, he wrote, "created man righteous." But then Adam sinned. Moreover, "we were all in that one man, since we all were that one man who fell into sin." Further, the "seminal nature" from which all humans were to be propagated already existed, in Adam. As a result, Augustine concluded, "when this was vitiated by sin and bound by the chain of death and justly condemned, man could not be born of man in any other condition." Man—in the person of Adam—was born with free will. But "from the evil use of free will there arose the whole series of calamities by which the human race is led by a succession of miseries from its depraved origin, as from a corrupt root, even to the ruin of the second death."[11] Left to themselves, humans were incapable of doing good. The first printed edition of Augustine's collected works was published early in the sixteenth century, and his thinking was widely under discussion just as the Reformation was getting under way.

Luther likewise regarded a negative assessment of the human character as an essential part of a believer's faith. "The moment you begin to have faith," he wrote, "you learn that all things in you are altogether blameworthy, sinful and damnable." Quoting from Paul's letter to the Romans—which in turn was citing Psalm 14—"None is righteous, no, not one."[12] (Whether the psalmist meant to imply inborn depravity in Augustine's sense is far from clear; instead of taking all men to be innately incapable of doing good, the psalm says "They are all gone aside."[13]) Luther went on to observe that while the commandments show man what he ought to do, they do not give him the power to do it. "They are intended to teach man to know himself, that through them he may recognize his inability to do good and may despair of his own ability."[14]

Calvin adhered even more closely to Augustine's harsh view of the human character. In his reading, the "miserable ruin, into which the rebellion of the first man cast us" implied "ignorance, vanity, poverty, infirmity and—what is more—depravity and corruption," not just of Adam and Eve themselves but of all men and women after them. Calvin went on to define original sin, which all humans acquired from Adam's sin, as "a hereditary depravity and corruption of our nature, diffused into all parts of the soul." Nor was original sin a matter of our being punished for what was merely our ancestors' error. "This is not liability for another's transgression," Calvin insisted. "We through his transgression have become entangled in the curse . . . not only has punishment fallen upon us from Adam, but a contagion imparted by him resides in us."[15]

The emphasis that Calvin in particular placed on this inborn depravity, and the strength of the language he used to describe it, were powerful. "This perversity never ceases in us," he wrote. "Our nature is not only destitute and empty of good, but so fertile and fruitful of every evil that it cannot be idle." Again, "so depraved is [man's] nature that he can be moved or impelled only to evil." In a passage that lends itself to a genetic reading in the post-Crick-and-Watson era, Calvin declared that even newborn infants "are guilty not of another's fault but of their own. For, even though the fruits of their iniquity have not yet come forth, they have the seed enclosed within them. Indeed, their whole nature is a seed of sin."[16]

The importance that Calvin attached to the doctrine of universal human depravity stemmed from its essential connection to the central Christian belief in redemption by Jesus's sacrifice on the cross. If some individuals were without sin, what would Christ's sacrifice be to them? But the Christian interpretation of the Fall implied a profound pessimism about man's ability to redeem himself apart from some act, some gift, from God. Because of the disobedience of Adam and Eve, and the hereditary depravity imputed to each of their descendants individually, no one was without sin. (One reminder of the essentially Christian nature of the doctrine is that the words "sin" and "fall" do not appear in the story as related in Genesis.[17]) As Paul wrote to the Corinthians, "since by man came death, by man came also the resurrection of the dead. For as in Adam all die, even so in Christ shall all be made alive."[18] As Calvin put it, "our lord came forth as true man and took the person and the name of Adam in order to take Adam's place in obeying

Giovanni di Paolo, *The Mystery of Redemption* (from Dante, *Paradiso,* circa 1450).
Adam and Jesus represent the bookends of human experience—
Fall and Redemption—with the Annunciation in between, as Beatrice explains
the mystery to Dante, with Justinian in the heaven before them.

the Father . . . and to pay the penalty that we had deserved."[19] Adam
and Jesus represented the bookends of humans' spiritual journey, the
one having corrupted all subsequent humanity and the other offering
redemption. Without the Fall, the Crucifixion loses its meaning. It is
no coincidence that Christian art of the period often portrayed the two
together. And often when Adam was not present in the picture in his
full flesh, his skull lay beside Christ's foot.[20]

The notion of humans' inborn depravity had implications beyond
the realm of theology, however. It provided an explanation for humans'
harmful, even disastrous, behavior toward one another, which persisted incorrigibly from one generation to the next. It had a particular
resonance for Europeans who had lived through the destruction and
cruel atrocities of the Thirty Years' War and the English Civil War. Secular thinkers concerned with the limits to human sociability, and the
challenge they posed to governance, likewise framed their inquiry in
these terms. For Hobbes, the potential war of all against all was the
greatest threat presented by fallen man. Pierre Nicole's description of
the "monster we harbor in our bosoms," which allows self-love to motivate so much of what we do, was even more directly an expression of
Calvin's idea of human corruption and depravity. (Nicole was a Roman
Catholic, but as a Jansenist he shared Calvin's radically Augustinian
theology.) He intended his analysis of how self-love "trim[s] itself up

with the appearances of charity" to explain how a society peopled by fallen men could nonetheless function with peace and order.[21] Adam Smith, following his teacher Francis Hutcheson, saw markets as an institution that disciplined individual behavior and that provided at least limited justice in the face of human imperfection.

Belief in Calvin's view of depravity and original sin acquired increasing dominance within English Protestantism, especially within the church hierarchy.[22] England under Henry VIII had broken away from the Roman Catholic Church in 1533, before Calvin had even left France. The immediate cause of the rupture, however, was not theological but political: Henry's desire to remarry, in the hope of providing England with a male heir, and the pope's refusal to annul his marriage to his longtime wife Catherine of Aragon (despite the approval of Thomas Cranmer, the Archbishop of Canterbury and therefore England's leading Catholic prelate). But the political origins of the separation notwithstanding, the newly independent English church now had to decide on its doctrine.

The process was chaotic, in part because after Henry's death whether England would remain Protestant or return to Roman Catholicism remained in dispute. Protestants and Roman Catholics each claimed that *they* constituted the true Catholic Church. The matter was firmly settled—in favor of an independent Protestant church—only after Henry's younger daughter took the throne as Elizabeth I, in 1558. The English church's Thirty-Nine Articles of Religion, drafted in Latin shortly thereafter but not officially promulgated in English until 1571, became and still today remains the codified doctrinal confession of Anglican (that is, the Church of England's, but today including the worldwide communion of which the Church of England is a part) belief.[23] While the church's Book of Common Prayer, originally based on pre-Reformation services but revised in 1552 to remove Roman Catholic elements, guides day-to-day and week-to-week worship and practice, the Thirty-Nine Articles are included in the Book of Common Prayer and historically the church has viewed the two as fully compatible. From 1571 on, every ordained minister was required by statute to subscribe to the confession.[24]

On the question of man's inherent nature, the Thirty-Nine Articles followed Calvin closely: original sin (also called birth-sin) "standeth not in the following of Adam ... it is the fault and corruption of the

Hans Memling, *The Last Judgment* (1467–1471).
Sorted at the final judgment, individual souls faced starkly different fates.
Images like Memling's brought believers face-to-face with
what they could wish or fear for their own everlasting destiny.

nature of every man." Man is "of his own nature inclined to evil."[25] Not surprisingly, it was the most Calvinistically inclined members of the sixteenth-century Church of England who pushed to give the Thirty-Nine Articles in their existing form as much authority as possible.

Nearly a century later, at the high tide of orthodox Calvinist influence in England, the doctrine was still the same. The Westminster Confession of Faith, agreed upon by a gathering of Puritan theologians convened by Parliament during the English Civil War, declared that "Our first parents . . . sinned in eating the forbidden fruit . . . and so became dead in sin." And what implication followed for Adam and Eve's descendants? "They being the root of all mankind, the guilt of this sin was imputed, and the same death in sin and corrupted nature conveyed to all their posterity." The continuing implications for human character were severe: "From this original corruption . . . we are utterly indisposed, disabled, and made opposite to all good, and wholly inclined to do all evil."[26]

·   ·   ·

In light of this inherently sinful and corrupted nature of all humans—
even newborn infants—what were Protestants to think about their
individual prospects for ultimate salvation? Did the depravity so
forcefully articulated by Calvin, and reconfirmed by both the Thirty-
Nine Articles and the Westminster Confession, condemn everyone to
eternal damnation? If instead some are to be saved, then who? And
by what means? Above all, for believers who are understandably concerned for their own ultimate spiritual prospects, can *any*body gain
access to those means?

On this question the Hebrew Bible was mostly silent, as were the
Gospels of the New Testament. Despite implicit references to some
kind of life after death in the earlier parts of the Bible—Jacob's concern
that his youngest son's death would bring down his gray hairs "to Sheol,"
rather than leaving him to be "gathered to his people" as Abraham and
Isaac were, and Saul's bringing up the long-dead Samuel (from where
is not stated) to seek his advice[27]—the notion of a resurrection and
subsequent afterlife did not explicitly enter the biblical texts until the
book of Daniel, a late addition dating to the second century before the
current era.[28] Envisioning the end of the world, but also some form
of renewed existence for those formerly living, the prophet foresees
that "many of them that sleep in the dust of the earth shall awake,
some to everlasting life, and some to shame and everlasting contempt."
And who would have which fate? "They that be wise shall shine as the
brightness of the firmament, and they that turn many to righteousness,
as the stars for ever and ever."[29] Daniel says nothing about the characteristics of those destined for shame and contempt.

The Gospel according to Matthew contains a similar reference,
although without explicitly identifying any specific attributes (like wisdom and righteousness in Daniel's account) of those who will enjoy
everlasting life. Instead, Jesus preaches a parable that begins, "The
kingdom of heaven is like unto a certain king, which made a marriage
for his son, and sent forth his servants to call them that were bidden
to the wedding, and they would not come." The apparent suggestion
is that human choice—in the parable, whether to attend the wedding
feast—matters for who will gain entry to the heavenly kingdom. But
the parable ends on a different note, as one guest who does attend "had
not on a wedding garment." Seeing him, the king instructs his attendants to "cast him into outer darkness," where there would be weeping

and gnashing of teeth, and Jesus concludes the parable with the cryptic summary, "many are called, but few are chosen." Hence human will alone is *not* sufficient.[30] The Apocryphal book of 4 Ezra likewise states that "The Most High made this world for the sake of many, but the world to come for the sake of a few."[31]

It was Paul, not the gospelists, who elaborated the sense in which only a few are chosen. In his letter to the Romans, often considered his most important work,[32] the apostle pondered whether God had turned away from the people of Israel. "Hath God cast away his people?" Paul asked. "God forbid," he answered. "At this present time also there is a remnant according to the election of grace." But the conclusion that the choice of this remnant was by grace bore an important implication: "if by grace, then it is no more of works; otherwise grace is no more grace."[33] Paul repeated the point in his letter to the Ephesians: "by grace ye are saved through faith, and that not of yourselves: it is the gift of God: not of works."[34] And to the Galatians, he wrote that "by the works of the law shall no flesh be justified."[35] Instead of choosing who will enter the kingdom of heaven according to their works—the righteous in Daniel, for example, or in Jesus's parable the wedding guests who did wear appropriate garments—for this purpose God acted purely out of his own grace. Salvation was not earned.

Several books of the Hebrew Bible far earlier than Daniel had given grounds for believing that God favors some individuals over others— and, moreover, that God's choice is not a consequence of human action—although unlike in what either Daniel or Paul wrote the context there does not explicitly bear on individuals' life after death. When Jacob and Esau struggle against one another as unborn infants, God tells their mother, Rebecca, "Two nations are in thy womb, and two manner of people shall be separated from thy bowels; and the one people shall be stronger than the other people, and the elder shall serve the younger."[36] God gives no reason for preferring Jacob over Esau in this way. More directly, for purposes of Paul's emphasis on the role of God's grace as opposed to choosing one individual instead of another on account of their respective works or other merits, after the escaping Hebrew slaves' sin of worshipping a golden calf during their flight from Egypt, God tells Moses, "I . . . will be gracious to whom I will be gracious, and will show mercy on whom I will show mercy."[37]

During the few centuries leading up to the emergence of Christianity, Jewish thinking imported from Plato and other Greek sources the idea of some kind of immortal soul that would outlive the physical body, perhaps eternally. As it did so, concern for that soul's individual fate acquired increased prominence. As in Daniel's contemplation of a physical resurrection, however, the emphasis was on the reward or punishment of each individual according to his or her personal merits. Even before Daniel, the prophet Ezekiel had stressed that a person's turning aside from sin might stave off whatever divine punishment he otherwise deserved.[38] This interest in personal salvation, and what would bring it about, became all the more intense once the destruction of the Jewish Temple, in the year 70, ended the animal sacrifice that was supposed to atone for the nation's sins as well as those of individuals.[39]

The Dead Sea Scrolls, many of which date to the period of the New Testament Gospels and Paul's letters, contain numerous references not only to an afterlife but to an idea of chosenness that clearly anticipates the direction taken by Paul. (The sectarian community that produced the Scrolls was presumably expressing its view of its own special destiny.) According to the Ages of Creation text, for example, "In accordance with God's compassion and in accordance with his goodness and the wonder of his glory, he has brought close some from among the sons of the earth . . . to be considered with him in the community of celestials, to be a holy congregation, standing in rank for eternal life, in one lot with his holy ones." There is a destiny for "each man according to his lot which God has cast for him."[40] The image of God's casting a lot (or a fate) for the chosen ones is a characteristic turn of phrase used frequently in the Scrolls. Another typical passage—in this case from the Thanksgivings, the set of psalm-like statements of praise for God that are unique to the Dead Sea Scrolls—links chosenness with rescue from depravity, referring to "the depraved spirit you have purified from great iniquity, that he might stand in rank with the host of holy ones and come into community with the congregation of the sons of heaven."[41] The sense of awe at having been cast in the lot of the elect, despite one's earthly impurity and unworthiness, is likewise a repeated theme.

Beyond emphasizing the crucial role of God's grace, Paul also introduced the parallel idea of *pre*destination: that since an individual's election did not depend on his or her actions, God could—and did—make the choice to confer grace not only without waiting to see how the person lived but before the person even lived at all. Paul wrote to the Romans, "For whom he did foreknow, he also did predestinate to be conformed to the image of his Son."[42] Writing to the Ephesians, Paul went further, explaining that God's choice predated not only the individual's life but even the creation of the world. "He hath chosen us in him before the foundation of the world, that we should be holy and without blame before him." Even before creating the world, God had "predestinated us . . . according to the good pleasure of his will, to the praise of the glory of his grace, wherein he hath made us accepted in the beloved."[43]

The early church fathers likewise regarded who was to be saved, and who not, as a central question. The most articulate on the subject was Augustine, who took up predestination and its relation to human depravity in his *Treatise on the Gift of Perseverance*, written in 428, just two years before his death. "This is the predestination of the saints," Augustine wrote, "the foreknowledge and the preparation of God's kindnesses, whereby they are most certainly delivered." Predestination of the saints was God's gift, which God "foreknew" that he would give to his chosen ones. In rejecting the possibility of human agency's being effective for this purpose, Augustine likewise echoed Paul's disclaimer that this gift was in any respect bestowed in anticipation of an individual's own worth or deeds. Rather, it is "the true grace of God, that is, that which is not given in respect of our merits."[44]

Eleven centuries later, Calvin elevated the doctrine of predestination, in the sense of both Paul and Augustine, to a place of paramount importance in his theology. With predestination, salvation—for those who were saved—was eternally secure; it was not contingent on human action. Moreover, Calvin was explicit about an aspect of the doctrine that Paul had left unspecified: what of those who were *not* predestined as saints? Were they simply passed over, as if by oversight or neglect? Or were they too the subject of God's purposeful judgment, only in their case a negative one?

According to Daniel those who did not awake to everlasting life were to suffer shame and everlasting contempt, and in Jesus's parable as related by Matthew the king instructed his attendants to cast the unwelcome guest into outer darkness, where there was weeping and gnashing of teeth. Calvin's view of predestination was similar. "It comes to pass by God's bidding," he wrote in the *Institutes*, "that salvation is freely offered to some while others are barred from access to it." All men are not born into equal condition. Some are to enjoy eternal life, others eternal damnation. God "does not indiscriminately adopt all into the hope of salvation but gives to some what he denies to others." Indeed, "by his just and irreprehensible but incomprehensible judgment he has barred the door of life to those whom he has given over to damnation."[45]

This explicitly two-sided rendering, in which both the salvation of the saved and the damnation of the damned are deliberate choices made by God, was not original to Calvin. As early as the seventh century, the Spanish archbishop Isidore of Seville had labeled it "double," or "twin," predestination: "There is a double predestination, of the elect to rest and of the reprobate to death." And Isidore in turn had attributed the doctrine to Augustine two centuries before.[46] But Calvin placed far greater emphasis on the two-sided purposefulness of God's decision to confer grace or not, and following the Reformation *double* predestination—often called that by critics—became associated with his thinking.

Crucially, Calvin strictly followed both Paul and Augustine in attributing the choice to save or to damn a person to God's own grace, not the person's actions. God, he wrote, "utterly disregarding works, chooses those whom he has decreed within himself . . . God of his mere good pleasure preserves whom he will." More specifically, "with respect to the elect, this plan was founded upon his freely given mercy, without regard to human worth." And he followed Paul and Augustine as well as in therefore dating this choice to before the person lived, indeed before there was a world at all. God "established by his eternal and unchangeable plan those whom he long before determined . . . to receive into salvation, and those whom, on the other hand, he would devote to destruction."[47] The concept of election, by divine grace alone, became central to Calvin's Reformed theology. Unconditional chosenness—of the children of Israel before the coming of Christ, and of the individual elect after—united human experience.[48]

As the German sociologist Max Weber famously emphasized, looking back on the Puritan experience in particular, knowing that they had been either saved or damned for all eternity—and with no opportunity to affect that determination, which had been made eons before their birth—was deeply troubling to many Calvinist believers.[49] Righteous conduct, even faith itself, might provide external signs that a person was among the elect, and pious Puritans sought reassurance in whatever inference they might intuit from their own attitude or conduct. But these potential indications were merely that; they were never causal, because for this purpose there could be no human cause. The sole determining factor was God's freely given grace. The resulting existential anxiety (a term used by Weber, and later by the mid-twentieth-century theologian Paul Tillich[50]) was no more than what Calvin anticipated. "All those who do not know that they are God's own will be miserable through constant fear," Calvin wrote.[51] Much of the fire-and-brimstone preaching of the Puritan clergy who taught the Calvinist doctrine exacerbated that fear (as no doubt it was meant to do).

Even so, Calvin argued that the doctrine of predestination was a *comfort* to believers. Knowing that they were utterly depraved and corrupt, as a consequence of Adam's sin and from it the Fall of all mankind, they understood that their own character deserved only damnation. But for no reason attributable to their own merit, merit that for this purpose was completely lacking, some few among them—Calvin often thought one in a hundred, but sometimes one in twenty or even one in five—would nonetheless be saved, simply by God's gracious choice. And anyone who is saved "is then relieved and set free not only from the extreme anxiety and fear that were pressing him before, but from every care." Hence while there was fear, there could be hope too. "In the very darkness that frightens them," Calvin wrote, "not only is the usefulness of this doctrine made known but also its very sweet fruit."[52]

As with the doctrine of depravity, here too official belief among the early English Protestants followed Calvin's thinking. The Thirty-Nine Articles stated that "Predestination to Life is the everlasting purpose of God, whereby (before the foundations of the world were laid) he hath constantly decreed . . . to deliver from curse and damnation those whom he hath chosen." As a result, predestination is "so excellent a benefit of God." It is "full of sweet, pleasant, and unspeakable comfort to godly persons . . . because it doth greatly establish and confirm their faith of eternal Salvation."[53]

The Westminster Confession followed Calvin's thinking more completely, making explicit both sides of double predestination. "By the decree of God, for the manifestation of his glory," the Confession stated, "some men and angels are predestinated unto everlasting life; and others foreordained to everlasting death." Also following Paul and Augustine, "Those of mankind that are predestinated unto life, God, before the foundation of the world was laid, . . . hath chosen . . . out of his mere free grace and love, without any foresight of faith or good works." And what of everyone else? "The rest of mankind God was pleased . . . to pass by, and to ordain them to dishonor and wrath for their sin, to the praise of his glorious justice."[54]

The depraved nature of humans, resulting from the Fall, likewise bore implications for why humans exist in the first place and therefore what is our purpose in living, questions just as fundamental as what happens to us after we cease to exist.

Numerous sections of the Hebrew Bible make clear that the creation—all of it—stands as a glory to God the creator. On each of the six days of the account of creation in Genesis, including the day on which the first man and woman are formed, God proclaims that the result is "good." The Psalms especially are full of exultant statements of God's resulting glory. Psalm 8 declares that God's glory is above the heavens. Psalm 24 repeatedly refers to God as the King of glory. Psalm 29 enjoins us to "give unto the Lord Glory and strength." Psalm 57, addressing God, proclaims "let thy glory be above all the earth." Psalms 72 and 108 repeat the same thought. Psalm 104 expresses confidence that the glory of the Lord will endure forever. Psalm 145, again addressing God, predicts that in future generations the saints "shall speak of the glory of thy Kingdom." Psalm 148, after a series of injunctions to praise God, again concludes that his glory is above the earth and heaven.

The idea of creation as glory to God also occurs repeatedly in the Bible's prophetic writings. Isaiah represents God as saying of his people, "every one that is called by my name . . . I have created him for my glory." Similarly, according to Isaiah God speaks of "my people, my chosen. This people have I formed for myself, they shall shew forth my praise." Most famously, the prophet declares that "the whole earth is full of his glory." Describing God, Habakkuk envisions that "His glory covered the heavens, and the earth was full of his praise."[55]

The New Testament repeatedly expresses the same theme. The Gospel according to John, for example, quotes Jesus as saying to God, "I have glorified thee on earth; I have finished the work which thou gavest me to do." Writing to the Corinthians, Paul instructed his followers, "Whether therefore ye eat or drink, or whatsoever ye do, do all to the glory of God." The image of God's glory is also integral to the more explicitly Christian pairing of creation with salvation. Using nearly identical language, both Matthew and Luke picture Jesus's return as "in the clouds of heaven with power and great glory."[56]

But why are humans, having been created only then to have fallen, enjoined to engage in this glorification? Does God somehow benefit from being glorified by such corrupt beings? Drawing on these and other biblical passages, Calvin consistently concluded that humans—depraved as they are—were created not for their own sake but for the sake of God's glory, and that that glory was the ultimate purpose of all creation including theirs.[57] Even the Fall itself glorified God, as do all things that come to pass. So too, therefore, does the salvation of some, as well as the damnation of others: "the pious mind realizes that the punishment of the impious and wicked and the reward of life eternal for the righteous equally pertain to God's glory."[58]

Addressing a contemporary critic, the Dutch Catholic theologian Albertus Pighius, Calvin pointed to the verse in Proverbs that states, "The Lord hath made all things for himself: yea, even the wicked for the day of evil."[59] He concluded that "God, though needing nothing to be added to Himself, yet created the race of men for his own glory." This was "the great and essential end of man's creation."[60] Here Calvin was again following Augustine, in this case Augustine's more personal statement addressing God in his Confessions: "You had no need of me. I do not possess such goodness as to give you help, my Lord and my God."[61] The chasm between God's righteousness and human depravity was too great.[62]

But if so, what then is the point of the repeated injunction that humans actively engage in glorifying God? According to Calvin, glorifying God is the only purpose fallen man has left. Writing in the Institutes, he explained that before Adam's sin, "Scripture attributed nothing else to him than that he had been created in the image of God." And afterward? "What, therefore, now remains for man, bare and destitute of all glory, but to recognize God for whose beneficence he could not be grateful when he abounded with the riches of his grace"—that is, before the Fall—"and at least, by confessing his own poverty, to glorify him in whom he did not previously glory."[63]

Further, Calvin firmly rejected any idea that humans were to glorify God merely for *their* benefit: "What! does God desire to be worshipped by us, more for our sakes, than for his own? Is His regard for His own glory so buried out of His sight, that He regards us alone?" And referring to the many biblical statements like those in the Psalms, "What then is to become of all those testimonies of the Scripture which make the glory of God to be the highest object and ultimate end of man's salvation?" Answering his own rhetorical questions, he concluded, "Let us hold fast this glorious truth;—that the mind of God, in our salvation, was such as not to forget himself, but to set his own glory in the first and highest place." Continuing in language that resonated with that of the prophet Isaiah, "He made the whole world, for the very end, that it might be a stupendous theatre whereon to manifest his own glory."[64] The image of all creation as a theater of God's glory became a central theme in Calvinist theology.

At the same time, the ultimate desire of each man or woman must be salvation, Calvin thought, and salvation would bring happiness beyond the human imagination. "Let us always have in mind," he wrote, "the eternal happiness, the goal of resurrection—a happiness of whose excellence the minutest part would scarce be told if all were said that the tongues of man can say." The Kingdom of God, as Calvin pictured it, "will be filled with splendor, joy, happiness, and glory."[65]

But Calvin was also clear that access to this happiness was not universal. Only those who are able to achieve humility and dependence before God will enjoy it, and only the elect—those who are so predestined—will succeed. All men and women can, indeed should, aspire to this supreme happiness; but only the saved, whom God has favored with grace, can achieve it. "If the Lord will share his glory, power, and righteousness with the elect," Calvin wrote, "nay, will give himself to be enjoyed by them and, what is more excellent, will somehow make them to become one with himself, let us remember that every sort of happiness is included under this benefit."[66]

In light of the repeated injunctions to glorify God in both the Hebrew Bible and the New Testament, Calvin was hardly alone in accepting this purpose as the essential intent underlying creation. But he uniquely made this theme central to his theology, in such a way as to suggest that everything God does, everything God makes happen, is ultimately for God's own glory. In the words of one modern interpreter, "Calvin, who was constantly overwhelmed by the majesty of God, consecrated himself and his theology to the glory of God." It was this "zeal for the glory of God" that gave his theology its distinctive character.[67]

Like his ideas of depravity and predestination, Calvin's view of the purpose of human existence became central to his followers' theology as well—and, soon after, to the belief of most English-speaking Protestants. Echoing Calvin's statements about God's self-sufficiency, the Westminster Confession declares that "God hath all life, glory, goodness, blessedness, in and of himself; and is alone and in and unto himself all-sufficient, not standing in need of any creatures which he hath made, nor deriving any glory from them, but only manifesting his own glory." Similarly, that glory was the exclusive purpose of creation: "It pleased God . . . for the manifestation of the glory of his eternal power, wisdom, and goodness, in the beginning, to create or make of nothing the world, and all things therein."[68]

And what, then, is the purpose of humans' existence? Again according to the Westminster Confession, "God, the great Creator of all things, doth uphold, direct, dispose, and govern all creatures, actions, and things, from the greatest to the least . . . to the praise of the glory of his wisdom, power, justice, goodness, and mercy."[69] The Westminster Larger Catechism, the instructional set of questions and answers written in 1646–1647 by the group of Puritan clergy who also drafted the Confession, followed the same line of thought. The Catechism begins by asking "What is the chief and highest end of man?" The stated answer: "to glorifie God, and fully to enjoy him for ever."[70]

Assault on Orthodox Calvinism

It is the greatest and justest discouragement in the world to all
endeavors of repentance and reformation, to tell men that they
can do nothing in it.

—JOHN TILLOTSON

We cannot, as moral agents, observe what is right and true, or
be righteous and holy, without our own free and explicit choice.

—JOHN TAYLOR

C alvin's ideas of depravity, predestination, and the purpose of human
existence spread rapidly within the expanding Protestant world, and
after his death in 1564 followers like Theodore Beza in Geneva and
William Perkins in Cambridge continued to elaborate these doctrines
and further their command over churchgoers' belief. In time, however,
questions arose even among the committed faithful. Not surprisingly,
the doctrine of predestination—intended by Calvin as a source of comfort but, to many of those faithful, ground for profound anxiety and
even despair—was a particular focus of concern.

Almost by accident, a Dutch theologian, Jacob Arminius, became
the fulcrum of the dispute. Born in 1560, Arminius had been a student first at Leiden and then at Geneva under Calvin's successor Beza.
He then returned to Holland, where he served as a minister in the
Reformed Church in Amsterdam. In 1589 a colleague asked him to
refute the ideas put forth by two ministers in Delft who had refused
to endorse Beza's view, following Augustine and Calvin, that the elect
who were to be saved were chosen before the Fall of Adam and Eve.[1] At
about the same time, the Amsterdam consistory (the governing body

of the local Reformed Church) asked Arminius to refute the views of another Dutch theologian who was critical of Calvinist doctrine more broadly. Especially in the latter dispute, two aspects of predestination were particularly at issue: Did those who were among the elect have to do anything, or even merely have to will something, to receive God's grace once it was given? Or were their actions and their will beside the point for this purpose? And once someone received God's grace, could he fall away from it? If so, how? On each set of issues, the question in short was whether human agency—choice or action, or both— mattered for an individual's salvation.

With Arminius's credentials as a former student of Theodore Beza, the presumption was that he would reaffirm the orthodox Calvinist doctrine. But despite his Calvinist pedigree, after study and reflection his answers to the questions given him took a different direction. Yes, he concluded, an act of human will *is* involved in receiving God's grace: God "foreknew" who would accept faith and who wouldn't, and extended his grace not arbitrarily but to those who he knew in advance would choose in this way. While grace alone was still what mattered for salvation, the giving of grace was not unconditional but rather in foreknowledge of who would choose faith.[2] Grace, therefore, *can* be resisted.

Further, Arminius concluded, individual humans can fall from grace after receiving it. True, those who have received this "life-giving Spirit" thereby have "sufficient powers to fight against Satan, sin, the world and their own flesh, and to gain the victory over these enemies." But this strength is not theirs unconditionally. Only if they "stand prepared for the battle, implore his help, and be not wanting to themselves," will God preserve them from falling.[3] Arminius's answer to each question put to him, therefore, was—in part—that human choice and agency matter.

Arminius made no attempt to publish his unexpected conclusions, and he was circumspect even in what he wrote but did not publish. After stating his view of the need for the saints to stand ready for battle and implore God's help, for example, he modestly opined that it would be useful for a church synod (a formal church gathering) "to institute a diligent inquiry from the Scriptures, whether it is not possible for some individuals through negligence . . . to decline from the sound doctrine which was once delivered to them," and thereby cause the divine grace they have received to be ineffectual. Even more cautiously, "Though I here openly and ingenuously affirm, that I never taught that a true believer can either totally or finally fall away from the faith, and perish; yet I will not conceal, that there are passages of Scripture which seem to me to wear this aspect."[4]

These departures from Calvinist orthodoxy had begun to influence Arminius's sermons, however, and in 1591 one of his senior colleagues in the Amsterdam ministry complained to the local consistory.[5] Arminius managed to satisfy the consistory that he was preaching nothing improper, and the matter remained quiet for more than a decade. But in 1603 he was appointed professor of theology at the university in Leiden and at this point the controversy became acute. Rival theologians, including Arminius's earlier accuser, publicly objected to university proceedings involving Arminius and others holding like views, and opposed the dissertations of their opponents' students. The dispute soon came also to involve matters of church authority and governance—in this case, whether only religious bodies or the civil authorities as well could remove an unorthodox minister or professor, or convene a national-level synod.

Arminius died in 1609 but the publication of his writings, beginning soon after his death, kept the controversy alive.[6] Less than a year later, his followers presented an official petition to the States-General of Holland, the highest Dutch civil authority, raising five specific points of disagreement with the prevailing Calvinist orthodoxy. Even though Arminius was no longer there to argue his views, his followers did so in his name and the position they advanced quickly acquired the label "Arminian." In time, for faithful Calvinists, Arminian became an all-purpose epithet referring not just to dissent concerning these specific aspects of predestination but to any form of disagreement with orthodox Calvinist doctrine. (Arminius was never as important for the Arminians as Calvin was for the Calvinists.)

In response to the Arminians' petition, those committed to the predestinarian view as laid out by Calvin and Beza responded with a counterpetition of their own, reaffirming the unconditional nature of God's grace and the impossibility of falling from it. As was typical of such doctrinal disagreements, each side claimed authority in the line of Paul and then Augustine. The dispute simmered for the better part of a decade until, in 1618, the Dutch Reformed Church convened a synod to settle the debate. Held in the southern Dutch city of Dordrecht—commonly, Dort—the gathering included representatives of the Dutch church's provincial synods and of the Dutch universities. Representatives of the Reformed churches in Switzerland, Britain, and Germany came as well. Throughout, the meeting was instigated, organized, and dominated by the orthodox Calvinist forces.

After six months of debate, the Dort Synod predictably rejected Arminius's views and reaffirmed the orthodox doctrine. The synod's official concluding statement, affirmed in April 1619 and issued in May, organized this accepted belief around five "points" that directly responded to the challenges raised by the Arminians, and that then formed the basis of orthodox Calvinism.[7] In time, at least among English-speaking Calvinists, it became popular to order these five points according to the convenient mnemonic TULIP:[8] Total Depravity, in the sense of extreme corruption and sinfulness of human nature following the Fall, so that humans cannot, without assistance, choose to have faith. Unconditional Election, so that God's choice of whom to save is by his will alone, not in respect of any decision or action, or any other merit, of those who are chosen—hence implying also the unlimited sovereignty of God in making this election, and in parallel the absence of any role in it for human choice or action other than that consequent on receiving God's grace. Limited Atonement, meaning that although Jesus's suffering and death were sufficient to atone for the sins of all humanity, they are nonetheless efficacious only for the elect. Irresistible Grace, so that—contrary to the Arminians (and perhaps to Arminius himself, depending on which of his statements one chooses)—the elect inevitably turn to faith, and do so only once, and no one who is chosen can resist either God's grace or the salvation it brings. And Perseverance of the Saints, meaning—again contrary to the Arminians—that the elect cannot fall away from faith (and anyone who appears to do so never really had faith to begin with).

The States-General accepted the Dort Synod's statement, and to enforce its content within the church sent it on to each of the country's provincial synods. Ministers who refused to sign it—roughly two hundred of them—were removed from office. Those who continued to speak out against the Dort principles were banished from the country. It was, for the time being, a total victory for the orthodox side.

Total depravity, unconditional election, limited atonement, irresistible grace, and perseverance of the saints continued to frame the central doctrine of orthodox Calvinist belief for at least the next three centuries, and in some quarters they still do today. (The phrase "five-point Calvinist"—or sometimes even TULIP Calvinist—still often refers to a believer in Reformed doctrine as laid down at Dort.) But the discomfort that these ideas caused among many of the would-be faithful did not disappear, nor did the debate that Arminius and his followers had initiated. By the time of Adam Smith and his contemporaries, more than a century after the Dort Synod, that debate remained intense within Protestant church circles, especially in Scotland. In the meanwhile, contention over religion, among other issues, had led to a civil war and a revolution.

In 1534, following his excommunication the year before, Henry VIII proclaimed himself head of the newly independent Church of England, and for the remaining thirteen years of his lifetime the English church was anti-Rome politically albeit not yet clearly Protestant in its the-

Martyrdom of George Marsh and William Flower, 1555.
The execution of hundreds of committed Protestants, often enacted as a public spectacle, during "Bloody" Mary's brief reign reinforced popular antipathy toward Catholicism in England.

ology. (Henry himself was firmly anti-Protestant.) But Henry's death led to a dozen years of turmoil. His nine-year-old son, who assumed the throne as Edward VI, never attained sufficient age or stature to be a governing force in his own right, and so others—often pursuing their own objectives—ruled, and disagreed, in his name. After just six years Edward died, succeeded by his older half-sister, Mary. Mary was Henry's daughter by his first wife, the Spanish Catherine. Like her mother, she was a staunch Catholic, and within a year of assuming the throne she married the Catholic prince Philip of Spain, son of the Holy Roman Emperor Charles V who had spent years fighting the Protestants on the continent. She quickly sought to return England to the Roman Church. But by then (Mary came to the throne twenty years after the initial separation under her father), increasing numbers of Englishmen were becoming accustomed to Protestantism and many had become committed Protestants.[9] Her effort to root them out, involving not just dismissals of clergymen from their posts but outright persecutions including public burnings—more than three hundred were killed—earned her the lasting sobriquet Bloody Mary. John Foxe's *Book of Martyrs,* recording many of these events, became England's most widely read book after the Bible.

Mary died in 1558, having reigned for only five years. Her younger half-sister, Elizabeth, was Henry's daughter by Anne Boleyn, his first wife after the break with Rome enabled him to remarry. Unlike Mary, Elizabeth had been reared as a Protestant. Moreover, the chief foreign threat that England faced during her forty-five-year reign was from Catholic Spain. Once she succeeded to the throne, Elizabeth was determined to maintain her kingdom's independence and with it that of the English church, beginning the very next year with an Act of Uniformity that reconfirmed her control over all church matters—including requiring all English persons to attend church weekly. The Thirty-Nine Articles, laying out the basic tenets of Anglican belief, were likewise a product of the effort to consolidate England's Protestant settlement. The queen officially sanctioned the Latin version of the new confession in 1563; the English translation in use today, including some minor changes, appeared eight years later. With the Articles' publication in English, an oath of conformity was required for all ordained clergy. Increasingly, predestinarian theology prevailed within the Church of England.[10]

As the separation between the English and Roman churches deepened, the Roman Church excommunicated the queen. In return, all Catholic priests in her realm were officially classified as traitors. Even so, whether England would survive as an independent and Protestant country remained in doubt until 1588, when a combination of lucky weather and Francis Drake's seamanship delivered a historic victory over the massive armada sent by Spain's King Philip II (who thirty years earlier had been king of England while he was married to Queen Mary).[11] In 1593 another act under Elizabeth specified capital punishment as the ultimate penalty for anyone refusing to worship within the Church of England.[12]

By this time, however, the contention facing English Protestantism came from not one front but two: not just the continual threat to the nation from Catholic Spain, but an increasingly intense dispute within Protestant ranks over matters of doctrine as well as observance. Given the essentially nontheological motivation for the English church's departure from Roman Catholicism in the first place, Protestant believers influenced by Calvin and his followers found the Church of England still too Catholic. At the same time, even though the dispute triggered by Arminius's followers and the consequent debate at Dort were yet to burst forth, among other English Protestants resistance to Calvinist doctrines such as predestination was also beginning to appear. Increasingly, the lines of contention were not Protestant versus Catholic, but within Protestantism.[13]

Although Elizabeth personally disliked Calvinism, in the interest of political stability she strove to keep open dissent firmly in check during her reign. When the influential theologian Richard Hooker attempted to articulate a middle way between Reformed Protestantism and Roman Catholicism, for example, drawing accusations that he diverged from the Thirty-Nine Articles, he was pressured to affirm predestinarian doctrine.[14] On Elizabeth's death in 1603, however, the competing factions became more vocal. The new king, James I (who was already James VI in Scotland), voiced support for what had by then become the orthodox Calvinist view. He also agreed to convene a conference—not a church-convened council with the authority to legislate, but merely an informal meeting—to debate these and related questions. The conference took place the next year, at Hampton Court outside London. The Puritan faction attempted to gain confessional status for a set of articles drafted some years earlier by the Archbishop of Canterbury (called the Lambeth Articles, from the archbishop's residence) after a prominent Cambridge theologian had challenged the doctrine of predestination, but which Queen Elizabeth had rejected. But James likewise declined to endorse them.

In the end, little came of the gathering for purposes of settling troublesome theological questions. Instead, the Hampton Court Conference is best remembered today for commissioning a new translation of the Bible into English. It took seven years for the appointed committees of scholars to complete their work, and the new Bible, duly named for the king who had convened the conference, appeared in 1611. The King James Bible stands as one of the grandest monuments of the English language, profoundly influencing literary usage as well as popular speech over more than four centuries.

The ongoing religious contention within English Protestantism did not disappear, however. (Nor did the threat from Catholic Europe. In 1605 the authorities in London foiled a plot to blow up the Houses of Parliament and assassinate the king; four hundred years later England still celebrates the fortuitous outcome each year on Guy Fawkes Day, named for the chief criminal.) Despite his early expression of support, at Hampton Court James declined to make the orthodox Calvinist position binding within the church that he now headed. And as time passed, although the Church of England remained Protestant, he continued to resist any firming of Calvinist doctrine—in part out of fear that doing so would heighten tensions with Catholic Europe, principally Spain. His stance remained unchanged after the Arminian controversy raised these doctrinal questions to further prominence, and even after the Dort Synod appeared to settle the matter, in favor of Calvinist orthodoxy, among the Reformed churches on the continent.

James continued to engage in England's ongoing religious controversy from time to time, however, and not in ways favorable to the nation's strict Calvinists—now often called (not by themselves but others, especially their opponents) Puritans. In 1618 James authorized a *Book of Sports* that clarified what activities were allowed on Sundays. The list was far more permissive than what the Puritans, and even many non-Puritans, would have tolerated.[15] In 1624 James publicly endorsed an irreverent and highly controversial book written by Richard Montagu, a Church of England priest, bearing the suggestive title *A New Gagg for an Old Goose*. Montagu was a fierce opponent of the papacy and its authority, but the book's argument highlighted similarities between Church of England and Roman Catholic theology.

Critical readers thought he had insufficiently distinguished the *true* Catholic church (of which the Church of England of course remained a part) from the false Roman Catholic church. In the same spirit, Montagu endorsed traditional Catholic practices that the English church had eliminated when it broke away, such as invocation of saints. At the time, in England, criticism of the papacy was sufficiently commonplace to attract little notice. By contrast, expressing adherence to Catholic theology, and even more so advocating Catholic practice, were highly controversial.[16]

The apparent threat of a movement closer to Catholicism became more acute the next year, when James died and his son, Charles, succeeded him as king. Just five weeks after assuming the throne, Charles married a French Catholic princess. The next year, he officially prohibited discussion of predestination within the Church of England. At the same time, he approved the appointment of prominent Arminians and their sympathizers to the church's clergy. (One appointment, which especially infuriated the Calvinists, elevated Richard Montagu to bishop.) In 1629, after the king dissolved Parliament following a dispute over predestination, Charles imposed a yet wider prohibition on theological debate within the church. And in 1633 he elevated William Laud, whom five years earlier he had made Bishop of London, to Archbishop of Canterbury and therefore the Church of England's highest-ranking prelate.

Laud turned out to be the catalyst for events that within a decade and a half cost Charles not only his kingdom but his life. The new archbishop quickly moved to place renewed emphasis on the role of the sacraments—introducing high altars in prominent churches, for example—thereby moving the Church of England visibly closer to Roman Catholic practice. He also restored the human and other images that the Church had earlier removed from places of worship in response to the offense they gave to Puritans and other dissenters. There were doctrinal changes as well. The prominently placed statement that "Thou hast delivered us from superstition and idolatry," widely understood as a reference to Roman Catholicism, was omitted from the reissue of a supplementary prayer book. At the same time, the church began to emphasize that the Roman Catholic Church was indeed a true church, suppressing anti-Roman views that some suspected might actually be directed at the Church of England itself.[17] With the Catholic forces at just this time gaining advantage in the ongoing religious wars on the continent (what we now call the Thirty Years' War), all of these actions created fear of a rapprochement with Rome.

Laud also began to enforce more strictly the requirement that Church of England worship use the official Book of Common Prayer, thereby thwarting the Puritans' desire for a simplified service with less formal liturgy. By contrast, at Laud's urging Charles republished the *Book of Sports* from a decade and a half earlier, relaxing the stricter consensus on Sabbath observance that had informally grown up in the meanwhile. Both steps further alienated England's orthodox Calvinists. Worse yet, Laud began to persecute "nonconformists" within the Church of England clergy, most of them Puritans, bringing many to trial in the infamous court that sat in the Palace of Westminster's Star Chamber (named that because of the ceiling painted to depict a starry sky).

Laud's actions triggered two responses from the Puritan community, each of profound importance. First, many English Puritans despaired of attempts to achieve their aims within either church or polity in England, choosing instead to create a new commonwealth elsewhere. In 1607 a group of Separatists, so called because they chose to remove themselves altogether from the Church of England, had emigrated to Leiden, an active Calvinist center in Holland; and in 1620 they had moved on to create a permanent settlement in the New World, which they named Plymouth. In 1630 a much larger group of nonseparating Puritans, gathered under the auspices of the recently formed Massachusetts Bay Company (at first called the New England Company), had settled in Boston. As Laud's actions became ever more threatening, this trickle became the Great Migration, with a thousand or more leaving for America each year. John Cotton, who emigrated in 1633 and became the second pastor of the church established in Boston, was among those who (in his words) "came to the judgment that by the free preaching of the word and the actual practice of our church discipline we could offer a much clearer and fuller witness in another land than in the wretched and loathsome prisons of London, where there would be no opportunity for books or pens or friends or conferences."[18]

By no means all of England's Puritans followed, however, and those that remained formed an increasingly forceful opposition not just to the archbishop but to the king.[19] Their opening came in 1640, when Charles, perpetually in fiscal straits, summoned a Parliament to autho-

Trial of Archbishop William Laud, 1644.
Laud's trial ended without a conviction, but within a year he was executed under an act of Parliament. His persecution of the Puritans helped trigger both revolution and civil war, as well as the migration to New England.

rize new revenues. The new Parliament was dominated by Puritans, and it quickly moved to oppose both Charles and his archbishop. While it took no direct action to confront the king, before the year was out Parliament had arrested Laud on the charge of treason and brought him to trial. For the time being there was no conviction, but the accused remained imprisoned nonetheless.

Execution of Charles I, 1649.
The regicide marked the point of no return in the Puritan revolution,
opening the way for eleven years of rule with no monarch.

The army, consisting for the most part of non-Puritans, sided with the king. In response, the Puritan parliamentary faction formed its own army under first Thomas Fairfax and later Oliver Cromwell. A decade of on-and-off military conflict ensued. Although the progress of the war was irregular, with each side achieving victories from time to time, on balance the parliamentary forces increasingly had the advantage and Parliament controlled ever more of the country. The fighting finally ended in August 1651 with the parliamentary forces' battlefield victory at Worcester.

In the meanwhile, Parliament—in reality, the House of Commons—had effected a revolution. In December 1648, the controlling faction (the Puritan army prevented the other members from participating) put Charles on trial for high treason. The judges convicted him, and on January 30, 1649, he was beheaded. (Hence it was Charles's elder son, whom his supporters proclaimed King Charles II, who led the last effort of the royalist forces at Worcester.) Parliament then abolished the monarchy altogether and created in its place an English Commonwealth, to be governed as a republic. Within two years, however, the republican government broke down and Parliament instead established a Protectorate, in reality a military dictatorship, with Cromwell as Lord Protector.

The revolution was religious as well as political. Almost as soon as the Puritans gained power, Parliament issued new laws enforcing tighter Sabbath observance: no games, no sports, no trade, no travel. All copies of the infamous *Book of Sports* were ordered to be burned. All printing, and all preaching too, had to be licensed by the state. In 1645, still during the first phase of the fighting but with the parliamentary forces establishing the upper hand, Parliament went forward to execute Archbishop Laud. The grounds were that he had "traitorously endeavored to alter and subvert God's true Religion . . . and instead thereof to set up Popish Superstition and Idolatry."[20] The next year Parliament abolished the office of bishops and archbishops altogether. The move was the culmination of a process begun five years before when a large group of Puritans had presented a petition, popularly called the Root and Branch Petition, calling for the elimination of episcopacy in all its "roots" and "branches." In 1650, with the king now gone, Parliament repealed the Elizabethan Act of Uniformity that had placed the English monarch at the head of the church (and had imposed a variety of liturgical practices to which the Puritans objected).

Getting rid of the king and the bishops resolved some issues, but hardly all. The Church of England's clergy and other concerned parties continued to debate matters of church governance and authority, with traditional Anglicans advocating a new hierarchy of bishops, some Puritans ("congregationalists") seeking effective autonomy for individual congregations and their appointed clergy, and even more ("presbyterians") preferring to rest authority in elected governing bodies. The church's theology was under dispute as well. In 1643, soon after the fighting began, Parliament had convened at Westminster an Assembly of Divines, including clergy and other interested parties, to debate the outstanding issues. Over the next few years, the group held nearly twelve hundred meetings. The chief product of their efforts was the Westminster Confession of Faith, agreed upon by the Assembly in November 1646, approved by Parliament in December, and publicly proclaimed early the following year.

It proved to be the high tide of orthodox Calvinism in England.

Cromwell died in 1658, and Parliament designated his son to succeed him as Lord Protector. But one-man rule could not survive the victorious general's absence. In 1660 the military regime fell apart, and Parliament reestablished the monarchy. Charles II, the elder son of the king beheaded eleven years before, was now king not just in name among his close group of loyalists but in reality.

England's turn away from Puritan practice was swift as well. In contrast to Cromwell's austerity, the new king openly displayed the luxury typical of European royal courts of the time. Once on the throne, Charles II immediately relaxed the laws prohibiting public entertainments of which the Puritans disapproved. The new dramas that quickly appeared in the London theaters (some "Restoration comedies" are still occasionally performed today) often took on a risqué tone that the Puritans would never have tolerated. In the same vein, many of the new puppet shows in the city streets mercilessly satirized the now defenseless Puritans.

But the Puritans' losses were more than a matter of popular culture. In his first year on the throne, Charles once again made the Book of Common Prayer the basis for all Anglican worship, thereby restoring the liturgy that the Puritans had abolished in the 1640s. The next year, with the king's approval, Parliament passed a new Act of Uniformity requiring all Church of England clergy to swear assent to the Book of Common Prayer before their congregations. Some 1,900 Nonconformists and dissenters—in other words, Puritans—refused and were therefore removed from their positions. (Enforcement was strict; subsequent legislation made it illegal for an ejected minister to approach within five miles of his former parish.) In parallel, Charles restored to their parishes the Church of England clergy who had been ousted first during the Civil War and then under Cromwell. The new act also required all Church of England priests and deacons to be ordained by the church's bishops, and all preachers who were not priests to be licensed by the bishops. The Restoration was therefore threefold: monarchy, liturgy, and clergy. Arminian theology was now increasingly taught as well; with some irony, Cambridge—earlier the training ground for many Puritan theologians—took up the new heterodoxy more so than did Oxford.[21] Following the Restoration, orthodox Calvinism held little sway within the church.[22]

In time, however, it became apparent that the 1662 legislation had not achieved the uniformity that the king and Parliament had sought. In 1673, therefore, Parliament enacted a new set of Test Acts requiring all civil and military officers to swear an oath to the Church of

England. (The requirement remained law for more than a century and a half.[23]) The country was now staunchly Protestant, though certainly not Puritan in practice and theologically no longer committed to Calvinist orthodoxy. Catholics and "dissenting" Protestants were allowed to worship, but they were denied full civil rights and Catholics in particular were subject to fines and imprisonment.

This new equilibrium unraveled on Charles II's death in 1685 and the accession of his younger brother, James. In contrast to the ambiguity that surrounded Charles's personal religious beliefs, James had converted to Roman Catholicism during the 1660s (he was living in France at the time), and after some years he openly became a practicing Catholic. Following passage of the Test Acts in 1673, he had resigned his office as Lord High Admiral rather than take the required oath. And although he had agreed long ago that his two daughters from his first marriage would be raised as Protestants—a choice that later turned out to be of great significance—after his first wife's death James married an Italian Catholic princess.

In the meanwhile, tensions with Catholic Europe were rising again, as they had a century before, only this time it was not Spain but France under Louis XIV that represented the principal foreign menace. With anti-Catholic sentiment mounting in England, and Charles II having no legitimate children, in the early 1680s the king had had to dissolve three Parliaments in a row because each was prepared to enact an Exclusion Bill barring his brother, James, from the succession. Throughout the last years of Charles's reign, frequent conspiratorial rumors, and some genuine conspiracies too, revolved around various alleged or actual Catholic plots to assassinate him and place James on the throne. In France Louis revoked the Edict of Nantes, which for nearly a century had protected the country's Protestants from persecution. Some 200,000 promptly fled, further intensifying anti-Catholic feelings in nearby Protestant countries including England.

On Charles's death, James, still a Catholic, took the throne as James II. His Catholic wife likewise became queen. Like his brother before him, James quickly moved to change—no doubt he would have claimed to *restore*—England's religious laws. But while Charles's aim had been to reverse Puritan influence within the Church of England while nonetheless maintaining the country's Protestantism, the new king's goal was to diminish the dominance of the Church of England altogether in order to make room for Roman Catholicism. James suspended the Test Act requirement of a Church of England oath, first for military officers and then for civilian government officials. Soon after, he began replacing Protestant high-officeholders by Catholics. In addition, he published in his own name several papers, supposedly belonging to his deceased brother, asserting the superiority of Catholicism to Protestantism. He also received a papal nuncio (ambassador), the first one England had had since the time of Bloody Mary more than a century before.

In 1687 James issued a Declaration of Indulgence, announcing his intention not only to repeal the Test Acts altogether but to abolish all laws disadvantaging either Catholics or dissenting Protestants. He then ordered all Church of England clergy to read the Declaration aloud in their churches; those who protested—including the Archbishop of Canterbury—were arrested. Meanwhile, he openly proceeded with plans to pack the next Parliament with members who would vote as he directed on religious questions.

Matters came to a crisis just three years into James's reign, triggered by the birth of a son to his queen in June 1688. Under England's succession based on male primacy, the newborn infant, not either of James's daughters from his first marriage, was now next in line for the throne. Instead of anticipating an eventual end to James's increasingly bold pro-Catholic actions, once he died and either of his Protestant daughters succeeded him, the country now contemplated a permanent Catholic monarchy in direct violation of the Elizabethan settlement. The strain proved too great. Three weeks after the child's birth, a group of prominent English Protestants appealed to William, Prince of Orange in the Netherlands, a grandson of Charles I but more importantly a Protestant and the husband of James's older daughter, Mary (at the time twenty-six years old). William came to England in November, and most of the army to which James might have looked to defend him and his kingdom instead gave its support to the foreign prince. In December James fled to France, and William allowed him to go unharmed.

In February 1689, in what was hailed as England's Glorious Revolution—sometimes called the Bloodless Revolution—Parliament declared that James had effectively abdicated, and William and Mary jointly assumed the throne as king and queen (William as William III). Later that year, Parliament enacted a Bill of Rights, which in time assumed its place as one of the landmark statements of English civil liberties. But the bill also reimposed the Test Acts, and it more specifically prohibited any future English monarch from either being a Roman Catholic or marrying one. On William's death (Mary had predeceased him), Mary's younger sister, Anne, became queen. And when Anne died, the throne therefore passed not to her half-brother, the so-called Old Pretender then living in France, but to her cousin the Duke of Hanover who became King George I; he was her closest Protestant relative.

Following the Glorious Revolution, England's new monarch—in this case, monarchs—moved promptly to reshape England's religious landscape. A new Act of Toleration, passed in William and Mary's first year on the throne, extended freedom of worship to all Protestants, including Puritans (both Congregationalists and Presbyterians) as well as Baptists and Quakers, though not to Catholics. The act's formal title explained its purpose: "an Act for Exempting their Majestyes' Protestant Subjects dissenting from the Church of England from the Penalties of certaine laws."[24] The Church of England remained the established church, supported by government-enforced tithes, payable by church-goers as well as others. But it was therefore no longer a *national* church in the sense of enjoying a monopoly on authorized worship.

William and Mary's new appointments within the Church of England, beginning with John Tillotson as Archbishop of Canterbury in 1691, likewise gave English Protestantism a more tolerant and theologically liberal face. Following the Glorious Revolution, the forces for Protestant unity stemming from the perceived threat of a return of Roman Catholicism were now gone. Tillotson and other new ecclesiastical officeholders, while clearly Protestants, mostly shared a broad, even lenient, stance on doctrine—certainly in contrast to any firm commitment to Calvinist orthodoxy. With their appointment, the English church in effect accepted a division between "high church" and "low church" theologies; clergy of both groups were now free to advance their views within the church. Moreover, neither embraced orthodox Calvinist doctrine. Even with the Thirty-Nine Articles still in place, ever since the Restoration the highest levels of the Church of England had been distinctly Arminian. With Tillotson's appointment, anti-predestinarian thinking now found clear expression at the highest levels of the Church of England. The Puritans had gained their freedom, but their revolution within the church had proved temporary.

The reasons were as much practical as theological. With memories still fresh of the Civil War, the beheading of the king, and the abolition of the monarchy, the traditional high-church faction—who by now had been opposing the Puritan movement for nearly a century—thought the preaching of predestination threatened to undermine the public's allegiance to the established order in both church and state. The newer low-church group, now led by Archbishop Tillotson, feared what they saw as the potential costs of ideological extremes more generally, as demonstrated all too vividly by the Civil War and the following eleven years of Puritan rule. In addition to the military casualties, during this period hundreds of women had been executed as witches, and many among the new liberal-thinking clergy were leading skeptics of witchcraft accusations.[25] Calling themselves "Latitude men" to reflect the deliberately liberal view that they embraced across a variety of issues, both liturgical and theological—the common term for them today is Latitudinarians—the low-church clergy were inclined on principle to oppose any uncompromising orthodoxy, instead remaining open to differing viewpoints.[26]

They were responding to broader intellectual currents as well. By the end of the seventeenth century the renewed commitment to the importance of reason that came to mark what we now call the Enlightenment had begun to take hold, and the Latitudinarians firmly embraced it. Within theological circles, the emphasis was on the presumed complementary relationship between revelation and reason, with new autonomy allowed to the latter component.[27] The goal of a revived interest in "natural theology" was to seek knowledge of the divine through the application of reason to observation of the world that God had created.[28] Following decades of discussion sparked by Hobbes, Shaftesbury, and others, the Latitudinarians also shared a new emphasis on individual virtue and morality as opposed to doctrine, especially when doctrine either was unconnected to individual behavior or, worse yet, threatened to undermine it. And, following the Glorious Revolution, the Latitudinarians were deeply committed to the value of individual liberty.

More than anyone else, the Englishman who embodied the new

Enlightenment thinking during the years leading up to the Glorious Revolution and then in its immediate aftermath was John Locke. Locke was best known in his own time, as he remains today, for a series of pathbreaking works of philosophy and political theory. In his widely read *Essay on Human Understanding* he elaborated at length on the centrality of reason to what makes us human. God had been bountiful, he wrote, in giving to all men "a mind that can reason." Further, God had given us "the light of reason," and "reason must be our last judge and guide in every thing."[29]

Locke was also an active participant in the practical political debates of his time, staunchly defending the parliamentary cause and welcoming the change in monarch that it had effected. His *Two Treatises of Government,* published in 1689 following his six years of exile in the Netherlands (he had been removed from his position at Oxford for advocating "pernicious books and damnable principles"[30]), was intended in part to justify the regime of the new king and queen. But it too based much of its argument on the universality of reason as the vehicle, accessible to all, through which we come to understand the natural law. Reason is "the common rule and measure God hath given to mankind," and it "teaches all mankind who will but consult it." Man's natural freedom, and his liberty of acting according to his own will, were grounded in his having reason; without it, man was "brutish."[31] Locke's famous *Letter Concerning Toleration,* also from England's first year under the new monarchs but written with Louis XIV's revocation of the Edict of Nantes in mind, similarly sought to ground England's new Act of Toleration in broader philosophical principles rejecting any coercion of religious conformity.

Locke was also a committed Christian, however, and he took a direct interest in religious matters and in the theology of the English church. In 1695, by which time the rule of William and Mary was solidly established—and, although Archbishop Tillotson had died the year before, the new monarchs' other ecclesiastical appointments were firmly in place—Locke published a book titled *The Reasonableness of Christianity as Delivered in the Scriptures.* In it Locke again emphasized the importance of reason as the distinguishing capacity of humans. But he also highlighted the role of God as the world's creator, and as his title suggested, he forcefully defended the compatibility of reason and religion. As he had argued in his *Essay on Human Understanding,* reason is itself a natural form of revelation, and "he that takes away reason, to make room for revelation, puts out the light of both."[32] Proceeding from this central role of reason, he also expressed what, to some, seemed a new, more benign view of the divine: "God had, by the light of reason, revealed to all mankind, who would make use of that light, that he was good and merciful."[33]

These views in turn led Locke to reject the Calvinist doctrines of depravity and salvation based on God's grace granted only to the elect. The same spark of the divine nature, and the same divinely bestowed knowledge that made someone a man, he argued, also showed him the path that as a man he was obliged to follow. It was reason, which God had given to all humans, that brought man into conformity with God's wishes. Invoking an image that in time became commonplace in Enlightenment-inspired religious discussion, Locke referred to man's reasoning power as a candle—in this case, a candle given to him by God. It was up to the individual whether to use it or not. "He that made use of this candle of the Lord, so far as to find out what was his duty, could not miss to find also the way to reconciliation and foregiveness, when he had failed of his duty; though, if he used not his reason in this way, if he put out or neglected this light, he might, perhaps, see neither."[34]

In contrast to the orthodox Calvinist view that only the elect can achieve faith, therefore, because God gave *all* men and women reason all have it within their power to find their way to God. Although historically "the multitude" had often failed to take sufficient advantage of this essential human faculty to discover true religion, "the rational and thinking part of mankind" succeed in finding the one, supreme, invisible God, once they use their reason to seek him out.[35] Reason had been given to humans by an act that one might well conceive as God's grace, but it was given to everyone, and it was each individual's choice whether to use it.

A second key underpinning of the new Latitudinarian thought was Newtonian science. As was also true a century later, in Adam Smith's and David Hume's time, scientists and clergymen lived together in a common culture. In the seventeenth century fellowships at Oxford and Cambridge normally required holders to be ordained (although Newton was granted a royal dispensation not to be[36]), and so most English academic scholars of whatever interest were at least formally clergymen.[37] In parallel, many clerics of what came to be known as Latitudinarian views had been active in founding England's Royal Society for the Improvement of Naturall Knowledge by Experiment, only months after the Restoration, and they eagerly embraced the era's flood of new scientific discoveries.[38] In their eyes the new science was favorable to religious belief, not hostile. God had written not one, but two books for man's benefit: the holy scriptures and the book of nature. As the theologian Richard Baxter (not a Latitudinarian churchman but a nonconformist Puritan) wrote in 1685, in his *Paraphrase on the New Testament,* "True Physicks is the Knowledge of the knowable Works of God, and God in them."[39] But the perceived scientific support for religion went beyond mere theorizing. The telescope and the microscope, both new inventions less than a hundred years before, were continually revealing new wonders that reinforced the argument for God as the designer of the universe.[40]

Newton likewise viewed his *Principia Mathematica,* published in 1687, just before the Glorious Revolution, as contributing to man's knowledge not only of the physical universe but also the God who had created it. He saw the universe as one in which God's presence and force are immanent, enforcing the natural laws that he had established for the world he created.[41] In contrast to Descartes, who depicted God as having created the mechanical world and given it an initial push, but then left it on its own, Newton's God was the clockmaker who continuously intervened to keep the mechanism moving according to the divine plan. In the *Principia,* he wrote of the planets' orbits needing constant adjustment; the finger of God did the adjusting.[42]

Newton's work taught people to believe that the behavior of the universe was regular, governed by laws that are knowable, and that the goal of science was to gain that knowledge. But believing that the universe is systematic and accessible to human understanding stood in opposition to any claim that God exercised his sovereignty in an arbitrary way. It therefore ran against the grain of orthodox Calvinist notions of unconditional election as an exercise of God's sovereignty according to no more than his own act of grace, not given in respect of any merit or other understandable characteristic of the individual who received it.

The vehicle that most prominently brought together English science and theological thinking in the period following the Glorious Revolution was a series of endowed public lectures established by the distinguished scientist Robert Boyle. Best known for the law (still named for him) relating the pressure exerted by a confined gas to the volume of the container that confines it, Boyle was the most respected member of the Royal Society in its early decades. He was also the son of Richard Boyle, Earl of Cork and Lord Treasurer of Ireland, and one of Ireland's richest men. On the younger Boyle's death, in 1691, his will provided funds to support an annual set of lectures aimed at establishing the existence of God via observation of the natural world according to scientific principles. The first set of lectures, given the next year by the classical scholar (and master of Trinity College, Cambridge) Richard Bentley, was an important step in calling attention to Newton's recently published *Principia*. Following Newton's theological views as well, Bentley described gravity as "the immediate Fiat and Finger of God."[43]

The best known of the early Boyle Lectures—although many attracted widespread attention in English intellectual and religious circles—were those given in 1704–1705 by the philosopher and Anglican clergyman Samuel Clarke. Consistent with Boyle's intent, Clarke sought to deploy Newtonian ideas about matter and space to establish the existence of a purposeful God who is continually involved in the working of the universe. Clarke's aim was to rebut both deists, who pictured God as having created the world but then absented himself from it, and atheists who denied that God existed to begin with. He argued instead that matter exists only by the will of God, and moreover that it has no power of self-motion. The key implication: the physical universe is not self-sufficient. Not only is God the cause of the world's existence, God remains involved in the world's everyday functioning. Moreover, God's actions are certainly not arbitrary; the functioning that they maintain follows regular laws, understandable through a combination of observation and reason.

But Clarke went on also to explore the role of humans in this universe of laws. The key question, as he put it, was "whether there be *at all* in Man any such Power, as a Liberty of Choice and of Determining his own Actions; or on the contrary his Actions be all as Necessary, as the Motions of a Clock." While he framed the question in philosophical terms of free will versus determinism, the issue clearly bore implications for the ongoing religious debates of the past century. Clarke concluded that even a world that is deterministic in the sense that God has foreknowledge of men's future actions is consistent with their nonetheless having freedom of choice over those actions. The necessity governing their actions was "only a *Moral*" necessity, which amounted to "*no Necessity at all*, in the Sense of the Opposers of Liberty." Indeed, this moral necessity was evidently "consistent with the most perfect *Natural Liberty*" of human choice and action.[44]

Against the background of these strong intellectual currents, and in the political climate of the Glorious Revolution as well, English Protestant theologians continued to challenge orthodox Calvinist doctrines. The questions at issue in this debate partly focused on Calvinist thinking specifically, but they also reflected the tension between God's sovereignty and humans' free will that arises in almost all Western religious thinking: What scope does any particular view of the divine leave for human independence of thought and action? And whatever that scope is, what moral value attaches to individual liberty? More problematically, if God's sovereignty is supreme, does that make God the source of the evil that is in the world? Even of the evil done by individual humans? If God created man in his image, are human failings then a reflection of divine imperfection?[45]

A more specific aspect of this inquiry was the perceived tension between predestination, as Calvin had preached the doctrine and his followers had elaborated it, and individual morality. If men and women know that they are predestined either to be saved or not, and that God's choice regarding their individual spiritual fate has been made before they were born (more than that, before the world existed), what incentive is left to motivate them to live moral lives? And if God's choice was to damn them, what does that imply about the nature of God? Especially on the presumption that the elect represent only a fraction of the human population—according to many Calvinists, merely a small fraction—does consigning the rest as reprobates contradict the idea of a benevolent God?

As in the Arminian debate on the continent, in England too the questioning had begun well before the events of 1688–1689. Even during the height of the Puritan ascendency, committed laymen often embraced "preparationist" thinking that emphasized steps faithful individuals could take to gain some measure of assurance about their salvation. Such thinking clearly downplayed the idea of predestination.[46] Once the Purtian regime collapsed, prominent members of the clergy took up the theme as well. Preaching at the university church in Oxford in 1661, just after the Restoration, Robert South anticipated what soon developed into a movement to sidestep doctrinal belief altogether in favor of a heightened emphasis on virtue and moral behavior. What we profess is only the badge of our religion, South declared, and what we believe only the beginning. What matters is what we practice and the custom we keep. South did not shy away from the bearing of his view on the all-important question of salvation: "The grand deciding question, at the last day, will be, not, What have you said? or believed? but, What have you done more than others?"[47]

Similarly directing his focus away from the doctrine of predestination, Isaac Barrow, a theologian and the master of Trinity College at Cambridge during the 1670s, chose to emphasize "the essential goodness of God, and his special benignity toward mankind." A key part of that goodness was the "common providence" that continually upholds us in our everyday lives, protecting us in dangers and rescuing us from many "mischiefs." God's laws for man were part of the "innumerable and inestimable benefits graciously conferred on us." In imposing those laws, God "plainly doth not so much exercise his sovereignty over us as express his kindness toward us."[48]

This kind of non- and even anti-predestinarian thinking became both more widespread and more open after the Glorious Revolution, especially once the new monarchs appointed John Tillotson as Archbishop of Canterbury. Now it was the clerical head of the Church of England himself who was openly challenging orthodox Calvinist belief. Although Tillotson was raised as a Puritan and educated at Cambridge, after his ordination in the Church of England his ideas took a more liberal direction emphasizing individual morality over adherence to strict theological doctrine. Like many of his contemporaries among the clergy, he was also interested in science and he became an early fellow of the Royal Society. In short, his intellectual tendencies were typically Latitudinarian.

With his deep concern for individual morality, Tillotson rejected the orthodox Calvinist view of utter depravity. It was true, he acknowledged, "that the nature of men is sadly corrupted and depraved; but not so bad as by vicious practices and habits it may be made." He went on, "it is a great mistake to argue the common condition of all mankind, from the descriptions that are given in the scripture of the worst of

men." Moreover, many people if not most—including the "unregenerate" (in modern evangelical language, those who have not been born
again)—have the capacity to understand what kind of life they should
seek to lead. "All unregenerate men are not equally devoid of a sense of
God, and spiritual things," he argued; instead, they are "very capable
of persuasion."[49]

It was this persuasion that Tillotson, as a clergyman, saw as the
church's purpose. The doctrines of depravity and predestination, however, took away the reason for even attempting it. Reflecting the practical orientation characteristic of most Latitudinarians, he concluded
that "it is the greatest and justest discouragement in the world to all
endeavors of repentance and reformation, to tell men that they can do
nothing in it." What should the clergy be telling their flocks instead?
The aim of the church's exhortations and promises should not be to tell
men what they were or weren't capable of doing, he argued, but what
they *should* do. By contrast, "it will be an hard thing to convince men,
that any thing is their duty, which at the same time we declare to them
to be out of their power."[50]

But if a moral life, and even salvation, were within the power of individual men and women to achieve, was divine grace still required? Tillotson, like other Arminians of his day, saw the need for human effort
and for divine grace together: without grace, men and women's effort
is doomed to failure. "We affirm the necessity of God's grace hereto,"
he confirmed, but along with it "the necessity of our co-operating with
the grace of God." Human choice and action—cooperation, as Tillotson put it—were not just possible but *necessary*. Citing both Paul and
the prophets, he boldly told his listeners, "*Work out your own salvation; repent and turn yourselves from all your evil ways; make ye new
hearts and new spirits.*" To him, these were all metaphors for persuading people that "we may and ought to do something toward repentance
and conversion." Summing up what amounted to the contemporary
Arminian view, "We say that without the powerful excitation and aid
of God's grace, no man can repent and turn to God; but we say likewise, that God cannot be properly said to aid and assist those, who do
nothing themselves."[51]

And what, then, of predestination as Calvin and his followers had
preached it? Tillotson rejected it bluntly: "The doctrine of *absolute reprobation* is no part of the Doctrine of the Holy Scriptures that I ever

saw." In his view, it also plainly contradicted the idea of a benevolent God. To believe "that God hath decreed, without respect to the Sins of Men, their absolute ruin and misery" overthrew all possible notion of God's goodness. "God is infinitely better than the best of Men," Tillotson argued, "and yet none can possibly think *that* Man a good Man, who should absolutely resolve to disinherit and destroy his Children, without the foresight and consideration of any fault to be committed by them." Indeed, "it is not an easy matter, to devise to say anything worse than this of the Devil."[52]

Tillotson died suddenly, in the fall of 1694, after leading the Church of England for only three and a half years. But his ideas about the essential importance of human agency, issuing from his position of authority within the church, long outlived him, and his writings continued to be read for decades after his death.[53]

Locke's tract on the *Reasonableness of Christianity*, published just the next year, was part of this attack on the Calvinist doctrines of depravity and predestination.[54] Locke acknowledged the centrality to Christianity of the biblical story of the Fall, but he rejected outright the claim that Adam and Eve's failing contaminated all humans forevermore. "It is obvious to any one, who reads the New Testament," he began, "that the doctrine of redemption . . . is founded on the supposition of Adam's fall. To understand, therefore, what we are restored to by Jesus Christ, we must consider what the scripture shows we lost by Adam."[55]

What Locke concluded from the biblical account, however, was not what orthodox Calvinists believed. "The doctrine of the gospel is, that death came on all men by Adam's sin," he continued. But what did this death amount to? Referring to orthodox Calvinists, "some will have it to be a state of guilt, wherein not only he, but all his posterity was so involved, that every one descended from him deserved endless torment." According to the Calvinist doctrine of depravity, the death that came to all men was "also a state of necessary sinning . . . in every action that men do."[56]

This belief is what Locke rejected. In contrast, he wrote, "I must confess, that by death here, I can understand nothing but a ceasing to be, the losing of all actions of life and sense. Such a death came on Adam, and all his posterity, by his first disobedience in paradise." Death here, in other words, meant clinical death, not moral or spiritual death. The lasting outcome of the Fall was not the depravity of Adam and all of his

descendants, but simply their physical mortality. Locke therefore concluded that the doctrine of depravity must have been a later (and false)
interpretation, not intended by original Christian scripture. Highlighting the absence of direct scriptural support for the orthodox interpretation, he archly observed that "If by death, threatened to Adam, were
meant the corruption of human nature in his posterity, 'tis strange, that
the New Testament should not any where take notice of it."[57]

Beyond arguing from his own close reading of scripture, Locke also
brought his expertise as a political theorist to bear on the question.
Drawing on Hobbes's well-known discussion in *Leviathan* of what justified one person's standing as a representative of someone else—an
issue that had been at the center of the conflict between king and Parliament in the 1640s (and that would figure again in the debates leading up to the American Revolution)—Locke asked what made Adam
a legitimate representative of the entire human race to such an extent
that his sin could affect all of his progeny.[58] In advancing the doctrine
of depravity, Calvin had written that "Adam was not merely the pro-
genitor but, as it were, the root of human nature; and that therefore in
his corruption mankind deserved to be vitiated."[59] His English disciple
William Perkins had likewise argued that "all his posteritie sinned"
because "Adam was not then a priuate [private] man, but represented
all mankinde."[60] The Westminster Larger Catechism closely followed
Perkins's formulation, declaring that "The covenant being made with
Adam as a publique person, not for himself only, but for his posterity,
all mankind descending from him by ordinary generation, sinned in
him, and fell with him in that first transgression."[61]

Rejecting all of these claims, Locke insisted that Adam could not
have represented all subsequent humans because the consent required
for that representation was necessarily absent. To have all of mankind
"doomed to eternal, infinite punishment, for the transgression of Adam,
whom millions had never heard of, and no one had authorised to trans-
act for him, or be his representative" was not consistent with the justice
or goodness of a great and infinite God.[62] The end point of Locke's
argument, like Tillotson's, was that since mankind is *not* depraved, and
humans *can* choose to accept God's grace, and their behavior *is* effective for their salvation, individual morality therefore matters.[63]

As the eighteenth century began, this emphasis on the importance
of moral behavior—and the ability of not just the elect but all men and

women to choose to act morally—spread rapidly among the Church of England's clergy. In 1710 Daniel Whitby, an Oxford-educated Anglican priest, published *A Discourse on the Five Points*, an obvious reference to the Calvinist principles enunciated at Dort nearly a century before.[64] Whitby was known for his antipathy to Roman Catholicism, but he was also a Latitudinarian in the mold of Tillotson and Locke. His treatise was a systematic attack on the principles of Dort Calvinism.

According to Whitby's account of how he came to write the *Discourse*, he "was bred up Seven Years in the University under Men of the *Calvinistical* Persuasion," and he "therefore had once firmly entertained all their Doctrines." But like Tillotson, he became disillusioned with the doctrine of depravity imputed from Adam's sin to all of his descendants, and from that starting point he then came to question each of the five Dort principles. Marking the path that the Calvinist-versus-Arminian debate was to take through much of the eighteenth century, he portrayed the question of depravity as inseparable from that of free will. Whitby argued, as many Puritans also believed, that God gave life to humans as a period of trial and probation. For the trial to be a genuine one, however, men and women must have the freedom to choose between obedience to God, and the eternal happiness obedience brings, and sin with the misery that inevitably follows from it. If humans are depraved as Calvin portrayed them, this "disability" prevents them from choosing obedience, and so the trial is not meaningful. Further, supposing that *God* imposed this disability on all men and women would be an injustice to God's benevolence.[65]

Instead, quoting from Deuteronomy, Whitby maintained that "God and his Servants have sufficiently confirmed the Liberty we contend for in this State of Tryal, by setting Life and Death, Good and Evil before our Eyes, and putting it to our choice." And he went on to echo Joshua's command to the Hebrews, "Chuse you this day whom ye will serve." But the choice had to be a real one: "*whosoever hath a Liberty to chuse, hath also a Liberty to refuse, & vice versa.*" If all men and women had become depraved by the imputation of Adam's sin, then "to offer Life unto them only upon impossible Conditions" only made it "certain and infallible that they shall fail of obtaining Life." Indeed, commanding them to choose life rather than death under these conditions amounted to hypocrisy, even an insult: "What is it in effect but to insult over the dreadful Misery of Men, and with an hypocritical Pretence of

Kindness, and a Desire of their Welfare, to condemn them to Eternal Death without a Possibility of having Life."[66]

As the century went on, the rejection of depravity and predestination, and in parallel the emphasis on moral behavior and the free will to choose it, became increasingly direct and explicit. In a widely read treatise of 1740 titled *Scripture Doctrine of Original Sin*, the prominent theologian John Taylor argued forcefully that the Calvinist doctrine of original sin was not just incorrect but inconsistent with accepted biblical teachings about God's goodness and justice—and, moreover, that the idea of depravity imputed from the Fall makes God the author of sin, in that God has then sent his creatures into the world with insuperably sinful inclinations. This rejection of original sin was a central part of Enlightenment thinking.[67] Taking phrases from the Westminster Confession, but turning them to the opposite conclusion, Taylor wrote that "If all Men are by Nature utterly indisposed, disabled, and . . . wholly inclined to all Evil," then "no Man is obliged to attempt the Reformation of the World, nor any, except Adam, blameable for whatever Wickedness is in it."[68]

The essential tension that Taylor highlighted was that our natural faculties are given us by an act of God's absolute power (as were Adam's), "without our Knowledge, Concurrence, or Consent." But moral virtue, by its very nature, implies "the Choice and Consent of a moral Agent." Are humans moral agents? If they are, Taylor believed, then their own free will must be paramount for these purposes. However God goes about engaging our wills, "we cannot, as moral Agents, observe what is right and true, or be righteous and holy, without our own free and explicit Choice."[69]

And the reason we are all moral agents? Following Locke and the profusion of Enlightenment thinkers after him, Taylor argued that God had given to all men, not just initially to Adam, the reason and understanding they need to distinguish between good and evil. Because of this gift, "their Wickedness must not be ascribed to a good, just, and holy God . . . but to themselves, who have abused the Goodness of God, blinded their own Minds, [and] misapplied their natural Powers." There was no ground for pointing to God as the source of evil in the world. To the contrary, "*God hath made Man upright.*"[70]

. . .

These challenges to belief in depravity and predestination, increasingly explicit as English theologians moved forward from Tillotson to Taylor, also bore implications for God's intentions for humanity. No one questioned that man's existence glorified God or even that, in Calvin's by-then famous phrase, the entire universe was a theater of God's glory. But increasingly, the assumption underlying the movement away from belief in orthodox ideas of depravity and predestination was that God's aims with respect to mankind had a further, benign dimension: God *intended* the men and women he created to enjoy happiness and well-being, and in more than the mere sense that participating in glorifying God should of course make them happy.

Samuel Clarke, the theologian and philosopher who had paved new ground in natural theology with his Boyle Lectures at the beginning of the century, spoke frequently on divinely intended human happiness in the sermons he delivered during his twenty-year tenure—from 1709 until his death in 1729—as rector of the church of St. James's, Westminster. (Isaac Newton served on the St. James's vestry during part of this period. Perhaps not by coincidence, when Newton died, in 1727, Clarke was offered his position as master of the Royal Mint; he declined.) Clarke saw human happiness as a deliberate part of the purpose behind God's creation of the world. The uniform intention of all God's commandments, he stated, was that "they always tend to the same regular End, the Order and Happiness of the whole Creation."[71]

Moreover, Clarke argued that this benevolence on the part of the creator plainly contradicted the orthodox doctrines of depravity and predestination. The universal happiness of "all reasonable Creatures," he thought, stemmed "from their acting according to that Nature which God has given them."[72] But if humans' nature led to happiness, that nature could not be one of depravity that inevitably sank them in sin and misery. Rather, God's goodness "moves him to diffuse upon All his Creatures . . . every good which either *They* are in their own Nature *capable* of *receiving*, or which for *Him*, in his All-wise Government of the Whole, is *fit* and *reasonable* to *give*." It followed from this line of argument that "there *is* not, there *cannot be* any such thing, as *absolute and unconditionate Reprobation*." Such a matter would be "wholly contradictory to all our Notions of Goodness." If the doctrines of depravity and reprobation were true, it would follow that divine goodness had no meaning at all, and that "it was neither *in itself* of any importance, nor of any consequence to Us, whether the Almighty God was Good or no."[73]

Clarke similarly rejected Calvin's claim that predestination was a source of comfort to depraved but therefore frightened beings. To the contrary, he argued, what gave good men comfort was "a right Notion of the Justice of God." Like Locke (although without invoking Locke's image of the candle of reason), Clarke thought that if good men sincerely strive to perform their duty, they will know that "with a just and righteous God there can be no secret Decree to exclude them from Happiness." It was the "*Happiness and Perfection* of rational Creatures" that constituted "the great *End and Design* of God's Creation."[74] Predestination, as Calvin had laid down the doctrine, was simply incompatible with this view.

Another prominent proponent of the idea of divinely intended human happiness was Philip Doddridge—unlike Clarke, not an Anglican priest but a "dissenting" minister of a congregation independent from the Church of England. Doddridge was best known as an energetic promoter of evangelical missionary efforts in the American colonies. Human happiness as the end of divine creation stood at the center of his devotional program. In his widely read treatise *The Rise and Progress of Religion in the Soul,* published in 1745, Doddridge addressed God as the "great Eternal Original, and Author of our Being and Happiness," going on to say, "From Thee proceed all good Purposes and Desires; and this Desire above all, of diffusing Wisdom, Piety, and Happiness in this World." Following Clarke, he pointed to God-given rationality as the intended means that enabled humans to attain happiness. God, "*so benevolent a Being,*" would naturally "take a peculiar Pleasure in communicating to such as humbly ask [blessings], *those gracious assistances*, which . . . fit them for that Happiness to which their Rational Nature is suited." That was the purpose for which this God-given human capacity was intended.[75]

For Doddridge, even the accoutrements of religion, like the Bible, were sources of happiness. To infer from the Bible that men and women should afflict themselves, and one another, was to learn the wrong lesson. It was the great design of the Gospel, he wrote, "to teach us to *abhor* all unnecessary *Rigour* and *Severity*, and to *delight*, not in the *grief*, but in the *Happiness* of our fellow creatures." The New Testament, in his view, was a "*Method to Happiness.*" The purpose of religion was to promote God's glory in the happiness of mankind.[76]

The logical train of thought running from God's benevolence to the intent for human happiness, and hence to our obligation to delight in the happiness of our fellow creatures, was influential beyond the scope of religious thinking. In 1731 John Gay, a philosopher and Anglican priest teaching at Cambridge (and a cousin of the John Gay who wrote *The Beggar's Opera*), published a treatise on "the fundamental principle of virtue or morality," in which he argued that because the happiness of mankind is willed by God, humans are obliged to act so as to maximize the happiness of their fellow creatures.[77] "It is evident from the Nature of God," Gay wrote, that "he could have no other Design in creating Mankind than their Happiness."[78] Before the century was out, Gay's *Dissertation* had become one of the foundational texts of the utilitarian philosophy of seeking the greatest happiness for the greatest number, as later developed by such intellectual giants as Jeremy Bentham and, in the nineteenth century, John Stuart Mill.

With some lag in time, these same themes of the benevolence of God, and therefore the inherent goodness of men and women endowed by God with the power of reason, took hold in Scotland as well. So too, especially under the influence of Francis Hutcheson at the university in Glasgow, did the new emphasis on the importance of individual virtue and morality, centered on human choice and agency. While the first led to a weakening of the Scottish clergy's belief in depravity, the second led many to even greater discomfort with the orthodox Calvinist doctrine of predestination.

As in England, for Scots the revolution of 1688 bore not just political but religious consequences. Scotland's religious history had been even more fiercely contended than England's. Calvinists—in Scotland, "Presbyterians" because of their form of church governance—had dominated the Church of Scotland since 1560. Charles I had attempted to impose an episcopal structure on the church, as well as to force its use of the Book of Common Prayer, but both moves provoked intense opposition from nearly all segments of Scottish society and they ultimately failed. The Scottish dimension of the Civil War in the 1640s had been especially bitter, with conflicting factions reflecting a complex blend of religious, political, and class loyalties even among opposing groups of Presbyterians. After the Restoration, Charles II briefly succeeded in imposing an episcopal structure and removed nearly a third of Scottish ministers from their parishes; the reaction was again violent, including the assassination in 1679 of James Sharp, Archbishop of St. Andrews. Under James II (who was titled James VII in Scotland), yet more Presbyterian clergymen had been removed from their pulpits. James also took steps to advance Roman Catholicism, as he had in England, turning the nave of the abbey at Holyrood into a Catholic royal chapel and installing a Catholic printing press as well as a Jesuit school in the palace itself.

Following the Glorious Revolution, most of these changes were reversed. The bishops were removed from office. (In time, they and their followers formed a separate Scottish Episcopal Church, not affiliated with the Church of Scotland and distinct from the Church of England.) The clergy deposed by James were reinstated. The Church of Scotland was also authorized to use the Westminster Confession, rather than the English church's Thirty-Nine Articles. To prevent separatist tendencies, however, an oath of allegiance to William and Mary was required for membership in the church's General Assembly. Although Anglican priests were allowed to remain within the Church of Scotland if they accepted the Westminster Confession, from the early eighteenth century onward Presbyterians again dominated the church. Even so, the same intellectual currents at work in England affected Scottish thinking as well. From 1707 on, Scotland was a part of the Kingdom of Great Britain, and so both the laws and the patronage that mattered now largely originated in London.

By the 1730s, when David Hume was still a young man and Adam Smith just a youth, a liberal-thinking group of self-labeled "Moderates"—close in their thinking to England's Latitudinarians— had emerged as the faction within the Scottish church most aligned with Enlightenment ideas. By the 1740s, a wide gulf had developed between these more liberal thinkers, who pointedly ignored the Calvinist doctrines in the Westminster Confession, and their more traditionally minded fellow clergy. Intellectually protégés of Francis Hutcheson, and in many cases his actual students, the Moderate clergy embraced their teacher's ideas of an inborn moral sense, which ran against the grain of orthodox thinking centered on depravity and predestination. In time they also developed close ties to Hume, Smith, and other secular thinkers of the Scottish Enlightenment.[79]

As time passed, the Moderates came to occupy the most significant positions within the Church of Scotland, as well as many university appointments over which the Church exerted influence if not outright control. Hugh Blair became a minister at a smaller Edinburgh church in 1754 and from 1758 until his death he was a minister of the High Church at St. Giles.[80] He also began lecturing at the University of Edinburgh in 1759, and three years later he became professor of rhetoric and belles lettres. In 1759 Adam Ferguson, not a regularly ordained pastor of a congregation but licensed to preach, became professor of natural philosophy at Edinburgh; from 1764 on he was professor of moral philosophy. William Robertson became principal (president) of the University of Edinburgh in 1762, and from 1763 on he was frequently the moderator of the church's General Assembly.

The Scottish Moderates saw themselves as the middle party in a three-way theological disagreement. On one side were the orthodox Calvinist Presbyterians—often called the Popular, or even the High-flying Party—committed to strict predestinarian doctrine.[81] Especially after the revivals of the early 1740s, this group was also increasingly associated with a more personal, emotional commitment to religious belief as well as practice (in the vocabulary of its detractors, "enthusiasm"). On the other side were the deists, who believed in a God who had created the universe but afterward played no ongoing role in it. For the deists, natural theology, based on systematic observation of nature, was sufficient to gain knowledge of God; their thinking left no place for revelation, either Christian or other.

Like the English Latitudinarians, the Scottish Moderates were also more interested in individual morality and virtue than in theological doctrine. As a result, their beliefs were at least implicitly Arminian. Many had some sympathy for deism too, and as their friendship with Hume demonstrated, in some cases they were even willing to tolerate agnostics and perhaps even atheists. As students of works by Hutcheson like his *Inquiry concerning Moral Good and Evil* (1726) and his *Essay on the Nature and Conduct of the Passions and Affections* (1728), they were above all concerned with questions of moral personal conduct in human relations. At an abstract philosophical level they, like their mentor, saw religion as the counter to Hobbesian materialism. At a more practical level, they thought the essential role of religion, centered on God's benevolence toward man, was to promote virtue in human behavior.

Hugh Blair, for example, in a sermon at St. Giles, assessed "what true religion is" within his and his colleagues' understanding.[82] His disdain for Calvinist orthodoxy was plain: "There is a certain species of religion, (if we can give it that name,) which has no claim to such high distinction; when it is placed wholly in speculation and belief . . . or in fiery zeal about contested opinions." That form of religion, he bluntly stated, "is not the religion which we preach."[83] Instead, "that religion consists in the love of God and the love of man." Reflecting the Moderates' emphasis on virtue, along with the stoic philosophy that many had also acquired from Hutcheson, Blair argued that *true* religion "consists in justice, humanity, and mercy; in a fair and candid mind, a generous and affectionate heart; accompanied with temperance, self-government, and a perpetual regard in all our actions to conscience, and to the law of God."[84] Depravity and predestination were simply not part of the story.

Indeed, according to Blair, religion of the kind that he and his fellow Moderates supported was essentially identical to virtue. "A religious, and a thoroughly virtuous character," he wrote, "I consider as the same."[85] Alexander Carlyle, a close colleague of Robertson's who served as moderator of the church's General Assembly in 1770, made the same claim: "To make men pious and virtuous, through the knowledge of the truth," was "the object of our ministry."[86]

Views like Blair's and Carlyle's, and underlying them the ideas that Locke and Tillotson and Clarke and the other English Latitudinarians had advanced decades earlier, were what Smith and Hume heard from friends in the clergy with whom they regularly associated at the Select Society and elsewhere. Smith also knew directly the thinking of many of the English Latitudinarians, including Locke (he owned copies of *Two Treatises of Government* and *An Essay Concerning Human Understanding*[87]), Bishop Butler, whom he labeled an "ingenious and subtile philosopher," and Josiah Tucker (whose works he also owned).[88] Moreover, these religious ideas—the natural goodness of man in contrast to inborn depravity, the central role of free human choice and action in contrast to predestination, and the design of the universe not solely for the glorification of God but to promote human happiness too— by extension carried implications for how to think about the secular world.

These further, secular implications were in turn closely aligned with the key elements of the new thinking that in time produced the Smithian revolution in economics and then shaped the evolution of modern economics ever since. To be sure, recognizing the logical connection between ideas, or even sets of ideas, is not the same as establishing historical influence.[89] But not only did the transition in thinking that set the foundation for modern economics closely follow the movement away from orthodox Calvinism in time, the two shared a logical coherence as well. To a large extent, in their thinking about both philosophy and what we now call economics, Smith and his contemporaries were secularizing the essential substance of their clerical friends' theological principles.[90]

The concept of utter depravity that was central to Calvin's theology meant that men and women were not reliably able to tell good from bad, right from wrong, or systematically able to act on whatever differences between them they might perceive. (Calvin referred to the "misshapen ruins" of man's ability to distinguish good from evil.[91]) It was not much of an extension therefore to conclude that they were also unable to distinguish whether their actions were good or bad in wider contexts. In the first instance, they were unlikely to understand what actions they might take would be in their own self-interest. Responding merely to the dictates of their depraved nature, they were even less likely to act in ways that would systematically render others better off.

By contrast, if whatever original sin humans might bear does not imply Calvinist depravity[92]—more specifically, if all men and women are endowed with reason, and if the human character is one of inherent goodness, as both the English Latitudinarians and the Scottish Moderates argued—then men and women *are* able both to make moral choices and to act with virtue. A natural extension of this distinctly more optimistic but still theologically based assessment of humanity is that men and women also have the ability to distinguish secular good from bad, including understanding their own self-interest. Further, there is nothing in their inborn nature that prevents them from systematically acting in ways that can, and under the right conditions will, result in outcomes beneficial to other people as well.

The doctrine of predestination, including unconditional election, irresistible grace, and inevitable perseverance in grace for those who receive it, meant that it was impossible for individuals to effect, or even contribute to, their salvation. But what else that mattered to them might they then be unable to influence? A person's incapacity to make any choice or take any action to promote his ultimate spiritual prospects bears a natural affinity to a parallel inability to make choices or take action to improve one's material well-being. Such a person's systematically acting in ways that made others better off would seem even less likely to the predestinarian way of thinking.

The concept of humans as morally conscious agents, with free will and choice, instead meant that individuals *are* able to help determine whether they are saved or not. Their ultimate destiny is, at least to some significant degree, within their control. In Locke's metaphor, they have the candle of the Lord by which to see and then act; in Tillotson's phrase, they are able to cooperate in achieving their salvation. By extension to the secular realm, people not only understand what is in their own interest; they are able to act on that understanding. And, again under the right conditions, even though driven by no more than their inborn nature they can act to improve the lives of others too.

Finally, if the sole purpose of creation is to glorify God, then human happiness per se carries no religious value and there is no reason that the world God created should be structured so as to foster it. By contrast, if human happiness—including the potential ability of each individual to achieve a moral life, and spiritual salvation once that lifetime ends—is also part of the intent of a benevolent God, then the world in which we live is one in which those ends are not just possible but likely. By extension to secular matters, human material needs and abilities are likewise such as to enable happy lives. Individual human nature, therefore, as well as human institutions, are also likely to give rise to material aspects of satisfaction.

These new ideas, advanced over the prior century in opposition to orthodox Calvinist thinking, formed an essential part of the worldview that Adam Smith and his contemporaries brought to their attempt to create a science of man analogous to what Newton had constructed for the physical world. Hutcheson's and Smith's ideas about human sympathy and the desire for fellow-feeling were, in effect, a secularization of the principle of Christian love (even though Hutcheson, who wrote in an explicitly religious vein as well, would certainly have been comfortable without the secularization), applied to men and women whose nature was not depraved but characterized by an innate goodness. The idea that people acting on no more than their own natural desires can nonetheless improve not only their own material lives but others' too mirrored the belief that all people, not just the elect few, can succeed in achieving a moral life. Smith's insight into the role of markets and competition in rendering what can happen into what *will* happen reflected the increasingly widespread belief that the benevolent God who created the world intended the human creatures he put in it to be happy, and therefore that God also endowed their world with the human institutions needed to channel their behavior accordingly.[93]

The worldview stemming from these new and fiercely contended ideas about God and God's relationship to mankind shaped the "pre-analytic Vision" that preceded the contribution of Smith and others of his day in the line of thinking that in time became economics. And as Max Weber later argued in a different context, these secular ideas initially spurred by religious thinking long outlived the religious impulse and controversy that initially prompted them.[94]

The Calvinist Controversy
in Colonial America

Man is not merely so much lumpish Matter, or a *mechanical
Engine*, that moves only by the Direction of an impelling Force . . .
he hath a Principle of Action within himself, and is an Agent in
the strict and proper Sense of the Word.

—EBENEZER GAY

A more shocking idea can scarce be given of the Deity, than that
which represents him as *arbitrarily dooming the greater part of the
race of men to eternal misery.*

—CHARLES CHAUNCY

The contention surrounding religious thinking in England and Scotland, marked at first by resistance to Calvinist ideas of depravity
and predestination, and in time by a growing dominance of non- and
even anti-predestinarian theology, traced a similar course in America,
and especially in New England.[1] But there were significant differences
too. In part because of these colonies' Puritan origins, in the eighteenth
century America saw a late-period resurgence of orthodox Calvinist
thinking. Once that resurgence ebbed, however, many of the new
republic's churches charted an even more liberal form of Protestantism
than either the English or the Scots had yet embraced.

The Massachusetts Bay Colony, established in 1630 and then peopled
from the Great Migration triggered by Archbishop Laud's persecutions
in England, was a Puritan enterprise from the beginning. The church
established by the colony's civil government adhered to orthodox Calvinist principles and practice, and no Anglicans or Roman Catholics

were permitted as residents.[2] Neither were other forms of deviant wor-shipers; Roger Williams, even though not yet recognizably a Baptist, was forced to leave the colony in 1636, but his experience there had been troubled since his arrival five years earlier. The court's order of expulsion accused him of having "broached & divulged diverse new & dangerous opinions," and having "maintained his objectionable opin-ions without hint of repentance or retraction."[3] (Four decades later, when Native Americans attacked Providence during King Philip's War, the expulsion order was revoked so that the elderly Williams, then liv-ing nearby, could take refuge in Boston.) Nor were Quakers permitted either. During 1659–1661 the colony executed four of them when they resisted banishment. (Since 1959 a statue of one, Mary Dyer, has stood immediately in front of the Massachusetts State House, just across from the site of her hanging on the Boston Common three hundred years before.)

The commitment to strict religious uniformity was a natural con-sequence of the Puritans' self-exile from England. Their purpose in coming to the New World was to establish an independent common-wealth to fulfill God's will as they saw it. Willingly to live alongside open nonbelievers—even Christians who believed in God but none-theless believed differently—would have seemed a mark of insincer-ity. Thomas Shepard, one of the first generation of Puritan ministers, rejected toleration of diverse forms of worship as "Satan's policy."[4] Urian Oakes, who followed Shepard as minister at the First Church in Cambridge and then became an early president of Harvard College, the seminary established to train clergy in the orthodox Puritan mold, denounced such toleration as the "first born of all *Abominations*."[5] In a short book modestly titled *The Simple Cobler of Aggawam*, Nathan-iel Ward, who arrived in 1634 and served as minister at the church in Ipswich, declared, "I dare take upon me, to bee the Herauld of New England so farre, as to proclaime to the world, in the name of our Colony, that all Familists, Antinomians, Anabaptists, and other Enthu-siasts shall have free Liberty to keepe away from us, and such as will come to be gone as fast as they can, the sooner the better."[6] The colony's strictly Puritan character stood for half a century.[7]

The colony was just that, however—a colony—and in time it too became subject to the changing political and religious tides in England. In 1684, amid concerns that some incorporated English towns were becoming too independent, Charles II revoked many royal charters including the one under which the Massachusetts Bay Colony had operated since its inception. On succeeding to the throne, James II forced the colony first to accept a Church of England priest and then, in 1688, to permit construction of an Anglican chapel. It was the colony's first non-Puritan church. (King's Chapel, still bearing that name, stands on the original site near the Boston Common.) The colony's new royal charter, granted by William and Mary in 1691, left in place the established Puritan, or Congregational, church. In keeping with the new Act of Toleration in England, however, it provided that "for ever hereafter there shall be a liberty of Conscience allowed in the Worship of God to all Christians (Except Papists)."[8] Anglican, Baptist, and Quaker worship were all now allowed, though not Roman Catholic. Moreover, under the new charter Puritans no longer exclusively exercised the franchise. Protestants other than Congregationalists were also able to vote.

As in England, the question soon became what beliefs Protestants, including those standing in the Puritan tradition, would hold and what religious practices they would follow. In 1699, prompted in part by revulsion at the trials in Salem six years earlier, which had resulted in twenty executions for witchcraft, a group of dissidents established the Brattle Street Church in Boston. The group's leader, John Leverett, was a layman; but as the grandson of a former governor of the colony, and a faculty member at Harvard (and soon to be Harvard's president), he lent prominence to the undertaking. Others involved in founding the new church were likewise from prominent Boston families. (In time its parishioners would include such luminaries as John Hancock and John and Abigail Adams.) Under its minister Benjamin Coleman, a strong advocate of natural theology, the new church accepted the Westminster Confession but followed a more Anglican form of worship. Coleman was also well known for imposing looser membership conditions than at other Puritan churches of the day, which typically required personal testimony of a "regenerative" (reborn) religious experience before an individual could qualify for full membership, or have his children baptized.[9] Unlike other Puritan churches, the Brattle Street Church did not limit baptism to the children of adults who were already members, and it also gave women members the right to participate in electing the church's minister.

At about the same time, Harvard College, still the only institution of higher education in New England, broadened its curriculum. Harvard students now read natural philosophy, including Shaftesbury's works, as well as the English Latitudinarians. Sermons by John Tillotson became required reading, as in time were Samuel Clarke's Boyle Lectures. (When the English revivalist George Whitefield, a firm predestinarian, visited Harvard in 1740 he complained that "Bad books are become fashionable among the tutors and students. Tillotson and Clark are read, instead of Shepard, Stoddard, and such-like evangelical writers."[10]) With a lively traffic in books and pamphlets, and private letters too, across the ocean—by the early 1700s most ships took only six or seven weeks from Southampton to Boston, and in the late-summer-to-early-fall sailing season nine or ten arrived in an average week[11]—religious debate in America and Britain was increasingly a transatlantic conversation.

The most dramatic break with Puritan tradition occurred, with some irony, not in Massachusetts but in Connecticut. Worried by the liberalizing tendencies under way in Boston, and fearful that Harvard in particular might go too far toward accepting the non-predestinarian theology that Archbishop Tillotson had recently articulated in England, and perhaps Anglican practice too, in 1702 a group of committed Calvinists led by Cotton Mather founded a new college. (Mather's having failed to become president of Harvard, a position that his father had held, may also have been a motivation.) Yale, located in New Haven, was to be an orthodox bulwark. Twenty years later, however, all seven members of the college's faculty jointly announced their conversion to the Church of England. The primary reason was their discomfort over predestination. The trustees discharged the college's rector, Timothy Cutler, and imposed a formal requirement that henceforth anyone serving as either rector or tutor not only declare assent to the Westminster Confession but further "give Satisfaction to them of the soundness of their Faith, in opposition to *Arminian* and Prelatical [a Puritan term of opprobrium referring to Anglicans] Corruptions."[12] But the damage was done, and the rapid growth of Anglicanism was increasingly seen as a threat to the dominance of the region's Congregational churches.

Samuel Johnson—a 1716 Yale graduate and at first a Congregational minister, but then in 1722 one of the "Yale Seven"—denied that he was an Arminian. But years later he nonetheless explained his objections to

Calvinist doctrine along lines that Tillotson had by then made familiar in England. Johnson echoed Tillotson's concern that there was nothing like belief in predestination that can "so effectually tend not only to tempt us to entertain hard and unworthy Thoughts of God, but also to cut the Sinews of all our Endeavours to repent and return to Him and our Duty." The straightforward reason was that "for ought we know, we may be absolutely excluded from all possibility of succeeding by a sovereign and inexorable Decree of Reprobation," and if so then all our labors in that direction would be in vain. Like Tillotson, Johnson flatly stated that predestination "appears to me infinitely impossible to be true." The doctrine was "plainly inconsistent with the very Notion of [God's] being a Moral Governour of the World."[13]

Instead, he believed that God made men "free, self exerting and self-determining Agents," and that this, not any doctrine of depravity or predestination, was "the Idea or Conception of Him which . . . the Holy Scriptures universally give us." What determined individual men's and women's salvation, Johnson argued, was not divine election but their own choices and actions. In the state of retribution after this life, individuals' fate would be decided not according to what they had arbitrarily received from God but "what Use and Improvement they shall have made of what they have received." In contrast to orthodox Calvinist notions of depravity and, for the nonelect, reprobation, "No Man is in fact laid under an absolute Necessity of being sinful and miserable." God had assured mankind that "none shall be miserable at last but for their own Fault."[14] Johnson went on to an active role in the Anglican clergy in America, and when King's College (later renamed Columbia University) was founded in New York City in 1752, he became the institution's first president.

As the eighteenth century moved on, open opposition to orthodox predestinarian doctrine spread beyond Tillotson-inspired Anglicans. The Congregational minister Experience Mayhew began his 1744 treatise *Grace Defended* with the summary statement that "What is principally insisted on in the Essay, is, *That the Offer of Salvation made to Sinners in the Gospel, does comprise in it an Offer, or conditional Promise, of the Grace given in Regeneration.*"[15] In other words, God's grace is offered, not simply granted, and the offer is not unconditional nor is its acceptance inevitable. Mayhew was best known as a missionary to the Wampanoag Indians on Martha's Vineyard, but his book was

John Wesley Preaching from the Steps of a Market Cross
at Epworth. Following the example of George Whitefield, Wesley turned to
outdoor preaching in 1739 as churches increasingly barred him from their pulpits
and as the crowds he drew became too large to fit inside even when churches
did allow him to preach. In time outdoor preaching became a trademark of
Methodism and of evangelicalism more broadly.

sufficiently widely read that Edward Wigglesworth, an orthodox Calvinist who served for more than four decades as professor of divinity at
Harvard, denounced it as "a Medley of Arminianism & Pelagianism."[16]

In a sermon preached in Boston in 1749, Lemuel Briant, the minister of First Church in Braintree, followed Tillotson's line of thinking
even more closely. Once again the sticking point was Calvin's denial of
individual men's and women's ability to influence their spiritual fate.
"Either our living with Righteousness is of some Use and Significance
in the Affair of our salvation, or it is not," Briant observed. If it was not,
then there was nothing to be said in favor of it. Instead, "the greatest

Advocates for Licentiousness may be the best Friends of Christianity, and the most Vicious the highest in the Grace of God."[17]

Yet a further spur to the movement away from predestinarian thinking, in America no less than in England, was the spread of Methodism. John Wesley, the English founder of this new approach to evangelical Protestantism, visited America only briefly—and not entirely successfully—in a missionary effort in the new colony of Georgia, in 1736. But his influence proved lasting, in America no less than in England, and it grew over time. Like other revivalists, Wesley was known for outdoor preaching and other efforts to bring a new form of religion directly to ordinary citizens. (When criticized for not taking a parish and sticking to it, he replied that all the world was his parish.) Far more than other popular revivalists, however, Wesley worked systematically to build a movement and he proved successful; although he never returned to America, Methodist preachers that he commissioned began arriving in the late 1760s. Wesley also did not shy away from what he saw as the implications of his ideas for the practical issues of the day. He was staunchly opposed to slavery, for example. (Georgia did not yet admit slaves when he was there.)

Wesley was also energetically Arminian in his theology.[18] In his sermon "Free Grace," in 1739, he took up the theme that if the Calvinist doctrine of predestination is correct, then all efforts like preaching have little point. They are needless both to the elect and to everyone else. "In either case, our Preaching is vain, as your Hearing is also vain." Moreover, contrary to Calvin's idea of the sweet comfort that belief in predestination provides to believers, he thought the doctrine "tends to destroy the Comfort of Religion." Wesley also expressed the by then familiar concern that belief in predestination undermines the motivation for moral behavior that religion traditionally seeks to encourage, concluding that "this uncomfortable Doctrine directly tends to destroy our Zeal for Good Works." Still worse, it, "destroy[s] our Love to the greater Part of Mankind."[19]

In contrast to predestinarian thinking, Wesley's lifelong efforts to convert the multitudes stemmed from his belief in the capacity of all men and women to determine their own salvation, not by means of "works" but through their active choice to accept God's grace. To his listeners who asked why were not all men saved, he replied that the answer was certainly not because of any arbitrary decree by God. All that stood in the way of their salvation—*anyone's* salvation—was their own lack of will: "What is the Cause why all men are not saved; namely, that they will not be saved." And to provide a scriptural basis for his argument, Wesley quoted Jesus's saying, as recorded by Matthew, "*How often would I have gather'd you together, and ye would not!*"[20]

What especially distinguished Wesley's writings on predestination was not so much his contrary theology—others had advanced these views before—but the directness and force with which he expressed his opposition. The doctrine of predestination, he bluntly stated, "is not a Doctrine of God, because it makes void the Ordinance of God." Indeed, "it directly tends to destroy that Holiness, which is the End of all the Ordinances of God." Its manifest tendency was "to overthrow the whole Christian revelation." It was therefore, as far as he was concerned, "a Doctrine full of Blasphemy . . . the Blasphemy clearly contained in *the Horrible Decree* of predestination." He concluded, "I abhor the Doctrine of Predestination."[21]

Especially in New England, however, with the region's Calvinist roots, predestinarian thinking was—for a time—more resilient than it had proved in the mother country. Indeed, as Weber and others later emphasized, popular predestinarian thinking in New England was, in some respects, even more firmly entrenched. Increase Mather, Boston's leading minister at the close of the seventeenth and beginning of the eighteenth centuries (following the Glorious Revolution in England, he negotiated the colony's new royal charter), followed Calvin in making explicit that only a small percentage of men and women were among the elect. The son of Richard Mather, a distinguished minister in the first generation of the migration to Massachusetts Bay (and in his turn father of the much more famous Cotton), and an early graduate of Harvard College, Increase Mather had an impeccable Puritan pedigree and his career followed in suit. Among other calls, he served as minister of Boston's North Church, one of the city's largest and most prominent, and as president of Harvard. (He was also closely involved in the Salem witch trials.) In a series of sermons he delivered in 1720, titled "Awakening Soul-Saving Truths," Mather bluntly declared that "*the Lord's Chosen are but Few.*" The world was divided into "*the Election and the rest,*" and what he called the Election were "but few compared with the rest of the World." In yet a different rendering, "the Lord's Chosen are a *little Flock*."[22] (Thomas Shepard, one of the first-generation Massachusetts clergy, had been more specific: "'Tis a thousand to one if ever thou bee one of that small number whom God hath picked out to escape this wrath to come."[23])

Mather went on to reconfirm the Calvinist doctrine that "the chosen of the Lord have been chosen *from the beginning*, from Eternity," and, moreover, that "that choice stands, it shall never be altered." He also took pains to rebut what he saw as the rising threat of the alternative belief that, as Wesley would soon be preaching, *all* men and women are born as potential candidates for salvation: "We may here see the Erroneousness of several Opinions that some have taken up," he wrote, including "*Universal Redemption*, that Christ has died to save all Men." To the contrary, Mather argued, "all Men whatsoever are not the Objects of his Redemption. He did not design His Blood should be shed for to make Atonement for the Sins of every one, but only for the Elect of God, His Chosen."[24]

Further, as orthodox doctrine held, God chose whom he will save "without any work of theirs, without regard to any desert of theirs, He chooses them from His Sovereign Grace." And because God had chosen them in this unconditional way, they could take no pride or even personal satisfaction in their status. "As for the Elect of God themselves, they are by Nature no better than the vilest Reprobates that lives on the face of the Earth." And what about the reprobates themselves—according to his thinking, the great majority of all humans—who had no less personal merit than the elect? Mather's conclusion, which in the printed version of his sermon he put entirely in italics, was that *"the greatest part of the Children of Men will perish Eternally."*[25]

Increase Mather's son Cotton was also educated at Harvard, and he followed his father to the pulpit of Boston's North Church. (Cotton Mather was also the grandson, on his mother's side, of the first-generation Puritan clergyman John Cotton: hence his given name.) The younger Mather was a prodigy of sorts, incisive in his thinking and enormously prolific in his writings. He was also a complicated figure in many respects, embracing Enlightenment ideas but only to the extent that they were compatible with orthodox Calvinist thinking. Like many among the Puritan clergy in America at that time, Cotton Mather admired the new wave of scientific discoveries such as Copernican astronomy and Newtonian physics, and he saw it as his responsibility as a pastor to educate his parishioners about them. He was also an early advocate of smallpox inoculation. Apart from his scientific interests, he advocated commercial reform, on the ground that commerce should be a benefit to everyone, not just a means for a few to acquire riches.[26] At the same time, like his father he was a vocal supporter of the witch trials at Salem.

Cotton Mather gave his best-known defense of what he called "the Illustrious Doctrine of Predestination" in his treatise *Free-Grace, Maintained & Improved*. His chief object was to defend the doctrine against the rising threat of Arminianism. Even some who profess to believe predestination, he wrote, nonetheless pervert the doctrine as if it were meant either to reassure or to discourage people who should repent. But this was not what the doctrine was about. Under its correct interpretation, focused not on any attempt to change individuals' lives but rather the inexorability of their spiritual fate, the doctrine was true and it merited belief and support. His aim was to defend it. Mather acknowledged that predestination had its mysteries, even its abstruse difficulties. But, he argued, men should not "pretend therefore, that it should be Silenced and Smothered & Shut out of Sermons." The doctrine was, he proclaimed, true and authentic, "Proposed by our Lord, and His Apostles." It was "no little part of the *Gospel*; and we do not fully Preach the *Gospel* . . . if there be nothing of this Declared."[27]

Although he denied that predestination was intended either to motivate repentance or not, Mather nonetheless rejected Tillotson's concern that belief in the doctrine discouraged either preaching by the clergy or moral behavior by the faithful. Instead, he argued, "it hath a wondrous Tendency to the *Edification* of the Faithful in their *most Holy Faith*, and the Ignorance of it mutilates the *Praise* of God, and cherishes the *Vice* of man." He therefore enjoined those who might aspire to think of themselves as among the elect, "Will you not Admire, O *Chosen of God*, Admire the *Absolute Sovereignty* of God in His Chusing of you?" But like his father, he also warned them not to ascribe their election (if indeed they had been chosen) in any way to their own merit, nor even to God's foresight of their personal worthiness. To think so was to put the matter backward. "Is the Fore-sight of our *Faith* and *Obedience*, the *Cause* why God has *Chosen* us? Then say, We *first* choose God before He chooses us!" To the contrary, "We are chosen TO *Faith* and *Obedi-*

ence; not chosen FOR our Foreseen *Faith* and *Obedience*. They are the *Effects* of our *Election;* they cannot be the *Causes* of it."[28] Mather's clear articulation of the doctrine, with his sharp logical distinction between what was cause and what was effect, framed not only the understanding of predestination in colonial America but the way in which scholars like Weber have understood it ever since.

The best known among the colonial clergy, and still regarded by many as the foremost theologian America has yet produced, was Jonathan Edwards.[29] Born in Connecticut in 1703 and educated at Yale, Edwards was, like Cotton Mather, the son and grandson of Congregational ministers. Having no qualms about embracing the conditions imposed by Yale's trustees after the faculty's group apostasy, he served briefly as a tutor at the college. Beginning in 1726 he became an assistant to his grandfather Solomon Stoddard, one of the "river gods" of the Puritan clergy in the Connecticut River Valley, and on Stoddard's death, three years later, Edwards took his place as minister in Northampton, Massachusetts.[30] But also like Mather, Edwards was a complicated personality, and in 1750 a dispute with his church over membership requirements led to his being dismissed. While his grandfather had allowed "unregenerated" children of church members to enjoy partial membership, Edwards sought to exclude them. The congregation refused to go along, discharging him instead.

After leaving Northampton, Edwards moved to nearby Stockbridge, where he served as a missionary to the local Mohican Indians. But he also continued to write prolifically, producing some of his most penetrating works during these years. In 1758 he took up an appointment as the second president of the College of New Jersey—subsequently Princeton University—filling the vacancy created by the death of his son-in-law Aaron Burr. (Burr was the father of the Aaron Burr who later served as vice president of the United States and, famously, killed Alexander Hamilton in a duel.) But after only two months in office, Edwards contracted smallpox from a failed inoculation and died.

It was Edwards's role in the revivals of the 1730s and early 1740s—the Great Awakening—that first brought him widespread public acclaim. Through no doing of his own, the movement began in his own backyard of Northampton and the other Connecticut River towns.

Edwards's conservative temperament initially rendered him suspicious of some of the revivals' more radical innovations, especially the emotional appeal directed toward large masses of mostly uneducated people, often in open-air and other informal settings. But he quickly came to value these new methods' ability to reach—more than that, to affect intimately—huge numbers who might otherwise not come to church, or if they came might remain unpersuaded at any more than a superficial level.

Edwards first came to international attention with his 1737 book *A Faithful Narrative of the Surprising Work of God in the Conversion of Many Hundred Souls in Northampton,* an account of the revivals in the Connecticut River Valley two years earlier. In part because his was one of the first accounts to be published, supporters of the Awakening soon looked to him as a leader of the movement even though he never enjoyed the preaching success of the Englishman George Whitefield, who regularly attracted massive outdoor crowds on his several visits to America. (Whitefield initially hoped that success in America would spur a similar revival movement in Britain.) Especially after the publication in 1742 of Edwards's treatise *Some Thoughts Concerning the Present Revival of Religion in New England,* which defended the movement to a large readership including skeptical clergy in Boston and other nearby places, as well as to interested laymen in locations where the meetings never reached, he became the Awakening's most prominent American proponent.

Along the way, Edwards's enormous body of writings—the Yale edition of his collected works runs to twenty-six printed volumes, or seventy-three online—combined with the universally recognized depth of his scholarship, especially in classic works like *Freedom of the Will* (1754) and *Original Sin* (1758), commanded a respect within his lifetime that has outlived him by two and a half centuries. By the time of his death, he was well known not just in America but among intellectual circles in both England and Scotland. There is no record of Adam Smith's owning any of Edwards's works, but he presumably knew very well who Edwards was.

At the height of the Great Awakening, on July 8, 1741, at a wooden meetinghouse in Enfield, Connecticut, Edwards preached what has become the most famous sermon ever delivered in America: "Sinners in the Hands of an Angry God." According to the later recollection of Eleazar Wheelock, another Yale graduate and Congregational minister (and later the founder of Dartmouth College), who had joined him for the revival in Enfield and the surrounding towns, the crowd inside the meetinghouse had been anything but quiet before Edwards spoke.[31] But once Edwards began to preach, his message quickly arrested their attention. As he continued, his words struck them as a message of doom, personally directed to each member of the congregation.

Edwards's subject was depravity and what it meant for ordinary men and women. There was embodied in the very nature of carnal men, he told the assembled crowd, "a foundation for the torments of hell." The corruption of men's hearts was something "immoderate and boundless in its fury." As a result, men "*deserve* to be cast down into hell . . . justice calls aloud for an infinite punishment of their sins." And confirming the elder Mather's argument that only few are saved, he noted that the majority of those who had lived before then, and were now dead, had "undoubtedly gone to hell."[32]

To make the resulting spiritual plight of most of mankind concrete, Edwards likened an individual human to a spider suspended over a fire, apt to fall in at any moment—but held up by God: they were held in the hand of God, over the pit of hell. (The biblical image of the bottomless pit would have been familiar to Edwards's listeners; in the Psalms those whom God has abandoned dwell there, and in Revelation that is where Satan will be confined.[33]) Mankind deserved to fall into the fiery pit. They were already sentenced to it. Heightening the intensity of this frightening image, "the pit is prepared, the fire is made ready, the furnace is now hot, ready to receive them, the flames do now rage and glow . . . and the pit hath opened her mouth under them." More than that, "hell is gaping for them, the flames gather and flash about them, and would fain lay hold on them, and swallow them up."[34]

Addressing the congregation directly, Edwards explained that it was only God's will that prevented each individual present that day from falling into this fiery pit: "Your wickedness makes you as it were heavy as lead, and to tend downwards with great weight and pressure toward hell; and if God should let you go, you would immediately sink and swiftly descend into the bottomless gulf." All their righteousness, he told them, would no more hold them up from the pit of hell than a spider's web would be able to stop a falling rock. Only God protected them. "'Tis nothing but his hand that holds you from falling into the fire every moment."[35]

As the doctrine of predestination implied, Edwards further

reminded his listeners that nothing within their power could influence God's choice of whether to continue to hold them up or let them fall. "You hang by a slender thread, with the flames of divine wrath flashing about it, and ready every moment to singe it, and burn it asunder," he told them. But "you have . . . nothing to lay hold of to save yourself, nothing to keep off the flames of wrath, nothing of your own, nothing that you ever have done, nothing that you can do, to induce God to spare you one moment." Far from being able to attract God's favor, because of their depravity "The God that holds you over the pit of hell, much as one holds a spider, or some loathsome insect, over the fire, abhors you . . . he looks upon you as worthy of nothing else, but to be cast into the fire." Indeed, "you are ten thousand times so abominable in his eyes as the most hateful venomous serpent is in ours."[36]

And, Edwards made clear, the threat—more than that, the overwhelming likelihood—of the damnation that he described in such vivid terms faced his listeners that day, in that very church, no less than anyone else. "God is a great deal more angry with great numbers that are now on earth, yea, doubtless with many that are in this congregation," he warned them, "than he is with many of those that are now in the flames of hell." There was no room for complacency. Even for a man who was in good health, and who perceived no threat that he should immediately leave this world by some accident, this was no evidence that such a person was not on the very brink of eternity, and that his next step would not be into another world. How many who were present that day would likely remember his sermon in hell?, he asked. "It would be a wonder if some that are now present, should not be in hell in a very short time, before this year is out. And it would be no wonder if some person that now sits here in some seat of this meeting house in health, and quiet and secure, should be there before tomorrow morning."[37]

Edwards presumably meant to frighten his listeners, and he succeeded. As Stephen Williams, another minister participating in the revival, recorded in his diary, "Before the sermon was done, there was a great moaning and crying out throughout the whole house. What shall I do to be saved? Oh I am going to hell." According to Williams, the "shrieks and cries were piercing and amazing"—so much so that Edwards was unable to finish the sermon.[38] It was printed in full shortly afterward, however, and since then anthologized countless times. It stands, rightly, as an example of what orthodox Calvinist preachers in America told their followers at the movement's last great height.

The fervor of the Great Awakening ebbed, however, and as it did the turn away from orthodox Calvinist belief became apparent. Surveying New England in 1726, Cotton Mather had observed, no doubt overconfidently, "I cannot learn, That among all the Pastors of Two Hundred Churches, there is *one Arminian*."[39] By the time Jonathan Edwards moved to Stockbridge nearly a quarter-century later, the situation was plainly different. In his farewell sermon to his Northampton congregation, Edwards warned that "you should watch against the encroachments of error; and particularly Arminianism, and doctrines of like tendency." Reflecting on the inroads that the supporters of such views had made just since the recent revivals, Edwards observed that "the progress they have made in the land, within this seven years, seems to have been vastly greater than at any time in the like space before." Looking forward, he worried that Arminians were "creeping into almost all parts of the land, threatening the utter ruin of the credit of those doctrines, which are the peculiar glory of the gospel." As a consequence, the rising generation was "doubtless greatly exposed."[40]

What Edwards had observed was the steadily increasing appeal of the challenges to depravity and predestination laid out by Tillotson, now more than a half-century before, and most recently in John Taylor's *Scripture Doctrine of Original Sin* (followed, in the same vein, by his *Key to the Apostolic Writings*). Of all the English theologians writing in opposition to orthodox Calvinist thinking, Taylor was the most widely read in New England.[41] During the last years of Edwards's missionary work in Stockbridge, in 1756 and 1757, he wrote a reply to Taylor which he titled *The Great Christian Doctrine of Original Sin Defended*. Edwards was unambiguous about whom he was debating. "I shall consider whether we have any evidence, that the heart of man is naturally of a corrupt and evil disposition," he wrote. "This is strenuously denied by many late writers, who are enemies to the doctrine of original Sin, and particularly by Dr. Taylor."[42]

After weighing the arguments and evidence, Edwards reaffirmed the orthodox view that he had rendered so vividly personal and direct in his famous revival sermon nearly two decades before. The natural state of mankind, he concluded, was such that "they universally run themselves into . . . their own utter eternal perdition, as being finally accursed of God, and the Subjects of his remediless wrath through Sin." Nor was this outcome the result of accident, or mere bad choices by individuals. Rather, the cause was "the natural state of the mind of man." At bottom, "their nature is corrupt and depraved with a moral depravity, that amounts to and implies their utter undoing."[43] Edwards's treatise was published in 1758, shortly after he died.

In a further work published still later after his death, in 1765, Edwards also addressed the purpose of God's creation. As among orthodox Calvinists before him, the glory of God was the central focus. "All that is ever spoken of in the Scripture as an ultimate end of God's works," he claimed, "is included in that one phrase, 'the glory of God.'" That was "the last end of God's works . . . the supreme and ultimate end of the work of creation."[44]

To a greater extent than most of his predecessors, however, Edwards also recognized the happiness of men and women—God's creatures— as an essential element of divine intent. His argument was that human well-being and God's glory are inseparable, because the human happiness that matters comes from people's relationship to God. "God's respect to the creature's good, and his respect to himself, is not a divided respect," he maintained. The two were united, in that the happiness at which God aims for his creature is "happiness in union with himself." Moreover, "The more happiness the greater union: when the happiness is perfect, the union is perfect."[45] At least in this respect, Edwards's theology left open a path for a key element of what after him became the dominant tendency of American Protestant thinking.

The mid-century resistance by Edwards and other remaining orthodox Calvinists could not prevail. As he understood by the time he left Northampton, Arminian thinking—rejecting depravity and predestination, and in any case concerned more with virtue and morality in behavior than belief in doctrine—was increasingly guiding the preaching in America's churches. Moreover, an additional force pushing Protestant thought in this direction was the growing attraction of natural theology. During the latter half of the eighteenth century, the natural theology movement combined with these changing interpretations of what scripture meant to foster yet a further departure in American Protestantism. Along the way, as had happened in Scotland and in

England, the process of change was surrounded by intense and protracted controversy.

Part of what gave the natural theology movement its appeal was the increasingly obvious inability of Protestant theologians, all grounding their arguments in revelation from the same scripture, to agree on what that revelation was. Did the New Testament show, as Calvin had argued, that humans were depraved and their fate predestined in a manner wholly apart from whatever merits they might hope to attain? Or, as Wesley and others now claimed, were those doctrines not only *not* implied by the New Testament, but inconsistent with it (even a blasphemy of it)? Especially after the bloody wars between Catholics and Protestants in Europe, and between one variety of Protestant and another in England, natural theology seemed reassuringly ecumenical.

Following the approach used to such good effect in John Locke's *Reasonableness of Christianity,* at the end of the previous century, but also in keeping with the Puritans' traditional emphasis on the importance of scripture, Arminian-thinking clergy in America often preferred to focus on scripture itself rather than more recent creedal statements like the Westminster Confession. If doctrines like depravity and predestination were really what the Bible said, as their more orthodox colleagues maintained, why not skip the creed and go directly to the Bible? The new, liberal clergy were convinced that a close reading would show that such ideas were unscriptural.

In addition, as knowledge of Newtonian science and the influence of the Enlightenment spread, especially among America's educated elite, the appeal of any kind of revelation lost ground to the attraction of arguments grounded in reason and systematic observation. Jonathan Mayhew (Experience Mayhew's son), a 1744 graduate of Harvard and beginning in 1747 minister at Boston's West Church, was one of the natural theology movement's early leaders in America. Mayhew emphasized the role of reason in a way that ran directly counter to orthodox Calvinist views of human depravity. "Men are naturally endowed," he preached in 1748, "with faculties proper for distinguishing betwixt truth and error, right and wrong." And because they possessed these abilities, "the doctrine of a total ignorance, and incapacity to judge of moral and religious truths, brought upon mankind by the apostasy of our *First Parents*, is without foundation."[46]

Instead, Mayhew asserted, invoking Locke's famous metaphor, "The *candle of the Lord* which was lighted up in man at first, when *the inspiration of the almighty gave him understanding* . . . has kept burning ever since." That understanding, not any native incapacity stemming from the disobedience of Adam and Eve, was the distinguishing characteristic of the human species. It was reason that exalted humans above the beasts of the field. Drawing also on the recent thinking of Francis Hutcheson, but likewise by Shaftesbury well before him, Mayhew went on to tell his congregation that the creator, in addition to endowing humans with the reason required to distinguish good from evil, had also given them another faculty: a moral sense. With this moral sense, inborn human nature was just the opposite of what Calvin and his followers meant by depravity. "By virtue of this faculty," he wrote, "moral good and evil, when they are objects to our minds affect us in a very different manner; the first according us pleasure, the other pain and uneasiness."[47]

In a line of argument that resonates with one of the central themes of Adam Smith's *The Theory of Moral Sentiments,* Mayhew also claimed that humans' inborn sociability, including the desire for others' approval, was key to their behavior.[48] "We desire to be thought favourably of, by mankind," he claimed; "to be thought so by the wise and good, yields no small satisfaction." Even so, he continued—now introducing the role of the divine—our desire for approval from our fellow men and women is not the most powerful impetus to our behavior. Using language strikingly like what would appear eleven years later in Smith's first book, Mayhew asserted that what men and women really desired was "the approbation of the great *Inspector* and *Censor* of that world whose esteem we court." For Mayhew, "God himself is a *Spectator* in this *theatre* of the universe." The desire to earn *God's* approval was the most powerful human motivation, offering the prospect of the greatest satisfaction to every person.[49] Smith's impartial spectator, in *The Theory of Moral Sentiments*, represents a person's sense of the moral judgment that a "disinterested" *human* observer would draw in any given situation; but the parallel is clear, as is the similarity in language. There is no record of whether Smith had read Mayhew's sermon, but it would not be surprising if some of his friends in the Scottish clergy had.

Mayhew departed from orthodox Calvinist doctrine not just in his view of a reasoning human nature, guided by a moral sense, but also

in emphasizing the benevolent character of the divine. Following Newton, he envisioned an eighteenth-century God of understandable laws,
not Calvin's God of inscrutable purposes.[50] But he also saw that God
as infinitely benevolent to the creatures he had created. It is because of
God's benevolence, he argued, coupled with humans' desire for God's
approval, that rational men and women act benevolently toward their
fellow creatures. Further, God's benevolence meant that humans are *by
nature* inclined to act in ways that promote one another's happiness.
"He that is wise as well as benevolent," Mayhew claimed, "will observe
those methods of acting, which are the most conducive to happiness."
And "the nearer we conform to the great law of benevolence, the nearer
we conform to the perfections of the Deity."[51]

A decade later, one of Mayhew's senior colleagues in the local clergy
took up the same ideas. Ebenezer Gay, a generation older than Mayhew, had graduated from Harvard when Increase Mather was still living and Cotton Mather was in his prime. But he long outlived both
(he outlived Mayhew too), and in 1759, having served as a Congregational minister for more than forty years, Gay delivered the Dudleian
Lecture at Harvard. These annual lectures, endowed by Massachusetts
Chief Justice Paul Dudley on his death in 1751, were to address subjects including natural and revealed religion. Gay's topic was "Natural
Religion as Distinguished from Revealed";[52] even the title signaled a
departure from orthodox thinking. Theology based also on reason and
observation, it suggested, was different from theology based solely on
reading the Bible. And depending on how one interpreted the Bible,
the two might conflict.

But Gay's interest was in more than methodology. His twin themes
were the ability to infer the nature of God by observing the world in
which we live, and the conclusion—on the basis of that observation—
that because God is benevolent, intending men and women to be
happy in their existence, they were created with both the ability and
the inclination to act morally toward one another. The character of the
divine, he stated, was clearly evident in the whole Creation around us.
By contrast, clearly referring to orthodox ideas of depravity and predestination, "No Doctrine, or Scheme of Religion, should be advanced,
or received as scriptural and divine, which is plainly and absolutely
inconsistent with the Perfections of God, and the Possibility of Things."
Turning to stronger language, Gay argued that "Absurdities and Con-

tradictions . . . are not to be obtruded upon our Faith. No Pretence of Revelation can be sufficient for the Admission of them." To do so would be to "set the Gifts of God at variance."[53]

As for humans' ability to know what constitutes moral behavior, our obligation to do what God in his perfection requires of us is "discernable in the Light of natural Reason," which God has given us. In contrast to any notion of inborn depravity, "There is an essential Difference between Good and Evil, Right and Wrong . . . which the Understanding (if made use of) cannot but discern." As a result, all men and women have a "Rule of Actions within their own Breasts"— just as Hutcheson's moral sense implied. All this was evident, Gay argued, through natural theology, based on observation of the world God had created, including ourselves: "Whoever observes the divine Workmanship in human Nature," he argued, "and takes a Survey of the Powers and Faculties with which it is endowed, must needs see that it was designed and framed for the Practice of Virtue." In a further use of the thinking of the time, Gay went on to invoke Newton's ideas of gravity to describe this universal human capacity: "There may be something in the intelligent moral World analogous to Attraction in the material System—something that inclines and draws Men towards God, the Centre of their Perfection and consummate Object of their Happiness."[54]

But the analogy to Newton went only so far. Given man's natural ability to know what is right to do, what then mattered was doing it. "There is doing, as well as knowing, by Nature, the Things contained in the Law of it," Gay claimed. "Knowing them is but in order to the doing of them." Following what John Taylor and others had argued, he vividly portrayed humans as fully developed moral agents, capable of choosing and acting on their own. Unlike an apple falling to the ground, "Man is not merely so much lumpish Matter, or a *mechanical* Engine, that moves only by the Direction of an impelling Force." Rather, "he hath a Principle of Action within himself, and is an Agent in the strict and proper Sense of the Word." Moreover, because this active moral feature of human nature stems from reason, it is part of what makes us human. The special endowment of man's nature that distinguishes him as human is "the Power of Self-determination, or Freedom of Choice." It was part of the "Spirit of Man." Under the direction of inborn human reason, that spirit was "an inward Spring of Motion and Action."[55]

A generation later, the natural theology movement was still strong among the intellectual elite of America's Protestant clergy. It was all the more so following the American independence movement of the 1770s and the consequent need to unify what had been separate colonies. Disputes over what scriptural revelation meant had been problematic enough when they were mostly contained within one region or even one denomination. But different colonies professed, and in many cases attempted to enforce, incompatible versions of what was supposed to be the same religion. The established church in every Southern colony was Anglican, while in New England it was Congregational. Many Marylanders were Roman Catholics. At least until the fighting broke out, most prominent Pennsylvanians were Quakers.[56] Once the "Americans" realized that their future path lay in political unity, the challenge presented by disparate theologies became more salient.

Charles Chauncy, whose great-grandfather was an early president of Harvard, had been a minister at Boston's First Church since 1727, shortly before Cotton Mather died. He was still in the same pulpit six decades later. In the 1740s, Chauncy had been best known as a critic of the Great Awakening revivals, which he saw as based on emotionalism and which he feared would lead to social disorder. In part, he thought the preaching of popular itinerants like Whitefield, and the "enthusiasm" it generated, undermined the public's confidence in their own local churches and the ministers who served them.[57] But like many others at the time, he also understood that colonial America was in upheaval in more ways than one. With the colonies' churches constituting one of the society's most fundamental institutions, it was only natural that the language of theology was the medium of controversy in other areas as well. It was dangerous to the civic order to allow it to be misused.

In a treatise apparently written in the 1760s but not published until after the Revolutionary War had ended, titled *The Benevolence of the Deity,* Chauncy laid out in blunt terms his opposition to doctrines like predestination and depravity, and his belief instead in a God that intended humans to enjoy happiness.[58] Divine benevolence toward mankind manifested itself in two related ways. The inanimate aspects of the world God had created—plants, the lower animals, minerals, the seas—were so arranged as to provide the physical means to support human happiness. And, as Jonathan Mayhew had earlier argued, humans are endowed with capacities that both enable and attract them to act in ways that promote their own happiness.

Moreover, for Chauncy, belief in God's benevolence was intimately connected to *dis*belief in orthodox Calvinism. It was precisely because God was benevolent that human depravity and predestination were unthinkable. It simply could not be that by God's own decree some men, perhaps even most, were free to choose only that which is sinful. "A more shocking idea can scarce be given of the Deity," he wrote, "than that which represents him as *arbitrarily dooming the greater part of the race of men to eternal misery.*" Even if God were "wholly destitute of goodness, yea, positively *malevolent* in his nature, a worse representation could not be well made of him." Yet this was "the true import of the *doctrine of absolute and unconditional reprobation.*"[59]

Following in what was by then a long line of anti-predestinarian argument, going back to Tillotson nearly a century before, Chauncy went on to point to the doctrine's inconsistency with the perception of man as a free moral agent, and to argue that "it totally destroys the idea of moral good and evil." Yet, referring to the remaining orthodox Calvinists among the contemporary clergy, "This is the scheme embraced by some at this day, and by some too who are called divines, and would be looked upon as the only orthodox ones among their brethren." But the doctrine was "so grossly false," and "so debasing to the nature of man, and so dishonorary to the perfectly benevolent God," that it was strange that anyone would continue to entertain a favorable opinion of it. By contrast, the intent of the God in whom Chauncy believed was "that we might perpetually carry in our own breasts a powerful motive to make ourselves happy."[60]

Although Chauncy's book remained unpublished until 1784, by then he and other like-minded colonial clergymen had been preaching about divine benevolence, and the resulting religious importance of human happiness, for at least two decades. One historically important consequence was that in place of Locke's classic formula framing the natural right to "life, liberty and property," which the First Continental Congress included in its Declaration of Colonial Rights in 1774, the Declaration of Independence adopted by the Second Continental Congress two years later wrote of "life, liberty and the pursuit of happiness." In America, it is the second version that has endured.

.   .   .

The central themes of the natural theology movement during this period were an emphasis on religion as a matter of morality as opposed to doctrine (what some advocates called "practical" religion), the grounding of virtuous behavior in reason, and the assumption that the world is structured in this way—and humans have reason to begin with—because the benevolent God who created it intended men and women to live together in happiness. At least in America, the movement also had an affinity for the belief that because all humans are endowed with reason, and are therefore able to act as free moral agents, all are potentially able to achieve salvation as well. (Another of Charles Chauncy's books, also published in 1784 but in this case anonymously, bore a long title that ended, *or, the Salvation of All Men the Grand Thing Aimed at in the Scheme of God.*) Natural theology also had an affinity with Unitarianism: the embrace of God but with it a rejection of the traditional Christian concept of that God as a Trinity consisting of Father and Son and Holy Spirit. By the end of the eighteenth century, these ideas too began to spread, especially in America, and especially among the new republic's intellectual elite.[61]

Unitarianism grew from origins at the core of the theological thinking that had flourished in England from early in the seventeenth century and had then been embraced by many in America. The English philosopher Samuel Clarke had followed up his renowned Boyle Lectures of 1704–1705 with a book titled *Scripture-Doctrine of the Trinity,* published in 1712.[62] (Clarke's book later served as the model for John Taylor's even more influential *Scripture-Doctrine of Original Sin.*) Although from its title the book could have been thought to defend Trinitarian belief, in fact the purpose was to attack it, and the book remained influential for two generations. The ideas in it found a comfortable home in America. The Puritans, following Calvin, had accepted the doctrine of the Trinity. But the doctrine was never a specific focus of their attention, and the absence of an explicit biblical foundation for it had always presented a conundrum (which some recognized and others ignored) for a movement so grounded in scripturalism.[63] For many in the colonies and then the new republic, Unitarian thinking was less a matter of rejecting the Trinity than simply leaving it aside.[64]

In many ways, Unitarian thinking represented a coming together of the natural theology movement and some elements of the parallel but more secular tradition of deism. By observing the wonders of the universe, Unitarians inferred that there must be a God who created it and went on to infer the character of that God. But nothing in the observable world provided evidence of a distinct Father, Son, and Holy Spirit. While deists, as the label implied, acknowledged the role of a deity as the creator of the universe, they rejected the notion of a God with a continuing active presence in that universe after the creation. Moral behavior, therefore, was what mattered to deists—not worship according to some set liturgy, and certainly not adherence to any specific theology based on biblical revelation. To the new Unitarians, just like convinced deists, the Calvinist doctrines set forth in the Westminster Confession were not just not believable; they were not even worthy of endorsement as a useful fiction.

By the latter half of the eighteenth century, deism was widespread in America as it was in Scotland and England, there too especially among the educated. Although Adam Smith was private about his personal religious beliefs, he was most likely a deist (in contrast to his friend Hume's agnosticism or even atheism).[65] So too were many of the founding fathers of the new United States, even though they had no objection to participating in religious services. When the delegates to the Constitutional Convention gathered in Philadelphia for four months in the summer of 1787, many of them attended services together each Sunday—not at any specific church, but at various of the city's churches on an informally rotating basis. On the first Sunday after many had arrived, they went together to mass at St. Mary's Chapel, a Roman Catholic church, even though no one in the group was a Catholic. (Washington, who rarely attended church services, did not join the group on that first Sunday but made a point of going to mass at St. Mary's the next Sunday.[66]) Once Unitarianism recognizably emerged, with many Congregational churches in particular embracing the new way of thinking and in time formally identifying themselves as Unitarian, the appeal among educated groups was not surprising.

With some historical resonance, the first church in America to have an openly Unitarian minister was King's Chapel in Boston—a century earlier, the Massachusetts Bay Colony's first non-Puritan church. Although the church had been Anglican since its founding, in 1782 the Unitarian-thinking Congregationalist James Freeman became its minister. Three years later the church's proprietors voted to remove all Trinitarian language from its prayer book, mostly adopting the revisions recommended by Samuel Clarke nearly three-fourths of a century before. Over the next twenty years, seven of Boston's other eight churches (all except the Old South Church) likewise became recognizably Unitarian, although no doubt many orthodox worshippers remained in their congregations. By just a few years into the new century, Massachusetts alone had thirty-nine Unitarian churches. By the mid-1830s there were well over a hundred. In 1822 Thomas Jefferson wrote to a friend, "I trust that there is not a young man now living in the United States who will not die an Unitarian."[67]

The Unitarians and their sympathizers plainly rejected the orthodox Calvinist doctrine of depravity. To be sure, they were painfully aware of human sinfulness. But like the Arminians who had shown the way before them, what they could not accept was that this imperfection was the consequence of Adam's sin irrevocably imputed to all humans thereafter. To the contrary, they took men and women to be free moral agents, neither tainted nor constrained by any ancestor's sinful action. Henry Ware, a well-known Unitarian and professor of divinity at Harvard, wrote in 1820 that "We have certainly no cause to feel ourselves humbled under a sense of anything that we are by nature. We have occasion to be ashamed only of what we have become by practice." We should condemn ourselves, Ware argued, only when we are conscious "of a course of life not answering to the powers, and faculties, and privileges of our nature."[68]

Because that nature was the creation of a benevolent God, the proper attitude toward it was not the self-loathing appropriate to innately depraved beings, which Jonathan Edwards had so vividly articulated in his famous sermon, but satisfaction in the dignity of man. "What God has made us, we should think of with unmingled satisfaction," Ware argued. It was only what we have made ourselves that should give us cause for regret and shame.[69] Fifteen years earlier, a protracted controversy surrounding his views had arisen over Ware's appointment at Harvard; until then the tradition had been to appoint only orthodox Calvinists as professors of divinity.[70] By 1820 the resistance to Unitarian thinking was well past. Ware helped found the Harvard Divinity School and twice served as acting president of the university. His son Henry Ware Jr., in time also a professor at the school, became the principal mentor of Ralph Waldo Emerson. Among many of the educated, especially in New England where much of the last century's controversy had been centered, the new way of thinking had become the mainstream. As the country moved on into the nineteenth century, it became even more so.

Unitarian thinking likewise rejected the doctrine of predestination based on God's sovereign and arbitrary decision to save some individuals while damning others. William Ellery Channing, for nearly four decades minister of Boston's Arlington Street Church and the city's leading Unitarian minister, explained in a widely reprinted sermon delivered in 1819 that "We cannot bow before a being, however great and powerful, who governs tyrannically." Instead, the God that men and women ought to worship "is infinitely good, kind, benevolent . . . not to a few, but to all; good to every individual, as well as to the general system." There was, in Channing's view, no tension between a God who administered justice and a God who acted benevolently. God's justice coincided with benevolence.[71]

In Channing's reckoning, what mattered was virtue in human behavior; and virtue in turn promoted happiness. (As a Unitarian, he saw belief in the Trinity as essential to neither.) As among the English Latitudinarians, it was having a religious character—as he had put it a few years earlier, "a mild, candid, and charitable temper"—that made someone religious, not subscribing to creeds expressing doctrines remote from everyday living.[72] A half-century before, the Scottish Moderate Hugh Blair had preached that "A religious, and a thoroughly virtuous character . . . I consider as the same."[73] By now Blair's view had become conventional wisdom, at least among the New England elites. In a court decision rendered in 1810, Massachusetts chief justice Theophilus Parsons ruled in favor of state sponsorship of the commonwealth's Congregational churches on the ground that the effect of religion was "to make every man submitting to its influence a better husband, parent, child, neighbor, citizen, and magistrate."[74]

In his much publicized sermon of 1819, Channing argued that the true love of God "perfectly coincides, and is in fact the same thing with the love of virtue, rectitude, and goodness." Moreover, there was no bar—no inborn depravity inherited from Adam or anyone else—that prevented any man or woman from achieving virtue. Instead, virtue had its place in the moral nature of every man. And because God was benevolent, the virtue that religion inspired was essential to human happiness. Virtue and happiness, though not identical, were "inseparably conjoined."[75]

The role of religion, as Channing saw it, was therefore to foster the aspiration to virtuous behavior that was the same as the love of God, and that would fulfill God's intent by rendering virtuous men and women happy (and also enhance the happiness of those among whom they lived). As Locke had argued, and then the Enlightenment thinkers who followed him, the reason that God had given them made this possible. What was required of each man or woman was to develop that reason. Righteousness was the product not of some deep personal religious experience—regeneration—but of education and training. Even regeneration was a product of intellectual development. "We look upon this world," Channing explained, "as a place of education."[76]

The emergence of Unitarianism did not end religious controversy in America, nor even in New England. (Within a generation what had been the Standing Order of Congregational Churches formally split between those still called Congregational and those now formally called Unitarian.) Thomas Jefferson's confident expectation that every young American then living would die a Unitarian proved false. The former colonies were now parts of a unified nation, governing itself under one Constitution, and what had been their established churches—that is, churches enjoying state support, either financial or other—were gradually disappearing. Jefferson in particular interpreted the Constitution's First Amendment to create "a wall of separation between Church and State," following from the fact that "religion is a matter which lies solely between Man & his God" so that "he owes account to none other for his faith or his worship."[77] But neither political unification nor the end to churches' competition for public revenues did away with disagreements over such essential matters as the human character, the ultimate spiritual destiny of individual men and women, and the divinely intended purpose of human life on earth. Those debates have continued, albeit in evolving form, through the nineteenth century and the twentieth, and on to the present day.

By the time of William Ellery Channing's famous sermon, Adam Smith had been dead for nearly three decades. But by then the new discipline that Smith and his contemporaries had created had taken on a new life—the label for it was now "political economy"—both in Britain and in America.[78] Just as Smith and his fellow Scots had drawn inspiration from a worldview influenced by the intense religious debates raging all around them, the thinking of this new discipline's American practitioners was similarly shaped by their own countrymen's ongoing religious controversies. Indeed, many of these early American political economists were themselves members of the clergy.

8

Visions of Human Progress

And I John saw the holy city, new Jerusalem, coming down from
God out of heaven.

—REVELATION

Mankind . . . in striving to remove inconveniencies, or to gain . . .
advantages, arrive at ends which even their imagination could not
anticipate.

—ADAM FERGUSON

Depravity versus innate goodness, predestination versus human
agency, glorification of God versus human happiness as the divine
intent: these intense debates about people's lives and their prospects
for the afterlife, carried on throughout the English-speaking Protestant
world, in the Old World as well as the New, were central to the intellectual culture in the midst of which Adam Smith and his contemporaries
worked out the ideas that became the basis of modern economics. At
the same time, a quite different set of questions provided yet another
battleground for protracted religious controversy during this period—
focused not on men and women, with their inborn character and individual destinies, but the future of the world as a whole. That debate too
had its reflection in the economic thinking of the time, and its influence has likewise continued to resonate within economics since then.

The book of Daniel, with its explicit reference to an afterlife involving different fates for different formerly alive individuals—"some to
everlasting life, and some to shame and everlasting contempt"—was a
late addition to the Hebrew Bible (and mostly written not in Hebrew
but Aramaic). Although the narrative is set during the period of Jewish
exile in Babylonia, six centuries before our era, the book was not writ-

ten until the middle of the second century. Along with the suggestion of an individual afterlife it offered the Bible's first, albeit highly meta-phoric, vision of the end of human history. In a passage mirroring the story in Genesis in which the imprisoned Joseph interprets Pharaoh's dream of seven lean cows devouring seven fat ones, the Hebrew cap-tive Daniel is asked to interpret a dream experienced by the Babylo-nian king, Nebuchadnezzar. In order to test Daniel's powers, however, the king requires Daniel first to tell him what his dream was before explaining its meaning.

Daniel replies—correctly—that in his dream Nebuchadnezzar had seen a great statue, of excellent brightness and terrifying appearance. According to Daniel's description, "This image's head was of fine gold, his breast and his arms of silver, his belly and his thighs of brass, his legs of iron, his feet part of iron and part of clay." As the dream contin-ued, a stone "was cut out without hands" and struck the image on its iron-and-clay feet so that they shattered. "Then was the iron, the clay, the brass, the silver, and the gold broken to pieces . . . and the wind carried them away." The stone, in contrast, "became a great mountain, and filled the whole earth."[1]

Daniel's interpretation of the King's dream was that the four parts of the statue—gold head, silver arms and breast, brass belly and thighs, and iron legs—represented four kingdoms that would each, in succes-sion, rule the world. (The gold head was Nebuchadnezzar's Babylonia.) Each in its turn would face destruction, giving way to the next. But after the destruction of the fourth and final earthly kingdom, then "shall the God of heaven set up a kingdom, which shall never be destroyed"; once established, "it shall stand for ever." The process of establishing this divine kingdom was not to be a smooth one, however. At the end of the book, the prophet warns that "there shall be a time of trouble, such as never was since there was a nation even to that time." But then God's own people "shall be delivered, every one that shall be found written in the book," and the resurrection leading to everlasting life for some, and shame and everlasting contempt for others, will take place.[2]

The Gospel according to Matthew, written more than two centuries later, elaborated on Daniel's vision of a time of trouble. In Matthew's account, "ye shall hear of wars and rumours of wars . . . nation shall rise against nation, and kingdom against kingdom: and there shall be famines, and pestilences, and earthquakes." (According to Mark,

Jesus similarly says, "in those days there shall be affliction, such as was not from the beginning of the creation which God created unto this time."[3]) But immediately after these tribulations, "then shall all the tribes of the earth mourn, and they shall see the Son of man coming on the clouds of heaven with power and great glory." What follows is the Rapture—the New Testament Greek also translates as seizing—in which "Then shall two [men] be in the field; the one shall be taken, and the other left. Two women shall be grinding at the mill; the one shall be taken and the other left."[4]

The final biblical account of the end of days is in the book of Revelation, dating to the last decade of the first century, during the reign of the emperor Domitian. In this closing book of the New Testament, John of Patmos relates his vision of not just the overthrow of an empire but the ending of the earth itself in a final battle between the forces of light and darkness—a familiar theme in Mesopotamian myth, dating to long before the Hebrew Bible, and then in Hellenistic imagery as well.[5] The highly symbolized narrative describes an angel, holding in his hand a chain and the key to a bottomless pit. The angel "laid hold on the dragon, that old serpent, which is the Devil, and Satan, and bound him a thousand years, and cast him into the bottomless pit, and shut him up, and set a seal upon him, that he should deceive the nations no more, till the thousand years should be fulfilled."[6]

But even this span of time would be only a temporary respite. "When the thousand years are expired, Satan shall be loosed out of his prison, and shall go out to deceive the nations which are in the four quarters of the earth." Those nations rise up, but "fire came down from God out of heaven, and devoured them." Then the devil "was cast into the lake of fire and brimstone," to be "tormented day and night for ever and ever." At the same time, the physical world as we know it is destroyed— but replaced by a new and glorious creation, with life everlasting for those who inhabit it. As John's vision continues, "I saw a new heaven and a new earth: for the first heaven and the first earth were passed away. . . . And I John saw the holy city, new Jerusalem, coming down from God out of heaven . . . and there shall be no more death."[7]

What were the faithful to make of all this? Did these texts constitute a prediction, carrying the Bible's authority, of actual worldly events to come? Or were their authors instead seeking to describe mankind's spiritual journey, resorting to concrete images as metaphors for future developments too shrouded in mystery for humans, with our limited knowledge, to delineate in plain language?

The early Christians, often persecuted by the Roman state, took the prediction literally, and many eagerly looked forward to the imminent overthrow of the Roman Empire. In their reading, the four kingdoms foretold by Daniel were the four great empires that the Mediterranean had known within recent centuries: the Babylonians, the Persians, the Greeks, and now the Romans.[8] True to Daniel's vision (supposedly foretelling these events but in fact not written until afterward), each of the first three had perished. Now it remained only to see Rome toppled as well—and Christian believers freed from oppression—which many early Christians thought would happen quickly. According to Matthew, after describing the appearance of the Son of man in heaven, and angels gathering his elect from the four winds, Jesus had proclaimed that "this generation shall not pass, till all these things be fulfilled."[9] He also told his disciples that "there be some standing here, which shall not taste of death, till they see the Son of man coming in his kingdom."[10] Nonetheless, according to Mark even Jesus himself did not know just when the predicted end would occur.[11] Many Christians also interpreted the specifics of John's vision in Revelation to refer to individual Roman institutions or personalities. (On some readings the frequently mentioned "beast" was the emperor Nero, on others Domitian himself.) Especially following the destruction of Jerusalem, in the year 70, anticipating that the end of Roman rule would involve widespread tribulation seemed only natural.[12]

As time passed, wars came and went but the Roman Empire did not collapse. Moreover, early in the fourth century, under Constantine, Christianity was legalized within the empire and whoever was emperor assumed personal control of the church.[13] In 380 Christianity became the empire's official religion, and in 391 all pagan temples were closed and pagan religion outlawed. No longer persecuted but now supported by the Roman state, Christians no doubt continued to yearn for the triumph of good over evil; but they had little practical reason to hope for the empire to collapse. Increasing numbers of Christians now adopted a new interpretation, most clearly articulated by Augustine in *The City of God* in 426: the biblical texts describing the end of the world, including especially Revelation, were an allegorical representation of humanity's future *spiritual* journey; they did not refer to actual worldly events to come. The new Jerusalem that would descend from heaven would be the redemption of fallen man. In time, this metaphoric reading became the accepted understanding, and it remained so for centuries.[14] As late as 1522, in the introduction to his translation of Revelation into German, Martin Luther declared the text "neither apostolic nor prophetic."[15]

But the biblical account of the end of days was one of the many issues on which Luther changed his mind, as he came to realize that his movement would not succeed in reforming the existing church but instead would establish a competing one.[16] The enhanced focus on scripture that came with the Protestant movement lent itself to a renewed focus on the Bible's apocalyptic texts as well. When the emperor Charles V's troops sacked Rome in 1527, he interpreted the city's destruction as the beginning of the church's punishment by God for its evil ways. Writing again about Revelation, in 1545, Luther concluded that the book was indeed a valid, even if highly symbolized, prophecy of actual events to come. Most Protestants, including not just Lutherans but those in Calvin's Reformed tradition as well, soon accepted this new—actually old (pre-Augustinian)—view. The question with which many Protestants have struggled ever since is precisely how then to connect the biblical narrative to expectations for the future of the world in which we live. How to interpret the millennium, the thousand years during which Satan is bound and contained in the bottomless pit before his release and then the world-ending conflagration, has been a particular focus of speculation.

Joseph Mede, a Cambridge-educated English theologian active in the early decades of the seventeenth century, followed Luther in accepting the Revelation narrative, including the description of the millennium, as real-world prophecy.[17] Mede's interpretation was a positive, optimistic one, however. With the image of the binding of Satan, he thought, the author of Revelation was foretelling the defeat of evil, and the realization of the Gospel, *within future human history*. Writing in the 1630s, Mede could look back to a long series of favorable events as grounds for this optimistic outlook: the invention of the printing press (early 1440s), the beginning of the Reformation (1517) and its step-by-step triumph in England, England's defeat of the armada sent by Catholic Spain (1588), the foiling of the "Gunpowder Plot" (1605) intended to assassinate the new King James I and establish Catholic rule following the death of Queen Elizabeth, and the onset of the Puritan revolution following the dissolution of Parliament by Charles I (1629).[18] These happy events suggested to Mede an inevitable progression toward a better world, specifically in the sense of realizing the Gospel on earth and within the lifetimes of men and women such as ourselves.[19]

The advance of the Puritan revolution and the Civil War, followed by the Commonwealth and Protectorate under Cromwell, spawned a profusion of popular, and often radically extreme, millennial thinking. John Milton, in his 1641 tract *Animadversions,* declared that "Thy Kingdome is now at hand . . . all creatures sigh to bee renew'd."[20] The Fifth Monarchy Men, a group that took its name from the story of Nebuchadnezzar's dream in Daniel, supported the Puritan cause but opposed the Protectorate on the ground that, as the story in Daniel made clear—the stone that destroys the four earthly kingdoms is cut "without hands"[21]—establishing the fifth and final kingdom was to be God's work, not man's. Other groups of the time, like the Ranters and the Levellers, did not place millennialism at the center of their popular appeal but frequently embraced millennialist ideas. Even after the collapse of the Protectorate and the restoration of the monarchy, millennialist fervor continued, inspired in part by the approach of the symbolic year 1666. (According to traditional numerology that assigns values to specific letters of the Greek alphabet, 666 corresponds to the beast that rises out of the sea, with ten horns and seven heads, as foretold in Revelation.[22])

Many American Puritans, equally committed to an intense scripturalism, engaged in similar thinking. The first-generation Boston minister John Cotton, father-in-law of Increase Mather and grandfather to Cotton Mather, held that the first beast described in Revelation represented the Roman Catholic Church and the second was the pope. On the basis of his own prophetic reading of the text, he predicted that a period corresponding to the millennium, brought about by the preaching of godly Puritans, would begin in 1655.[23] (Cotton died in 1652, too early to reflect on whether he had been correct.) His grandson, while avoiding the troublesome matter of a date, confidently noted that "There are many Arguments to perswade us, That our Glorious LORD, will have an HOLY CITY in AMERICA; a *City,* the STREET whereof will be *Pure* Gold."[24]

By the last decades of the seventeenth century, however, different intellectual currents began to influence ideas of what the biblical prophecies meant. The same tide of Lockean rationalism that shaped English Protestant thinking about depravity and predestination during this period also affected debates about the meaning of the millennium. Richard Baxter, another English theologian and a Noncomformist minister of the latter half of the seventeenth century, accepted Joseph Mede's optimistic reading. He too argued that progress toward a millennium was inevitable, and that it would occur within future human history. Even more so than Mede, Baxter saw the advent of the millennium in abstract, metaphorical terms: no physical resurrection of saints or appearance of Christ in the air, and no Rapture of living persons, but rather the establishment of a righteous, earthly kingdom in the spirit of God.

In Baxter's view, however, the advance toward this righteous kingdom would not be steady. Progress toward the millennium would instead occur by distinct stages. Other millennialists, he argued, "say oft, that Christ's Kingdom begins at the *Millennium*, as if he had done none before." Their error, in his judgment, was to "distinguish not the several Gradations of his Kingdom, as from the Conception and Embryo to its maturity." He then went on to list fourteen steps along the way to the millennium, beginning with the Promise to Adam and concluding with "convincing and converting the World."[25]

The influence of Enlightenment ideas of the power of human reason was even more evident in the thinking of Thomas Burnet, chaplain to William III following the Glorious Revolution, but also a physician and a scientist. All things concerning the world in which we live, he argued, are susceptible to humans' ever expanding range of knowledge. "Whatsoever concerns this Sublunary World," he wrote—meaning the earthly world in which we humans live (literally, the world under the moon)—"in the whole extent of its duration, from the Chaos to the last period, this I believe Providence hath made us capable to understand, and will in its due time make it known."[26] Referring even more specifically to the eventual end of the world, Burnet invoked an image similar to Locke's famous candle: "when the End of all Things approaches, Truth, being revived, may shine with double Lustre."[27]

Like Mede and then Baxter before him, Burnet believed that the millennium foretold in the Bible referred to future real-world events, so that progress toward the millennium was therefore inevitable, and moreover that this progress would occur not continuously but in distinct stages. In keeping with the ideas of Locke and other more

contemporary thinkers, however, he also argued that this earthly progression would take place *via natural forces*—importantly including
human agency—rather than by divine intervention. "If we would have
a fair view . . . of Natural Providence," he wrote, "we must not cut the
chains of it too short"; appealing unnecessarily to explanations such as
a supernatural First Cause, or to miracles, was, in effect, to denigrate
the majestic capacities of the divine. "We think him a better Artist,"
Burnet argued, "that makes a Clock that strikes regularly at every hour
from the Springs and Wheels which he puts in the work, than he that
hath so made his Clock that he must put his finger to it every hour to
make it strike."[28] Even more so than Mede or Baxter, Burnet's ideas
became part of popular culture.[29]

Together with the optimistic reading of the millennium that Joseph
Mede and others had popularized earlier in the century, the idea that
natural forces including the actions of humans themselves were the
force propelling our world toward the millennium bore a powerful
implication. *Human efforts* to achieve a better world now carried a
religious, specifically a millennialist, connotation. And, following
both Locke and Burnet, the spread of knowledge was essential to this
effort. William Whiston, a theologian and mathematician who gave
the Boyle Lectures in 1707, two years after Samuel Clarke, joined in this
new, millennialist interpretation of advancing knowledge. The end to
be sought, he claimed, was a "happy time," when all human doubts are
removed and all objections to proper religious thinking are obviated
by the improvement of our knowledge, and when "the Conduct of the
Divine Providence, Reason and Revelation, shall reciprocally bear Witness to, and embrace, each other."[30]

In David Hume's and Adam Smith's day, many of the Moderate
clergy in their circle of friends likewise embraced an allegorical millennialism. Hugh Blair, minister at St. Giles but also a professor at the University of Edinburgh, looked forward to "that happy period foretold by
ancient prophecy; *when there shall be one Lord over all the earth, and
his name one.*" For him too, expanded knowledge was central to the
millennial vision: "*there shall be nothing to hurt nor destroy in all the
holy mountain of God* . . . and *the earth shall be full of the knowledge of
the Lord as the waters cover the sea.*"[31]

In America, Jonathan Edwards likewise embraced the idea that the
Kingdom of God advances by stages. In Edwards's thinking, however,
perhaps no stage was the final one. Rather, there is, in *each* of these

successive comings of God, "an ending of the old heaven and earth and a beginning of a new: accompanying each an end to a temporal state and a beginning [to] an eternal state."[32] Human history was a moral continuum, a series of fulfillments, each in some way embodying elements of the end state. The coming of the millennium, therefore, was a perpetual process; human happiness came from union with God, and "happiness will be increasing to eternity [as] the union will become more and more strict and perfect."[33] Edwards took the Great Awakening of the 1730s and early 1740s as a sign that the millennium was imminent. Writing in 1743 about the recent revivals, he speculated that "'Tis not unlikely that this work of God's Spirit, that is so extraordinary and wonderful, is the dawning, or at least a prelude, of that glorious work of God, so often foretold in Scripture, which in the progress and issue of it, shall renew the world of mankind."[34]

More specifically, Edwards concluded that the millennium was likely to arrive first in the New World—indeed, in America, and near his own Northampton: "we can't reasonably think otherwise, than that the beginning of this great work of God must be near. And there are many things that make it probable that this work will begin in America." After laying out his reasons, both scriptural and historical, for pointing to the American colonies as the millennium's initial place of arrival, he went on, "And if we may suppose that this glorious work of God shall begin in any part of America, I think, if we consider the circumstances of the settlement of New England, it must needs appear the most likely of all American colonies, to be the place whence this work shall principally take its rise."[35]

The ideas that Edwards expressed—and that predecessors as far back as John Cotton had voiced as well—were influential well beyond the realm of the religiously conscious faithful. Writing in his diary in 1765, the religiously unorthodox John Adams regarded the settlement of America with reverence and wonder, describing it as "the Opening of a grand scene and design in Providence for the illumination of the ignorant and the emancipation of the slavish part of mankind all over the earth."[36]

The crucial question that this developing consensus failed to resolve, however, was the timing of the millennium—the period during which evil is banished from the earth, and metaphorically, Satan is bound and confined in the bottomless pit—vis-à-vis the existence of humans. Would the advent of the millennium mark the end of the world as we know it? Or would the earth continue to exist in its current form, and humans such as ourselves continue to inhabit it untroubled by evil, right through the foretold thousand years (however long that might be in time as we conventionally measure it), until the conflagration marking the final defeat of Satan and the descent from heaven of the New Jerusalem?

The difference was more than merely a matter of timing. If the world will end, and Christ return, before the millennium, then there is less scriptural basis for improvement of the world in which we live: human life as we know it will continue until the Second Coming, and then end. The thousand years (or however long) without evil will occur, as foretold, but those who enjoy that better state will not be men and women such as ourselves. This view—often labeled *pre*millennialism to signify the ending of the world *before* the millennium—spawned a rich interpretative tradition that continues vigorously among many Protestant groups, especially in America, to the present day.[37]

Under this often exactingly literalist interpretation of scripture, the precise timing of the future events foretold is naturally a matter of intense interest. Relying on specific elements of the pertinent biblical texts, especially in Daniel and Revelation, both scholarly and popular commentators have frequently sought to draw out the intended parallels connecting what the Bible says and what will happen to the world. The final verses in Daniel, for example, refer first to "a thousand two hundred and ninety days" and then to "the thousand three hundred and five and thirty days."[38] The sequence of events recounted in Revelation refers (twice each) to "forty and two months" and to "a thousand two hundred and threescore days."[39] Those too may well not be actual twenty-four-hour days, or standard lunar months;[40] but if not, what time units do they signify? And dating from when?

Speculations of this kind have proliferated over the years, often with great exactitude. Looking to the concept of the millennium in Revelation, many people thought the world would end in the year 1000, but many such predictions have involved more complicated reasoning. John Cotton's calculation that a form of millennium would begin in 1655 resulted from equating the forty-two months mentioned in Revelation to 1,260 days, then taking each "day" to represent one year, and

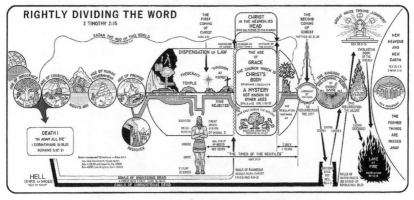

Dispensational timeline charts.
Top: John G. Hall, *God's Dispensational and Prophetic Plan* (1985).
Bottom: Clarence Larkin, *Rightly Dividing the Word* (circa 1920).
Each represents the entire span from the creation to the apocalypse.

finally beginning the count from the year 395, when (at least by some traditions) the Roman emperor Theodosius recognized the Bishop of Rome as head of the state religion.

Such efforts began to attract even more widespread popular interest in the early nineteenth century after John Nelson Darby, an Anglo-Irish Bible teacher, began publicizing his view that the divine will works through human history in distinct and discernible stages, or "dispensations." The most spectacular such prediction was that of William Miller, a Baptist preacher from upstate New York, who concluded that the world would end within the year following March 21, 1843. No doubt the hardships created by the Panic of 1837 and then the protracted economic depression that the financial collapse triggered, including widespread unemployment and the disappearance of individual wealth as the prices of land and other assets fell, added to the popular appeal of Miller's prediction. As the year-end date approached, many of his followers disposed of their possessions, donned white robes, and went to hilltops to await the Rapture. After several postponements, the episode became known as the Great Disappointment.

William Miller's Great Disappointment, 1843.
The anticipation of the apocalypse by Miller's followers, and its failure to occur
on the schedule he had predicted, became one of the most widely noted religious
events in America between the Second Great Awakening and the Civil War.

But many Americans continued to embrace this kind of dispensational premillennialism, and such ideas received a further boost with
the publication in 1878 of *Jesus Is Coming* by William Blackstone, a
layman from Illinois. The book, which by now has sold tens of millions
of copies in scores of languages (and remains in print), drew on scattered biblical passages to chart the entirety of world history, from the
creation to the Second Coming—which Blackstone saw as imminent.[41]
Nearly a century later, Hal Lindsey's *The Late, Great Planet Earth* (actually written by Carole Carlson) followed much the same theme but
without the historical context, instead tracing out the biblical end-time
prophecies in current-day events and anticipating the Second Coming
sometime in the 1980s. The book was the top-selling nonfiction book
of the 1970s. Beginning in the 1990s, the *Left Behind* novels by Tim
LaHaye and Jerry B. Jenkins rendered the biblical image of the Rapture
("then shall two be in the field; the one shall be taken, and the other

Times Square, May 2011.
Predictions of the imminent apocalypse have remained a staple of
millennialist thinking for centuries, including in our own time.

left") into modern-day fiction. These books too have sold, and continue to sell, millions of copies, and they remain central to large parts
of American popular culture.

And more specific prophecies, like William Miller's, have continued
to appear from time to time as well. Most recently, a group sponsored
by Family Radio, a U.S.-based religious broadcasting network, widely
publicized its founder Harold Camping's prediction that the world
would end on May 21, 2011.[42]

By contrast, if the world will not end until *after* the millennium (and
if the scriptural texts foretell actual earthly events), then the Bible predicts a period when human life *as we know it* will be free from evil.
Together with the naturalist interpretation of the millennium associated with Baxter and Burnet and their followers, this *post*millennialist
view is more often associated with allegorical rather than literal readings of the biblical texts. But whether allegorical or literal, it attaches
to human efforts to improve the world an additional dimension of
religious value: the millennium, though a continuation of the existing
world, will nonetheless be a better world—better in terms of knowl-

edge, social conditions, politics, international relations, and in a host of other ways as well. And men and women such as ourselves will be here to enjoy it.

This kind of thinking, and the imagery that went with it, pervaded the American popular imagination as well. Joseph Mede had seen the defeat of the Spanish Armada as a milestone on the way toward the millennium that would occur in this world; in 1758, during the Seven Years' War, many New Englanders hailed the dramatic capture of the French fortress at Louisburg, in Nova Scotia, as an event of millennial significance. In his widely read call to arms, *Common Sense,* Thomas Paine predicted that with the American Revolution the "birth-day of a new world [was] at hand." With the victory that was theirs to win, the Americans would be able "to begin the world over again."[43] And following the Philadelphia convention in 1787, Benjamin Rush, who had signed the Declaration of Independence eleven years before, predicted "a millennium of virtue and happiness as the necessary consequences of the proposed Constitution."[44]

Under a *post*millennialist interpretation of the account in Revelation, not only is human history a story of improvement; the improvement itself is human-caused. The millennium is not only the moral government of God; it is the ultimate triumph and symbol of human effort, brought about through ongoing exertion. Early in the nineteenth century Joseph Emerson, a Congregational minister in Beverly, Massachusetts (and a distant cousin of Ralph Waldo), wrote that "The wonderful and amazing events that will introduce the Millennium will be principally effected by human instrumentality." Invoking the by then familiar clockwork imagery, Emerson argued that "Tho the Spirit of God must move the wheels, yet he makes use of human agents at every turn." The crucial implication was the need for human effort: "most urgently are we required to apply our hearts, our tongues, our counsels, our property, our influence, our prayers, our talents, our utmost exertions, our every effort, to the blessed work."[45] A few years later, in a work titled *Harbinger of the Millennium,* William Cogswell, another Congregational minister and also secretary of the American Education Society, similarly declared that "Those individuals who desire, pray, and labor for the advancement of this blessed day, are co-workers with [God] in bringing it forward."[46] In 1835 Charles Grandison Finney, by then the most prominent Presbyterian minister in the United States, even hoped that "If the church will do all her duty, the millenium may come in this country in three years."[47] A half-century later Josiah Strong, a leader of the Social Gospel movement that was then gaining strength in America, wrote that it was "fully in the hands of the Christians of the United States, during the next fifteen or twenty years, to hasten or retard the coming of Christ's kingdom in the world by hundreds, and perhaps thousands, of years."[48]

The postmillennial vision therefore linked the destiny of mankind as a whole with the effort of each individual. Under this view, the antislavery movement in the nineteenth century, the temperance movement then and through the early decades of the twentieth century, and continuing efforts to eradicate poverty and to establish world peace since then all have value not just on their own terms but as ways of hastening the arrival of the Kingdom of God. So too does education. Technological advances, especially including improvements in communications, likewise assume a religious, specifically a millennialist, resonance. Just as Joseph Mede attached a religious connotation to Gutenberg's printing press, many Protestants two hundred years later viewed the telegraph and then the telephone in a similar way. Because it enabled mass communication between nations, and with it the spreading of the Gospel, the first transatlantic telegraph cable, completed in 1858, was widely hailed as an event heralding the imminent arrival of the millennium.

Samuel Hopkins, a student of Jonathan Edwards who went on to become a distinguished Congregational minister in his own right (and Edwards's first biographer), extended this postmillennial line of thinking to entertain the possibility that the millennium had already begun. Like Edwards, Hopkins thought the Second Coming would occur within the world as we know it. It was both reasonable and desirable, he wrote, "that Jesus Christ, who suffered shame and reproach in this world . . . should have this reproach wiped off in the sight of all men, and that the cause in which he suffered and died, should prevail and be victorious in this same world."[49]

Even more so than Baxter and Burnet in England, Hopkins interpreted the approach of the millennium in terms of the spread of human knowledge. Knowledge and holiness were "inseparably connected," he argued, and in some respects, the same. As a consequence, "a time of eminent holiness, must be a time of proportionably great light and knowledge." Hopkins's view of the rapidly approaching millennium also extended to the practical consequences of advancing human knowledge, including the material convenience and comforts delivered by the new labor-saving inventions that were then beginning to become widely available as a result of the Industrial Revolution.[50]

During the course of the nineteenth century, especially in America, optimistic millennial thinking of this kind was prevalent even among groups who were technically premillennialist in their theology and therefore thought the Second Coming would occur before the millennium rather than after. Some thought it had already happened. The Shakers in their communities scattered across the Eastern and Midwestern states, the Fourierists living in their "phalanxes," and the Perfectionists who settled in Oneida, New York, all saw themselves as establishing the Kingdom of God on earth. The Shakers—formally the United Society of Believers in Christ's Second Appearing—believed that Christ had already returned in the person of Mother Ann Lee, beginning with her vision in a Manchester jail cell before her emigration to America. According to the society's official creed from 1823, "Here commenced the real manifestation of Christ's second appearance."[51] Charles Fourier's followers likewise hailed him, personally, as "the second coming of Christ."[52] The Boston Fourierist Charles Dana, who served as head waiter at the utopian Brook Farm community in Concord, wrote that "Our ulterior aim is nothing less than Heaven on Earth, the conversion of this globe."[53] John Humphrey Noyes, whose Perfectionist movement sought to usher in the millennium by practicing the communal living that they associated with the earliest Christians, at one point had his followers officially vote that "The Kingdom of Heaven has come."[54]

Although explicit postmillennialism eventually faded away, as most people who were inclined toward more allegorical readings of the Bible no longer believed in anything that could be called a millennium as such (by the 1850s even the Baptist journal *Christian Review* was expressing its hope for a "social millennium"),[55] more general ideas stemming from postmillennial thinking increasingly influenced domestic reform movements in predominantly Protestant countries as well as their international politics and their popular culture. Just as the abolition movement and commitment to America's Manifest Destiny in the West had been expressions of postmillennialism earlier on, in the first half of the twentieth century the common perception of both the world wars, and of the creation of the United Nations following the Second, assumed millennialist rhetoric and symbolism. (British use of apocalyptic symbolism was especially explicit during World War I, the "War to End All Wars.") So too did the civil rights movement in the second half of the twentieth century. All were widely understood as ways of establishing the Kingdom of God on earth.

Secularized expressions of postmillennial thinking continued to pervade popular culture as well, especially in America. The Chicago World's Fair, held in 1893 to mark the four hundredth anniversary of Columbus's arrival in the New World, featured a White City designed to have visibly millennialist overtones. The exposition, which attracted 26 million visitors representing forty-six countries, showed off the latest technological marvels including the new American Bell telephone (visitors witnessed the first long-distance call from the Midwest to the East Coast) and the first all-electric kitchen. It also hosted numerous conferences. The largest, held in September, was the World Parliament of Religions.

Writing that same year, the Social Gospel leader Josiah Strong stated that "Science, which is a revelation of God's laws and methods, enables us to fall into his plans intentionally and to co-operate with him intelligently for the perfecting of mankind, thus hastening forward the coming of the kingdom."[56] The distinguished theologian and former abolitionist James Freeman Clarke (named for his grandfather, the James Freeman who had led the transition of King's Chapel in Boston to Unitarianism) offered a "new theology" structured around five points, the fifth of which was "the *Continuity of Human Development* in all worlds, or the *Progress of Mankind* onward and upward forever."[57] As the scientific organizing principle for social thought increasingly shifted from Newton's physical mechanics to Darwin's biological evolution, the idea of ongoing positive development seemed only natural. But neither the idea that scientific progress fostered moral progress nor its expression in grand world expositions was uniquely American. At the Exposition Universelle held in Paris in 1900, the centerpiece of one of the major pavilions was an allegory, placed in a giant basin with shooting fountains and illuminated by colored lights, representing Humanity advancing toward the Future, led by Progress.[58]

Both the sentiment and its expression in similar settings have continued, again especially in America. The General Electric pavilion at the 1964 New York World's Fair housed a Carousel of Progress that displayed the company's latest consumer products, under the slogan "Progress Is Our Most Important Product." In the spirit of Samuel Hopkins, who had hailed labor-saving devices as promoting religious and moral development, most visitors understood the implication that housewives would devote the time freed from daily chores to improving either their families or the world. Disney World's EPCOT (the acronym stands for Experimental Prototype Community of Tomorrow), built in 1982 in Orlando, Florida, and still in operation, features an eighteen-story-tall geodesic sphere covered in silver—named Spaceship Earth—that has become the attraction's most easily recognizable symbol. The ride inside presents a history of technological advances in communication, a traditional millennialist theme going back to the role of the printing press in spreading knowledge of the Gospel.

Adam Smith and his contemporaries lived more than two hundred years after Luther redirected Protestant thinking toward associating biblical accounts of the millennium in at least some loose way with the unfolding path of actual human history, and following also the subsequent contributions to this line of thought by English theologians such as Mede and Baxter and Burnet. By Smith's day several key assumptions were well established in English Protestant thinking, especially of the postmillennialist stripe. To begin, human advance over time was widely viewed as not just spiritual, but moral and material as well. Men and women had ascended from paganism to belief, but much of their spiritual journey remained ahead. In just the same way, the physical character of their society, and of the lives they led within it, had changed from what their ancestors knew. It too would continue to advance in the future.

Especially following Mede's writings more than a century before, this advance was seen to be inevitable. As Baxter in particular had argued, however, inevitable did not mean continual. Human progress, presumably in both the spiritual and the material realms, occurred in distinct stages. In between each new advance, matters might well stagnate or even retrogress. But each new stage carried human society to a higher level than before. The past had advanced discontinuously. So would the future.

Further, not only did the advance from one stage to the next rely on natural forces, rather than miraculous divine intervention, those propelling forces importantly included human agency. What men and women do mattered for moving their society forward. And because knowledge both motivates and enables human action, the advance of knowledge was central to this process. Greater knowledge was valuable in itself, for religious reasons. But according to millennialists like Baxter and Burnet, and in America Edwards and Hopkins, increasing knowledge played an instrumental role in human progress too, making possible society's advance from each stage to the one that followed.

The conception of human progress adopted by Adam Smith, including in particular Smith's theory of economic progress, embodied each of these closely connected elements. Not surprisingly, Smith's starting point was the unfortunate fact of scarcity, made acute over time by the human tendency to reproduce in ever larger numbers. As he went on to elaborate at length in *The Wealth of Nations,* human institutions provided a partial remedy for the problem that this scarcity created. Commerce, combining specialized production and voluntary exchange, was an astonishingly efficient way of meeting human needs and desires on the basis of limited resources. Further, commerce provided at least some modicum of justice—imperfect, to be sure, but under most circumstances greater than under any other practicable set of economic arrangements.

But where did these institutions—especially commerce—come from? By the middle of the eighteenth century, the common understanding was that they had evolved over time. (The notion of evolution at work, however, was not Darwinian; Darwin did not propose his idea of natural selection until a century later.[59]) Further, the common view among Smith's contemporaries was that the evolution of different human institutions was connected. As Smith illustrated with his account of the development of town life in *The Wealth of Nations,* advances in economic institutions brought about advances in political institutions: the rise of towns, where people produced nonagricultural goods and therefore had need to engage in trade, led to physical security and political liberty superior to what had existed under rural feudalism. Hence economic advance mattered for politics too. And standing behind both was the advance of knowledge. "Scientific" progress led to economic progress, which in turn led to progress in politics as well.

David Hume, writing in 1741 when Smith was still a teenager, laid out this integrated view of human progress in an essay titled "Of Refinement in the Arts," aimed at rebutting the increasingly popular claim (especially following the South Sea Bubble episode) that commerce merely led to luxury and decadence. "*Industry, knowledge,* and *humanity,* are linked together by an indissoluble chain," Hume wrote, "and are found, from experience as well as reason, to be peculiar to the more polished, and, what are commonly denominated, the more luxurious ages." As the inclusion of humanity in his italicized trio suggested, the point Hume was making was about more than just a society's material standard of living. "Industry, knowledge, and humanity, are not advantageous in private life alone," he explained. "They diffuse their beneficial influence on the *public,* and render the government as great and flourishing as they make individuals happy and prosperous." Contemplating the prospects for what he considered to be primitive societies, he rhetorically asked, "Can we expect, that a government will be well modelled by a people, who know not how to make a spinning-wheel, or to employ a loom to advantage?"[60] Clearly he thought not.

Hume's main point, however, was about political liberty. Progress of this kind in "the arts," he summarized, is "favourable to liberty, and has a natural tendency to preserve, if not produce a free government." Hume even offered an explanation for how the link between economic and political progress came about—indeed, one that seems strikingly modern in its focus on the role of the middle class: "where luxury nourishes commerce and industry, the peasants, by a proper cultivation of the land, become rich and independent; while the tradesmen and merchants acquire a share of the property, and draw authority and consideration to that middling rank of men, who are the best and firmest basis of liberty."[61]

At the same time, Hume saw liberty as the foundation of economic progress. In a companion essay published a year later, he argued (and in italics) that "*it is impossible for the arts and sciences to arise, at first, among any people unless that people enjoy the blessing of a free government.*" His reasoning was straightforward. "From law arises security: From security curiosity: And from curiosity knowledge." As a result, the initial emergence of the basis for economic industry and advancement could never be expected under despotic governments.[62]

Hence knowledge led to economic advance, which led to liberty and security, which in turn led to further advances in knowledge. The process was mutually reinforcing, and therefore potentially cumulative. But the question still remained: what started this process in the first place? Hume offered no answer.

As part of his teaching as professor of moral philosophy at the University of Glasgow, well before he began writing *The Wealth of Nations,* Adam Smith presented a set of lectures on natural jurisprudence— meaning not just what the prevailing laws were, and when and by whom they were enacted, but through what broader human process society's institutions more generally came to be. Smith never wrote down the content of these lectures, at least not in any form that survived him. Two students, however, did just that: one who heard the lectures during 1762–1763, the other in 1763–1764. Each left a detailed record of what Smith had said. The existence of neither document was publicly known for well over a century. Scholars first became aware of the notes from 1763–1764 in 1895, and their contents were published the following year. The 1762–1763 account turned up only in 1958; it was not published until 1978.[63] The resulting book, combining both sets of student notes, bears the title *Lectures on Jurisprudence.*

Like many before him, in the *Lectures on Jurisprudence* Smith described a now familiar stylized representation of the evolution of human economic activity: "There are four distinct states which mankind pass thro: 1st, the Age of Hunters; 2dly, the Age of Shepherds; 3dly, the Age of Agriculture; and 4thly, the Age of Commerce."[64] Smith was hardly the first to delineate these distinct ways of producing what people need in order to live, in what is now often labeled the Four Stages theory.[65] Nor was he the first to connect these successive stages of economic development to changes in governance and legal institutions. The Dutch legal theorist Hugo Grotius in the first half of the seventeenth century, the German philosopher Samuel Pufendorf in the later seventeenth century, and in France Montesquieu's *Spirit of the Laws* as recently as 1748, had all articulated similar historical schematics based on the same four stages, and in the same order. Smith was well aware of all of these works. In 1750 Anne-Robert-Jacques Turgot, the French economist and politician whom Smith met during his stay in Paris in 1766, described a three-stage version of "the advances of the human race" (the usual first three, but without commerce) in lectures that he gave at the Sorbonne.[66] In Scotland, John Dalrymple relied on the full four-stage sequence in his 1757 history of British property law, and Henry Home, Lord Kames, did so in his legal history published in 1758. (So too, most famously, did Smith's contemporary Edward Gibbon, in *The Decline and Fall of the Roman Empire*; but Gibbon's great work appeared only after Smith was lecturing on the subject.)

As Hume's essay from 1741 illustrates, Smith was also not alone in thinking that these different modes of earning the population's subsistence carried different implications for law, especially for laws regarding the holding and use of property.[67] In his multivolume *History of America,* their friend William Robertson wrote that "In every inquiry concerning the operations of men when united together in society, the first object of attention should be their mode of subsistence. Accordingly as that varies, their laws and policy must be different."[68] In the *Lectures on Jurisprudence,* Smith simply took for granted that "Property and civil government very much depend on one another." Indeed, "Till there be property there can be no government."[69]

What was new in Smith's account—although Turgot had advanced the same idea in his Sorbonne lectures[70]—was a dynamic, self-contained theory of how the transition from each of these economic stages to the next came about. The driving force, he explained, was the scarcity created by human fecundity: specifically, the pressure of expanding population against a society's limited productivity *within any given mode of subsistence.* Beginning in the Age of Hunters (a more modern rendering would call them hunter-gatherers), small bands of humans initially could have supported themselves adequately from whatever edible fruits or vegetables they found growing naturally, together with any live game they were able to catch. As people had recognized at least since biblical times, however, when resources are plentiful population increases ("When goods increase, they are increased that eat them"[71]). Nourished by an ample supply of food, a band's numbers would have increased, in time growing beyond their ability to feed themselves by such limited means.

According to Smith, the solution that emerged, in order to prevent hunger and starvation, was to capture some animals but not immediately kill them for meat, keeping them instead for milk and to breed—hence the Age of Shepherds. But with continually growing population, that mode of subsistence too in time proved inadequate. The response then, following the sequence, was to plant seeds and raise edible crops.[72] In time, however, even with both pastured animals and crop-based agriculture, the expanding population again outstripped the capacity to supply food, clothing, shelter, and other necessities. For reasons that Smith apparently understood very well but would not clearly articulate until more than a decade later, in the opening pages of *The Wealth of Nations,* the way to increase productivity then was for different individuals to specialize in different production activities. Further, this division of labor in turn required that they exchange what they produced. What resulted was Commerce.[73]

The key driver in this progression, from each stage to the next, was scarcity. But a further necessary ingredient was expanding knowledge. Maintaining domesticated animals required knowing which animals were suitable, and how to maintain them. (Even today, sheep and cows are kept for milk and meat; tigers and deer are not.) The next transition required knowing which seeds to plant, when to harvest them, and what to do with the produce to render it edible. (Humans cannot eat wheat and most other grains in the form in which they grow; they need to be ground and then cooked.) Agriculture also required the development of tools such as hoes, spades, the plow, and, in time, the wheel.[74] Commerce required yet a further increase in knowledge, including techniques of specialized production as well as the mechanics of exchange.

Crucially for this purpose, advances in knowledge are normally *cumulative* (unless the society suffers some severe cultural disruption). Once people had learned how to keep animals, or grow plants, they were not going to forget. The movement from one mode of subsistence to another that advancing knowledge enabled, according to Smith's rendering of the Four Stages theory, was therefore irreversible. Human society did not oscillate from hunting to shepherding to agriculture and back again. Each step of the process was a once-for-all change. In short, what Smith offered was a theory of *progress.*

And, in keeping with Hume's ideas along with those of numerous other writers on the subject, this theory of economic progress provided a theory of progress in political institutions as well. As Smith put it, "It is easy to see that in these severall ages of society, the laws and regulations with regard to property must be very different." Hunter-gatherers have few possessions and require little in the way of laws or governance.[75] Shepherding, however, requires establishing ownership claims to animals and rights to pasturage. It also raises the burden of communal defense. (People might not fear anyone's attacking them merely to inflict malicious harm, but stealing their animals could provide a sufficient motive.) As a result, "The age of shepherds is that where government properly first commences."[76]

Settled agriculture in turn requires agreeing on the rights and obligations of planting and harvesting, land use, and the defense of harvested produce. Because of the time lag between planting and harvesting, these arrangements are inherently more complex. (Not coincidentally, in Roman mythology Ceres—whose name gives the root of the English word cereal—was the goddess not only of agriculture but of laws and lawgiving.) Plant-based agriculture also enables a group of people to settle in one place, thereby introducing a further need for legal structures and government having nothing directly to do with economic production per se.[77]

Finally, commerce, especially in its exchange component, requires the entire institutional infrastructure necessary to support ongoing market activity, including accepted weights and measures, means of contract enforcement, and, in all known commercial economies, money.[78] Moreover, the market-centered nature of commerce leads to yet further physical agglomeration of people—not just villages and some towns, scattered through the agricultural countryside, but cities and even major metropolitan areas (think London, with a population approaching one million during Smith's lifetime)—thereby presenting even greater demands on government such as crime control and provision of public necessities like water and sanitation. At each step of the way, as one of the four stages followed another, the burden placed on laws and governance increased, and the concept of personhood and the rights it embodied expanded.

Smith's theory was therefore a self-contained, dynamic theory of *integrated progress*, in which advances in knowledge enabled the economic transitions that scarcity motivated, while the resulting economic progress, once achieved, in turn created the basis for political progress. Smith invoked no external influence, no mysterious change in human nature or behavior. At each step forward, the process required nothing more than self-interest enabled by increased knowledge. But over time—presumably very long periods of time—the cumulative effect of actions by countless individuals, each merely responding to the exigency of circumstances, changed society as well. The law of unintended consequences was at work here as elsewhere.

With his theory's focus on scarcity in feeding a growing population as the force driving economic transitions, Smith in effect anticipated—but answered very differently—the problem of overpopulation that Thomas Robert Malthus would famously raise a generation later. The assumption that human population grows geometrically, unless somehow stopped, was already widely familiar. In his *Essay on the Principle of Population*, first published in 1798, Malthus further assumed that the supply of food increases only arithmetically, and on that basis he envisioned a never-ending pressure of population against available resources, leading to perpetual deprivation and misery that would hold population in check. Smith instead invoked expanding knowledge, and the increase in food supply that it enabled, as humanity's solution to the problem. In the revised version of his *Essay*, published in 1803, Malthus considered a form of Smith's idea but rejected it. Omitting the key role of expanding knowledge, he argued that mere hunger was insufficient to spawn new customs.[79]

More than two hundred years later, it is clear that Smith was right. With expanding knowledge, food production has increased vastly beyond anything Malthus (or Smith too) could have imagined.[80] And even while living standards have risen, in one country after another, population growth has slowed—notwithstanding the absence of pressure from Malthus's predicted misery. In most high-income countries today, populations are stable or even declining (apart from immigration). The world's total population continues to rise, but entirely because of growth in the poorest countries.[81] Despite the rising overall population, the number of people in the world who suffer hunger and malnutrition is falling.[82] Malthus's insight may turn out to be correct for some resource that he did not contemplate, such as the ability of the earth's ecosystem to maintain its climate in the face of unlimited emission of greenhouse gases, but at least to date it has been wrong about food. There Smith was the more prescient.

Even so, Smith fell short of providing a full-fledged theory of economic growth in today's sense. In the *Lectures on Jurisprudence* he explained how each of a series of one-time transitions took place: from hunting to shepherding, then to settled agriculture, and then to commerce. But commerce was the end of the sequence. Once an economy had achieved a commercial state, further increases in productivity could only come from ever greater specialization in production, and for just this reason Smith assigned division of labor pride of place in *The Wealth of Nations*. (He also expressed concern over the human consequences of ever increasing division of labor, and, as we have seen, suggested universal public education as the solution.[83]) Despite the importance he attached to the accumulation of capital, he displayed no awareness—neither in the *Lectures on Jurisprudence* nor in *The Wealth of Nations*—of the possibility of ongoing technological progress that is the basis of the modern understanding of economic growth. He simply lived too early to come to that insight.[84]

Smith's theory of the irreversible advance from one mode of subsistence to the next, with resulting improvement in governance and liberty, represented a striking departure from the vision of human progress—rather, the lack of it—that had characterized Western historical thinking for much of the past two thousand years. The Greeks and the Romans had mostly conceived of human history as the reverse of progress. Following Hesiod, they believed human society had *des*cended from a long-ago Golden Age. Otherwise, thinkers of the classical era mostly held a cyclical view of human development: improvement in some eras, followed by decline in others. They agreed with Aristotle and Lucretius that the advance of knowledge was cumulative; but this one-way intellectual advance bore no practical consequences.[85] Throughout the Middle Ages, most thinkers on the subject similarly saw human history as merely cycling between periods of advance and regression.[86]

The Renaissance marked a return to the classical belief that human history was a story of decline—in this case, not from some mythical Golden Age but from the classical period itself. Beginning in the fourteenth century, western Europeans rediscovered Greek learning and with it a new awareness of the achievements of pagan antiquity. Especially with the influence of Petrarch, interest exploded in regaining the cultural heritage of not just classical Greece but Rome as well.[87] By the fifteenth century, for educated Europeans, the era of ancient

Raphael, *The School of Athens* (1509–1511).
The two central figures are Plato (left) and Aristotle (right).
Other representatives of the classical age portrayed include Socrates; Pythagoras;
Euclid; and Hypatia, a late-fourth- and early-fifth-century mathematician and
philosopher, and the only woman included in the picture.

Greece and Rome represented the apex of human development, and the motivation underlying much of their own remarkable effort in literature and the arts was to glorify that longed-for past. Raphael's early-sixteenth-century fresco *The School of Athens*, which brought together in one scene figures as separated in time as Pythagoras from the sixth century before our era and Hypatia who lived nearly a thousand years later, epitomized the Renaissance view. So too did Thomas More's *Utopia*, from almost the same date as Raphael's painting, which sought to blend the theology of the Roman Catholic Church with the glories of pagan antiquity.[88] (More's title, from the Greek, means "no such place.") The very label Renaissance—*re*birth—signified the desire to return to what was before.

New secular thinking that admitted the prospect of progress in human history came only with the eighteenth century. By then the Renaissance was well over. It was important for this purpose that the Renaissance had happened, since it was the Renaissance that rekindled the Europeans' awareness of their history and without a sense of history no notion of progress is possible. But it was important too that the Renaissance, and with it the yearning for a lost world, the desire to regain the perfection of an idealized past, was over. Belief in the superiority of all things ancient leaves little room to contemplate ongoing human progress. In the Renaissance humanists' attempt to recover Europe's past, they had in effect become enslaved to it.[89] But by the eighteenth century, getting back to the achievements of two thousand years before was no longer the height of human aspiration.

Another reason for new thinking was the increasing pace of advance in human knowledge: not just the sweeping scientific revolutions brought about by Copernicus and then Newton, but the ongoing series of more specific discoveries due to Galileo, Leibniz, Boyle, Kepler, Pascal, Priestley, Hooke, Huygens, and a host of others. Just as important, by the eighteenth century it was becoming ever more evident that advancing knowledge did have practical implications. Gutenberg's printing press, from three hundred years before, was not a unique event. The steam engine, first developed by Thomas Newcomen in 1712, opened the way to applying to practical use nonhuman (and nonanimal) power not constrained by the location of wind or flowing water. By the end of the century James Watt had adapted Newcomen's invention to rotary motion, then as well as now the standard design for machinery of all sorts. In the meanwhile, even without requiring nonhuman power, James Hargreaves's spinning jenny had enabled a single worker to spin yarn onto multiple spools at once. With the subsequent invention of Richard Arkwright's water frame, and then Edmund Cartwright's power loom, power-driven mechanical textile production—in time the heart of the Industrial Revolution—was under way.

A further influence on thinking about the course of human history was the Europeans' reaction to the discovery of the New World. The sixteenth-century Spanish historian Francisco López de Gómara wrote that "The greatest event since the creation of the world, apart from the birth and death of its creator, is the discovery of America."[90] Even more than the existence of unsuspected continents, what in time drew the Europeans' attention was the exotic peoples they found there—their housing, their clothing (or lack of it), their foodstuffs, their seeming aversion to permanent towns or villages (which the Europeans greatly overestimated), above all their novel forms of governance.[91] The question that quickly arose was what relation "the Americans" bore to the Europeans themselves, and therefore what light, if any, observing them might shed on the Europeans' past. Had the Europeans' ancestors once lived like these strange peoples, so that in them modern men were now able to glimpse their own origins?

Locke's answer, at the very end of the seventeenth century, was yes. His interest in the subject was motivated in part by seeking to establish a justification for the Europeans' claiming possession of land in the New World; the rationale he offered was that by erecting permanent structures and farming establishments they had "improved" the land, while the Native Americans had not. But this inquiry inevitably led him to consider what accounted for such fundamental differences between the two societies. The explanation, he concluded, was evolution (again, not in Darwin's sense) over time. "In the beginning," Locke wrote, "all the world was *America*." More specifically, America was still "a pattern of the first Ages in Asia and Europe."[92]

The implication was that the Europeans could indeed learn about their own history by observing how these strange people, who presumably lagged behind them in the path of human development, currently lived—just as astronomers today study the origins of our own galaxy by observing others located sufficiently far away that the light we receive from them was emitted billions of years ago. By the first half of the eighteenth century, Locke's view of "the Americans," and their relationship to the Europeans of his own time, had become widely accepted.[93] But the assumption implicitly underlying such philosophical history (as its proponents called it) was that human history was *not* a descent from some earlier higher state, nor even an endless course of cyclical ups and downs. It was progress.

And, finally, there was the influence of millennialism. The two hundred years leading up to Hume's "Of Refinement in the Arts" and Smith's *Lectures on Jurisprudence* had seen a revival of belief in the apocalyptic biblical texts as prophecies of real-world events, along with the ensuing debate over whether the promised millennium (however long it might actually last) would occur within or beyond human history. Under the postmillennial view that the world would not end until after the foretold era of freedom from evil, human history was inevitably one of advance to a higher state. Moreover, under most renderings of this religiously inspired view, by the middle of the eighteenth century the advance was seen to be not a once-for-all jump to earthly bliss but a series of upward steps—in short, progress.[94]

Smith's conception of the Four Stages sequence, with its self-contained dynamic explanation of how an economy advances from one way of meeting human needs to the next, was strikingly congruent with the postmillennialist thinking put forward by a series of English theologians over the prior two centuries: Propelled by human scarcity, the advance is inevitable. It proceeds by stages. The mechanism driving it relies only on natural forces, importantly including human agency. Increasing knowledge is essential to this active human role. And the economic progress that advancing knowledge enables brings progress in other dimensions of human life as well.

In keeping with the thinking of Smith and others of his era, this theory of human progress also had no need to rely on deliberate intent on the part of the individuals whose actions brought it about. (If it did, the advance would not be inevitable.) Adam Ferguson, Smith's counterpart as professor of moral philosophy at the University of Edinburgh, stated the more general principle several years after Smith gave his lectures on the subject at Glasgow: "Mankind . . . in striving to remove inconveniencies, or to gain . . . advantages, arrive at ends which even their imagination could not anticipate." He went on, "Every step and every movement of the multitude, even in what are termed enlightened ages, are made with equal blindness to the future; and nations stumble upon establishments, which are indeed the result of human action, but not the execution of any human design."[95] As in so much of the era's thinking, the law of unintended consequences was at work.

Just as with the theory that explained the beneficial consequences of self-interested behavior under conditions of competitive markets, which Smith later developed in *The Wealth of Nations,* there is no reason—nor any need—to think that he or Hume, or most of their contemporaries, embraced postmillennial thinking as a matter of personal religious belief. They did not have to. These ideas were all around them, not just in religious thinking but more broadly. As the eighteenth century moved on, this line of thinking provided support for an ever wider embrace of the idea of unified progress across the different dimensions of human existence: Turgot's "On the Successive Advances of the Human Mind" (the second of the *Two Discourses* that he delivered at the Sorbonne in 1750), William Robertson's *A View of the Progress of Society in Europe* (1769), Gilbert Stuart's *A View of Society in Europe, in its Progress from Rudeness to Refinement* (1778), most famously Condorcet's *Sketch for a Historical Picture of the Progress of the Human Mind* (1795). Economic progress was a key part of the process. As Auguste Comte would write, early in the next century, "All human progress, political, moral, or intellectual, is inseparable from material progression."[96]

What was still missing was the central ingredient of the modern understanding of economic growth: not just occasional one-time technological improvements, which by then were familiar in both agriculture and manufacturing, but *ongoing* technical progress. That too came early in the nineteenth century—not in Scotland or England, but in the new United States.

Political Economy
in the New Republic

The history of mankind in all ages of the world, shows, that they
will never labour for subsistence, so long as they can obtain it by
plunder—that they will never labour themselves, so long as they
can compel others to labour for them.

—DANIEL RAYMOND

Equality of conditions not only ennobles the notion of labor, but
raises the notion of labor as a source of profit.

—ALEXIS DE TOCQUEVILLE

A dam Smith died in July 1790, at the age of sixty-seven. By then his
great friend and intellectual mentor David Hume had been dead
for fourteen years. William Pitt, who became prime minster after Britain's North American war collapsed, and who lionized Smith as a valued policy advisor and a national asset more generally, had been in
office for seven years. Across the ocean, George Washington had been
serving as president of the new United States of America for sixteen
months.

That new nation presented a starkly different economic setting from
what Smith and Hume had known in Britain, and it therefore raised
new questions for the still developing field of inquiry that was coming
to be known as "political economy." With fewer than four million U.S.
citizens strung out along the Atlantic seacoast, from Georgia to what
would later become Maine, the fear of overpopulation that prompted
Malthus to write his famous *Essay* was simply absent. (Even Malthus

acknowledged that settler society in North America offered the best known conditions for human increase.[1]) By the turn of the nineteenth century, the U.S. population had grown to more than five million, but the country's settled area had expanded more than in proportion. As of 1800, sixteen states plus the officially organized U.S. territories filled the continent as far as the Mississippi River, except for the Florida peninsula. Jefferson's purchase of Louisiana from France three years later would add much of the rest. For the foreseeable future, too many people on too little land was not going to be a problem.[2]

The fact that the new republic was just that—new, and a republic—mattered too. Part of Smith's motivation in writing *The Wealth of Nations* had been to urge Britain to abolish the array of stifling monopolies that blocked competition in the country's markets for many goods. These long-standing arrangements were mostly either gifts from Britain's monarchs or the by-product of a corrupt political system, in which only a small minority of British subjects voted in parliamentary elections and both votes and influence were readily for sale. By contrast, the events that brought the United States into being had mostly swept away whatever such impediments to economic competition had built up during America's colonial past. Just a month before signing the Declaration of Independence, John Adams wrote that "The Decree is gone forth . . . that a more equal Liberty, than has prevailed in other Parts of the Earth, must be established in America."[3] Especially in the wake of their successful revolution, citizens were optimistic that their new republic would be free of the corruption that they identified with the Old World's monarchies. The makings of American exceptionalism, the notion of a special role for their country in the course of world history and future developments, were already in place.[4]

Further, the new nation had little ambition for conquest or empire outside North America. Compared to traditional European powers, therefore, there was less ground to construe the objectives of economic development in terms of fostering military strength. A growing population, stemming from natural increase as well as ongoing immigration, was important for settling the vast continent—not for maintaining a standing army or manning foreign military adventures. Improving living standards were their own attraction, not a means of affording arms and mercenary troops.

The economic issues confronting the United States in these early decades were different: westward expansion to settle the continent; the ongoing evolution from subsistence farming to a market economy; canals and turnpikes, and later railroads—internal improvements in the vocabulary of the day, infrastructure in more modern language—to facilitate the westward movement, and also to bring produce to market and goods back to where people lived; tariffs to allow the new nation's "infant industries" to grow, protected from already mature competitors overseas; arrangements for the nation's public debt, including obligations left over from the Revolutionary War as well as financing for whatever internal improvements the new government would support; banking institutions to facilitate ordinary commercial payments and enable regularized borrowing and lending. Each of these issues was the subject of intense debate in the new republic's early years. Each presented not just political considerations but fundamental economic questions. It was only natural for the new political economists to seek to analyze and understand them.

And, too, there was the question of slavery. By the time of the Revolution, the Northern states had mostly abolished the "peculiar institution." The Southern states had not, and with much of their agriculture organized on the basis of slave labor they were unlikely to do so.[5] The issue was fundamentally a moral one, but it had economic dimensions too. In the absence of slavery, plantation labor would need to be supplied either by former slaves as free workers or by some new workforce. In addition, slaves were capital assets to those who owned them, typically representing a sizable part of a slaveholder's wealth. Delegates at the Constitutional Convention in Philadelphia in 1787 had understood the issue, but found themselves unable to agree on an acceptable resolution. In the end they not only ducked the matter but took it off the nation's agenda for the next twenty years. The Constitution's Article I provided that "The Migration or Importation of such Persons as any of the States now existing shall think proper to admit, shall not be prohibited by the Congress prior to the Year one thousand eight hundred and eight." (Careful drafters, in Article V the framers also protected against the possibility of overcoming this bar by amending the Constitution itself.) The constitutional shield lasted only twenty years, however, and afterward the slavery debate became ever more heated until it erupted in the greatest crisis in the nation's existence, before or since.

While economic matters engaged much of the everyday attention of most citizens, underlying the entire national agenda were the broader implications of building—for the first time, anywhere—a new democratic republic, one on a grand scale in terms of both geography and population. The American Revolution had created not just an independent political entity but a radically altered set of attitudes toward human society and individuals' role in it.[6] Citizens now had to work out, under circumstances never before encountered, the balance between elite and popular opinion in charting their society's course. They also had to confront questions about the kind of society in which they were going to live, and what to think about its future.

Following the successful war for independence, and the establishment of their dramatically new polity, most were optimistic about that future. But just what did optimism mean in this setting? Like people everywhere, Americans in the early federal period approached such questions with attitudes shaped at least in part by their religious beliefs.[7] For most, the questions In what kind of society do we now live? and What is the future of our new nation? were inseparable from the question What kind of God created us?

The first treatise on political economy written in the United States was Daniel Raymond's *Elements of Political Economy,* initially published in 1820. Raymond was born in Connecticut into an old New England family with long-standing Puritan roots. The ideas about economics that he set forth reflected the religious origins of his region and his forebears.

Politically, Raymond was a Whig, committed to the principles laid out first by Alexander Hamilton and more recently Henry Clay. He saw industrial development as essential to the young nation's economic future.[8] On those grounds, he advocated internal improvements and other public works, and he favored a public debt to support them. He also favored tariffs to protect new industries from foreign competition. In some cases he thought the government should grant monopolies to protect key firms in these young industries from domestic competition as well. Among Raymond's writings was a defense of the Whig program, which (taking Clay's name for it) he titled *The American System.*[9]

Like most New Englanders, Raymond opposed slavery. (The Whigs, who sought support in both North and South, avoided taking a position; as late as 1848 the party's platform was silent on the subject.) He had gained initial acclaim—in the South, notoriety would have been more accurate—from his antislavery tract *The Missouri Question,* published in 1819 when he was in his mid-thirties.[10] The Constitution had protected slavery only among the Union's original thirteen states, and by then the provision had lapsed anyway. Whether to allow slavery in states to be admitted subsequently was left undecided. The decision mattered not only for those living in the newly admitted states, but because it affected the balance of slave- versus non-slave-state representation in Congress. Each new state admitted would add two members to the U.S. Senate, plus some number to the House of Representatives based on its population.

In 1819 the cutting edge of nationwide political debate focused on whether to admit Missouri as a new state, and if so under what conditions: slave or free. Raymond's book attracted widespread attention, especially for his bringing statistical analysis to bear in attacking slavery. (In part, he relied on Malthus's assumption of geometrical increase, which he applied to the slave population, warning that eventually there would be no land left for free labor to farm.) Congress resolved the immediate dispute the next year with the Missouri Compromise, admitting Missouri as a slave state balanced by nonslave Maine. But the slavery debate continued, and Raymond's analysis remained relevant.

In 1820 Raymond published an early version of his *Elements of Political Economy,* followed by a revised text in 1823.[11] His book was the first comprehensive and systematic work on economics published in the United States, and it quickly drew praise, especially from New Englanders. Former president John Adams, still living nearly a quarter-century after leaving office, hailed the book as having national significance. "I have never read any Work upon political Economy with more satisfaction," Adams wrote. It represented "a proud monument of American literature." He went on, "I shall warmly recommend it to the perusal of every Man of Letters that I see."[12] Two decades later John Quincy Adams, by then serving in the House of Representatives after his own term as president, presented a copy to the Library of Congress.[13]

The central themes in Raymond's economics harked back to the earliest days of America's Puritan settlement. John Winthrop, chosen in 1629 as governor of the Massachusetts Bay Colony, was an English lawyer and landowner, educated at Trinity College, Cambridge. He was also a devout Puritan. According to tradition, as the departing settlers gathered in Southampton in March 1630, preparing to sail for the New World, Winthrop preached to his fellow colonists on board their lead ship, the *Arbella*. His lay sermon, "A Model of Christian Charity," remains one of the most famous sermons ever delivered in the English language.[14]

Winthrop warned his new countrymen not to expect an egalitarian society. God almighty, he told them, "in his most holy and wise providence hath so disposed of the condition of mankind, as in all times some must be rich, some poor, some high and eminent in power and dignity, others mean and in subjection." In the new colony they too would experience inequality, in income and in rank. But applying orthodox Calvinist principles not just to their spiritual but also their secular state, he cautioned them not to presume any merit to themselves if they happened to be among the rich (whatever that might mean in the wilderness to which they were going) or one of the officers wielding authority: "No man is made more honorable than another or more wealthy . . . out of any particular and singular respect to himself, but for the glory of his creator and the common good of the creature, man."[15] Material well-being, like salvation, was a gift from God. And that gift stemmed purely from God's gracious act, not recognition of any merit in the individual recipient.

The practical implication of this predestinarian understanding of life's disparities, Winthrop then argued, was the need for a communitarian stance toward one another—in attitude and in action as well—reminiscent of the mutual charity advocated by Paul and the early Christian church. Self-interested individualism might be good enough in the already established world of the England they were leaving, but conditions in their new home rendered other considerations essential. "Every man might have need" of one other, he explained, and so it was important that "they might be all knit more nearly together in the bonds of brotherly affection" and "that every man afford his help to another in every want or distress." And how should they help a fellow colonist in economic distress? With a loan? Or simply by giving him what he might need? Winthrop was exactingly specific: "Thou must observe whether thy brother hath present, or probable, or possible means of repaying thee. If there be none of these, thou must give him according to his necessity, rather than lend him as he requires."[16] (Referring to a potential borrower as "thy brother" recalled the language of the prohibitions against taking interest in Leviticus and Deuteronomy, with which his listeners would have been amply familiar.[17])

But the governor's call for communitarianism in the colonists' new home extended beyond the matter of loans versus gifts. "The care of the public must oversway all private respects," Winthrop explained, and this public-over-private ranking of priorities called for a more general willingness of those with more than they needed to support any whose resources might be insufficient. "We must be willing to abridge ourselves of our superfluities, for the supply of others' necessities," he concluded. Moreover, this injunction regarding how the colonists should live together was not just a matter of practical human need. It carried divine significance. "Thus stands the cause between God and us," he warned. "We are entered into covenant with him for this work." And he went on to invoke the image from Matthew for which his sermon is today so famous: "we shall be as a city upon a hill. The eyes of all people are upon us."[18]

The communitarianism to which John Winthrop called his fellow colonists became a staple of the American Puritans' economic thinking.[19] Pursuing one's interest was entirely acceptable; doing so to the exclusion of concern about others was not. Self-interest was not the same as selfishness. Nearly a century later, Cotton Mather wrote, "*Let no man seek* (only) *his own, but every man anothers Wealth. . . .* Be willing that your *Neighbour* should be Benefited, and Encouraged, as well as Your Self."[20] A century later still, Daniel Raymond placed such communitarian thinking at the core of his analysis of political economy.

Raymond's starting point in *Elements of Political Economy* was the centrality of labor to economic production, and hence the eternal (as he saw it) tension between the necessity for labor and human attempts to avoid it. The history of mankind, he wrote, "shows, that they will never labour for subsistence, so long as they can obtain it by plunder—that they will never labour themselves, so long as they can compel others to labour for them." Opposition to slavery, the subject of his prior book, now framed his approach to economic relations more generally. Why had this propensity to force others to do our work for us "so universally

characterized the human race"? What explained "this obstinate perseverance in a course of conduct, so manifestly unjust, and so totally
inadequate to the accomplishment of the object for which it appears to
be adopted?"[21] Slavery, as he believed he had already shown, was not
just morally wrong but economically inefficient.

To explain this conundrum, Raymond looked to the traditional Calvinist origin of human depravity: the Fall. "The solution of this seemingly strange perversity in the human character, may be found in the
following sentence of condemnation, pronounced upon fallen man by
his Creator, 'And unto Adam he said. . . . In the sweat of thy face shalt
thou eat bread.'" For Raymond, the curse in Genesis was the "express
sentence of God himself, pronounced upon his fallen creature man."
It was "the irrevocable law of nature." But because of their depravity,
inherited from Adam, men did not simply accept God's curse and turn
to their decreed labor. "Unfortunately for humanity," attempts to live
off of *others'* labor "had always been the distinguishing characteristic
of man whenever he possessed adequate power."[22]

Here too Raymond was following squarely in the American Puritan tradition. While Cotton Mather had warned against pursuing one's
own interest to the exclusion of (worse yet, at the expense of) others', he
had also emphasized the need for labor on its own grounds. "'Tis not
Honest, nor *Christian,*" he had written, "that a *Christian* should have
no *Business* to do." In addition to such behavior's defying the curse
of God on fallen man, Mather also regarded not laboring as equivalent to stealing: "To be without a *Calling* . . . 'tis against the *Eighth
Commandment;* which bids men seek for themselves a comfortable
Subsistence."[23]

Even so, Raymond concluded, "from the time the sentence was
pronounced to the present day, mankind have been struggling against
it, and striving by every means in their power to extricate themselves
from its operation." But this decree of God was the irrevocable law of
nature, and so escape was impossible. As a result, "all their struggling
has been and will be in vain," and not just in vain but perverse, as
the example of slavery in America had shown. "Every unlawful effort
only plunges them deeper and deeper into the abyss of misery."[24] Cotton Mather, likewise referring to Adam's expulsion from Eden and his
need to work in the new life outside the garden, had argued that "the
Curse is become a *Blessing,* and our *Sweat* has a tendency to keep us

from abundance of *Sin*."[25] Alas, Raymond observed, there were people everywhere who "instead of supporting themselves by their own
industry, contrive to supply themselves with the necessaries and comforts of life, from the industry of others."[26]

But while it was possible for some individuals within any community to exploit others in this way, Raymond pointed out that *the community as a whole* had no choice but to supply its own labor. In making
this argument, Raymond anticipated by some decades the analytical
distinction that economists later came to draw between propositions
that held for individuals and those that held for entire economies.[27]
Writers on political economy, he lamented, had fallen into error "by
pretending to reason from individuals to nations, without taking into
consideration the different circumstances in which they are placed."
They failed to recognize that "A principle may be true, when applied to
an individual or part of a nation; but it may be untrue when applied to
the whole nation as an unity."[28]

Despite his writing in America of the 1820s, therefore—a time when
most people interested in economic matters thought in terms of disparate regions (New England; the South; the West, meaning Ohio and
Illinois)—Raymond therefore took the proper unit of analysis to be
the nation as a whole. "A nation is one, and indivisible," he wrote, "and
every true system of political economy must be built upon this idea, as
its fundamental principle." His reasoning turned on the essential need
to supply labor. Individual men and women might be able to subsist
without working. But "in regard to nations, mankind are brought very
nearly within the operation of the sentence pronounced on them by
the Almighty, so that nations are obliged almost exclusively to rely on
their own industry, for their enjoyment of the necessaries and comforts
of life." Indeed, "A nation never can, therefore, eat bread, but in the
sweat of its own face." As a result, he concluded, "Individual interests
are perpetually at variance with national interests."[29] In the particular
example that he had foremost in mind, slaveholders might be serving
themselves individually, but they were harming America.

The difference mattered for purposes of political economy because
Raymond followed Adam Smith in gauging *a nation's* wealth according to its population's living standard, not its military power, or its
holdings of gold and silver, or the expanse of territory that it claimed.
Physical property constituted wealth for an individual, but not for a

nation. One person could sell property to another; the population collectively could sell its property to no one. "What is the true definition of national wealth?" he asked. "I shall define it, *a capacity for acquiring the necessaries and comforts of life*." And for this purpose, labor—commanded under God's curse—was essential. More than anything else, the capacity to produce those necessaries and comforts depended on "the industrious habits of the people."[30]

Raymond also followed Smith—and in this case, Winthrop too—in his disapproval of economic inequality so extreme as to depress the living standard of the general public beyond a comfortable level. Smith had written that no society could be flourishing and happy if most of its members were poor and miserable.[31] Raymond likewise was clear that what was important was the standard of living of the people *as a whole*. "When we speak of national wealth," he wrote, "we speak, or at least should speak, of the condition of the whole nation, and not any constituent part of it." He therefore rejected the merit of a society characterized by inequality like that of the American South under plantation slavery. "If the whole territory, and all the property of a nation is engrossed by a few, while a much greater number are sunk into a state of hopeless poverty and wretchedness, it matters not how great the sum total of individual wealth may be." As long as the nation was considered as a unit, composed of all its citizens, such a society could "never be said to enjoy a high degree of national wealth."[32]

But economic thinking in America followed a different path. While Daniel Raymond's successors continued to accept the economy as a whole as the relevant unit of analysis, the emphasis on labor and the communitarian spirit that Raymond took from his Puritan forebears constituted a road not taken. Religious thinking remained a strong influence on the ideas that became dominant among American political economists of the pre–Civil War era. But that religious thinking was different from Raymond's predestinarian, Fall-centered Calvinism. So too were the economic ideas that it fostered.

Part of the reason was the ambivalent and then evolving attitude toward self-interest among American religious thinkers themselves. Cotton Mather had cautioned that no man should look out for *only* his own interest, but he had accepted that pursuing self-interest, in an explicitly commercial setting, was morally legitimate—indeed, morally required. "A Christian should follow his *Occupation,* with *Industry,"* Mather enjoined. "Let your *Business* Engross the *most* of your Time." Writing four years before Mandeville first published the poem that became the basis of his *Fable of the Bees,* Mather used the same imagery but with a different message: "Let there be no *Drone* in the *Hive."*[33]

Jonathan Edwards had likewise endorsed the pursuit of self-interest—within proper limits. A Christian spirit, he argued, "is not contrary to all self-love. It is not a thing contrary to Christianity that a man should love himself, or what is the same thing, that he should love his own happiness." Like Adam Smith, Edwards saw the pursuit of self-interest as merely part of human nature. "That a man should love his own happiness is necessary to his nature," he stated. Further, this aspect of human nature was not some lamentable consequence of Adam's sin. "Self-love in this sense is no fruit of the Fall," Edwards wrote, "but is necessary and what belongs to that nature of all intelligent beings which the Creator hath made." Even the saints loved their own happiness. The imperative of religion was not to banish self-interest but to limit and regulate it. The self-love to which a Christian spirit was contrary was only "an inordinate self-love," what amounted to selfishness. "The alteration which is made in a man when he is converted and sanctified is not by diminishing his love to happiness, but only by regulating it."[34]

Others in the Puritan tradition adopted views toward self-interest similar to Edwards's. Samuel Cooper, for more than thirty years minister at Boston's Brattle Street Church, addressed the topic of "disinterested Benevolence" in a sermon he preached in 1753 to the city's Society for Encouraging Industry. "We are not indeed to imagine that the benevolent Man divests himself of all Regard to his own Interest," Cooper assured his listeners. To the contrary, "Self-Love is at least as necessary to the Support and Happiness of the World as social: both were design'd by the Author of Nature to exert themselves in us to a certain degree." Like Mather, Cooper maintained that self-interest was not just acceptable but religiously mandated: "our Lord has taught us to make the Love of ourselves, the Measure and Standard of Love to others: *Thou shalt love thy Neighbor as Thy self."*[35] Without a proper regard for one's own person, there would be no regard for other people.

How, then, were religiously motivated individuals to act so as to advance the well-being of other people? Not, Cooper claimed, by abandoning their concern for themselves: "the charitable Man is not destitute of a prudent Regard to his own Interest." Again like Mather before him, Cooper drew a direct link to economic activity and initiative. "The large-hearted and disinterested Patriot," he argued, "forms Designs of enlarging the Wealth and Power of his Country." And this, his audience in the Society for Encouraging Industry were no doubt pleased to hear, meant "introducing and encouraging the most useful Arts and Manufactures." Moreover, this kind of economic enterprise was not just useful in material terms, it was necessary to human happiness: "nothing but Industry, and a full Employment of such as have Ability for Work, can make Plenty and Happiness circulate thro' a whole Community."[36]

Another colonial-era clergyman who argued in the same vein was Thomas Clap, a Congregationalist and president of Yale from the mid-1740s to the mid-1760s. In an essay on "Moral Virtue and Obligation" that he offered as "a Short Introduction to the Study of Ethics," Clap attributed self-interest to the God-given nature not just of humans but all living beings. "God has implanted a Principle of *Self-Love* and Self-Preservation in all Animals," he stated. He too therefore concluded that the proper aim of religion was not to abolish this self-interest but to confine it within proper bounds. "Since therefore this Principle of Self-Love is implanted by God, and answers many good Ends, it is not to be eradicated; but regulated by, and made subservient to a Principle which is infinitely higher and better." That principle was "Conformity to the moral Perfections of God."[37]

The line of religious thinking articulated by Mather, Edwards, Cooper, Clap, and many others as well, accepting the moral legitimacy of self-interest while seeking a means of limiting and regulating it, was fully congruent with the view of competitive markets soon laid out by Adam Smith in *The Wealth of Nations*. In time that way of thinking, not Daniel Raymond's guilt-ridden focus on man's unending effort to escape God's curse by exploiting others' labor, formed the basis for the development of economic thinking in the new American republic.

But there was a departure too. Smith's insight was that competitive markets were the device that usefully, even necessarily, regulated self-interest. Smith would have little to say, however, about where the market as an institution of human society came from. To these clergymen, the answer would have been obvious: if markets were essential to enabling society to function so as to foster human happiness, they must therefore be the creation of an actively benevolent God. The political economists who took over Smith's thinking and adapted it to the economic situation of America in the early nineteenth century thought just that.[38]

By then, however, America's religious landscape was changing. The differences were partly a consequence of the new democratic ethos spawned by the Revolution, partly a product of the country's westward expansion, and partly the influence of the increasingly rapid evolution toward a market economy. From the perspective of American religious thinking, and religious practice too, the heart of the matter was a new relationship between elite and popular opinion.

Alexis de Tocqueville, the French lawyer and minor aristocrat who visited America in the early 1830s, and on the basis of what he saw wrote what many admirers still take to be "at once the best book ever written on democracy and the best book ever written on America,"[39] commented at length on the extraordinary sense of equality that he observed among citizens of the still new nation. "Among the novel objects that attracted my attention during my stay in the United States," Tocqueville wrote, "nothing struck me more forcibly than the general equality of condition among the people."[40]

He of course did not mean that everyone enjoyed the same material standard of living, or had equal physical strength or mental acuity, or worked at the same profession. By equality of condition Tocqueville meant a civic status, one in which—unlike in his native France—there were no legal distinctions based on birth, and all male citizens stood on the same plane before the law and in their relation to the republic in which they lived.[41] In Tocqueville's assessment, this new form of equality was no mere philosophical abstraction. It exerted a "prodigious influence" on the entire course of the new American society. "It creates opinions, gives birth to new sentiments, founds novel customs, and modifies whatever it does not produce."[42]

The religious sphere of American life could hardly stand apart from this prodigious influence. Tocqueville, coming from a traditionally Roman Catholic country, was struck as well by the peculiar character of religious life in a country with no established church but where religion nonetheless played a powerful and pervasive role in the society. "On my arrival in the United States," he wrote, "the religious aspect of the country was the first thing that struck my attention; and the longer I stayed there, the more I perceived the great political consequences resulting from this new state of things." Unlike in most European countries, "Religion in America takes no direct part in the government of society." Even so, "it must be regarded as the first of their political institutions." The key to this apparent contradiction was that while he thought religion exercised little influence on the country's laws, nevertheless "it directs the customs of the community." More fundamentally, he found that in America "the spirit of religion and the spirit of freedom . . . were intimately united." As he described their mutual interaction, "The Americans combine the notions of Christianity and of liberty so intimately in their minds that it is almost impossible to make them conceive the one without the other."[43]

Under the influence of the new spirit of equality and freedom that Tocqueville observed, the face of religion in America had changed radically within just the few decades since independence. At the time of the Revolution, there had been some 1,800 Christian ministers in the thirteen colonies, almost all of them formally trained in theology and other aspects of their professional calling. By the early decades of the new century, many had no seminary training, and sometimes little formal education of any kind. Even in Boston, perhaps the most traditional community in this regard, ten of the nineteen men who served as ministers in the city's non-Congregational churches at the end of the eighteenth and beginning of the nineteenth centuries had attended neither a college nor a seminary.[44] Moreover, the number of those acting as clergy increased dramatically. By the mid-1840s the United States had nearly forty thousand Christian ministers. The population had grown, but the number in the clergy had grown three times as fast.[45]

Much of this expansion occurred outside the long-established denominations. The early decades of the new century saw a disproportionate increase among those like the Methodists, and various separatist Baptist groups, that had previously been regarded as heterodox sects. Entirely new denominations also emerged: the Disciples of Christ, the Latter-Day Saints (Mormons), among African Americans the African Methodist Episcopal (AME) church, those simply calling themselves Christians. America, at the end of the eighteenth century and for the first few decades into the nineteenth, experienced a Second Great Awakening, comparable in some ways to the revivals of the 1730s and 1740s but now marked by a new, pluralistic efflorescence. Members of these new or previously heterodox denominations, which—unlike the Congregationalists and the Episcopalians—had never known the benefit of being any state's established religion, typically had a skeptical attitude toward government more generally.[46] Many Baptists and other "dissenters" had opposed ratification of the Constitution that created the new country in 1789.[47] From the earliest days of the republic, these groups' resistance acted as a brake on the development of state authority (and as time passed their opposition persisted, with profound effects on the nation's politics).[48]

These changes in the conduct of religious life in America were therefore of a piece with the democratic consequences of the Revolution, which by the time of Tocqueville's visit had evolved past the initial forms and attitudes of the post-independence period to full-fledged Jacksonian democracy. In one area of the nation's life after another— not just politics, but newspaper publishing, banking, the practice of law, even medicine—the authority of established elites eroded while new groups lacking professional training and credentials, often lacking any formal education, gained sway. Religion was a part of this democratic movement. Even before the Revolution, democratic spokesmen had attacked the privileged position and the aristocratic tendencies among the clergy in the established churches.[49] In the early republic the deference previously paid to seminary-trained clergy, in effect granting them a monopoly over organized religious life, gave way in many quarters to a form of anticlericalism that regarded untrained, self-proclaimed leaders as more genuine mediators guiding the way to what believers sought. Learning from books in seminaries, many people thought, blocked the influence of the Holy Spirit.[50]

Religious practice changed as well. The average age of converts in the First Great Awakening was the mid-twenties; now most were in their late teens.[51] Modes of religious expression that appealed to ordinary citizens—what intellectuals of an earlier era had often denigrated as "enthusiasm"—became normal practice, not just a phenomenon reserved for occasional revivals like those led long ago by White-

Edward Williams Clay, *Camp Meeting on the Western Frontier* (1836).
As the country moved westward, and as new denominations flourished—
especially the Methodists—religious life in America increasingly
took on an outdoors character.

field and Edwards. Instead of insisting that the faithful come to them, in well-built and even elegant church buildings, the new preachers, many of them itinerant travelers with no real home base, took religious participation to the public with tent revivals and camp meetings extending right up to the country's rapidly expanding frontier. As new technology made printing cheaper (and with a higher rate of literacy in America than elsewhere), religious tracts aimed at a popular audience similarly spread the traditional religious commitment to the written word among a far broader audience than ever before.

These developments were often the product of sustained individual efforts by charismatic and innovative new religious leaders: John Leland, a Baptist minister active in his native Massachusetts as well as, for many years, in Virginia; Lorenzo Dow, a Methodist widely renowned for his near-hysterical style of preaching; Charles Grandison Finney, the commanding Presbyterian leader of the mid-century decades, who served for fifteen years as president of Oberlin College while simultaneously leading revivals and spearheading efforts for the abolition of slavery. Some of these energetic leaders—Richard Allen of the AME church, Joseph Smith and then Brigham Young who led the Mormons, later in the century Mary Baker Eddy of the Christian

Science movement—created entire new denominations. Even William Miller, whose expectation of the apocalypse was so publicly "disappointed" in 1843 and 1844, ended up fathering a new sect, today's Seventh Day Adventists.

Along with this individual entrepreneurship, however, the profusion of religious activity and diversity was the product of yet another feature of the new American society that had also caught Tocqueville's eye: citizens' eagerness to form themselves into voluntary groups to accomplish some specific purpose. "As soon as several of the inhabitants of the United States have taken up an opinion or a feeling which they wish to promote in the world," he observed, "they look out for mutual assistance; and as soon as they have found one another out, they combine." As a result, voluntary associations were established to promote a host of diverse causes, including public safety, commerce, industry, morality and religion, among many others.[52] The inclination to form associations extended to "Americans of all ages, all conditions, and all dispositions," Tocqueville reported, and he saw it as a further expression of the new country's democratic quality in contrast to European society. "Wherever at the head of some new undertaking you see the government in France, or a man of rank in England, in the United States you will be sure to find an association."[53]

Religion was no different, especially in a country with no established church. Each denomination's funding to sustain itself had to come from its own supporters. But the religious impulse, mobilized by private associations of just the kind Tocqueville observed, went well beyond merely supporting the country's churches. In a sermon preached in 1827, just a few years before Tocqueville's visit, the prominent Presbyterian minister Lyman Beecher hailed the "voluntary associations of Christians" that were undertaking religious work across a wide swath of diverse activity: Bible societies, tract societies, education societies, "societies to aid in the support of the Gospel at home, to extend it to the new settlements, and through the earth," and "associations of individuals who make it their business to see that every family has a Bible, and every church a pastor, and every child a catechism."[54]

The American Temperance Society, founded in 1826 by Beecher and Justin Edwards, another Presbyterian minister (likely a relative of Jonathan Edwards but not a close one), was especially active. The average American at that time drank the equivalent of seven gallons of pure alcohol each year.[55] Reformers appropriated the Fourth of July—for the past half-century a day of national celebration, but by then also an occasion for widespread public drunkenness—as an occasion for proclaiming the virtues of temperance, hosting alcohol-free picnics, preaching the dangers of strong drink, and urging participants to take "dry oaths" and other pledges. Within a few years, temperance weddings had also become fashionable in some areas, with coffee replacing the more traditional wine not to mention harder beverages. Many towns staged temperance processions on the Fourth of July. Activists wrote temperance songs for these occasions, some for adults but many for children ("This youthful band/Do with our hand/The pledge now sign/To drink no wine").[56]

This energetic activity among America's increasingly diverse religious groups was in part a mark of the recognition of the public importance of private morality that came with the Second Great Awakening.[57] It also reflected the continuing movement away from orthodox Calvinist thinking. The presumption was that just as individual men and women, with proper help, were able to achieve spiritual salvation, so too they would be able to give up their earthly vices. Just as the clergy's task was to convert them to religious faith—and had it within their ability to do so—religiously inspired self-improvement associations took up the challenge of reforming their behavior in more secular matters. For individuals to accept their social as well as private responsibility was to help usher in the Kingdom of God. Private morality was therefore an apt subject of public responsibility. It was no coincidence that the most Arminian-thinking groups, like the Methodists, were the most active in many of these endeavors. But especially in the wake of the "disappointment" of Millerism in the early 1840s, many Baptists and Presbyterians who had been attached to dispensational premillennialism gravitated toward a more postmillennial outlook, and with it an embrace of active reformist engagement.[58]

Tocqueville also believed that the political freedom and equality he so admired in America fostered a spirit of economic initiative he had never before seen. In America, he concluded, freedom was "especially favorable to the production of wealth."[59] Equality of condition (as he called it) created the belief that *anyone* could get ahead; and while not everyone would succeed in doing so, this belief fostered an attitude that *everyone* should at least try. In effect, the awareness of economic opportunity created a parallel sense of obligation to economic effort.

Coming from a very different country, Tocqueville remarked at length on how this widely felt obligation shaped the behavior of ordinary citizens. "It is strange to see with what feverish ardor the Americans pursue their own welfare," he remarked. "Everyone wants either to increase his own resources or to provide fresh ones for his progeny." Nor did he observe any pervasive attempt, along the lines Daniel Raymond claimed, to escape work by exploiting the labor of others. "Perhaps there is no country in the world where fewer idle men are to be met with," Tocqueville wrote, "or where all who work are more eager to promote their own welfare." Such tendencies were all aspects of how "equality suggests to the Americans the idea of the indefinite perfectibility of man."[60] Other visitors from abroad commented on the same eager economic effort. In 1839 *The Sporting Review*, a British monthly, wrote that very few even of the country's wealthiest citizens were "wholly untrammeled by business of a professional or mercantile nature."[61]

The universal opportunity that early-nineteenth-century Americans perceived (universal among while males, that is) was also in part the product of an economy that was rapidly expanding, as population increased and settlement moved westward. Even before the establishment of the republic, Washington and others among the new nation's founders had identified development westward as essential to its success.[62] In the first half of the nineteenth century that aspiration became a reality. Before 1820 the Appalachian Mountains constituted the country's western frontier for most practical purposes. As of 1810, fewer than one citizen in seven lived farther west. Now steamboats on the rivers, and canals and turnpikes where there were no natural water routes, made accessible areas ever farther from the coast. The Erie Canal, completed in 1825, reduced by a factor of ten the cost of transporting agricultural produce from western New York State and beyond into New York City. The result was an explosion of growth in the country's upper Midwest.[63] Just five years later, the first section of the Baltimore and Ohio Railroad opened. From 1820 on, the frontier moved inland by about twenty miles each year. By mid-century, half of the country's 23 million inhabitants lived west of the Appalachians.[64]

The economy was not just expanding but changing as well, and the changes also brought new opportunities. The American economy was still primarily agricultural. In the early nineteenth century, however, the country's agriculture was beginning to shift from subsistence farming to production for the market economy. In the past a family working an individual farm, or perhaps a whole village together, had typically sought to be self-sufficient to whatever extent it could. People produced most of what they needed—most obviously food, but also their own clothing as well as implements forged by the local blacksmith—and they looked to itinerant peddlers or occasional visits into town to supply the little they could not make for themselves. By the 1830s, however, American farmers were beginning to specialize, growing as much as they could of one crop like wheat or corn and selling most of their harvest. In return, they increasingly relied on the market economy to provide what they no longer grew or made for themselves. Writing in 1860, Ralph Waldo Emerson recalled that "When men now alive were born, the farm yielded everything that was consumed on it. The farm yielded no money, and the farmer got on without. . . . Now, the farmer buys almost all he consumes."[65] Economic engagement with the broader world was no longer a matter of superfluous niceties but essential to survival.

This accelerating structural change enormously expanded individual opportunities and therefore the scope for individual choice in the economic sphere. Unlike subsistence farming, commercial agriculture created incentives for large-scale production, and therefore accumulation of wealth (typically in the form of land). It also exposed many of the country's citizens, as never before, to economic risks. Farmers had always faced the possibility of adverse weather and poor harvests, but an independent family farm grew many crops and raised animals as well, and it was unlikely that all of its varied productive activities would fail in the same year. Farms producing for sale to the market mostly relied on a single crop.

Beyond the vagaries of the harvest, commercial agriculture also exposed farmers to a whole new range of market risks. The harvest might be ample, but what if the market price for the single crop they grew turned out to be low? Large-scale production also required large acreage, and many owners financed their expanded holdings by borrowing. Fluctuations in the credit market therefore mattered too. The sharp constriction of lending that followed the Panic of 1837 created widespread distress for half a decade, driving down prices, wages, and profits throughout the economy including the farm sector. And, as always, the development of financial markets provided opportunities for speculative behavior that exposed those who engaged in it, as well as many who simply relied on these markets to carry out their ordinary business dealings, to risks that had little to do with the underlying non-financial economic activity.

At the same time, new industries were starting up outside agriculture, providing wage-based employment not just on the now much larger commercial farms but in what over time would grow into a mass urban workforce. American manufacturing activity was initially centered in New England, but in time it spread westward. Similarly, what had started out primarily as textile production, under the highly mechanized factory model pioneered in America by Francis Cabot Lowell, expanded into hard goods as well. The development of manufacturing created yet further opportunities for initiative and entrepreneurship. It also provided jobs for many among the growing numbers of workers no longer needed on the farms, as population in older agricultural areas continued to expand. What were once comfortably sized family farms, a century or more earlier, had by now been divided three or even four times in order to accommodate successive generations' independence. By the 1830s that process had reached its practical limit. Farm families with more than one son now increasingly saw their adult children either move to employment in the growing cities and towns or join the movement westward.[66] One reflection of the profusion of new and different opportunities was a popular handbook published in 1836 titled *The Panorama of Professions and Trades;* the telling secondary title was *Every Man's Book.*[67]

To Tocqueville, the individual effort driving all this economic churning was a product of the equality and freedom that characterized the new republic. "There is therefore a close bond and necessary relation between these two elements, freedom and productive industry," he wrote. In other settings, the need for labor might seem to be a curse laid by God on sinful man. In the America he observed in the early 1830s, "Equality of conditions not only ennobles the notion of labor, but raises the notion of labor as a source of profit." Labor in the pursuit of wealth, under conditions of equality and freedom, was no curse.

It was part of men's and women's quest to improve, even to perfect, the world in which they lived. "The idea of perfectibility," Tocqueville wrote, is "as old as the world; equality did not give birth to it, but has imparted to it a new character."[68]

This vigorous economic activity bore implications for religious thinking too. The awareness of ever wider opportunities, in a setting of political equality, heightened many early-nineteenth-century Americans' sense that their economic destiny was in their own hands. This new attitude, spreading among ever larger parts of the population, was not conducive to predestinarian religious thinking. The role of individual human agency in the economic sphere was becoming more tangibly evident than ever before, as increasing numbers of Americans took control of their own paths. To suppose that their individual spiritual destinies were completely out of their hands—decided eons ago, with no regard to their efforts or conduct or success—contradicted their everyday intuitions. Just as changed religious attitudes about the possibilities of human agency had influenced thinking about economic questions for more than a century, now the reality of expanded economic opportunity shaped Americans' receptiveness to different religious precepts.

As Tocqueville pointed out, with no established church the practical need for American religious groups to compete for adherents and funding constrained most religious thinking in the new country to run along lines that would meet believers' spiritual needs without seeming to oppose their worldly endeavors or otherwise make them feel too uncomfortable. "The more the conditions of men are equalized," he observed, the more important it was for religion "not needlessly to run counter to the ideas that generally prevail or to the permanent interests that exist in the mass of the people."[69]

More concretely, as the shift to commercial agriculture created new opportunities, and as the country's mercantile and manufacturing elite grew—including in both cases many who had come from only modest origins—prospering farmers and businessmen, together with their families, were unlikely to choose to attend churches where they would regularly hear themselves denigrated and their moral character deplored from the pulpit. Dwelling on humans' innate depravity, inherited from the long-ago sin of their first parents, did not fit the spirit of the times. Even outside the realm of the more established denominations, the Shakers, who reached their peak of support around 1840, denounced the doctrine of depravity as "one of the most destructive errors that ever proceeded from the powers of darkness."[70] As the nineteenth century went on, the overall tendency was not only a continuing embrace of religious beliefs centered on human agency as opposed to predestination, but the "embourgeoisement" of groups like the Methodists that had begun with a more distinctly working-class outlook.[71] For these denominations to have done otherwise would have set them at odds with the spirit of creative economic enterprise that characterized the young republic.

The anti-predestinarian spirit of the times naturally favored denominations like the Methodists and Baptists. John Wesley, the founder of Methodism, had been outspoken in his opposition to the doctrine. Beginning with the Second Great Awakening, most (though certainly not all) Baptist groups likewise rejected it.[72] Both the Methodists and the non-predestinarian Baptist denominations experienced explosive growth during this period. From virtually no presence in America at the time of the Revolution, the number of Methodist congregations grew to approximately twenty thousand by the time of the Civil War; Baptist congregations went from 450 to over twelve thousand.[73] But denominations long committed to predestinarian thinking—even the Presbyterians, who also stood in a direct line of succession from Jonathan Edwards—tempered their commitment to orthodox Calvinist doctrine as well.

In the 1830s, the Presbyterian minister Charles Grandison Finney led one of the era's most successful revivals, in upstate New York. Lecturing on the subject of revivals soon afterward, Finney did not explicitly reject predestinarian doctrine, as Wesley had. Instead, he simply contradicted it, portraying the individual sinner as an active agent in his or her own conversion. "Men are not mere *instruments* in the hands of God," he argued, and it was impossible that the conversion of a sinner "should take place without his agency." In contrast to the orthodox doctrine of irresistible grace, Finney explained that "What sinners do is to submit to the truth, or to resist it." The choice was theirs. "Sinners cannot be converted without their own agency, for conversion *consists in* their voluntary turning to God."[74]

While he accepted that others among his church's clergy might believe in predestination, Finney nonetheless thought that when they did it was better—for the purpose of effective revivals—to leave that belief unspoken. "If election and sovereignty are too much preached," he warned, "sinners will hide themselves behind the delusion that they can do nothing." The difficulty with preaching predestination was that then "Sinners have been commanded to repent, and told that they could not repent, in the same sermon." As a result, the message a prospective convert received was, "You can and you can't, you shall and you shan't, you will and you won't, and you'll be damned if you don't." The underlying problem, as Finney saw it, was that many believers often "supposed God's sovereignty to be something very different from what it is." They had "got behind a perverted view" of the doctrine, thinking of it as "such an arbitrary disposal of events, and particularly of the gift of his Spirit, as precluded a rational employment of means for promoting a revival of religion."[75] And anything that impeded revival was to be avoided.

Religious values and economic values were therefore in harmony, not opposed, in America of the early nineteenth century. The new nation's revolutionary origins, evolving into Jacksonian democracy, had heightened the sense of importance attached to individual human agency in the realm of politics, just as the movement away from orthodox Calvinism in the previous century had done so in religion. Now the combination of rapid national expansion and new commercial horizons was fostering that same sense of opportunity and self-driven destiny in the realm of economics as well: productive activity, undertaken by individuals acting in their own perceived interest, produced favorable consequences not just for themselves but for the country too. Americans who sought to analyze economic behavior and its outcomes—the country's "political economists"—took these presumptions as their starting place.

The Clerical Economists

> To forbid trade among nations, is, therefore, a very unwise
> thing; but it is also a very wicked thing, for it is contrary to
> the will of God.
>
> —JOHN McVICKAR

> If it be asked, how far may this increased productiveness of
> human industry be carried, we answer, it is impossible to tell,
> unless we can ascertain how great are the blessings which
> God has in reserve for man.
>
> —FRANCIS WAYLAND

Unlike David Hume and Adam Smith, many of the key figures who charted the path of political economy in the United States in the decades before the Civil War approached their work from a perspective of personal religious commitment. Some were clergymen. Others, while not ordained, had strong religious ties nonetheless. Their religious orientation, however, differed from Daniel Raymond's Puritanism. They were mostly Protestants,[1] but they had little interest in doctrines like depravity and predestination. The God they worshipped was a benevolent one, and they believed human happiness was fully consistent with—indeed, it was the principal means of—God's glorification. While they paid little attention to the prospect of the end of days, they mostly shared a secular optimism consistent with what by then had become recognizable as postmillennial thinking.

The first college in America to offer a course in political economy, starting in the 1820s, was Columbia. John McVickar, the instructor for this new discipline, was a professor of moral philosophy, just as Smith had been at Glasgow. But in keeping with Columbia's origins—established by royal charter from George II, it was originally called King's College but renamed after the Revolution—he was also an Episcopal priest. Like Raymond, McVickar was a Hamilton-Clay Whig who favored "internal improvements" to foster the advance of commerce as the country expanded westward. But in addition to supporting the expansion of trade domestically, McVickar also advocated free trade internationally. He saw the arguments for encouraging commerce among the disparate regions of the United States as applying to commerce among countries too.

McVickar first published his thoughts on economics in 1825. The work, titled *Outlines of Political Economy,* presumably contained his lectures for the course he was then giving at Columbia.[2] Several years later, he separately published a thirty-eight-page *Introductory Lecture to a Course of Political Economy; Recently Delivered at Columbia College, New York.*[3] By then his title at the university had changed; he was now professor of moral philosophy *and political economy.* McVickar also wrote a highly simplified version of his lectures aimed at spreading his ideas on the subject among New Yorkers and other Americans—at that time, the great majority—who would never enroll at Columbia or any other institution of higher education. This short book, printed in large type and full of concrete examples that sometimes strike the modern reader as amusing ("How is it when two boys *swop* knives? Can both gain?"), not to mention moral lessons from the Bible as well, was published in 1835 as *First Lessons in Political Economy, for the Use of Primary and Common Schools.*[4] By then McVickar's title at Columbia had changed again. The book identified its author simply as professor of political economy.

McVickar of course recognized the importance of labor in the production of everyday goods and services. But rather than assign labor the unquestionably central role that Raymond had given it in his slavery-motivated treatise written just a few years before, McVickar portrayed economic activity as a process that integrated labor with knowledge as well as other human attributes. And instead of resting his conception on biblical foundations, as Raymond had done, McVicker turned to Newtonian images. "In the language of this science," he told students in his *Introductory Lecture,* "man is but a machine for the creation of value; yet still is that machine shewn to be perfect in its proportion to skill, knowledge, temperance, industry, and the whole train of personal virtues." And what if a worker failed to exhibit these virtues? "Destitute of these, man is a machine out of order."[5]

Even more so than Adam Smith, who had regarded what he called the road to virtue and that to fortune as very nearly the same for most people (though not for those occupying "the superior stations of life"),[6] McVickar endorsed the pursuit of wealth as a positive force contributing to the development of moral and religious virtue. The pursuit of wealth, he told his students, was "decidedly favourable to the formation of moral character," at least when judged from a national point of view. To be sure, wealth was not the same as virtue. Yet neither was it virtuous to despise wealth. Instead, "the pursuit of it is favourable to moral conduct, and in the mass of men, necessary to it."[7]

Moreover, just as pursuing wealth brought nonmaterial benefits by enhancing individuals' moral character, at the aggregate level economic dealings *between nations* fostered peaceful relations. Anticipating a line of argument that British writers like Norman Angell would popularize early in the twentieth century, and Americans like Thomas L. Friedman toward that century's end,[8] McVickar pointed to trade as a practical force preventing international conflict. Political economy, he argued, teaches among nations "the all-important lessons of peace and mutual benefits. It does more than forbid war; it takes away those false opinions on which war arises." More specifically, international trade "unites nations, not by treaties or federations, which may be broken or evaded, but by the laws of mutual interest, which when once fully understood, no member is inclined to break or evade."[9]

Among both individuals and nations, therefore, economic activity in pursuit of wealth harnessed human self-interest to deliver unintended but beneficial consequences. "If political economy is listened to," McVickar proclaimed, "it would make nations and states a brotherhood of love." Wealth and peace therefore went together. In an echo of what David Hume had written about a nation's domestic trade, but now brought to the international context, "the voice of all history declares, without foreign commerce no civilization, no wealth; with it, riches, power, and refinement."[10] Nor did McVickar see any need for action by government to guide this foreign commerce. Repeating what Smith had said about foreign investment in *The Wealth of Nations,* but now applying the idea to international commerce more generally, he maintained that "the trading of merchants with foreign countries will always regulate itself."[11]

But McVickar departed from Smith in one significant way. For McVickar, approaching the subject as not just a religiously commit-

ted man but a member of the clergy, unintended but beneficial consequences of human actions occur because a benevolent God makes it so.
The study of political economy, he wrote, "shews that to be their interest, which religion has shewn to be their duty." Why? "If you ask how
it happens that this accordance should thus happily exist between religion and science in matters of mere human policy, I can only answer
by referring you to the will of that wise and good Providence which has
made our duty and interest the same."[12]

The argument for free trade, therefore, was not just a practical one;
it was at its core a *religious* imperative. "I cannot but reverence the
claims of free commerce as something *holy*," he concluded, "something
allied to the policy of a higher power than man."[13] By the 1830s the
question of tariffs versus free trade had become the most pressing economic policy issue the United States faced, and in McVickar's view the
advocates of free trade had God on their side: "To forbid trade among
nations is, therefore, a very unwise thing; but it is also a very wicked
thing, for it is contrary to the will of God."[14]

McVickar's reasoning went beyond the simple claim that because
free trade fostered international peace it must therefore be divinely
intended. Two decades earlier, the English economist David Ricardo
had explained the theory of comparative advantage in international
trade. Because of either natural or man-made resources, nations differ
in their productive capacities. If each nation focuses its production
on the goods it is more easily able to produce, and then they trade
among one another so that each acquires the mix of goods it wants
to consume, each will end up with more than if it shunned trade and
merely consumed what it made on its own.[15] (The label *comparative*
advantage reflects the conclusion that even if one country is more
efficient than another in producing *every* good, as long as the differential in their productivity is uneven across different goods there are
still gains to both countries from specialization and trade.) In effect,
Ricardo's principle was an application of the advantages of specialized
production—Smith's division of labor—to countries rather than individuals. McVickar was clearly aware of the British economist's work.
He referred to Ricardo frequently in his *Outlines,* and mentioned him
in his *Introductory Lecture* as well; he did not pretend to originality in
this respect.

But the question still remained—it would not have occurred to

Ricardo to ask—why did different countries have different resources to begin with? Why do agricultural conditions vary from north to south, for example, and why are deposits of certain minerals found in some countries but not others? To a clergyman like McVickar, the answer was obvious: because God created the world in that way. But why had God done that? Here political economy provided the explanation: "For what other reason," he asked in his *First Lessons* for schoolchildren, "do you suppose, has he given to different countries such different soils and climate and productions, but that they should freely exchange with each other, and thus all be happier and more comfortable?"[16]

This same application of political economy even explained a basic feature of the earth's geography: the pattern of land and water on the planet's surface. By the nineteenth century it was well understood that transportation of both people and goods was cheaper by water than over land. Moreover, the Erie Canal had just fully opened in 1825 and so for McVickar, living in New York City, the lesson was fresh. The extension to an international setting was straightforward. If international trade fostered peaceful relations, and the oceans made trade more convenient, it must be that God had created the oceans as a means of facilitating economic exchange and thereby promoting peace among the world's countries. "Such no doubt was the intention of our Heavenly Father, in forming our earth out of land and water," he wrote—not to separate nations, as some people had claimed, "but to unite them like brothers." And precisely how? The oceans would "make them mutually useful, by each exchanging its own productions for those of others, and thus to make all happier by giving them more enjoyments and more comforts than they could otherwise have had."[17]

The direction for political economy to which Raymond's treatise pointed did not fit the intuitions of a new nation that by the early nineteenth century had mostly moved beyond orthodox Calvinism, and McVickar's book proved insufficient as an alternative view of the discipline. The person who most successfully filled the resulting vacuum was Francis Wayland. Born in New York City, and educated at Union College, Wayland studied medicine before being called to the clergy. After studying at Andover Seminary in Massachusetts, he became a Baptist minister and initially served at Boston's First Baptist

Church. In 1827, however, at the age of thirty-one, he became president of Brown University in Providence. Reflecting the continuing legacy of Roger Williams's Rhode Island—the original name was The College or University in the English Colony of Rhode Island and Providence Plantations—most of the college's founders had been Baptists and its charter required that a majority of the trustees be Baptists as well. Wayland served as Brown's president for nearly three decades, playing an important role in steering the institution's development from a colonial college to a national university.

In the nineteenth century it was typical for the president of an American college to teach a course on religion or moral philosophy to the school's senior class, and Wayland did so at Brown. He also produced a book from his course, which instructors at many other colleges used as well. His *Elements of Moral Science,* published in 1835, sold more than 100,000 copies.[18] But he also introduced other subjects to Brown's curriculum, including "Evidences of Revelation" and "Political Economy."

Wayland's views on the economic issues of the day were much like McVickar's, favoring commerce and internal improvements domestically as well as free trade internationally. (He distinguished between the two, however, for purposes of financing; while he supported public funding of projects like harbors that would enable international commerce, he thought internal improvements like roads and canals should mostly rely on private initiative.) In 1837 he published a second book, *The Elements of Political Economy.* The introduction explained that "The following work contains, in substance, the Lectures on Political Economy which have been delivered, for some years past, to the Senior Class in Brown University."[19] Wayland's book became the most widely used political economy text in America before the Civil War, eventually selling fifty thousand copies.[20] In an effort to spread his views still more widely, a decade later he also published a simplified version "abridged and adapted to the use of schools and academies."[21]

Like McVickar, Wayland saw political economy as an application of Newtonian science, taking for granted that scientific laws and principles are what they are because God made them so. "By Science," he began, "we mean a systematic arrangement of the laws which God has established." The notion of fixed laws played a prominent role in Wayland's thinking more generally, and this foundational principle applied to economics no less than other lines of inquiry. It was obvious, he

wrote, that "the Creator has subjected the accumulation of the blessings of this life to some determinate laws."[22]

As Raymond had done, Wayland recognized the need for labor as
one of these immutable laws. "Neither physical comforts, nor even
physical necessities," he pointed out, "can be obtained, unless labor first
be expended to procure them." And, again like Raymond, he explained
this necessity by referring to God's curse on Adam: "The universal law
of our existence, is, 'In the sweat of thy face shalt thou eat thy bread,
until thou return to the ground.'" Seeking to avoid labor led to punish-
ments, and in specific forms. "He who refuses to labor with his mind,
suffers the penalty of ignorance. . . . He who refuses to labor with his
hands, suffers, besides the pains of disease, all the evils of poverty, cold,
hunger and nakedness."[23]

But rather than dwell on the need for labor as a manifestation of
humanity's moral shortcomings, or assume some universal effort to
escape God's curse by exploiting the labor of other people, Wayland
simply accepted that labor and the act of performing it in order to
satisfy human wants were both practically understandable and morally
legitimate. God created the world so that "the universe around us is
composed of objects suited to gratify our desire, and thus minister to
our happiness." Human agency, in the form of labor applied to these
objects, therefore works hand in hand with divine creation in enabling
these objects to serve human ends. Wayland divided the qualities of
natural substances (like grain, or iron ore) that are necessary to render them useful to humans into two categories: "first, those which are
imparted to the substance by the immediate act of God; and secondly,
those that are imparted to it through the intermediate agency of man."
The second were no less a gift from God than the first. Both together
were the basis of the "capacity to gratify desire" that was "the first element that enters into our notion of wealth."[24]

Wayland had clearly read Smith,[25] and he followed closely Smith's
explanation of the basis for commerce in specialized production
together with voluntary exchange. Echoing the opening sentence of
The Wealth of Nations, he wrote that "the productive result of human
power is greatly increased by union of effort and division of labor."
The twofold reason was that "every man has his preference for some
particular kind of labor," and "every man can succeed better by con-
fining his labor to one thing." As Smith had also explained, division of

labor then required exchange of goods. With specialized production, "every man is desirous of exchanging the value created by himself, for that created by others." The result was "the necessity of universal and ceaseless *exchange*."[26]

Importantly, however, in this process as in other aspects of a world created by a benevolent God, the law of unintended consequences— specifically, *beneficial* consequences—resulted in benefits, shared among people in general, stemming from individual actions motivated merely by self-interest. "In political economy, as in morals, every benefit is mutual; and we cannot, in the one case, any more than in the other, really do good to ourselves, without doing good to others; nor do good to others, without also doing good to ourselves." In the end, "the benefit of one is the benefit of all . . . he who is honestly promoting his own welfare, is also promoting the welfare of the whole society of which he is a member."[27]

Like Smith, Wayland went beyond merely asserting the principle of mutual benefit from self-interested behavior, displaying a well-articulated understanding of the market mechanism. In explaining the central role of prices, he wrote that "It is the operation of these principles that keeps the supply of any article . . . always equal to the demand: and, it is surprising to observe, with what accuracy this effect is produced." Referring to the supply of food and other necessities, for example, "in the largest cities, there is always just enough butcher's meat, and vegetables, and clothing, to supply the wants of the inhabitants, and no more." The reason for this happy state of affairs was the effect of price movements in steering productive effort: "The moment the price of an article falls below cost, it ceases to be produced, until the price rises. As soon as it rises above ordinary profit, capital and labor are directed to it, and it is produced in sufficient quantity to meet the unusual demand."[28] Wayland's exuberant embrace of the price mechanism exceeded Smith's often more nuanced description. The laws of economics were an expression of God's unity and perfection, no less than the laws governing the physical universe, and so standing in awe of the scope and precision of their operation seemed only appropriate.

Wayland then explained commerce among the different regions of the United States, or among different countries, as simply another application of the gains to productivity from specialized production. "I have thus far considered the division of labor, as it exists among the inhabitants of the same place," he wrote. "The same principle, however, applies to people of *different districts*." In this case, however, specialization arose not merely from individuals' differing talents and tastes for work but also, as Ricardo had shown, from physical resources that differed from one location to another. "No district possesses advantages for producing every thing," but "almost every district possesses peculiar facilities for producing something." Hence "by each district's devoting its labor to that kind of production, for which it has the greatest natural facilities, the production of the whole country will be increased."[29]

Given this line of argument, the extension to commerce among countries was direct. So was the attribution to a benevolent deity. "God has bestowed upon different districts of the same country, different advantages," Wayland summarized. "But every one may see, that the same principles apply to different nations inhabiting different parts of the globe." The gains from specialization therefore applied internationally as well. "Every individual will be richer and happier, when each portion of the globe devotes itself to the creation of those products for which it has the greatest natural facilities."[30] The result was an expression of the harmony in the universe, imposed by a benevolent deity.

In the case of trade among nations, however, Wayland followed McVickar in arguing that God intended something beyond mere economic improvement. He took it to be readily evident that "Every man needs, for the gratification of his innocent desires, nay, for his conveniences and even necessaries, the productions of every part of the globe." He therefore inferred that "it is evidently the will of our Creator, that but few of these objects, every one of which is necessary to the happiness of every individual, should be produced except in particular districts." The reason, he concluded—the "final cause of all this"—was also evident: "God intended that men should live together in friendship and harmony." God's way of realizing this intent was "to render it no less the interest, than the duty of every one, to live in amity with all the rest."[31] The benign consequences of free trade embodied the notion of harmony in the universe, which Smith had taken from the stoics as a fundamental aspect of nature, but which McVickar and Wayland attributed to the will of a benevolent God. And the prospect of advancing peace among the world's nations resonated as well with the postmillennialist spirit of the time.

Elijah Smith, Jr., *The Boston Manufacturing Company* (1823).
Francis Cabot Lowell's textile mill, located in Waltham, Massachusetts,
and relying on water power, pioneered the integration of spinning
and weaving in a single factory.

Moreover, Wayland went beyond McVickar (and Ricardo too) in one important respect. Observing the rapid economic changes taking place in the new United States, he understood that over time it was possible for a country to change the set of "advantages" that it brought to the production of various goods and therefore to its participation in international trade. The new Erie Canal was only one recent example. Although the waterway from Albany to Buffalo was internal to the United States, by connecting to the Hudson River it enabled produce from inland regions to reach New York City's seaport, from which it might then be exported. More immediately relevant for Wayland, living in Providence, by the 1830s manufacturing industries that had barely existed at the beginning of the century were rapidly developing in many parts of New England including Rhode Island. In time, they too might compete for sales overseas.

Wayland therefore intended his account of the benefits flowing from international trade, based on countries' differing advantage in producing one good or another, "by no means to assert that such arrangements and relations are to be permanent." Clearly having in mind the rapid pace of industrial development then under way in America, he inferred that "As a country accumulates fixed capital, it creates its own facilities for creating almost every kind of manufactured product." If a country's citizens are unhappy with whatever comparative advantage (to use Ricardo's term for it) they are currently able to bring to trading, they have it within their power to change those conditions. With this insight Wayland anticipated, by nearly two centuries, what economists now call the theory of *dynamic* comparative advantage.[32] Further, anticipating theories of economic development that economists would explore in depth more than a century later, he also speculated that "One nation will naturally begin to do this at the same point of accumulation at which another began to do it."[33]

Advocates of international trade like John McVickar and Francis Wayland grounded their arguments in their perception of the will of a benevolent God who had structured the world in such a way that meeting man's basic economic needs brought nations together in commerce and thereby fostered peaceful relations among them. But the appeal to the benevolent intent behind divine creation was not limited to free traders. Political economists who sought to shield America's new industries from foreign competition likewise claimed that their arguments were no more than recognition of how the divine creation was intended to work.

Like the tension over slavery, the free trade controversy in antebellum America was in large part a sectional dispute. New England, home to much of the nation's emerging manufacturing, mostly favored protection. America's early mills and foundries made little that foreign producers did not make as well, and often better or more cheaply. For most manufacturers, winning export business was not a serious prospect. Their interest was in protecting their ability to sell to domestic markets, not just in New England but all along the Atlantic coast and into the rapidly developing interior. Tariffs, which made imported manufactures more expensive to domestic buyers, were therefore in their interest. (So were canals and turnpikes, to enable their goods to reach many of those domestic buyers.) Following the end of the War of 1812, and the removal of the trade embargo imposed under President Madison, the textile mill owner Francis Cabot Lowell personally traveled to Washington to lobby for tariffs to protect American manufacturers from renewed British and East Indian competition.

By contrast, plantations in the Southern states produced cotton, tobacco, rice, and other crops that Europeans in particular needed to obtain from elsewhere. For Southerners, buying manufactured goods from abroad served just as well as, and often better than, relying on what might be more expensive (and often lower-quality) goods made domestically. At a more fundamental level, the South and New England were now united in a single country, and no nation can indefinitely export without importing. If Southern planters were going to continue to sell their cotton and tobacco abroad, Americans had to buy from abroad as well.

Although Francis Wayland lived as an adult in Rhode Island, and therefore might well have allied himself with New England's manufacturing interests, his exposure to American business was mostly different. Wayland was originally from New York City, then as always one of America's most active trading ports. In Rhode Island, most of the families who had founded the university he led, and who provided much of its ongoing support, were likewise more involved with shipping and trade than manufacturing. The Brown family, in honor of whose donations the university's name was changed in 1804, had long been associated with trade in rum and slaves (although some family members were abolitionists).

The political economist who most publicly championed the interests of the New England manufacturers was Boston-born Francis Bowen. An 1833 graduate of Harvard, Bowen was briefly an instructor at Phillips Exeter Academy and then at Harvard. Unlike McVickar and Wayland, he was not an ordained clergyman. But like most New Englanders at Henry Ware's Harvard, Bowen was a firm Unitarian. Ralph Waldo Emerson delivered his classic "Divinity School Address," setting forth the principles of what became known as transcendentalism (a further offshoot of Unitarianism), at the school's commencement ceremony in 1838. Bowen was teaching at Harvard at the time.

Beginning in 1843 Bowen served as the editor of—also chief contributor to—the *North American Review,* a literary and political magazine founded some decades earlier by prominent New Englanders. More so than any other publication of the time, the *North American Review* represented a national-level outlet for informed criticism and opinion. (Other distinguished figures who served as the *Review*'s editor during the nineteenth century included Edward Everett, James Russell Lowell, Charles Eliot Norton, and Henry Adams.)[34] In 1850 the Harvard faculty invited Bowen to return as professor of history. Some of the university's overseers objected, however, presumably on account of stances he had taken in the *Review,* and the board declined to approve his appointment. Three years later, this time with little if any apparent objection, he became "professor of natural religion, moral philosophy and civil polity." Among other subjects, he taught political economy.

Bowen was a protectionist, fully aligned with New England's manu-facturing interests, and opposition to unrestricted trade among nations was central to his teaching and his writing. In 1856 he published a polit-ical economy text, *The Principles of Political Economy: Applied to the Condition, the Resources, and the Institutions of the American People.*[35] The book's subtitle was meant to imply that earlier American works on the subject—most prominently, Wayland's 1837 best-seller—had erred in uncritically embracing Adam Smith's ideas without taking proper account of the differences between Britain and the new United States. Most importantly, Bowen thought, while Smith's claims for the merits of free trade perhaps made sense for a well-established manufactur-ing center like England, they did not apply to the conditions of a new country only just building its industrial capability.[36]

Like McVickar and Wayland before him, Bowen made explicit that the basis for humans' behavior in the economic sphere, as elsewhere, was their creation by a benevolent God operating through Newtonian laws of nature. Society, he wrote, is "a complex and delicate machine, the real Author and Governor of which is divine. Men are often his agents, who do his work, and know it not." This by now familiar princi-ple applied in particular to individuals' pursuit of their economic inter-est. The worldly machine's divine author and governor "turneth their selfishness to good; and ends which could not be accomplished by the greatest sagacity, the most enlightened and disinterested public spirit, and the most strenuous exertions of human legislators and governors, are effected directly and incessantly, even through the ignorance, the willfulness, and the avarice of man."[37]

For Bowen, the unintended but beneficial consequences of men's and women's behavior, following from their creation by a benevo-lent God, stood at the heart of economic analysis. These designs, as revealed by the principles of political economy, "manifest the contriv-ance, wisdom, and beneficence of the Deity, just as clearly as do the marvellous arrangements of the material universe." Even the lowest passions of mankind, such as ostentation, petty rivalry, and the love of gain, were "overruled for good in their operation upon the interests of society." They were the most efficient means of advancing the society's welfare. Following Smith, Bowen concluded that "We are all servants of one another without wishing it, and even without knowing it." And echoing Mandeville, "we are all cooperating with each other as busily and effectively as the bees in a hive."[38]

This interpretation of private economic activity based on divine intent carried over to matters of economic policy as well. By the 1850s the phrase "laissez-faire" was becoming familiar in English-language discussions of political economy.[39] Bowen defined the concept for his readers in a way consistent with his own religiously oriented view of the discipline: "*Laissez-faire;* 'these things regulate themselves,' in common phrase; which means, of course, that God regulates them by his general laws, which always, in the long run, work to good."[40]

Trade *between nations,* however, did not regulate itself. And if left to itself, it did not necessarily work to the common good. Bowen's argument for protection rested in the first instance on economic self-sufficiency as a key requisite of the national independence for which Americans of an earlier generation had fought, and which his contemporaries still prized. In contrast to economic dependence among the various states of the union, which was to be encouraged on the ground that it strengthened their political ties, for the nation as a whole "political independence—that is, the enjoyment of distinct institutions and laws, chosen and established by ourselves" required that "we should not be entirely dependent upon foreigners."[41]

True independence, he acknowledged, did not require a nation to forgo all commercial intercourse with others. Even so, "it does require that each nation should be able to exercise, within its own limits, all the great branches of industry designed to satisfy the wants of men." Further, to be independent did not mean actually making everything the country needed, merely having the ability to do so. But an independent nation "must be able to practice all the arts which would be necessary for its own well-being, if it were the only nation on earth."[42] Bowen's argument, grounded in this specific concept of economic independence, echoed the case that Malthus and others had made for maintaining Britain's Corn Laws, which discouraged grain imports even at the cost of economic inefficiency.[43] It also anticipated the ideas that, more than a century later, guided the economic policies of the Soviet Union under Stalin and then China under Mao.

But the argument had a moral component as well, focused not on the nation as a political entity but rather the people who comprised it. "If it be restricted to agriculture alone," Bowen wrote, "or to manufactures alone, a portion of the energies of its people are lost, and some of its natural advantages run to waste." Such a loss, he claimed, was a moral concern as well as economic, and it was up to protectionist measures—most obviously, tariffs—to prevent it. "To be so limited in its sphere of occupation, to be barred out from some of the natural and necessary employments of the human race, through the overwhelming competition of foreigners, is a serious evil, which it is the object of a protective policy to obviate or redress."[44]

Moreover, just as Bowen saw protectionism as preserving economic freedom rather than restricting it—implicitly valuing the freedom of domestic producers over that of whoever might prefer to buy goods from abroad—he construed protectionist policies as reinforcing, rather than limiting, laissez-faire economic arrangements. "On whatever other grounds this policy may be objected to," he argued, "it is surely not open to the charge of being an infringement of the *laissez-faire* principle, or a restriction of every man's right to make such use as he pleases of his own industry and capital." Again invoking the intent of a benevolent creator, the object of a protectionist policy "is not to narrow, but to widen, the field for the profitable employment of industry, and to second the working of the beneficent designs of Providence in the constitution of society, by removing all artificial and unnecessary checks to their operation." In Bowen's reasoning, the chief artificial check to be resisted was not government-imposed tariffs, but foreign competition.[45] Eliminating the hindrances created by competition from abroad opened room for a laissez-faire economic system to operate at home.

Further, just as McVickar and Wayland had argued in favor of free trade by claiming an economic underpinning for peaceful international relations grounded on what they took to be God's intent, Bowen now made an analogous claim in support of protection. "By treating the human race as one great family," he warned, "we are not following, but departing from, the apparent design of Providence." In contrast to

Wayland's vision of the world's oceans as a device for knitting countries together through commerce, Bowen concluded that "the Deity seems to have stamped on the features of nature and of humanity, in unmistakable characters, that nations shall remain separate and distinct, each pursuing . . . its own separate interests." Unrestricted trade, he thought, upset the natural state of affairs that God had intended for the world. Whether advocating free trade or protection, American political economists in the pre–Civil War period anchored their views in religious argument.[46]

Beyond their positions either for or against free trade, and their understanding of market competition as the means of harnessing self-interest for the common good, political economists in America before the Civil War arrived at yet another important new insight—in this case one that Adam Smith and his contemporaries had failed to grasp. Significantly, they grounded it too in the intent of a benevolent God.

Smith had lived too early to see the possibility that productivity, and therefore living standards, might continue to improve indefinitely over time. As both he and Turgot laid out in their dynamic version of the traditional Four Stages theory, each transition along the way from hunting to pasturage to settled agriculture to commerce brought a discrete improvement in material living standards. But commerce was the final step in this progression. An already commercial nation like England or France could achieve further improvement by abolishing monopolies and other impediments to competitive markets, and advocating that path was a large part of the motivation underlying *The Wealth of Nations*. But this gain too would be a once-for-all advance. Thereafter, further improvement could come only from ever more intensive division of labor, and this process was presumably subject to diminishing returns. Moreover, as Smith emphasized, ever greater specialization caused working people's aptitudes and moral character to atrophy.

As late as the 1820s, although many people realized that they were living better than their parents and grandparents had, there was still no awareness of the possibility of improvement that would go on indefinitely—or, if this were possible, what might bring it about. In England, the up-and-down economic consequences of the Napoleonic

Wars had largely obscured the longer-run trend of rising output and improving living standards. In America the war for independence, then the creation of the new republic, then the interruption of foreign commerce due to Jefferson's 1807 trade embargo, and then the War of 1812, had had the same effect.

By the 1830s matters were different. The United States was not just expanding westward, improvements in transportation were rendering the new areas of settlement ever closer. In 1800 it had taken three days to travel from New York to either Boston or the new capital in Washington, D.C. One week would only take a traveler to the Appalachians. Going on to the new states on the other side of the mountains, like Kentucky and Tennessee, or territories like today's Ohio and Indiana, took three to four weeks. Reaching the Mississippi River took five weeks or longer.[47]

Over the next thirty years the efficiency of river steamboats quadrupled,[48] while the nation built not only roads but a network of canals linked to the country's rivers and the Great Lakes. The Erie Canal ran full across New York State, the Chesapeake & Ohio Canal led westward from Washington, and the Ohio & Erie Canal would soon connect Lake Erie to the Ohio River. By 1830 one week's travel from New York was sufficient to reach eastern Kentucky or Ohio, and the Mississippi was only another week away—even though the introduction of railroads was just beginning.[49]

Agriculture was becoming more productive as well—no small matter in a country that still remained predominantly agrarian. American farmers were the first to power their reaping machines with steam, and between 1800 and 1840 productivity in growing and harvesting wheat increased by 60 percent. Importantly, the productiveness of the new lands cultivated as the country expanded westward was no less than in the areas Americans had farmed before: the improvement in productivity was the same whether measured by how many hours of labor it took to farm an acre of land or how many hours it took to produce a bushel of wheat.[50] The problem that had so concerned Malthus, and then in a more sophisticated way Ricardo—declining per-acre production as new lands came into use—did not apply. The combination of greater productivity and ever more land under cultivation led to a vast increase in harvests. Cotton production, for example, multiplied fairly steadily from 70,000 bales in 1800 to 730,000 in 1830, and more than 1.3 million by 1840.[51]

With increased agricultural productivity, along with expanding population (the country grew from five million people in 1800 to seventeen million by 1840), farms in already established areas no longer needed all of the available labor. But industrialization was expanding rapidly as well, providing ample new employment opportunities. As in Britain, the textile industry was initially the heart of the expansion. Mills relying on new technology opened rapidly, especially in New England. The region's production of cotton textiles rose from 30,000 yards of cloth in 1805 to more than 300 million yards by 1840.[52] By then Lowell, Massachusetts—named for textile entrepreneur Francis Cabot Lowell—had twenty-two cotton mills and 20,000 people, making it the state's second largest city behind Boston. Seven thousand of those residents, mostly young women, worked in the mills, processing 16 million tons of raw cotton into nearly 50 million yards of finished cloth.[53] Because industrialization inevitably led to urbanization, along the way the character of many Americans' daily lives also changed. More now lived in cities, or at least in sizable towns.

Above all, living standards were improving rapidly. Under the burden of Jefferson's trade embargo and then the War of 1812, Americans' average income had increased little during the first two decades of the nineteenth century. But the remaining time until the Civil War saw rapid gains. The average income, adjusted for changing prices, increased by 24 percent over the 1820s, and by another 19 percent over the 1830s (despite the depressing effects, toward the end of the decade, of the 1837 financial panic).[54]

By the 1830s, therefore, it was becoming evident that the improvement in productivity and living standards, compared to the latter part of the eighteenth century, was not merely the upswing of yet another "long wave" that would soon reverse itself. And, with ever more widespread application of new technologies—in transportation, in agriculture, in industry—it was becoming evident too that more stood behind this ongoing improvement than just increasing division of labor (although that clearly mattered as well).

Francis Wayland was the first political economist, not just in America but anywhere, to realize—and to articulate clearly, in a form that has survived—the possibility of ongoing economic growth propelled indefinitely by technological progress. Wayland ascribed this phenomenon too to the intent of a benevolent God. "If it be asked, how far may this increased productiveness of human industry be carried," he

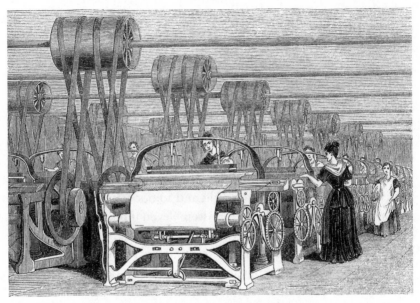

Interior of a powered textile factory (1844).
Powered by steam, rods running below the ceiling used belts to impart
rotary motion to large numbers of machines in a single location,
making possible mass production of textiles.

Winslow Homer, *Bell Time* (1868).
Large textile mills created the need for an urban workforce,
in turn enlarging the towns that grew up around them.

pondered in his 1837 *Elements of Political Economy,* "we answer, it is impossible to tell, unless we can ascertain how great are the blessings which God has in reserve for man." Making clear that the blessings he had in mind included the economic fruits of advancing technology, he continued, "Who can estimate the benefits conferred on man by the magnet, or by steam, or by the printing press?"[55] It was the magnet that enabled generation of electricity, it was steam that powered the textile mills and the steamboats and now the railroads, and it was the printing press that made knowledge of these new technologies available to anyone who wished to exploit them.

Most importantly, economic growth could continue, *indefinitely,* because technological advance not only could continue but *would* if God so willed—which Wayland, embracing the era's postmillennialist outlook, was fully prepared to believe. He therefore saw the new technologies driving the expansion of economic activity not as a one-time occurrence but an ongoing process. "What reason have we," he challenged any doubters, "to assume that the gifts of God are exhausted, or that there are not other and more excellent natural agents to be discovered, or other modes of using those we are already acquainted with, that shall produce yet more surprising results than any which we have yet witnessed?"[56]

Looking back, he understood how people had failed to foresee the progress that had now become reality. Before the discovery of such advances as electricity and the steam engine, "the most vivid imagination could never have conceived of the benefits which they have already conferred upon society." But the doubters had been wrong—because of their limited imagination and, more fundamentally, because they had not understood the practical import of God's benevolence. Doubters would likewise be wrong about the future as well. "There is no reason," he concluded, "to suppose that we are now more capable of fathoming the goodness of God, than our ancestors were, three or four hundred years ago."[57]

Wayland was right—about the remaining three decades of his lifetime (he died in 1865) and, for that matter, about the century and a half since then as well. Westward expansion continued. The economy continued to industrialize. The country's population continued to increase, from natural growth and from immigration. Productivity continued to improve, in industry and on the farms. Americans' living standards continued to rise.

By the 1840s advances in the technology of ocean sailing, taking advantage of the new clipper ships, were adding to the earlier gains in the efficiency of river steamboating. California, which the gold discoveries at the end of the decade made a magnet for westward migration, was soon only three weeks' travel from the country's Eastern Seaboard. Just as important, railroads were now spreading across the country. Between 1830 and 1860 American companies laid fifty thousand miles of track—enough to cross the continent more than a dozen times (although there was still no complete transcontinental route) and representing somewhat more than a tenth of the total railroad mileage the country would eventually put in place.[58] By the time of the Civil War, an integrated rail network covered much of eastern Pennsylvania and New York, and all of New England up to southern Maine. Another, not yet as fully developed, covered much of Ohio, Indiana, and Illinois. There were also tracks across some parts of Virginia, the Carolinas, and Georgia, and extending into central Alabama. (The North-South difference in railroad development would soon play a major role in the Union victory.) One week's travel from New York City was now sufficient to reach anywhere east of the Mississippi River. Boston, Philadelphia, Washington, Richmond, and Cleveland were all within one day.[59]

New technology brought improvements in communication too. Building on a series of inventions from the prior two decades, in Europe as well as America, Samuel F. B. Morse first publicly demonstrated his version of the electric telegraph in 1844. Within ten years there were nearly seven hundred telegraph offices spanning most of the United States east of the Mississippi, as well as southern Canada.[60] In 1858 a transatlantic cable linked the U.S. network with those in Britain and in Europe, and the first telegraph cable spanning the North American continent followed in 1861. (The original transatlantic cable broke within two months of operation, and replacing it would take until 1866.)

From 17 million in 1840, America's population rose to 31 million in 1860. Agricultural output expanded explosively, but so did industrialization. From 300 million yards of cotton cloth in 1840, textile production in New England reached one *billion* yards by 1860.[61] Moreover,

U.S. manufacturing was increasingly moving beyond textiles to produce other goods as well: shoes, finished lumber, ironware, and many others besides.

With this robust economic activity, living standards improved dramatically. Following on the strong gains of the 1820s and 1830s, Americans' average income, adjusted for changing prices, rose by another 10 percent in the 1840s and a further 24 percent in the 1850s.[62] In 1851 *The Independent,* a New York–based religious weekly, declared that "A grand feature of our times is that *all* is *Progress.*" Expressing the growing spirit of postmillennialism, the editors looked forward to a "grand consummation of prophecy in a civilized, an enlightened, and a sanctified world."[63] By the time Abraham Lincoln was elected president, per capita income was double what it had been forty years before. Especially

Home Sweet Home (1880).
With rising living standards spreading throughout ever more
of the population, middle-class domesticity became a possibility for
increasing numbers of families and an ideal for many more.

in the nation's growing cities and towns, Americans saw themselves as developing a middle-class culture. As in England, family domesticity, grounded in orderliness and a comfortable material standard of living, increasingly became the accepted ideal.

Public awareness of this economic improvement and the expanded opportunity that came with it further reinforced the tendency toward non-predestinarian thinking within American Protestantism. Americans were cultivating new territories, redirecting established farms to new production, starting new businesses, seeking out new professions. In these decades before the Civil War, it often seemed that just about anyone—any white male, that is—could rise into the country's economic elite.[64] Lincoln, speaking in Milwaukee in 1859, expressed a widespread view of the remarkable opportunities his countrymen faced in the modern era. "If any continue through life in the condition of the hired laborer," he told his audience, that must be "because of either a dependent nature which prefers it, or improvidence, folly, or singular misfortune."[65] But if individual initiative and effort so reliably brought material success, why could men and women not achieve spiritual salvation through their own efforts as well?

The astonishing expansion and improvement of these pre–Civil War decades also influenced how Americans, including their religious leaders, thought of their new nation and the society they were creating within it. As early as the mid-eighteenth century, religious thinkers like Jonathan Edwards and then Samuel Hopkins had embraced post-millennial notions of the prospects for future human progress. Some, Edwards in particular, had seen a special role for the new society, not yet an independent country, being created in what had been a wilderness unknown to Europeans. Toward the end of the eighteenth century, the idea of a millennial role for America gained additional force with the creation of the new democratic republic. Urging his fellow citizens on to war, in 1776, Thomas Paine declared that "We have it in our power to begin the world over again. A situation, similar to the present, hath not happened since the days of Noah."[66]

After the Revolution ended successfully, John Murray, pastor of the Presbyterian church in Newburyport where George Whitefield was buried, asked, "Are not we the children of Israel too—a professing covenant-people, in a land peculiarly privileged with gospel-light?"[67] Ezra Stiles, president of Yale, hailed the new republic as "God's American Israel."[68] Many American towns' names—New Canaan, Connecticut; Promised Land, South Carolina; Zionsville, Indiana; together with countless others—expressed the same idea. In popular American writings on the new U.S. Constitution, the most frequently cited book (even exceeding Montesquieu's *Spirit of the Laws*) was Deuteronomy.[69]

The notion of a special, millennial role for America gained yet further force in the early decades of the nineteenth century, as the new republic not only survived but thrived and expanded. Preaching in Plymouth, Massachusetts, in 1827, Lyman Beecher expressed "the hope, that this nation has been raised up by Providence to exert an efficient instrumentality in this work of moral renovation" of the world. What the world needed was "a new creation," and this project in turn required an example. "Some nation, itself free, was needed, to blow the trumpet and hold up the light." Nor (even though Beecher was a Presbyterian) was this role to be grounded in "the presumptuous hope of grace without works." Action was necessary, and Americans were the best able to undertake it. America's self-government, intellectual culture, and religious commitment made the nation fit for the task. "The history of our nation is indicative of some great design to be accomplished by it," Beecher determined. It was "the purpose of God to employ this nation in the glorious work of renovating the earth."[70]

By the 1830s the country's vast physical expansion and rapid economic development caused such thinking to be even more widely embraced, and more central to Americans' conceptions of themselves and their society. Moreover, by now many millennial thinkers of this stripe increasingly looked to the West as the nation's future. Although he was a Yale-educated New Englander who began his career in Connecticut and in Boston, in 1832 Beecher moved to Cincinnati to serve as minister at the city's Second Presbyterian Church and to establish what became Lane Theological Seminary. In "A Plea for the West," originally a sermon that was part of his fundraising campaign for the new seminary, he declared that it was "plain that the religious and political destiny of our nation is to be decided in the West." The West—by which he meant the new states of Ohio, Indiana, Illinois, and Missouri—was "destined to be the great central power of the nation, and under heaven, must affect powerfully the cause of free institutions and the liberty of the world."[71]

In making this argument, Beecher echoed Edwards's postmillennial theme, highlighting the parallel between progress in the spiritual and the worldly realms. "All great eras of prosperity to the church have been aided by the civil condition of the world," he observed. Referring to a passage from the final chapter of Isaiah, in which the prophet acknowledges that the earth was not made to bring forth in one day, nor a nation born at once, he told his listeners, "I consider the text as a prediction of the rapid and universal extension of civil and religious liberty, introductory to the triumphs of universal Christianity." And he agreed that God had assigned America a special role in how this blessed development would come about. America was "destined to lead the way in the moral and political emancipation of the world." Jonathan Edwards had thought that the millennium would commence in America, he reminded his listeners, and "all providential developments since, and all the existing signs of the times, lend corroboration to it."[72] The orthodox Calvinist doctrine of individual predestination was losing ground, but its transposition to the national level was gaining strength, with the spread of democracy now linked to the spread of the Gospel. The American experiment, as people called it, was clearly of divine origin.

A generation later, Horace Bushnell likewise took up the theme that the human race "exists under laws of progress." Also educated at Yale, but a quarter-century after Beecher, Bushnell was pastor at Hartford's North Congregational Church. Like many Protestants of his day, he believed in a benevolent, loving God, whom he saw as savior rather than judge or punisher. He also believed in the innate goodness of men and women, viewing them as active participants in their own redemption. And his thinking reflected a strong postmillennial optimism. "The whole object of God, in our training," he wrote in 1858, "is to develop in us a character of eternal uprightness." But the consequence was more than merely individual; it involved "grand possibilities of social order and wellbeing."[73] Other prominent religious leaders, like Charles Grandison Finney, offered similar pronouncements.

The attraction of postmillennial thinking, including in particular a special role for America in redeeming the world, was hardly limited to religious figures. In his Annual Message to Congress in 1830, Andrew Jackson took pride in the nation's rapid progress from "a country covered with forests" to "our extensive republic, studded with cities, towns, and prosperous farms, embellished with all the improvements which art can devise, or industry execute," and "filled with all the blessings of liberty, civilization, and religion." Both population and civilization were moving westward, he noted; moreover, this westward expansion had a moral dimension. It was "a source of joy that our country affords scope where our young population may range unconstrained in body or in mind, developing the power and faculties of man in their highest perfection."[74] Jackson's theme of the new nation's mission to spread civilization and democracy through westward expansion would soon acquire a label. In 1845 an unsigned article in the *Democratic Review* hailed the admission of Texas as the twenty-eighth state as "the fulfill-ment of our manifest destiny to overspread the continent allotted by Providence for the free development of our yearly multiplying mil-lions."[75] Just after the Civil War (and after purchasing Alaska from Rus-sia), Secretary of State William Seward told an audience in Boston, "Nature designs that this whole continent, not merely these thirty-six States, but that this whole continent, shall be, sooner or later, within the magic circle of the American Union."[76] The concept of the nation's Manifest Destiny helped to shape American thinking throughout the remainder of the century and beyond.

George Bancroft, the author of the first history of America to have genuinely national scope and importance, expressed the same nearly religious awe at what the new nation was accomplishing. After grad-uating from Harvard in 1818, Bancroft was among the first of what in time became a wave of nineteenth-century Americans—including such figures as Henry Wadsworth Longfellow, Horace Mann, and James Russell Lowell—who studied in Germany. Returning to Boston four years later, he became an instructor at Harvard, contributed to the *North American Review* and other publications, and began work on the *History of the United States,* for which he is best remembered. Beginning in the 1830s, Bancroft also took up a series of increasingly significant political appointments, serving as customs collector for the port of Boston and then, in the administration of President James Polk, successively secretary of the navy, acting secretary of war, and minister to Great Britain. But he broke with the Democrats over slav-ery, in time becoming an active spokesman for the Union during the Civil War. After the war he served as minister to Prussia (after 1871, to the newly united imperial Germany) under Presidents Andrew Johnson and Ulysses Grant. Throughout, however, he was working on his monumental history, which eventually ran to ten volumes—the last published in 1874.

Bancroft began this work when Andrew Jackson was president, and the image of America that he set forth was largely the same as what Jackson portrayed in his 1830 Annual Message. (For that reason, what he wrote annoyed his fellow Bostonian and Harvard graduate John Quincy Adams, whom Jackson had defeated in 1828.[77]) In his introduction to the opening volume, published in 1834, Bancroft hailed the "equal rights . . . sovereignty of the people . . . prosperity . . . even justice" and "domestic peace" that by then marked this remarkable new political democracy. "Every man may enjoy the fruits of his industry," he wrote (obviously referring only to whites); "every mind is free to publish its convictions." Like Jackson, he saluted the country's ongoing physical and economic expansion. "New states are forming in the wilderness; canals . . . open numerous channels to internal commerce; manufactures prosper along our watercourses; the use of steam on our rivers and railroads annihilates distance." In the process, both wealth and population were increasing exponentially. Bancroft also admired the new nation's ability not just to attract immigrants from abroad but to make Americans out of them. "An immense concourse of emigrants of the most various lineage is perpetually crowding to our shores," he wrote, "and the principles of liberty, uniting all interests by the operation of equal laws, blend the discordant elements into harmonious union."[78]

What especially impressed Bancroft, writing in 1834, was how rapidly all this was being accomplished. "It is but little more than two centuries since the oldest of our states received its first permanent colony," he pointed out. "Before that time the whole territory was an unproductive waste" where "the arts had not erected a monument," and the continent's soil "was lavishing its strength in magnificent but useless vegetation." What had enabled this remarkable progress was that "a favoring Providence, calling our institutions into being, has conducted the country to its present happiness and glory."[79] The idea that divine Providence especially favored America was by then long familiar, among not just religious figures but the nation's political leaders too. Reflecting on the events leading up to the creation of the new republic

George Caleb Bingham, *Daniel Boone Escorting Settlers
Through the Cumberland Gap* (1851–1852). The religious imagery in
Bingham's painting resonated with the millennialist connotations
of westward movement in America.

as they were unfolding, Washington had expressed the view that its
success would demonstrate the role of "the finger of Providence" as
visibly as any event in the course of human affairs ever could.[80] By
Jackson's and Bancroft's day, that Providential aspiration had become
a reality.

The new nation's art and literature likewise reflected the theme of
America as a place of fresh beginning, creating a world free from the
corruption that marred the old one. George Caleb Bingham's 1851–52
painting of *Daniel Boone Escorting Settlers Through the Cumberland
Gap* recalled classic images both of Moses leading the Israelites to the
Promised Land (with Boone's rifle taking the place of Moses's staff) and
of the flight of the Holy Family into Egypt (with the settlers' wives rid-
ing in place of Mary). Significantly, Boone and his party are shown—as
they would have been in reality—traveling from east to west; and the
light is shining from the west.

Nor did the introduction of new manufacturing industries, or even the railroad, alter the image of America as a renewed Eden. George Inness's 1856 depiction of the Lackawanna Valley shows the Delaware, Lackawanna & Western railroad chugging its way through a pastoral landscape with the engine leaving a trail of steam. In the nearby town of Scranton, shown in the distance, the railroad's roundhouse (the first that the DL&W built) is clearly visible. So is a working industrial plant, with smoke issuing from a tall stack. None of these marks of human activity and technology disrupts the harmony of Inness's scene. To the contrary, the image of a new Eden that was both agrarian and semi-industrialized presented a visible contrast to the horrors of the slave economy to the south.[81]

Writing at mid-century, Herman Melville also articulated the millennial self-conception of Americans of the time. In *White-Jacket*, a novel based on his experiences serving in the U.S. Navy (the book he wrote immediately before undertaking *Moby-Dick*), Melville echoed Tocqueville's theme of "a country like ours, boasting of the political equality of all social conditions." But, invoking biblical language, he

George Inness, *The Lackawanna Valley* (circa 1855).
In Inness's representation, neither the clearing of woodland nor the arrival of industrialization, including the railroad, overcomes the Edenic quality of the America that continual westward movement was settling and developing.
(The painting's dominant tone is a lush green.)

drew as well on his Puritan ancestors' sense of religious mission in the New World. "We Americans," he declared, "are the peculiar chosen people—the Israel of our time; we bear the ark of the liberties of the world." The predestination in which the Puritans had believed might not apply to individual men and women, but it did to nations and especially to America. "God has predestinated, mankind expects, great things from our race; and great things we feel in our souls."[82]

Moreover, the country's mission was not for Americans alone. America's destiny was to lead other nations into the long awaited new era. Before long, Melville concluded, "the van of the nations must, of right, belong to ourselves." The feat of mastering a previously untamed wilderness, recounted in fiction of the time like James Fenimore Cooper's *Leatherstocking* novels and portrayed in images like Bingham's Daniel Boone, carried over to the advance of civilization more broadly. "We are the pioneers of the world," Melville proclaimed, "the advance-guard, sent on through the wilderness of untried things, to break a new path in the New World that is ours." What mattered was that Americans' world was new, free of Europe's corruption. "In our youth is our strength; in our inexperience, our wisdom." The new nation's mission, if it would only live up to it, was no less than millennial. "Long enough have we been sceptics with regard to ourselves, and doubted whether, indeed, the political Messiah had come. But he has come in *us,* if we would but give utterance to his promptings."[83]

There was a problem, however. The equality of conditions that Tocqueville hailed as the hallmark of democracy in America might prevail among white men, but women's status under the law was restricted in a variety of ways such as voting and property holding, and as of 1860 thirteen of the thirty-three states still had chattel slavery. As the reformist impulse of the early nineteenth century demonstrated— the American Temperance Society, the Home Missionary Society, the American Peace Society, the American Education Society, the American Sabbath School Union, among many others—there was no lack of causes, or of enthusiasm for them.[84] But it was slavery that Americans of the day increasingly saw as inconsistent with their nation's millennial mission.

Even at the time of Tocqueville's visit in the 1830s, the tension was becoming widespread. In a petition to Congress that circulated widely at the time, inviting individual towns and other groups to insert their name and forward a copy on to Washington, signers declared themselves "deeply convinced of the sinfulness of Slavery, and keenly aggrieved by its existence." Appealing to "the holy cause of Human Freedom," it called on Congress to abolish slavery altogether in the District of Columbia, and to end the slave trade throughout the United States.[85]

Not surprisingly, both Francis Wayland and Francis Bowen were opposed to slavery. In his moral philosophy textbook, Wayland condemned slavery as a "violation of Personal Liberty," and in his political economy text he cited the slave trade as the only form of ongoing international commerce that impoverished the trading nations.[86] A decade later, he represented the antislavery position in a pamphlet coauthored with a pro-slavery minister from South Carolina.[87] Bowen's textbook mentioned slavery only briefly, and without moral comment. Years later, however, commenting on the Civil War, he made his view clear: "We may not fear the judgment of posterity about the recent war of the Rebellion; for the abolition of slavery alone, which it has brought about, is a great good and a possession forever, not for this country only, but for the civilized world."[88]

The publication in 1851 of Uncle Tom's Cabin, written by Lyman Beecher's daughter Harriet Beecher Stowe, put a human face on the evil of slavery for many readers. (Several of Lyman Beecher's other children were prominent in their own right as well, including the Congregational minister Henry Ward Beecher, perhaps America's best known preacher in the decades following the Civil War, and Catharine Beecher, who founded several schools for women and wrote popular tracts on religious and moral issues.) Although Stowe minimized the bloody scenes of whipping and other torture typical of many other antislavery tracts, the book unmistakably portrayed slavery as a sin and a social evil. Years later, Henry James wrote that the novel "knew the large felicity of gathering in alike the small and the simple and the big and the wise." It had, he recalled, "above all the extraordinary fortune of finding itself, for an immense number of people, much less a book than a state of vision, of feeling and of consciousness, in which they didn't sit and read and appraise and pass the time, but walked and talked and laughed and cried . . . in a manner of which Mrs. Stowe was the irresistible cause."[89] Within its first year the book sold 300,000 copies in the United States, and far more abroad, making it the most widely read novel of the time.[90]

The impetus behind the abolition movement, first in England and then in America, had long been a religious one. In the 1830s and 1840s, the controversy led three of America's largest Protestant groups—the Baptists, the Methodists, and the Presbyterians—to split into Northern and Southern denominations. For many in the North, the war that followed was a holy war, a ritual of religious purification, aimed at removing the moral stain that blocked the nation from fulfilling its millennial mission.[91] Julia Ward Howe's stirring "Battle Hymn of the Republic," first published in *The Atlantic Monthly* in February 1862, captured the religious spirit of this trial by arms with its imagery of "the fateful lightning of [God's] terrible swift sword" and "the fiery gospel writ in burnished rows of steel." Especially in Howe's original version, the final verse—"As He died to make men holy, let us die to make men free"—made explicit the connection of the war's human sacrifice to the salvation that Christians saw in Jesus's death. (Modern renditions often change the closing words to "let us *live* to make men free.") Within just a few years, following the bloody encounters at Antietam and Gettysburg, the nation had acquired a new understanding of "the glory of the coming of the Lord."[92]

George Bancroft, who lived until 1891, brought out a final revision of his *History of the United States of America* in 1882. Looking back on the nation's experience since he had begun his great work, he chose to add only two sentences to the introduction to the first volume, published in 1834: "The foregoing words, written nearly a half-century ago, are suffered to remain, because the intervening years have justified their expression of confidence in the progress of our republic. The seed of disunion has perished; and universal freedom, reciprocal benefits, and cherished traditions bind its many states in the closest union."[93]

Slavery—the evil seed, analogous to the original sin to which earlier religious thinking had traced mankind's wretched depravity—was indeed gone. The nation had sacrificed in blood to remove it. But Americans after the Civil War faced new challenges, to their self-image not less than their material circumstances. In these challenges too, economic factors loomed large and the political economists of the day, soon to be simply "economists," were eager to address them. Once again, the influence of religious thinking would shape how they did so.

Competing Gospels

The future fortunes of America will be fabulous. . . . I look forward into that "golden" future, literally, which is opening before
us, and marvel whether the most poetic dreams of growing wealth
may not fall short of the reality.

—HENRY WARD BEECHER

Men learned to make wealth much faster than they learned to
distribute it justly. Their eye for profit was keener than their ear
for the voice of God and humanity. That is the great sin of modern
humanity, and unless we repent, we shall perish by that sin.

—WALTER RAUSCHENBUSCH

The challenges confronting Americans in the decades that followed
the Civil War were, to a large extent, economic. By then economic
growth—meaning not just an ever larger population expanding across
the continent, but ongoing improvement in the living standard of
ordinary citizens—was an established fact. With one significant hiatus, in the 1880s and the first half of the 1890s, that improvement continued on into the early twentieth century. The country's population
nearly tripled between the end of the Civil War and America's entry
into World War I, and per capita living standards more than doubled.
The American economy was changing in other ways too. Internally,
what had been disconnected regional or even local centers of economic activity were increasingly becoming integrated throughout the
country. In 1890 the annual report of the superintendent of the census announced that the country no longer had a frontier line; the era
of westward expansion into empty territory was over.[1] Externally, the
United States was a growing presence in commerce overseas, not yet
the world's leading economic power but well on the way.

What role the national government would play in this vigorous economic development remained to be determined. The canals, and now

increasingly the railroads, that made westward expansion possible were in significant part the product of government initiative. In the 1860s and early 1870s alone, more than $100 million in government bonds and loans, and more than 100 million acres of government-owned land, went to support railroad expansion. But what other economic functions should the government assume? For example, farmers in many sections of the country now depended on rail transport to bring their crops and livestock to market. Surely no one had intended to empower the railroads to squeeze out all of the farmers' profit. But what restraints on freight charges were consistent with America's form of government? And via what mechanism might the government impose those restraints?

With the continuing advance of industrialization, similar questions arose in other areas of the economy as well. American manufacturing was no longer mostly a matter of small producers who naturally competed among themselves and against foreign imports. In many industries—steel, machinery, shipbuilding—big firms, engaged in heavy production, were becoming the norm. For the first time since the Revolution, Americans now confronted economic institutions of a sufficiently large scale to call into question the effectiveness of individual self-initiative.[2] The essential assumption underlying the laissez-faire thinking of Francis Wayland and other antebellum political economists was that businesses would naturally have to compete. Was that notion still plausible? And if not, was a government organized on laissez-faire economic principles sufficient to make competition happen?

A parallel set of questions surrounded these business giants themselves. They too were in significant ways the creation of government action: corporate charters that enabled joint ownership by large numbers of stockholders who might not even know one another; laws limiting liability, so that stockholders stood at risk of losing their initial investment but nothing more; patent protection for new kinds of machines like McCormick's reaper, Otis's elevator, and Singer's sewing machine. The huge firms that emerged in the decades following the Civil War presented challenges well beyond the concerns that Adam Smith had expressed about the collusiveness and self-seeking political meddling of merchants a hundred years before. No one envisioned these firms as sovereign entities, but just what role were they supposed to play in a democratic society?

Yet a further new challenge, especially in the latter decades of the nineteenth century, was the growth of the urban workforce—and with it the emergence of large-scale urban poverty. To be sure, there had always been impoverished, in some cases even destitute, citizens. But in a largely agrarian economy, and moreover one with seemingly unlimited new lands to put into cultivation, the problem remained limited. Now the frontier was gone, and advancing mechanization was eating away at the need for farm work. The combination of gains in agricultural productivity and accelerating industrialization led ever more Americans to move from rural areas into the country's rapidly growing cities, and large numbers of new immigrants arriving from abroad gathered there as well. Further, as large-scale manufacturing steadily replaced small shop-based production, most urban workers no longer enjoyed any significant prospect of ever going into business on their own. In contrast to how Lincoln had described working for someone else, on the eve of the Civil War, wage employment was now increasingly a permanent status. And those who had no job at all often suffered deprivation on a scale previously unknown in America.

Economic activity in the United States flourished in the years following the Civil War. With the completion of the first transcontinental rail link—the westbound Union Pacific and eastbound Central Pacific lines joined up in Promontory Point, Utah, in May 1869—the country's center of gravity was moving westward. The area of agricultural cultivation was expanding, but so were inland cities like Cleveland, Chicago, and St. Louis. Especially with the new possibilities opened up by the railroad, the development of commercial agriculture that had begun well before the war now gained further momentum. But the railroads not only facilitated economic expansion, to a large extent they led it. By the early 1870s the United States was laying six thousand miles of new track per year, three times the average rate in the decade before the war.[3] One out of ten nonfarm workers was now directly engaged in railroad construction.

Further, railroad expansion required iron and steel. Taking advantage of the new Bessemer process, first developed in the 1850s and adopted by Andrew Carnegie's Pittsburgh works soon after the Civil War ended, American steel mills went from just 69,000 tons of output in 1870 to 1.5 million tons a decade later.[4] The ready availability of

Meeting of the Central Pacific and the Union Pacific
at Promontory Summit, Utah, May 10, 1869.
The first transcontinental rail link, combined with the ending of the Civil War
just four years before, gave the country a new sense of geographic unity.

iron and steel in turn enabled large-scale manufacturing, especially of machinery. By 1880 machinery production was the country's leading industry.[5] Cities from Pennsylvania across the Midwest—Pittsburgh, Cincinnati, Detroit, Indianapolis, Milwaukee, Minneapolis—were becoming major manufacturing centers. Moreover, new homegrown technologies were pointing the way to a profusion of possibilities soon to come. In 1875 Alexander Graham Bell first demonstrated how electricity could carry sound, and the next year he patented the first working telephone. In 1879 Thomas Edison produced the first commercially successful electric lamp.

The end result of this burgeoning economic activity was an especially rapid advance in Americans' living standards. Across the country as a whole, per capita income, adjusted for price changes, rose by more than 50 percent between the late 1860s and the early 1880s—the most rapid sustained increase on record for the United States, either before or since.[6] True, Americans shared unequally in this advance.

The owners of new, large-scale businesses acquired wealth on a previously unimagined scale, while many of their fellow citizens continued to work for low pay and under hardship conditions. Even so, in a time of such extraordinary growth most Americans enjoyed significant economic gains. Further, many now benefited from new efforts by government, especially at the state and local level. Public spending on education in particular increased rapidly during this period, as the movement to provide universal free public education through grammar school (usually meaning eighth grade) gained momentum. Improved sanitation, including a clean water supply in the cities, was dramatically cutting the death rate from disease.

Growth slowed in the 1880s and early 1890s under the weight of a worldwide agricultural depression together with a series of financial crises both in America and abroad. Expanded production from new lands under cultivation—in Canada, in Argentina, in Australia—pushed down crop prices around the world. Wheat fell from $1.25 per bushel in the early 1870s to less than 50 cents by the mid-1890s, corn from 52 cents a bushel to 21 cents, cotton from more than 10 cents per pound to less than 7.[7] Failures of both banks and ordinary firms proliferated irregularly between one crisis and the next. By the early 1890s the Erie Railroad, the Northern Pacific, the Philadelphia & Reading, and the Atchison, Topeka & Santa Fe were all bankrupt, along with nearly five hundred banks and more than fifteen thousand other businesses.[8] Jobs became hard to find too. In the mid-1890s unemployment reached 17 percent of the nonfarm labor force, compared to just 4 percent in the economy's healthy years.[9] By 1895 per capita income, even adjusted for falling prices, stood below the level of a decade and a half before.

But growth resumed after the mid-1890s and then continued robustly through World War I. A run of poor harvests in Europe reversed the worldwide decline in agricultural prices. The new cyanide method for processing ore greatly increased production from South Africa's gold fields, triggering what amounted to an expansionary monetary policy in countries, including the United States, that were on the gold standard. By the end of the 1890s new finds along the Klondike River in Alaska, and in Canada's Yukon Territory, further expanded the world's gold supply. In the meanwhile, the ongoing rush of new technologies provided continuing impetus to economic expansion.

In part, the resumed expansion after the mid-1890s represented a renewal of America's growth from the early post–Civil War years. Steel production continued to increase. By 1913 American mills, having switched from the Bessemer converter to the Siemens open-hearth furnace, and now vertically integrated with their own minefields in Michigan and their own shipping fleets to carry the iron ore across the Great Lakes, were producing 31 million tons of steel per year. Railroad construction, which had fallen below 2,000 miles of track per year during the economy's depressed period, returned almost to the 6,000-plus rate of the 1870s. By the end of the century, nearly three-fifths of the country's eventual total of rail mileage was in place.[10] The manufacture of railroad cars, including Pullman sleeping cars for passengers and the newly developed refrigerator cars for shipping meat products, had also grown into one of the country's leading industries.

Other industries that had been part of the economic landscape for decades, but on a smaller scale, now expanded rapidly as well. By the 1890s American manufacturers were making more than one million of the new "safety bicycles" each year. By the turn of the new century, manufacturing output overall had tripled since the early post–Civil War years. By the eve of World War I it had doubled yet again, with explosive growth not just in consumer goods such as food and clothing and tobacco products but industrial machinery as well. And there was the automobile. As late as 1905, the value of horse-drawn passenger vehicles produced was nearly double that of motor cars. But Ford's Model T first appeared on America's roads in 1908, and by 1914 Ford Motor alone was producing a quarter-million cars per year and the value of motor car output exceeded that of horse-drawn vehicles by more than ten to one.[11] Overall, more than one-fifth of American workers were employed in some form of manufacturing (compared to well under one-tenth today). By then the Midwest was clearly the heartland of American manufacturing.

With the increased manufacturing activity, urbanization continued as well. By 1910 more than one in five Americans lived in cities or towns larger than 100,000, and nearly two in five lived in places larger than 10,000. Urbanization allowed yet new industries to develop too. The new "skyscrapers" made possible by advances in building technology (together with the development of electric elevators) changed the appearance of most American cities. New York's oddly shaped Flatiron

Flatiron Building, New York City (1903).
Completed in 1902, the twenty-story Fuller Building (as it was
originally named) quickly became a symbol both of New York City
and of the new era of urban development.

Building, built in 1902 on the narrow triangular space formed where
Broadway, Fifth Avenue, and East 22nd Street come together, set the
style for urban construction in other cities as well. Large urban-based
retailing—Macy's and Gimbel's in New York, Wanamaker in Philadelphia, Marshall Field in Chicago, Woolworth and the Great Atlantic
and Pacific Tea Company (the A&P for short) in almost every city of
any size—changed the way people shopped. But so too did mail-order
firms, like Sears Roebuck, especially for Americans living outside
urban areas. Electrification, not just inside buildings but outside too as
street lights changed over from gas to electricity, created another whole
new industry. Thomas Edison had patented the incandescent electric
light in 1879 and the electric power station in 1882. Thirty years later,
on the eve of World War I, parts of many American cities looked the
way they did until nearly a century later.

And the standard of living continued to improve. Between the mid-1890s and America's entry into World War I, per capita income, adjusted for price changes, rose yet again by more than 50 percent—as it had in the decade and a half immediately following the Civil War. The average income now stood at two and a half times the level of a half-century earlier. With economic inequality still widening, once again not all citizens participated equally in these gains. Even so, the sense of progress was clear enough for the large majority of the population. By the time the United States entered World War I, Ford had reduced the price of a standard touring car to less than half a year's wages for the average American manufacturing worker.

It did not take long after the Civil War for America's Protestant clergy to take note of the economic progress under way all around them. One of the first to hail the new economic era was Henry Ward Beecher, a son of Lyman Beecher and brother of the author of *Uncle Tom's Cabin*. The younger Beecher was educated at the Boston Latin School and then Amherst College, while his father was still preaching in New England, and he then followed his father west to take his clerical training at Lane Theological Seminary in Cincinnati. He soon made his way back east, however, in 1847 becoming pastor at New York's Plymouth Congregational Church, located in Brooklyn Heights. By the time of the Civil War, Henry Ward Beecher had become one of the best known clergymen in America, preaching each week to a congregation that numbered three thousand. Among the regular members were Arthur and Lewis Tappan, scions of a Boston mercantile family and active abolitionists before the war; Alfred Beach, a publisher and inventor who designed an early precursor of New York's subway system; John Tasker Howard, who along with his father started the first New York–to–California steamship line; and many other men of wealth and prominence. In keeping with his congregation's prosperous economic status, Beecher was also America's best paid clergyman, earning an annual salary of $100,000 (roughly $1,600,000 in today's dollars).[12]

Like his father, Henry Ward Beecher was a theological moderate, taking little interest in long-past doctrinal disputes over such matters as predestination, and instead emphasizing the benevolence of God and therefore the innate goodness of man. (One fellow clergyman observed that the Christianity preached by Beecher and others of the younger generation bore so little relation to the orthodoxy of the past that it was "substantially another religion" from that preached a half-century earlier.[13]) Like his sister, and many of his parishioners, he had been an active abolitionist before the Civil War. Now that slavery was gone, he emerged as a vigorous spokesman for America's political and economic structure, viewing his country with a strongly optimistic, postmillennial outlook. Early to recognize the new era of renewed prosperity, he declared in 1867 that "Boundless wealth is open before us. . . . We are entering upon an era of wealth."[14]

Moreover, Beecher made clear that this newly developing wealth was good for both individuals and society. He was not a believer in poverty, he wrote; nor did he consider poverty any kind of condition of holiness. No doubt bearing in mind the munificent standard of living enjoyed by many of his parishioners—not to mention his own—he explained that "A man can as well labor for and benefit the community in which he dwells when living in a royal mansion, as when living in a hovel. In order to live for others, it is not necessary to live in squalid misery." Beecher enjoined his fellow citizens that they too should be comfortable in this new wealth, and also in its pursuit. "You need not be ashamed to be rich," he told them, and "you need not be ashamed to be thought to be seeking riches." To the contrary, wealth was "one of the most important powers that is committed to the hand of man." It was a power for good when rightly employed.[15]

The country's post–Civil War economic expansion did not disappoint him. Three years later, in a Thanksgiving Day sermon that he titled "The Tendencies of American Progress," Beecher further developed the theme that the country's increasingly evident prosperity was welcome not just for its own sake but as a necessary underpinning to a morally sound society. There must be prosperity in material things, he told his congregation, if there is to be prosperity in moral things. His reasoning closely resembled what David Hume had said about what he called refinement in the arts more than a century before. "It is impossible to civilize a community without riches," Beecher stated. "No nation ever yet rose from a barbarous state except through the mediation of wealth earned."[16] Commercial prosperity was "indissolubly connected with public morals."[17]

America in this new age was amply achieving this essential prerequisite for civilization and morality. "The mass of our working population," Beecher observed, "were never so well clothed, so bountifully fed and so well housed, as they are now." Moreover, along with the obvious wealth and conspicuous consumption of the economic elite, he saw that even those Americans at the bottom of the economic scale were participating in the country's prosperity. "The lowest material conditions are working upward, and not downward," he concluded.[18]

Even more important, from his postmillennialist perspective Beecher assumed—correctly, as subsequent decades bore out—that what he was witnessing was more than just a temporary economic boom. "The future fortunes of America will be fabulous," he predicted. "I look forward into that 'golden' future, literally, which is opening before us, and marvel whether the most poetic dreams of growing wealth may not fall short of the reality."[19] Moreover, this prospect was more than just a matter of material living standards; there was a moral dimension to it as well. On the eve of the Civil War, Emerson had observed that "A dollar is not value, but representative of value, and, at last, of moral values . . . wealth is moral."[20] Following Emerson, and also taking a metaphor from Melville's prewar *White-Jacket*, Beecher drew a direct connection between the fabulous wealth that he foresaw and America's millennial role. "Nowhere else does wealth so directly point towards virtue in morality, and spirituality in religion, as in America," he asserted; "we have been put in the van among nations."[21]

Another ten years later, reflecting on America's continuing economic expansion and improvement, Beecher remained committed to the central importance of prosperity and wealth for national development more broadly. "Men talk about plain living and high thinking," he observed. "You never saw a nation that lived plain and thought high." And again echoing Hume, he declared that "no community can be civilized except through riches. You cannot civilize poverty."[22]

In time others took up Beecher's theme, often invoking the assumed connection between wealth and morality to posit not merely a justification for seeking wealth but a moral imperative to do so. In the latter decades of the nineteenth century, the Baptist minister Russell Conwell offered what may have been the most vigorous argument along these lines, and certainly the most widely heard. While most Protestant clergymen of the day (and earlier too) began their ministry at a young age—Beecher and his father had each been twenty-four, Francis Wayland twenty-five, and Charles Grandison Finney, twenty-eight—Conwell did not enter the ministry until his mid-thirties. After graduating from Yale, with wartime service in the Union army along the way, he first pursued a career as a lawyer and real estate promoter and then as a newspaper writer and publisher. He also wrote campaign biographies of Republican presidential candidates who had served in the war, including Grant, Hayes, and Garfield, and in time he acquired a significant reputation as a world traveler and professional lecturer. But he then decided to attend Newton Theological Seminary in Massachusetts (later Andover-Newton) and in 1879, at the age of thirty-five, he was ordained.[23]

Three years later Conwell became pastor of Philadelphia's ten-year-old and financially troubled Grace Baptist Church, which under his leadership—and his phenomenal talent for fundraising—developed into America's first institutional church, embodying far more than Christian worship.[24] By 1891 the church had a new building, popularly called the Baptist Temple (which soon became the popular name for Grace Church itself), large enough to accommodate three thousand congregants. It was the largest Protestant church in America. Soon the church was also sponsoring three hospitals. In the meanwhile Conwell had started a nighttime school offering instruction to working-class students. By 1887 it had become Temple College (in time, Temple University). For nearly four decades, ending only with his death, Conwell served simultaneously as pastor at the church and president of the college.

As part of his tireless fundraising efforts for Grace Church and its institutional affiliates, Conwell traveled extensively, lecturing wherever he went. Rather than vary his address, he repeatedly—according to some accounts, between five and ten thousand times over the years—delivered what amounted to the same lecture. Titled "Acres of Diamonds," it began with a parable of a young man who went off in search of wealth only to return home, after a lifetime of hardship and no success, to find that the riches he had been seeking were beneath the ground beside his original home. Drawing the story's moral, Conwell would then continue, "the opportunity to get rich, to attain unto great wealth, is here in Philadelphia [or whatever city in which he was speaking] now, within the reach of almost every man and woman who hears me speak tonight."[25]

The inspiration Conwell sought to impart to his audience, however, went beyond the message that no one needed to leave home to find material success. In his telling, the story became a vehicle for promoting the moral value of wealth itself, and therefore the moral imperative to seek it. "I say that you ought to get rich," he told his listeners, "and it is your duty to get rich. . . . If you can honestly attain unto riches in Philadelphia, it is your Christian and godly duty to do so."[26] A half-century before, Tocqueville had observed that Americans' widespread perception of the opportunity to achieve economic success created a sense of moral and social obligation to seek it. For Conwell, that obligation was religious as well.

The rationale that he gave loosely drew on Adam Smith's conception of the benefits of a market economy, as set forth in *The Wealth of Nations*. But there was an important difference. Consistent with other Enlightenment thinking, Smith represented the beneficial consequences for others that followed from individual economic initiative as unforeseen, and certainly unintended. The butcher, the baker, and the brewer give us our dinner not from any concern for our welfare but in order to make a living. In Conwell's rendering, the beneficial effects of individual economic action became a matter of deliberate design, motivated on moral and religious grounds. And the profit individuals earned along the way corresponded to how much they benefited others. "You can measure the good you have been to this city by what this city has paid you," he argued. "A man can judge very well what he is worth by what he receives."[27]

Men and women (Conwell was early to embrace the idea of economic initiative by women) of course had a religious obligation to work to benefit others, and the way to know how best to do so was therefore to seek out the best way to make money. Using the example of a woman who prospered from opening a button shop, once she realized that her neighbors needed buttons but had nowhere to buy them, Conwell told his audience, "if you will just take only four blocks around you, and find out what the people want and what you ought to supply . . . and figure up the profits you would make if you did supply them, you would very soon see it. There is wealth right within the sound of your voice." Making a profit, and thereby benefiting others, was nothing less than a religious act: "to make money honestly is to preach the gospel."[28]

. . .

Conwell may have been the preacher who most forcefully articulated (many today would say he caricatured) the idea of an imperative to strive for riches based on the assumed beneficial effects for society of individual wealth-seeking, but he was hardly alone. At the turn of the twentieth century, William Lawrence, the Episcopal bishop of Massachusetts, took up the same theme that Henry Ward Beecher had articulated thirty years before. As in Beecher's day, a renewed period of economic prosperity was becoming evident. Lawrence welcomed it not just on its own account but for the broader benefits that followed from it. Material prosperity, he observed, was "helping to make the national character sweeter, more joyous, more unselfish, more Christlike."[29]

Even more than Conwell, Lawrence drew a direct connection between wealth-seeking and individual morality. "In the long run," he wrote, "it is only to the man of morality that wealth comes."[30] (Conwell had asserted that ninety-eight out of a hundred of the rich men of America were honest; that was why they were rich.[31]) The reason, Lawrence concluded, was that wealth-seeking was part of man's intended role in a world designed by a benevolent God. "We believe in the harmony of God's universe," he stated. "We know that it is only by working along His laws natural and spiritual that we can work with efficiency."[32] Conwell had argued that the foundation of godliness and the foundational principle of success in business were "both the same precisely."[33] Lawrence put it more simply: "Godliness is in league with riches."[34]

Not surprisingly, many of those who were amassing the greatest wealth concurred. In addition to the implicitly Smithian idea that if a person sought riches the actions required to attain them would end up benefiting others, Conwell had also pointed to the possibilities for using wealth once a person acquired it. "Money is power," he had argued, echoing Beecher, "and you ought to be reasonably ambitious to have it. You ought because you can do more good with it than you could without it."[35] As America's economic expansion continued, and the new industrial age enabled individual economic success on a scale previously unimagined, the nation's moral attention moved beyond the mere acquiring of wealth to the subsequent question of how those who had done so should use it.

In 1889 Andrew Carnegie, by then perhaps the richest man in America from the vast empire he had built out of his Pittsburgh steel works, laid out his vision of the obligations that went along with wealth such as his. The duty of the man of wealth, he explained, was to live modestly, "shunning display or extravagance," and after his small living expenses "to consider all surplus revenues which come to him simply as trust funds, which he is ... strictly bound as a matter of duty to administer in the manner which, in his judgment, is best calculated to produce the most beneficial results for the community." By acting in this way, the man of wealth would become "the mere agent and trustee for his poorer brethren, bringing to their service his superior wisdom, experience, and ability to administer, doing for them better than they would or could do for themselves."[36]

Carnegie's paternalistic argument, claiming for the super-rich the ability and the obligation to administer economic resources on behalf of their fellow citizens better than they might possibly manage for themselves, was of course a justification for allowing individuals to amass wealth such as his. For purposes of motivating and guiding economic activity, it accepted, indeed it welcomed, "the present most intense individualism." But for purposes of allocating the ultimate fruits of that activity, it looked to "an ideal state, in which the surplus wealth of the few will become, in the best sense, the property of the many." The end result would be a better society—better for everyone—because "wealth, passing through the hands of the few, can be made a much more potent force for the elevation of our race than if it had been distributed in small sums to the people themselves."[37]

To achieve this end Carnegie looked in the first instance to private initiative among those who had acquired wealth, and in his own life he sought to fulfill that ideal through his many and varied philanthropies: most visibly, the creation of free public libraries in cities and towns across America, but also the Carnegie Institute of Technology (today Carnegie Mellon University), a nationwide pension and insurance system for college teachers (Teachers Insurance and Annuity Association), the Carnegie Endowment for International Peace, and a host of other initiatives. But he also saw a role for the government, in case men of wealth failed to do as he did. He therefore urged that a share of a rich man's estate "should go at his death to the public through the agency of the state," and he called for a graduated inheritance tax reaching 50 percent for amounts over $1 million. He dismissed the concern that such a tax would dull the incentive motivating individual commercial enterprise. To the contrary, "to the class whose ambition it is to leave great fortunes and be talked about after their death, it will attract even more attention, and, indeed, be a somewhat nobler ambition to have enormous sums paid over to the state from their fortunes." In the absence of such a tax, "the man who dies leaving behind him many millions of available wealth, which was his to administer during life, will pass away 'unwept, unhonored, and unsung.' . . . Of such as these the public verdict will then be: 'The man who dies thus rich dies disgraced.' "[38]

At a time when incomes, and even more so wealth, were reaching a degree of concentration not previously seen in America, Carnegie saw his concept of accumulation and disposition of wealth as an effective antidote for its unequal distribution, which would then prove only temporary. A man or woman who acquired wealth was to be a trustee for the poor, "intrusted for a season with a great part of the increased wealth of the community" and administering its use for the broader good. "Such, in my opinion, is the true Gospel concerning Wealth, obedience to which is destined some day to solve the problem of the Rich and the Poor, and to bring 'Peace on earth, among men Good-Will.' "[39]

There was, however, a less evidently humanitarian side to the ideas of the clergymen and other thinkers who propounded what, following Carnegie's widely read statement, became known as the Gospel of Wealth. Henry Ward Beecher consistently exhibited little sympathy for the poor, declaring at one point, "no man in this land suffers from poverty unless it be more than his fault—unless it be his *sin*."[40] And if they felt overworked, so be it. He repeatedly condemned the movement for an eight-hour workday. Russell Conwell told his audiences across the country that "the number of poor who are to be sympathized with is very small." Like Beecher, he justified this seemingly heartless view on the ground that "there is not a poor person in the United States who was not made poor by his own shortcomings, or by the shortcomings of some one else."[41]

With the emergence of mass urban poverty in the decades after the Civil War, the dual question of responsibility for the poor—who was responsible for their condition, and who therefore should assume responsibility for addressing it—was taking on ever greater importance. Horatio Alger's hugely popular novels, beginning with *Ragged*

Dick in 1867, always featured some morally deserving young city lad
who came to success because a chance incident brought him to the
attention of an already prosperous older man.[42] The title of the Alger
series, "Luck and Pluck," highlighted the twin elements that many
Americans saw driving individuals' fortunes. By contrast, Emerson
dismissed luck altogether. "There is always a reason, *in the man,* for his
good or bad fortune," Emerson wrote. Good luck was merely "another
name for tenacity of purpose."[43] Conwell squarely sided with Emerson.
Embracing the view of poverty implicit in Calvin's precept that adver-
sity is a sign of God's absence, and prosperity of God's presence,[44] he
warned that "To sympathize with a man whom God has punished for
his sins, thus to help him when God would still continue a just punishment, is to do wrong, no doubt about it."[45]

Many others in the clergy expressed a similar disregard for either
inequality or even outright poverty. Henry Ward Beecher was con-
temptuous of calls for greater equality. "Men who bring less manhood
into the market ought, in spite of all the insane theories which have
come from abroad, to have the lowest wages; and men who bring the
most manhood into the market ought, by a celestial edict, to have the
highest place, the most honors and the largest remunerations, since
they have the causes of them in themselves." Even more dismissively,
"It is absurd to claim that an industrious versatile man should stand no
higher and have no more than the man who drinks beer three times a
day, and spends half his time in sleep, and the rest of his time grumbling and saying that he is as good as the next man."[46]

Beecher saw as a particular threat the new ideas of economic equality that in his day were beginning to come to America from Europe.
Dismissing what he called the theories of German socialists and the
political economy of French communes—but indirectly targeting the
nascent American labor movement as well—he defiantly declared that
"The workingmen of Europe, whether leaders or followers, are not fit
to be teachers of Americans in the matter of political economy and
instituted liberty." When it came to matters of human rights and individual liberty, Americans had nothing to learn from Europeans and
much to teach them. What he objected to in particular was the claim
"that it is the duty of government to be paternal, to look after the welfare of its subjects, to provide them with labor, and to see to it that they
are happy." Such ideas would only lead to "Tzarism . . . Caesarism . . .

absolute monarchy." Economic inequality, Beecher concluded, was inevitable: "there is a great law by which little being must appear to be less, and must have less, than much being, and more being must appear to be more and must have more than even much." It was a matter of God's will. "He has meant that great shall be great and that little shall be little. Men are distributed on a long scale; and no equalizing process will take place till you can make men equal in productive forces."[47] The poor must heed God's will and reap the misfortunes of their inferiority.

Phillips Brooks, the longtime rector of Boston's Trinity Church, and William Lawrence's predecessor as Episcopal bishop of Massachusetts (Brooks also wrote the lyrics to "O Little Town of Bethlehem"), likewise preached mostly about personal religion. In an early letter to his father, he accepted "the rebuking of sins, and public sins as well as private," as what he felt he had been ordained to preach, but he nonetheless stood apart from most social reform efforts other than abolishing slavery.[48] Brooks dismissed concerns for the poor on the ground that "Excessive poverty, actual suffering for the necessities of life, terrible as it is, is comparatively rare."[49] He was even harsher in his attitude toward those who objected to the era's widening economic inequalities. "The instinct which asks for equality is a low one," he claimed; "equality, if it were completely brought about, would furnish play only for the lower instincts and impulses of man." Indeed, *in*equality—even inequality that stemmed from no difference whatever in individuals' talent or effort or intelligence—was for Brooks part of what made life worthwhile. "It is the fact of privilege, the inequalities among men for which they do not seem to be responsible, which makes a large part of the interest and richness of human existence."[50]

The hardships caused by the economic depression that lasted from the early 1880s to the mid-1890s rendered such views increasingly out of step with the sympathies of many Americans, and especially uncomfortable for many in the Protestant clergy. The ceaseless fall of agricultural prices left increasing numbers of farmers unable to eke out a decent living. Spreading urban labor unrest and the violence that it triggered—the 1886 Haymarket riot in Chicago, the Homestead steel strike near Pittsburgh in 1892, the Pullman strike across much of the nation's rail system in 1894—similarly drew the public's attention to the plight of oppressed industrial workers.

In 1889 *Scribner* magazine published an illustrated article by news-

Jacob Riis, *Street Arabs—Night Boys in Sleeping Quarters* (1890).
Riis's shocking photographs of life in New York's tenements highlighted the
prevalence of urban poverty during the country's prolonged economic depression.

man Jacob Riis, featuring his intentionally disturbing photographs of
the urban poor in the tenements of New York's Lower East Side. Riis's
photographs attracted especially widespread attention for his use of the
new technology of mobile flash photography, and the next year he published a book-length version titled *How the Other Half Lives*.[51] It was
becoming impossible to ignore the dire straits in which many Americans now found themselves, and hard to accept that so many were
destitute solely on account of what Russell Conwell called "their own
shortcomings." The claim that their plight was no more than divine
punishment for their sins increasingly rang of hypocrisy, if not outright disregard for humanity.

The reaction took multiple forms. Farm organizations like the
Patrons of Husbandry (popularly, the Grange), and in the South both
the all-white Southern Farmers' Alliance and the Colored Farmers'
Alliance, grew into popular protest groups. In the cities the struggling
American labor movement gained new momentum. Union activist

Samuel Gompers, expanding his activity from his original base in the New York cigar makers' union, founded the American Federation of Labor in 1886. In 1894, following President Grover Cleveland's decision to call in the U.S. Army to protect the railroads during the Pullman strike, seventeen different "industrial armies" marched on Washington seeking one or another form of federal assistance, typically in the form of jobs working on new road construction or other public projects.

Political parties, both old and new, also took on new agendas. The newly formed People's Party (also known as the Populist Party) enjoyed significant success in the 1892 elections, winning several governorships and seats in Congress, before descending into the fringe monetary mania and anti-Semitic bigotry for which it eventually became known. Although William Jennings Bryan ran for president in 1896 as a Democrat, the heart of his platform—and the subject of his famous "Cross of Gold" speech at the party's nominating convention that summer— was the Populists' call for free coinage of silver. By soon after the turn of the new century, Theodore Roosevelt's trust-busting campaign and then Woodrow Wilson's broad-based progressive movement framed the agenda of the two major parties. By the time Wilson ran for president (with Roosevelt competing unsuccessfully as a third-party candidate), there was no significant party in American politics that did not endorse a reformist program.

America's religious establishment could hardly stand apart from this movement. Many in the clergy found it increasingly difficult to ignore the spreading urban and rural poverty among those without jobs, as well as the increasingly visible exploitation of those who had them: low wages, unsafe working conditions, child labor, a workday that seemed too long for everyone but especially for women. Few thought the problem was wealth per se. If anything, there was too little of it. The issue that many in the Protestant clergy chose to address was the ever more disparate distribution of that wealth. As the nation's economic problems deepened, these religious leaders increasingly chafed for the church to play a more active role in addressing them. Many saw the church's complacency as the root of the problem.

The first national-level leader of the clergy's reaction to this perceived complacency was Washington Gladden. Educated at Williams College,

Gladden had become a Congregational minister in 1860, at age twenty-four. But he also initially pursued a newspaper career, serving as religion editor of the *New York Independent* and from that perch helping to mobilize opposition to the corruption of the city's notorious Boss Tweed. In his preaching Gladden deliberately set a humble tone, most famously expressed in the words he wrote for what in time became a widely popular hymn: "O Master, let me walk with Thee, In lowly paths of service free." But he also took a strong interest in the broader social and economic issues facing the country. As early as 1875, well before the economic depression of the 1880s and early 1890s set in, he signaled the future direction of his interests with a book titled *Working People and Their Employers.*

It was in the 1880s, however, as the hardships of the protracted business downturn became evident, that Gladden's work achieved full strength. By then minister at the First Congregational Church in Columbus, Ohio, where he remained until his death, Gladden published a series of widely read books bringing a religious perspective to the nation's economic problems and calling on the church to take up an active role in resolving them. Even the books' titles indicated his increasingly explicit focus on economic issues: *Applied Christianity: Moral Aspects of Social Questions* (1887); *Tools and the Man: Property and Industry under the Christian Law* (1893); and *Social Facts and Forces: The Factory, the Labor Union, the Corporation, the Railway, the City, the Church* (1897).

Gladden's goal, building on the postmillennial vision of laboring to create a new heaven on earth, was to broaden the concerns of his fellow Protestants to encompass not only the earthly conduct and spiritual salvation of individual men and women but also the character of the society within which they lived.[52] "The end of Christianity is twofold," he wrote in *Tools and the Man:* "a perfect man in a perfect society." The two were equally important. "The law and the gospel address themselves to the conscience and the affection of the man, but they address him as a member of the social organism." Though a Congregational minister, Gladden harked back to the preaching of pre–Civil War Unitarians like William Ellery Channing in believing that the concept of sin was not just individual but collective as well, and it was necessary to confront it at both levels. America's churches therefore needed to speak to the structure and condition of society, along with the beliefs and behavior of individuals. "There is need among us, then, of emphasizing the social side of our Christian work," Gladden stated. "Christianity gives a law to society as well as to the individual. We are called to convert men, as we are called at the same time and with equal authority to furnish them a Christian society to live in after they are converted."[53]

And what would constitute such a Christian society? For Gladden, the term meant more than simply one where churches were available for parishioners' worship and sermons for their personal edification. Individuals' behavior depended on the society in which they lived. There were certain forms of social organization, he believed, that tended to "promote the worth and goodness of men themselves." And there were "other outward conditions which tend to belittle and discourage personal worth and goodness."[54]

The choice, he argued, was clear. "We need to encourage those forms of social organization in which the value of character shall be rightly estimated, and men shall not be reckoned merely as counters in the great game of material exchanges." This choice, Gladden thought, was precisely what America now confronted. And it was incumbent on the church to bring the force of religion to bear on making that choice. "The problem now before us," he wrote in 1893, "is, whether any higher power can be invoked to save the good that the greed of gain has brought forth upon the earth. This is the problem that confronts those of us who labor for the christianization of society."[55]

Moreover, Gladden was specific about the central economic problem that the church should lead society to rectify: spreading poverty together with widening inequality. In contrast to what his contemporaries like Russell Conwell and Phillips Brooks had to say on the matter, Gladden's view of economic inequality recalled the attitude of earlier Americans going back to John Winthrop: "The enormous inequalities of condition and possessions existing and constantly increasing among us foster, on both sides of the great gulf,—among the rich as well as among the poor,—tempers and sentiments which are the reverse of Christian. Contempt on the one side, envy on the other, fill the social atmosphere with feverish and inflammable influences."[56]

This situation, Gladden believed, could not persist in the modern world, and especially not in America. Inequalities perhaps as great had existed in other ages, he acknowledged, "but never before such inequalities in a society founded on the doctrine that all men are created equal," and "never before in a society in which the poor had the spelling-book and the newspaper and the ballot in their hands."[57] Literacy, a free press, and electoral democracy—the combination, he believed, rendered the country's current economic posture unsustainable. The question was how to bring about the change America so urgently needed.

Walter Rauschenbusch, a generation younger than Gladden, called even more explicitly on America's Protestant churches to lead the way in bringing that change about. Born a year after Gladden was ordained, to a family of German immigrants living in Rochester, New York, Rauschenbusch was educated first in Germany and then at Rochester's recently founded Baptist-sponsored university and the associated Baptist seminary. For more than a decade he served as pastor at New York City's Second German Baptist Church, before returning to Rochester as a professor at the seminary. Rauschenbusch also applied his enormous energies beyond either the church or the seminary, however, in 1892 founding the Brotherhood of the Kingdom (originally called the Society of Jesus). The Brotherhood was a nondenominational Protestant group committed to what its members saw as the social teachings of Christianity, including in particular teachings concerning wealth and its distribution.

Like Gladden, Rauschenbusch was a prolific writer, and his books forcefully advanced the message of what was coming to be called the Social Gospel: *Christianity and the Social Crisis* (1907); *Prayers for the Social Awakening* (1910); *Christianizing the Social Order* (1912); *A Theology for the Social Gospel* (1917).[58] In *Christianity and the Social Crisis* he took up Gladden's argument that America's current economic situation was untenable, and that unequal distribution of the nation's growing wealth was the heart of the matter. "Western civilization is passing through a social revolution unparalleled in history for scope and power," he wrote; "this social crisis is the overshadowing problem of our generation." Pointing to the corrosive social and moral consequences of extreme economic inequality, Rauschenbusch was clear too about the threat of divisive political struggle that this widening division posed for a democratic society. "The vastness and free sweep of our concentrated wealth on the one side, the independence, moral vigor, and political power of the common people on the other side," he warned, "promise a long-drawn grapple of contesting forces."[59]

These fears were hardly new, even in America. Tocqueville, struck by the widening gulf between the owners of manufacturing establishments and their hired hands that he observed even in the very early stage of the country's industrialization, in the 1830s, had seen a potential threat to the equality of condition that he identified with American society as a whole. "The master and the workman have then here no similarity," he noted, "and their differences increase every day." He went on to caution that if America's democracy ever gave way to a permanent aristocracy, this industrially grounded social inequality would be the gate by which it entered.[60] Seven decades later, Rauschenbusch saw that the further advance of industrialization, now extending to massive mills and factories, and railroads spanning the nation in all directions, was making the social gap between rich and poor vastly greater. The extremes of wealth and poverty had grown much further apart, he wrote, and therefore the poor had become poorer in relative terms. America was becoming a society of separate social classes. "There is a rich class and a poor class, whose manner of life is wedged farther and farther apart, and whose boundary lines are becoming ever more distinct."[61]

Rauschenbusch's analysis focused squarely on the question of distribution, and like Gladden he placed the era's widening inequality in the context of a collective concept of sin. "Men learned to make wealth much faster than they learned to distribute it justly," he concluded. "Their eye for profit was keener than their ear for the voice of God and humanity. That is the great sin of modern humanity, and unless we repent, we shall perish by that sin." It was now the responsibility of religion and the church to bring that repentance about. As Gladden had argued before him, the church's focus must encompass not just individual faith and acts but the structure of the society in which men and women lived. "It is the function of religion to teach the individual to value his soul more than his body, and his moral integrity more than his income," Rauschenbusch declared. "In the same way it is the function of religion to teach society to value human life more than property, and to value property only in so far as it forms the material basis for the higher development of human life."[62]

Rauschenbusch understood that the emphasis he and Gladden and other proponents of the new Social Gospel were placing on *society,* rather than merely focusing on the saving of individual souls, represented a departure from recent American Protestant thinking. But he argued that they were actually taking Christianity back to its historical roots. Both the Gospels and the early church fathers, as he read them, had displayed an abiding concern for the poor. They had likewise embraced such ideas as communal ownership of property. "The manhood of the poor," he noted, "was more sacred to it [referring to the Hebrew Bible] than the property of the rich."[63] Once Christianity became the official religion of the Roman Empire, the individualism characteristic of Hellenistic thinking gradually displaced the early emphasis on reshaping human society and bringing about the Kingdom of God. (Constantine had ruled not from Rome, but the Greek city of Byzantium—renamed Constantinople.) The Social Gospel, as Rauschenbusch saw it, represented a return to those original roots.[64] As he put it in one of his later books, the Social Gospel sought to bring men under repentance for their *collective* sins. It called them to the faith of the old prophets, who believed in the salvation *of nations.*[65]

Motivated also by a robust postmillennialism, Rauschenbusch had high hopes for the ability of America's Protestant churches to achieve this objective if they would only bend themselves to the task. Their purpose should be not just to save individual men and women's souls but to reform the society in which men and women lived. "Jesus worked on individuals and through individuals," he acknowledged, "but his real end was not individualistic, but social, and in his method he employed strong social forces." More succinctly, "his end was not the new soul, but the new society; not man, but Man."[66]

In light of the enormous challenge, there was no room for complacency, much less inaction. Given a choice like what society now faced, there was also no such thing as neutrality. The church was one of the most potent forces in Western civilization, he asserted. As a result, "It cannot help throwing its immense weight on one side or the other. If it tries not to act, it thereby acts." If America's churches would only place themselves actively on the side of social change, none of society's existing institutions would be able to resist their force. Invoking metaphors that at once personified how he saw religion and acknowledged the rush of change in the modern age, Rauschenbusch foresaw that "Under the warm breath of religious faith, all social institutions become plastic." More than that, the active force of religion was *necessary* for change to occur. "Unless the economic and intellectual factors are strongly reenforced by religious enthusiasm, the whole social movement may prove abortive, and the New Era may die before it comes to birth."[67]

What urgently mattered was for the nation's religious leaders to reframe the scope of their efforts. Rauschenbusch urged them forward in the direction to which the Social Gospel pointed. "Religious men have been cowed by the prevailing materialism and arrogant selfishness of our business world," he lamented. He now called on them to abandon their deference. His colleagues in America's clergy should have the courage of their religious faith. They should make clear that "the life of a nation 'consisteth not in the abundance of things' which it produces, but in the way men live justly with one another and humbly with their God."[68]

The movement that Gladden and Rauschenbusch spearheaded reflected not just a reaction to America's glaring economic and social shortcomings in the present age but also the postmillennialist outlook toward the future that increasingly characterized the nation's mainline Protestant churches at the turn of the twentieth century.[69] As Rauschenbusch summarized the objective of so much of his work, both within the church and more broadly, "It is not a matter of getting individuals to heaven, but of transforming the life on earth into the harmony of heaven."[70] In the spirit of pragmatism that marked so many other dimensions of American life as well, in the closing decades of the nineteenth century and at the opening of the twentieth, advocates of the Social Gospel were unwilling to rely on individual conversion alone to bring about the social change the nation required.[71]

Like postmillennialist thinking more generally, the Social Gospel also drew confidence from the increasingly apparent advance of science, with its ever more apparent practical applications. Josiah Strong, another of the movement's major figures, observed that "Science, which is a revelation of God's laws and methods, enables us to fall into his plans intentionally and to co-operate with him intelligently for the perfecting of mankind, thus hastening forward the coming of the kingdom."[72] The divinely decreed end was inevitable; but it was urgent nonetheless to work for its achievement. Postmillennialism united ideas of human progress with the symbols of the apocalypse.[73] Both the content and the rhetoric of the Social Gospel reflected the combination.

The movement continued to gain momentum even as the American economy returned to a trajectory of sustained but irregular growth in the early years of the new century. A wave of popular literature brought Social Gospel ideas to many Americans who were not regular churchgoers, or whose own ministers perhaps displayed less enthusiasm. Charles Sheldon's novel *In His Steps,* published in 1896, traced out what happened in a fictional town after the local minister persuaded his congregation to take no action for an entire year without first asking themselves "What would Jesus do?" The book eventually sold more than fifty million copies, and well over a century later Sheldon's arresting question still appears on bracelets and bumper stickers throughout America.[74] Other Social Gospel novels, like *The Inside of the Cup* and *The Dwelling-Place of Light,* written by Winston Churchill (an American cousin of the British prime minister of later years), likewise reached a broad public.

By the time of World War I, the Social Gospel had gained sufficient acceptance among mainline American Protestants for Walter Rauschenbusch, then just fifty-six but only a year from the end of his life, to write that it had become "no longer a prophetic and occasional note." It was now unfamiliar only in "backward" communities. The Social Gospel had become orthodox. "All those social groups which distinctly face toward the future," he proudly claimed, clearly showed "their need and craving for a social interpretation and application of Christianity." He went on to reaffirm the movement's core belief that "The establishment of a community of righteousness in mankind is just as much a saving act of God as the salvation of an individual from his natural selfishness and moral inability."[75] In time Rauschenbusch's confidence proved overly optimistic. But it was a fair representation of the growing consensus of the day.

With the beginning of the twentieth century, the Social Gospel movement's momentum took institutional form as well. In 1904 Washington Gladden became moderator of the National Council of Congregational Churches. In 1908 a group of clergy drawn from thirty-three Protestant denominations, with collectively eighteen million members, formed a Federal Council of Churches (in 1950 renamed the National Council of Churches).[76] The group represented most of the so-called mainline denominations, though not typically those that identified themselves as evangelical. Advancing the Social Gospel stood at the center of the new organization's agenda.

That meant putting religious principles into daily application, in the economic sphere no less than elsewhere. The driving impetus for change was to be the nation's Protestant churches, but everyone understood that implementing these ideas would require an active economic policy carried out by government. In his 1907 book, *Christianity and the Social Crisis,* Rauschenbusch had urged churches to establish kindergartens (another German innovation), playgrounds, children's centers, and other educational facilities; but he doubted whether the churches had the financial base to accomplish even these limited ends, much less effect the broadly based economic redistribution he thought necessary. The task was one for public policy.

The official report of the new FCC's first meeting prominently embraced Social Gospel thinking. "Rich and poor, capitalist and laboring man, are not classifications and distinctions made by the Church of Christ," the group declared. "It is the Church of America which must deal with the social and industrial problems of America." The centerpiece of the agenda was that "practice must be made to conform to the essential standards of the Gospel, which are themselves the highest ideals of social righteousness." The focus was on what should be, not what was, and there was no excuse for passivity in the face of harmful inequality. "Multitudes are deprived, by what are called economic laws, of that opportunity to which every man has a right. When automatic movements cause injustice and disaster, the autonomy should be destroyed."[77] Different strands of Christianity had been adopting religious creeds for nearly two thousand years. In 1912, the FCC formally adopted a new *social* creed, earlier endorsed by the Methodists—now called The Social Creed of the Churches—stating just these principles.

The new Social Creed was a statement of principles. What specific, concrete steps public policy should pursue to achieve them was a question for the discipline of political economy—now increasingly just called "economics."

Economics for
Social Improvement

The ultimate end of political economy is not, as is generally assumed, the mere quantitative increase of wealth. Society, as an organic unit, has a higher economic end.

—JOHN BATES CLARK

Some earnest men have formed the American Economic Association, to investigate problems of social science, in order thereby to contribute to human progress.

—RICHARD T. ELY

The Gospel of Wealth and the Social Gospel: by the end of the nineteenth century, American religious thinking offered two competing visions for the nation's economy and how—more fundamentally, whether—public policy should guide it. Each reflected a powerful postmillennial sense of mission for the future, viewing material improvement as a necessary foundation enabling mankind's spiritual advance. Each recognized a special role for America to lead the way on this journey, both materially and spiritually. But the two movements translated their shared aspiration into concrete terms differently, especially on questions of power and decision making in the economy.

The difference in economic thinking was not a matter of liberal versus conservative theology, nor of disagreement over traditional doctrinal issues like depravity and predestination.[1] The Unitarians, for example—before the Civil War the most theologically liberal of the country's major Protestant denominations—mostly preached the Gospel of Wealth during much of this period, and they did so in language reflecting an economic elitism even greater than among other churches that expressed similar views.[2] Moreover, while advocates of the Gospel of Wealth and of the Social Gospel agreed that material prosperity was essential if mankind was to achieve spiritual progress, their respective ideas about how to achieve that prosperity—in particular how to enable the broad majority of America's citizens to share in the nation's growing wealth and, on that basis, join in the spiritual progress that it fostered—nonetheless differed sharply. So too, therefore, did the implications of their thinking for economics.

Proponents of the Gospel of Wealth saw private initiative as the principal source of economic advance, and therefore of progress in civilization as well. Prominent spokesmen like Henry Ward Beecher and Russell Conwell urged their followers to start businesses and create wealth. They embraced the myriad efforts of the nation's churches— hospitals, orphanages, shelters, provision of food and clothing to the needy—aimed at relieving whatever human suffering private wealth creation temporarily failed to eliminate. Other forms of economic initiative, however, by either government or workers, they saw only as impediments. As labor unrest began to develop in the late 1870s, Beecher offered a spirited opposition to calls for regulation of either hours or working conditions. "The liberty of the individual is destroyed where men are not allowed to work when they please, where they please, as long as they please," he argued. He similarly opposed any attempt to introduce European-style labor unions in the United States, declaring that "The importation into America of European emissaries and European theories and European methods for the relief of labor I look upon as an importation of abominations." More generally, "'Hands off!' we say to government. 'See to it that we are protected in our rights and in our individuality, but do not go a step further than that.'"[3]

Washington Gladden and Walter Rauschenbusch, and their growing cohort of followers in the Social Gospel movement, had no such reservations. Rauschenbusch was explicit in rejecting the deference that placed private companies above the reach of government regulation. "A private business that employs thousands of people, uses the natural resources of the nation, enjoys exemptions and privileges at law, and is essential to the welfare of great communities, is not a private business," he declared. "It is public, and the sooner we abandon the fiction that it is private, the better for our good sense."[4] The era's antitrust legislation—beginning with the Sherman Act of 1890, which has provided the principal basis of U.S. antitrust law ever since, and reinforced by the Clayton Act and the creation of the Federal Trade Commission, both in 1914—was a concrete expression of this sentiment. So was the wave of "trust-busting" litigation initiated by Theodore Roosevelt. The Social Gospel movement likewise supported efforts to create an organized labor movement, and in time the Federal Council of Churches found broad areas of cooperation with the nation's rapidly expanding trade unions.

Importantly for the development of the field of economics, at just this time two other influences—one organizational, the other methodological—were also reshaping the subject as an intellectual discipline. In the latter half of the nineteenth century, the social sciences in the United States began to emulate the professionalization that these disciplines had already achieved a generation or more before in Europe, especially in Germany.[5] The motivation, in part, was to reestablish intellectual authority following the popular democratization that had swept through so many areas of American life a half-century earlier.[6]

In 1865 scholars from a variety of subject areas had formed the American Social Science Association. Two decades later, what had been closely allied lines of inquiry within this broad umbrella began to go their separate ways. In 1884 historians from across the country founded the American Historical Association. (George Bancroft served as the group's second president.) The following year a group met in Saratoga Springs, New York, to create the American Economic Association, recognizing that what practitioners now increasingly labeled "economics" was not merely a part of what had been political economy.[7] In turn, other groups of social scientists soon went on to found similarly named associations: for political science, for sociology, and for anthropology. Each new organization was separate from the others, and each has continued since then as the flagship organization for its discipline in the United States.

In a reflection of the same movement toward intellectual professionalization, American universities were then beginning to organize their faculties into divisions and departments along subject-based lines. By 1890 Chicago, Columbia, Harvard, Johns Hopkins, Michigan, Pennsylvania, Princeton, Wisconsin, and Yale all had recognizable departments of economics. A century and a quarter later, they remain among the country's leading centers of teaching and research in the field. A further expression of professionalization was the establishment of dedicated scholarly journals as outlets for new thinking. In 1886 economists at Harvard began publishing *The Quarterly Journal of Economics,* and those at Chicago followed with the *Journal of Political Economy* (still using the older name for the discipline) in 1892. Both remain today among the top journals in the field. Early in the new century the American Economic Association launched its own journal, *The American Economic Review,* which over time became preeminent.

The methodological revolution was the introduction of mathematics, not yet in explicit equations and symbols—that would come later—but as a conceptual framework for economic analysis.[8] Adam Smith's loose notion of the "effort of every man to better his condition" now became a more formal assumption that households act to maximize their well-being, and that firms maximize their profits, subject to the prices they face (importantly including wages as the price of labor) and whatever other constraints the market presents. Within this more explicit framework of optimization, economic decisions were now portrayed as pursuing some activity, such as buying goods for households or hiring workers for firms, to the point at which the value of the next unit bought, or the next worker hired, just balanced the market cost. Households would buy any particular good until the "marginal value" of their having it equaled the price they had to pay for it, and firms would hire workers until the "marginal product" of their labor equaled the going wage. Firms likewise would produce for sale until the "marginal cost" of making their product equaled the price they could charge for it in the market. Each of these so-called marginal relations was no more than the standard mathematical condition for some form of optimization. Recognizing them as such revolutionized economic analysis.

By the late nineteenth century, economics was a sufficiently mature discipline that its susceptibility to influence from the broader culture of the society at large no longer extended to basic theoretical concepts in the way it had in Adam Smith's time, or even Francis Wayland's. The scope for influence stemming from the set of external attitudes and presumptions that economic thinkers brought to their work—their worldview in Einstein's phrase, their preanalytic Vision in Schumpeter's—was now more a matter of application and method. Smith's fundamental insight into the competitive market mechanism remained the conceptual backbone of the discipline, and it now acquired the expanded analytic capacity provided by the mathematics of the marginalist revolution. But to what end? At this level, the religious thinking of the day continued to exert a strong influence.

And, in light of the deep division that now marked American Protestantism, which line of religious thinking? Beecher, Conwell, William Lawrence, and others who preached the Gospel of Wealth assumed that existing economic and political institutions, relying on largely unrestricted markets for both goods and labor, delivered the maximum benefit, and to the broadest public interest, that economic activity could achieve. Total income and wealth nationwide, not just in America but in Britain and some western European countries as well, had reached levels never before seen. These clergymen believed, as Andrew Carnegie had argued and was demonstrating through his own philanthropy, that the increasingly unequal distribution of the fruits of the economy's production was merely a temporary phenomenon that empowered those who were financially successful, with their demonstrated superior administrative and other abilities, to act as trustees on behalf of their fellow citizens. People should therefore seek to earn economic success on their own, as best they could. Government should stand back and let them achieve it when and where they could.

By contrast, Social Gospel thinkers like Gladden and Rauschenbusch regarded the highly unequal distribution of individual incomes and wealth, and the differential command that this skewed distribution created over the economy's resources and over political influence in what was supposed to be a democracy, not as an annoying side phenomenon but the center of the story. The protracted economic depression of the 1880s and early 1890s only deepened their concerns. In their eyes the material hardships imposed by economic inequality, and even more so pathologies like extreme poverty and the exploitation of labor to which it gave rise, were an outright violation of religious principles as well as a threat to the stability of any democratic society. While the Gospel of Wealth justified a laissez-faire stance for government in the economic sphere, the Social Gospel called for state intervention. The federal government had already become an important driver of initiatives in many other areas of the nation's life, ranging from abolition of slavery to the creation of public land-grant universities (even though once established they were then under the control of the various states) to the building of railroads that now spanned the continent. Why not in the economy as well?

Some economists of the time took intellectual positions consistent with Gospel of Wealth thinking. Arthur Latham Perry, a professor of history and political economy at Williams, wrote in his 1891 textbook of "The fine old Bentham principle of laissez-faire, which most English thinkers for a century past have regarded as established forever in the nature of man and in God's plans of providence and government." Perry's was not the era's dominant strain of thinking, however, at least not among the new generation of economists, and he went on to complain that his contemporaries who had recently founded the profession's new association were casting laissez-faire principles aside.[9]

The men (no women were present) who gathered at Saratoga Springs in September 1885 to found the American Economic Association were predominantly followers of the Social Gospel movement. Washington Gladden was among the group.[10] Many of the others had seriously considered entering the ministry before deciding to pursue economics instead. Many had written books or articles about religion and the church before they took up writing about economics. Their religious understanding formed a central part of their sense of the world in which they lived. Their eagerness now to form a new organization for economists reflected the broader professionalization of the social sciences that was then under way in America, but it was also a response to the increasingly evident trauma of the ongoing economic depression.

Social Gospel leaders like Gladden and Rauschenbusch looked to government to redress the moral wrongs inherent in the country's prevailing economic situation, but they had little to say about just what policies the government should adopt. That was a matter for the new science of economics, and it was a challenge that the founders of the new association took up within the worldview that the Social Gospel of their time imparted to them. Economics was a field of inquiry well worth undertaking for its own sake. Applied to addressing the nation's economic difficulties, it was also morally instrumental, showing the route to the material prosperity that was essential for moral advance.

.   .   .

Their foremost intellectual leader was John Bates Clark. Descended from an old New England family—two of his great-grandfathers had fought in the American Revolution—Clark grew up in Providence, Rhode Island, and attended Amherst College. His father's illness forced him to leave college for several years to run the family business, however, and he was twenty-five by the time he graduated. He had intended after college to enter the Yale Divinity School to study for the Congregational ministry. But in his senior year he encountered economics, which Julius Seelye, a Dutch Reformed minister, taught as a branch of Mental and Moral Philosophy.[11] (After serving a term as a U.S. congressman, a few years after Clark graduated, Seelye returned to Amherst as the college's president; he also served as president of the Congregational Home Missionary Society.) Under Seelye's influence, Clark abandoned his plans for the ministry and instead chose economics.

In the early post–Civil War decades American universities were not yet prepared to offer graduate-level instruction, but many of those in Europe, and in Germany in particular, were. Clark therefore went abroad for graduate study, first in Heidelberg, then Zurich, and then back to Heidelberg. The formative influence on his thinking was studying under Karl Knies, one of the founding figures in the then dominant German historical school of economics.[12] Closely aligned with nineteenth-century trends in liberal Protestantism within Germany, the historical school placed human institutions at center stage in accounting for political and social developments including those in the economic sphere. Human behavior was subject to influence from the environment in which people lived, above all from their material environment and the legal and social institutions that societies put in place. The key implication was to reject any deterministic view that social outcomes, either past or present, were inevitable. Rather, human outcomes were the consequence of human action, and therefore within the scope of human effort to change.[13] Such thinking had implicitly underpinned much of the reformist activity in America throughout the nineteenth century, including the temperance movement and the high value placed on education. Clark's work in economics reflected this set of fundamental presumptions.

After returning to America in 1875, but then losing more than a year to illness, Clark taught for twenty years at a series of institutions (including Amherst) before becoming a professor at Columbia, where he then remained for nearly three more decades. He was one of the principal founders of the American Economic Association, and he served as one of the organization's early presidents. Working in parallel with Stanley Jevons and Alfred Marshall in England, and Léon Walras in France, he was also the foremost American contributor to the marginalist revolution in economic methodology. More generally, Clark was the first American to gain recognition as an original economic theorist, not just a follower of ideas developed abroad or a knowledgeable applied thinker about practical economic problems at home.[14]

The early influence of Clark's introduction to the field under his teacher Seelye, together with his exposure to the ideas of the German historical school, proved durable. In his book titled *The Philosophy of Wealth,* Clark was open about the religious basis of his economic thinking. "The church," he wrote, "diffuses the spiritual impulses that are communicated to it; and while this work still has, as its chief end, the moulding of character itself, it has, as a secondary end, the improvement of the economic relations of men." Echoing the view that Gladden and other proponents of the Social Gospel were then beginning to set forth, he was also explicit about the role that he looked to the church to play in this regard. "The church wields a primary force in the new economic system, and is, to that extent, an arbiter of men's earthly fortunes." Not only was this role in the economy consistent with the church's traditional spiritual purpose, the two reinforced one another. While the church "may hasten the advent of earthly peace by gathering men more rapidly into its spiritual fold," he explained, "it may also hasten the spiritual work by promoting outward harmony" in earthly affairs. "For the sake of every interest entrusted to its keeping the church is called upon to use the economic power entrusted to it."[15]

Just as he embraced an economic role for the church, Clark defended a role for spiritual concerns in the study of economics. Notwithstanding his position as the leading American contributor to the marginalist revolution, with its more formal mode of analysis, he resisted any attempt to narrow the scope of the field by excluding important human dimensions that might be difficult to fit within the new mathematical framework. In *The Philosophy of Wealth* he expressed his concern that the image of man that economists were now constructing as the object of their discussion "may or may not resemble the man whom God has created"; in his view, "the latter only is the true subject of political economy." Anticipating criticisms of economic thinking that became far more prevalent a century later (and that persist today), he complained that "The assumed man is too mechanical and too selfish to correspond with the reality." Men and women, as God created them, were human in all respects. "What is true of a laboring machine requiring only to be housed and clothed, and to be fed . . . will certainly not be altogether true of a laboring *man* in modern society."[16]

What was particularly missing from any such bare-bones mathematical representation, Clark worried, was the value men and women attach to their personal sense of moral worth, what Adam Smith had called praise-worthiness. For Clark, "in the last analysis the sense of right in men is a supreme motive." This inborn desire for moral worth often ran counter to people's material objectives, and so it was important for economists' theorizing to take it into account. "The desire for personal worthiness opposes self-interest as an equal antagonist," he maintained. "Under the influence of such motives, man can never be a being striving solely for personal advantage, and society can never be wholly given over to an ignoble scramble for profit."[17] It followed that any economic theory that excluded intangible considerations like the desire to do what is morally right was at best incomplete.

The direction in which Clark proceeded from this insight paralleled Gladden's (and later Rauschenbusch's) call for the church to focus not just on individuals but on the society in which they lived. Reflecting the thinking of the German historical school that he had absorbed as a graduate student at Heidelberg, Clark grounded his argument in the belief that the conditions of society shape individuals' attitudes and behavior. Influences stemming from society as a whole, he explained, were capable of transforming individual nature. An individual man or woman became "higher and better" by being a part of a well-designed society. Best of all, under the right conditions men's "higher wants"—including the ingredients of "intellectual, aesthetic and moral growth"—could expand without bound, resulting in "a limitless outlet for productive energy." There was no reason, therefore, to anticipate the kind of stationary state about which John Stuart Mill and others had theorized earlier in the century. In Clark's evaluation, the extent to which this limitless human energy is utilized was "the gauge of genuine economic progress."[18]

More than any other human institution, Clark saw the church as able to establish the conditions needed to bring about this genuine economic progress, and foremost among those conditions was a more just and equal distribution of what the economy produced. "The securing of the greatest quantity, the highest quality, and the most equitable distribution of wealth is the rational goal of economic society," he declared. He readily acknowledged that there might be a trade-off among these ends, but if so the price was worth paying. "A better division of the results of industry might atone for some diminution in the amount produced," he argued.[19] The guiding principle was that "the ultimate end of political economy is not, as is generally assumed, the mere quantitative increase of wealth. Society, as an organic unit, has a higher economic end." And, as both Gladden and Rauschenbusch repeatedly emphasized, a key reason the problem remained unsolved was that "Religion has held itself too much aloof from this particular work."[20]

With time, Clark's ideas continued to advance along these lines. By the outset of World War I, he thought the case for government intervention in the nation's economic affairs required little elaboration. "The rule that would bid the State keep its hands off the entire field of business, the extreme *laissez-faire* policy once dominant in literature and thought, now finds few persons bold enough to advocate it or foolish enough to believe in it," he observed. Mere creation of wealth was not sufficient. The primary goal was instead to "Develop in these economic contests the sense of justice—let both parties seek to follow a rule of right—and men's hearts, at least, will not need to be embittered."[21]

With the proper intervention by government, Clark believed, the "capacity for further improvement" was "in sight," and the opportunities it provided were enormous. From his postmillennialist perspective, he welcomed those opportunities in openly scriptural language. "We may build a new earth out of the difficult material we have to work with," he wrote, "and cause justice and kindness to rule in the very place where strife now holds sway." With the right guidance, "A New Jerusalem may actually rise out of the fierce contentions of the modern market. The wrath of men may praise God and his Kingdom may come, not in spite of, but by means of the contests of the economic sphere."[22] Economics, properly conceived and implemented, was the route to the millennium.

. . .

Richard T. Ely, more than anyone else the person responsible for establishing the American Economic Association, came from a background similar to Clark's. Born to a family of strict Presbyterians, Ely concluded early on that predestinarian doctrine made God too absolute and left too little to human will. Although troubled by his family's distress at his rejection of their strongly held beliefs, he briefly considered the Universalist ministry and then became an Episcopalian.[23] His early attitude toward these contrasting religious outlooks turned out to be indicative of his intellectual orientation more generally, including his approach to economics. In his professional thinking as well as his personal beliefs, Ely resisted any kind of determinism, emphasizing instead the capacity of human agency to shape not only individuals' spiritual destiny but conditions in the material world.[24]

Ely's education took an indirect route as well. He began as an undergraduate at Dartmouth, but had to withdraw from college when his father lost his job in the economic crisis of 1873. He then finished his undergraduate education at Columbia, where he could attend without any tuition obligation and minimize other expenses by living with an uncle in New York City.[25] Like Clark, he then went to Germany for graduate training. At first he studied philosophy at the university in Halle, long known as a center of the Pietist movement within the Lutheran Church. But after a short time he decided to take up economics and political science. He therefore moved to Heidelberg where he too studied under Karl Knies and absorbed the anti-deterministic ideas of the German historical school.[26]

Even more so than for Clark, the emphasis on human institutions and their influence on individual behavior, and via that behavior on social outcomes, became central to Ely's worldview, and it shaped his approach to economics throughout his career.[27] Laissez-faire thinking, to his mind, was just as opposed to moral freedom as predestination. It was a surrender to yet another form of determinism—in this case, the determinism of the market under whatever economic institutions happened to be in place—and on that ground he opposed it. There was no reason to allow the institutions that had grown up in the past to govern the present, much less the future. He instead saw the economic condition of society as the outcome of human decisions and human actions. The key implication was that people bear a moral responsibility for how they and their fellow citizens live.

In contrast to Clark, however, Ely's interest was in practical application, not theory. His ambition for his chosen discipline was that it actively identify real problems and contribute to solving them. Laissez-faire economics, he believed, was an impediment to achieving those aims. The statement of principles that he wrote, providing the initial impetus for the creation of the American Economic Association, flatly declared, "we hold that the doctrine of *laissez-faire* is unsafe in politics and unsound in morals." What was the alternative? Ely's answer was action by government: "We regard the state as an educational and ethical agency whose positive aid is an indispensable condition of human progress."[28] Some years later, he wrote that "God works through the State in carrying out His purposes more universally than through any other institution."[29]

Ely completed his PhD work at Heidelberg, and after a year of further study in Berlin he returned to the United States. In 1881 he joined the faculty of the recently founded Johns Hopkins University (where one of his graduate students was Woodrow Wilson). Inspired by the example of a colleague there who had taken the lead in establishing the American Historical Association the year before, in 1885 Ely launched the initiative that led to the founding of the American Economic Association.[30] Working with a small committee that included both academic economists and others—Washington Gladden was part of this initial group too—he drafted the statement of principles for the larger group that he then brought together at Saratoga Springs to create the new association. He then served as the organization's secretary for the first seven years of its existence, and some years later he became its president.

Along the way, Ely also brought his organizational energy to bear in advancing his religious interests. In 1891 he helped to organize the Christian Social Union of the American Episcopal Church, and two years later he and several associates founded the American Institute of Christian Sociology to provide lecture-based summer programs for both laymen and the clergy. He frequently contributed articles to *Christian Union* magazine, of which Henry Ward Beecher had earlier served as editor, and he was especially active as a lecturer in the Chautauqua movement, both at the society's annual summer program and in other venues. (His economics textbook, which eventually became the leading economics text in the United States, with more than a million copies sold, originated as the book for his Chautauqua summer course and was first published by Chautauqua Press.) Over time, Ely became one of the leading lay spokesmen for the Social Gospel, and his books were part of the required training for ministers in several denominations including both the Methodists and the Episcopalians.[31]

In 1892 Ely moved from Johns Hopkins to the University of Wisconsin, as director of the university's School of Economics, Political Science, and History. He soon began to assemble around himself a group of economists and other scholars committed to the institutional and historical approach to economics that he had seen in Germany. The effort did not pass without opposition. Two years after Ely's arrival at Wisconsin, Oliver Wells, the state superintendent of public instruction (and therefore an ex officio member of the university's Board of Regents), wrote an open letter in *The Nation* accusing him of supporting strikes and boycotts, seeking to justify physical attacks on both people and property, and otherwise advocating socialism and even anarchism. In his letter, Wells called for Ely's removal from the university's faculty. After holding public hearings on the matter, however, the board instead exonerated Ely and censured Wells, issuing a strong defense of freedom of speech in the academy. (Ely's most prominent student among economists, John R. Commons, who likewise became a leading academic spokesman for the Social Gospel, encountered similar difficulties. Commons was fired from the University of Indiana, and then Syracuse, and finally came to join Ely at Wisconsin where after Ely retired he led the school's efforts in institutional economics until well into the 1930s.[32])

Ely remained at Wisconsin for more than three decades, and during much of this period he was the university's most widely known faculty member. The institutional approach to economics that he instilled there continued to distinguish the university for the next two generations. In the 1920s he and the group of economists and other scholars he had assembled served as a private think tank for Wisconsin's reformist Senator Robert La Folette Sr., especially during La Folette's run for president on the Progressive Party ticket in 1924.

.   .   .

Ely's personal religious commitment remained firm through his successive changes in denominational affiliation. The statement of principles that he drafted for the proposed American Economic Association declared, "We hold that the conflict of labor and capital has brought to the front a vast number of social problems whose solution is impossible without the united efforts of Church, state and science."[33] In 1889, not long after spearheading that effort and while he was still teaching at Johns Hopkins, he published two books: *Social Aspects of Christianity* and *An Introduction to Political Economy*. The respective titles suggested that one was a tract on religion, specifically the Social Gospel, while the other might be a conventional economics textbook.[34] In fact the two were intertwined, with significant elements of economic thinking entering the book on Christianity while Ely's religious attitudes importantly shaped his economic thinking.

In both books, however, Ely made clear his goal for economics to broaden from an endeavor oriented primarily toward describing and analyzing existing economic relations to one also concerned with improving them. In part, the change he sought would be a return to Adam Smith's motivation, in *The Wealth of Nations*, not merely to present his insights into the competitive market mechanism but on that basis to indicate how a country like eighteenth-century Britain could achieve a higher standard of living. But Smith's recipe had been largely a matter of what *not* to do—no monopolies, no interference with foreign trade, no guilds to restrict who could do what work—and his American followers like Francis Wayland had largely followed that approach. Under the influence of America's late-nineteenth-century Social Gospel movement, Ely now sought to give economics a more active, interventionist orientation, seeking out positive steps by which public policy, implemented *by government,* could improve on the status quo. The origins of individual economic suffering in particular were subject not just to analysis but correction.

But Ely's opposition to laissez-faire economics was also consistent with his desire for *the church* to take on a significant role in fostering the improvement society needed. Agreeing with Gladden, and later Rauschenbusch, he was firm that "The Church must gain leadership" in addressing the country's economic challenges.[35] Ely saw the Social Gospel movement as a continuation of the reformist tendency in American Protestantism that dated to the founding of the republic, and that had manifested itself earlier in the nineteenth century in the church's involvement in promoting abolition, temperance, education, literacy, and missionary work both at home and abroad. In light of that rich reformist tradition, he was frustrated by the tendency of the Protestant churches of his own day to accept the status quo as inevitable and immutable. The church, he complained, had in recent years "contented herself with repeating platitudes and vague generalities which have disturbed no guilty soul, and thus she has allowed the leadership in social science to slip away from her."[36] Laissez-faire thinking, in his judgment, was in large part to blame for this moral abdication.[37]

Ely laid out the new desired orientation for the discipline of economics most directly in *Social Aspects of Christianity*, bluntly asking, "Why should economic science concern itself with what ought to be?" (as opposed to merely analyzing what is). His solidly nonpredestinarian answer was that "The germs of a better future always exist in the present, but they require careful nursing"; contrary to what proponents of laissez-faire assumed, "They do not develop spontaneously." Emphasizing the role of human choice and agency, he argued that the economic life of man was to a large extent the product of the human will. Moreover, because material prosperity was the foundation of spiritual progress, as both the Social Gospel and the Gospel of Wealth proclaimed, economists had a positive obligation to show how to achieve that prosperity. "The categorical imperative of duty enforces upon each rational being perfection 'after his kind,'" Ely declared, and "the economic life is the basis of growth of all the human faculties."[38]

Squarely in step with the Social Gospel movement, Ely pointed to the distribution of income and wealth as the specific problem most in need of economists' attention. "With the inventions and discoveries of modern times," he wrote, "we seem almost to have solved the problem of production: but the problem of an ideal distribution of products still awaits a satisfactory solution."[39] Like Clark, he both understood and accepted that it might be necessary to sacrifice some production to achieve a more desirable distribution.[40] "To show that a practical measure will create wealth is not enough to recommend it," he argued. "The main question is, What effect will it have on the entire life of the nation, also of humanity?"[41]

The goal for economists, therefore, was clear: to achieve "such a production and such a distribution of economic goods as must in the highest practicable degree subserve the end and purpose of human existence for all members of society." That ideal combination of production and distribution would be different from what currently prevailed. But it would be "in harmony with the ethical ideal of Christianity," and for Ely this was what mattered most. "The true starting-point in economic discussions," he wrote, "is the ethical community, of which the individual is a member." Washington Gladden was already preaching (and would soon write, in *Tools and the Man*) about the harmful effects of extreme inequality on both the rich and the poor. Ely similarly lamented that present conditions within society did not satisfy the demands of ethics. "On the one hand, we see those who are injured by a superfluity of economic goods; and on the other, those who have not the material basis on which to build the best possible superstructure." The result, in both cases, was a "waste of man."[42]

Ely fully understood that paying low wages to workers, or even forcing them to work under blatantly exploitative conditions, might be a spur to greater production. As John Bates Clark and his fellow marginalists had shown, with a lower wage—that is, a lower marginal cost of labor—employers would optimally take on more workers (up to the point that, with greater output, their marginal product declined to the level of the lower wage). But like Clark, Ely believed that accepting less production in exchange for an improved distribution was a trade worth making. "It is argued that low wages increase possible production," he acknowledged. "Even if this be so, such wages diminish the power of the recipients to participate in the advantages of existing civilization, and consequently defeat the end and purpose of all production." And the conclusion applied more broadly than just to wages. "Child labor, female labor, and excessive hours of labor, fall under the same condemnation."[43]

For Ely, these concerns were not peripheral; they were central to what economics *should be* about. "The essential characteristic of the new political economy," he stated, "is the relation it endeavors to establish between ethics and economic life." Indeed, "it is precisely in our economic life that ethical principles of any real validity must manifest themselves." The goal, therefore, was for economists' intellectual efforts to be "brought into harmony with the great religious, political, and social movements which characterize this age." The key to achieving that alignment was a new conception of social ethics, which "places society above the individual, because the whole is more than any of its parts."[44] Either Gladden or Rauschenbusch could have penned the same sentences.

This was also the purpose for which Ely and his colleagues, just a few years before, had established the new organization to promote their field. As he later described the initiative, "Some earnest men have formed the American Economic Association, to investigate problems of social science, in order thereby to contribute to human progress." The purpose of the new association, he explained, was "to study seriously the second of the two great commandments on which hang all the law and the prophets, in all its ramifications, and thus to bring science to the aid of Christianity."[45] His reference was to Jesus's saying, as reported in the Gospel according to Matthew, "Thou shalt love the Lord thy God with all thy heart, and with all thy soul, and with all thy mind. This is the first and great commandment. And the second is like unto it, Thou shalt love thy neighbor as thyself. On these two commandments hang all the law and the prophets."[46] The explicitly stated project of bringing economics to the aid of Christianity was reflected in the presence of twenty-three Protestant ministers (again including Gladden) among the association's 181 original members.[47]

Just as he considered what the study of economics should be about in his book on Christianity, Ely did not hesitate to write about religion in his economics text. In *An Introduction to Political Economy* he observed that "the economic activity of civilized man is, to-day, chiefly social." As a result, "we are not concerned merely with the material life of men in its narrow sense, for there can scarcely be a phase of the life of society which does not come within the province of the economist." And for purposes of that broad aspiration for his field of study, "Christianity offers us our highest conception of a society which embraces all men, and in that conception sets us a goal toward which we must ever move."[48]

Following Smith and other thinkers of the Enlightenment, Ely grounded this focus on *society* in the basic fact of humans' economic dependence on one another. Further, he argued, this interdependence had deepened as the economy had changed over the hundred-plus years since Smith's time: "*This economic dependence of man upon man thus increases with the progress of industrial civilization*" (his italics). But dependence of any kind could be either healthy—as Pufendorf,

Hume, and Smith all thought regarding the economic dependence that brought humans together in a society—or not. Ely thought the difference hinged on at least some rough degree of equality in the resulting economic relations, and he expressed this idea too in religious language. "When the dependence of one person upon another takes the form of mutual obligation between equals in strength, it is often not felt as a hardship at all," he noted. "It was evidently meant by the Governor of the universe that man should seek union with his fellows. This is his salvation."[49] The chief implication for the field of economics was again that the distribution of society's economic product, not just its aggregate total, was what economists should study and seek to improve.

Importantly for the future direction of the still evolving field, Ely went beyond merely exhorting his fellow economists to add an ameliorative dimension to their descriptive and analytical work. By the latter decades of the nineteenth century, systematic statistical data—on production, prices, trade flows, employment, and a wide variety of other dimensions of economic activity—were increasingly becoming available, in the United States, in Britain, and in many other countries as well.[50] For purposes of simply understanding the basic facts, economists were therefore able to go well beyond the crude, in retrospect often merely anecdotal, information on which Smith and Malthus and others of their time had relied. The availability of better data, ranging across so many aspects of economic behavior, now spurred economists to look more carefully for documentable regularities that might either support or disconfirm their theories. But Ely also saw in this new form of inquiry an opportunity to think systematically about how to *improve* economic conditions as well.

Drawing on his graduate training in the thinking of the German historical school, Ely now suggested for this purpose a new methodology based on the use of explicit cross-country comparison as a way to gain a deeper understanding of whatever behavior was under study, as well as to introduce the possibility of deliberate ameliorative intervention. "We can observe certain regularities and tendencies in all social phenomena," he wrote. What should economists conclude from them? When people observed that many of the social phenomena that mattered appeared to recur regularly, year after year, "a feeling akin to fatalism arose, and some statisticians were inclined to look upon these

regularities as . . . beyond the control of man." But such an attitude contradicted Ely's worldview in a number of ways: not just the lessons of
his graduate education but likewise his non-predestinarian sense of the
possibilities for human agency and his postmillennialist aspiration for
improvement, both of which were characteristic of intellectual circles
in America in his day more generally. In Ely's hands, data-based cross-
country comparison came to the rescue. A deeper inquiry, he pointed
out, revealed differences in these regularities between one country and
another. And still further analysis showed that these differences "could
be brought about by the action of man."[51]

In this methodological aspect of his work, Ely's approach not only
drew on the economics he had learned in Germany but also mirrored parallel contemporary developments in biblical studies. In the
nineteenth century, German scholars had led the way in what came
to be known as "higher biblical criticism"—using close philological
study to understand scriptural texts as human-written, even if divinely
inspired, and therefore as reflections of the time and place in which
they originated. The leader in this effort was Julius Wellhausen, a professor successively at several German universities and also the son of a
Lutheran pastor. Wellhausen's book *The History of Israel,* which created
an immediate sensation, was first published in 1878 when Ely was a student at Heidelberg.[52] The best known aspect of Wellhausen's hypothesis
(still familiar today, although by now much elaborated by subsequent
scholarship) was the identification, from literary and lexical evidence
in the texts themselves, of four separate components of what became
the Pentateuch, attributed to different groups writing at different periods, and assembled only later into the first five books of the Hebrew
Bible as we have them today.[53]

The historical and institutional approach to economics that Karl
Knies and others of his school were pursuing during Ely's years of
study at Heidelberg emphasized the same kind of new, empirically
based orientation. The guiding principle was that there were few or no
universal economic regularities, valid at all times and in all places. Economic behavior, like every other aspect of human life, was conditional
on the prevailing social arrangements. The methodology that Ely now
advocated, comparing specific economic outcomes across different
countries with their distinct laws and other institutions, reflected this
empirical and institutional orientation.[54]

The concrete example that Ely used to illustrate his point was smuggling. "Self-interest induces some men to smuggle, but induces others not to smuggle," he wrote. "We observe the proportion between smugglers and non-smugglers. Now let us change the laws. . . . Lo! The proportion between smugglers and non-smugglers has changed." In short, human institutions, subject to deliberate political choice—in this example, laws regarding tariffs, border enforcement, and punishment of smugglers when apprehended—mattered for economic behavior. Self-interest was presumably always present, but it was not a constant force. Along with individual motives, the prevailing laws and institutions shaped how those motives turned into action.[55] (An economist today would put it differently: self-interest may be a constant force, but the way in which that force directs individual behavior depends on existing conditions and constraints. But the point is the same.) Conceiving as universal those regularities that are in fact fundamentally contingent was a scientific error. And when the contingency that matters rests on human choices, disregarding the possibility of change was a moral failing.

Here too, Ely's thinking in large part amounted to reintroducing—but also showing how to make scientifically operational—insights that Smith, and Hume as well, had emphasized right at the inception of modern economics. While he placed at center stage the universal and unending desire on individuals' part to better their condition, Smith also consistently highlighted the importance of laws and institutions, repeatedly drawing out their role in shaping incentives. Hume too acknowledged that "as 'tis impossible to change or correct anything material in our nature, the utmost we can do is to change our circumstances and situation."[56]

In Ely's time and milieu, both Washington Gladden and Walter Rauschenbusch likewise emphasized the role of the society in which people lived, including especially the economic relations it imposed on them, in shaping their individual behavior for better or worse. This was the basis for their thinking that sin was collective as well as individual, including in economic behavior, and therefore for their seeking changes in the structure of society in order to elevate humanity both materially and spiritually. Gladden had vigorously argued that some social institutions "promote the worth and goodness of men" while others "discourage personal worth and goodness."[57] Now Ely was offering a concrete way to determine which was which. Which laws and government policies led to smuggling, and which to honest trade? Which fostered broadly shared prosperity, and which resulted in morally corrosive inequality of income and wealth? Which helped draw humankind toward the millennium (be it corporeal or metaphoric), and individuals to salvation, and which kept vast numbers of men and women mired in misery and sin? Because the laws and other social institutions that mattered for such purposes were devised by humans, they were subject to change. Comparisons across different countries, each with its different set of laws and institutions, offered a means to discover the way forward.

The methodology that Ely now advocated therefore served a purpose beyond the already valuable one of better understanding why economic behavior was what it was. It sought also to enable economic science to concern itself with "what ought to be." Exploiting cross-country comparisons to understand the behavioral consequences of different economic policies and other institutional arrangements led directly to considering which policies, and what sets of institutions, would foster a better society. The fundamental point was that human outcomes, in economics no less than elsewhere, were not predetermined. "The will of man is a main factor in all politico-economic phenomena."[58]

Not all elements of Ely's vision for economics (nor Clark's, for that matter) have survived. But two that have done so remain readily visible in the discipline more than a century later.

Economics today continues to be a policy-oriented inquiry, aimed not just at understanding observed behavior but exploring potential avenues for improvement in society-wide outcomes. Although some publications do specialize in either pure economic theory or statistical methods, the great majority of articles published in the field's scholarly journals motivate whatever question is under study by pointing to its bearing on economic policy, or conclude by drawing policy implications from the analysis presented, or both. This pattern is even more prevalent, with the policy content of the analysis bulking still larger, in books about economics aimed at a broad public audience. The educated public today expects discussion of economics to be about public policy. It largely is. Before Ely's time, it was not.

Second, the methodology of cross-country (or, within any one country, cross-state or -city or -province) investigation, grounded in precisely the logic that Ely laid out more than a century ago, remains standard. Why, for example, do most Americans save so little? Is our low saving rate a response to low returns available on the available investment assets? Or perhaps to high tax rates? Or to the fact that with Social Security and Medicare to provide for our basic needs in old age, we simply see no need to save on our own? Comparison with other countries, where asset returns or taxes or pension and medical arrangements are different, is a standard source of insight.

Or, to take a broader question, why has productivity growth, and with it the improvement of the population's average standard of living, slowed in most advanced economies in recent decades? Observing that this slowdown has not been uniform across countries, and taking account of potentially relevant differences among them—differences in education, or investment rates, or industrial policies—is likewise a standard way of seeking policy-oriented answers. The effect of immigration on wages, of patent laws on innovation, of social welfare programs on poverty, of monetary policy on inflation, of tariffs on trade flows, of taxes on the allocation of investment, are all questions that economists today regularly address by comparing policies and other institutions across different countries and observing the resulting outcomes. The underlying logic that structures the analysis is identical to Ely's. So is the usual objective of such work: to infer what pattern of taxes, or pensions, or education, or industrial policy, would lead to improved economic and social outcomes.

The policy orientation that Richard T. Ely's economics represented, and in many respects John Bates Clark's as well, reflected not only their intellectual training in the German historical school but also the broader cultural influence of the Social Gospel movement in the America of their day.[59] The presumptions that Clark and Ely took from the religious ideas swirling around them shaped their professional thinking no less than their personal religious commitments and their career trajectories. The institutional-comparative methodology that entered economics via Ely's work in particular stands as the primary expression of the Social Gospel's influence on the field.

By contrast, the ameliorative ambition for economics that both Clark and Ely shared was consistent with a worldview (in Einstein's sense) that American Social Gospelists like Gladden and Rauschen-busch and adherents of the Gospel of Wealth like Beecher and Law-rence and Conwell preached in common. None of these prominent religious leaders believed in predestination. Despite their differences, thinking on both sides continually emphasized the enormous possi-bilities that each group saw for human choice and human action. And while they differed in their presumptions about economics—existing American institutions either were or were not the best one could have, economic inequality either was or was not a problem in need of recti-fying, laissez-faire either was or was not sound policy—the worldview that they shared, and that they helped create among other Americans in their time, embraced these expansive possibilities for choice and action as well. Further, both sets of religious thinkers shared a robustly postmillennialist outlook toward human society, and toward America's unique role in advancing it. Improving the world, whether through individual action or public policy, was more than a practical, material goal. It had religious significance.

Conflict and Crisis

We must be able to think our modern life clear through in Christian terms, and to do that we also must be able to think our Christian faith clear through in modern terms.

—HARRY EMERSON FOSDICK

What the liberal theologian has retained after abandoning to the enemy one Christian doctrine after another is not Christianity at all, but a religion which is so entirely different from Christianity as to belong in a distinct category.

—J. GRESHAM MACHEN

The creation of the Federal Council of Churches in 1908, encompassing most of the country's mainline Protestant denominations, represented a coming together of the Social Gospel and the Gospel of Wealth. Both lines of religious thinking embraced a postmillennialist belief that material progress and spiritual progress were intertwined and inevitable, that efforts to hasten that progress had religious value regardless of whether the ensuing millennium was to be physical or metaphoric, and that America bore a God-given responsibility to lead the world toward the better future to come. American institutions— economic, political, and religious—were the example other nations should follow.

By the time of World War I, mainline Protestants largely accepted the existing system of market-based competition (not yet called "free enterprise"[1]) hailed by adherents of the Gospel of Wealth, but subject to elements of government guidance and even paternalism advocated by the Social Gospel: antitrust policy to ensure that the competition was genuine, regulation of working conditions to protect employees' safety, and product regulation to guard consumers. In a further victory for the Social Gospel, labor unions became part of the generally accepted American order. So too did a federal income tax, introduced by constitutional amendment in 1913. Even so, in keeping with Gospel of Wealth thinking, no massive redistribution of either incomes or wealth took place. Nor did the United States adopt national-level old-age pensions, or insurance against sickness and unemployment, all of which Germany had implemented years earlier under Bismarck.

The spirit of openness and compromise extended to religious matters as well. Mainline Protestants now accepted the "higher criticism" of the Bible pioneered by Wellhausen and other German scholars in the previous century, as well as the theory of evolution—crucially including the evolution of the human species—set out by Charles Darwin and Alfred Russel Wallace.[2] While each denomination continued to witness its own particular faith, mainliners mostly downplayed doctrinal disputes of the kind that in the past had led to sharp divisions. As large-scale immigration continued to broaden America's demographic makeup, some aspects of this ecumenicalism also extended to groups other than Protestants. Mainline Protestants played little role in the vituperative bigotry directed against New York Catholic Al Smith's run for president in 1928, and many spoke out against it. A year earlier, Charles Evans Hughes, previously a Supreme Court justice and soon to return to the Court as chief justice, led the way in founding the National Conference of Christians and Jews.

Prominent spokesmen for this new mainline consensus forcefully articulated its modernist, ecumenical, nondoctrinal orientation. Shailer Mathews, for example, became dean of the University of Chicago Divinity School in 1908, just as the FCC was coming into being. Educated at Colby College and then Newton Seminary, Mathews was a theologian, not an ordained member of the clergy. But he became a leading voice of liberal Protestantism in the years after World War I, remaining dean at Chicago for twenty-five years. He was also active in the Baptist Church, helping to establish the Northern Baptist Convention in 1907 and later serving as the group's president.

Mathews's best known book, published in 1924, laid out what he aptly called *The Faith of Modernism*. He was plain in rejecting the way not just Protestants but all monotheistic religions had defined themselves for centuries. The modernist movement did not seek to organize a specific system of theology or draw up a written confession, he wrote.

Indeed, "The religious affirmations of the Modernist are not identical with any theology. They represent an attitude rather than doctrine." Nor did he shy away from contrasting the open stance of modernism to other forms of religious thinking, which he dismissed as dogmatic. "If the temptation of the dogmatic mind is toward inflexible formula," he declared, "that of the Modernist is toward indifference to formula." Moreover, everyone should understand that much of the concrete religious imagery invoked by Protestants of an earlier era was merely metaphor: "the Modernist cannot think of a literal hell with fire and burning."[3]

Mathews felt free not merely to regard prior generations' ideas and images as metaphors, but to leave them behind altogether if they had become unhelpful. The essence of what he called modernism was that its mode of thought adapted itself to the age. He felt no allegiance to many of the doctrinal patterns that had expressed the convictions and attitudes of Christians who lived in different circumstances and were governed by different social practices. Instead, "We shall shape new patterns whenever they are needed, from life itself." To this end, he proposed to draw not on faith and tradition alone, but to look as well to empirical guidance, from wherever it might come. The modernist would not stake his or her faith on untested traditions, but would ground it on literary criticism, history, and the individual's own experience. Although Mathews did not personally contribute to the higher biblical criticism (he was not a Bible scholar), he embraced it fully. Taking account of the legal, social, and philosophical presumptions of the societies from which the holy texts came, at the specific times in which they were written, would give us a fuller understanding of the Bible and a greater ability to use it as a source of religious inspiration and guidance.[4]

While Mathews was the principal intellectual force behind the modernist Protestant theology in America, the popular face of mainline religious practice following World War I was Harry Emerson Fosdick. Also a Baptist, but unlike Mathews an ordained minister, Fosdick was educated at Colgate and then the nondenominational Union Theological Seminary in New York. He soon became active in the organizational life of mainline Protestantism, serving (along with Mathews) on the FCC's Committee on the War and the Religious Outlook. Constituted while World War I was still under way, the committee produced a series of publications bearing on how the conflict affected Americans' personal experience, how it challenged the nation's Protestant churches, and what changes were therefore appropriate in the churches' teachings and in their responsibility for the "social problems of the time." Its most prominent work was a book-length report titled *The Church and Industrial Reconstruction,* published in 1920. Reacting to the lingering economic dislocations in the United States and elsewhere—and noting as well the war, the collapse of the governing regime in Germany and other defeated countries, the Bolshevik Revolution in Russia, and other upheavals—the report began with the inspiring proposition that "The world-wide industrial unrest . . . is not simply the rumbling of empty stomachs; it is the stirring of the soul of man."[5]

In keeping with his ecumenical seminary training, by the time of the FCC committee's report Fosdick, though ordained as a Baptist, was pastor at New York's First Presbyterian Church. He soon joined Shailer Mathews as a leading public spokesman for the new, modernist incarnation of mainline Protestantism. In contrast to Mathews's focus on theology, however, Fosdick echoed many of the Unitarians of the late eighteenth and early nineteenth centuries in emphasizing the religious imperative to both individual and collective action. Often drawing on sayings originally by others when he preached, he was frequently identified with the ethos expressed by the French poet and novelist Anatole France that "It is by acts and not by ideas that people live."[6]

While of course accepting the bedrock Social Gospel principle that the structure of society crucially shapes the lives of people within it— this, after all, was central to what both the Social Creed of the Churches and *The Church and Industrial Reconstruction* were about—Fosdick had no patience for any kind of fatalistic determinism. "Life consists not simply in what heredity and environment do to us," he objected in one of his books, "but in what we make out of what they do to us."[7] With his firm postmillennial outlook, he called on American Protestants to strive to improve the world in which they lived. Another saying often associated with Fosdick was that "Christians are supposed not merely to endure change, nor even to profit by it, but to cause it."[8] Norman Vincent Peale, a similarly oriented Protestant preacher a generation younger, attributed to Fosdick the aphorism that "The world is moving so fast these days that the one who says it can't be done is generally interrupted by someone doing it."[9]

Not all American Protestants accepted Mathews's liberal theology, however, nor Fosdick's postmillennialist activism. Moreover, Fosdick's appointment at First Presbyterian Church had always been controversial within the denomination. Embroiled in controversy once his modernist vision of Protestantism came under attack, and increasingly attracting nationwide attention as he vigorously defended his views, in the mid-1920s he resigned from First Presbyterian and accepted the pulpit at New York's Park Avenue Baptist Church.

The move ended up bringing him all the more prominence. Fosdick had long been close to philanthropist John D. Rockefeller Jr. (son of the oil tycoon), serving on the board of the Rockefeller Foundation as well as advising Rockefeller on his personal philanthropy.[10] In turn, Rockefeller, a longtime backer of liberal Christian causes (when the FCC was founded, he promised to underwrite at least 5 percent of the first year's budget), had been one of Fosdick's leading supporters. Now he was a congregant as well. Before Fosdick's move to Park Avenue Baptist, the two had discussed his becoming the pastor of a new, ecumenical church that Rockefeller would fund. Now the plan was for him to go to Park Avenue Baptist, for that church (with Rockefeller's support) to build a grand new church overlooking the Hudson on New York's Upper West Side, and for the Park Avenue Baptist congregation to move there once the new church was ready.[11] Designed to look like a medieval cathedral, but nondenominational Protestant in its practice, Riverside Church opened in October 1930. *Time* magazine featured Fosdick on its next cover, hailing him as "without doubt the most famed living Protestant preacher."[12]

The opposition to Mathews's modernism and Fosdick's ecumenicalism reflected a long-standing tradition of American Protestant thought that had stood apart from both the Gospel of Wealth and the Social Gospel. Evangelical revivalism, in the spirit of Presbyterian Charles Grandison Finney as well as other charismatic leaders often associated with Methodism before that movement in America took on a more prosperous, middle- or even upper-middle-class character, had persisted right through the nineteenth century. But the revivalist impulse was hardly limited to Americans of modest economic means. One of its foremost proponents was Dwight Moody, a Chicago-based publisher and philanthropist. Originally from Northfield, in central Massachusetts, Moody moved to Boston as a teenager and while there became religiously devout. Relocating to Chicago shortly before the Civil War, still in his late teens, he began preaching as a revivalist despite never having been ordained. As he often described his experience, "I look on this world as a wrecked vessel. God has given me a lifeboat and said to me, 'Moody, save all you can.' "[13]

Unlike Finney, Moody was firmly *pre*millennialist in his theology. While Finney had sought not only to convert individual men and women but to reform society as well—he played a significant role in both the abolition movement and the temperance movement—Moody's focus was squarely on the individuals to be saved. In an article he wrote in 1879, Moody complained that "There is a great deal of talk about reform. It is reform in politics, and reform in religion, reform in business, and reform in this, that, and the other, until I am tired of the word." He summarized his own priorities: "We don't want reformation so much as we want regeneration. We don't want the pest-house repainted; we want the disease out."[14] The way to address social or economic problems was not politically based reform but religious revival.

Amassing significant wealth from his publishing business, Moody became close to other rich industrialists, and he used both his own resources and those he could attract from his friends not for secular philanthropy like Andrew Carnegie's but explicitly evangelical projects such as the Moody Bible Institute in Chicago (then and now, a major center of dispensational premillennialism[15]) and the Mount Hermon School for boys (today the coed Northfield Mount Hermon School) in his hometown in Massachusetts. The Moody Church, which grew out of the Sunday school he sponsored, in time became one of Chicago's largest and most influential Protestant churches.

Moody's evangelical Protestantism resembled neither the Gospel of Wealth nor the Social Gospel, and when those two lines of thought came together in the Federal Council of Churches the differences from what Moody preached became all the more visible. Unlike the mainliners who created the FCC, Moody's followers rejected the higher biblical criticism, continuing to view the holy scriptures as not just divinely inspired but of purely divine origin, and therefore not influenced by the specific human society into which they were committed nor the specific time at which that happened. They similarly rejected any notion of evolution, for either humans or lower animals (or even plants), as hypothesized by Darwin and Wallace. The account of creation given in Genesis meant precisely what the words said, and if evolutionary theory said something different it must be mistaken. Many evangelicals further subscribed to the detailed chronology put forth in 1654 by the Anglican bishop James Ussher, who concluded, on the basis of careful study of the details set forth in the Hebrew Bible, that the world had been created on the evening of October 22 in the year 4004 before the current era.[16]

In contrast to the mainliners' postmillennialism, the eschatology to which Moody and other revivalist Protestants subscribed was mostly premillennialist. They lent little support to most of the ideas for ameliorative government action initially proposed by the Social Gospel and then embraced by the FCC, including most forms of market regulation as well as new government programs to ease the life of the indigent. (Calls for government to restrict private behavior were another matter; banning the sale and consumption of alcohol was an objective the revivalists and the Social Gospelers shared.[17]) Reforming society, in the hope of hastening the millennium, was also not part of their program. Their aim was to convert individual souls, in anticipation of a millennium that would come at God's chosen time, and mostly to rely on traditional Protestant voluntarism to improve needy citizens' lives in the meanwhile. Along the same lines, they also mostly opposed any role in the economy for organized labor. The antidote to urban poverty, or unequal distribution of wealth, or oppressive working conditions, was voluntary adherence to Christian principles promoted by Christian charity.[18]

The revivalists also opposed the adaptive and ecumenical theology that modernist mainline Protestants were already beginning to embrace, as soon to be articulated at the national level by leaders like Mathews and Fosdick. In the 1890s the New York pastor and author Daniel Gregory, a graduate of the conservative Princeton Theological Seminary, wrote that "Christ's ethical principles have never changed, and will never change. They will never be accommodated to human society or development; but must shape that society and development if it is not to end in decay and destruction."[19] Early in the new century, the hugely popular revival preacher Billy Sunday was telling his audiences, "I do not believe in this twentieth-century theory of the universal fatherhood of God and the brotherhood of man. . . . You are not a child of God unless you are a Christian."[20]

The establishment of the Federal Council of Churches in 1908 crystallized the opposition of these revivalist Protestants who had mostly accepted neither the Gospel of Wealth nor the Social Gospel. In response, a group of conservative theologians organized by the recently established Bible Institute of Los Angeles (consciously modeled on the Moody Bible Institute) produced a set of ninety essays, published between 1910 and 1915 in twelve volumes titled *The Fundamentals*.[21] These statements spanned a wide range of topics, laying out the grounds for rejecting such modern religious developments as higher biblical criticism and ecumenicalism along with secular movements like socialism and Darwinism. One common theme cutting across many of the positions taken was a skepticism of the sufficiency of human reason for attaining moral and religious truths; the alternative was the necessity of faith, including faith in the Bible as a transcendent source of authority. Another frequent theme was opposition to reformist social activism. (One contribution to *The Fundamentals* referred to "a so-called 'social gospel' which discards the fundamental doctrines of Christianity and substitutes a religion of good works," concluding that "The hope of the world is not in a new social order instituted by unregenerate men; not a millennium made by man; not a commonwealth of humanity organized as a Socialistic state; but a kingdom established by Christ which will fill the earth with glory at the coming of the King."[22]) Many of the essays also expressed conservative Protestants' opposition to the beliefs of other American religious groups including Catholics, Mormons, and Christian Scientists.

A further aspect of *The Fundamentals*, which in time proved especially important, was the building of a closer connection between these varied expressions of theologically conservative Protestantism and premillennialist eschatology.[23] In 1909, just a year before the first of the *Fundamentals* volumes appeared, Oxford University Press had published a new edition of the King James Bible presenting the original 1611 text together with annotations and commentary. Written by Cyrus Scofield, an American Congregational minister associated with several of Dwight Moody's initiatives (he served as pastor at Moody's church in Northfield, Massachusetts), the commentary followed the "dispensational" interpretation of human history and the biblical end times advanced nearly a century before by John Nelson Darby.[24] Sco-field also provided a handy key allowing readers to cross-reference related verses, including tying the specific prophecies in Revelation to the Hebrew Bible as well as earlier books of the New Testament. Pub-lished as the *Scofield Reference Bible,* the book had a large impact in popularizing dispensational premillennialism, especially in America. (With an estimated ten million copies sold—the best-selling book in the five-hundred-year history of Oxford University Press—it is still in print.[25])

The Fundamentals, following so shortly after, built on this momen-tum.[26] Although some conservative Protestant theologians at the time subscribed to postmillennial eschatology, both the funding and the energy behind *The Fundamentals* came from convinced premillenni-alists. Lyman Stewart, president and one of the founders of Union Oil Company, instigated the project and put up most of the money, and created his own publishing company to publish the volumes. Two years earlier Stewart had helped found the Bible Institute of Los Angeles and had installed as the first dean the nationally known dispensational premillennialist William Blackstone.[27] (Several years later, Blackstone was succeeded by R. A. Torrey, who had been the superintendent of the Moody Bible Institute and pastor at the Moody Church.) A con-vinced premillennialist himself as well as conservative in his theol-ogy more generally, and strongly opposed to alternative views that he considered incorrect, Stewart not only chose the volumes' editors but exerted increasing control over the choice of content when some of the essays in the earliest volumes failed to conform to his thinking.[28] In the end, as he intended, the establishment of premillennialism as one of the central tenets of conservative Protestantism in America was one of the project's most significant consequences.[29] Again with Stewart's support, more than three million volumes were quickly printed and, mostly, given away to churches, seminaries, missions, and individual families.[30]

The influence on evangelical thinking stemming directly from *The Fundamentals,* and especially from the near-universal embrace of pre-millennialism within the evangelical community (itself largely a con-sequence of *The Fundamentals*), proved enormous. Instead of seeking their own approach to addressing the visible problems of the day, based on traditional Protestant notions of voluntarism, many American evangelicals now began to turn away from new political or social or economic thinking altogether, rejecting the entirety as one more facet of a worldly menace to be avoided and, if possible, resisted. As a result, during much of the early twentieth century many evangelical Protestants continued to embrace a social message essentially identical to the dominant ideas of the 1870s and early 1880s—before the economic and other challenges of the late nineteenth century gave rise to new thinking in a variety of quarters, including the Social Gospel.[31]

By the 1920s, fundamentalists—as those who adhered to the ideas set forth in *The Fundamentals* were now often called—presented an increasingly vigorous opposition to the liberal Protestantism represented by Mathews and Fosdick, together with a resistance to the growing influence of the FCC among America's business and political elite.[32] In a 1923 book titled *Christianity and Liberalism*, J. Gresham Machen, a Presbyterian theologian and a professor at Princeton Seminary, cast the new trends in Protestant thinking as a failed attempt to reconcile traditional Christianity with modern science—"the enemy who ever lies in ambush." This effort, Machen argued, was doomed to failure. "The liberal attempt at rescuing Christianity is false," he declared. Moreover, it was based on "a grossly exaggerated estimate of the achievements of modern science."[33]

Modernist views might or might not merit discussion, Machen claimed, but they represented some other religion—not Christianity. "What the liberal theologian has retained after abandoning to the enemy one Christian doctrine after another is not Christianity at all, but a religion which is so entirely different from Christianity as to belong in a distinct category," he argued. More specifically, "the liberal attempt at reconciling Christianity with modern science has really relinquished everything distinctive of Christianity, so that what remains is in essentials only that same indefinite type of religious aspiration which was in the world before Christianity came upon the scene." If liberal thinking were to prevail, "Christianity would at last have perished from the earth and the gospel would have sounded forth for the last time." The result, not just in the religious sphere but in Western society more broadly, had already been "an unparalleled impoverishment of human life."[34] Looking to his own institution, Machen urged Princeton Seminary to discipline any of its faculty members who compromised with even modestly more liberal views.

The fundamentalist attack in turn evoked a vigorous reaction from the mainliners. Most prominently, Fosdick, still at First Presbyterian, delivered a sermon provocatively titled "Shall the Fundamentalists Win?" He was unsparing in his rebuke. "You cannot fit the Lord Christ into that Fundamentalist mold," he declared. The intention of those who sought to do so was "to drive out of the evangelical churches men and women of liberal opinions." Their program was both illiberal and intolerant. "Has anybody a right to deny the Christian name to those who differ with him," he asked, "and to shut against them the doors of the Christian fellowship? . . . The Fundamentalists say that this must be done."[35]

Fosdick argued that excluding the new, modernist line of Protestant thinking was not just illiberal, it would block the church from fulfilling its mission. "We must be able to think our modern life clear through in Christian terms," he argued, "and to do that we also must be able to think our Christian faith clear through in modern terms." Nor was this the first time changing circumstances had created a need for the church to rethink its beliefs and its practice. There was nothing new about the situation, he explained. It had happened again and again. Although the specifics changed from one era to another, the need for fresh thinking—not in opposition to what had come before, as Machen's reference to "the enemy" implied—but made to fit in harmony with it, was a constant. "Whenever such a situation has arisen, there has been only one way out: new knowledge and the old faith had to be blended in a new combination." In the present crisis, as Fosdick saw it, this was precisely what he and his fellow mainliners were striving to accomplish. The fundamentalists were on a campaign to shut them out. The question American Protestants now faced was "Shall they be allowed to succeed?"[36]

Fosdick also thought what he labeled the "illiberality" of the fundamentalists' effort was harmful on its own account. "Has intolerance any contribution to make to this situation?" he asked. "Will it persuade anybody of anything? Is not the Christian church large enough to hold within her hospitable fellowship people who differ. . . . When will the world learn that intolerance solves no problems?" His own view was clear: "The worst kind of church that can possibly be offered to the allegiance of the new generation is an intolerant church."[37]

The sermon cost Fosdick his pulpit. It was the catalyst for the controversy that led to his resigning from First Presbyterian Church two years later.[38] But it enormously bolstered his national reputation. Within a month the sermon had been published in several respected outlets, including *Christian Century* and *Christian Work,* and with funding from Rockefeller and the assistance of a publicist he employed, 130,000 copies of a slightly abridged version were distributed nationwide.[39] The effort made Fosdick the country's most visible public opponent of fundamentalism and the foremost defender of the liberal, modernist, ecumenical ideas that by then characterized mainline American Protestantism. In time he became a popular cultural symbol transcending the sphere of religion. In 1942 cartoonist Al Capp's long-running comic strip *Li'l Abner* introduced a new character, police detective Fearless Fosdick, the "ideel" of every "100% red-blooded American boy," and in 1952 NBC featured a weekly *Fearless Fosdick* television series. A year after delivering his career-changing sermon, the real Fosdick reflected, "I am profoundly sorry that the sermon has been misinterpreted; I am profoundly sorry that it has caused a disturbance; but I cannot honestly be sorry at all that I preached the sermon. When I get to heaven I expect it to be one of the stars in my crown."[40]

The opposition of Fosdick and his mainline colleagues to the rising tide of fundamentalism was predictable. The year after Fosdick's move to Park Avenue Baptist, however, the fundamentalist movement suffered a more devastating setback, and from an unexpected source: a trial court. In 1925 the state of Tennessee enacted a statute prohibiting any teaching in the state's public schools that contradicted the biblical account of the creation of man. To challenge the new law, the American Civil Liberties Union arranged for John Scopes, a young teacher in the small town of Dayton, Tennessee, to admit that he had reviewed with his high school biology class a textbook chapter on evolution (ironically, from the state's own mandated textbook). What was in question, therefore, was not Scopes's actions but the validity of the statute, and the trial attracted nationwide attention (as it was intended to—many in Dayton's local establishment had deliberately promoted the action as a way of attracting business to the town). At the behest of the World Christian Fundamentals Association, William Jennings Bryan, the former secretary of state and presidential candidate but also a staunch fundamentalist believer, agreed to come to Dayton to serve as counsel to the prosecution. In turn, the ACLU recruited Clarence

Darrow, the country's most famous criminal lawyer, as counsel for the defense.

The trial, conducted in a carnival atmosphere, gathered all the publicity it was meant to. In the end it proved a disaster for the fundamentalist movement. The jury convicted Scopes—given the admitted facts, it would have been hard not to—but Darrow managed to make the fundamentalist argument against evolution look foolish. His public ridicule of Bryan, who took the stand himself as an expert witness, became all the more sensational in retrospect when Bryan died only five days after the trial ended. In a further letdown for the anti-Darwin forces, the judge sentenced Scopes merely to a $100 fine, the Tennessee Supreme Court overturned even that modest penalty (on the ground that the jury should have fixed the amount), and the local prosecutor declined to retry the case.

The adverse publicity generated by the Scopes trial, followed closely in the press and on the radio by large numbers of Americans who never would have heard Harry Emerson Fosdick preach or read a book by Shailer Mathews, put Protestant fundamentalism into retreat for a generation.[41] At the same time, the movement's remaining energy turned increasingly toward divisive internal conflict. Princeton Seminary, founded in 1812 to resist the drift toward liberalism at Harvard and other institutions, had from its inception been associated with conservative Presbyterian theology. In the denomination's 1837 schism the seminary had stood firmly on the old-school side, opposed to the new measures employed by revivalists like Finney as well as the demands of Presbyterian abolitionists. Since then it had resisted much of the modernist, increasingly ecumenical trend of the late nineteenth and early twentieth centuries. "Princeton theology" had come to connote predestinarian Calvinist orthodoxy, an emphasis on the centrality of human sinfulness, suspicion of evolution and higher biblical criticism, belief in the Bible's inerrancy, and an exclusive view of what Christianity was all about. Even so, at the end of the 1920s, when a reorganization of the seminary's supervisory boards presented the possible prospect of tolerating other points of view, longtime professor J. Gresham Machen led a conservative revolt, taking half of the faculty with him to found a new seminary (Westminster Theology Seminary) and a new church (the Orthodox Presbyterian Church).

.   .   .

Before long, however, the mainline establishment represented by Fosdick and Mathews encountered its own setback—one from which it never fully recovered. In this case too, the origin lay outside the realm of religion per se. This time the shock was economic.

The American economy had moved forward irregularly in the years following World War I. Production expanded in many of the leading industries that had accounted for the nation's economic growth before the war; wages rose, especially in manufacturing and other rapidly expanding sectors; and businesses invested in new factories and machinery. In industries that now increasingly relied on assembly lines, firms were able to lower their prices and thereby make their products more widely available. The Model T Ford, introduced at $850 in 1908, sold for only $260 in 1925.[42] The ongoing rise in the stock market lent the 1920s a further feeling of heightened prosperity, as many Americans amassed new paper wealth. But economic downturns interrupted the expansion four times—not just in 1918–19, in response to postwar demobilization and the influenza epidemic, but again in 1921–1922, 1923–1924, and 1926–1927—and of the 129 months between November 1918 and August 1929, the economy was contracting in fifty-two.[43] In the latter half of the 1920s, although stock prices continued to climb, several important sectors of economic activity went into decline. Homebuilding peaked in 1925, and by 1929 the rate of new construction had fallen by half. Business investment topped out in 1926.

Even so, no one anticipated the depression that began in 1929. The downturn, which lasted until 1933, was unprecedented in both length and severity. Production overall declined by one-third. In the industrial sector, output fell by one-half. In many industries the decline was far worse. Steel production fell from 62 million tons per year to 15 million, iron ore extraction from 74 million tons to 10 million. Automobile manufacturing dropped from 4.5 million cars in 1929 to just over one million in 1932. New investment nearly disappeared. Even with the decline in the latter half of the 1920s, investment of all kinds in the United States—including new factories, machinery, houses, and business inventories—totaled $17 billion in 1929. By 1932 total investment was less than $2 billion. In 1929 American firms had manufactured 2,300 new railroad cars (already down from a peak of 2,900 three years earlier), including both passenger and freight. In 1933 the industry's entire output was seven passenger cars and two freight cars.

The human dimension of the Depression was extraordinary as well, and for many, devastating. The decline in the stock market wiped out $75 billion of household wealth—equivalent to three-fourths of the total national income in 1929—bankrupting tens of thousands of speculators who had bought on margin, but also annihilating the wealth of countless ordinary Americans who simply owned stocks. As factories and mines and retail stores shut down, millions of Americans had no work. In 1929 fewer than 3 percent of Americans who wanted to work had no job. By 1933 one of every five would-be workers—more than 10 million nationwide—was unemployed. Outside the farm sector, where many hands lived on the farms they worked and therefore remained in place even when there was no work to do, unemployment reached 30 percent of the labor force.[44] Moreover, even these astonishing rates of joblessness excluded millions of "emergency workers" across the country employed by federal relief programs like the Civilian Conservation Corps and the Works Progress Administration.[45] (At their peak, in 1936, these new relief agencies employed 3.7 million workers.[46])

The consequences were shocking, even to the most casual observer. In the downtowns of most cities, crowds of well-dressed job seekers jammed the few operating employment offices, while more haggard-looking throngs lined up at soup kitchens operated by churches and the Salvation Army. As families faced eviction for not paying their rent, and homeowners lost their houses when they could no longer keep up their mortgages, makeshift camps of the homeless (popularly called

Depression soup line, New York City (1932).
The Great Depression brought to America personal economic deprivation
on a scale not approached in the nearly nine decades since.

Hoovervilles after the nation's curiously inactive president) cropped up on the outskirts of many cities. By 1933 home mortgage foreclosures were running at a thousand a day nationwide. In some cities—Cleveland, Indianapolis, Birmingham—more than half of all home mortgages were in default.

The farm sector was even more depressed. The most pervasive problem was a steep fall in the prices of crops and livestock, well beyond the declines elsewhere in the economy. Between 1929 and 1933 retail prices throughout the country fell on average by 24 percent, and wholesale prices by 32 percent; prices of farm products fell on average by 52 percent. As a result, the average income of American farmers went from $960 a year to $280. In some areas of the country, most obviously the Midwest Dust Bowl, the distress was even greater. In 1932 alone, a quarter of a million farmers lost their land as banks foreclosed on their unpaid mortgages. By 1933 more than half of all farm debt owed in the United States was in default.

Foreclosures did not mean that banks and other lenders recovered their investment, however, as the market value of homes as well as farms had also fallen. Thousands of banks closed down, wiping out the assets of unlucky depositors and at the same time shutting off the economy's supply of credit. Businesses went bankrupt too, defaulting not just on their bank loans but on bonds held by investors including insurance companies, pension funds, and many individuals. State and local governments likewise struggled to meet their obligations. Three states and more than thirty of the country's three hundred largest cities defaulted on their debts. At several points during the Depression—the final months of 1930, the spring of 1931, and the winter of 1933—the nation's banking system was on the brink of collapse.

Recovery began only in 1933. The one-week Bank Holiday imposed by Franklin Roosevelt as he assumed the presidency marked the turning point. Even so, the recovery was slow and incomplete. It took until 1936 for the economy's total output to regain the 1929 level, and then a new downturn began in the spring of 1937, lasting through midyear 1938. By 1940, even with 2.8 million "emergency workers" still on the federal payroll, unemployment remained at nearly 10 percent of the American labor force (nearly 14 percent outside the farm sector). Not until 1943, when the nation had nine million men and women in uniform fighting World War II, did unemployment recede to the 1929 level.

The Depression was a worldwide phenomenon.[47] While the specific circumstances differed from one country to another, mass unemployment, sharp and persistent declines in production, business bankruptcies, widespread failure of banks and other financial institutions, and destruction of asset values and wealth were prevalent across the industrialized world. The two countries hardest hit were the United States and Germany, but France, Britain, Japan, and smaller nations everywhere suffered economic declines as well. Especially coming so soon after the dislocations of World War I, the resulting strains were more than many of these societies could sustain.

In most countries, albeit in widely divergent ways, the Depression triggered consequences far beyond the realm of economics. Germany took a path that led to dictatorship, mass murder, war, and, finally, total destruction. Fascist governments assumed control in Italy and Spain, and in France as well once the country collapsed in the face of German aggression. Similar fascist movements, though not successful in coming to power, emerged in Britain and numerous other countries. Internationally, a new world order—the United Nations, the World Bank, the International Monetary Fund, and a host of military alliances—grew from the wreckage of the Depression and then World War II. In America, the Depression reshaped the country's political landscape and fundamentally altered the role citizens looked to their government to play.

Religion could hardly remain immune to this onslaught that so upended widely held assumptions and reoriented popular thinking. Nor could economics.

As an intellectual discipline matures, its conceptual core normally becomes less subject to external influence—from worldly events, from thinking in other areas of inquiry, from the culture of the day. Fundamental thinking within a mature discipline more and more tends to follow its own momentum, while the role of such outside forces becomes increasingly a matter of application and method.[48] Economics, in the century and a half beginning with Adam Smith, had traced a path consistent with just such an evolution. The movement away from orthodox Calvinism in much of the English-speaking Protestant world gave moral philosophers like Smith and his contemporaries an expanded vision of the potential for good inherent in human agency and human institutions. This new worldview (in Einstein's sense) fostered the emergence of a creatively different understanding of how, within the setting of competitive markets, actions motivated by no more than individual self-interest systematically result in improvements to human welfare more broadly, and this understanding has formed the conceptual core of Western economic thinking ever since.

In the first half of the nineteenth century, British political economists like David Ricardo and John Stuart Mill extended this foundational base to derive insights into more specific aspects of economic life such as land rents, patterns of international trade, and the accumulation of physical capital, in each instance going well beyond Smith's analysis but remaining nonetheless within the same basic theoretical conception of individually self-interested behavior operating subject to the constraints of market competition. Their counterparts in America, like Francis Wayland and Francis Bowen, likewise accepted the basic Smithian conceptual framework and devoted their efforts to drawing out implications for laissez-faire economic policies (which both men favored) as applied to practical issues of the day like free trade (which Wayland favored but Bowen did not, though in each case on laissez-faire grounds).

In the nineteenth century's later decades, the discipline evolved in several further ways—none of which, however, represented a departure from the fundamental conceptual foundation established by Smith's contribution a century before. Economists including Stanley Jevons and Alfred Marshall in Britain, Léon Walras in France, and John Bates Clark in America gave new mathematical precision to the Smithian idea of self-interested households and firms interacting in a competitive market environment, framing the decisions of both sets of actors as the outcome of an explicit optimization for which the solution took the form of a "marginal" relation between some market-given price or wage and some incremental value subject to the household's or firm's control. This methodological advance gave the discipline a fully articulated theoretical apparatus, capable of addressing a potentially infinite variety of applied questions in specific settings. But the underlying conceptual basis remained that established by Smith a century before.

At the methodological level, Richard T. Ely, inspired by the American postmillennialism of the time and drawing too on his graduate training in the thinking of the German historical school, pushed the discipline to exploit the growing base of economic statistics to draw empirically grounded inferences about the many ways in which the environment in which households live and firms operate shapes how they pursue their self-interest. Under the leadership of Ely and his followers, this new empirical focus on the constraints society imposes on choices made by both individuals and firms led in turn to an emphasis on institutional choices to be made by the society itself—in other words, economic policy. The consequence was a new, ameliorative direction for economics as a discipline, seeking now not just to understand and explain observed patterns of behavior but also to reshape the prevailing environment that produced those patterns, and thereby improve on the outcomes.

In response to the 1930s Depression, economists expanded enormously the range of actual and potential policy measures to which they applied this new methodological orientation, while at the same time retaining the same conceptual basis grounded in the working of self-interested behavior subject to both market and institutional constraints. In the United States the Roosevelt administration attacked the economic crisis with an openly experimental attitude, introducing a wide variety of government interventions. Apart from the activist spirit, there was little attempt at consistency, and some of the measures taken ran at cross-purposes with others.[49] The objective was to discover what worked and what didn't. As Roosevelt put it in his inaugural address, "This Nation asks for action, and action now."[50] Measures implemented just within the new administration's famous first hundred days included creation of the Civilian Conservation Corps to provide jobs, the Federal Emergency Relief Administration to buttress urban incomes, and the Agricultural Adjustment Administration to support farm prices and refinance farm mortgages. Congress appropriated more than $3 billion (compared to the size of the economy, equivalent to nearly $1 trillion today) for new public works, and the administration took numerous other steps to shield both farmers and urban homeowners from mortgage foreclosures.

Further anti-Depression measures, as time passed, spanned wide areas of economic activity: the Farm Credit Administration (also to refinance farm mortgages), the Home Owners' Loan Corporation (for residential mortgages), the U.S. Housing Authority (housing for low-income families), the Works Progress Administration (jobs for millions of workers building projects all over the country), the Glass-Steagall Act (separating investment banking from commercial banking), Social Security (old-age and disability pensions), the Federal Deposit Insurance Corporation (guaranteeing individual accounts up to $5,000), the Securities and Exchange Commission (reforming the issuance and trading of stocks), the Food, Drug and Cosmetic Act (consumer product regulation), and the Tennessee Valley Authority (bringing electricity to rural areas in seven states). These measures were not just numerous and varied, they were massive in scale. During the 1930s one American in five, not counting their families, directly benefited from one or another form of federal assistance.

Each of these measures, along with many proposals that never came to fruition, became the subject of economic analysis. During the Depression the U.S. government became the world's largest employer of economists, as both traditional government departments and new agencies added to their staffs. At the same time, economists in universities and in many affected industries turned their energies to analyzing the effects of the many policies newly put in place, as well as even more that remained mere proposals. The spirit and the method of Richard T. Ely pervaded these efforts.

There was also a more basic departure in economic thinking in response to the Depression, one that did extend to the discipline's conceptual core. Fluctuations in economic activity, whether agricultural or industrial, had long been familiar. So had banking crises. Chronic mass unemployment, persisting for a decade and more, was a new phenomenon, however, and existing economic theory was incapable of either explaining it or devising a remedy. Under the standard theory, why would would-be workers, especially those suffering the hardships that were so easily visible during the Depression, not simply accept a lower wage in order to find employment? Why would firms not cut prices in order to attract customers and maintain their production? In fact, wages and prices did fall during the Depression. Why, then, did these declines not put both people and factories back to work? Was the problem merely that wages and prices hadn't fallen enough? Would further declines do the job?[51]

A parallel line of questioning challenged the conventional theory of how monetary policy works. As prices and wages fell, the money in people's pockets and in their bank accounts gained in purchasing power. Why did people not feel richer and therefore spend more? And if consumers' response to the enhanced value of their monetary holdings was insufficient to spur the economy back to full employment, why couldn't the central bank simply create more money? After doing without a central bank from 1836 to 1914, the United States had established the Federal Reserve System not only to prevent banking crises—in addition to memories from the nineteenth century, the repeated crises of 1901, 1907, and 1913 greatly increased support for the initiative—but also to keep blocked-up financial markets from impeding nonfinancial economic activity. Now America had a central bank, but it seemed impotent to achieve either task.

At the most basic level, established economic theory going back to Smith, Ricardo, and Mill, and not contradicted by any of their successors in either Britain or America held that the overall level of economic activity was determined by the availability and cost of relevant inputs to production—most importantly labor and capital, and in an agricultural economy land too—in conjunction with the technology and organization used to combine them. In the 1930s there were no fewer available workers than before, and the lines at employment offices made clear that they still wanted to work. The factories were still there, and their owners complained bitterly about not being able to run them. People had not forgotten the technologies that were in use just a few years before. Why, then, were output and employment so far below what they had been in 1929?

The contribution of the English economist John Maynard Keynes, quickly taken up by Alvin Hansen and other followers in America, was to recognize that the supply of inputs to production was only half of the story.[52] There had to be demand for the output as well. The concept of an economy's *aggregate supply* of goods and services, based on its available human and physical resources together with its level of technology and its degree of specialization (division of labor), had implicitly been central to economics since Smith, and explicitly so since Ricardo. But there was no parallel concept of *aggregate demand*. The standard assumption was that prices would adjust so that consumers bought what firms produced. If prices fell far enough, some firms might cut back on production; but in the end consumers would buy what the firms produced, and markets would clear.

Keynes introduced the parallel notion of aggregate *demand,* determined by a variety of influences such as interest rates, investors' expectations, businessmen's optimistic or pessimistic "animal spirits," and the taxing and spending done by the government. The level of aggregate demand mattered because firms would not hire labor to produce what they could not sell, and households could not buy what they had no income to afford. Without jobs, households had no income and therefore could not buy firms' products. Without customers, firms could not sell their output and therefore had no need for workers.

Instead of the smoothly efficient functioning of competitive markets conceived by Smith, and largely accepted by his successors up until the 1930s Depression, the conditions now prevailing constituted a crippling failing of coordination. Workers wanted jobs, and if they had them they would buy goods and services. Firms wanted customers, and if they had them they would hire labor and produce goods and services. But neither group acting on its own—much less any single worker or any individual firm—could move forward without the other side's doing so as well. Smith's great contribution had been to show how competitive markets coordinated participants' diverse and sometimes inconsistent intentions. Now the market economy was manifestly failing at that task.

Introducing the concept of aggregate demand, together with a theory of what determined it, opened the way for an entirely new dimension of economics: *macro*economics, meaning analysis of the behavior of entire economies. Most of what had before been simply "economics" now became *micro*economics, meaning analysis of the behavior of individual households and firms. Any economy's aggregate output is of course merely the total of the goods and services produced by all of the firms within it, and at the same time the total of the purchases made by all of its households (plus the government). Similarly, any economy's aggregate employment is the result of all of the decisions that firms make to offer jobs and that individuals make to take them. But the fundamental basis of macroeconomics, stemming from Keynes, was the insight that features of the *interaction* of these firms and individual workers and consumers, in a market setting coordinated by nothing other than Adam Smith's competitive price system, can render the behavior of the aggregate economy different from simply the sum of what each firm and each person acting individually would choose to do. The goal of this new line of thinking, ever since, has been to understand what the essential features of this economic interaction are, and to establish the conditions under which actual economy-wide outcomes differ from what simply adding up the relevant individual would-be behavior, on a stand-alone basis, would imply. In the spirit of economics as an ameliorative discipline, macroeconomists have also sought to explore potential policy remedies for the resulting pathologies, most prominently the failure to sustain full employment (or, in parts of the period since the Great Depression, a tendency toward overfull employment which leads to price inflation).

Keynes's contribution, and the development of macroeconomics to which it led, marked the kind of fundamental conceptual departure not often prompted by external forces in a mature discipline. But in this respect as in so many others, the Great Depression was an exception.[53] Not only in the United States but throughout the industrialized world, economies were not behaving as Smith and Ricardo and Mill— together with Wayland and Clark and Ely—thought. And the resulting human trauma was too great to ignore.

Especially in America, the Depression had a lasting effect on religious attitudes as well. Viewed from one perspective, the hardships of the 1930s might have led to a reinforcement of support for the activist ideas that were central to the Social Gospel, and that became part of mainline establishment thinking with the creation of the Federal Council of Churches. In the latter decades of the nineteenth century, even the periods of general prosperity were leaving behind large numbers of the nation's citizens.[54] Now, with prosperity a distant memory, the down-and-out families and homeless children that Jacob Riis had photographed in New York City were visible all across the country. The activist remedies that Washington Gladden and Walter Rauschenbusch had sought even then, and that the FCC had embraced in its Social Creed just before World War I, seemed more evidently needed than ever.

Roosevelt's moral education had been squarely within the Social Gospel wing of modern Christianity, and many of his administration's New Deal programs merely added specifics to the more general decla-

rations of purpose made not long before by mainline Protestant organizations.[55] Others in his administration, most notably Labor Secretary
Frances Perkins (the first woman to serve as a U.S. cabinet officer) and
Commerce Secretary Harry Hopkins (who also supervised a number
of key agencies like the Federal Emergency Relief Administration and
the Works Progress Administration), also came from active Social
Gospel backgrounds. The new macroeconomic policy advocated by
Keynes—that the government should spend beyond its revenues if
necessary to bolster insufficient aggregate demand—likewise bore an
affinity to the active, interventionist ethos expressed first by the Social
Gospel and then by the FCC and its supporters.

But the trauma of the Depression, and then the lingering mass
unemployment through the long years of the recovery, eroded citizens' confidence in established authority at all levels, religious as well
as civil. For many religious believers, it also called into question the
confident postmillennialism that had underpinned both the Social
Gospel and the Gospel of Wealth in the previous century, and that now
ran through much of mainline Protestant thinking. The carnage in the
trenches of the world war—even more so, the evident failure of the
"War to End All Wars" to achieve that purpose—had increasingly rendered optimistic visions of secular progress suspect.[56] So too had the
worldwide influenza epidemic that immediately followed, killing more
people than the war had. As reflected also in the shifting tide of the
nation's electoral politics, Social Gospel ideas in particular lost their
appeal in American culture. The war had undermined the assumption
of human rationality and basic human decency on which the movement had rested.[57]

Now the Depression had further undermined public optimism.
The world in which many Americans lived had become visibly worse,
not better, within their lifetimes. At the bottom of the Depression
the country's per capita income stood below where it had been thirty
years earlier. Even just restoring the living conditions of a decade or
two decades before seemed little more than a fond hope.[58] Far fewer
Americans than before found themselves still able to embrace Walter
Rauschenbusch's optimism, expressed during the war, that "It is for us
to see the Kingdom of God as always coming, always pressing in on the
present, always big with possibility."[59] By the 1930s better times did not
seem to be coming. Few big possibilities for the future were apparent.

Events abroad further compounded the sense that the world was moving away from, not toward, any kind of New Jerusalem. By the end of the world war, Russia had fallen victim to the Bolshevik Revolution and then a communist dictatorship. Germany managed to overcome first anarchy and then hyperinflation, establishing a new republican government to replace the Kaiser; but under the weight of the Depression the country now turned to Nazism. Fascists were in charge in Italy, Spain, and Portugal. The Austro-Hungarian Empire had collapsed at the end of the war, and since then many of its component pieces had struggled even to survive as independent nation-states, much less deliver any improvement in their citizens' lives. The very idea of progress leading to a future earthly millennium seemed increasingly fanciful. As fundamentalist Presbyterian minister J. Vernon McGee later summarized the impact of these varied disasters, looking back after World War II and the beginning of the Cold War, "two world wars, a worldwide depression and then the atomic bomb put the postmillennialists out of business."[60]

Despite their doubts about any postmillennial future, under the pressure of the times Americans during the Depression looked in increasing numbers to their religion for comfort in the face of personal privation, either real or threatened, and in outright fear for the stability of the world in which they lived. For many, the vague and idealistic abstractions of the mainline churches seemed simply inadequate. Modernist thinking that rejected any fixed creed, and liberal principles that emphasized the church's tolerance for divergent points of view, required a certain base of assured confidence. During the twentieth century's first three decades, mainline Protestant spokesmen had been appealing to a public who mostly enjoyed that confidence.[61] Now it was gone. Allegiance to the mainline churches, and to their ideas, withered as well.

Uniting Religious and Economic Conservatism

The century's most blatant force of satanic utopianism is communism.

—WILLIAM F. BUCKLEY JR.

Communism is not only an economic interpretation of life—Communism is a religion that is inspired, directed, and motivated by the Devil himself who has declared war against Almighty God.

—BILLY GRAHAM

Many Americans, both clergy and laymen, saw the Great Depression as a form of divine punishment. The Hebrew Bible portrays the frequent disasters that afflicted the ancient Israelites—plagues, invasion by foreign powers, the destruction of the first Jewish Temple, the forced exile in Babylonia—as God's response to the people's repeatedly straying into idolatry. Many Americans now viewed the Depression as the all too inevitable consequence of their own nation's moral failings, some of which seemed to constitute new forms of idol worship. The Jazz Age had introduced new social customs along with new ideas about sexual morality. The decade's stock market boom had brought sudden wealth to investors who, in the eyes of many fellow citizens, were mere "speculators" who had done nothing to earn it. The Eighteenth Amendment, prohibiting the manufacture, sale, or transportation of alcoholic beverages, had promised to fulfill a long-held aspiration of American Protestant reformers. The result instead was pervasive gangsterism, violence, and corruption, with perhaps even more drunkenness than before.

President Herbert Hoover's treasury secretary, Andrew Mellon, welcomed the financial panic that brought on the Depression as the means to "purge the rottenness out of the system." Instead of resisting the economic decline that followed, Mellon recommended letting the destruction run its course, like a fever killing germs that had invaded the body. His advice to Hoover was "Liquidate labor, liquidate stocks, liquidate the farmers, liquidate real estate."[1] Many in the clergy agreed. Preaching at New York's Grace Episcopal Church while visiting from England, on the Sunday immediately following the October 1929 stock market crash, the Bishop of Winchester acknowledged that the financial crisis had no doubt brought distress to many innocent people. But, he continued, "I shall not be sorry it has come if it has administered a severe blow to that gambling spirit which attempts to get something for nothing, to obtain larger profits at the ruin of others. The gambling craze practically means an attempt to get something for nothing, to secure a far higher reward for an investment than it really deserves." At All Angels Episcopal Church, Reverend George Trowbridge said that while he was desperately sorry at the defeat and humiliation so many had suffered, nonetheless "I do not believe it is morally or economically sound to gamble as men and women have been doing with ever increasing fervor, and . . . I cannot help but feel that they have in a sense received their just deserts."[2] Franklin Roosevelt, a senior warden (the highest lay office) in the Episcopal Church and also at the time governor of New York, likewise criticized the "fever of speculation."[3]

Once Roosevelt became president, however, he swiftly moved from gloating over the speculators' losses to trying one policy after another in the attempt to put ordinary Americans back to work.[4] In his first inaugural address, a speech rife with biblical language and allusions— "We are stricken by no plague of locusts," "The money changers have fled from their high seats in the temple"—he framed this effort in moral terms as much as material.[5] "Happiness lies not in the mere possession of money," Roosevelt declared; "it lies in the joy of achievement, in the thrill of creative effort. The joy and moral stimulation of work no longer must be forgotten in the mad chase of evanescent profits."[6]

Many Americans, however, even those who agreed with Roosevelt about the moral value of work, did not accept his urgent call for "action, and action now" if that meant action by the government. Religious conservatives in particular increasingly lumped activist government together with the organized labor movement and the liberal Social Gospel as not just wrongheaded in practical terms but precursors of a politically statist Antichrist. Writing during World War I, Walter Rauschenbusch had hailed the Social Gospel as "the moral power in the propaganda of Socialism."[7] By contrast, in a volume of *The Fundamentals* published just two years before, Charles Erdman, a Presbyterian minister and a professor at Princeton Seminary, denounced "the endeavor which many are making to identify Socialism with Christianity." Socialism, he bluntly stated, was not only no substitute for religion, it was "antagonistic to Christianity." Christianity, in the true form that he and his Princeton colleagues like J. Gresham Machen taught, "is something other than a social propaganda and far more than an economic theory."[8] Such disputes within the Protestant clergy may have appeared parochial in 1917. By 1933 the stakes were far greater.

Events abroad heightened the sense of urgency. Many Americans feared that the rise of fascism in Germany and Italy, and the Bolshevik dictatorship in Russia, pointed to where this country too might be heading. Some conservative clergymen—including the young Harold Ockenga, who would go on after World War II to become one of the foremost leaders of American evangelical Protestantism—speculated that Hitler, Mussolini, Stalin, and Roosevelt were conspiring to establish a confederacy to be ruled by the Antichrist.[9] Within months of Roosevelt's taking office, the fundamentalist *Moody Monthly* explicitly compared the president to Hitler and warned that his actions were preparing the way for "the big dictator, the superman, the lawless one at the head of the ten kingdoms of the prophetic earth."[10] When the new administration officially recognized the USSR later that year (a step none of its predecessors since the Bolshevik Revolution had been willing to take), the move seemed to provide conclusive evidence.

A few years later, other conservative religious figures interpreted the Blue Eagle sign, which businesses participating in the short-lived National Recovery Administration program were asked to display, as a precursor to the "mark of the beast" foretold in Revelation. Billy Sunday described the NRA and other anti-Depression initiatives as "serpentine coils of this communistic, socialistic, atheistic, monster."[11] Louis Bauman, a minister in the fundamentalist Brethren Church in

Los Angeles, but with a large nationwide following as well, wrote in 1936 (again referring to Roosevelt) that "dictators do not long remain benevolent! Benevolent dictator; then, tyrannical dictator; then, Antichrist."[12] The president's seemingly endless series of economic initiatives seemed to some the harbinger of a biblically foretold political despotism. Fundamentalist Baptist preacher J. Frank Norris, who had already labeled Roosevelt a communist before his election, now wrote that the New Deal was "no more or less than the American name for Russian Communism."[13]

In time, the moral fervor earlier directed at speculators and bootleggers developed into a full-scale religiously based opposition to the Roosevelt administration's policies.[14] By 1937 James Fifield, pastor at First Congregational Church in Los Angeles, was proclaiming that "The President of the United States and his administration are responsible for the willful or unconscious destruction of thrift, initiative, industriousness and resourcefulness which have been among our best assets since Pilgrim days."[15] Fifield was not an insignificant figure. His was the largest Congregational church in the world. Spiritual Mobilization, a nationwide organization he founded in 1935 and then led as its president, sponsored lectures, conferences, and retreats across the country, all directed toward mobilizing religious commitment to free market economic principles and laissez-faire policies.

Fifield was a theological moderate who attached little importance to doctrine. Like Dwight Moody and other revivalists of an earlier era, however, he viewed the aim of Christianity as saving individuals, not rectifying the ills of society along Social Gospel lines. If citizens were in distress, traditional Protestant voluntarism would assist them. The government's usurping that role amounted to "pagan statism."[16] Fifield was also unsympathetic to government efforts to reduce racial discrimination, criticizing "efforts of minorities to push in where they are not wanted."[17] In parallel, his economic views were intensely conservative, and he saw the government as the greatest threat now facing America's capitalist system. He directed his preaching and his organizational energies to mounting a religious opposition to Roosevelt's program. "I speak of the intimate, personal observations I have made of individuals who have lost their ideal, their purpose, and their motive through the New Deal's destruction of spiritual rootage," Fifield wrote. "Every Christian should oppose the totalitarian trends of the New Deal."[18]

Fifield was not alone in his sentiments, and in time other conservatives in the clergy joined his effort. George Benson, who served for ten years as an unordained missionary in China and then became president of church-sponsored Harding College in his native Arkansas, likewise became a nationally prominent critic of the Roosevelt administration's policies. He was especially critical of the government's deficit spending, calling instead for balanced budgets. Benson spoke widely throughout the country at the behest of conservative groups, and he wrote a regular column that eventually spread to 2,500 newspapers across the country. He also started the National Educational Program, based at Harding College, to foster "godliness and patriotism" and to resist "pernicious" government policies imposing market regulation.[19]

Charles Fuller, a Baptist minister, reached an even broader audience—in time estimated at twenty million—through his weekly radio broadcast, *The Old Fashioned Revival Hour,* in which he too championed free market economic policies. Shortly after World War II, Fuller established the conservative Fuller Theological Seminary in California. Wilbur Smith, a product of the Moody Bible Institute and later a theology professor at Fuller Seminary, was even more specific in identifying Roosevelt as a dictator, arguing that his election, along with the sudden rise of dictatorships throughout Europe, served as "preparation for the coming of a great world dictator."[20]

These conservative clergymen and theologians who opposed the activist direction taken by American economic policy enjoyed the support of powerfully motivated and financially well-endowed members of the country's business community—so much so that in many instances the ideas and initiative seemed to come not from the clergy but from businessmen, who recruited sympathetic preachers to advance their opposition to the New Deal. Conservative businessmen had already been active in opposing Roosevelt's policies, albeit not from any explicit religious perspective. As early as 1934, the three DuPont brothers (of the DuPont chemical company family), each of whom had earlier supported Roosevelt, started the American Liberty League to oppose his administration's new direction. But now many anti-Roosevelt businessmen turned to the clergy to advance their agenda.[21]

J. Howard Pew, whose family had founded Sun Oil and who served as the company's president, was especially active in opposing Roosevelt, becoming a leading force in the DuPonts' new organization as well as other secular groups like the National Association of Manufacturers. But Pew helped finance many elements of the religiously based opposition too, lending financial and organizational support to both James Fifield and George Benson, and taking a leadership role in numerous other efforts. (Later, in the 1950s, Pew helped to found the Christian Freedom Foundation, which published the biweekly conservative magazine *Christian Economics,* and he also helped fund the more broadly oriented *Christianity Today.*) George Pepperdine, the founder of Western Auto Supply Company, likewise lent both money and activism to the anti–New Deal campaign. In 1937 he established Pepperdine College, in Los Angeles, as an institution dedicated to teaching "under conservative, fundamental Christian supervision."[22]

Part of what was new in these initiatives was the deliberate deployment of religious arguments, articulated by clergymen and other prominent religious figures, to advance a specifically *economic* agenda: conservative, laissez-faire economic policies. In the early and middle decades of the nineteenth century, religious thinking had influenced American economic ideas, and the resulting markets-based economic theorizing naturally bore a positive affinity with the religious thinking that had inspired it. Later in the century, and on into the 1920s, Social Gospel spokesmen and then the Federal Council of Churches had advocated a different direction in economic policy, also on religious grounds. Now this development had come full circle, as people who were neither economists nor clergymen encouraged and even recruited preachers to argue—on religious grounds—for the laissez-faire policies that they favored.

What was also new was the campaign to bring the force of religion to bear on how the general public thought about these issues. This development too marked a significant further progression in the historical influence of religious thinking on economic thinking. Some anti-Roosevelt activists did enlist economists in their efforts. Alfred Haake, for example, who had been chairman of Rutgers's economics department and then went on to work as a prominent consultant to General Motors and other industrial companies, became director of the Chicago regional office of James Fifield's Spiritual Mobilization. But the primary focus of Fifield's efforts, like Pew's and Pepperdine's and the DuPonts', was not influencing the thinking of economists. Their target was ordinary citizens.

Both of these changes proved lasting. American clergymen, often with support from the business community and from conservative political groups as well (themselves frequently business-funded), have often since then been at the forefront of activism on behalf of conservative economic policies. And as economics has become ever more mature as a discipline, and therefore progressively more insulated at the basic conceptual level from influences originating outside the field,[23] the bearing of religious thinking has increasingly been a matter of shaping the attitudes of the public at large. Because most ordinary citizens are primarily interested in how economic realities affect their lives—not theories about how economies behave, or the methodologies that economists apply in their research—in the modern era the influence of religious thinking on economic thinking has therefore been most visible in affecting public attitudes regarding economic policy.

The effort to deploy religiously based arguments in the service of conservative economic policies—spearheaded by clergymen, funded and sometimes initiated by interested businessmen, and aimed mostly at the general public—resumed after a half-decade hiatus in which the nation mobilized its full energy for World War II. The aim now was to prevent the New Deal programs that Roosevelt had implemented a decade earlier, to combat the Depression and spur the subsequent recovery, from becoming permanently entrenched in America's political framework and possibly evolving into a full-fledged socialist welfare state. In 1946 the Methodist minister Abraham Vereide (who later established the National Prayer Breakfast) organized the National Council for Christian Leadership to bring politically conservative senators and congressmen together with economically conservative business leaders, under a religious umbrella.

The next year Presbyterian minister J. Vernon McGee became pastor of the Church of the Open Door, founded three decades earlier by oilman Lyman Stewart's Bible Institute of Los Angeles (which just a few years before had organized publication of *The Fundamentals*). McGee soon started a daily radio broadcast in which he regularly denounced Keynesian economic policies and government interference in the economy. A firm premillennialist, as was Stewart, McGee looked instead to the millennium to bring justice for the poor. But it was not the church's role, and certainly not government's, to bring the millennium about. "The Kingdom of God will *not* be established by man's efforts, by human ability," he argued. "It's not our business to build a Kingdom. . . . The Kingdom is never established by the church, never by an organization, never by a movement. The world will not grow into the Kingdom of Heaven."[24] And until the millennium came, he maintained, economic policies that prevented individuals from exercising free choice in the market impaired their freedom in matters of faith as well.[25]

Many of the key figures from business and the clergy who had led the anti–New Deal campaign during the Depression and the recovery years continued to be active in the postwar period as well. In 1949, with financial support from conservative backers in the business community, Spiritual Mobilization began broadcasting a weekly radio commentary by Reverend Fifield. Titled *The Freedom Story,* it soon aired on more than eight hundred stations across the country. Later that same year, Spiritual Mobilization started publishing a monthly magazine, *Faith and Freedom,* which consistently attacked not only the continuing New Deal policies but also the more liberal Protestant clergymen who supported them. Howard Pew's new magazine, *Christian Economics,* started publishing in 1950. Its masthead read, "We stand for free-enterprise—the economic system with the least amount of government and the greatest amount of Christianity."

Concerns about the government's role in the economy had gained significant intellectual heft, toward the close of the war, from the publication of Friedrich Hayek's highly influential tract *The Road to Serfdom.* The Austrian philosopher and economist had earlier done pathbreaking theoretical work showing how decentralized markets processed countless bits of information from widely dispersed sources, bringing them collectively to bear on resource allocation and other economic decisions far more efficiently than what any system of centralized planning could achieve. In his 1944 book he argued that the progressive encroachment of government on private economic decision making threatened not only to undo those efficiencies of the market economy but ultimately to impinge on personal liberties as well. Hayek's widely publicized American speaking tour, later that year, further spread the book's message in the United States, as did publication of a condensed version in *Reader's Digest*. Many of the clergymen who were actively campaigning for conservative economic policies helped to push the book as well. Fifield's Spiritual Mobilization, for example, advertised the book and also distributed it. (These sources of support notwithstanding, Hayek's thinking on policy questions was not as consistently conservative as the commonplace perception of him might imply; among other noteworthy departures, he favored nationalized health care.[26])

With some irony, conservatives' fears of continuing government intervention in the American economy took on even greater urgency after Dwight Eisenhower was elected president—and with a Republican majority in the U.S. Senate—in 1952. Many Republicans had embraced the World War II hero with no prior political affiliation as their opportunity to recapture the presidency after twenty uninterrupted years of Democratic administrations under Roosevelt and then Truman; and they proved right. But soon after taking office Eisenhower made clear that he had no interest in repealing key 1930s innovations like Social Security, deposit insurance, and banking and securities regulation, all of which Reverend Fifield and others had labeled socialist.[27] While he made no direct public statement on the subject, Eisenhower consistently declined to support efforts to reverse these essential New Deal programs. Privately, he explained that "Should any political party attempt to abolish social security, unemployment insurance, and eliminate labor laws and farm programs, you would not hear of that party again in our political history."[28]

Along with the mobilization of economically conservative members of the nation's Protestant clergy, theologically conservative groups had been organizing themselves as well. The recovery from the embarrassment of the 1925 Scopes trial had been a slow process. Leaders of conservative denominations continued to adhere to the principles set forth in *The Fundamentals,* but now they increasingly embraced a more inclusive concept of Christian fellowship in place of the narrower vision articulated by earlier intellectuals like Machen and preachers like Billy Sunday. Like the theologically liberal mainliners, who had managed to look beyond their denominational differences in order to come together in the Federal Council of Churches a generation before, many theological conservatives now likewise became willing to cooperate across denominational boundaries. Perhaps most important, in the wake of not only the Scopes trial but also the lengthy Depression and then the advent of World War II, they were now increasingly willing to engage with modern secular culture.

Religious conservatives had also come to understand the advantages—in visibility, in political clout, in public appeal—that their more liberal counterparts drew from having the FCC as a national-level umbrella organization. A further, related spur to their joining together was a recent decision by the major national radio networks not to sell airtime for religious broadcasts but to allot it for free to "recognized" religious communities, which for Protestants meant in practice denominations that belonged to the FCC. Evangelicals therefore saw themselves at risk of losing access to commercial radio, which by then had become one of their principal avenues for reaching a broad public audience.

In 1941 a group centered around the Moody Bible Institute agreed to form a nationwide body for evangelical denominations.[29] At the group's first official gathering, held the next year in St. Louis, participants agreed on the need for a permanent organization, which they named the National Association of Evangelicals for United Action (soon shortened to simply the National Association of Evangelicals). Harold Ockenga, the pastor of Boston's Park Street Church, became the NAE's first president. Ockenga had been a student at Princeton Theological Seminary at the time of J. Gresham Machen's revolt, and along with some of his more conservative classmates he had followed Machen to the new Westminster Seminary. He remained a staunch conservative, not only in his theology but in politics and economics too. The dual threat that the nation's evangelical churches faced, he argued in his keynote address at the St. Louis meeting, was Roman Catholicism on one side and "that terrible octopus of liberalism, which spreads itself throughout our Protestant Church," on the other. At the same time, he deplored the "revolution in our political form" that had come with the increasing role of the nation's government, a phenomenon he attributed to the "disintegration of Christianity" in America.[30]

In rallying his fellow evangelicals to the need for unity, Ockenga pointed to these and other "ominous clouds of battle which spell annihilation unless we are willing to run in a pack." Following decades of dissension among denominations, he admitted, "Evangelical Christianity has suffered nothing but a series of defeats." As a result, secularism had permeated our society, leading to "the break-up of the moral fibre of the American people." The need for unity was therefore urgent. "Satan's greatest stronghold," he told his listeners, was "the division of Christians into denominations as they are today."[31] In a follow-up address to the group a year later, he warned that "the kingdom of heaven is drawing to a close" and "the kingdom of hell is at hand. . . . We are almost in the age of the beast." The immediate problem confronting evangelicals was that the church, and with it the country's spiritual development, was being overwhelmed by material and ideological forces. But the impending crisis America faced was not just moral, it was political and economic too. Once World War II ended, the new age would be "one of famine, of pestilence, unemployment and of crisis that will outstrip that following World War I many times."[32] Under Ockenga's leadership, the NAE quickly established itself as the conservative counterpart to the FCC.

Even so, it took time for the NAE to gain widespread acceptance among theologically conservative American Protestants. Many of the denominations that had sent representatives to the founding conference in Chicago declined to join, and Ockenga's Conservative Congregational Conference ended up supplying a disproportionate share of the organizational energy and leadership. By 1945 only fifteen denominations had signed up, representing fewer than half a million parishioners. (The FCC at that time had only twenty-four member denominations, but they represented more than 27 million parishioners; the Methodist Church alone accounted for eight million.[33]) By the mid-1950s there were forty member denominations in the NAE, including the Assemblies of God and the National Association of Free Will Baptists, each with about 400,000 members. Even so, most, like Ockenga's, were small. Most significantly, the Southern Baptist Convention, then with five and a half million members, followed traditional Baptist doctrine in rejecting such interdenominational groups as having no legitimate authority and potentially even threatening Baptist distinctiveness. (Today the country's largest Protestant denomination, with fifteen million members, the Southern Baptist Convention still belongs to neither the NAE nor the FCC.) Both the National Baptist

Convention, then with four million members, and the Northern Baptist Convention, with one and a half million, remained in the FCC.

While Ockenga did much of the organizational work, the NAE's principal intellectual leader was Carl Henry, a Baptist minister and a graduate of Wheaton College and the Northern Baptist Theological Seminary.[34] Henry's theology was premillennialist, but he was sharply critical of the apathy that many who shared that outlook had traditionally shown toward efforts to improve conditions in society. He too wanted to convert individual men and women, but he sought as well to inject Christian values in the modern world more broadly. He therefore challenged his fellow evangelicals to move beyond their resistance to public engagement.

Henry's 1947 book, *The Uneasy Conscience of Modern Fundamentalism*, was a manifesto for just this kind of new, activist evangelicalism. "The church needs a progressive Fundamentalism with a social message," he wrote. "If historic Christianity is again to compete as a vital world ideology, evangelicalism must project a solution for the most pressing world problems. It must offer a formula for a new world mind with spiritual ends, involving evangelical affirmations in political, economic, sociological, and educational realms."[35] In a follow-up article published the next year, Henry was expansive in laying out the areas of focus that he deemed appropriate for this new evangelical effort: "the political and economic oppression of smaller nations, race tensions, the struggle between capitalism and the leftist economies, the communist bid for world supremacy, the tension between management and labor, the widespread longing for world peace, the growing inevitability of another war."[36] Henry's approach to this broad range of problems, however, consistently held to revivalist tradition; the answer was not government regulation but Christian morality. In effect, Henry took up Harry Emerson Fosdick's action-oriented challenge, but within J. Gresham Machen's traditional theology.

Under the prodding of Henry and other like-minded, more modern evangelicals, in 1951 the NAE established a Forum on Social Action, which in time led to a permanent NAE Commission on Social Action. In the meanwhile, in 1948 Henry had become the first professor of theology at the new Fuller Seminary. In 1956 he became the founding editor of *Christianity Today,* a new conservative evangelical magazine started by revivalist Billy Graham and funded in large part by Howard

Pew. In the late 1960s, however, Henry resigned his position in protest against what he deemed excessive interference by Pew, who opposed his desire for evangelical Protestants to engage with the social issues of the day, and in particular wanted the magazine to take a more explicitly critical view toward the mainline churches' stance on many of these issues. Henry, hoping to win mainliners to his cause, disagreed. Pew prevailed.[37]

By mid-century, however, the focus of America's political attention had shifted. The change carried far-reaching implications for the way in which the nation's renascent Protestant evangelicalism took up Carl Henry's challenge to engage with the secular world of affairs, as well as for how religious thinking influenced the American public's views of economics and economic policy. The catalyzing force was the threat of world communism, backed up by a Soviet Union that now had atomic weapons. The impact in America of this new challenge was to unite religious conservatism and economic conservatism in ways that went well beyond the earlier cooperation of businessmen and clergymen in opposing the New Deal. It now brought together, for purposes of public participation in national affairs, what had earlier been distinct lines of conservative political thinking.

Two different conservative philosophies were—and, to a great extent, still are—prominent in American approaches to politics. Traditionalism, stemming in large part from the writings of the eighteenth-century Irish-English politician Edmund Burke, emphasizes the value of continuity in both the forms and the substance of governance, as well as everyday life. As Burke stated the central principle in his widely read reaction to the French Revolution, "it is with infinite caution that any man ought to venture upon pulling down an edifice which has answered in any tolerable degree for ages the common purposes of society."[38] In spirit, Burkean conservatism is communitarian and often paternalistic. For purposes of economic policy, it is often interventionist. Traditional religious institutions and practice are normally considered part of the continuity to be valued and preserved.

By contrast, libertarianism, in America largely associated with Friedrich Hayek's *The Road to Serfdom* but also with roots in the earlier thinking of John Locke and other political philosophers who empha-

sized individual rights, is strongly individualistic. Its economic implications normally favor laissez-faire policies. Libertarianism naturally
favors freedom of religious choice, and to many this principle extends
to the freedom to choose no religion at all. Especially in contrast to
Burkean traditionalism, libertarian thinking often therefore carries
atheistic overtones.

The force that brought these disparate lines of conservative thinking
together in the public sphere, and at the same time united America's
religious conservatives and economic conservatives, was the existential threat posed by the seemingly inexorable spread of communism.
Communism had the unique feature of simultaneously representing the mortal enemy of three different sets of principles central to
Western societies, and especially to America. With its "dictatorship of
the proletariat," which in practice meant placing all authority under
the direction of the Communist Party, communism was the antithesis of political democracy. With socialized ownership of factories,
machinery, and other "means of production," together with resource
allocations determined by top-down central planning, communism
was the antithesis of free market capitalism. And as both Karl Marx
and Friedrich Engels had explained—Marx famously labeled religion
"the opium of the people"; Engels wrote that communism "makes all
existing religions superfluous and supersedes them"—and as the open
hostility of communist governments from China to Russia to Poland
now made clear, communism was the antithesis of Western religion.[39]

The opposition of communism to democracy was alone sufficient to
mobilize nearly universal antipathy among Americans. But the other
two features, in tandem, now played a crucial role as well. Because it
opposed free market capitalism, not only businessmen and other owners of capital but everyone who had a stake in the market system—or
who even merely believed in the economic advantages that competitive
markets convey—saw communism as a threat to people's daily way of
life. And because it opposed religion in the form that nearly all Americans knew, all those for whom religious belief and practice played an
important role in their lives saw communism as a threat to their spiritual well-being too. What made the opposition to communism such
a powerful force, not just mobilizing the country for the decades-long
Cold War against the Soviet Union but profoundly affecting American
society domestically, was the realization by these two only partially
overlapping groups that they were fighting the same battle.

More than anyone else, the person who brought together religious conservatism and economic conservatism under the banner of anticommunism was William F. Buckley Jr. The scion of a wealthy Roman Catholic family from Connecticut (his father had made his fortune in the oil business in Mexico), Buckley was born in New York but grew up partly in Paris and London.[40] After wartime military service he attended Yale, graduating in 1950. The next year, at age twenty-five, he published a harsh denunciation of the ideas to which he had been exposed there. Titled *God and Man at Yale*, the book was a broad attack on liberal ideas that he claimed were then dominant not just at this one university but in intellectual circles throughout much of America.[41] In contrast, Buckley embraced purer forms of individualism and free market economics, along with traditional (not necessarily Catholic) religion. The book attracted broad public attention, and it immediately made the young author a celebrity in conservative circles.

Buckley continued to write prolifically on the twin themes of religion and free market economics, forcefully arguing that the two realms of thinking were closely intertwined. In a reply to one of his critics, the year after *God and Man at Yale* appeared, he emphasized that "religion must inform the individual in *all* his activities." Specifically including the economic sphere of life, he wrote, "I feel that religion must guide the individual when he faces such questions as what are honorable and what are dishonorable means of amassing wealth, and what are responsible and irresponsible means of disbursing this wealth."[42]

Any spokesman for the Social Gospel would surely have agreed. But Buckley went on, as he had in his book, to make clear that the economic policies favored by the Social Gospel in the early years of the century, and implemented by Roosevelt in the 1930s and now defended by most liberals in the 1950s, were not what he had in mind. Instead, he believed that what he called "the great American adjustment—economic freedom" had earned "highly convincing credentials as a basically humanitarian, dignified, and realistic system of economic behavior . . . a system that has maximized individual freedom and individual prosperity." And, as he also had done in *God and Man at Yale*, he rejected the interventionist policies associated with the Social Gospel and then the New Deal, and now 1950s liberalism, dismissing them all as not just ineffective but so counterproductive as to undermine their own aims. "Our march down the primrose path of collectivism," he wrote, "far from alleviating the social evils of Manchesterism [a British term for unfettered market capitalism], will ultimately aggravate them, and nail down the coffin-lid on individual freedom besides."[43]

Buckley followed up *God and Man at Yale* with a second book in 1954, coauthored with his brother-in-law Brent Bozell (who a few years later wrote Barry Goldwater's best-selling *Conscience of a Conservative*). The new book sought to defend Senator Joseph McCarthy from the intense criticism he was by then receiving for the methods he used in his investigation into alleged communist infiltration of the U.S. government and the army.[44] The effort was unsuccessful—later that year the Senate formally censured McCarthy, and he ended his career in isolation and disgrace—but the book further solidified Buckley's status as a conservative stalwart as well as an exceptionally talented writer.

A year later Buckley launched a new weekly magazine, *National Review,* dedicated to advocating the blend of free market economics and libertarian politics, buttressed by a serious commitment to traditional religion, that he had first laid out in *God and Man at Yale.* In the "Publisher's Statement" announcing the new magazine, he was searing in his critique of contemporary American society. "The inroads that relativism has made on the American soul are not so easily evident," he wrote. "One must recently have lived on or close to a college campus to have a vivid intimation of what has happened. It is there that we see how a number of energetic social innovators, plugging their grand designs, succeeded over the years in capturing the liberal intellectual imagination."[45] His aim was to mount a countervailing and equally energetic opposition.

At the same time, Buckley was also critical of the often self-serving efforts of the existing conservative establishment in contemporary American politics, especially on the part of the business community that had been leading the opposition to interventionist economic policies since the 1930s. To him, these business interests constituted "the well-fed Right, whose ignorance and amorality have never been exaggerated for the same reason that one cannot exaggerate infinity." He therefore saw his own initiative as a wholly new movement, firmly opposed to the left but also different from the right in its current form: "We begin publishing . . . with a considerable stock of experience with the irresponsible Right, and a despair of the intransigence of the Liberals."[46] But on the fundamental issues at stake, he knew on which side he stood. "The profound crisis of our era," he wrote, was "the conflict between the Social Engineers, who seek to adjust mankind to conform with scientific utopias, and the disciples of Truth, who defend the organic moral order . . . we are, without reservations, on the conservative side."[47]

What now made this conflict urgent, Buckley argued, was the communist threat. "The century's most blatant force of satanic utopianism is communism," he declared. And because communism was a force of and for evil, there was no room for compromise. Some Americans, including political figures as well as many thoughtful citizens who held no public office, were arguing that the United States should now accept the fact that the Soviet Union was a nuclear power, that Mao's communists had won in China, and that communism would continue to prevail over the European "satellites" that had fallen under Soviet domination in the aftermath of World War II. In an echo of J. Gresham Machen's attitude toward liberal Protestants, but now directed against a foreign enemy, Buckley made clear that the *National Review* would have none of it: "We consider 'coexistence' with communism neither desirable nor possible, nor honorable; we find ourselves irrevocably at war with communism and shall oppose any substitute for victory."[48]

National Review was an immediate success, and although it soon slowed its publication schedule from weekly to every other week it became a major force within American conservatism. In the meanwhile, Buckley continued to write, not just for his own magazine, and to speak in the service of the blend of economic and religious conservatism for which he became ever better known. His books from this period included *Up from Liberalism* (1959) and *Rumbles Left and Right* (1963). (Later in life, he wrote two memoirs, one a "literary autobiography" and the other an "autobiography of faith.") While his commitment to free markets and individual freedoms remained strong, he rejected calls to take the country back to where Franklin Roosevelt had found it. Adopting the same attitude toward the essential New Deal programs that Eisenhower would assume on becoming president, he wrote in *Up from Liberalism* that "if we permit ourselves to go on saying the same things about the imminence of catastrophe—if we become identified with the point of view that the social security laws toll the knell of our departed freedoms, or that national bankruptcy will take place the month after next—we will, like the Seventh Day Adventists, who close down the curtain on the world every season or so, lose our credit at the bar of public opinion."[49]

Beginning in 1966 Buckley also hosted a weekly television program,

Firing Line, on which he conducted live interviews with a wide range of guests, but especially with prominent conservatives like Barry Goldwater and Ronald Reagan. The show continued until well after China had abandoned Maoist economics in favor of a more market-oriented system, the Soviet Union had collapsed, and the USSR's European satellites had achieved independence.

The anticommunist crusade attracted vigorous support from America's religious activists as well, especially among the recently reenergized Protestant evangelical community. Opposition to "godless communism" had been a continual drumbeat since well before World War II. (The phrase itself dates to long before; in 1851 Augustus Thompson, a Congregational minister in Roxbury, Massachusetts, warned against the appeal of "a new social regimen, a godless communism."[50]) In an address to a meeting of the Federal Council of Churches in 1933, the Methodist Bishop of Zurich, visiting from Switzerland, praised the newly elected German chancellor Adolf Hitler for having "turned the current that was sweeping Germany into the chaos of Godless communism."[51] But the usage was not limited to Nazi sympathizers. In 1941 the Catholic journal *Commonweal* reacted to Germany's invasion of Poland and the Soviet Union's subsequent annexation of the eastern part of that country by arguing that "Hitler's treachery against his comrade in crime in the joint attack upon Catholic Poland is the perfect symbol and proof of the nazi basic philosophy and is not to be regarded as a holy crusade against godless Communism."[52]

America's political leaders now joined as well in the rejection of communism as godless. In his speech to the Democratic National Convention in the summer of 1940, accepting the party's nomination for an, unprecedented third term as president, Franklin Roosevelt warned that new forces let loose in the world were forcing one of the great choices of history. The decision facing America, together with the country's allies, was not merely a choice of government by the people versus dictatorship, or even freedom versus slavery. It was "the continuance of civilization as we know it versus the ultimate destruction of all that we have held dear—religion against godlessness; the ideal of justice against the practice of force; moral decency versus the firing squad."[53]

After the war, in 1948—earlier that year the Soviet Union had carried out a coup d'état to cement its control over Czechoslovakia—Harry Truman similarly declared, "I hate communism. I deplore what it does to the dignity and freedom of the individual. I detest the godless creed it teaches."[54] The point was a continual theme for Truman. As his time as president neared an end, in his public remarks the night before the 1952 election, he hailed the effort to bring "the united power of the free nations to overcome the conspiracy of godless communism."[55] And in his farewell address, two months later, he said of the communist world, "Theirs is a godless system, a system of slavery."[56] The theme long outlasted Truman. In 1959, addressing the opening session of the North Atlantic Council's ministerial meeting in Washington, President Eisenhower explained that in deciding to create NATO, "the stake was not merely the security of our nations from military onslaught; the true issue was our ability to protect the spiritual foundations of Western civilization against every kind of ruthless aggression, whether the attack should be military, economic or political."[57]

The uniting of religious conservatism and economic conservatism that Buckley and his colleagues at the *National Review* worked to bring about was likewise a dominant theme among the evangelical Protestant clergy. In an article titled "Christianity and the Social Crisis," published in 1955, Carl Henry wrote that "It is more than a matter of poor judgment to discuss the conflict between Communism and Capitalism solely on the economic level." To the contrary, the antireligious dimension of communism was central to its anticapitalism. "What Communism says about God, man, and the world is the fundamentum from which its economic theory is forged," he explained. "Only because Communism rejects supernatural providence, can it champion economic determinism. . . . The anti-spiritual framework of Communism is the very basis on which Communist economics rests."[58]

The implication was that adherence to traditional Western religion— for Henry, evangelical Protestantism—was a *necessary* element of the struggle against communism. "Christian theism alone is the indispensable guarantee of the well-being of man," he argued, "in the economic zone of life as well as every other." The origin of the crisis now facing the Western world, the economic challenge included, was the widespread rejection of its religious roots under the influence of both social scientists and liberal forces in the clergy. "The fact that the West surrendered the radical Biblical judgment on history and took Hegel and

Darwin rather than Jesus and Paul as its guides, and substituted the optimistic 'social gospel' for the redemptive good news, opened this door for a radical critique of the social order from the Marxist rather than Christian sources."[59] The Hebrew Bible had repeatedly attributed ancient Israel's worldly travails to the people's worship of false gods. Henry now linked the threat facing the entire Western world to the public embrace of modern social theory and, among Protestants, the mainline denominations' embrace of the Social Gospel rather than traditional evangelicalism. These perverse beliefs opened the way to communist atheism, together with all the other evils communism brought.

The way forward, therefore, was obvious. The aim of the Marxist program was unmistakable, Henry argued. Communism "insists that the suppression of belief in God and the supernatural is the fundamental basis on which a just economic order is to be reared." It followed that the essential first step in the effort to save capitalism was to return to traditional evangelical religion. "It is not Capitalism, therefore, which is the guardian of Christianity," he declared, "but Christianity which alone can safeguard free enterprise from perversion."[60]

The nexus linking communism as the antithesis of capitalism and communism as the antithesis of religion was a theme taken up by conservative political theorists as well. John Hallowell, a prominent political scientist who taught at Duke for more than four decades, likewise pointed to communism's rejection of religion as the basis for its economic program. To Hallowell, however, communism was itself a form of religion. That is what made its appeal so powerful. But it was a very different religion from traditional Western religion, and therefore one that competed with and ultimately opposed the Western version. In his book *The Communist Credo and the Christian Creed*, published the same year as Carl Henry's "Christianity and the Economic Crisis," Hallowell offered the view that communism "is something more than an economic doctrine, something more than an economic system opposed to capitalism . . . something more than a political or economic theory." It was, he argued, "a complete philosophy of life, a world view." In his analysis, "the passion which informs it is religious in character." Indeed, "it might well be described as a religion."[61]

Hallowell went on to elaborate the idea that communism was an alternative form of religion, one that offered a substitute for key aspects of what people had traditionally sought in Western religion, and therefore drew strength on just this account. "It is a gospel of salvation by revolution and therein lies its most powerful appeal," he wrote. Communism offered the promise of redemption—not for the individual, but collective redemption for all, in a new society. "It is nothing less than the redemption of mankind from corruption and evil that is its professed aim." At a more philosophical level, "Marxism offers a complete explanation of existence," and therefore "The communist, like the Christian, is a man of faith confident of the ultimate triumph of righteousness as he understands it."[62] A few years later, Paul Tillich, one of the foremost theologians in America in the early post–World War II decades, observed that as a matter of objective historical influence Karl Marx was "the most successful of all theologians since the Reformation."[63]

The idea that communism offered a different economic system *because it was an alternative religion* further helped to galvanize religious opposition not only to actual Soviet communism but to any policies that resonated with the interventionist, nonmarket economics that communism represented. John Foster Dulles, Eisenhower's secretary of state, summarized the connection in his remark that "For us there are two kinds of people in the world. There are those who are Christians and support free enterprise, and there are the others."[64] To be sure, some elements of the anticommunist movement—Disciples of Christ minister Gerald L. K. Smith ("the dean of American anti-Semitism"[65]), journalist and sometime academic Russell Kirk, businessman Robert Welch (who in 1958 founded the John Birch Society)—represented the far-right fringe of American politics. But they too mostly sprang from conservative religious origins, and nearly all embraced economic ideas that were not merely anticommunist but deeply conservative.

The American clergyman who most effectively took up the anticommunist crusade was Billy Graham. Born to Presbyterian parents in North Carolina, Graham attended a series of religious institutions before being ordained as a Southern Baptist minister at age twenty-one.[66] An engaging personality and an inspiring speaker, he soon established himself as one of America's leading revivalists, spurring countless individuals to accept "the call" at hugely attended revivals across the country as well as on radio and television. Some of the cru-

Billy Graham preaching in Trafalgar Square, London, 1954.
Both in America and abroad, Graham's engaging personality and powerful
style of preaching attracted enormous crowds, often in outdoor settings
that recalled the great revivals of an earlier era.

sades that he organized and led—at Madison Square Garden, at Yankee Stadium, at London's Trafalgar Square—were mammoth events that assumed historic significance in themselves. As time passed, Graham came to assume a role in American society that transcended evangelical Protestantism, and even the realm of religion per se. For decades he consistently ranked at or near the top of the annual Gallup survey asking who was the most admired man or woman in America.

Especially in his early career, Graham strongly pushed the conservative economic ideas that fellow clergymen like James Fifield and Charles Fuller had advocated in their opposition to the New Deal, and he often relied on support from many of the same businessmen who had supported their efforts. Graham first met Dwight Eisenhower, while the general was still in the army, through the efforts of Texas oil baron Sid Richardson. Several years later, it was Graham who persuaded Howard Pew to support *Christianity Today,* promising him that

"Instead of being liberal, like so many are, it will be conservative, evangelical, and anti-Communist. I sincerely believe it is the greatest possible investment an American businessman can make in the Kingdom of God at this moment."[67] (Graham's father-in-law, the former China missionary L. Nelson Bell, served as the magazine's executive editor from 1956 to 1973.) Later on, along with Harold Ockenga he enlisted Pew's support to establish the Gordon-Conwell Theological Seminary outside Boston—combining two existing schools, one named for Russell Conwell—as an East Coast counterpart to Fuller Seminary in California. George Champion, at the time executive vice president of Chase Manhattan Bank (and later the bank's CEO), chaired Graham's record-breaking New York crusade.

Graham consistently embraced the business community more generally and welcomed its support, writing in the magazine of the U.S. Chamber of Commerce that "Thousands of businessmen have discovered the satisfaction of having God as a working partner."[68] By contrast, in his early years he was hostile to organized labor, criticizing strikes as well as other union efforts to increase wages or improve working conditions. At the revival meetings that he led in Greensboro, North Carolina, in the fall of 1951—during the revival Graham preached thirty-five times, to audiences totaling nearly 400,000 people—he repeatedly offered the thought that the paradise of Eden had had "no union dues, no labor leaders, no snakes, no disease."[69]

By contrast, despite a halting start and frequent ambiguity—the Greensboro revival was segregated, and almost no blacks attended—Graham was early to express liberal views on matters of race, always one of the greatest points of tension in American society, and especially then and especially in his native South.[70] Even before the Supreme Court's 1954 Brown v. Board of Education decision, Graham made his opposition to racial segregation clear. At a revival in Chattanooga the year before, he threatened to leave unless the organizers took away the rope set up to separate blacks and whites in the congregation; when no one did so, he removed the rope himself.[71] In 1956 he published articles in both Life magazine and Ebony (thereby reaching both white and black audiences) explicitly labeling racism a sin and deploring segregation in the nation's churches. Later, he publicly demonstrated his support for Martin Luther King Jr., inviting King to give the invocation one evening at his 1957 Madison Square Garden crusade, and posting bail for him following one of his many arrests. In 1960, Graham published an article in *Reader's Digest*—another outlet that reached large numbers of evangelical Protestants—deploring segregation in America's churches.[72] He explained that while the societies portrayed in the Bible included people of different races, there was no scriptural basis for segregation. All people, blacks as well as whites, were equal in the sight of God.

Graham was also ecumenical in his theology, as well as in his conception of the aims of the revival movement. Despite his Presbyterian roots, he was a Baptist and he maintained that "*anyone* can be saved" (his italics).[73] From very early on, his preaching rejected the importance of denominational differences among Protestants. When the NAE criticized him for associating with nonfundamentalist Christian groups, he replied that he intended to "go anywhere, sponsored by anybody, to preach the gospel of Christ if there are no strings attached to my message."[74] In time he embraced a broader ecumenical stance, welcoming collaboration with Catholics, Jews, and believers in non-Judeo-Christian faiths as well. While he took the immediate mission of the revivals he led to be converting individual men and women, he also accepted the Social Gospel principle that the church played a crucial role in reforming society. Among the "tremendous social implications" that he explicitly attributed to past revivals, he included abolition of slavery, the end of child labor, reduced working hours, "our great trade unions," educational institutions, "most of our charity organizations," slum clearance programs, and women's suffrage.[75]

As time passed, and Graham acquired ever greater prominence and admiration, he made a point of publicly seeking friendships with politicians from both parties. Beginning with Eisenhower, he famously enjoyed a personal relationship with every American president for more than a half a century. (Not with Truman, however: after privately meeting with the president for the first time, at the White House, Graham knelt down on the front lawn to pose for press photographers; from then on Truman dismissed him as a publicity seeker.[76]) As his close ties to the conservative business community would suggest, however, his early career was more partisan. In his preaching he opposed most initiatives associated with the Democratic Party, not just on labor issues but including most welfare programs, and in 1951 he complained from the pulpit about "our debt-ridden inflationary economy with its fifteen-year record of deficit finance and with its staggering national debt."[77] He also opposed U.S. economic aid to Europe, like that deployed under the Marshall Plan, arguing that in the wake of the destruction of World War II the Europeans' "greatest need is not more money, food, or even medicine; it is Christ."[78]

More generally, Graham thought, government involvement in the economy smacked of socialism.[79] Revival was his preferred alternative to government intervention, in the economy or more broadly. But he sometimes argued for a more limited focus for religious bodies too. In his book *World Aflame,* published in the mid-1960s, he repeated the long-familiar conservative complaint that the church had been "trying to solve every ill of society." Instead, "if the church went back to its main task of preaching the Gospel and getting people converted to Christ it would have far more impact on the social structure of the nation than it can have in any other thing it could possibly do." In the same vein, he criticized religious figures on either the left or right who offered pronouncements about "disarmament, federal aid to education, birth control, the United Nations, and any number of social and political issues."[80]

Graham was early to move to the forefront of the anticommunist movement. In a sermon that he preached in Los Angeles in September 1949, within days of the Soviet Union's revealing that it now possessed an atomic bomb, he interpreted this new development in apocalyptic terms. "I am persuaded that time is desperately short!" he warned. Just a few months before, he noted, a British member of Parliament had concluded that "we have only five or ten years and our civilization will be ended." But "That was before he heard that Russia has the atomic bomb." Referring to the "devastated cities of Germany and the wreckage of war," which he had seen firsthand on his visits to Europe, Graham foresaw that "An arms race, unprecedented in the history of the world, is driving us madly toward destruction!" And he did not hesitate to bring the threat home to his listeners, urging them therefore to reform their lives and to seek salvation. "God Almighty is going to bring judgment upon this city unless people repent and believe," he warned. Later in the sermon he returned to the same theme: "I can see the judgment hand of God over Los Angeles. I can see judgment about to fall." And yet again, near the sermon's end, "this may be God's last call to Los Angeles!"[81]

The root of the threat, he explained, was that communism "has decided against God, against Christ, against the Bible, and against all religion." Anticipating the argument that Carl Henry and others would soon advance in greater depth, he went on to explain that communism was itself a form of religion. But to Graham it was the ultimate *anti*-religion: "Communism is not only an economic interpretation of life— Communism is a religion that is inspired, directed, and motivated by the Devil himself who has declared war against Almighty God." The Soviets' new weapon, he thought, made obvious the parallel to the end-of-time battles between the forces of light and the forces of darkness, as foretold in Revelation. The destruction of their city was inevitable if the citizens of Los Angeles did not repent and seek faith. "I warn you to repent of sin and turn to Jesus Christ as a city before it is too late," he told them. "If Sodom and Gomorrah could not get away with sin; if Pompeii and Rome could not escape, neither can Los Angeles! . . . Unless God's people turn to Him and the city repents, we are going to see the judgment of God come upon us."[82]

The threat of communism—both the material danger and the spiritual—remained a constant theme of Graham's preaching through-out the Cold War years. So did the association of communism with the devil, and so too did the vision of pending Armageddon. In a 1954 arti-cle titled "Satan's Religion," he wrote that "It is a battle to the death— either Communism must die, or Christianity must die, because it is actually a battle between Christ and anti-Christ."[83]

Communism, he explained, had falsely appropriated the tenets of Christianity: falsely because although it arrived at many of the same precepts, it did so without their divine origin and inspiration. Communism—Satan's religion, with Marx as its prophet, Lenin as the leading saint, and now Georgy Malenkov (who briefly took over after Stalin's death in 1953) as the high priest—had secularized almost every doctrine of Christianity that pertained to man. "For example, they boast that they believe in sharing and equal distribution. The doctrine of sharing was never more eloquently preached and practiced than it was by Jesus Christ." (As often, Graham's views on the subject departed from conservative thought as laid out in *The Fundamentals*. Accord-ing to theologian Charles Erdman's essay, "The fundamental economic problem relates to the division of wealth; and as to that Christ refused to speak."[84]) What was at issue in the imminent communist threat was the claim over mankind's most basic moral principles. "A war of ideologies is being waged throughout the world, a war of the secular against the spiritual," Graham proclaimed. "The actual battles in the areas of combat are only material manifestations of the larger battle that rages in the hearts of men throughout the earth."[85]

Importantly, however, there were what Graham called the actual battles. As William Buckley was arguing from a different perspective, the threat that communism posed was also a material one, indeed existential. The route forward, Graham believed, was not compromise, or coexistence, but confrontation. "With the forces of Communism now in possession of modern nuclear weapons," he wrote, "it behooves Americans to gird on the whole armor of God that we may be able to stand in the evil day."[86]

Graham was still advancing the same opposition to communism fifteen years later. In an appearance on Buckley's television show *Firing Line,* in 1969, he answered one question by explaining that "Communism, you see, has an eschatology. Marxism has an eschatology. They say that they can build a new world. They can bring about a social order, a new social order. . . . They can bring about heaven on earth. This is the ultimate teaching of Communism." Nor had the threat of nuclear war diminished in importance in his assessment. In answering another of Buckley's questions, he stated, "I think, for example, in the Bible it would have been very difficult to understand the 18th Chapter of Revelation [describing in detail the destruction of the future Babylon] 50 years ago. But since the advent of the atomic bomb and the hydrogen bomb, we now see that man has at his disposal weapons that could bring all of these prophetic things about . . . we live under the shadow of the bomb."[87] As the title of Graham's 1983 book indicates— *Approaching Hoofbeats: The Four Horsemen of the Apocalypse*—the theme remained a centerpiece of Graham's thinking throughout the Cold War years.[88]

Graham's apocalyptic vision proved a popular one among American conservatives. Speaking in 1961, a half-decade before he began to seek the governorship of California, Ronald Reagan reflected that "There can be only one end to the war we are in. . . . Wars like this one end in victory or defeat." Moreover, time was short. "One of the foremost authorities on communism in the world today, a former medical missionary, has said that we have ten years, not ten years in which to make a decision, we have ten years to decide the verdict because within this decade, the world will become either all free or all slave."[89] That same year, Barry Goldwater declared, "Nor is there such a thing as peaceful coexistence."[90] Running for president three years later, Goldwater made the same statement, this time making explicit the religious roots of the conflict. There could be "no existing with" Communist powers as "long as they do not believe in God."[91]

Two decades later, speaking now as president, Reagan elaborated on the theme that religion—and the communists' opposition to it—stood at the heart of the conflict. In an address to the National Association of Evangelicals, he reminded his listeners of his observation, in his first press conference as president, that "as good Marxist-Leninists, the Soviet leaders have openly and publicly declared that the only morality they recognize is that which will further their cause, which is world revolution." Their morality, he asserted, "is entirely subordinate to the interests of class war." Western morality, as members of the NAE well understood, was different. "We will never compromise our principles," the president assured his audience. "We will never abandon our belief in God."[92]

Reagan went on to relate the story of a young father whom he had heard some years earlier, at the height of the Cold War, addressing a large gathering in California. In Reagan's account of the incident, after telling the audience that "I love my little girls more than anything," the young man said, "I would rather see my little girls die now, still believing in God, than have them grow up under communism and one day die no longer believing in God." Reagan made clear his approval—more than that, his admiration. "There were thousands of young people in that audience," he recalled. "They came to their feet with shouts of joy. They had instantly recognized the profound truth in what he had said."[93]

Economics in
the Public Conversation

To relieve the sick, the destitute and the helpless, is a religious
duty, and therefore should, like every other religious duty, be a
voluntary service.

—FRANCIS WAYLAND

A society that responds voluntarily to its needs is superior to one
in which the welfare of humanity becomes the sole responsibility
of government.

—CARL HENRY

The Soviet Union ceased to exist as of Christmas Day 1991. The union's
fifteen erstwhile republics went their separate ways as independent
nations, some closely aligned but others not. In Russia, from the outset
the largest of the republics, and now again under its historic name,
the Communist Party survives only as a tiny remnant with no political influence. The country has adopted the forms of a parliamentary
democracy, but what was the rule of one party has in fact given way to
the rule of one man. Outright state ownership and central planning of
economic enterprise are gone, and many markets (for individual labor,
for example) do function freely, but important economic decisions as
well as a substantial share of the country's wealth are under the control of either the government or a small number of private "oligarchs."
Russia continues to challenge the United States—politically, diplomat-
ically, in a few areas economically—but the resulting tensions now follow the traditional channels of competition among great powers. The

existential threat once posed by the world's leading communist nation is past. And with communism gone, the Russian government again supports the country's Orthodox Christian Church.

China has followed a different path, and presented a different ongoing challenge, but there too the threat once posed by the determined advance of world communism is gone. China remains a military dictatorship under the sole control of the country's Communist Party. The party continues to be hostile to most forms of religion, though less on fundamental philosophical grounds than from concern that religious groups—for that matter, organized groups of any kind outside the control of the state—might undermine its exclusive political dominance. In the economic sphere, any remaining connection to communism as delineated by Marx and Lenin is weak at best. Mao Zedong died in 1976, and two years later Deng Xiaoping launched the country on a new economic path built around functioning markets and private enterprise (although many firms, especially the larger ones, remain partly state-owned). Since Deng's reforms, China has mounted the most rapid sustained economic growth ever recorded anywhere, as the economy has increasingly modernized and the population's average living standard has doubled and then redoubled and then doubled yet again. China now competes with the United States for influence and for markets, particularly in Asia and increasingly in other parts of the world as well such as Africa and South America. But this competition too mostly follows routes familiar from great power interactions in the past.[1]

In short, the threat posed by world communism, which galvanized conservative religious leaders like Billy Graham as well as lay figures like William F. Buckley throughout the latter half of the twentieth century—not to mention countless politicians ranging from Reagan and Goldwater to lesser figures at all levels of government—is gone. Even the last two remaining genuinely communist countries do not fit the description. Cuba, in earlier decades a sponsor of insurgencies in many developing countries, and once even the cause of a nuclear standoff between the United States and the Soviet Union, achieved such poor economic performance, over so many years, that it is now a threat to no one. North Korea, with which the United States, South Korea, and other allied nations remain technically at war, represents a military threat not because it is communist but because it is a rogue state with nuclear weapons.

Even so, the melding of religious conservatism and economic conservatism led by Buckley and Graham, in large part in response to the communist threat, remains in place. The pattern is familiar. Max Weber, seeking the historical roots of what he called the Protestant Ethic, argued that the modes of thought and behavior that he attributed to predestinarian Calvinism and other forms of ascetic Protestantism had long outlived the religious beliefs that originally gave rise to them. The longing for external signs to indicate whether an individual was or was not among the elect, Weber claimed, led believers to attach religious value to practical virtues like industriousness and thrift, as well as to commercial success per se. Over time, that religious value evolved into a more general moral appreciation of these "Protestant" forms of behavior, separate from any specific spiritual content and free-standing from any theological basis. As a result, Weber concluded, in countries where ascetic Protestantism had been prevalent, respect for these personal traits survived the weakening appeal of the religious beliefs that had first catalyzed them. In effect, the attitudes these beliefs spawned had become secularized.

The continuing religious connotation attached to conservative economic ideas, especially those bearing on public economic policy, has followed a similar course. In this case the historical catalyst was the existential threat that communism posed, simultaneously, to free market economics *and* to Western religion. Under that dual threat—and spurred on by the forceful leadership of Buckley and Graham, together with many others—the opposition to the New Deal, and then to the continuation of the government's role in the economy under Eisenhower's brand of moderate Republicanism and then Lyndon Johnson's Great Society, acquired a deep resonance with conservative Protestant beliefs. In this case, what atrophied was not the religious beliefs but the external threat. But the affinity that that threat created between conservative Protestantism and conservative economic attitudes has survived the demise of communism and therefore the disappearance of the threat itself.

As had been true all along, beginning with the reaction to Roosevelt's grab bag of New Deal programs during the Great Depression, the force of this religious resonance now bears primarily on popular opinion rather than the theorizing of professional economists. Economics has long since become sufficiently mature as an intellectual discipline that the great majority of its practitioners no longer shape their professional thinking according to external influences of this kind. The field has acquired its own internal momentum. Ordinary citizens, however, are a different story. And, like ordinary citizens everywhere, most Americans are interested not in the abstract theories of professional economists but practical questions regarding the economy in which they live and the policies that govern it.

This continued bearing of religious thinking on economic thinking—now focused on public opinion about the economy and economic policy, rather than economists' theorizing—is especially relevant in America. The United States is an outlier in the religiosity of its population. Most countries around the world (apart from majority-Muslim oil producers) follow a regular pattern in which higher living standards go along with less prevalent religious belief, as well as less frequent religious observance among those who do believe. In higher-income countries like Sweden, France, Canada, and Japan, a smaller share of the population reports believing in a supernatural deity, or in a life after death, or in a heaven or hell. Even among those who hold such beliefs, the frequency with which people go to church or take part in other religious observances, or even just have some ongoing association with a church or other religious institution, is smaller than elsewhere. (The phenomenon is not new: more than half a century ago, the British religious writer C. S. Lewis famously complained of the "unchristening of Europe."[2]) In middle-income countries like Mexico, Chile, and Lebanon, the prevalence of both belief and participation is substantially greater. In lower-income countries like India, Brazil, Nigeria, and Indonesia, the overwhelming majority of the population are believers, and most participate in formal religious activities on a regular basis.

The United States is a clear exception. Although Americans' per capita income exceeds that of any of the other large high-income countries—$64,000 per person in the U.S. versus the equivalent of $56,000 in Germany, at second place among the G7 countries, and an average of $46,000 among the other five[3]—Americans' prevalence of churchgoing and belief in God are far greater. When asked in surveys, 69 percent of Americans say they consider themselves to be religious, versus just 51 percent on average among the other G7 countries, and 35 percent attend a church or synagogue or mosque at least once a week, compared to only 15 percent on average in the other six countries.[4] In America 53 percent say religion is very important in their lives, compared to only 15 percent in the other six countries. Fifty-five percent of Americans pray at least once a day; elsewhere in the G7, on average just 17 percent do.[5] In each of these respects, as well as other standard measures of religiosity, Americans more nearly resemble citizens of countries with far lower incomes, such as Mexico (per capita income of $20,000) or Lebanon ($16,000).

Especially in America, therefore, religious influence on what *the general public* thinks about matters of economics and economic policy has the capacity to be powerful. And as the analogy to Weber's account of the origins of the Protestant Ethic suggests, it is not surprising that this influence continues to be widespread even though the force that brought the relevant aspects of religious thinking and economic thinking together in the first place—in this instance, the threat of world communism—has disappeared. Americans' exceptional religiosity shapes many aspects of the nation's popular culture, ranging from education to politics to popular literature.[6] There is no reason to expect attitudes toward economic questions, and issues of economic policy, to be different.

A puzzle that has attracted broad attention among observers of American politics in recent decades is the increasing tendency of large numbers of lower- and even middle-income Americans to vote, in national elections and often at the state and local levels too, in ways that run counter to their individual economic interest.[7] In 2015 *The New York Times* wrote, "It is one of the central political puzzles of our time: Parts of the country that depend on the safety-net programs supported by Democrats are increasingly voting for Republicans who favor shredding that net." Lower-income states like Mississippi, Kentucky, and Maine are prime examples. What the article labeled "this political disconnect among lower-income Americans" only became more pronounced in the 2016 election.[8] A further article in 2018, titled "The Government Check Disconnect," documented that on average across the United States, in counties where people receive the *most* government assistance, *higher* percentages vote Republican. The state highlighted in the article was Kentucky, where one resident in seven receives food stamps (one of the highest dependency rates in the country) and 62.5 percent of voters went for Trump.[9]

Attitudes toward taxes are a typical case in point. As of 2020, the top-bracket rate of individual income tax that Americans pay was 37 percent.[10] But that rate applied only to couples with combined income, after deductions, greater than $622,000, or for single taxpayers, greater than $518,000. As a result, fewer than one percent of all taxpayers were subject to the 37 percent rate. Including the tens of millions who earned too little to pay any tax at all, the percentage was even smaller. Yet more than one-third of all Americans—38 percent in one typical survey—say they are opposed to raising taxes on top-bracket incomes.[11] Thirty-three percent oppose a significantly increased tax rate on incomes above $10 million.[12] Candidates who favor such increases typically find that doing so hurts them at the polls.

An even more extreme example is estate taxation (the "death tax"). The amount that any individual can leave to others at death, free of any federal estate tax, is currently $11.6 million. (Before 2018 the amount was smaller by half, scaled for price inflation; in 2017 it was just under $5.5 million.) Each member of a married couple is individually entitled to this exemption, and transfers from one spouse to the other are exempt from tax altogether; the tax-free bequest limit for the two together is therefore $23.2 million. In addition to this fairly generous (for most people) amount, gifts made while a person is alive are tax-free up to some limit, and trusts and other legally structured vehicles can further reduce exposure to taxation.

As a result, even before the doubling of the exemption in 2018 fewer than one-fourth of one percent of deaths in America triggered any estate tax liability.[13] Yet surveys consistently show that nearly half of all Americans—48 percent in one typical poll—favor abolishing the estate tax altogether, rather than leaving it as a levy that only the richest families would have to pay.[14] (During the 2020 Democratic presidential primaries, some candidates advocated a wealth tax—in other words, doing what an estate tax does, but without waiting for a person to die—and the proposal seemed to attract some popular support,[15] but the candidates who advocated it did not prevail and the issue then disappeared from the campaign; it is too early to judge whether support for the idea will persist, and if so whether it will extend to estate taxation as well.)Attitudes toward a wide variety of other public policies, on familiar issues such as health care and benefits for unemployed workers, consistently display similar patterns as well.

One potential answer to this puzzle is that perhaps people believe it to be in their interest in the longer run—or if not their interest, then their children's—to keep top-bracket income tax rates low and not to tax estates at death. Most people know full well that their incomes today are not above $600,000, and that their wealth is far from $23 million. But perhaps they think they will become rich, and therefore face those higher tax rates, at some point in the future. Or if they do not become that rich themselves, perhaps their children will.

The evidence is clear, however, that for the overwhelming majority of Americans such beliefs would be mistaken. Apart from a small number of highly successful entrepreneurs, and an even smaller number of people who strike it rich playing the lottery, most people's lifetime income trajectory is well established by the time they reach their late twenties or early thirties.[16] People who have a significant probability of going on to earn large incomes and accumulating substantial wealth—business executives, sports stars, entertainment celebrities, some doctors and lawyers—may not have achieved that success yet, but by that age they are already in careers in which these outsized financial rewards are a possibility. By contrast, by their late twenties or early thirties most Americans are set in careers in which they know, or at least should know, that income and wealth on this scale are out of reach. Possibilities for one's children are more uncertain, but patterns of mobility make it unlikely as well that most Americans who are not already in the top income brackets themselves will see their children achieve such financial success either.[17] Most Americans who oppose higher tax rates on top-bracket incomes, or who call for abolishing estate taxes, are therefore resisting what other people pay.

It is also possible that people think they, or their children, will benefit indirectly from the economic effect of lower taxation at the top of the scale. Perhaps lower tax rates will lead those with top-bracket incomes to start new businesses, or invest to expand going concerns, thereby creating new jobs and making existing ones more productive. If so, wages would rise and everyone else would benefit too. This story had a plausible ring four decades ago, when Ronald Reagan proposed reducing the top individual income tax rate from 70 percent and the estate tax exemption was only $600,000. But with the top tax rate fluctuating between 30 and 40 percent ever since 1987, and the estate tax exemption now more than $23 million for a married couple, the prop-osition is far less persuasive.

Moreover, the experience of recent decades has lent little support to this line of thinking. When President Clinton proposed raising the top-bracket tax rate from 31 percent to 39.6 percent, in 1993, opponents of the measure predicted that doing so would choke off the then strug-gling recovery from the 1990–1991 economic downturn, and in partic-ular would stunt investment in new factories and machinery. Instead, after the tax rate went up the U.S. economy experienced the longest sustained expansion then on record, ending only in 2001, as well as one of the most rapid, with average growth of 3.7 percent per annum over the eight years following the tax increase. Business investment, far from showing any weakness, led the expansion.

The explanation for the behavior of lower- and middle-income vot-ers most frequently offered by political scientists—and many others as well, most prominently journalist Thomas Frank in his best-selling book *What's the Matter with Kansas?*—points to the joint implication of two salient features of how democracy works in America.[18] First, as a constitutional matter, the United States is a representative democracy, not a direct democracy. At the federal level, and for the most part at the state and local levels too, citizens vote for candidates, not for pol-icies. The use of referendum procedures, which can constitute direct democracy, varies widely from state to state. Some have binding votes on specific policy questions, some have nonbinding votes, and some have no referendum procedure at all. The procedure does not exist at the federal level. The U.S. Constitution has no referendum provision.

Second, not because of the Constitution but as a practical matter, the number of realistically competitive candidates in the general election for most federal or state offices is limited to two. No formal require-ment specifies the number of political parties; the U.S. Constitution is silent on the role of parties altogether. But in fact the United States has historically followed a two-party system, and this structure has displayed considerable stability over time. By now the Democrats and the Republicans have been in place as the country's two major politi-cal parties for more than a century and a half. Sometimes numerous candidates for any one office run in each party's primary, but in the great majority of cases the general election offers only two plausibly competitive candidates: one Democrat and one Republican.

The joint consequence of having a representative democracy and offering a limited choice of candidates is that voters are necessarily choosing among candidates who represent *combinations of policies,* some of which they may favor and others not. If only one issue mattered to voters in any election, the availability of two candidates might give them a complete choice: one candidate could take one position on that issue, and the other the opposite position. But as soon as there are even just two issues that matter, a ballot with only two candidates cannot provide a full choice. With two issues there are four possible combinations of policies, and so having a full range of choice would require a minimum of four candidates. With many different policy issues under debate, as is normally the case, the fact of having only two candidates between whom to pick renders the fact of having to choose between candidates who represent combinations of policies essential.

In the contemporary alignment, the two major parties tend to represent fairly stable combinations of policies. Republican candidates mostly advocate economic policies favorable to upper-income citizens (low taxes, especially for top-bracket taxpayers, limited support for the unemployed and others with low incomes, limited provision of social services, and the like), together with more conservative social policies (restriction or outright prohibition of abortion, for example, or opposition to same-sex marriage). Democrats typically advocate the opposite: economic policies more favorable to those with lower incomes, along with more liberal social policies. A voter who prefers economic policies favoring upper-income groups *and* conservative social policies therefore has little difficulty deciding to vote Republican. In the opposite direction, a voter who prefers economic policies favoring lower-income groups together with liberal social policies is highly likely to vote Democratic.[19]

The focus of the by now conventional explanation for the apparent voting puzzle is instead the voter whose self-interest lies with economic policies favoring *lower*-income groups but who also prefers *conservative* social policies. The evidence from opinion surveys indicates that nearly a third of American voters—29 percent according to one recent study—fall into this category.[20] What choice should someone make who would benefit from more generous unemployment benefits and welfare programs, and who has little chance of ever earning enough to pay tax at top-bracket rates, but who, on moral grounds, opposes abortion and same-sex marriage? In most elections, neither the Republican nor the Democratic candidate satisfactorily represents such a voter's preferences.

The familiar claim is that lower-income voters with conservative attitudes on social issues are increasingly voting Republican.[21] One reason might be that with rising incomes over time, economic issues have become less important to much of the population, even including those whose incomes are low compared to contemporary standards in an increasingly affluent society. Another reason might be that the movement to center stage of highly divisive issues like abortion and same-sex marriage has rendered social issues more salient than in the past. Yet another possibility, suggested by Thomas Frank—although many would disagree—is that the two parties have moved sufficiently close together on economic issues that social issues are now, for practical purposes, all that distinguishes them.[22] Whatever the reason, the standard argument is that lower-income voters' preference for conservative social policies is what has led them to vote, in ever greater numbers, in ways counter to their economic interest.

The claim that lower-income Americans increasingly vote against their personal economic interest because under the U.S. two-party representative system that is the only way they can register their preference for conservative social policies has a certain plausibility. In the 1950s John Hallowell described communism as more than just an economic system opposed to capitalism, indeed more than a mere political or economic theory. It was "a complete philosophy of life, a world view," and on that ground a threat not only to American business but Western democracy as well, and of course Western religion too.[23] Billy Graham likewise warned that communism was not just an economic arrangement but its own religion: "a religion that is inspired, directed, and motivated by the Devil himself."[24] For this reason Graham concluded that "either Communism must die, or Christianity must die."[25]

As the threat of world communism ebbed, conservative Protestant clergymen shifted their perception of the enemy to focus closer at hand. Francis Schaeffer, a Presbyterian pastor and theologian whose writings assumed great prominence especially in the 1970s and 1980s (Schaeffer was in some ways a successor to Carl Henry, although his books had broader popular appeal than Henry's), now framed "secular humanism" as the all-encompassing worldview that threatened both the spiritual and the temporal aspects of Western civilization.[26] Especially once evangelical Protestants joined Roman Catholics in their opposition to abortion—a move that came surprisingly late—secular humanism took the place of communism as the intellectual and cultural enemy in the nation's internal political battles.[27]

Some evidence from public opinion surveys does support the idea that many lower-income Americans vote against their economic interest as a by-product of their greater eagerness to vote for conservative social policies. In recent years social issues have become more important to voters at all income levels, and they especially appear to matter for purposes of voter turnout. The evidence also suggests that lower-income voters on average have more conservative views on social issues than either middle- or upper-income voters.[28] Given the existing two-party alignment, the conflict between lower-income voters' preferences over social policies and their self-interest in economic policies is therefore all the greater.

Nonetheless, there are grounds for skepticism. On closer inspection, key features of voting patterns contradict the idea that such conflicts are what drive the behavior of lower-income voters. The share of white voters in the lower half of the income distribution who reported that they voted Republican in national elections exhibits no consistent increase or decrease since the 1950s. Until the 2016 election, the same was true for whites who do not have a college education, and even for those whose incomes are below average among the noncollege-educated— the group that is usually at the center of the supposed conflict created by a preference for conservative social policies together with economic policies favorable to those with low incomes. On average in the first four presidential elections beginning in 2000, only 51 percent of low-income noncollege-educated whites who voted cast their ballots for the Republican candidate, compared to a very steady 58 percent of this group that did so in 1952, 1956, and 1960. In 2016, 62 percent of this group voted for Donald Trump, only slightly above the Republican share six decades earlier.[29] Americans without a college education, and especially those whose incomes are below average for that group, are the ones most likely to benefit from government support programs. They also pay less in taxes. The fact that they have displayed no consistent trend toward voting Republican in recent years therefore stands as a significant contradiction to the conventional explanation for the lower-income voting paradox.

Evidence from opinion surveys over the last four decades likewise contradicts the idea of increasing polarization on social issues, and therefore potentially greater salience of social issues in voters' decision. Instead, the gap between views on social issues held by voters living in normally Republican-majority states and those in states where Democrats normally have a majority modestly *narrowed* over this period. Even more surprising—and also contrary to the conventional explanation for the apparent tendency of lower-income groups to vote against their own economic interest—the analogous gap in views on *economic* issues has *widened*.[30] In addition, the evidence suggests that social issues matter more to *more highly* educated voters, and to those with *greater* education, neither of whom have much to do with the puzzle over why so many lower-income voters tend to vote against their economic interest. Similarly, while the importance of social issues has increased among all groups, the increase has been greater among *more highly* educated voters.

A second factor that complicates any attempt to draw inferences along these lines from observed voting patterns is the reversal of the two parties' respective positions on race and civil rights. Until the 1960s, Republicans—historically, the party of Lincoln—had mostly favored expanding the civil liberties of black Americans, including outlawing racial segregation. Democrats, especially in the "solid South," had mostly resisted. In the mid-1960s, however, President Lyndon Johnson pushed Congress to pass both the Civil Rights Act of 1964 and the Voting Rights Act of 1965, firmly establishing Democratic leadership on this issue. In turn, the "Southern strategy" adopted by Richard Nixon in his 1968 presidential campaign pivoted the Republican Party in the opposite direction.[31] Ever since, most Americans have identified the Democrats as the party of civil rights, and the Republicans as the opposition on this issue.

This historic reversal is relevant to the lower-income voter puzzle because incomes in the South are lower on average than elsewhere in the country, and because the South has been the chief center of voters' movement from Democrat to Republican. In 1960 all twenty-two senators representing the eleven states that were part of the Confederacy during the Civil War were Democrats. By 2020, only three were Democrats and nineteen were Republicans. In 1960 these states' delegations in the House of Representatives consisted of one hundred Democrats and only six Republicans. By 2020 there were forty-eight Democrats and eighty-nine Republicans.[32] These shifts have accounted for *more than all* of the nation's move from what once was a seemingly permanent Democratic majority in both houses of Congress to the more competitive balance of the most recent decades, with the Republicans in the majority more often than not. In recent presidential elections, Southern electoral votes have mostly gone to Republican candidates as well.

Continuing resistance to protecting and expanding civil rights for black Americans, and in some settings Hispanics too, is one of the "conservative" social policies that proponents of the conventional explanation for the puzzling voting behavior of lower-income white Americans have in mind. In some respects, therefore, pointing to the South's shift of allegiance from Democrat to Republican is consistent with the overall argument. But particularizing the argument to one issue, in one section of the country, is not what those who advance this explanation normally have in mind. (The title of Thomas Frank's book refers to *Kansas*.) The outsized share of the South in the nation's electoral shift over the last half-century is therefore another cause for hesitation.[33]

Yet a third reason for skepticism about the claim that the representative nature of American democracy in conjunction with the prevailing two-party system explains lower-income voters' puzzling behavior comes from more direct evidence on what these voters think. True, in the United States citizens do not vote directly for policies on a one-by-one basis. They instead vote for candidates who typically represent many policy positions, among which any given voter may agree with some and disagree with others. But opinion surveys do ask people for their views on individual policy issues, and on a stand-alone basis. There is no requirement that someone who expresses a particular view on one question must on that account respond in a particular way on any other.

Opinion surveys therefore provide evidence that voting behavior alone cannot, including evidence on what people think about policy questions considered one by one. And repeated findings from these surveys—such as 38 percent of the population opposing higher top-bracket income tax rates that fewer than one percent would pay, or 48 percent favoring elimination of the estate tax for which only a small handful of families are liable—make clear that large numbers of Americans do prefer policies that run against their own economic interest. It is not the case that they merely go along with such policies as the necessary counterpart of voting for something else.

There is also substantial evidence that Americans' voting behavior, and their stand-alone views on questions of economic policy as well, are closely related to their *religious* beliefs and participation—a pattern that the standard story based on representative democracy with too few candidates to provide a full range of policy choices would not explain.

In the 2004 election, for example, it was not surprising that voters with higher incomes were more likely to vote Republican. But their tendency to do so depended strongly on their frequency of religious participation. Among those who reported that they never went to church, about the same share—roughly 40 percent—voted for George W. Bush, regardless of their incomes. Among those who attended church once or twice a month, however, income mattered. Fifty-eight percent of higher-income churchgoers voted for Bush, compared to 53 percent of those with middle-range incomes, and only 45 percent of those with lower incomes. And among voters who attended church more than once a week, income was even more important for how they voted. Among this especially religious group, 75 percent of those with higher incomes voted for Bush, versus 70 percent of those with middle-range incomes, and just 52 percent of those with lower incomes. In short, income mattered, but it mattered much more when voters were more religious.[34]

Although the specifics were different, a similar pattern emerged in 2016. Among voters who said they never went to church, the same 29 percent voted for Donald Trump regardless of their incomes. Among those who went once or twice a month, 55 percent of higher-income churchgoers voted for Trump, compared to only 46 percent of those with lower incomes. Among voters who attended church more than once a week, 61 percent of those with higher incomes voted for

Trump, versus just 47 percent of those with lower incomes. Once again, income mattered more when voters were more religiously active.[35]

The importance of voters' religion shows up clearly as well in people's opinions on economic policy issues. It is hardly surprising that opposition to higher taxes, for example, is greater among higher-income groups. But opposition to taxes also turns out to vary systematically with people's religious affiliations, and sometimes in ways that contradict what their personal economic situation would suggest. The same pattern, in which views on economic issues go along with people's religious affiliations, also appears regarding other policy issues such as government spending and regulation of business. It appears too on more basic philosophical questions about our economic system, like whether hard work is what stands behind success in life. What is striking is that in each of these cases the group that primarily stands out is evangelical Protestants.[36]

In one 2008 survey, for example, 44 percent of Americans favored abolishing the estate tax altogether (a somewhat smaller share than the more recent 48 percent). On the basis of income alone, the gap between Republicans and Democrats on this issue was not surprising. Republicans on average have incomes distinctly above the national average, and a greater share of Republicans than of the general population (62 percent) favored eliminating the tax. Democrats on average have incomes somewhat below the national average, and a lower percentage (33 percent) favored eliminating the tax. Members of mainline Protestant denominations followed the expected pattern too. Mainline Protestants on average have incomes slightly above the national average, and 49 percent favored abolishing the tax. By contrast, members of *evangelical* Protestant denominations presented a sharp departure. Evangelicals on average have incomes well below the national average—even below the average income for Democrats. Yet 53 percent of white evangelicals (again, compared to 44 percent for Americans overall in this survey) favored abolishing estate taxes altogether.[37]

Evangelical Protestants likewise stand out in their attitudes toward the role of government more generally.[38] Americans are fairly evenly divided over whether their government should do more or do less. Fifty-one percent say they would prefer a smaller government, providing fewer services, over a bigger government providing more services. (In this poll, preferring the same size government as today was not an option offered.) Among mainline Protestants, the share preferring less government is larger: 59 percent. But among evangelical Protestants it is 64 percent. And among evangelicals who also say they want their denominations to preserve traditional beliefs and practices rather than adjust them in light of new circumstances, the share that prefer less government is 69 percent. Not surprisingly, these differences in attitudes carry over to questions of the effectiveness of government safety net programs—another area in which Americans overall are evenly divided. Exactly half of Americans say they agree that "government aid to the poor does more good than harm, because people can't get out of poverty until their basic needs are met." Among mainline Protestants the share is 46 percent; among evangelicals 38 percent, and among traditionalist evangelicals just 33 percent.[39] On yet another dimension of the role of government in the economy, Protestants who say they are not born again favor increasing their state's minimum wage (to $12 an hour in this poll) by 69 percent to 31, virtually the same as the general population. Born-again Protestants also favor the proposal, but only by 57 percent to 43.[40]

And the same differences across religious affiliations apply to policy choices concerning taxes and spending. When asked how the federal government should reduce its budget deficit, members of mainline Protestant denominations again voice opinions that are indistinguishable from those of Americans as a whole. Thirty-seven percent of Americans overall would prefer cuts to nondefense spending over either a tax increase or cuts in defense spending. Among Protestants who identify themselves as neither evangelical nor born again, the percentage that prefer cuts to nondefense spending is the same 37 percent. Among members of evangelical denominations, however, 46 percent prefer cutting nondefense spending, and among those who consider themselves born again 49 percent—despite the fact that with their lower-than-average incomes, evangelicals are more likely to benefit from many of the programs that might be cut.[41] Whether the subject is taxes and spending, or government safety net programs, or government regulation of business, or preferences more generally for larger versus smaller government, the pattern is consistent.

More casual associations often confirm this connection as well. At least until the election of Donald Trump in 2016, a typical response to the question of which presidents since World War II people most associated with opposition to taxes and government regulation was to point to either Ronald Reagan or George W. Bush, or perhaps both. And when people were asked which presidents they most identified as in sympathy with the nation's evangelical Protestant churches, the typical response was usually the same: Reagan and the younger Bush—more so even than Jimmy Carter, who when he was president was a born-again Southern Baptist. (In 2000 Carter announced that he was leaving the Southern Baptist Convention, largely because of the denomination's refusal to ordain women; he remains a Baptist, however, attending a church with dual Southern Baptist and Cooperative Baptist affiliation.[42]) Trump, who drew 75 percent of the vote among white Protestants who consider themselves born again (versus only 48 percent of white Protestants who had not had that religious experience), now appears to be continuing the pattern.[43]

What is especially striking is that despite their typically lower incomes, evangelical Protestants are more likely than other Americans to believe that economic success in life is the result of individual effort. During the nineteenth century preachers of the Gospel of Wealth like Henry Ward Beecher and Russell Conwell repeatedly told their congregations that diligent effort, thoughtfully applied, leads to economic success. In his book on the Protestant Ethic, early in the twentieth century, Max Weber observed that Americans have always stood out in their commitment to this belief, arguing that the nation's Calvinist origins, even though long since secularized, were the root of the connection. In the 1950s another sociologist, Seymour Martin Lipset, sought to explain the contradiction that although intergenerational economic mobility in America was not measurably greater than in other Western democracies (since Lipset wrote, the evidence has become clear that there is *less* mobility in America[44]), the prevalent image of American society held by both Americans and foreigners nonetheless placed substantial emphasis on America's supposedly greater mobility. Today Americans and foreigners alike *over*estimate mobility in the United States and *under*estimate it elsewhere.[45]

The association of individual effort and economic success remains typical of Americans today. Among citizens of European Union countries, 54 percent say they believe that what determines a person's income is mostly luck. Only 30 percent of Americans subscribe to that view. Conversely, while only 26 percent of Europeans say they think the poor are poor because they are lazy, 60 percent of Americans say they believe this is so. Beliefs about opportunities for mobility exhibit parallel differences. In Europe, 60 percent of citizens say they think the poor are trapped in their poverty. Only 29 percent of Americans think the poor are stuck where they are.[46] According to another recent survey (for the U.S. only), although the percentages have narrowed over the past two decades, 61 percent of Americans still agree that "most people who want to get ahead can make it if they're willing to work hard," while only 36 percent think "hard work and determination are no guarantee of success for most people."[47]

Beyond these cross-country differences, however, in America opinions on such matters also depend on individuals' religious affiliations. Among mainline Protestants, the share who say they believe that work leads to success is 61 percent—the same as for the American population as a whole. But among Protestants who consider themselves born again, 71 percent think so. Conversely, 27 percent of born-again Protestants, but 37 percent among mainliners, think "hard work and determination are no guarantee of success for most people."[48] In a different survey, 46 percent of those who belonged to any Christian faith (either Roman Catholic or any Protestant denomination), and 53 percent of white evangelicals thought a lack of effort was generally to blame for a person's poverty, while only 29 percent of all non-Christians thought so.[49] In the same vein, today's Prosperity Gospel, which in the United States teaches that God bestows material blessings on people who prove their faithfulness by following the Bible, is largely associated with Pentecostal denominations, which are mostly considered evangelical.[50]

Parallel differences also describe people's understanding of how problems in society arise. More than four-fifths of Americans who identify themselves as religiously conservative say they think that "if enough people had a personal relationship with God, social problems would take care of themselves." Fewer than one-third of self-identified religious progressives agree, and fewer than one-fifth of those who consider themselves nonreligious.[51] Similar differences apply to attitudes toward economic policy as well. Among mainline Protestants, 71 percent of those who regard their denominations as "modernist" favor taxing wealthy citizens in order to fight poverty, while only 50 percent of those in "traditionalist" denominations are in favor. Evangelicals overall are less supportive of such a policy, but the pattern across different evangelical denominations is the same: 69 percent of those in modernist denominations favor higher taxes on the wealthy in order to fight poverty, but only 46 percent of those in traditionalist denominations do. (Among non-Christians, approval of such a policy is noticeably higher: for example, 80 percent among Jews.)[52]

These systematic differences in how people belonging to different religious groups think about economic questions matter for the low-income voter puzzle because it is primarily among evangelicals and other conservative Protestants that the movement toward more conservative voting patterns over the last half-century has occurred. Mainline Protestants, on the whole, have moved modestly in the opposite direction; several decades ago mainliners were more likely than Americans overall to vote Republican in national elections, but over time this difference has largely disappeared. Nor has there been much of a persistent trend among non-Protestant voters. Apart from the 1960s, when John F. Kennedy's presence on the ballot drew an outsized share of the Catholic vote, there has been little consistent movement one way or the other in the voting pattern of American Catholics over the past half-century.[53] The share of white non-Hispanic Catholics voting Republican rose modestly in 2012, and again in 2016, but it is too soon to judge whether these two elections marked a new trend; Hispanic Catholics (who are becoming a larger share of Catholics overall) have been trending toward voting more Democratic. While Jews have historically voted disproportionately Democratic compared to Americans overall, despite considerable volatility from one election to the next there has been little apparent trend in their behavior either. By contrast, throughout this lengthy period evangelical Protestants have displayed an irregular but nonetheless pronounced trend toward voting more Republican in national elections.[54] Not coincidentally, the South, where the shift from Democrat to Republican has been most pronounced, is the section of the country where evangelicals make up the greatest proportion of the population.[55]

These connections between Americans' views on matters of economic policy and their individual religious affiliation, especially among evangelical Protestants, no doubt reflect a variety of influences. Three, however, stand out.

First, the continuing influence of the historical turn away from pre-destinarianism, which laid the basis for the Smithian revolution in economic thinking in the eighteenth century, remains readily apparent in the American public's attitudes toward matters of economics and economic policy. In Adam Smith's day the most significant consequence for economics stemming from this change in religious thinking was an expanded vision of the possibilities for human choice and human action—under the right conditions, which Smith centered in competitive markets. By now the general public has largely absorbed that insight. In addition, especially among Americans, beliefs about the possibilities for *individual* economic success strongly conform to a non-predestinarian view as well. Most Americans reject the idea that some factor apart from their own ability and efforts—divine election in Calvin's thinking, simple luck in the more modern secular vocabulary—determines their individual destinies. In today's secularized context, the belief that anyone can achieve spiritual salvation has its parallel in the belief that anyone can get ahead economically through talent and hard work.

The predominance of non-predestinarian thinking, and its reflection in attitudes toward opportunities for individual economic success, are all the more striking in light of the continuing belief in a divinely intended destiny for America as a nation. Few Americans now speak of Manifest Destiny, and only a small fraction of Protestants belong to denominations that place predestination, in anything like the form spelled out in the Westminster Confession, among their creeds. (The largest ones that do are the Presbyterian Church (USA), with one and a half million members, and the Presbyterian Church in America, with fewer than 400,000.) Yet most Americans, including most Protestant evangelicals, do believe that the United States, with the country's long-standing democratic political institutions and its historical tradition of civil freedoms, has a special role to play in the world. Many see this role as a divinely ordained mission to lead the world toward freedom and democracy—or if not that, then as the inspired consequence of some kind of historical Providence. On the eve of World War II, Harold Ockenga mused that "it is almost as though God pinned His last hope on America."[56] Forty years later Ronald Reagan spoke for more than just his own political supporters when he asked, in accepting his party's nomination for president in 1980, "Can we doubt that only a

Divine Providence placed this land, this island of freedom, here as a refuge for all those people in the world who yearn to breathe freely?"[57]

For the great majority of Americans, however, this special character and preordained role attributed to the nation as a whole does not carry over to predestined fates for individuals, especially in matters of economics.[58] As a result, Americans continue to believe that the United States has greater economic mobility than other countries, even in the face of increasingly contradictory evidence. More to the point, Americans mostly support economic policies—for example, a welfare system that is strictly limited compared to what other high-income countries have—that make the most moral sense if people's economic destinies are indeed in their own hands. Similarly, they support policies, like lower tax rates and less government regulation than in otherwise similar countries, designed to give broad scope for individual economic initiative and to reward its success. Moreover, Americans' attitudes toward such economic policies depend in part on their individual religious commitments, with evangelical Protestants offering the greatest support even when their own economic interest lies elsewhere.

Second, many of these attitudes, especially among evangelicals, reflect the strong historical tradition of Protestant voluntarism.[59] Even before the American Revolution, leading clergymen like John Witherspoon made clear that they saw robust religious institutions as a precondition underlying their belief in the argument for limited government that they took from political theorists like Locke and Montesquieu. Witherspoon was himself an influential figure in the debate over the creation of the new United States—he signed the Declaration of Independence—and his influence was even greater through his student James Madison, whom he mentored while serving as president of the College of New Jersey (later renamed Princeton). But he was also active in church affairs, convening the Presbyterian Church's first General Assembly in the United States and serving as the body's moderator.

According to Witherspoon and others who shared his viewpoint, religious institutions were essential to a polity like the new democratic republic they were establishing. Strong religious institutions cultivated the civic virtue that made individual liberty possible, and they therefore filled the vacuum that limited government necessarily left as the counterpart to that liberty.[60] The argument was analogous to Adam Smith's assumption—at just the same time—that the individual moral behavior about which he wrote in *The Theory of Moral Sentiments* underpinned the functioning of the market economy as laid out in *The Wealth of Nations*. (As the twentieth-century economist Kenneth Arrow put it, "a great deal of economic life depends for its viability on a certain limited degree of ethical commitment. Purely selfish behavior of individuals is really incompatible with any kind of economic life."[61]) In Witherspoon's thinking, religious institutions filled a dual role: circumscribing individual behavior so as to enable people to live together amicably, and providing for the material needs of those who for one reason or another failed to provide for themselves—in both cases, so that government would not have to do so.

The numerous religiously based voluntary societies that so struck Tocqueville in the 1830s—the American Bible Society, the American Tract Society, the American Temperance Society, the American Anti-Slavery Society, to name just a few—grew out of attempts during the early federal period to fill just that vacuum. In his *Elements of Political Economy*, written just a few years after Tocqueville's visit, Francis Wayland likewise recognized the importance of institutions other than government to address the needs of those whom the free markets that he advocated would inevitably leave behind, and he pointed to religious institutions in particular for this purpose. "To relieve the sick, the destitute and the helpless, is a religious duty," he wrote, "and therefore should, like every other religious duty, be a voluntary service." In a moral and religious community, charity should mostly come from individuals out of their own resources, or from the resources of voluntary associations, not from the government.[62] Just as Witherspoon was not merely an American founding father but also a Presbyterian minister, Wayland was America's leading political economist of the first half of the nineteenth century as well as a Baptist minister.

This deep-rooted commitment to the role of religious institutions has continued to underpin much of American Protestant thinking ever since, especially among evangelicals.[63] The revivalism of Charles Grandison Finney and Dwight Moody bore a strong relation to concepts of political liberty, and Moody in particular displayed a deep distrust of government. A free society required a moral core, and it was the church's role to provide it. The Social Gospel's call for *government* action, at the end of the nineteenth century and in the early decades of the twentieth, was a departure in this regard, prompted in part by the emergence of large-scale production in an increasingly national, even international, economy. Even so, its proponents were never clear just what balance they looked to achieve between the respective roles of government and of the churches in meeting the needs that this new economy created.

During the Depression of the 1930s, the religious opposition to Roosevelt's New Deal initiatives was in part based on a more general antipathy to activist government, but it also reflected a particular resistance to the prospect of government's usurping what many thought was properly the social mission of the nation's churches. Later on, the energetic mobilization of America's religious communities in opposition to the threat posed by world communism drew in part on the same religiously based antistatism. In the 1980s, Carl Henry argued that "A society that responds voluntarily to its needs is superior to one in which the welfare of humanity becomes the sole responsibility of government."[64] Also in the 1980s, in his widely read "Judeo-Christian defense" of free enterprise, the evangelical theologian Harold Lindsell insisted that while God demanded protections like fair treatment of employees, safe working conditions, and provision for the sick and the injured and the elderly, those steps were legitimate only if employers implemented them voluntarily.[65] In light of this history, it comes as no surprise that today more than two-thirds of white evangelical Protestants in the United States say they think the government is performing services that should be left to religious groups and private charities.[66] It is also no surprise that even among evangelicals who stand to benefit most from various forms of government regulation, many are nonetheless opposed to it.[67]

And third, a continuing part of what distinguishes American evangelicals not only from mainline Protestants but from other Americans more generally is their almost unanimous premillennialism.[68] Americans' views of eschatology have changed asymmetrically over the last century. Today the explicit postmillennialism that attached religious significance to secular progress in earlier times has mostly disappeared. Most mainline Protestant churches take no official stance on the millennium, or even a Second Coming. But ever since their initial embrace of *The Fundamentals,* just over a century ago, conservative American Protestants have been premillennialist in their eschatology, at least at an informal level. The Statement of Faith of the National Association of Evangelicals includes Jesus's "personal return in power and glory." Most Adventist, Pentecostal, Holiness, and fundamentalist denominations, altogether representing sixteen million members, officially embrace the prediction of a Second Coming and many have an official premillennialist interpretation.[69] Most Baptist denominations— including the Southern Baptist Convention (fifteen million members) and the National Baptist Convention USA (seven million)—likewise insist on the belief that Jesus will personally return to the earth, but take no official position on the millennium; the great majority of their members, however, apparently understand this future event through a premillennialist theology. The Mormon (LDS) Church, with more than six million members, is not formally Protestant but it too officially embraces premillennialist doctrine.

Moreover, for many evangelicals these are not predictions of some indefinite or far-off event. A survey taken in 2010 found that 41 percent of all Americans expect that Jesus will either definitely (23 percent) or probably (18 percent) have returned to earth by the year 2050. Here too, evangelicals stand out. Fewer than one-third of Catholics hold this belief, and little more than one-fourth of mainline Protestants do. But 58 percent of evangelical Protestants think the Second Coming either definitely or probably will happen by 2050.[70]

The prevalence of premillennialism among evangelical Protestants has numerous easily visible reflections in American culture, ranging from the continuing popularity of Hal Lindsey's 1970 book *The Late Great Planet Earth,* to Tim LaHaye and Jerry Jenkins's subsequent series of *Left Behind* novels, to the ready embrace of religiously based conspiracy theories surrounding one after another contemporary development. Just as the threat of communism—and especially the news that the Soviets had acquired atomic weapons—spawned widespread apocalyptic interpretations a half-century ago, the atrocities of September 11, 2001, the unending wars in Afghanistan and Iraq, and the seemingly permanent threat of religious-based terrorism continue to do so in the current era. Nonmilitary threats to social stability have drawn similar reactions. In the 1930s many Americans interpreted the Great Depression in eschatological terms.[71] In the 1960s many interpreted the urban riots and other upheavals associated with the civil rights movement in the same way.[72] Some saw the 2008 financial crisis that way.[73] Most recently, nearly half of Americans surveyed thought the COVID-19 pandemic and the associated economic collapse represented either a wake-up call to faith or a sign of God's coming judgment, or both.[74]

As has been true since the nineteenth century, belief that human history in its current form will end with the Second Coming, and that this event will precede the thousand years of blissful existence foretold in Revelation—which therefore will not occur within human history as we know it—has often proven inimical both to acceptance of the possibility of progress in society and to attempts to achieve that progress before these end-of-days events occur. The tension between such theologically grounded temporal pessimism and the urge nonetheless to bring about reform has long been a central feature of American evangelical thinking. Nineteenth- and early-twentieth-century evangelicals stood apart from many efforts to improve living conditions and society more generally. Even so, they not only worked alongside mainline Protestants to eliminate specific evils like slavery and drunkenness but energetically sought government intervention in the effort to do so, culminating first in abolition and later in Prohibition.

At the middle of the twentieth century, Carl Henry lamented that "evangelical Christianity stands divorced from the great social reform movements," and he laid the blame on what he argued was a widespread misuse of premillennialism.[75] Harold Ockenga likewise called for a more activist evangelicalism, preaching that "It is the Christian's duty to occupy till Christ comes. This means that we shall be engaged in humanitarian activity as well as evangelism and missions."[76] Henry's and Ockenga's shared concern was a key element motivating the founding of the National Association of Evangelicals and, soon thereafter, the group's Commission on Social Action. Billy Graham, while certainly looking to the government to resist communism, mostly preached revivalism as an alternative to government attempts to reshape domestic society at home. "The government may try to legislate Christian behavior," he wrote in the 1960s, perhaps recalling the failure of Prohibition, "but it soon finds that man remains unchanged."[77]

As a result, not only do two-thirds of evangelical Protestants think the government is carrying out functions better left to religious groups and other private charities, but religiously committed Americans of nearly all faiths see less need for government services and government intervention than do most citizens of other high-income countries. In conjunction with the far greater share of Americans who identify with one or another religion, and who participate in church services and other religious activities, the implication for the public discussion of economics and economic policy—and ultimately for actual economic policy too—is profound.

From its inception as a recognizable intellectual discipline, economics has been influenced by religious ideas. At first that influence had a narrow circumference, bearing mostly on the thinking of the moral philosophers and then political economists who were working out the subject's fundamental theory and structure. Over time, following the usual pattern, as the discipline matured its professional thinking became less subject to such external influences. But in the meanwhile, as America's modern economy took shape, and as the government grew to play a larger role in it, matters of economics and especially economic policy took on ever greater importance for the public at large, and the influence of religious ideas on economic thinking bore increasingly on popular opinion rather than the work of professional economists. Americans, with their far greater religiosity than citizens of other countries at a comparable stage of economic development, have been particularly subject to this influence, and the public discussion of economics and economic policy in America shows it. The non-predestinarian and voluntarist orientation of American Protestantism in general, and the premillennialism of evangelical Protestants in particular, today mark its most powerful substantive features.

Thomas Carlyle famously called economics the dismal science.[78] It is a pity that the label stuck. Carlyle was writing at the end of the 1840s, when Britain's growing population seemed to be outrunning the country's ability to produce food—the period was popularly called the Hungry Forties—and Karl Marx's "immiserated" urban labor force was crowding the country's cities and manufacturing centers. John Stuart Mill, in what would become the world's best-selling economics textbook for the remainder of the nineteenth century, was analyzing the economic "steady state" characterized by zero growth and no other form of progress either.[79] But by the 1840s, and especially in Britain, such thinking was hardly new. By then secular pessimism about economic matters had dominated British political discussion for half a century—ever since Malthus had warned of the supposedly inevitable pressure of population, growing at a geometrical rate, against food supply which he thought grew only arithmetically.[80] To Carlyle, it seemed all too true.

But economics, as an intellectual discipline, remains at its core a child of Enlightenment thinking, with all the optimism about the human enterprise that that epochal movement entailed. Moreover, neither Malthus's nor Mill's nor Marx's analysis bore much relation to the very different situation of America anyway. Instead of too many people pressing up against too little available land, America was (and to this day largely remains) a continent with vast uninhabited areas to be filled. Far from embracing any notion of a steady state, the American ethos has from the beginning been one of progress, specifically including improvement in material living standards. And for most of the nation's existence, the combination of technological advance and physical expansion—at first expansion of agricultural land under cultivation, and later expansion of the stock of factories and machinery— has delivered on that promise. (At times when it has not, the public has dramatically manifested its disappointment, often with predictably unfortunate social and political consequences.[81]) Far from becoming immiserated, America's growing workforce doubled its standard of living roughly once every forty years over nearly two centuries.

Along the way, economic thinking has mostly reflected the expansive vision of human possibilities that this experience of growth and improvement has validated, together with an optimism about the world's future that the dominant religious thinking of the English-speaking world has imparted to it ever since the time of Adam Smith and David Hume. The historical image of economics as a product of the Enlightenment is accurate. The idea that because of this parentage economics has been uninfluenced by religious thinking is not. The era in which Smith and Hume lived, and from which modern Western economics sprang, was also one of fundamental transition in the religious presumptions shared by much of the population. Especially during the extended period while this transition in religious thinking was in progress, the contention surrounding it was sufficiently fierce to attract the attention of the public at large, including those like Hume (certainly) and Smith (probably) who self-consciously took little interest in such matters. The basic religious ideas at issue in those long-ago debates profoundly affected their view of the world. What they thought about economic questions reflected that influence.

Even the very notion of economic *policy*, as we know it today, is in large part a consequence of these ongoing changes in religious thinking. The point of any public policy is, consciously and deliberately, to change aspects of society for the better. Economic policy is no different. But the idea that such improvement is even possible rests on very basic presumptions about the world in which we live, and our capacity to shape it by the actions we collectively choose. The new religious thinking of the late seventeenth and then the eighteenth century, and in America on into the nineteenth, provided the cultural soil in which men and women could contemplate such possibilities. That creative thinkers would then direct this endeavor to such a central feature of everyday life as the economy in which they lived and worked and earned their livelihood was only natural. With the passage of time, and ever greater availability of information and ever broader opportunities for public participation, it was natural as well that the general public took up an interest in the debate. But that engagement has likewise rested in part on a worldview shaped by the era's prevailing religious presumptions. It does so today.

Economics is far from the only subject of human thought and debate that religious thinking has influenced, and continues to influence, in this way. But focusing on economics in this context is important, for two reasons. Because it is true that economics emerged from the Enlightenment, and because the conventional image of the Enlightenment downplays the importance attached to religion in favor of humanistic thinking, the commonplace assumption is that economics in turn likewise stands apart from religious ideas. This is not true, nor has it been, ever since the inception of economics as a modern intellectual discipline. Taking account of the influence of religious thinking is essential to a full understanding of one of the great areas of modern human thought.

And because practical matters of economic policy are so pervasively important for most citizens, today far more so than in Adam Smith's time because of the more national character of the economy and the greatly expanded role of government in it, public engagement with the ongoing debate over whatever are the economic policy questions of the day—taxes and government spending, support for industry and job creation, incentives to undertake research, impediments to international trade, regulation of the workplace for purposes of safety and of products for purposes of consumer protection, environmental restrictions, what degree of economic inequality is acceptable and what to do when prevailing inequities are excessive, even how to preserve economic activity in the face of a disease pandemic—is increasingly central to modern political life in a democratic republic.

Ordinary citizens, however, likewise bring to this debate whatever worldview *they* hold. Whether consciously or not (and in most cases not), that worldview too rests on presumptions that originate in the religious thinking of either today or sometime in the past. No one in a democratic society is going to tell citizens that their religious presumptions are wrong, or that the implications that follow from them for economic policy are flawed. But clearly understanding the substance and origins of the worldview that underlies our fellow citizens' participation in this essential part of our democracy is sure to make it work better.

Acknowledgments

I'm an economist, and so it's no surprise that this is a book about economics. But the story I tell in it is largely about influences on economic thinking stemming from outside the discipline, even from before there was such a discipline as economics: most centrally, theology and the history of religious thinking and religious institutions, but also political history, social history, and the theory of politics. Learning from scholars in disciplines other than my own has therefore been essential to this effort. Living and working in a university community provides a cornucopia of opportunities to do just that, and I am fortunate that the scholars among whom I happen to live amply possess the wide-ranging knowledge on which I needed to draw. They have also been remarkably generous in sharing it with me.

My greatest debt is to two fine young scholars, both graduates of the Harvard Divinity School, whose diligent and untiring support bookended this project. David Smith worked with me at the outset, educating me on subjects theological and historical about which I had little prior knowledge. Erik Nordbye filled the same role in the project's latter years. I could not have done this work without their help. And, at a personal level, I have enormously valued their friendship. In addition to them, other Harvard students who helped with my research on this project include Chris Chaky, Brian Chen, Jamin Dowdy, Lev Menand, Jeremy Patashnik, Kip Richardson, and Rebecca Wagner. I am grateful to them all. I also appreciate the administrative assistance of Kristen Lynch and Aden Gideon of the Harvard Economics department.

Numerous friends and colleagues, some at Harvard but many elsewhere, discussed my ideas with me, or read early drafts of individual chapters, or helped me in other ways. Richard Tuck patiently listened to the argument of many of the book's chapters over the course of several years of our leading a graduate seminar together. Anthony Waterman gave me incisive comments on many of the chapters once they were written and provided a steady flow of further insights besides. Daniel Finn did likewise. Frank Schott read the entire manuscript and provided helpful comments throughout (and even did me the honor of likening what I was writing to the work of his Princeton dissertation superviser, Jacob Viner). Other friends and colleagues who read draft chapters, or discussed ideas with me, or patiently answered my questions, include Alberto Alesina,

Stephen Ansolabehere, Harold Attridge, Jeffrey Barneson, Bradley Bateman, Stephen Bergman, David Bock, Michael Boudin, Adam Broadbent, Filippo Cesarano, Sarah Coakley, Stefan Collignon, Steven Coy, Robert Darnton, Charles Donahue, James Engell, Niall Ferguson, Charles Freeman, Charles Fried, Mary Fuhrer, Edward Glaeser, Claudia Goldin, Charles Goodhart, Peter Gordon, Robert Gordon, William Graham, Stephen Greenblatt, David Hall, David Hempton, Gerald Holton, Daniel Howe, Lawrence Katz, Carl Kaysen, Hans-Helmut Kotz, David Laibson, Michael MacDowell, Charles Maier, Gregory Mankiw, Stephen Marglin, Robert Margo, George Marsden, Rachel McCleary, Justin Muzinich, Eric Nelson, Robert Nelson, Akiva Offenbacher, Paul Oslington, Richard Parker, Nicholas Phillipson, Matthew Price, Melinda Rabb, Michael Rosen, Emma Rothschild, James Simpson, Robert Solow, Jonah Steinberg, Michael Szenberg, Peter Temin, Mark Valeri, Camillo von Mueller, Richard Whatmore, James Wible, John Winthrop, and Stephen Woolman. I am grateful to them all. None of them is responsible for any errors I may have made; those are entirely mine.

One element of sadness, perhaps inevitable in carrying out a project like this over a span of years, is that some of the colleagues and friends who were most supportive and helpful along the way are no longer here to see the final product. It is too late to thank them for their encouragement and their friendship. But I do remember, with gratitude and affection, Daniel Bell, William Hutchison, John Olcay, Frank Schott, and Robert Silvers. I miss them all.

Initial funding for the project came from the Bowen H. and Janice Arthur McCoy Charitable Foundation. A grant from the John Templeton Foundation then enabled me to continue the work. I am grateful to Buzz McCoy, and to Kimon Sargeant from Templeton, for their encouragement and their confidence in what I set out to do. Harvard University also provided two sabbatical semesters during which I was able to focus on this effort without classroom obligations.

I am delighted to have worked once again with Jonathan Segal, my editor at Knopf. I appreciate his interest in what I have done and his support for it. The entire team at Knopf, including Fred Chase, Andrew Dorko, and Erin Sellers, was consistently helpful as well as easy to work with throughout the publication process. I am also grateful to Robert Barnett for again handling arrangements with Knopf on my behalf.

I have written before that the support of my wife and my sons has served as a moral anchor, a fixed star, in my life. This remains true. And over the years my family has expanded, including now a new generation. They are all a blessing. But above all, there is Barbara. This book is again for her.

Notes

ABBREVIATIONS

EMPL David Hume, *Essays Moral, Political, and Literary* (Indianapolis: Liberty Fund, 1987).

EPE Francis Wayland, *The Elements of Political Economy* (New York: Leavitt, Lord & Company, 1837).

FB Bernard Mandeville, *The Fable of the Bees: Or, Private Vices, Publick Benefits.* 2 vols. (Oxford: Clarendon Press, 1924).

ICR John Calvin. *Institutes of the Christian Religion.* 2 vols. (Louisville: Westminster John Knox Press, 1960).

IPE Richard T. Ely, *An Introduction to Political Economy* (New York: Chautauqua Press, 1889).

LJ Adam Smith, *Lectures on Jurisprudence* (Oxford: Oxford University Press, 1978).

OPE John McVickar, *Outlines of Political Economy* (New York: Wilder & Campbell, 1825).

PPE Francis Bowen, *The Principles of Political Economy: Applied to the Condition, the Resources, and the Institutions of the American People* (Boston: Little, Brown, 1856).

PW John Bates Clark, *The Philosophy of Wealth: Economic Principles Newly Formulated* (Boston: Ginn & Company, 1894).

SAC Richard T. Ely, *Social Aspects of Christianity: And Other Essays* (New York: Thomas Y. Crowell, 1889).

TMS Adam Smith, *The Theory of Moral Sentiments* (Oxford: Oxford University Press, 1976).

WJE Jonathan Edwards, *Works of Jonathan Edwards.* 26 vols. (New Haven: Yale University Press, 1957–2008).

WN Adam Smith, *An Inquiry into the Nature and Causes of the Wealth of Nations.* 2 vols. (Oxford: Oxford University Press, 1976).

INTRODUCTION

1. Keynes, *General Theory*, 383. Elsewhere Keynes wrote that although most of us have not read authors such as Hobbes, Locke, Hume, and Adam Smith, "Nevertheless we should not, I fancy, think as we do, if [they] had not thought and written as they did"; Keynes, *End of Laissez-Faire*, 15–16.
2. Stern, "German History in America," 133.
3. The concept of religion I have in mind is the traditional notion of a unified system of beliefs about what is sacred that unites believers into a moral community, as in Émile Durkheim, rather than the more modern (and particularly American) notion of the feelings and experiences of solitary individuals, as in William James. See Durkheim, *The Elementary Forms of the Religious Life*, 47, and James, *Varieties of Religious Experience*, 31–32.
4. Phillipson, *Adam Smith*, 190.
5. Wood, "Rhetoric and Reality," 16; 23.
6. Tawney, *Religion and the Rise of Capitalism*.
7. For a concise summary of Bailyn's view, see Wood, "Rhetoric and Reality," 23; see also Bailyn and Garret, eds., *Pamphlets of the American Revolution*.

CHAPTER 1: ECONOMICS, POLITICS, AND RELIGION

1. Paine, *American Crisis*, in *Rights of Man*, 63.
2. Lai, *Adam Smith Across Nations*. The acclaim accorded *The Wealth of Nations* was also amplified by the influential series of lectures given at the University of Edinburgh in 1800–1801 by Dugald Stewart, the professor of moral philosophy and also Smith's first biographer, as well as by Stewart's 1794 biography of Smith; Stewart, "Plan of Lectures on Political Economy," xvii–xx; and "Account of the Life and Writings of Adam Smith, LL.D."
3. On the influence of Newtonian science on Scottish Enlightenment thinking, see, for example, Wilson, *Seeking Nature's Logic*, 1–68; Wood, "Science in the Scottish Enlightenment"; and Grabiner, "Maclaurin and Newton." Dugald Stewart was clear about the influence on Smith's work.
4. Hume, *Treatise of Human Nature*, 185.
5. Stephen Greenblatt, for example, wrote of "the programmatic, devastating disbelief expressed in Diderot, Hume, and many other Enlightenment figures"; Greenblatt, *The Swerve*, 262.
6. Robertson, letter to Margaret Hepburn (f. 235r).
7. Einstein, "Motive des Forchens." Translation from Holton, "On Einstein's *Weltbild*," 3.
8. Indeed, the concept has become commonplace in referring to people's thought processes. For a recent example in the economics literature, see Galperti, "Persuasion."
9. Erikson, *Toys and Reasons*, 148.
10. Holton, *Scientific Imagination*, 70.
11. Holton, "Einstein and the Cultural Roots of Modern Science," 1; and "On Einstein's *Weltbild*," 1, emphasis added.
12. Merton, *Science, Technology and Society*, 238.
13. Nelson, "What Kind of Book?," 151; 148; 155–56. Referring to the evolution of political ideas, Nelson argued that such influences are "radically understudied"; 169. And he

pointed to "historical experience, both political *and religious*" as their origin; 171, emphasis added.

14. Emerson, *Journals and Miscellaneous Notebooks*, Vol. 9, 253, and *Representative Men*, 30–31, 189; also cited in Reynolds, *Beneath the American Renaissance*, 4–6.

15. Marshall, *Principles of Economics*, 332.

16. Whitehead, *Science and the Modern World*, 48.

17. Holton, *Advancement of Science*, xiv.

18. Einstein, "The Problem of Space, Ether, and the Field in Physics," in *Ideas and Opinions*, 276.

19. Holton used Einstein's original German for world image: *Weltbild*.

20. Donald Winch referred to this process as "strategic selection designed to distil from the chaos of ordinary observation the kind of assumptions and variables which would, when deductively connected, shed a penetrating light on the main causal factors at work in a situation"; Winch, "Introduction," in Ricardo, *Principles of Political Economy and Taxation*, xviii.

21. Samuelson, "Liberalism at Bay," 20.

22. Schumpeter, *History of Economic Analysis*, 41, emphasis added.

23. Galbraith, *Economics in Perspective*, 1.

24. Kuhn, "History of Science," 109, 118 (the article originally appeared in the *International Encyclopedia of the Social Sciences*, 1968, Vol. 14, 74–85).

25. The Scottish Enlightenment was far from independent of the "Enlightenments" under way, then and earlier, on the continent—for example, in France and Germany. Key figures of this time in Scotland drew especially on the French, and both Hume and Smith spent time in France. See Haakonssen, *Natural Law and Moral Philosophy*, as well as several of the contributions in Porter and Teich, *Enlightenment in National Context*.

26. Cockburn outlived both Hume and Smith. See her letters and memoir, published long after her death: *Letters and Memoir of Her Own Life*.

27. The literature hailing the importance of the Scottish Enlightenment is vast. Some highly readable examples include Sher, *Church and University in the Scottish Enlightenment*; Broadie, *Scottish Enlightenment*; Herman, *How the Scots Invented the Modern World*; and Buchan, *Crowded with Genius*.

28. "Dinner" was the main meal of the day, and at various times and places during the eighteenth century it began any time between noon and late afternoon. In Jane Austen's novels it was normally at four.

29. Emerson, "Social Composition of Enlightened Scotland."

30. *LJ*, 540–41.

31. *WN*, 97–98.

32. See Goodspeed, *Legislating Instability*.

33. Smith, *Correspondence of Adam Smith*, 162.

34. Smith predicted that if the American colonies did remain within the British Empire—and were granted representatives in Parliament ("of which the number ought from the first to be considerable")—within "little more than a century" the "seat of the empire" would shift to America; *WN*, 625–26.

35. See, for example, Carroll, *Christ Actually*, 156.

36. Waterman, "Mathematical Modeling as an Exegetical Tool," 558.

37. Wood, *Friends Divided*, 44.

38. Rae, *Life of Adam Smith*, 12–13.

39. David Hume, *Letter from a Gentleman*.
40. Mossner, *Life of David Hume*, 162.
41. MacCulloch, *The Reformation*, 160, citing in turn Bornkamm, *Luther in Mid-Career*, 635–36.*Cuius regio, eius religio* was first proposed in 1526, at the Diet of Speyer. Especially in northern areas of Europe, the tradition dating back for centuries had instead been that many aspects of the law to which an individual was subject depended on the ethnic group to which he belonged, rather than the place in which he lived; see, for example, Le Goff, *Medieval Civilization, 400–1500*, 30.
42. Needless to say, not all opinion regarded Laud's actions in this way. Even many Englishmen not committed to the established church had a more favorable view; see, for example, Hume, *History of England*, Vol. 5, 460.
43. See Gaunt, *English Civil Wars*, 8.
44. Swift, *Gulliver's Travels*, 120.
45. Some accounts imply even larger numbers of deaths. See, for example, Schmidt, *Dreissigjahrige Krieg*.
46. The Czech Protestant Church, which revived when Bohemia became a part of the new Czechoslovakia after World War I, is very much an exception.
47. See, for example, Sher, *Church and University in the Scottish Enlightenment*, esp. 35.
48. *WN*, 810.
49. The analogy is not exact: in Newton's law the function of distance in the denominator is distance squared, while in economists' trade models the function is some power of distance but not necessarily the square.
50. The most influential early work on gravity equations in the context of international trade was Tinbergen, *Shaping the World Economy*. For a recent survey of work in the field, see Head and Mayer, "Gravity Equations."
51. A seminal paper on financial "contagion" that predated the crisis is Allen and Gale, "Financial Contagion." For a postcrisis survey of work in this area, emphasizing "fire sales" (another physical analogy) as the mechanism that propagates the contagion, see Shleifer and Vishny, "Fire Sales in Finance and Macroeconomics." Scott, *Connectedness and Contagion*, exploits the idea of financial contagion to address a variety of policy issues.
52. See, for example, Gort and Klepper, "Time Paths," and Parente and Prescott, "Barriers to Technology Adoption and Development." For a survey comparing the empirical performance of different mechanisms of technological diffusion, see Comin and Hobijn, "Cross-Country Technology Adoption." For a specific application to one familiar technology (computers), see Caselli and Coleman, "Cross-Country Technology Diffusion."
53. The seminal modern work is by Simon Kuznets; see, most famously, "Economic Growth and Income Inequality," and, in much greater detail, "Quantitative Aspects of the Economic Growth of Nations," especially Section III. Other familiar work on the subject includes Sjaastad, "Costs and Returns of Human Migration"; Lewis, *Evolution of the International Economic Order;* and Stark and Bloom, "New Economics of Labor Migration."

CHAPTER 2: THE ROAD TO ADAM SMITH

1. Deuteronomy 11:13–15. Unless otherwise noted, all Bible translations are from the King James Version (the translation that Smith and his contemporaries knew).

2. Matthew 5:9.
3. Matthew 6:19.
4. 1 Timothy 6:9.
5. Notwithstanding the biblical prohibition, as a practical matter even the medieval church tolerated interest on loans other than to individuals, such as loans to the king or for commercial purposes.
6. Matthew 19:23.
7. Mayhew, *Malthus*, 195; also see Chs. 7 and 8.
8. Mun, *England's Treasure by Forraign Trade*, 173.
9. Slack, *Invention of Improvement*, 144.
10. Fletcher, *Two Discourses Concerning the Affairs of Scotland*, esp. 8–18.
11. Smout, *History of the Scottish People, 1560–1830*, 242.
12. Hume, "Of the Jealousy of Trade," in *EMPL*, 331.
13. There were some earlier expressions of this idea. Jean Bodin, a sixteenth-century French political philosopher, wrote that "it is more seemly for a prince to be a merchant, than a tyrant; and for a gentleman to trafficke, than to steale." Bodin, *Six Bookes*, 660.
14. *WN*, 96; 99.
15. See Pocock, *Machiavellian Moment*, Part III.
16. See, for example, Whatmore, "Luxury, Commerce, and the Rise of Political Economy," and Slack, *Invention of Improvement*, Chs. 5–6.
17. Mun, *England's Treasure by Forraign Trade*, 180.
18. Sidney, *Discourses Concerning Government*, 254; Sidney's essay was first published in 1698.
19. MacCulloch, *The Reformation*, 643.
20. See, for example, Addison, in *The Spectator*.
21. Whiston, *England's State Distempers*, 13; 3.
22. Bailyn, *Ideological Origins of the American Revolution*, 51.
23. "An act to prevent the infamous practice of stock-jobbing" (7 George II, c.8). See Ross, "Emergence of David Hume as a Political Economist," 36.
24. Swift, *The Bubble*, 5–6.
25. On Hogarth's engraving, see Stratmann, *Myths of Speculation*, 132–37.
26. For a useful overview, see Brooke, *Philosophic Pride*, Ch. 5.
27. Hobbes, *Leviathan*, 97; *De Cive*, 49.
28. Norris, *Theory and Regulation of Love*, 55. Here, and below, emphasis (italics) in all quotations is from the original unless otherwise noted.
29. Brown and Morris, *Starting with Hume*, 107. More generally on Shaftesbury's focus on sentiments, including those focusing on our own sentiments, see Baier and Luntley, "Moral Sentiments and the Difference They Make," 15–45; and Frazer, *Enlightenment of Sympathy*, 17–25.
30. As we shall see, Adam Smith, by contrast, saw the development of town life as a positive force for public morality in the sense of liberty and good governance.
31. Defoe, *Review of the State of the English Nation*, 17–18.
32. Hume, *Treatise of Human Nature*, 316.
33. On Jansenism, see Van Kley, "Pierre Nicole, Jansenism, and the Morality of Enlightened Self-Interest," and Orain, "Second Jansenism."
34. Several historians of economics have written extensively on the influence of Jansenist thinking on the development of the field. See, for example, Faccarello, *Foundations of Laissez-faire*; Waterman, "Changing Theological Context of Economic Analysis"; and Orain, "Second Jansenism."

35. For a useful summary, see Force, *Self-Interest Before Adam Smith*. See also the insightful reaction by Faccarello, "Tale of Two Traditions."

36. Nicole, *Moral Essays*. Nicole's name did not appear on the title pages; the essays were identified as "Written in French, by Messieurs du Port Royal."

37. Yolton, *Locke as Translator*.

38. Nicole, "Of Charity and Self-Love," in *Moral Essays*, Vol. 3, 123–76. The essay first appeared in French in 1675 and in English translation in 1680. Although some writers on this subject distinguish between "self-interest" and "self-love"—see, for example, Force, *Self-Interest Before Adam Smith*—for purposes here the two are effectively equivalent. As Anthony Waterman put it, "*Self-love* . . . is simply *self-interest* in theological disguise"; Waterman, "How Did Economics Get Its Shape?," 13–14.

39. Nicole, "Of Charity and Self-Love," 123.

40. Nicole, "Of Charity and Self-Love," 125; 134–35; 145; 148.

41. Nicole, "Of Charity and Self-Love," 126; 128. For a useful discussion, see Faccarello, "Tale of Two Traditions," esp. 708.

42. Nicole, "Of Charity and Self-Love," 128.

43. Pierre Nicole, "Of Grandeur: Part I," in *Moral Essays*, Vol. 2, 165–67. Faccarello gives a different translation; *Foundations of Laissez-Faire*, p. 28.

44. Nicole, "Of Charity and Self-Love," 124.

45. On Boisguilbert's contribution, see especially Faccarello, *Foundations of Laissez-faire*. See also Force, *Self-Interest Before Adam Smith*; Faccarello, "Tale of Two Traditions"; Faccarello and Philippe Steiner, "Religion and Political Economy," and Waterman, "Changing Theological Context of Economic Analysis."

46. Boisguilbert, *Le Detail de la France*, Vol. 2, 581–662. Boisguilbert's works have never been translated into English. The title used in the text here is from McCollim, *Louis XIV's Assault on Privilege*, 148.

47. Boisguilbert, *Traite de la nature*, Vol. 2, 827–78. The translation of the title is from Maifreda, *From Oikonomia to Political Economy*, 180.

48. Boisguilbert, *Traite de la nature*; translation from Faccarello, "Tale of Two Traditions," 709.

49. Boisguilbert, *Traite de la nature*; translation from Faccarello, *Foundations of Laissez-faire*, 97.

50. Cantillon, *Essay on the Nature of Trade in General*.

51. van den Berg, "Cantillon on Profit and Interest."

52. Mizuta, *Adam Smith's Library*, 45; *WN*, 85.

53. For an overview of Mandeville's life and work, see Hundert, *Enlightenment's Fable*; Kaye, "Introduction," in *FB*; and Cook, "Bernard Mandeville and the Therapy of 'The Clever Politician.'" Dekker, "'Private Vices, Public Virtues' Revisited," provides a useful discussion of the political circumstances behind Mandeville's emigration.

54. *Henry V*, Act I, Scene 2. Interestingly, the Archbishop's comment also hints at an early understanding of what Adam Smith would later call the division of labor: "Therefore doth heaven divide / The state of man in diverse functions, / Setting endeavor in continual motion."

55. Bees were also used as symbols in private contexts. Rome's Barberini family used a shield with three bees. In part because of Maffeo Barberini's papacy as Urban VIII, some ten thousand bees supposedly decorate the city's buildings.

56. For example, Hartlib, *Reformed Common-wealth of Bees*.

57. Hundert, *Enlightenment's Fable*, 23; Le Goff, *Your Money or Your Life*, 11.

58. *FB*, 87.
59. *FB*, 261.
60. *FB*, 86; 91.
61. *FB*, xlvi; 18; 24.
62. *FB*, 25.
63. *FB*, 26.
64. Macaulay, *History of England*, Vol. 1, 397. For useful overviews of attitudes toward improvement during this time and somewhat before, see Appleby, *Economic Thought and Ideology in Seventeenth-Century England*, Ch. 7, and, more recently, Slack, *Invention of Improvement*.
65. Some part of Mandeville's defense of such criminals may have been genuine, however. In 1724 he published separately a pamphlet calling for publicly maintained and supervised houses of prostitution. See *FB*, 19; 86. Also see his anonymous pamphlet, published as Phil-Porney, *Modest Defense of Publick Stews*.
66. *FB*, "A Search into the Nature of Society," 355.
67. Houghton, *Collection for the Improvement of Husbandry and Trade*, 382–83; 389.
68. *FB*, 34–35.
69. See again Cook, "Bernard Mandeville and the Therapy of 'The Clever Politician.'"
70. *FB*, 36–37.
71. Friedrich Hayek, for example, hailed Mandeville as an economic "master mind," emphasizing his deep understanding of human nature and giving him credit for having "provided the foundations on which David Hume was able to build"; Hayek, "Lecture on a Master Mind," 138. But even Hayek acknowledged that Mandeville "probably never fully understood what was his main discovery" (127).
72. For a discussion of the pre-Newtonian origins of this concept, see Greenblatt, *The Swerve*, Ch. 3, esp. 74.
73. It was retranslated in 1803 (with an American revision in 1848), and again in 1934, and most recently in 1999.
74. Cook suggested that what led Mandeville to this idea was the analogy between how the "skillful Politician" manipulated the various "passions" within society and how a physician (of Mandeville's day) manipulated his patient's passions; see again Cook, "Bernard Mandeville and the Therapy of 'The Clever Politician.'"
75. Hundert, *Enlightenment's Fable*, 7; 154.
76. Hayek wrote, referring to Mandeville's *Fable*, that "There is perhaps no other comparable work of which one can be equally confident that all contemporary writers in the field knew it, whether they explicitly refer to it or not"; Hayek, "Lecture on a Master Mind," 128.
77. Mandeville's writings also apparently influenced Smith's views on another subject: the evolution of human institutions (see Chapter 8 below). For discussion of this aspect of Mandeville's contributions, see Rosenberg, "Mandeville and Laissez-Faire" and "Adam Smith on the Division of Labour: Two Views or One?"
78. Writing nearly two centuries later, the English critic Leslie Stephen referred to Mandeville's argument as "a cynical system of morality" that "was made attractive by ingenious paradoxes." Stephen, "Mandeville, Bernard," 21.
79. Hundert, *Enlightenment's Fable*, 16.
80. Hundert, *Enlightenment's Fable*, 8.
81. Butler, *Fifteen Sermons*, 9; 54; both passages are cited in Waterman, "Changing Theological Context of Economic Analysis," 129, with somewhat different wording.

Butler, *Fifteen Sermons,* 2nd ed., 153. The biblical reference is to Matthew 22:39. On Butler's influence more generally, see Waterman, *Political Economy and Christian Theology.*

82. See Price, "Liberty, Poverty and Charity."
83. For an overview, see Tennant, *Conscience, Consciousness and Ethics.*
84. Hutcheson, *Inquiry into the Original of Our Ideas of Beauty and Virtue,* 104. In the book Hutcheson praised Butler.
85. Hutcheson, *System of Moral Philosophy,* Vol. 1, 321. The book was published (by Hutcheson's son) only after his death; but it was apparently circulating among his friends as early as the late 1730s.
86. Charles Rollin, *Histoire ancienne,* Vol. 12, 360–61, cited in Orain, "Second Jansenism," 467.
87. Pope, *Essay on Man,* 18.
88. David Hume, "Of Refinement in the Arts," in *EMPL,* 269. The essay was titled "Of Luxury" in the original 1752 edition.
89. Samuel Johnson, "Luxurious," *Dictionary of the English Language.*
90. See Berry, *Idea of Luxury.* Slack, *Invention of Improvement,* 146, refers to the "demoralization of luxury."
91. Aristotle, *Politics,* Bk. 6, Ch. 5, 375.
92. Hume, "Of Refinement in the Arts," 302; 313; 306. Hume also argued that consumption of luxuries makes the nation stronger because the labor mobilized for this purpose can, if needed, be directed to the "public service" (307). For an analysis of Hume's views on luxury, see Berry, "Hume and Superfluous Value."
93. Tucker, *Brief Essay on the Advantages and Disadvantages,* 126.
94. On Tucker's economic writings and their influence, see again Price, "Liberty, Poverty and Charity," and Waterman, *Political Economy and Christian Theology.*
95. Josiah Tucker, "A Preliminary Discourse, setting Forth the natural Disposition, or instinctive Inclination of mankind toward Commerce," in *Elements of Commerce,* 6–7.
96. Tucker, *Seventeen Sermons,* 139.
97. Mizuta, *Adam Smith's Library,* 256–58. See also Waterman, "Changing Theological Context of Economic Analysis," 129.

CHAPTER 3: PHILOSOPHICAL UNDERPINNINGS

1. For Smith's biography, see Ross, *Life of Adam Smith,* and Phillipson, *Adam Smith.*
2. Edward Reynolds, a seventeenth-century bishop but also a Puritan, drew the distinction as follows: "there is a knowledge of God *natural* in and *by his works:* and a knowledge *supernatural* by revelation out of the Word"; cited in Miller, *New England Mind,* 82. Not everyone agreed that it is possible to draw inferences about God from observing his creation. David Hume, in his posthumously published *Dialogues Concerning Natural Religion,* explicitly rejected the idea; see Hume, *Dialogues,* Pt. 2, 17–28.
3. Adam Smith, "To Dr. Archibald Davidson," in *Correspondence,* 309.
4. Baxter, *A Paraphrase on the New Testament,* I Corinthians, Ch. II, "Annotations."
5. Ray, *Wisdom of God.*
6. Newton, *Four Letters,* 1.

7. See Hetherington, "Isaac Newton's Influence."

8. Smith, "History of Astronomy," in *Essays on Philosophical Subjects,* 98; 105.

9. Smith, "History of Astronomy," 105.

10. Smith, *Lectures on Rhetoric and Belles Lettres,* Lecture 24, 145–46. See also the discussion in Weingast, "Adam Smith's 'Jurisprudence.'"

11. Mizuta, *Adam Smith's Library,* 179.

12. *WN,* 761.

13. Ross, *Lord Kames and the Scotland of His Day,* 374–77.

14. Hume, *Treatise of Human Nature,* 4. Hume's *Treatise* was first published in 1739. Hume's intellectual program is often described as "a Newtonian science of the mind"; see Grune-Yanoff and McClennen, "Hume's Framework for a Natural History of the Passions," 102.

15. The opening sections of Hume's *Treatise of Human Nature* identify the imagination (along with memory) as one of two mechanisms through which people's impressions become ideas, and much of the *Treatise's* first book focuses on four faculties— understanding, reason, the senses, and the imagination—arguing that the operation of the first three is grounded in the fourth; see Fogelin, "Hume's Scepticism," 101. Many Enlightenment thinkers emphasized reason as the distinguishing human characteristic, but Hume differed; Book 1, Part 4, Section 1 is titled "Of skepticism with regard to reason." Numerous writers on Smith's work have emphasized the importance he attached to the imagination; see, for example, Griswold, *Adam Smith and the Virtues of Enlightenment,* and Otteson, *Adam Smith's Marketplace of Life.*

16. See Haakonssen's introduction to *Theory of Moral Sentiments,* xii–xiii.

17. *TMS,* 9. Smith's ideas of putting ourselves in others' shoes comports surprisingly well with modern research on the "theory of the mind"; see, for example, Dennett, *Consciousness Explained.* Evidence from experiments with children indicates that this ability apparently develops at about age four.

18. *TMS,* 13.

19. *TMS,* 116.

20. The capitals may merely have reflected the English printer's conventions of the day. For example, in Josiah Tucker's *A Brief Essay on . . . Trade,* published ten years before, all nouns are capitalized. Still, in *The Theory of Moral Sentiments* these particular nouns are capitalized while most others are not.

21. *TMS,* 235–37. All of these passages are from the material that Smith added for the book's sixth edition, published shortly before his death in 1790. But elsewhere in *The Theory of Moral Sentiments,* Smith also wrote that "we may admire the wisdom and goodness of God even in the weakness and folly of man," and so the basic thought was presumably not a new turn of mind; *TMS,* 106. The question of theological content in Smith's thinking has been the object of much attention. See, for example, Hill, "Hidden Theology of Adam Smith"; Graham, "Adam Smith and Religion"; and, more generally, Waterman, "Economics as Theology," and Oslington, *Political Economy as Natural Religion,* Ch. 4

22. *TMS,* 149; 23. The importance of interaction for life satisfaction was also an old idea. The Greek philosopher Philodemus wrote that pleasure in life is impossible "without living prudently and honorably and justly, and also without living courageously and temperately and magnanimously, *and without making friends,* and without being philanthropic" (emphasis added); quoted in Greenblatt, *The Swerve,* 77. Here once again Smith's thinking was aligned with that of Hume, who wrote that "friendship

is the chief joy of human life" and that "the two greatest and purest pleasures of human life [are] study and society"; *Enquiry Concerning Human Understanding*, 102; *Dialogues Concerning Natural Religion*, 4.

23. Hume, *Treatise of Human Nature*, 206. Hume likewise praised the benefits of conversation: "The blood flows with a new tide: The heart is elevated: And the whole man acquires a vigor, which he cannot command in his solitary and calm moments"; *Treatise of Human Nature*, 228.

24. David Haig, a biologist, has offered an evolutionary interpretation of Smith's ideas about "sympathy." Haig, "Sympathy with Adam Smith and Reflexions on Self."

25. *TMS*, 9; 21; 10; 13.

26. *TMS*, 25.

27. *TMS*, 200.

28. Here too Smith took his lead from Hume: see, for example, *Treatise of Human Nature*, Book 3, Part 3, Section 1 (esp. 368–69). His concept of the impartial spectator also drew on thinking by Joseph Butler, whom he called "a late ingenious and subtile philosopher"; *TMS*, 43.

29. Burns, "To A Louse, On Seeing One on a Lady's Bonnet at Church," in *Poems*, 192–94.

30. *TMS*, 24.

31. *TMS*, 25.

32. John Rawls, referring to both Hume and Smith, postulated an "impartial sympathetic spectator" and argued that "A rightly ordered society is one meeting the approval of such an ideal observer"; Rawls, *Theory of Justice*, 184.

33. See again Haakonssen, xii–xv.

34. *TMS*, 114–19. Joseph Butler had earlier referred to a "Law of Reputation," which enforces various civil laws by rendering certain vices "every where infamous," and contrary virtues "of good Report"; Butler, *Sermon Preached before the House of Lords*, 6.

35. *TMS*, 115–17.

36. *TMS*, 185.

37. *TMS*, 184.

38. *TMS*, 184–85.

39. Gibbon, *Decline and Fall*, Vol. 1, 68.

40. Tucker, in his book published just two years before (a version of which Smith owned at the time of his death), wrote that "the Self-Love and Self-Interest of each Individual will prompt him to seek such Ways of Gain, Trades and Occupations of Life, as by serving himself, will promote the public Welfare at the same Time"; Tucker, *Instructions for Travellers*, 31–32.

41. *TMS*, 184–85.

42. See, for example, Martin, "Economics as Ideology": "The famous 'Invisible Hand' was only another of Smith's references to God" (279). More recently, Harrison, "Adam Smith and the History of the Invisible Hand," has shown that references to invisible or hidden hands were a commonplace of sermons and other religious writings at an earlier time. See also von Mueller, "The Invisible Hand and the Case of the Additional Tamquam."

43. See, for example, Weisskopf, "The Method Is the Ideology," 877.

44. *TMS*, 87; 236.

45. *TMS*, 185.

46. As a partial explanation, in the *Wealth of Nations* Smith observed that consumption choices become careless when items absorb only a small fraction of a person's budget; see Hollander, "Making the Most of Anomaly," 19.

47. *TMS*, 180.

48. *TMS*, 61; 181; 64.

49. *FB*, 25.

50. *TMS*, 183.

51. *TMS*, 149.

52. For different views on the question, see, for example, Easterlin, "Does Economic Growth Improve the Human Lot?" and "Income and Happiness"; Inglehart, *Culture Shift in Advanced Industrial Society*, Ch. 1; Sacks et al., "New Stylized Facts."

53. Doing so is commonly called "rational adaptation." See Constantinides, "Habit Formation"; Campbell and Cochrane, "By Force of Habit"; Becker and Murphy, "Theory of Rational Addiction."

54. The idea was hardly new with Mandeville, however: "Then I saw that all toil and all skill in work comes from man's envy of his neighbor"; Ecclesiastes 4:4 (in the Revised Standard Version; the translation in the King James Version is different). As Amartya Sen has noted, in some contexts even such basics as the notion of required minimum nutrition are socially based; Sen, *Poverty and Famines*, 12.

55. *FB*, 127; 128.

56. *TMS*, 50.

57. *WN*, 869–70.

58. *WN*, 870.

59. See Veblen, *Theory of the Leisure Class*. Veblen's idea continues to be a focus of economic research, although the more modern term is "status goods"; see, for one recent example, Burstyn et al., "Status Goods."

60. *TMS*, 182.

61. *WN*, 421.

62. *WN*, 99.

63. *TMS*, 304.

64. *TMS*, 63.

65. Nunn and Qian, "The Potato's Contribution," 594; data from Chandler, *Four Thousand Years of Urban Growth*, and Bairoch, *Cities and Economic Development*.

66. Montesquieu, *De l'esprit des loix*. Translation by Hirschman, *Passions and Interests*, 60.

67. Boyd, "Manners and Morals," 67.

68. Price, "Liberty, Poverty and Charity," 765. See also Price, "Sociability and Self-Love."

69. Butler, *Sermon Preached before the Incorporated Society*, 12.

70. Tucker, *Seventeen Sermons*, 138–39.

71. Priestley, *Lectures on History and General Policy*, 386.

72. Mizuta, *Adam Smith's Library*, 205–6; 216.

73. Robertson, "A View of the State of Europe," in *Works*, Vol. 4, 97.

74. Hume, "Of the Rise and Progress of the Arts and Sciences," in *EMPL*, 119.

75. Rush, "Thoughts upon the Mode of Education Proper in a Republic," 689.

76. Jefferson, Franklin, and Adams, "American Commissioners to De Thulemeier, March 14, 1785," 28; cited in Wood, *Friends Divided*, 157.

77. Paine, *Rights of Man*, 266.

78. For an account of this idea and its origins, see Hirschman, *Passions and Interests*.

79. Hume, "Of Refinement in the Arts," in *EMPL*, 280.
80. C. A. Helvétius, *De L'esprit*. Translation by Hirschman, *Passions and Interests*, 28.
81. Baron d'Holbach, *Système de la Nature ou Des Lois du Monde Physique et du Monde Moral*. Translation by Hirschman, *Passions and Interests*, 27.
82. See James Madison, "No. 51", and Alexander Hamilton, "No. 72" in Hamilton et al., *Federalist Papers*, 256–60; 354–58.
83. According to Max Weber, for example, "capitalism is identical with the pursuit of profit, and forever *renewed* profit, by means of continuous, rational, capitalistic enterprise"; Weber, *The Protestant Ethic and the Spirit of Capitalism*, xxxi–xxxii.
84. Hume, "Of the Rise and Progress of the Arts and Sciences," in *EMPL*, 113. The thought was not limited to philosophers. Writing to James Madison in 1784, George Washington observed that "The motives which predominate most in human affairs is self-love and self-interest"; *Papers*, Vol. 2, 166.

CHAPTER 4: THE COMPETITIVE MARKET MECHANISM

1. *LJ*, 5.
2. *LJ*. For another version of these lectures, based on another set of notes, see Smith, *Lectures on Police, Revenue, and Arms*.
3. See Goodspeed, *Legislating Instability*.
4. See Stewart, "Account of the Life and Writings of Adam Smith, LL.D.," 52.
5. As one historian has speculated, "Had Louis given Turgot his full confidence and accepted all his advice without question, it is just possible that he might have spared his country a revolution"; Norwich, *History of France*, 187.
6. Peter Groenewegen carefully examined the similarities in Smith's and Turgot's writings, together with the opportunities Smith had to draw on Turgot's thinking, and concluded that while Smith no doubt learned from Turgot, there was little direct influence; see Groenewegen, "Turgot and Adam Smith."
7. See, for example, Skinner, "Adam Smith: The French Connection," and many of the references cited there.
8. Nearly two centuries later, Quesnay's *Tableau* exerted a strong influence on the development of input-output analysis by Wassily Leontief.
9. Quesnay, *Physiocratie*.
10. *WN*, 678.
11. Phillipson, *Adam Smith*, 194.
12. See Faccarello, *Foundations of Laissez-faire*, and Faccarello and Steiner, "Religion and Political Economy." For a recent overview of the influence of Smith's stay in France, see Blomert, *Adam Smiths Reise nach Frankreich*.
13. "To David Hume, Jul. 5, 1764," *Correspondence of Adam Smith*, 102. According to Nicholas Phillipson, whether the book he said he was beginning to write was in fact *The Wealth of Nations* "remains a matter of controversy and speculation"; Phillipson, *Adam Smith*, 188.
14. Keynes, *End of Laissez-Faire*, 12.
15. The scholarly literature commenting on *The Wealth of Nations* (and Smith's other work too) is vast. Hollander, *Economics of Adam Smith*, Winch, *Riches and Poverty*, Griswold, *Adam Smith and the Virtues of Enlightenment*, and Fleischacker, *On Adam Smith's Wealth of Nations*, are just of a few of the most prominent contributions

during the last half-century. See also many of the entries in Haakonssen, *Cambridge Companion to Adam Smith,* Berry et al., *Oxford Handbook of Adam Smith,* and Hanley, *Adam Smith,* and the many further references cited there. Finally, see Campbell and Skinner, "General Introduction," *WN,* 1–60.

16. *WN,* 341. Although there is presumably no connection, Smith's view of the desire of bettering our condition curiously parallels the ancient rabbinic view of the "evil inclination"—without which "no man would build a house, or take a wife, or beget children, or engage in business"; the "evil inclination" in this sense is innate from birth, while the "good inclination," often interpreted as the soul, develops only later (age twelve for girls, thirteen for boys). Genesis Rabba 9:7.

17. Haakonssen, "Introduction" to *Cambridge Companion to Adam Smith,* 16–17.

18. *WN,* 341.

19. Rousseau, *Social Contract,* 45. Similarly, Hume had argued that "Sovereigns must take mankind as they find them, and cannot pretend to introduce any violent change in their principles and ways of thinking"; Hume, "Of Commerce," in *EMPL,* 260.

20. *WN,* 343.

21. *WN,* 13.

22. *WN,* 13; 660; 25.

23. By one estimate, textiles accounted for at least half of all productivity growth in England during the Industrial Revolution; Clark, *Farewell to Alms,* Table 12.1. By contrast, in *The Wealth of Nations* Smith did comment on the dramatic fall in the price of watches over the previous century (p. 260); see Kelly and Ó Gráda, "Adam Smith, Watch Prices, and the Industrial Revolution."

24. For a contrary view, see Appleby, *Relentless Revolution,* Ch. 5. See also Slack, *Invention of Improvement.*

25. Smith also presumably understood the increase in agricultural productivity that had followed such improvements as enclosed fields, crop rotation, iron plows, and selective breeding of livestock. But as his reaction to the physiocrats indicated, his interest was not in agriculture.

26. *WN,* 28–29. Smith's example recently inspired a book title: Peart and Levy, *The Street Porter and the Philosopher.*

27. Smith's friend Adam Ferguson had earlier expressed similar concerns; see Ferguson, *Essay on the History of Civil Society,* 276–87.

28. *WN,* 781–82.

29. Smith's concerns have resonated in the industrialized world ever since. Perhaps the most famous depiction in popular culture is Charlie Chaplin's 1936 film *Modern Times.*

30. *WN,* 782. Smith went on to express concern that such a worker becomes "equally incapable of defending his country in time of war." Richard Sher suggested that what he may have had in mind was the failure of the Lowlanders to put up much defense in the 1745 Jacobite rebellion; Sher, *Church and University in the Scottish Enlightenment,* 40.

31. *WN,* 25.

32. *WN,* 26. Smith's analysis is of commercial society—not, for example, the inner workings of the family or other family-like communities. See, for example, Folbre, *Invisible Heart,* and Morse, *Love and Economics.*

33. *LJ,* 347.

34. James Steuart had already introduced the vocabulary of supply and demand nearly

a decade earlier: see Steuart, *Inquiry into the Principles of Political Oeconomy*. It was Thomas Malthus, in the second, expanded edition of his *Essay on Population*, who first offered an arithmetical demand function, but he implicitly assumed fixed supply; see Malthus, *Essay on the Principle of Population* (1803).

35. *WN*, 83.

36. *WN*, 26–27. Smith had made the same point, and almost in the same language, in the lectures he gave at Glasgow in the early 1760s that became *Lectures on Jurisprudence*: "When you apply to a brewer or butcher for beer or for beef you do not explain to him how much you stand in need of these, but how much it would be your [the student note-taker presumably meant to write "his"] interest to allow you to have them for a certain price. You do not address his humanity, but his self-love." See *LJ*, 348.

37. *WN*, 343.

38. *WN*, 266.

39. Not all thoughtful readers have agreed that by the "invisible hand" Smith intended no more than a metaphor. See, for example, Viner, *Role of Providence in the Social Order*, 82; Evensky, "Two Voices of Adam Smith"; Martin, "Economics as Ideology"; Grampp, "What Did Smith Mean by the Invisible Hand?"; Rothschild, *Economic Sentiments*, Ch. 5.

40. Hume, *Treatise of Human Nature*, 316; *WN*, 341.

41. Nearly two hundred years later, Daniel Bell wrote that "Smith here laid down a proposition that was almost entirely new in the history of civil society: in a free exchange, both parties to a transaction could gain." Bell, *Coming of Post-Industrial Society*, 303.

42. *TMS*, 183–84; *WN*, 419–22.

43. This aspect of Smith's argument did not attract universal agreement, then or afterward. A long-standing tradition—in America associated with Thomas Jefferson, for example—has regarded agrarian life as morally superior to urban. James Madison wrote, "'Tis not the country that peoples either the Bridewells or the Bedlams. These mansions of wretchedness are tenanted from the distresses and vices of overgrown cities. . . . The greater the proportion of [husbandmen] to the whole society, the more free, the more independent, and the more happy must be the society itself." Madison, "Republican distribution of Citizens," 147.

44. See Hume, *History of England*, Vol. 6, 223–28; and Smout, *History of the Scottish People*, 199. Hume referred to the "very imperfect notions of law and liberty" that prevailed, in contrast to the "government perfectly regular, and exempt from all violence and injustice" that emerged following the Act of Union (233). Waterman provides a useful summary in "David Hume on Technology and Culture."

45. *WN*, 418; 421; 412. The harsh view of country life under feudal law was hardly unique to Smith. In 1765 John Adams had expressed much the same view, also writing that the common people had lived "in a state of *servile* dependence on their lords"; Adams, "Dissertation on the Canon and Feudal Law."

46. *WN*, 422.

47. *WN*, 429; 431; 660.

48. Josiah Tucker's 1755 *Elements of Commerce* had included a lengthy appendix detailing "the inslaving of Commerce by exclusive Patents, and monopoly Corporations," with copious examples of the harm they had done and were doing; Tucker, *Elements of Commerce*, 136.

49. *WN*, 84; 267. On the surface, Smith's negative views of merchants seem to contradict those of his mentor Hume, who referred to merchants as "one of the most useful

races of men"; Hume, "Of Interest," in *EMPL*, 300. But Hume's explanation of the "usefulness" of merchants is fully consistent with Smith's description of the workings of commerce in *The Wealth of Nations*.

50. By contrast, writers on politics of the time more typically thought of the English constitution as "a fine, a nice, a delicate machine," so that "the perfection of it depends upon such complicated movements, that it is as easily disordered as the human body." John Adams, *Boston Gazette*, February 8, 1773; *Papers*, Vol. 1, 292.

51. *WN*, 842; 725; 888–91; 893.

52. See, for example, Roth, "Repugnance as a Constraint on Markets."

53. Robert Solow made this point about Smith in his "Remembering John Kenneth Galbraith."

54. *WN*, 540; 606; 343.

55. As much as a hundred years after Smith wrote, many British investors still regarded even the United States as an unsafe place for investment. See, for example, Pagnamenta, *Prairie Fever*, 135.

56. *WN*, 456.

57. One prominent example is Paul Samuelson's reference to "the ancient statement by Adam Smith that a competitive market system, concerned with atoms pursuing only their own narrow self-interests, would be led 'as if by an invisible hand to achieve the good of all." Samuelson, "Liberalism at Bay," 20. For a historical survey of the mistaken insertion of "as if" into what Smith wrote, and an analysis of how this insertion changes its meaning, see von Mueller, "The Invisible Hand and the Case of the Additional Tamquam."

58. *WN*, 456; Mandeville, "An Essay on Charity and Charity-Schools," in *FB*, 261.

59. Hume, "Of the Balance of Trade," in *Political Discourses*.

60. *WN*, 75. The use at this time of Newtonian language in contexts far removed from physics was hardly limited to Smith, or to thinking about economic questions. In 1774 the American legal theorist James Wilson (soon to become a signer of the Declaration of Independence and then the U.S. Constitution) wrote about the British system of government, "To the King is entrusted the direction and management of the great machine of government. He therefore is fittest to adjust the different wheels, and to regulate their motions."; Wilson, *Considerations on the Nature and the Extent of the Legislative Authority of the British Parliament*, 33.

61. Winch, "Introduction," in Ricardo, *Principles of Political Economy and Taxation*, vii.

62. To recall, as an undergraduate Smith had studied Nicole and Arnauld's logic text. In contrast to Mandeville, however, Smith never referred to Nicole, neither in *The Wealth of Nations* nor in any other of his other writings that have survived. Nor were any of Nicole's works in Smith's personal library when he died.

63. Smith's library included works by Cantillon, Ferguson, Tucker, and Steuart—and, of course, Hume; Mizuta, *Adam Smith's Library*. There are also examples of much earlier thinking that paralleled Smith's, such as Ibn Khaldun in the fourteenth century, but there is no way to know whether Smith was familiar with their writings.

64. On the influence of stoicism on Smith's thinking, see Brown, *Adam Smith's Discourse*, and Force, *Self-Interest before Adam Smith*, esp. Chs. 2, 3. Also see Gilbert Faccarello's review of Force's book; Faccarello, "Tale of Two Traditions." The same belief in natural harmony likewise underlay the preference of contemporary figures like Thomas Jefferson for minimal government: see Wood, *Friends Divided*, 328.

65. See Viner, "Adam Smith and Laissez Faire," 117.

66. Exactly a half-century before, for example, Joseph Butler—whose work Smith knew and admired—had invoked the "hands of Providence" in describing the favorable working of the law of unintended consequences: "by acting meerly from Regard (suppose) to Reputation, without any Consideration of the Good of others, Men often contribute to publick Good . . . they are plainly Instruments in the Hands of another, in the Hands of Providence, to carry on Ends, the Preservation of the Individual and Good of Society, which they themselves have not in their View or Intention"; Butler, *Fifteen Sermons,* 12.

CHAPTER 5: PREDESTINATION AND DEPRAVITY

1. See Simpson, *Burning to Read,* 32; 54.
2. Buckley, *Canons and Decrees of the Council of Trent,* 19. The Council met from 1545 to 1563, to consolidate the church's response to the Reformation (in what became known as the Counter-Reformation), but the stance it took toward Bible translation expressed a much longer-standing view.
3. There was greater controversy surrounding biblical translations in England than elsewhere. John Wyclif's translation, done between the 1370s and 1390s by a team that began work under his supervision, was banned by church officials in England in 1409. William Tyndale's translation of the New Testament was first printed in 1526, soon after the Reformation began; it too was banned, until after the English church separated from Rome. The most famous translation to come out of the Reformation was Luther's. He published his New Testament translation in 1522, and the complete Bible in 1534.
4. de Hamel, *Meetings with Remarkable Manuscripts,* 506.
5. Similarly, after the Reformation gained momentum the church's effort to suppress heterodox views via its Index of Prohibited Books, instituted in 1557, mostly proved ineffective.
6. For an account of the history, see Massing, *Fatal Discord,* Ch. 14.
7. Massing, *Fatal Discord,* 304; 309; 448.
8. Genesis 2:15, 1:26, 2:17.
9. Genesis 3:14–19.
10. Genesis 1:27.
11. Augustine, *City of God against the Pagans,* 555–56. Augustine's view is consistent also with writings in the Dead Sea Scrolls, roughly contemporaneous with the beginnings of Christianity. For example, the speaker of the Thanksgiving Hymns proclaims "I am a creature of clay mixed with water, the essence of shamefulness and a fountain of impurity, a smelting pot of transgression and constructed of sin, a spirit of error and depravity." (1QHa Thanksgiving Hymns, col 9:23–25); translation from Kugel, *Great Shift,* 198. In the same vein, the medieval Zohar, the central work of mystical Kabbalistic Judaism, "bears a strong sense that humankind, and the universe with it, exists in a fallen state"; Green, *Guide to the Zohar,* 152.
12. Luther, "Freedom of a Christian," in *Works,* Vol. 31, 346–47.
13. Psalm 14:3. Paul likewise wrote "They are all gone out of the way"; Romans 3:12.
14. Luther, *Freedom of a Christian,* 348.
15. *ICR,* 36; 251. Even before Calvin, in the "Prologue" to his 1525 translation of the New Testament into English, William Tyndale had labeled all men "chyldren of wrath"

and "heyres of the vengeannce of god by byrth"; even in their mothers' wombs, they are "full of the naturall poyson where of all synfull deds sprynge and cannott but symme outwards (be we never so yonge) yf occasion be geven." Tyndale, "Prologue," in *The New Testament*.

16. *ICR*, 251–52; 296.

17. The word "satan" (or any equivalent) also does not appear in the Genesis account. The text merely says that "the serpent was more subtle" than any of the other animals (3:1). One tradition of biblical exegesis follows this line, suggesting that the serpent merely showed Adam and Eve the way to knowledge, with no evil connotation. In a similar usage, Matthew (10:16) quotes Jesus as enjoining his followers, "be ye therefore wise as serpents, and harmless as doves." See Kugel, *Great Shift*, 59–66.

18. 1 Corinthians 15:20–21.

19. *ICR*, 466.

20. For a discussion of traditional artistic representations of the link between Adam and Jesus, see Greenblatt, *Rise and Fall of Adam and Eve*.

21. Pierre Nicole, "Of Charity and Self-Love," in *Moral Essays*, Vol. 3, 135. For a useful discussion, see Grewal, "Political Theology of Laissez-Faire."

22. See, for example, Simpson, *Permanent Revolution*, Chs. 1–4. As Simpson explains, after 1571 predestination was "the official doctrine of the Anglican Church," and "Anglican polity was centrally Calvinist and predestinarian" (26–27). Original sin and depravity were less controversial because these ideas were already part of Catholic theology, and consensus on them mostly prevailed as well. Diarmaid MacCulloch, for example, refers to the "constant emphasis on the incomparable majesty of God and the total 'fallen-ness' of humankind"; MacCulloch, *Later Reformation in England*, 73. Also see Todd, *Christian Humanism and the Puritan Social Order*, 18.

23. An earlier version, completed in 1552 under Elizabeth's brother Edward VI, had forty-two articles. The standard treatise on the history and interpretation of the *Thirty-Nine Articles* is Bicknell, *A Theological Introduction to the Thirty-Nine Articles of the Church of England*. Simpson, *Permanent Revolution*, labels the Thirty-Nine Articles "the official doctrinal statement of the English Church" (66).

24. For an overview of the history, see Benedict, *Christ's Churches Purely Reformed*.

25. Article IX, *Thirty-Nine Articles*, in Leith, *Creeds of the Churches*, 269.

26. Chapter VI, Articles I, III, and IV, *The Westminster Confession of Faith*, in Leith, *Creeds of the Churches*, 201.

27. Genesis 42:38, 25:8; 1 Samuel 28:15. The King James Version reads "bring down my gray hairs to the grave," but most other translations more accurately render the word as "Sheol": a reference not to an individual grave but some otherwise unspecified kind of underworld. There are also implicit references to an eternal afterlife in the Psalms and other later writings. In Psalm 16, for example, the psalmist says, "thou wilt not leave my soul in hell [again the better translation is "Sheol"] . . . Thou wilt show me the path of life . . . at thy right hand there are pleasures for evermore." Similarly, Psalm 73 declares, "Thou shalt guide me with thy counsel, and afterward [after death?] receive me to glory. . . . My flesh and my heart faileth; but God is the strength of my heart and my portion for ever." In Ecclesiastes Koheleth says of death, "Then shall the dust return to the earth as it was; and the spirit shall return to God who gave it" (12:7). (Under some interpretations, Koheleth's statement is a reflection of Genesis 2:7.)

28. The discussion of God's causing "breath to enter into" "dry bones" in the book of

Ezekiel is sometimes read to refer to the resurrection of individuals, but the prophet is clear that the bones in his vision symbolize the nation collectively: "these bones are the whole house of Israel." Ezekiel 37: 4, 5, 11.

29. Daniel 12:2–3.

30. Matthew 22:1–14. Elsewhere Matthew quotes Jesus as saying that God will "gather his wheat into the garner: but will burn up the chaff with unquenchable fire" (3:12).

31. 4 Ezra 8:1–3. The passage continues, "Just as, if you were to ask the earth, it would tell you that it provides very much clay, from which earthenware is made, but only a little dust from which gold comes, so in the course of the present world many have been created, but few shall be saved"; translation from Kugel, *Great Shift*, 297.

32. For example, Carroll, *Christ Actually*, 223.

33. Romans 11:1–6. The meaning is perhaps easier to read in a translation like the New Revised Standard Version: "there is a remnant, chosen by grace . . . if it is by grace, it is no longer on the basis of works; otherwise grace would no longer be grace."

34. Ephesians 2:8–9.

35. Galatians 2:16.

36. Genesis 25:23.

37. Exodus 33:19. An alternative translation would be "I will love whom I will love"—or "nurture," or even "hold close" (the root of the verb being translated refers to the womb).

38. Kugel, *Great Shift*, 278.

39. See, for example, Stroumsa, *End of Sacrifice*, 85.

40. Dead Sea Scrolls, 4Q181 1, II, 3–6. For an overview of the discussion of election and predestination in the Dead Sea Scrolls, see Schiffman, *Reclaiming the Dead Sea Scrolls*, Ch. 9.

41. Dead Sea Scrolls 1QH9(a) XI, 19–25.

42. Romans 8:29.

43. Ephesians 1:4–6.

44. Augustine, *Treatise on the Gift of Perseverance*, 539–40.

45. *ICR*, 921; 926; 931. For a concise overview of the historical development of predestinarian doctrine, see Thuesen, *Predestination*, Ch. 1.

46. A later statement of "double predestination" (*gemina praedestinatio*), but still long before the Reformation, was in the work of Gottschalk of Orbais, a ninth-century Saxon monk. See Isidore of Seville, *Sententiae*, 2, 6, 1; also see McGrath, *Iustitia Dei*, 161. On Gottschalk, see Otten, *Manual of the History of Dogmas*, Vol. 2, 67–72.

47. *ICR*, 921–922; 931.

48. In the section of the *Institutes* on predestination, immediately after the preface Calvin began his exposition of the doctrine with a discussion of the "offspring of Abraham"; *ICR*, 926–29.

49. Weber, *The Protestant Ethic and the Spirit of Capitalism*, 56–80.

50. Weber, *The Protestant Ethic and the Spirit of Capitalism*, 67; see, for example, Tillich, *Courage to Be*, esp. 40–54, but really throughout the book.

51. *ICR*, 922.

52. *ICR*, 224; 921.

53. Article XVII, *Thirty-Nine Articles*, in Leith, *Creeds of the Churches*, 272.

54. Chapter III, Articles III–VII, *Westminster Confession*, in Leith, *Creeds of the Churches*, 198–99.

55. Isaiah 43:7, 43:20–21; 6:3; Habakkuk 3:3. Many centuries later, the glorification of God by the grandeur of the universe was likewise a major theme of the Zohar.

56. John 17:4; 1 Corinthians 10:31; Matthew 24:30 (and see also Luke 21:27).

57. In this regard both Lutherans and Calvinists agreed. The Augsburg Confession of 1530, the initial codified statement of Lutheran belief promulgated after Luther and his followers had clearly separated from the Roman Catholic Church, stated that "good works should and must be done, not that we are to rely on them to earn grace but that we may do God's will and glorify him." See Article XX, *The Augsburg Confession*, in Leith, *Creeds of the Churches*, 77.

58. *ICR*, 43.

59. Proverbs 16:4.

60. Calvin, *Treatise on the Eternal Predestination of God*, 69.

61. Augustine, *Confessions*, 273.

62. Kadane, "Original Sin and the Path to the Enlightenment," 110.

63. *ICR*, 256.

64. Calvin, *Treatise on the Eternal Predestination of God*, 69.

65. *ICR*, 1004.

66. *ICR*, 1005.

67. Hesselink, "Calvin's Theology," 90; 85.

68. Chapter II, Article II; Chapter IV, Article I, *Westminster Confession*, in Leith, *Creeds of the Churches*, 197; 199.

69. Chapter V, Article I, *Westminster Confession*, in Leith, *Creeds of the Churches*, 200.

70. *Humble Advice Of the Assembly Of Divines*, 3.

CHAPTER 6: ASSAULT ON ORTHODOX CALVINISM

1. See W. R. Bagnall, "A Sketch of the Life of the Author," in *The Works of James Arminius*, Vol. 1. In an illustration of the complexity of the arguments surrounding Calvinist theology at the time, the two ministers from Delft were actually attempting to defend Beza against his critics; but they nonetheless argued that certain amendments to his thinking were necessary.

2. Arminius later wrote (in "A Declaration of the Sentiments of Arminius"), "This decree has its foundation in the foreknowledge of God, by which he knew from all eternity those individuals who would, through his preventing grace, believe, and, through his subsequent grace would persevere." The notion of prevenient grace, in approximately this sense, goes back at least to Augustine. Later Arminians—most notably John Wesley—likewise distinguished between two kinds of grace: "prevenient" grace (what Arminius called "preventing" grace), given to everyone, which restores (after the Fall) a person's ability to choose salvation; and "saving grace" (Wesley called it "justifying grace," or "sanctifying grace"), extended only to those who accept this choice and persevere in it until their death. See Arminius, *Works*, Vol. 1, 248 . Also see, for example, *Book of Discipline of the United Methodist Church*, 50.

3. Arminius,*Works*, Vol. 1, 254.

4. Arminius, *Works*, Vol. 1, 254.

5. Benedict, *Christ's Churches Purely Reformed*, Ch. 10.

6. The most complete exposition of his views, a critique that he had written in 1600 of an earlier work by the English Calvinist William Perkins, was first published in 1612. See Arminius, *Examination of A Treatise, Concerning the Order and Mode of Predestination and the Amplitude of Divine Grace*, in *Works*, Vol. 3, 279–525.

7. Formally, the statement was titled (in English) *The Decision of the Synod of Dort on the Five Main Points of Doctrine in Dispute in the Netherlands*. It was popularly called the *Canons of Dort*.

8. The TULIP mnemonic gained widespread use thanks to a popular Calvinist theology textbook published in 1936: Boettner, *Reformed Doctrine of Predestination*, 60–61. In Boettner's rendering, the *T* was Total Inability (which bore the same meaning as Total Depravity).

9. Recent scholarship indicates that this process advanced more slowly than traditional thinking assumed, and that loyalty to Roman Catholic worship and piety remained widespread. See Duffy, *Stripping of the Altars*.

10. Some scholars have even claimed a "Calvinist consensus." See, for example, Lake, *Moderate Puritans and the Elizabethan Church;* Tyacke, *Anti-Calvinists;* and Collinson, *Birthpangs of Protestant England*.

11. Garrett Mattingly also emphasizes Drake's effective logistical preparation in the years preceding 1588; Mattingly, *The Armada*.

12. Simpson, *Permanent Revolution*, 26.

13. See, for example, Tyacke, *Anti-Calvinists*.

14. Richard Hooker, "Notes toward a Fragment on Predestination" and "The Dublin Fragments," in *Works*, Vol. 4, 81–167; for Hooker's apparent affirmation of predestination, see 167.

15. Parker, *English Sabbath*, 139–216 (esp. 158–60). Sabbatarianism was not limited to Puritans, although it became especially identified with that faction following publication of the *Book of Sports*. Even non-Puritans attempted to enforce stricter codes of Sabbath discipline.

16. In his later position as a bishop, beginning in 1628, Montagu demonstrated leniency toward English Catholic "recusants," advanced the careers of Arminian sympathizers within the Church of England, and generally opposed the orthodox Calvinists.

17. Seaver, *Wallington's World*, 158.

18. See John Cotton's preface to John Norton's *Answer to the Whole Set of Questions*, 11.

19. For a first-person account of the lives of those who remained, see Seaver, *Wallington's World*.

20. "Articles presented against Laud by Henry Vane," quoted in Laud and Wharton, *History of the Troubles and Tryal of the Most Reverend Father in God, and Blessed Martyr, William Laud*, 156.

21. Howe, "Cambridge Platonists of Old England," esp. 471; and Collie, *Light and Enlightenment*, x.

22. See, for example, Spurr, *Restoration Church of England*, and Hampton, *Anti-Arminians*. But the effort to move beyond the strife of the Civil War and Interregnum was broader than just the religious dimension. The splendidly named Act of Free and General Pardon, Indemnity, and Oblivion, adopted in 1660, discouraged words "tending to revive the memory of the late differences or the occasions thereof" and urged Englishmen "to bury all Seeds of future Discord and remembrance of the former"; Rabb, "Parting Shots," 120–21.

23. The Test Acts were abolished for purposes of holding political office in 1828 and 1829. But for some purposes they lasted even longer. The requirement for students and dons at Oxford and Cambridge was not removed until 1871. Such religious restrictions had a long history; in the late Roman Empire, under an act of 597, nonorthodox believers were barred from all civil and military offices.

24. Simpson, *Permanent Revolution*, 153.
25. Wootton, *Invention of Science*, 459.
26. In this respect, the Latitudinarians followed in the tradition of Erasmus, more than a century before, who indirectly suggested that what people believe is less important than that peace in the world is maintained; Massing, *Fatal Discord*, 672.
27. See, for example, Sorkin, *Religious Enlightenment*, esp. 161, 231.
28. The idea of natural theology in this sense goes back at least to the stoics of ancient Greece. But Psalm 19 conveys the same idea: "The heavens declare the glory of God; and the firmament sheweth his handywork." In the medieval period both Judaism (Maimonides) and Islam (Averroes, Avicenna) embraced it. The Christian Raymond of Sabunde wrote his *Theologica Naturalis* in the 1430s. By contrast, David Hume argued that since cause cannot be inferred from observation, nothing can be known of the watchmaker from the watch; Waterman, "Changing Theological Context of Economic Analysis," 134.
29. Locke, *An Essay concerning Human Understanding*, in *Works*, Vol. 2, 244; 269; 280.
30. Quoted in Loconte, *God, Locke, and Liberty*, 59.
31. Locke, *Two Treatises of Government*, in *Works*, Vol. 4, 344; 341; 373; 436.
32. Locke, *An Essay concerning Human Understanding*, in *Works*, Vol. 2, 273. Elsewhere in the *Essay*, Locke summarized, "the existence of one God is according to reason; the existence of more than one God, contrary to reason; the resurrection of the dead, beyond reason" (261).
33. Locke, *The Reasonableness of Christianity*, in *Works*, Vol. 6, 133. Hume later picked up the same theme, dwelling on the importance of reason in his *Natual History of Religion*.
34. Locke, *The Reasonableness of Christianity*, in *Works*, Vol. 6, 133.
35. Locke, *The Reasonableness of Christianity*, in *Works*, Vol. 6, 135–36.
36. Newton refused a position in the established church because of his heterodox views on the Trinity. With the help of Isaac Barrow, master of Trinity College, he received a royal dispensation from this requirement. See Force, "Sir Isaac Newton, 'Gentleman of Wide Swallow'?," in *Essays*, 124.
37. Wootton, *Invention of Science*, 31.
38. See Merton, *Science, Technology and Society*, esp. Ch. 6; and Webster, *Great Instauration*. Even so, there were also suspected atheists among the early members of the Royal Society—perhaps most prominently Edmond Halley. (In a parallel to David Hume's experience six decades later, in 1691 Halley failed to become professor of astronomy at Oxford, apparently on account of his disbelief.)
39. See Baxter, *Paraphrase on the New Testament*, I Corinthians, Ch. II, "Annotations."
40. See Dolnick, *Clockwork Universe*, 117.
41. The Dutch-Jewish philosopher Spinoza had earlier emphasized the idea of God as immanent in the physical universe, but there were significant differences. For Spinoza, God is not the creator or all things; rather, God *is* all things. God therefore has no being apart from nature. The two also differed on the interpretation of "miracles." For Spinoza, a miracle is simply some phenomenon that has a natural explanation that humans do not understand. By contrast, Newton maintained that God can and sometimes does suspend nature's laws: God is "constantly cooperating with all things according to accurate laws, as being the foundation and cause of the whole of nature, *except where it is good to act otherwise*"; Newton, quoted in Force, *Essays*, 87 (emphasis added).

42. Brooke, *Science and Religion*, 148.

43. Bentley, *Eight Sermons*, 127.

44. Clarke, *Demonstration of the Being and Attributes of God*, 180; 207. In a work published just a few years later, Clarke also provided what became one of the key early texts opening the way to Unitarianism; see Clarke, *Scripture-Doctrine of the Trinity*.

45. These questions were hardly new. As early as the 1530s Philipp Melanchthon, Luther's principal disciple, had questioned whether the doctrines of depravity and predestination made God the author of evil in the world.

46. See, for example, Seaver, *Wallington's World*, 104.

47. South, "False Foundations Removed," in *Discourses on Various Subjects and Occasions*, 45.

48. Barrow, "On the Love of our Neighbor," in *Works*, Vol. 1, 256; 257.

49. Tillotson, "Of the Nature of Regeneration," in *Works*, Vol. 5, 306–7.

50. Tillotson, "Of the Nature of Regeneration," in *Works*, Vol. 5, 307–8.

51. Tillotson, "Of the Nature of Regeneration," in *Works*, Vol. 5, 308–9; 320 (these are two different sermons, both bearing the same title). Significantly, Tillotson's emphasis on an individual's "cooperating" with God in achieving his or her salvation echoes Thomas Aquinas's ideas in the *Summa Theologica* from more than four hundred years before. Well before Calvin, Luther had harshly dismissed Aquinas's ideas on the subject. By contrast, Erasmus had embraced the importance of human agency. See Massing, *Fatal Discord*, 80; 307; 346.

52. Tillotson, "The Goodness of God," in *Works*, Vol. 7, 33–34.

53. As a student at Harvard, in the 1750s, John Adams copied out by hand many of Tillotson's sermons and other writings; see Wood, *Friends Divided*, 40.

54. Because Tillotson's sermon quoted above was not published until 1697, three years after his death, it is not clear whether Locke had read it when he wrote his *Reasonableness of Christianity*; but he presumably was familiar with Tillotson's views.

55. Locke, *Reasonableness of Christianity*, in *Works*, Vol. 6, 4.

56. Locke, *Reasonableness of Christianity*, in *Works*, Vol. 6, 6.

57. Locke, *Reasonableness of Christianity*, in *Works*, Vol. 6, 7.

58. See Nelson, *Royalist Revolution* and "Representation and the Fall."

59. *ICR*, 248.

60. Perkins, *Golden Chaine*, 16.

61. *Humble Advice Of the Assembly Of Divines*, 7.

62. Locke, *Reasonableness of Christianity*, in *Works*, Vol. 6, 4–5.

63. See, for example, Spellman, "Locke and the Latitudinarian Perspective on Original Sin," 215–28.

64. The book's full title was more explicit: Daniel Whitby, *A Discourse Concerning: I. The True Import of the Words Election and Reprobation II. The Extent of Christ's Redemption III. The Grace of God IV. The Liberty of the Will V. The Perseverance or Defectibility of the Saints.*

65. Whitby, *Discourse*, 305; 313.

66. Whitby, *Discourse*, 339–41. The biblical references are to Deuteronomy 30:15–19 and Joshua 24:15.

67. See, for example, Kadane, "Original Sin and the Path to the Enlightenment." Kadane quotes Isaiah Berlin: "What the entire Enlightenment has in common is a denial of the central Christian doctrine of original sin" (105).

68. Taylor, *Scripture Doctrine of Original Sin,* 169.

69. Taylor, *Scripture Doctrine of Original Sin,* 179–80.

70. Taylor, *Scripture Doctrine of Original Sin,* 184–85. Taylor's views of man's "upright" nature followed not only Locke and Tillotson and others in the English-speaking world but also Leibniz (slightly younger than both Locke and Tillotson) in Germany. Later on, Kant (an exact contemporary of Adam Smith) shared a similar view, likewise based on the human capacity for reason.

71. Clarke, "Sermon VII: Of the Immutability of God," in *Sermons on the Following Subjects, Viz: Of Faith in God,* 152.

72. Clarke, "Sermon XIII: Of the Wisdom of God" in *Sermons on the Following Subjects, Viz: Of Faith in God,* 298.

73. Clarke, "Sermon XIV: Of the Goodness of God," in *Sermons on the Following Subjects, Viz: Of Faith in God,* 327–28.

74. The sermons were published only posthumously: See Clarke, "Sermon XVII: Of the Justice of God," in *Sermons on the Following Subjects, Viz: Of Faith in God,* 414; Clarke, "Sermon I, II: Of the Glory of God," in *Sermons on the Following Subjects, Viz: Of the Glory of God,* 18.

75. Doddridge, *Rise and Progress of Religion in the Soul,* 9; 147.

76. Doddridge, *Rise and Progress of Religion in the Soul,* 69; 98; 214.

77. Gay, "Preliminary Dissertation concerning the Fundamental Principle of Virtue or Morality," in King, *Essay on the Origin of Evil.* Gay's "Dissertation" was published as a preface to the English translation of William King's treatise *On the Origin of Evil.* (King, who had only recently died, had been Archbishop of Dublin; his book, originally published in 1702, was in Latin.) See also Waterman, "William Paley," 215.

78. Gay, "Preliminary Dissertation," xix.

79. For recent scholarship on the Church of Scotland Moderates of this period, see Ahnert, *Moral Culture of the Scottish Enlightenment.* See also Sher, *Church and University in the Scottish Enlightenment.*

80. The High Church was one of four congregations (all Presbyterian) that used St. Giles as their church. Blair was not the principal minister but a "Collegiate" or "Second Charge" minister.

81. On the labels for the Moderates' opponents, see Ross, *Life of Adam Smith,* 395. Today the typical term for them is evangelicals, but that was not the contemporary usage.

82. The sermon, titled "On the True Honour of Man," was published in 1790 as part of a collection of Blair's sermons; but it was presumably delivered some years earlier (Blair's introduction to the collection says "a great many years ago"). See Blair, "To the Reader," in *Sermons,* Vol. 5, vii.

83. Blair, "On the True Honour of Man," in *Sermons,* Vol. 3, 4–5.

84. Blair, "On the True Honour of Man," 5.

85. Blair, "On the True Honour of Man," 5.

86. Carlyle, *Usefulness and Necessity of a Liberal Education for Clergymen,* 30.

87. Mizuta, *Adam Smith's Library,* 151.

88. *TMS,* 43. Tucker in turn drew his Arminianism in part from his well-known correspondence with Clarke; see Tennant, *Conscience, Consciousness and Ethics,* 19–37.

89. See the useful discussion in Brown, *The Nature of Social Laws,* 18–23.

90. Orain makes a similar argument for the French Jansenists; Orain, "Second Jansenism," esp. 466. As the discussion earlier in this chapter should have made clear, the influence of theology on the thinking of Smith and his contemporaries is not incon-

sistent with the "reverse" influence of Enlightenment thinking—including thinking about economic questions—on the thinking of current and later theologians.

91. *ICR*, 270.

92. Some English Latitudinarians and Scottish Moderates simply reinterpreted original sin so that the doctrine did not imply depravity in Calvin's sense, while others rejected original sin altogether. Kadane, for example, argues that rejecting original sin brought together a number of strands of Enlightenment thinking; Kadane, "Original Sin and the Path to the Enlightenment."

93. For a different, but not contradictory, view of the relationship between these religious ideas and Adam Smith's work, see Waterman, "Economics as Theology," 907–21.

94. See Weber, *The Protestant Ethic and the Spirit of Capitalism.*

CHAPTER 7: THE CALVINIST CONTROVERSY IN COLONIAL AMERICA

1. In the Southern colonies, where the established church was the Church of England, the debate was naturally different. For an argument that New England historically played an outsized role in American intellectual and political development overall, see Baltzell, *Puritan Boston and Quaker Philadelphia.*

2. Much of subsequent American literature dwelled on the Puritan character and politics of early New England. Nathaniel Hawthorne's novels and stories—for example, "The Minister's Black Veil," "Endicott and the Red Cross," "Young Goodman Brown," above all *The Scarlet Letter*—are perhaps the most frequently read examples. As literary critic Lawrence Buell describes the beginning of *The Scarlet Letter,* "The opening sketch of the Puritan community reinforces the impression of an already fallen world. This utopian venture is almost new, but it already has a cemetery, a jail, a crime problem." Buell, *Dream of the Great American Novel,* 77.

3. Gaustad, *Liberty of Conscience,* 38.

4. Shepard, *Eye-Salve or A Watch-Word From our Lord Jesus Christ unto his Churches,* 14.

5. Oakes, *New England Pleaded with,* 54.

6. Ward, *Simple Cobler of Aggawam,* 3.

7. Antipathy to Roman Catholicism lasted far longer. In 1775 John Adams wrote of "the worst tyranny that the genius of toryism has ever yet invented; I mean the Roman superstition"; Adams, *Political Writings,* 28.

8. "Charter of the Province of the Massachusetts Bay, 1691," 22. Non-Puritan worshippers remained at a disadvantage, however, in that they continued to be responsible for taxes to support the established church (in addition to whatever they paid voluntarily for their own churches). Some towns also levied fines for not attending the established church. Quakers were also subject to penalties for refusing militia duties.

9. Since 1662, under the "Halfway Covenant," children of church members who had not yet undergone regenerative experiences were accepted as partial members of the church.

10. Whitefield, *Journals,* 301.

11. Data from Steele, *English Atlantic.*

12. Wright, *Beginnings of Unitarianism in America,* 18.

13. Johnson, *Letter from Aristocles to Authades,* 2–3.

14. Johnson, *Letter from Aristocles to Authades*, 3–4, 9.

15. Mayhew, *Grace Defended*, iii.

16. Edward Wigglesworth, quoted in Goodwin, "Myth of 'Arminian-Calvinism,' " 236.

17. Briant, *Absurdity and Blasphemy of Depretiating Moral Virtue*, 26.

18. Whitefield too was at first considered part of the founding group of Methodists, despite his predestinarian theology. He and Wesley were friends and allies at Oxford. But Whitefield's version of Methodism was strictly Calvinist. In time his branch of the movement and Wesley's parted ways, and Wesley's group, with its Arminian theology, won out in the struggle over the name. (The exception was Welsh Methodism, which remained Calvinist.)

19. Wesley, *Free Grace*, 10; 13; 16.

20. Wesley, *Free Grace*, 20–21; the reference is to Matthew 23:37.

21. Wesley, *Free Grace*, 10–11; 17; 22; 25–26.

22. Mather, *Awakening Soul-Saving Truths*, 3; 70; 75.

23. Shepard, *The Sincere Convert*, 94.

24. Mather, *Awakening Soul-Saving Truths*, 80–84.

25. Mather, *Awakening Soul-Saving Truths*, 91; 95.

26. Peterson, *City-State of Boston*, 240.

27. Mather, *Free-Grace, Maintained & Improved*, 1–2.

28. Mather, *Free-Grace, Maintained & Improved*, 2; 11.

29. The secondary literature discussing Edwards's life and work is vast. See, for example, Marsden, *Jonathan Edwards*, and the extensive references there to other literature.

30. See Sweeney, "River Gods and Related Minor Deities."

31. Wheelock's account of the day's events, as well as that of Stephen Williams, is summarized at length in Marsden, *Jonathan Edwards*, 220–21.

32. Edwards, "Sinners in the Hands of an Angry God," in *WJE*, Vol. 22, 405–8.

33. For example, in Psalm 28:1, "if thou be silent to me, I become like them that go down into the pit." Alternatively, God can rescue someone from the pit: "He brought me up also out of an horrible pit" (Psalm 40:2). See also Revelation 20:3.

34. Edwards, "Sinners in the Hands of an Angry God," 406; 409.

35. Edwards, "Sinners in the Hands of an Angry God," 410; 412.

36. Edwards, "Sinners in the Hands of an Angry God," 411–12.

37. Edwards, "Sinners in the Hands of an Angry God," 406–7; 416.

38. Williams, Diary, July 8, 1741. Also see Marsden, *Jonathan Edwards*, 220.

39. Mather, *Ratio Disciplinae Fratrum Nov-Anglorum*, 5.

40. Edwards, "Farewell Sermon," in *WJE*, Vol. 25, 486.

41. Wright, *Beginnings of Unitarianism in America*, 76.

42. Edwards, *Original Sin*, in *WJE*, Vol. 3, 107–8.

43. Edwards, *Original Sin*, in *WJE*, Vol. 3, 113.

44. Edwards, *Dissertation I: Concerning the End for which God Created the World*, in *WJE*, Vol. 8, 526–27.

45. Edwards, *Dissertation I: Concerning the End for which God Created the World*, in *WJE*, Vol. 8, 533.

46. Mayhew, *Seven Sermons*, 38.

47. Mayhew, *Seven Sermons*, 39; 97.

48. A much earlier Congregational minister, John Wise, had emphasized the role of human sociability: Because man is "extremely desirous of his own preservation," but "unable to secure his own safety and maintenance without the assistance of his

fellows . . . it is necessary that he be sociable." Indeed, it is "a fundamental law of nature, that every man, as far as in him lies, do maintain a sociableness with others." Wise, "Vindication of the Government of the New England Churches," 1216. Wise's text was originally published in 1717.

49. Mayhew, *Seven Sermons*, 101.

50. Wright, *Beginnings of Unitarianism in America*, 123.

51. Mayhew, *Seven Sermons*, 120; 125. Mayhew was also a strong opponent of the Calvinist doctrine of predestination, denouncing it as "most false and unscriptural, horrible to the last degree, to all men of an undepraved judgment, and blasphemous against the God of heaven and earth"; Mayhew, *Two Sermons on the Nature, Extent and Perfection of the Divine Goodness*, 66.

52. For purposes, here, "natural religion" is a synonym for "natural theology"; see, for example, the editor's note in Hume, *Principal Writings on Religion*, 200.

53. Gay, *Natural Religion as Distinguished from Revealed*, 6; 21–22.

54. Gay, *Natural Religion as Distinguished from Revealed*, 6; 8; 10–13. Mayhew had likewise appealed to Newtonian imagery: "Love is the spirit that cements mankind together; and preserves that order and harmony amongst them, which is requisite in order to the general safety and welfare; just as the regular motions and harmony of the heavenly bodies depend on their mutual gravitation towards each other"; Mayhew, *Seven Sermons*, 126.

55. Gay, *Natural Religion as Distinguished from Revealed*, 12–13.

56. See Baltzell, *Puritan Boston and Quaker Philadelphia*, 240–41, on the movement of Quakers to Anglicanism triggered by the war.

57. He also thought little of many of the revivalists: "Men who, though they have *no Learning*, and but *small Capacities*, yet imagine they are able, and without Study too, to speak to the *spiritual Profit* of such as are willing to hear them." Chauncy, *Seasonable Thoughts on the State of Religion in New-England*, 226.

58. Wright, *Beginnings of Unitarianism in America*, 174.

59. Chauncy, *Benevolence of the Deity*, viii.

60. Chauncy, *Benevolence of the Deity*, 131–32.

61. Although there was a Unitarian movement in Britain as well, Unitarianism in America was mostly homegrown. See Wright, *Beginnings of Unitarianism in America*, 6. On Unitarianism appealing to "the higher social circles" while Calvinism "occupied the lower social position," see Adams, *New England in the Republic*, 355. In the early decades of the nineteenth century, some of Boston's elite families even sent their daughters to a Roman Catholic convent school rather than expose them to the Trinitarian orientation of the public schools; Peterson, *City-State of Boston*, 366.

62. Clarke, *Scripture-Doctrine of the Trinity*.

63. Clarke had opposed Trinitarian doctrine, in part on just that ground, writing "the *Books of Scripture* are to Us Now not only *the Rule*, but *the Whole and Only Rule of Truth* in matters of Religion"; Clarke, *Scripture-Doctrine of the Trinity*, v.

64. To be sure, there were also opponents who defended Trinitarian thinking—for example, both Jonathan Edwards and his son-in-law Aaron Burr, the first president of the College of New Jersey; see Burr, *Supreme Deity of Our Lord Jesus Christ*.

65. In *The Wealth of Nations*, Smith wrote of "that pure and rational religion, free of every mixture of absurdity, imposture, or fanaticism, such as wise men have in all ages of the world wished to see established; but such as positive law has perhaps never yet established, and probably never will establish in any country; because, with

regard to religion, positive law has always been, and probably always will be, more or less influenced by popular superstition and enthusiasm"; *WN,* 793.

66. Larson, *Return of George Washington,* 116–18.

67. Thomas Jefferson to Doctor Benjamin Waterhouse, in *Works,* Vol. 12, 243.

68. Ware, *Letters Addressed to Trinitarians and Calvinists,* 52.

69. Ware, *Letters Addressed to Trinitarians and Calvinists,* 52.

70. One indication of the intensity of the controversy was the statement, believed to be by Jedidiah Morse, a conservative Congregationalist minister, that "the people of *Massachusetts,* except in a few instances, are not so revolutionized and deluded that they will commit their children to the loose and erroneous hand of Unitarians for an education"; "Affairs of the University," *Columbian Centinel,* vol. 42, no. 26 (November 24, 1804). See also Morse's pamphlet, published after Ware's election became effective, *True Reasons on which the Election of a Hollis Professor of Divinity in Harvard College, was Opposed.*

71. Channing's sermon, often called the "Baltimore Sermon," was preached in Baltimore at the ordination ceremony of Jared Sparks, who in turn became a well-known Unitarian minister in his own right. Sparks was also the first editor of George Washington's papers, and he served for several years as president of Harvard. See Channing, *Sermon Delivered at the Ordination of the Rev. Jared Sparks,* 16.

72. Channing, *Remarks on the Rev. Dr. Worcester's Second Letter to Mr. Channing,* 42.

73. Blair, "On the True Honour of Man," in *Sermons,* Vol. 3, 5.

74. Wright, *The Unitarian Controversy,* 23; 132.

75. Channing, *Sermon Delivered at the Ordination of the Rev. Jared Sparks,* 16; 21–22.

76. Channing, *Sermon Delivered at the Ordination of the Rev. Jared Sparks,* 17. At the end of his life, in the introduction he wrote for the first complete edition of his works, Channing wrote that nothing distinguished his writings more than "the high estimate of . . . human nature"; Channing, *Works,* Vol. 1, vi.

77. Thomas Jefferson, "To the Danbury Baptist Association" (January 1, 1802), in *Papers,* Vol. 36, 258.

78. Smith referred to "different theories of political oeconomy" in the introduction to *The Wealth of Nations,* and Book IV, laying out those various theories, was titled "Of Systems of Political Oeconomy"; *WN,* 11; 428. The first use of the phrase was by the French author Antoine de Montchrestien, in his *Traicté de l'oeconomie politique* in 1615.

CHAPTER 8: VISIONS OF HUMAN PROGRESS

1. Daniel 2:31–35.

2. Daniel 2:44, 12:1.

3. Mark 13:19.

4. Matthew 24:6–7, 29–30, 40–41. Paul, in his first letter to the Thessalonians (4:17), confirms this account of the Rapture: "Then we who are alive and remain shall be caught up together with them in the clouds to meet the Lord in the air." These accounts are the basis for the hugely popular *Left Behind* novels by Tim LaHaye and Jerry B. Jenkins; see, for example, LaHaye and Jenkins, *Left Behind.*

5. Carroll, *Christ Actually,* 160. Some scholars, however, have speculated that the author was a refugee from Jerusalem, which had been destroyed by the Romans in

70, and that parts of the narrative were an attempt to describe what he had seen there as the city fell. Other parts of the narrative appear to be describing the eruption of Mount Vesuvius in 79. See Pagels, *Revelations*.

6. Revelation 20:1–3.

7. Revelation 20:7–10, 21:1–4. Much of the symbolism in these chapters of Revelation (though not the narrative) draws on phrases from the Hebrew Bible, most often from the book of Daniel and from Isaiah Chapter 65. The most obvious example is Isaiah 65:17, "For behold, I create new heavens and a new earth: and the former shall not be remembered, nor come into mind."

8. The imagery of the four kingdoms, often with the fourth identified as Rome, was prevalent in other Jewish writings of the time as well: for example 4 Ezra 12:11–36, 2 Baruch 39:2–6, and 1 Enoch 89–90. It also appeared in some of the Dead Sea Scrolls: for example, 4Q552 and 553. For a list of scholarly references, see Kugel, *Great Shift*, 394.

9. Matthew 24:30–34.

10. Matthew 16:28.

11. "But of that day and that hour knoweth no man, no, not the angels which are in heaven, neither the Son but the Father" (Mark 13:32). In a similar vein the Talmud, originally dating from roughly the same period, condemns the attempt to predict the coming of the messiah: "Blasted be the bones of those that calculate the end-time" (B.T. Sanhedrin 97a).

12. In contrast to widespread interpretations of what followed soon after in the New Testament, there is little or no evidence that Jews of the time were anticipating the end of the world. See, for example, Wright, *The New Testament and the People of God*, 333; cited in Carroll, *Christ Actually*, 128.

13. See Freeman, *Closing of the Western Mind*, 154–77; also Freeman, *A.D. 381*.

14. The most prominent exception was Joachim of Fiore, a twelfth-century monk who held the pre-Augustinian view that the millennium and apocalypse described in Revelation did refer to real-world events to come. See McGinn, *Visions of the End*, 126–41.

15. Luther, "Preface to the Revelation of St. John," in *Luther's Spirituality*, 47.

16. Ernest Tuveson in particular advanced this view. See Tuveson, *Millennium and Utopia*, 24–25.

17. See Mede, *Key of the Revelation*. An earlier precursor of Mede's thinking was William Perkins, *Godly and Learned Exposition or Commentarie*. Perkins's argument was much less clear, but he offered a literal interpretation of the texts holding that the state of the world would improve between the present and the world's end. See also Gribben, *Evangelical Millennialism in the Trans-Atlantic World*, 35.

18. Mede would not have called it the Puritan revolution, however. That usage did not appear until 1826; Simpson, *Permanent Revolution*, 24.

19. For an overview of thinking about such matters in England at this time, see Christianson, *Reformers and Babylon*.

20. Milton, *Animadversions*, 38–39.

21. The translation in the Revised Standard Version is more explicit: "by no human hand."

22. Revelation 13:1.

23. Cotton, *Exposition upon the Thirteenth Chapter of the Revelation*, 93. Cotton's posthumously published treatise was first delivered as a series of lectures, in Boston, in 1639–1640. See also Toon, *Puritans, the Millennium and the Future of Israel*, 34–36.

24. Mather, *Theopolis Americana*, 43. In the same sermon, Mather went on to highlight the millennial implications of such projects as commercial market reforms, abolishing the slave trade, missionary work, and education. (He also apologized for the earlier persecution of Quakers and those accused of witchcraft.)
25. Baxter, *Glorious Kingdom of Christ*, 13–14. In parts of Baxter's writing, however, it is unclear just what he meant by "the millennium." From some of his statements, it appears that he thought the millennium had already occurred, beginning with the Edict of Milan legalizing Christianity within the Roman Empire (313) and ending with the fall of Constantinople to the Ottomans (1453)—very close to the biblical one thousand years.
26. Burnet, *Theory of the Earth*, 4.
27. Burnet, *Doctrina Antiqua de Rerum Originibus*, 246.
28. Burnet, *Theory of the Earth*, 215; 72.
29. More than a century after Burnet's death, Herman Melville would refer to "Burnet and the best theologians" in his novel *White-Jacket* (329).
30. Whiston, *New Theory of the Earth*, 81.
31. Blair, "On the Importance of Religious Knowledge to Mankind," in *Sermons*, Vol. 2, 457–58.
32. Edwards, *History of the Work of Redemption*, in *WJE*, Vol. 9, 353.
33. Edwards, *Two Dissertations: I. Concerning the End for Which God Created the World and II. On the Nature of True Virtue*, in *WJE*, Vol. 8, 533.
34. Edwards, *Some Thoughts Concerning the Revival*, in *WJE*, Vol. 4, 353.
35. Edwards, *Some Thoughts Concerning the Revival*, 353–58.
36. Adams, "THURSDAY. FEBRUARY 21ST. 1765," in *Diary and Autobiography*, Vol. 1, 257. Some later renderings of this statement refer to a grand "scheme"; see, for example, Wood, *Friends Divided*, 73; but the Massachusetts Historical Society digitization of the original makes clear that "scene" is correct.
37. There is a large literature on the origins and history of premillennialism. See, for example, Weber, *Living in the Shadow of the Second Coming*; Boyer, *When Time Shall Be No More*; and Wacker, *Heaven Below*.
38. Daniel 12:11–12.
39. Revelation 11:2–3, 12:6, 13:5.
40. Psalm 90:4 provides a scriptural basis for distinguishing time units in the Bible from conventional human reckoning: "For a thousand years in thy sight are but as yesterday when it is past, and as a watch in the night." The pseudepigraphical testament of Peter explicitly equates one day in God's time with a thousand earthly years (2 Peter 3:8).
41. See Noll, "Jekyll or Hyde?"
42. Identification of current-day individuals or groups with apocalyptic symbols has continued as well. During the Cold War, for example, it was not uncommon for premillennial Christians to identify the Soviet Union with the beast in Revelation (or with Magog in the book of Ezekiel, or with the threatening powers from the north frequently mentioned in Jeremiah).
43. Paine, *Common Sense*, in *Rights of Man, Common Sense, and Other Political Writings*, 53.
44. Rush, "The Pennsylvania Convention, Wednesday, 12 December," in Jensen, *Documentary History*, 592–93, cited in Larson, *Return of George Washington*, 194.
45. Emerson, *Lectures on the Millennium*, 243–45.
46. Cogswell, *Harbinger of the Millennium*, iii.

47. Finney, "Hinderances to Revivals," in *Lectures on Revivals of Religion*, 282.
48. Strong, *Our Country*, 180. The book was sponsored by the American Home Missionary Society. When the society brought out a new edition of the book in 1891, Strong edited the text to read "the next ten to fifteen years," thereby keeping his expected time frame unchanged.
49. Hopkins, *Treatise on the Millennium*, 40.
50. Hopkins, *Treatise on the Millennium*, 57; 71–72.
51. Green and Wells, *Summary View of the Millennial Church*, 10. Also see Jennings, *Paradise Now*, 29. Stephen Stein, the foremost current scholar of the Shakers, argues that the labels pre- and postmillennialist do not fit for them. See Stein, "American Millennial Visions."
52. Crowe, *George Ripley*, 181, cited in Jennings, *Paradise Now*, 220.
53. Delano, *Brook Farm*, 372.
54. Jennings, *Paradise Now*, 321.
55. Taylor, "Society's Future"; Taylor, one of the publication's editors, was a Southern Baptist minister. On the decline and eventual disappearance of explicit postmillennialist thinking, see, for example, Moorhead, "Between Progress and Apocalypse," and "Erosion of Postmillennialism in American Religious Thought."
56. Strong, *The New Era*, 30.
57. Clarke, "Five Points of Calvinism," in *Vexed Questions in Theology*, 15–16.
58. MacMillan, *War That Ended Peace*, 9.
59. Up through the first half of the nineteenth century, people used "evolution" to refer to a process by which one form gave rise to a different (presumably higher) form; but the Darwinian notion of randomness of mutations was absent; Haig, *From Darwin to Derrida*, Ch. 1. See also Bowler, "Changing Meaning of 'Evolution.'"
60. Hume, "Of Refinement in the Arts," in *EMPL*, 271–73.
61. Hume, "Of Refinement in the Arts," 277.
62. Hume, "Of the Rise and Progress of the Arts and Science," in *EMPL*, 115, 118.
63. See Meek et al., "Introduction," in *LJ*, 4.
64. *LJ*, 14.
65. See Meek, "Smith, Turgot, and the 'Four Stages' Theory." In recent years this historical evolution—especially the introduction of agriculture—has attracted renewed interest. For one recent contribution, together with extensive references to other work, see Matranga, "The Ant and the Grasshopper."
66. Turgot, "On Universal History." Turgot is best known within economics for his *Reflections on the Formation and Distribution of Wealth*, a significant treatise published in French in 1776 and in English translation in 1795. The book provided the first account of what later became known as the "iron law of wages." See Turgot, *Reflections on the Formation and Distribution of Riches*, esp. 46–49.
67. Smith did not use the descriptive phrase "modes of subsistence," but it has subsequently become familiar in the scholarly literature surrounding his work in this area. Ronald Meek in particular popularized its use; see Meek, *Social Science and the Ignoble Savage*, 6 and elsewhere. For a genealogy of the phrase in this context, see Lieberman, "Adam Smith on Justice, Rights, and Law," 230. Following Karl Marx, who wrote a hundred years after Smith's lectures, the more modern phrase would be "modes of production"; the meaning is the same.
68. Robertson, *History of America*, Vol. 1, 324. Robertson used the phrase "mode of subsistence" elsewhere in the book as well (e.g., 305–6).

69. *LJ*, 404.

70. Smith presumably met Turgot during his stay in Paris, but that was after his years of teaching at Glasgow. Whether Smith was aware of Turgot's 1750 Sorbonne lectures, when he gave his own lectures that became the *Lectures on Jurisprudence,* is not known. See Groenewegen, "Turgot and Adam Smith," and Skinner, "Adam Smith: The French Connection."

71. Ecclesiastes 5:11.

72. One factor in the transition to agriculture that modern scientists emphasize, but of which Smith was unaware, is climate change. See, for example, Suzman, *Affluence Without Abundance,* Ch. 14.

73. Smith's admirer and popularizer Dugald Stewart famously called this kind of thinking "conjectural history," and hailed it as "the peculiar glory of the latter half of the eighteenth century"; Stewart, *Works,* Vol. 7, 31, and *Dissertation First,* 86.

74. As usual in such developments, causation can run in both directions. For an argument that the development of private property led to the emergence of agriculture, see Bowles and Choi, "Neolithic Agricultural Revolution."

75. In contrast to this traditional view, however, modern anthropologists have reported a fairly sophisticated division of labor in some hunter-gatherer societies. See Hooper et al., "Skills, Division of Labour and Economies of Scale."

76. *LJ*, 16; 202. Smith's account of this process is often regarded as a response to Rousseau's ideas; see, for example, Force, *Self-Interest Before Adam Smith,* and Hont, *Politics in Commercial Society.*

77. The origins of agriculture, and the consequences of that development for human settlement, have attracted enormous attention from archaeologists, anthropologists, and others. For a recent discussion that supports Smith's account based on population growth leading to hunger, see Cline, *Three Stones Make a Wall,* Ch. 7.

78. Money, contract enforcement, and weights and standardized measures are all extremely ancient. The Bible mentions all three; for example, "Just balances, just weights, a just ephah, and a just hin, shall ye have" (Leviticus 19:36).

79. Malthus, *Essay on the Principle of Population* (1803), 37–43. Still later, Malthus acknowledged technological improvement in food production—such improvements had occurred throughout the eighteenth century—but he did not see that this possibility could avert the problem about which he was writing.

80. See Cohen, "Hunger Does Not Pay."

81. See United Nations, *World Population Prospectus.*

82. See, for example, Deaton, *Great Escape.*

83. Smith's contemporary Adam Ferguson likewise warned against the consequences of excessive division of labor, although his emphasis was more on the resulting division in society: Ferguson, *Essay on the History of Civil Society.*

84. Some scholars have argued that Smith, especially in *The Wealth of Nations,* did provide what amounts to a theory of economic growth. See, for example, Samuelson, "A Modern Theorist's Vindication"; Kurz, "Technical Progress, Capital Accumulation and Income Distribution"; and Waterman, "Is There Another, Quite Different 'Adam Smith Problem.'" The case is unconvincing. A more accurate reading recognizes what Robert Solow called "the famous failure of the great classical economists . . . to reflect at all adequately the significance of the Industrial Revolution and the several technological breakthroughs that drove it"; Solow, "Stories About Economics and Technology," 1113. Nathan Rosenberg noted that even in discussing agricultural

improvements, in *The Wealth of Nations*, Smith's focus was on "capital formation, rather than invention"; Rosenberg, "Adam Smith on the Division of Labour," 129, 132.

85. See Greenblatt, *The Swerve*, on the impact of the rediscovery, early in the fifteenth century, of Lucretius's *De Rerum Natura*.

86. Joachim of Fiore was exceptional; see again McGinn, *Visions of the End*.

87. Greenblatt, *The Swerve*, 116.

88. See Jennings, *Paradise Now*, 248–53.

89. Massing, *Fatal Discord*, 43.

90. Quoted in Parker, *Emperor*, 342.

91. Religious believers were also interested in how "the Americans" got there. The Bible did not mention a separate creation of humans, and it seemed implausible that they were somehow descendants of any of the various lineages indicated. In light of the lack of clothing among many living in tropical areas (which Columbus and other early explorer encountered first), there was even speculation about whether they might be inhabitants of a second Garden of Eden.

92. Locke, *Two Treatises of Government*, in *Works*, Vol. 4, 352–67; 402. Locke's specific interest, in writing Chapter 5 of the *Second Treatise*, was vindicating the colonial project in Carolina; see Nelson, *Theology of Liberalism*, 135.

93. See, for example, Lafitau, *Customs of the American Indians*. Lafitau's book was originally published (in French) in 1724, the year following Smith's birth.

94. Paul Slack likewise emphasizes the religious underpinnings of the sense of progress developed in England during the period immediately prior to Smith's lifetime; see again Slack, *Invention of Improvement*.

95. Ferguson, *Essay on the History of Civil Society*, 119.

96. Comte, *Positive Philosophy of Auguste Comte*, Vol. 2, 118.

CHAPTER 9: POLITICAL ECONOMY IN THE NEW REPUBLIC

1. Bashford and Chaplin, *New Worlds of Thomas Robert Malthus*, 70.

2. Jefferson, for example, cited "the immense extent of uncultivated and fertile lands" as ground for believing that food production could match population in increasing geometrically; Jefferson, letter to Jean-Baptiste Say (February 1, 1804), *Works*, Vol. 4, 526–27. For reviews of early American impressions of Malthus's essay, see Cady, "Early American Reaction to the Theory of Malthus," and Cocks, "Malthusian Theory in Pre–Civil War America."

3. Adams, "To Patrick Henry, June 3, 1776," in *John Adams: Revolutionary Writings*, 78.

4. Gordon Wood has argued that Thomas Jefferson, more than anyone, laid the foundations of belief in American exceptionalism; Wood, *Friends Divided*, 325.

5. See Freehling, *Road to Disunion*, Vol. 1, Ch. 12.

6. Wood, *Radicalism of the American Revolution*.

7. See Lynerd, *Republican Theology*, Ch. 4.

8. Not everyone at the time welcomed industrial development in the new nation. Thomas Jefferson famously preferred an agrarian society. For a review of the contemporary debate, see Hofstadter, *Age of Reform*, Ch. 1.

9. Raymond, *American System*. A later and more prominent defender of Hamilton's policies was Henry Carey, who rejected David Ricardo's analysis of trade, as well as laissez-faire polities more generally; Carey, *Principles of Political Economy*.

10. Raymond, *Missouri Question.*
11. Raymond, *Thoughts on Political Economy,* and *Elements of Political Economy.*
12. Adams, "From John Adams to Daniel Raymond, 8 February 1821."
13. "House of Representatives, Tuesday, June 23, 1840," 479; see Lee, *Slavery, Philosophy, and American Literature, 60.*
14. For a recent evaluation, see Rodgers, *As a City on a Hill.* Rodgers expresses skepticism that Winthrop preached the sermon on board the *Arbella.*
15. Winthrop, "Model of Christian Charity," 82–83.
16. Winthrop, "Model of Christian Charity," 83–85.
17. Leviticus 25:35–37; Deuteronomy 23:19–20.
18. Winthrop, "Model of Christian Charity," 89–91; the reference is to Matthew 5:14.
19. It entered their practice too. A visitor to Boston, a century later, reported seeing "a corn house in which a large quantity of corn is stored every year when prices are lowest and where, when food gets expensive in the winter and people begin to starve, they can buy the corn they need for the price at which it was bought," along with a hospital and four schools for orphans; "Travel Diary of Commissioner Von Reck," cited by Peterson, *City-State of Boston,* 244.
20. Mather, *Theopolis Americana,* 16–17.
21. Raymond, *Elements of Political Economy,* Vol. 1, 13; 18. Putting aside the religious and moral context, even many slave owners agreed with Raymond's observations. In the 1780s Thomas Jefferson famously wrote that "in a warm climate no man will labour for himself who can make another labour for him"; Jefferson, *Notes on the State of Virginia,* 163.
22. Raymond, *Elements of Political Economy,* Vol. 1, 18–19; 16.
23. Mather, *A Christian at his Calling,* 39–41; the eighth commandment prohibits stealing.
24. Raymond, *Elements of Political Economy,* Vol. 1, 19.
25. Mather, *A Christian at his Calling,* 41.
26. Raymond, *Elements of Political Economy,* Vol. 1, 27.
27. The best known example is probably the "paradox of thrift" emphasized by John Maynard Keynes and given that label by Paul Samuelson; Keynes, *General Theory,* 84; Samuelson, *Economics,* 269–72.
28. Raymond, *Elements of Political Economy,* Vol. 1, 44–45.
29. Raymond, *Elements of Political Economy,* Vol. 1, 44–47; 26.
30. Raymond, *Elements of Political Economy,* Vol. 1, 47–48.
31. *WN,* 96.
32. Raymond, *Elements of Political Economy,* Vol. 1, 52.
33. Mather, *A Christian at his Calling,* 46; 48; 42.
34. Edwards, "Charity Contrary to a Selfish Spirit," in *WJE,* Vol. 8, 254–55.
35. Cooper, "Sermon Preached in Boston," 2–3.
36. Cooper, "Sermon Preached in Boston," 3; 7–8.
37. Clap, *Essay on the Nature and Foundation of Moral Virtue and Obligation,* 15–16.
38. See Davenport, *Friends of the Unrighteous Mammon.*
39. Mansfield and Winthrop, "Editors' Introduction," Tocqueville, *Democracy in America,* xvii. Tocqueville was hardly the only European who visited the new United States in the 1830s and wrote a book about what he saw. Another prominent example, was Charles Murray's *Travels in North America,* which the author, an Englishman, dedicated to Queen Victoria.

40. Tocqueville, *Democracy in America,* Vol. 1, 3.
41. Tocqueville's focus on male citizens—specifically, excluding women and slaves—was consistent with the definition of democracy in classical times. See, for example, Beard, *SPQR,* 188.
42. Tocqueville, *Democracy in America,* Vol. 1, 3.
43. Tocqueville, *Democracy in America,* Vol. 1, 308; 305; 304; 306.
44. Wright, "Ministers, Churches, and the Boston Elite," in *Unitarian Controversy,* 43–44.
45. Hatch, *Democratization of American Christianity,* 4.
46. Gaustad, *Liberty of Conscience,* 211.
47. Klarman, *Framers' Coup,* 391; 484.
48. See Porterfield, *Conceived in Doubt.*
49. Wright, *Beginnings of Unitarianism in America,* 249.
50. This anti-intellectual current, both within the clergy and in how the public at large regarded the clergy, drew reinforcement from the interest of nineteenth-century Americans in dispensational premillennialism (see again Ch. 8), itself an anti-academic understanding of the Bible. See Noll, "Jekyll or Hyde?" See also Hatch, *Democratization of American Christianity,* Chs. 2, 6.
51. Fuhrer, *Crisis of Community,* 66.
52. In the years before Tocqueville's visit, Boston alone had its Marine Society, the Boston Athenaeum, the American Academy of Arts and Sciences, the Society for Propagating the Gospel, the Humane Society, the Massachusetts Congregational Charitable Society, the Episcopal Charitable Society, the Massachusetts Charitable Society, the Medical Society, the Agricultural Society, the Massachusetts Historical Society, the Massachusetts Charitable Fire Society, the Society for the Information of Strangers, the Indian Society, the Society for the Aid of Immigrants, the Massachusetts Missionary Society, the Massachusetts Bible Society, the Society for Promoting Christian Knowledge, and a separate (and competing) Society for Promoting Christian Knowledge, Piety, and Charity—and this list is not complete. Wright, "Ministers, Churches, and the Boston Elite," in *Unitarian Controversy,* 42; 54–57.
53. Tocqueville, *Democracy in America,* Vol. 2, 109; Vol. 1, 192; Vol. 2, 106. Numerous historians have argued for the origins of this voluntarism in Calvinist religious principles. For two recent examples, see Lynerd, *Republican Theology,* 50, and Fea, *Bible Cause,* 59–60. Less recent but also on point are Young, *Bearing Witness Against Sin,* and Hirrel, *Children of Wrath.*
54. Beecher, *Memory of Our Fathers,* 18. The year before, on election day, Beecher had delivered a version of the sermon to the Connecticut state legislature.
55. Chernow, *Grant,* 10.
56. Fuhrer, *Crisis of Community,* 155–68.
57. Lynerd, *Republican Theology,* 2; 102; 109–10.
58. Smith, *Revivalism and Social Reform,* 236.
59. Tocqueville, *Democracy in America,* Vol. 2, 140.
60. Tocqueville, *Democracy in America,* Vol. 2, 136; 153; 142; 33. Some contemporary writers attempted to argue a religious basis for this sense of obligation (see, for example, Hunt, *The Book of Wealth*), but that was not central to Tocqueville's account.
61. *The Sporting Review* (June 1839), 425; quoted in Pagnamenta, *Prairie Fever,* 108. *The Sporting Review* was a magazine devoted to fox hunting, steeplechasing, and other outdoor sports, and the import of the observation was to explain why so few Americans engaged in these pursuits.
62. Larson, *Return of George Washington,* 246.

63. See Bernstein, *Wedding of the Waters*.
64. Frieden, *Lessons for the Euro*, 18.
65. Emerson, "Wealth," in *Conduct of Life*, 102–3.
66. Fuhrer, *Crisis of Community*, 77–80.
67. Hazen, *Panorama of Professions and Trades*.
68. Tocqueville, *Democracy in America*, Vol. 2, 140; 152; 33.
69. Tocqueville, *Democracy in America*, Vol. 2, 26.
70. Green and Wells, *Summary View of the Millennial Church*, 99. On the Shaker population, see Brewer, *Shaker Communities, Shaker Lives*, 217, and Bainbridge, "Shaker Demographics," 355.
71. Howe, "Decline of Calvinism."
72. The disagreement within the denomination continues today, including within the largest Baptist group in America, the Southern Baptist Convention.
73. Lynerd, *Republican Theology*, 104–5.
74. Finney, *Lectures on Revivals of Religion*, 15–17; 259.
75. Finney, *Lectures on Revivals of Religion*, 188; 190; 18; 186; 19.

CHAPTER 10: THE CLERICAL ECONOMISTS

1. Prominent exceptions were Mathew Carey and his son Henry, both Roman Catholics.
2. *OPE*.
3. McVickar, *Introductory Lecture*.
4. McVickar, *First Lessons*, 24.
5. McVickar, *Introductory Lecture*, 5.
6. *TMS*, 63.
7. McVickar, *Introductory Lecture*, 6–8.
8. Angell, *Great Illusion*; Friedman, *The Lexus and the Olive Tree*. The argument also bears a similarity to Kant's prediction, in his 1795 essay on "perpetual peace," that political democracies would not wage war against one another; see Kant, "Toward Perpetual Peace," in *Toward Perpetual Peace and Other Writings*.
9. McVickar, *Introductory Lecture*, 8–9.
10. McVickar, *Introductory Lecture*, 9; 34.
11. McVickar, *First Lessons*, 28–29.
12. McVickar, *Introductory Lecture*, 9. Three-quarters of a century earlier, Josiah Tucker—not coincidentally, also a clergyman—had likewise put the point in religious language, writing that "Providence intended that there should be mutual dependence and connection" between people, and going on to apply the principle to trade between nations; Tucker, *Essay on Trade*, ii. By McVickar's day, the providentialist reading of Smithian economics was dominant in Britain as well; see, for example, Whately, *Introductory Lectures on Political Economy*.
13. McVickar, *Introductory Lecture*, 34.
14. McVickar, *First Lessons*, 31.
15. Ricardo, *On the Principles of Political Economy and Taxation*, 128–49.
16. McVickar, *First Lessons*, 31.
17. McVickar, *First Lessons*, 32.
18. Wayland, *The Elements of Moral Science*. Wayland also published an abridged and simplified version for students not yet in college: Wayland, *Elements of Moral Sci-*

ence: Abridged and Adapted to the Use of Schools and Academies by the Author. Wayland is often considered America's most popular nineteenth-century moral philosopher; see, for example, Marsden, "The Gospel of Wealth, the Social Gospel, and the Salvation of Schools," 15. The other text on moral philosophy widely used in American colleges before the Civil War was a half-century older, and by an English clergyman: William Paley, *Principles of Moral and Political Philosophy*.

19. *EPE*, v.
20. The most widely used text in the U.K. during this period was John Stuart Mill's *Principles of Political Economy*, first published in 1848. Wayland's text appeared in the same year as Henry Carey's, but it was Wayland's that attracted the broader readership; Carey, *Principles of Political Economy*.
21. See Wayland, *Elements of Political Economy: Abridged and Adapted to the Use of Schools and Academies*. An earlier abridgment, not done by Wayland himself, appeared in 1838.
22. *EPE*, 3.
23. *EPE*, 107–9.
24. *EPE*, 3–4; 7.
25. In the course that he taught at Brown, during the years before he published his own book, the text that he assigned was not *The Wealth of Nations* but a later work that Smith's book had influenced: J. B. Say's *Treatise on Political Economy*, first published (in French) in 1803. The fourth edition of Say's book was translated into English and published in the United States in 1821. See Heyne, "Clerical Laissez-Faire."
26. *EPE*, 15. (In later editions of the book, he modified the statement to say that "every man is desirous of exchanging some portion of the value created by himself.") Wayland's text mentions Smith by name five times—three of them in the context of his discussion of the division of labor.
27. *EPE*, 186–87; 429.
28. *EPE*, 11.
29. *EPE*, 86–88. Unlike McVickar, Wayland did not mention Ricardo by name.
30. *EPE*, 88–89.
31. *EPE*, 88–90.
32. See Krugman, "The Narrow Moving Band"; Grossman and Helpman, *Innovation and Growth in the Global Economy*, Ch. 7; and Redding, "Dynamic Comparative Advantage," 15–39.
33. *EPE*, 91. On Wayland's ideas as reflected in the subsequent theory of economic development, see, for example, Rostow, *Stages of Economic Growth*.
34. Following a hiatus from the early 1940s to the mid-1960s, the *North American Review* is still published today.
35. *PPE*.
36. Although Bowen gained particular prominence because of his textbook, he was not the only, nor the first, American economist to advocate protectionist tariffs. Friedrich List, who emigrated from Germany in 1824, did so as an extension of the Hamilton-Clay "American System."
37. *PPE*, 22–23.
38. *PPE*, 27.
39. The phrase, applied to an economic context, dates from the late seventeenth century; see Keynes, *End of Laissez-Faire*, 18. It first appeared in English in a treatise by the Englishman George Whatley (apparently coauthored in part by Whatley's friend, Benjamin Franklin); Whatley, *Principles of Trade*, 33–34. Its use became widespread

only in the nineteenth century, however, after James Mill used it in an article on "Economists" in the 1824 supplement to the *Encyclopaedia Britannica*; Mill, "Economists," 708.

40. *PPE*, 23.
41. *PPE*, 26.
42. *PPE*, 26.
43. In the fifth edition of his *Essay on the Principle of Population,* published in 1817, Malthus added a new chapter titled "Of Corn-Laws, Restrictions upon Importation."
44. *PPE*, 26–27.
45. *PPE*, 27.
46. *PPE*, 473. For a further discussion of the influence of religious thinking on pre–Civil War American political economists, beyond the three whose views are summarized here, see Davenport, *Friends of the Unrighteous Mammon.* For a further overview, see Noll, ed., *God and Mammon.* On the influence of religious thinking on American thought more generally during this period, see Noll, *America's God.*
47. Paullin, *Atlas of the Historical Geography of the United States,* Plate 138A.
48. Mak and Walton, "Steamboats and the Great American Surge in River Transportation," Appendix Tables 1 and 2.
49. Paullin, *Atlas of the Historical Geography of the United States,* Plate 138B.
50. Cooper, *Progress of Farm Mechanization,* 3.
51. *Statistical Abstract of the United States,* 594.
52. Atack and Passell, *New Economic View of American History,* Fig. 7.2 (based on underlying series compiled by Lance Davis and Louis Stettler, and by Robert B. Zevin).
53. Bigelow, *Statistical Tables: Exhibiting the Condition and Products of Certain Branches of Industry in Massachusetts, for the Year Ending April 1, 1837,* cited in Peterson, *City-State of Boston,* 473.
54. David, "Growth of Real Product in the United States Before 1840."
55. *EPE*, 53.
56. *EPE*, 53.
57. *EPE*, 53–54. Nearly two hundred years later, the ability to foresee technological advances that have not yet happened remains a subject of debate among economists. For opposing conclusions, see, for example, Brynjolfsson and McAfee, *Second Machine Age,* and Gordon, *Rise and Fall of American Growth.*
58. *Historical Statistics of the United States Colonial Times to 1970,* Series Q321 and Q329.
59. Here and above, see Paullin, *Atlas of the Historical Geography of the United States,* Plate 138C.
60. See map by Chas. B. Barr, entitled "Telegraph Stations in the United States, the Canadas, and Nova Scotia."
61. See again Atack and Passell, *New Economic View of American History,* Fig. 7.2.
62. See again David, "Growth of Real Product in the United States Before 1840."
63. "The Coming Age," *The Independent* 3 (January 16, 1851): 10.
64. Freehling, *Road to Disunion,* 42.
65. Lincoln, "Address to the Wisconsin State Agricultural Society," 98.
66. Paine, *Common Sense,* in *The Rights of Man, Common Sense, and Other Political Writings,* 53.
67. Murray, *Jerubbaal,* 32.
68. Engell, "The Other Classic," 345–46.
69. Levinson and Berman, "King James Bible at 400," 8.
70. Beecher, *Memory of Our Fathers,* 7; 12–14; 16; 19–20.

71. Beecher, *Plea for the West*, 11.
72. Beecher, *Plea for the West*, 8–11. The biblical reference is to Isaiah 66:8.
73. Bushnell, *Nature and the Supernatural*, 221–23.
74. Jackson, "Message to Congress," 60–61.
75. [O'Sullivan], "Annexation," 5. Authorship of the article is typically attributed to John O'Sullivan, an editor for the publication.
76. "Summary—This Day: American," 2.
77. Gaustad, *Liberty of Conscience*, 212.
78. Bancroft, *History of the United States*, Vol. 1 (1834), 1–3.
79. Bancroft, *History of the United States*, Vol. 1, 3–4. Tocqueville, whose book was published the following year, gave a similar account: "North America was inhabited only by wandering tribes, who had no thought of profiting by the natural riches of the soil; that vast country was still, properly speaking, an empty continent, a desert land awaiting its inhabitants." Tocqueville, *Democracy in America*, Vol. 1, 291. But the dim view of what Bancroft called "useless vegetation" was hardly new. A half-century before, following his famous visit to Scotland, Samuel Johnson had written of the "sullen power of useless vegetation"; Johnson, *Journey to the Western Islands of Scotland*, 59.
80. Washington, "To Lafayette," in *Papers*, Vol. 6, 299.
81. Jennings, *Paradise Now*, 89.
82. Melville, *White-Jacket*, 117; 153.
83. Melville, *White-Jacket*, 153.
84. By the time of the Civil War, Boston had a Female Anti-Slavery Society, a Society for the Prevention of Pauperism, a Society for Propagating the Gospel Among the Indians, an Infidel Relief Society, a Temperance Association, a Female Moral Reform Society, a Total Abstinence Society, and the Trustees for Donations for Education in Liberia (and see as well those founded earlier, listed in Ch. 9 above). In total, there were at least forty-six voluntary societies active in Boston. Volo and Volo, *Antebellum Period*, 68.
85. One example of the petition's use was by the women of the town of Boylston, in Massachusetts, in 1836; see Fuhrer, *Crisis of Community*, 235. See also *Annual Report of the Boston Female Anti-Slavery Society*, 32.
86. Wayland, *Elements of Moral Science*, 220; *EPE*, 186.
87. Fuller and Wayland, *Domestic Slavery Considered as a Scriptural Institution*.
88. Bowen, *Gleanings from a Literary Life*, 83.
89. James, *Small Boy and Others*, 159.
90. See Buell, *Dream of the Great American Novel*, Ch. 7, on the novel and its impact.
91. Even Thomas Jefferson, himself a slaveholder, had referred to slavery as a "fatal stain"; Jefferson, letter to Ellen Randolph Coolidge, 27 August 1825, in *Family Letters of Thomas Jefferson*, 457.
92. Howe, "Battle Hymn of the Republic," 145. See also Smith, *Revivalism and Social Reform*, 232. Also see Noll, *America's God*, Part V.
93. Bancroft, *History of the United States of America*, Vol. 1 (1882), 3.

CHAPTER 11: COMPETING GOSPELS

1. This finding was the spur to Frederick Jackson Turner's "frontier hypothesis" and the subsequent movement in American historiography to which it in turn led; see Turner, "Significance of the Frontier in American History."

2. Bateman, "Make a Righteous Number," 70.
3. *Historical Statistics of the United States: Earliest Times to the Present, Millennial Edition*, Series Df882–85.
4. Rogers, *Economic History of the American Steel Industry*, 16.
5. Atack and Passell, *New Economic View of American History*, Table 17.4.
6. Here and below in this chapter, figures for per capita income are based on total U.S. income from Gallman, "Real GNP, Prices of 1860, 1834–1909," and total U.S. population from Mitchell, *International Historical Statistics*.
7. *Historical Statistics, Millennial Edition*, Series Da719, Da697, and Da757.
8. For bank suspensions, see *Historical Statistics of the United States, 1789–1945*, Series N 135. For business failures, see *Historical Statistics, Bicentennial Edition*, Series V 24.
9. *Historical Statistics, Millennial Edition*, Series Ba475.
10. *Historical Statistics, Millennial Edition*, Series Df931. (Previously published estimates sometimes indicated a higher completion rate. See, for example, Atack and Passell, *New Economic View of American History*, Fig. 16.1, which shows a completion figure of approximately three-fourths based on Series Q321 and Q329 in the 1975 *Historical Statistics, Bicentennial Edition*.)
11. *Historical Statistics, Millennial Edition*, Series Dd309, 334, 336, 347, 348.
12. Beecher also attracted attention in a less favorable way. In 1874 a parishioner, Theodore Tilton, sued him for adultery with Mrs. Tilton. (Beecher had officiated at the couple's wedding.) The trial became a public scandal, attracting nationwide publicity. For a recent account, see Fox, *Trials of Intimacy*.
13. Mayo, "Liberal Christianity in Western Massachusetts," 65.
14. Beecher, "Administration of Wealth," 225.
15. Beecher, "Administration of Wealth," 225–27.
16. Beecher, "Tendencies of American Progress," 203; 211.
17. Beecher, "Lessons from the Times," 98.
18. Beecher, "Tendencies of American Progress," 205.
19. Beecher, "Tendencies of American Progress," 211.
20. Emerson, "Wealth," in *Conduct of Life*, 89.
21. Beecher, "Tendencies of American Progress," 215; 218.
22. Beecher, "The Strike and its Lessons," 114.
23. On Conwell's life, see Burr, *Russell H. Conwell and His Work*, and Bjork, *Victorian Flight*.
24. Conwell's talents for organizing and fundraising were evident even before he was called to Grace Church. While studying at Newton Seminary, he successfully took on the reorganization and financial rescue of an all but defunct Baptist church in Lexington, Massachusetts; Bjork, *Victorian Flight*, 16–17.
25. Conwell, *Acres of Diamonds*, 17. Conwell's parable bears some surface resemblance to Adam Smith's account of "the poor man's son" in *The Theory of Moral Sentiments*, but the end of the story is different and so is the intended point. In Smith's story the son spends his life in a series of hardships, striving to attain wealth. "It is then, in the last dregs of life, his body wasted with toil and diseases, his mind galled and ruffled by the memory of a thousand injuries and disappointments . . . that he begins at last to find that wealth and greatness are mere trinkets of frivolous utility" (*TMS*, 181). In "Acres of Diamonds" the young man's mistake is not his desire for material wealth but thinking he needs to leave home to find it.
26. Conwell, *Acres of Diamonds*, 18; 20.
27. Conwell, *Acres of Diamonds*, 25.

28. Conwell, *Acres of Diamonds,* 25; 18.
29. Lawrence, "The Relation of Wealth to Morals," 290.
30. Lawrence, "The Relation of Wealth to Morals," 287.
31. Conwell, *Acres of Diamonds,* 19.
32. Lawrence, "The Relation of Wealth to Morals," 287.
33. Conwell, *Acres of Diamonds,* 26.
34. Lawrence, "The Relation of Wealth to Morals," 287.
35. Conwell, *Acres of Diamonds,* 20.
36. Carnegie, "Wealth," 661–62.
37. Carnegie, "Wealth," 660.
38. Carnegie, "Wealth," 659–60; 664.
39. Carnegie, "Wealth," 660; 664.
40. Beecher, "Economy in Small Things," 263.
41. Conwell, *Acres of Diamonds,* 21.
42. Alger, *Ragged Dick.* (The book was first serialized in *Student and Schoolmate,* in 1867.)
43. Emerson, "Wealth," 86.
44. Calvin, *Commentary on Genesis,* Vol. 2, 39:1, 292. Christian acceptance of inequality (though without Calvin's attribution of divine presence or absence) is far older. The late-sixth-century pope and saint Gregory I wrote that "Providence has established various degrees and distinct orders . . . That creation cannot be governed in equality is taught us by the example of the heavenly hosts; there are angels and there are archangels, which are clearly not equals"; see Duby, *Three Orders,* 35.
45. Conwell, *Acres of Diamonds,* 21.
46. Beecher, "The Strike and its Lessons," 113–4.
47. Beecher, "The Strike and its Lessons," 112.
48. "Phillips Brooks to his Father," included in Allen, *Life and Letters of Phillips Brooks,* Vol. 1, 523. See also the discussion of Brooks in May, *Protestant Churches and Industrial America,* Ch. 3. James F. Woolverton gave a different view of Brooks, placing him more in the Social Gospel tradition; Woolverton, *A Christian and a Democrat,* 37; but May's treatment is more consistent with Brooks's own writings, as well as his long experience of preaching in the effort to effect personal spiritual change in his listeners, rather than contribute to bringing about social reform. Consistent with that view, Brooks remarked that he thought Beecher was "the greatest preacher of America and the Century"; May, *Protestant Churches and Industrial America,* 67.
49. Brooks, "Sermon XI: The Man with Two Talents," in *Twenty Sermons,* 194–95.
50. Brooks, "The Duties of Privilege," in *New Starts in Life,* 88.
51. Riis, *How the Other Half Lives.*
52. On the influence of postmillennialism on the Social Gospel, see Smith, *Revivalism and Social Reform,* esp. Ch. 14.
53. Gladden, *Tools and the Man,* 1; 4.
54. Gladden, *Tools and the Man,* 5.
55. Gladden, *Tools and the Man,* 5; 26.
56. Gladden, *Tools and the Man,* 26.
57. Gladden, *Tools and the Man,* 26–27.
58. Long after the Social Gospel movement had begun its decline, Rauschenbusch's books continued to be influential both in America and abroad. In the midst of World War II, William Temple, the Archbishop of Canterbury, published a book with a

title that echoed Rauschenbusch: *Christianity and Social Order.* The economist D. L. Munby later described the book as "one of the foundation piers of the Welfare State" in Britain; Munby, *God and the Rich Society,* 157.

59. Rauschenbusch, *Christianity and the Social Crisis,* xi-ii.
60. Tocqueville, *Democracy in America,* Vol. 2, 159; 161.
61. Rauschenbusch, *Christianity and the Social Crisis,* 249.
62. Rauschenbusch, *Christianity and the Social Crisis,* 218; 372. Failing to foresee the future consequences of Communism in Russia, and then in eastern Europe and in China, Rauschenbusch also observed that "It is hardly likely that any social revolution, by which hereafter capitalism may be overthrown, will cause more injustice, more physical suffering, and more heartache than the industrial revolution by which capitalism rose to power" (218).
63. Rauschenbusch, *Christianity and the Social Crisis,* 21.
64. Hanson, *Political History of the Bible in America,* 79–80. Also see Freeman, *Closing of the Western Mind.*
65. Rauschenbusch, *Theology for the Social Gospel,* 5.
66. Rauschenbusch, *Christianity and the Social Crisis,* xii, 60–61.
67. Rauschenbusch, *Christianity and the Social Crisis,* xii.
68. Rauschenbusch, *Christianity and the Social Crisis,* 372.
69. On the "hegemony" of postmillennialism in this period, see Moorhead, "Between Progress and Apocalypse," 525.
70. Rauschenbusch, *Christianity and the Social Crisis,* 65.
71. See, for example, Buell, *Dream of the Great American Novel,* 266–67.
72. Strong, *New Era,* 30. Viewed from the perspective of later developments, Strong became a controversial figure because of the racism he expressed in his best-known book, *Our Country.*
73. Moorhead, "Between Progress and Apocalypse," 525.
74. Great Christian Books, http://greatchristianbooks.storenvy.com/products/1526181 -in-his-steps.
75. Rauschenbusch, *Theology for the Social Gospel,* 2–3; 139–40.
76. Bateman, "Make a Righteous Number," 67.
77. Sanford, *Report of the First Meeting of the Federal Council,* 228–30; 233.

CHAPTER 12: ECONOMICS FOR SOCIAL IMPROVEMENT

1. Marsden, "The Gospel of Wealth, the Social Gospel, and the Salvation of Souls in Nineteenth-Century America."
2. See Howe, *Unitarian Conscience,* Ch. 5. Also see Marsden, "The Gospel of Wealth, the Social Gospel, and the Salvation of Souls in Nineteenth-Century America," 19, note 4. Marsden in particular notes that while earlier histories claimed that Unitarianism was the source of the Social Gospel movement, "The evidence for this claim establishes exceptions rather than the rule."
3. Beecher, "Strike and its Lessons," 112.
4. Rauschenbusch, *Christianizing the Social Order,* 427. In a lecture that he gave at Oxford a dozen years later, John Maynard Keynes echoed Rauschenbusch's views, referring to "the trend of Joint Stock Institutions, when they have reached a certain age and size, to approximate to the status of public corporations rather than that

of individualistic enterprise," and arguing that "One of the most interesting and unnoticed developments of recent decades has been the tendency of big enterprise to socialize itself"; Keynes, *End of Laissez-Faire,* 42.

5. Stern, "German History in America," 131–32.
6. See Haskell, *Emergence of Professional Social Science,* and Dorothy Ross, *Origins of American Social Science.*
7. For an account of the organizational efforts that led to the founding of the association, see Ely, "Founding and Early History of the American Economic Association," and Dorfman, *Economic Mind in American Civilization,* Vol. 3, 205–12.
8. The publication of Paul Samuelson's *Foundations of Economic Analysis,* in 1947, marked the inflection point for the use of mathematics in economic theory. For an account of the proliferation of mathematics in both theoretical and empirical work beginning in the 1950s, emphasizing the role of the Cowles Foundation's institutional sponsorship, see Lurie, *Cowles Catalyst.*
9. Perry, *Principles of Political Economy,* 251–52.
10. Ely, "American Economic Association, 1885–1909," 58. On the influence of the Social Gospel movement in the founding of the American Economic Association more generally, see also Bateman and Kapstein, "Between God and the Market," 249–58.
11. For an account of Seelye's instruction and his influence on Clark, see Everett, *Religion in Economics,* Ch. 2.
12. On Knies's influence on Clark as well as other economists of the period, see Papadopoulos and Bateman, "Karl Knies and the Prehistory of Neoclassical Economics."
13. Max Weber, who also studied at Heidelberg during this period, wrote in 1904 that the institutions under which people live govern even the psychological processes at work in determining their behavior, so that human institutions are also prior to human psychology. See Weber, *Die "Objektivität" sozialwissenschaftlicher und sozialpolitischer Erkenntnis;* for an English translation, see "The 'Objectivity' of Knowledge in Social Science and Social Policy," in *Max Weber: Collected Methodological Writings,* 100–138.
14. Again see Everett, *Religion in Economics,* Ch. 2. See also, more generally, Henry, *John Bates Clark.*
15. Clark, *The Philosophy of Wealth* (1894), 236. These statements did not appear in the book's first printing, published in 1886; they were added for all subsequent printings, beginning in 1887.
16. *PW,* 34–35.
17. *PW,* 48; 44.
18. *PW,* 42; 40; 95. Here Clark was echoing yet another leader of the Social Gospel. In his widely read book *Our Country,* published just the year before Clark's, Josiah Strong had written, "The World is to be Christianized and civilized. . . . And what is the process of civilizing but *the creating of more and higher wants?*"; Strong, *Our Country,* 14. Strong's writings on economics in turn showed the influence of the earlier work of Francis Wayland, illustrating the two-way interaction between economic thinking and religious thinking during this period; see, for example, Hanson, *Political History of the Bible in America,* Ch. 6.
19. In some of his writings, especially on the properties of marginal relationships, Clark suggested that the purely competitive market distribution had an aspect of justice. In his 1899 book *The Distribution of Wealth,* for example, he wrote that "free competition tends to give to labor what labor creates, to capitalists what capital creates,

and to *entrepreneurs* what the coordinating function creates." This kind of claim, however, runs counter to the main body of Clark's work. See Clark, *Distribution of Wealth*, 3.

20. *PW*, 58; 107; 205; 157.

21. Clark, *Social Justice Without Socialism*, 4–5; 46.

22. Clark, *Social Justice Without Socialism*, 47–48.

23. In his autobiography Ely explained, "I always rejected the idea of a good God creating the human race and then tolerating arrangements which sent a large part of it to eternal torture. How is this compatible with the omnipotence of God and the all-embracing love that Christ taught? . . . I finally went over to the Protestant Episcopal Church which I thought offered a fuller and richer life"; Ely, *Ground Under Our Feet*, 16.

24. Ely, *Ground Under Our Feet*. Also see Frey, "Impact of Liberal Religion on Richard Ely's Economic Methodology," and Handy, *Social Gospel in America*, 173–83.

25. In his autobiography, Ely did not explain why his tuition was free; he apparently received some form of merit-based scholarship. Ely, *Ground Under Our Feet*, 31.

26. In addition to Clark and Ely, several others among the principal founders of the American Economic Association had studied in Germany and absorbed the thinking of the German historical school. Henry Carter Adams taught for many years at the University of Michigan. Edwin R. A. Seligman was Clark's colleague at Columbia and also, in later years, the editor of the *Encyclopedia of the Social Sciences*. Simon N. Patten and Edmund J. James were both then at the University of Pennsylvania's Wharton School. (After first moving to the University of Chicago, James later became president of Northwestern University, and then of the University of Illinois.)

27. In a 1901 letter to Alfred Marshall, Ely wrote, "I suppose the connection, today, between the German economists and the Americans is closer than that between the American and the English writers. I am speaking about the personal connection as much as the connection of thought." Coats, "Alfred Marshall and Richard T. Ely," 192.

28. See "Report of the Organization of the American Economic Association," 16; 6.

29. Ely, *Social Law of Service*, 162–63. In another statement to the same effect, Ely wrote, "Now it may rationally be maintained that, if there is anything divine on this earth, it is the state, the product of the same God-given instincts which led to the establishment of the Church and the Family"; Ely, "Recent American Socialism," 303.

30. In 1884 Simon Patten and Edmund James had begun a preliminary effort to establish a Society for the Study of the National Economy, modeled after a similar association associated with the historical school in Germany; see Dorfman, *Economic Mind in American Civilization*, Vol. 3, 205. In 1889 the two founded another professional organization, the American Academy of Political Social Science. Years later, Ely contrasted their proposed platform with his; Ely, "Founding and Early History of the American Economic Association," 144.

31. Rader, "Richard T. Ely," 61–74. Also see Everett, *Religion in Economics*, Ch. 3, and Handy, *Social Gospel in America*, 173–83.

32. Commons's 1934 book *Institutional Economics* became the classic text for much of what he and Ely had taught.

33. "Report of the Organization of the American Economic Association," 7.

34. Ely's *Introduction to Political Economy* was a precursor to his best-selling textbook *Outlines of Economics*, first published in 1893. In the preface to the first edition of the *Outlines*, Ely explained the intended relationship between the two as follows: "The

present book was begun as a revision of my *Introduction to Political Economy*, but it has become practically a new book, and the publishers will retain the older work on the market. . . . In any future revision of the two books an effort will be made to develop still further the peculiar characteristics of each; the aim of the Introduction being to furnish chiefly historical and descriptive material; the aim of the Outlines being to give a systematic sketch of the theory"; Ely, *Outlines of Economics*, v–vi. The two books were very similar in structure, and sections of the *Introduction* were used without alteration in the *Outlines*. *Introduction to Political Economy* was republished in 1894 and again in 1901. *Outlines of Economics* was republished five times, with the last edition in 1937. On the two books' influence and sales, see Tabb, *Reconstructing Political Economy*, 117.

35. *SAC*, 147. An earlier book, on the labor movement, had likewise emphasized the essential role Ely thought the church needed to play in social and economic reform; Ely, *Labor Movement in America*.

36. *SAC*, 11.

37. Frey, "Impact of Liberal Religion on Richard Ely's Economic Methodology," 306.

38. *SAC*, 119; 121; 123–24.

39. *SAC*, 121.

40. It is not clear, however, to what extent Ely and other economists of this time had yet absorbed the new thinking of the marginal revolution associated with Jevons, Walras, and Clark. One historian's view is that "most of them seem to have been completely unaware in the 1880s of the 'marginal revolution' taking place at that very time." Heyne, "Clerical Laissez-Faire," 260.

41. *IPE*, 84.

42. *SAC*, 124; *IPE*, 84; *SAC*, 127.

43. *SAC*, 126–27.

44. *SAC*, 127; *IPE*, 68; *SAC*, 128–29.

45. *SAC*, 24–25. The explicitly Christian purposes of the association in its early years attracted some opposition; see Coats, "First Two Decades of the American Economic Association," 555–74.

46. Matthew 22:37–40 (Mark 12:29–31 is similar); the underlying texts are Deuteronomy 6:5 and Leviticus 19:18. A statement like Ely's—close but not quite word for word—appears in Washington Gladden's later (1893) book, *Tools and the Man*. But Gladden had been both preaching and writing on this aspect of economics since the mid-1870s and he and Ely had known one another since the mid-1880s, and so it is far from obvious who had influenced whom. See Gladden, *Tools and the Man*, 1.

47. Coats, "First Two Decades of the American Economic Association," 562. Coats notes that the number of ministers peaked at thirty-nine in 1894, by which time the total membership had reached eight hundred. See also "List of Members."

48. *IPE*, 21; 25; 14.

49. *IPE*, 26; 29.

50. For the history of one outgrowth of the new availability of such data, see Bateman, "Make a Righteous Number."

51. *IPE*, 126–27. The general idea was present in Ely's writings even earlier. Just two years after beginning to teach at Johns Hopkins, he wrote that political economy "is not regarded as something fixed and unalterable, but as a growth and development, changing with society. . . . the political economy of to-day is not the political economy of yesterday; while the political economy of Germany is not identical with that of England or America"; Ely, "Past and the Present of Political Economy," 45–46.

52. Wellhausen, *Geschichte Israels* see also Wellhausen, *Prolegomena zur Geschichte Israels.*
53. For a review and discussion, see, for example, Friedman, *Who Wrote the Bible?* Although the four-part division is still used as a convenient shorthand, more modern scholarship conservatively estimates that there were seventy-five to one hundred authors and editors of the Hebrew Bible, and possibly many more; see Friedman, *The Exodus,* 102. The path of scholarship that Wellhausen developed, relying on close reading of the biblical texts in the light of knowledge of grammar, philology, and history, followed a tradition first introduced in Protestant Europe in the sixteenth century by Erasmus. Hume's writings were also influential in this regard; see the editor's introduction to Hume, *Principal Writings on Religion,* xii.
54. See Frey, "Impact of Liberal Religion on Richard Ely's Economic Methodology."
55. *IPE,* 125–26.
56. Hume, *Treatise of Human Nature,* 344.
57. Gladden, *Tools and the Man,* 5.
58. *SAC,* 119; *IPE,* 126.
59. Clark and Ely, and the other economists who studied in Germany during this period, were hardly the only Americans directly influenced by the German historical school. Herbert Baxter Adams, a historian who taught for many years at Johns Hopkins (his students there included Woodrow Wilson and Frederick Jackson Turner), and John W. Burgess, a longtime professor of law at Columbia, were among the many others. See Stern, "German History in America," 131–63.

CHAPTER 13: CONFLICT AND CRISIS

1. Use of the phrase became popular only in the 1930s. One of the earliest American appearances in print was Johnson, "Fetich of Free Enterprise."
2. Darwin's *Origin of Species* had set out the theory of evolution by natural selection, but had carefully avoided explicitly applying the theory to humans; that came only with his later book, *The Descent of Man.*
3. Mathews, *Faith of Modernism,* 169; 171; 172; 177.
4. Mathews, *Faith of Modernism,* 176–77; 170.
5. Committee on the War and the Religious Outlook, *The Church and Industrial Reconstruction,* 287; 1.
6. France, "Sérénus," 14. The statement is attributed to Fosdick in popular secondary sources like *The Ultimate Book of Quotations,* 203; and *Daily Bread for Your Mind and Soul,* 154; but these do not provide citations to an original source for Fosdick's actually saying or writing it.
7. Fosdick, *On Being a Real Person,* 5.
8. One such attribution (without an original source) is in Brown, *He Came from Galilee,* 148. Others are common in books like *The Westminster Collection of Christian Quotations,* 31. None of these gives an original source.
9. Peale, *You Can If You Think You Can,* 116. The statement is also attributed to Fosdick in popular books like the *Treasury of Spiritual Wisdom,* 365. Again, none of these gives an original source.
10. Fosdick served on the board of the foundation from 1916 to 1921. When he left the board his brother Raymond took his place. See Miller, *Harry Emerson Fosdick,* 106. On Fosdick's relationship with Rockefeller, see also Dochuk, *Anointed with Oil,*

Ch. 4; Dochuk emphasizes the intermediary role of Frederick Gates, a senior official at Standard Oil.

11. The congregation sold its Park Avenue building to help finance the new church. It moved to temporary quarters in October 1929, and remained there until the new church was ready the next year.

12. "Religion: Riverside Church." Also see Coffman, *The Christian Century and the Rise of the Protestant Mainline*, 19.

13. Moody, "Second Coming of Christ," 279.

14. Moody, "Regeneration," 695.

15. On the role of the Moody Bible Institute, see Gloege, *Guaranteed Pure*.

16. Ussher, *Annales Veteris Testamenti*, 1.

17. The campaign for prohibition stands at the center of Charles Sheldon's best-selling Social Gospel novel, *In His Steps*. See Lynerd, *Republican Theology*, for an analysis of the evangelical Protestant tradition of shunning most forms of government economic regulation while simultaneously looking to government to enforce standards of private behavior in the personal realm.

18. See, for example, Hanson, *Political History of the Bible in America*, Ch. 6.

19. Gregory, "Review: *Christian Ethics*, by Newman Smith," 353.

20. The date of Sunday's statement is uncertain; it was published in 1914, in a collection of his sermons and other writings. See Sunday and Ellis, *Billy Sunday*, 360.

21. *The Fundamentals*.

22. Charles R. Erdman, "The Church and Socialism," in *The Fundamentals*, Vol. 12, 116; 119.

23. Paul D. Hanson has attributed the erosion of American Protestant support for the Social Gospel to the rise of premillennialism at this time; Hanson, *Political History of the Bible in America*, Chs. 6–7. See also Ch. 14 below.

24. Scofield, *Scofield Reference Bible*. A new edition, published in 1917, proved even more successful.

25. Wright, "Music Publishing, Bibles, and Hymnals," 464; Pietsch, *Dispensational Modernism*, 249–50, note 31.

26. On the advance of premillennial thinking during this period, see Sandeen, *Roots of Fundamentalism*; Weber, *Living in the Shadow of the Second Coming*; Boyer, *When Time Shall Be No More*; Moorhead, *World Without End*; Marsden, *Fundamentalism and American Culture*; and Sutton, *American Apocalypse*.

27. Contrary to postmillennialist ideas of improvement, Blackstone argued that "this wicked world, which is so radically opposed to God, and under the present control of His arch enemy, is not growing better." Also, "The cultured and scientific atheist is as surely in the service of Satan as the thief or the murder." Blackstone, *Jesus Is Coming*, 148; 150.

28. Gloege, *Guaranteed Pure*, 183–88.

29. On the predominance of premillennialism among American evangelicals, see again Weber, *Living in the Shadow of the Second Coming*. On the decline of the Social Gospel, see again Hanson, *Political History of the Bible in America*, Ch. 6.

30. *The Fundamentals*, Vol. 12, 4, cited in Marsden, *Fundamentalism and American Culture*, 119.

31. Marsden, "The Gospel of Wealth, the Social Gospel, and the Salvation of Souls in Nineteenth Century America," 10–21; esp. 18. See also Marsden, *Fundamentalism and American Culture*.

32. Matthew Avery Sutton also emphasizes "the impact of global events on fundamen-

talist theology and politics" in the United States. Sutton, "Was FDR the Antichrist?," 1053.

33. Machen, *Christianity and Liberalism,* 6; 8.
34. Machen, *Christianity and Liberalism,* 5–7; 9.
35. Fosdick, "Shall the Fundamentalists Win?," 713–15. Attacks of this kind on liberal American Protestants were not new. In 1822, exactly one hundred years before Fosdick's sermon, the *Unitarian Defendant* published a series of articles titled "On the Attempt to Deprive Unitarians of the Name of Christians," complaining that "exclusive and intolerant religionists" and "violent Partizans" were seeking to impose "cruel and preposterous injustice" in a "spiteful play of calling and refusing names"; *Unitarian Defendant,* Vol. 1, No. 2, 5–8; No. 3, 9–10; No. 4, 13–15. Even earlier, the opponents of Henry Ware's election to the professorship of divinity at Harvard argued that he and others in the more liberal clergy had so far departed from the true faith that they should be excluded from Christian fellowship; see Wright, *Unitarian Controversy,* 115.
36. Fosdick, "Shall the Fundamentalists Win?," 713.
37. Fosdick, "Shall the Fundamentalists Win?," 713–14; 716.
38. One critic within the Presbyterian Church, Clarence Macartney, published a sermon titled *Shall Unbelief Win?* When the church's General Assembly investigated Fosdick, John Foster Dulles, an active Presbyterian and future secretary of state, led his defense.
39. *Christian Century,* June 8, 1922; *Christian Work,* June 10, 1022.
40. Miller, *Harry Emerson Fosdick,* 117; Miller, "Harry Emerson Fosdick and John D. Rockefeller, Jr.," 300.
41. For a different view, see Sutton, *American Apocalypse.* Sutton argues that "historians have exaggerated the significance of the Scopes trial" in this regard (xiii).
42. Winchester, *The Perfectionists,* 167.
43. Based on the business cycle dating of the National Bureau of Economic Research.
44. Unemployment data from *Historical Statistics: Earliest Times to the Present, Millennial Edition,* Series Ba475–76.
45. Darby, "Three-and-a-half Million U.S. Employees Have Been Mislaid," and Weir, "A Century of U.S. Unemployment."
46. *Historical Statistics of the United States, Millennial Edition,* Series Ba477.
47. See, for example, Eichengreen, *Golden Fetters,* and Temin, *Lessons from the Great Depression.*
48. Thomas Kuhn theorized that "Early in the development of a new field . . . social needs and values are a major determinant of the problems on which its practitioners concentrate. Also during this period, the concepts they deploy in solving problems are extensively conditioned by contemporary common sense." By contrast, "The insulation of a mature scientific community . . . is an insulation primarily with respect to concepts." See Kuhn, "History of Science," 118–19.
49. See, for example, Hofstadter, *Age of Reform,* Ch. 7, and Brinkley, *End of Reform,* Chs. 1–5.
50. Roosevelt, "Inaugural Address."
51. This line of questioning became especially prominent once the Roosevelt administration launched the National Recovery Administration, which aimed at preventing further declines in prices in many industries. Part of the object of Keynes's 1936 book was to argue that further declines in wages and prices would *not* help the recovery. See Keynes, *General Theory.*

52. Keynes, *General Theory.*
53. See Friedman, *The Moral Consequences of Economic Growth,* Ch. 7. When Schumpeter wrote that a new version of what he called preanalytic Vision "may re-enter the history of every established science each time somebody teaches us to see things in a light of which the source is not to be found in the facts, methods, and results of the pre-existing state of the science," the primary example he had in mind was Keynes's response to the Great Depression; Schumpeter, *History of Economic Analysis,* 41.
54. Hence the significance of the title of Henry George's best-selling book: *Progress and Poverty.* By the late 1870s, at least some Americans were beginning to question the presumption that economic progress would eliminate poverty.
55. On Roosevelt's moral education, including the large role played by Endicott Peabody, Episcopal priest and headmaster of Groton School, see Woolverton, *A Christian and a Democrat,* Ch. 2.
56. See, for example, MacMillan, *The War That Ended Peace,* 640.
57. Bateman, "Make a Righteous Number," 73–74.
58. In 1930 Nelson Bell, a Southern Presbyterian missionary, and the future father-in-law of Billy Graham, wrote of "the mirage of a world getting better and better." See Sutton, "Was FDR the Antichrist?," 1058–59.
59. Rauschenbusch, *Theology for the Social Gospel,* 141.
60. McGee, "The Millennium," 222.
61. See, for example, Coffman, *The Christian Century and the Rise of the Protestant Mainline.*

CHAPTER 14: UNITING RELIGIOUS AND ECONOMIC CONSERVATISM

1. Hoover, *Memoirs,* 30.
2. "Calls Stock Crash Blow at Gamblers." See also James, "1929."
3. Galbraith, *Great Crash of 1929,* 107. Roosevelt served as senior lay warden of his home parish from 1928 until his death.
4. As late as his election campaign in 1932, Roosevelt had criticized Hoover for allowing the government to run a budget deficit rather than cutting spending to balance the budget as falling incomes reduced tax revenues.
5. See Isetti, "Moneychangers of the Temple."
6. Roosevelt, "Inaugural Address."
7. Rauschenbusch, *Theology for the Social Gospel,* 3.
8. Charles R. Erdman, "The Church and Socialism," in *The Fundamentals,* Vol. 12, 108; 111.
9. Sutton, "Was FDR the Antichrist?," 1063.
10. "Dictatorships," 480; also cited in Sutton, "Was FDR the Antichrist?," 1063.
11. Sutton, *American Apocalypse,* 242. For the original, see Sunday, "Sermon Notebook," Sunday Papers, folder 10, box 31.
12. Bauman, "1935—A Prophetic Review," 92. Also see Sutton, *American Apocalypse,* 255.
13. Norris, "The New Deal Uncovered," 11. On Norris's labeling Roosevelt a communist before the election, see Hankins, *God's Rascal,* 96; cited in Sutton, "Was FDR the Antichrist?," 1062.
14. For accounts of this development, see Phillips-Fein, *Invisible Hands;* Dochuk, *From Bible Belt to Sunbelt;* and Kruse, *One Nation Under God.*

15. Kruse, *One Nation Under God*, 12; see Fifield, "Religious Ideals and the Government's Program."

16. Dochuck, *From Bible Belt to Sunbelt*, 117.

17. Phillips-Fein, *Invisible Hands*, 73.

18. Kruse, *One Nation Under God*, 12.

19. See Dochuk, *From Bible Belt to Sunbelt*, 65–66.

20. Sutton, "Was FDR the Antichrist?," 1063.

21. To be sure, many in the clergy supported the Roosevelt administration and its policies. One prominent example was Monsignor John A. Ryan—often called "The Right Reverend New Dealer"—who gave the invocation at Roosevelt's 1937 inauguration (the first Roman Catholic priest to perform that function).

22. See Dochuk, *From Bible Belt to Sunbelt*, 71.

23. See again Kuhn, "History of Science," 80–81.

24. McGee, "The Millennium," 218; 229.

25. Dochuk, *From Bible Belt to Sunbelt*, 188.

26. Hayek, *Road to Serfdom*, 148–49.

27. Fifield, *Spiritual Mobilization*, 13. Also see Roy, *Apostles of Discord*, 292.

28. Eisenhower, "Letter to Edgar Newton Eisenhower," 1147. The statement is frequently quoted, albeit often without citing the source; see, for example, Thernstrom, *History of the American People*, Vol. 2, 804.

29. The proposed name was the National Conference for United Action Among Evangelicals. This was not the first attempt to form such a group. In 1846 American representatives attended a meeting in London aimed at establishing a worldwide Evangelical Alliance. But the British evangelicals running the meeting refused to admit American slaveholders. The next year, the Americans established their own Evangelical Alliance for the United States of America. This group collapsed in 1850, again over the slavery controversy. After the Civil War, Northern evangelicals revived the group and it continued until 1898. See Jordan, *Evangelical Alliance for the United States of America*. Although the focus of EAUSA then bore as much resonance with the Social Gospel–inspired FCC (founded in 1908) as with the mid-twentieth-century NAE, today it is the NAE that belongs to the Evangelical Alliance (since renamed the World Evangelical Alliance).

30. Ockenga, "Unvoiced Multitudes," 26; 29.

31. Ockenga, "Unvoiced Multitudes," 20; 24; 29; 33.

32. Ockenga, "Christ for America," 4; 3; 4.

33. Data from Landis, *Yearbook of American Churches*.

34. The Northern Baptists (today called the American Baptist Churches) never left the Federal Council of Churches. Henry's leading role in the National Association of Evangelicals is a useful reminder of the looseness of the prevailing denominational boundaries, then as well as now.

35. Henry, *Uneasy Conscience of Modern Fundamentalism*, 65.

36. Henry, "Vigor of the New Evangelicalism," 32.

37. For Henry's account of the disagreement, see his autobiography: Henry, *Confessions of a Theologian*, 161–62; 264–78.

38. Burke, *Reflections on the Revolution in France*, 153.

39. Marx, *Critique of Hegel's "Philosophy of Right,"* 131; Engels, "Draft of a Communist Confession of Faith," 103.

40. See Bogus, *Buckley*, and Kimmage, "Buckley Jr., William F."

41. Buckley, *God and Man at Yale.*
42. Buckley, "Father Fullman's Assault," 330.
43. Buckley, "Father Fullman's Assault," 330–31.
44. Buckley and Bozell, *McCarthy and His Enemies.*
45. Buckley, "Publisher's Statement," 5.
46. Buckley, "Publisher's Statement," 5.
47. Buckley, "Magazine's Credenda," 6. (This second piece by Buckley, also in the original issue, is often combined with the "Publisher's Statement" and the two are jointly called the "Mission Statement.")
48. Buckley, "Magazine's Credenda," 6.
49. Buckley, *Up from Liberalism,* 161.
50. Thompson, *Last Hours,* 200–201.
51. "Rebuke to Rolph Is Seen." Roosevelt also gave an address at the same meeting.
52. Williams, "Views and Reviews," 303.
53. Speaking in 1940, Roosevelt presumably had Nazi Germany in mind as well. But earlier in the speech he noted that "In Europe, many nations, through dictatorships or invasion, have been compelled to abandon normal democratic procedures." In light of the Soviet invasion of Finland and the joint invasion of Poland by both Germany and the USSR, both the previous year, it seems clear that his reference was at least in part to Soviet communism. Roosevelt, "Radio Message Accepting 3rd Term Nomination."
54. Truman, "Address at Mechanics Hall in Boston," 884. Joseph Martin, speaker of the U.S. House of Representatives, reacted to the coup in Czechoslovakia by declaring that the "fate of civilization is at stake"; Steil, *Marshall Plan,* 251.
55. Truman, "Radio and Television Remarks on Election Eve," 1047.
56. Truman, "President's Farewell Address to the American People," 1201.
57. Eisenhower, "Remarks at the Opening Session of the Ministerial Meeting," 306–7.
58. Henry, "Christianity and the Economic Crisis," 14.
59. Henry, "Christianity and the Economic Crisis," 14–15.
60. Henry, "Christianity and the Economic Crisis," 43–44.
61. Hallowell, *The Communist Credo and the Christian Creed,* 1–2. The idea of communism as itself a form of religion has since become familiar in popular Western culture. Writing in English, Josef Joffe, the publisher and editor of the German weekly *Die Zeit* (roughly, the German counterpart to *Time* magazine), referred to communism as "Soviet Russia's ersatz religion," and argued that "Lenin's most brilliant invention was a secular religion: Communism"; Joffe, "Godfather of Post-Truth Politics," 18. Yale historian Marci Shore similarly described Bolshevism as "a millenarian sect with an insatiable desire for utopia struggling to reconcile predestination with free will"; Shore, "Unbreakable Broken," 10.
62. Hallowell, *The Communist Credo and the Christian Creed,* 2; 4–5. More recent research has provided some evidence that elements of communist eschatology were directly borrowed from Christian thinking; according to Halfin, *From Darkness to Light,* "the Marxist concept of universal History was essentially inspired by the Judeo-Christian bracketing of historical time between the Fall of Adam and the Apocalypse" (40).
63. Tillich, *History of Christian Thought,* 476. The book was published posthumously (Tillich died in 1965), based on lectures he had given in 1962–1963.
64. Morgan, *The United States and West Germany,* 54; Dulles's statement was recalled by the French foreign minister at the time, Christian Pineau.

65. Several prominent authors have applied this phrase to Smith. See Lipset and Raab, *Politics of Unreason,* 244; and Ribuffo, *Old Christian Right,* 177.
66. On Graham's life, see McLoughlin, *Billy Graham;* Aikman, *Billy Graham;* and Wacker, *America's Pastor.*
67. Lichtman, *White Protestant Nation,* 215.
68. Graham, "God Before Gold," 34; also cited in Kruse, *One Nation Under God,* 37.
69. From a firsthand report by Warren Ashby and William Parker, cited in McAllister, "Evangelical Faith and Billy Graham," 23. (The reference to snakes is puzzling.)
70. See Wacker, *America's Pastor,* 120–36, for an overview of Graham's evolving stance on race and civil rights. *Christianity Today* was slower to embrace desegregation. By contrast, *Christian Century,* the chief mainline Protestant counterpart, was quick to do so.
71. Wacker, *America's Pastor,* 123–24.
72. Graham, "Why Don't Our Churches Practice the Brotherhood They Preach?"
73. Graham, "We Need Revival," 62.
74. Aikman, *Billy Graham,* 152.
75. Graham, "We Need Revival," 79.
76. In return, Graham was scathing in his criticism of Truman's conduct of the Korean War: "One of the great tragedies of all time was the division of Korea. Our nation must assume some responsibility for the division at the 38th parallel. I am certain that some of our leaders are going to have to answer to Almighty God for the terrible suffering and death of this land. Every soldier we have lost, every civilian who has died or been murdered is the result of the scandalous decision by the men who sold us down the river in the secret agreements at the peace tables." Graham, *I Saw Your Sons at War,* 34.
77. Graham, *America's Hour of Decision,* 144.
78. Graham, "Three Minutes to Twelve," 7:23–7:32.
79. For a more specific example of Graham's concern about the possibility of government programs leading to socialism, see Graham's radio program, *Hour of Decision,* June 8, 1952, cited in McLoughlin, *Billy Graham,* 102. Also see Kruse, *One Nation Under God,* 38.
80. Graham, *World Aflame,* 154–56.
81. Graham, "We Need Revival," 73; 70–71; 75.
82. Graham, "We Need Revival," 72–75.
83. Graham, "Satan's Religion," 41.
84. Charles R. Erdman, "The Church and Socialism," in *The Fundamentals,* Vol. 12, 110.
85. Graham, "Satan's Religion," 42–44.
86. Graham, "Satan's Religion," 42.
87. *Firing Line* (transcript pp. 23; 2–3).
88. Graham, *Approaching Hoofbeats.*
89. Reagan, "Encroaching Control." The former medical missionary to whom Reagan was referring was most likely Walter Judd, a Congregationalist who served as a medical missionary in China in the latter half of the 1920s and again in the latter half of the 1930s. Judd was a U.S. congressman from 1942 to 1963, known for his strident anticommunism and especially his opposition to Mao's China. Judd had used the phrase "half slave and half free" (famously due to Lincoln) in a speech to the Abraham Lincoln Club the previous year.
90. Goldwater, "How to Win the Cold War," 17.
91. Mohr, "Goldwater Met Warmly in South," 10.

92. Reagan, "Remarks at the Annual Convention of the National Association of Evangelicals."
93. Reagan, "Remarks at the Annual Convention of the National Association of Evangelicals."

CHAPTER 15: ECONOMICS IN THE PUBLIC CONVERSATION

1. See Allison, *Destined for War*, for an analysis of Sino-American competition within the classic great-power framework.
2. Lewis, *De Descriptione Temporum*, 7. For a similar view from about the same time, see Casserley, *Retreat from Christianity in the Modern World*.
3. Data, from the World Bank's *World Development Indicators*, are for 2018.
4. Data are from the *World Values Survey*. Also see Gelman, *Red State, Blue State*.
5. Data are from the Pew Foundation, "Age Gap in Religion Around the World."
6. See, for example, Buell, *The Dream of the Great American Novel*, 97.
7. The literature analyzing this phenomenon is large and growing. For a recent example, see Mettler, *Government-Citizen Disconnect*.
8. MacGillis, "Who Turned My Blue State Red?"
9. Porter, "The Government Check Disconnect." Data on food stamp (Supplemental Nutritional Assistance Program) use are from the U.S. Department of Agriculture, Food and Nutrition Service.
10. From 1993 through 2017 it was 39.6 percent; for some taxpayers, in some years, features like the loss of up to one-fifth of itemized deductions and the additional Medicare tax on income above the payroll tax cutoff made the overall top marginal rate a few percentage points higher.
11. See "Americans' Views of the Economy and the State of the Country," CBS News/*New York Times* Poll, 2008. In 2008 the top-bracket rate was only 28 percent, payable by couples with income above $200,300 or individuals with income above $164,550.
12. "Republicans Lower Expectations for a 2020 Trump Victory," *Economist*/YouGov Poll.
13. Estimate from the Tax Policy Center, "Briefing Book." According to Internal Revenue Service data, only 5,219 estate tax returns filed in 2016 (the most recent year for which data are available) involved any tax liability. Of those, 3,012 were for estates of under $5 million—none of which would be subject to tax under the new exemption. See Internal Revenue Service, Statistics of Income Division, "Estate Tax Returns Study."
14. Quinnipiac University Poll, "November 15, 2017." A similar Quinnipiac poll in May 2017 found the identical 48 percent for abolition. There is some evidence that explicitly informing people how few families pay the estate tax does increase support for it. (By contrast, the degree of support for other redistributive policies, such as income taxes or the minimum wage, does not respond to such influence.) See Kuziemko et al., "How Elastic Are Preferences for Redistribution?"
15. See, for example, Tankersley and Casselman, "Many Voters Are in Favor of Taxing the Wealthy" and "Voters Back Warren Plan to Tax Rich, Poll Shows."
16. See, for example, Gottschalk and Moffitt, "Growth of Earnings Instability in the U.S. Labor Market."
17. See, for example, Solon, "Intergenerational Income Mobility in the United States"; Mazumder, "Fortunate Sons"; and Chetty et al., "Where Is the Land of Opportunity?"

18. Frank, *What's the Matter with Kansas?* For two of the many critiques of Frank's argument, see Bartels, "What's the Matter with What's the Matter with Kansas?," and Wuthnow, *Red State Religion.*

19. Thinking of political choices within this kind of two-dimension frame is long familiar. Keynes, for example, observed that in a democracy any political party has to win voters' confidence by persuading them "either that it intends to promote their interests or that it intends to gratify their passions"; Keynes, "Am I a Liberal?," 295. (The statement does not appear in the first published version of the essay, in 1925, nor in the original 1931 edition of *Essays in Persuasion;* it was, however, in the typescript of a talk that Keynes gave to the Liberal Summer School in 1925, which then became the basis for the essay.)

20. Drutman, "Political Divisions in 2016 and Beyond," Fig. 2. For the other three groups, Drutman's study found 45 percent preferring economic policies favoring lower-income groups along with more liberal social policies, 23 percent preferring economic policies favoring higher-income groups and more conservative social policies, and 4 percent preferring economic policies favoring higher-income groups together with more liberal social policies. For a similar analysis, in which the two measured lines of distinction are income and education, see Kitschelt and Rehm, "Secular Partisan Realignment in the United States."

21. See again, Frank, *What's the Matter with Kansas?* Another recent example is FitzGerald, *The Evangelicals.*

22. Frank, *What's the Matter with Kansas?*, 175–78.

23. Hallowell, *Communist Credo and the Christian Creed,* 1–2.

24. Graham, "We Need Revival," 72–75.

25. Graham, "Satan's Religion," 41.

26. Schaeffer, *A Christian Manifesto,* in *Complete Works,* Vol. 5, 479.

27. FitzGerald, *The Evangelicals,* 358–61.

28. Ansolabehere et al., "Purple America," Fig. 3.

29. Based on data updating and expanding Bartels, "What's the Matter with What's the Matter with Kansas?," Fig. 3. Data from "Time Series Cumulative Data File, 1948–2016." Organizing the data somewhat differently—specifically, including the bottom *two-thirds* of the noncollege-educated group—Kitschelt and Rehm found a sharper shift toward Republican voting in 2012 and especially 2016; "Secular Partisan Realignment in the United States," Fig. 3. But they also reported that when they aligned the income divisions differently, to conform more with Bartels's approach, they too found less evidence of a shift from Democratic to Republican voting among genuinely low-income noncollege whites; see their note 48.

30. Ansolabehere et al., "Purple America," Fig. 2.

31. See Phillips, *Emerging Republican Majority.*

32. The 2020 total is larger than that for 1960 because these states have gained in population relative to the rest of the country.

33. For a recent view of the role of racial attitudes in American electoral politics, see Tesler, *Post-Racial or Most-Racial?*

34. Gelman, *Red State, Blue State,* Fig. 6.10.

35. Based on data from the 2016 post-election Cooperative Congressional Election Study poll, updating Gelman, *Red State, Blue State,* Fig. 6.10. Data from Ansolabehere and Schaffner, "Cooperative Congressional Election Survey Common Content, 2016," Harvard Dataverse, V4.

36. James Bratt referred to "economic conservatives . . . and American evangelicals, who assume an automatic affinity between their respective positions"; Bratt, *Abraham Kuyper*, 224.

37. Based on data from the 2008 CBS/*New York Times* Poll on the economy. In a more recent poll, only 18 percent of respondents who self-identified as born-again Protestants favored the estate tax, versus 38 percent of Protestants who said they were not born again (and 30 percent for the survey overall); Burns, "CCES 2014, Team Module of University of Michigan (UMI)."

38. See again Lynerd, *Republican Theology*, 26–33.

39. Pew Research Center, "2014 Religious Landscape Study."

40. Schaffner et al., "CCES Common Content, 2018."

41. Based on data from the 2017 Cooperative Congressional Election Study poll. Data from Ansolabehere and Schaffner, "2017 CCES Common Content."

42. Sengupta, "Carter Sadly Turns Back on National Baptist Body." For Carter's current church's affiliations, see http://www.mbcplains.org/.

43. Voting shares from American National Election Survey data; see Aldrich et al., *Change and Continuity in the 2016 Elections*, 146. For a broad overview of the historical background to evangelical support for Donald Trump, see Kidd, *Who Is an Evangelical?*

44. See, for example, Solon, "Cross-Country Differences in Intergenerational Earnings Mobility," 59–66; Corak, "Inequality from Generation to Generation"; and Corak, "Income Inequality, Equality of Opportunity, and Intergenerational Mobility."

45. Lipset and Bendix, *Social Mobility in Industrial Society*. Alesina et al., "Intergenerational Mobility and Preferences for Redistribution."

46. Alesina et al., "Why Doesn't the United States Have a European-Style Welfare State?," Table 13. Data are from the World Values Survey.

47. Pew Research Center, "Political Typology 2017." At the peak, in the late 1990s, the split was 74 percent versus 23 percent.

48. Pew Research Center, "Political Typology 2017."

49. Zauzmer, "Christians Are More than Twice as Likely to Blame a Person's Poverty on Lack of Effort."

50. Although most scholars of the international Prosperity Gospel would say that it remains individualistic in essential ways, some Pentecostals outside the United States draw a more collectivist lesson from the Prosperity Gospel, taking it to refer to nations rather than individuals; see Hummel, "The New Christian Zionism." At the same time, even within the U.S., Christian Zionists frequently appeal to the collectivist notion that God will bless the nation that blesses Israel. Another example of a highly individualistic movement, embracing Calvinist ideas about the connection of poverty to original sin and depravity, is Christian Reconstructionism; see Ingersoll, *Building God's Kingdom*, esp. 73–77.

51. Jones et al., *Do Americans Believe Capitalism and Government Are Working?*, 35.

52. Based on data from the Fourth National Survey of Religion and Politics, Bliss Institute, University of Akron. See Green, "American Religious Landscape and Political Attitudes," Table 12.

53. The increase in Democratic voting among Catholics was not limited to 1960; it continued to 1964, when Kennedy's 1960 running mate, Lyndon Johnson, was the Democratic presidential candidate.

54. Gelman, *Red State, Blue State*, Fig. 6.9; Aldrich et al., *Change and Continuity*, Fig.

5-5. On the voting difference between Hispanic and non-Hispanic white Catholics, see Aldrich et al., 145; 161–62.

55. The Southern Baptist Convention, with just over fifteen million members as of 2017, is the country's largest Protestant denomination. As the name suggests, the SBC's churches and membership are disproportionately located in the Southern states. But there are many evangelical churches in the United States beyond the Southern Baptists—one recent categorization classifies sixty-one denominations, and groups of denominations, as evangelical Protestant; see Green, *Faith Factor,* Appendix A—and many of those are also disproportionately centered in the South. According to the National Association of Evangelicals website, the group currently has "nearly forty" member denominations.

56. Ockenga, *God Save America,* 15. A few years later, speaking as president of the National Association of Evangelicals, Ockenga was more explicit: "I believe that the United States of America has been assigned a destiny comparable to that of ancient Israel"; Ockenga, "Christ for America," 3.

57. Reagan, "Address Accepting the Presidential Nomination at the Republican National Convention in Detroit." In his farewell address, in January 1989, Reagan returned to his familiar theme (from Matthew via John Winthrop) of America as a shining city on a hill, stating "And if there had to be city walls, the walls had doors and the doors were open to anyone with the will and the heart to get there"; Reagan, "Farewell Address to the Nation."

58. Solon, "Cross-Country Differences in Intergenerational Earnings Mobility"; Corak, "Inequality from Generation to Generation"; Corak, "Income Inequality, Equality of Opportunity, and Intergenerational Mobility."

59. The voluntarist tradition in American Protestantism dates to the very beginning; see Winthrop, "Model of Christian Charity." George Whitefield, preaching during the Great Awakening of the late 1730s and early 1740s, emphasized faith that God providentially provides through voluntary charity. Whitefield's ideas on the subject in turn reflected the thinking of the German Pietist August Hermann Francke.

60. Lynerd, *Republican Theology,* 85–86.

61. Arrow, "Social Responsibility and Economic Efficiency," 314.

62. *EPE,* 461.

63. See again Lynerd, *Republican Theology.* See also Porterfield, *Conceived in Doubt.*

64. Henry, *Christian Mindset in a Secular Society,* 23.

65. Lindsell, *Free Enterprise,* 118–20. Among other places where he taught, Lindsell was on the original faculty at Fuller Theological Seminary.

66. Jones et al., *Do Americans Believe Capitalism and Government Are Working?,* 12. In another survey, 52 percent of Protestants who regard themselves as born again agreed with a similar proposition (versus 40 percent of other Protestants and 36 percent of Americans overall); Jones and Cox, *Attitudes on Child and Family Wellbeing.* Evangelicals' opposition to the role of government in implementing social and especially redistributional programs stands in tension with their support for government enforcement of private morality on matters such as alcoholic beverages as well as homosexuality and abortion; see again Lynerd, *Republican Theology,* and Porterfield, *Conceived in Doubt.* Kruse, *One Nation Under God,* argues that although "Christian libertarianism" began as an antistatist movement, it unintentionally ended up sacralizing the federal government. An older study of evangelicals' economic views is Gay, *With Liberty and Justice for Whom?*

67. For one striking example, environmental regulation, see Hochschild, *Strangers in Their Own Land.*
68. Weber, *Living in the Shadow of the Second Coming,* and Wacker, *Heaven Below.*
69. See again Weber, *Living in the Shadow of the Second Coming,* and Wacker, *Heaven Below.*
70. *Life in 2050,* 15.
71. See, for example, Hanson, *A Political History of the Bible in America,* 89–94.
72. For example, in his 1965 book *World Aflame,* Billy Graham quoted Jesus from Matthew 24:12 ("As lawlessness spreads . . ."), and also 2 Timothy 3:1–5, and went on to write: "Notice that this passage teaches explicitly that these are characteristics of the last days. Our newspapers are filled with accounts of the rebellion of youth, the overthrow of governments, and riots in almost every country on earth. We have only to quote the crime records to show that lawlessness is increasing at a frightening rate around the world. Jesus taught that just before the end, lawlessness would be worldwide. He said: 'You shall hear of wars and commotions' (Luke 21:9). This word 'commotions' carries with it the idea of rebellion, revolution, and lawlessness, indicating that this was a sign of the approaching end of the age." Graham, *World Aflame,* 189.
73. See, for example, Seigle, "Growing Economic Crisis," and Malkin, "Global Financial Crisis an 'Act of God.'"
74. Dias, "The Apocalypse as an 'Unveiling.'"
75. Henry, *Uneasy Conscience of Modern Fundamentalism,* 27. See also Sutton, *American Apocalypse,* 293.
76. Harold Ockenga, "When the Time Is Short Turn to God" (1947), unpublished sermon quoted in Sutton, *American Apocalypse,* 315.
77. Graham, *World Aflame,* 155.
78. Carlyle, "Occasional Discourse on the Negro Question," 672–73.
79. Mill, *Principles of Political Economy.*
80. Malthus, *Essay on the Principle of Population* (1798). On the effect of Malthus on British political thinking in the first half of the nineteenth century, see Hilton, *Age of Atonement.*
81. Friedman, *The Moral Consequences of Economic Growth,* Chs. 5–8.

Bibliography

Adams, James Truslow. *New England in the Republic, 1776–1850*. Boston: Little, Brown, 1926.

Adams, John. "To the Printer." *The Boston Gazette* (February 8, 1773). In *Papers of John Adams*, Vol. 1, 292. Edited by Robert J. Taylor, Mary-Jo Klein, and Gregg L. Lint. Cambridge: Harvard University Press, 1977.

———. *The Diary and Autobiography of John Adams*. Edited by Mary-Jo Klein and Gregg L. Lint. Cambridge: Harvard University Press, 1961.

———. "A dissertation on the Canon and Feudal Law." *The Boston Gazette*, August 12, 1765.

———. "From John Adams to Daniel Raymond, 8 February 1821." *Founders Online*, National Archives. Accessed February 9, 2018. http://founders.archives.gov /documents/Adams/99-02-02-7463.

———. *John Adams: Revolutionary Writings, 1775–1783*. New York: Library of America, 2011.

———. *The Political Writings of John Adams*. Edited by George W. Carey. Washington, DC: Regnery, 2000.

Ahnert, Thomas. *The Moral Culture of the Scottish Enlightenment, 1690–1805*. New Haven: Yale University Press, 2014.

Aikman, David. *Billy Graham: His Life and Influence*. Nashville: Thomas Nelson, 2007.

Aldrich, John H., et al. *Change and Continuity in the 2016 Elections*. Thousand Oaks, CA: CQ Press, 2019.

Alesina, Alberto, Edward L. Glaeser, and Bruce Sacerdote. "Why Doesn't the United States Have a European-Style Welfare State?" *Brookings Papers on Economic Activity* (No. 2, 2001): 187–277.

Alesina, Alberto, Stefanie Stantcheva, and Edoardo Teso. "Intergenerational Mobility and Preferences for Redistribution." *American Economic Review* 108 (February 2018): 521–54.

Alger, Horatio. *Ragged Dick, or, Street life in New York with the Boot-Blacks*. Boston: Loring, 1868.

Allen, Alexander V. G. *Life and Letters of Phillips Brooks*. New York: E. P. Dutton, 1901.

Allen, Franklin, and Douglas Gale. "Financial Contagion." *Journal of Political Economy* 108 (February 2000): 1–33.

Allison, Graham. *Destined for War: Can America and China Escape Thucydides's Trap?* Boston: Houghton Mifflin Harcourt, 2017.

"Americans' Views of the Economy and the State of the Country." CBS News/*New York Times* Poll. April 3, 2008. Accessed January 31, 2018. http://www.cbsnews.com/htdocs /pdf/Mar08c-economy.pdf.

"An act to prevent the infamous practice of stock-jobbing." In *The Statutes at Large*, Vol. 16, 443–48. Cambridge: Joseph Bentham, 1765.

Angell, Norman. *The Great Illusion: A Study of the Relation of Military Power in Nations to Their Economic and Social Advantage*. New York: Putnam, 1910.

Annual Report of the Boston Female Anti-Slavery Society. Boston: Boston Female Anti-Slavery Society, 1836.

Ansolabehere, Stephen, and Brian Schaffner. "Cooperative Congressional Election Survey Common Content, 2016." Harvard Dataverse, V4. Accessed June 20, 2019. https://doi.org/10.7910/DVN/GDF6Zo.

———. "2017 CCES Common Content." Harvard Dataverse, V2. Accessed June 20, 2019. http://doi.org/10.7910/DVN/3STEZY.

Ansolabehere, Stephen, Jonathan Roden, and James Snyder. "Purple America." *Journal of Economic Perspectives* 20 (Spring 2006): 97–118.

Appleby, Joyce O. *Economic Thought and Ideology in Seventeenth-Century England*. Princeton: Princeton University Press, 1978.

———. *The Relentless Revolution: A History of Capitalism*. New York: W. W. Norton, 2010.

Aristotle. *The Politics*. New York: Penguin, 1992.

Arminius, James. *The Works of James Arminius, DD*. 3 vols. Auburn and Buffalo: Derby, Miller & Orton, 1853.

Arrow, Kenneth J. "Social Responsibility and Economic Efficiency." *Public Policy* 21 (July 1973): 303–317.

Atack, Jeremy, and Peter Passell. *A New Economic View of American History: From Colonial Times to 1940*. 2nd ed. New York: W. W. Norton, 1994.

Augustine. *The City of God against the Pagans*. Cambridge: Cambridge University Press, 1998.

———. *Confessions*. New York: Oxford University Press, 1991.

———. *A Treatise on the Gift of Perseverance*. In *A Select Library of the Nicene and Post-Nicene Fathers of the Christian Church*. Vol. 5. New York: Charles Scribner's Sons, 1908.

Baier, Annette C., and Michael Luntley. "Moral Sentiments and the Difference They Make." *Proceedings of the Aristotelian Society, Supplemental Volumes* 69 (January 1995): 15–45.

Bailyn, Bernard. *The Ideological Origins of the American Revolution*. Cambridge: Harvard University Press, 1992.

Bailyn, Bernard, and Jane N. Garrett, eds. *Pamphlets of the American Revolution, 1750–1776, Volume I: 1750–1765*. Cambridge: Harvard University Press, 1965.

Bainbridge, William Sims. "Shaker Demographics, 1840–1900." *Journal for the Scientific Study of Religion* 21 (December 1982): 352–365.

Bairoch, Paul. *Cities and Economic Development: From the Dawn of History to the Present*. Chicago: University of Chicago Press, 1988.

Baltzell, E. Digby. *Puritan Boston and Quaker Philadelphia: Two Protestant Ethics and the Spirit of Class Authority and Leadership*. New York: Free Press, 1979.

Bancroft, George. *A History of the United States*. Boston: Charles Bowen, 1834.

———. *History of the United States of America*. New York: D. Appleton & Company, 1882.

Barr, Chas. B. "Telegraph Stations in the United States, the Canadas, and Nova Scotia." Pittsburgh: Barr, 1853.

Barrow, Isaac. *The Works of Isaac Barrow*. 3 vols. New York: John C. Riker, 1845.

Bartels, Larry M. "What's the Matter with What's the Matter with Kansas?" *Quarterly Journal of Political Science* 1 (April 2006): 201–26.

Bashford, Alison, and Joyce E. Chaplin. *The New Worlds of Thomas Robert Malthus: Rereading the "Principle of Population."* Princeton: Princeton University Press, 2016.

Bateman, Bradley W. "Make a Righteous Number: Social Surveys, the Men and Religion Forward Movement, and Quantification in American Economics." *History of Political Economy* 43 (annual supplement, 2001): 57–85.

Bateman, Bradley W., and Ethan Kapstein. "Between God and the Market: The Religious Roots of the American Economic Association." *Journal of Economic Perspectives* 13 (Fall 1999): 249–58.

Bauman, Louis S. "1935—A Prophetic Review." *Kings Business* (March 1936).

Baxter, Richard. *The Glorious Kingdom of Christ, Described and Clearly Vindicated*. London: T. Snowden, 1691.

———. *A Paraphrase on the New Testament*. London: B. Simmons, 1685.

Beard, Mary. *SPQR: A History of Ancient Rome*. New York: Liveright, 2015.

Becker, Gary S., and Kevin M. Murphy. "A Theory of Rational Addiction." *Journal of Political Economy* 96 (April 1988): 675–700.

Beecher, Henry Ward. "The Administration of Wealth." *Herald of Health and Journal of Physical Culture* 10, no. 5 (November 1867): 225–27.

———. "Economy in Small Things." In *Plymouth Pulpit*. New York: J. B. Ford, 1875.

———. "Lessons from the Times." In *New Star Papers; or, Views and Experiences of Religious Subjects*. New York: Derby & Jackson, 1859.

———. "The Strike and its Lessons." *Christian Union* 16, no. 6 (August 8, 1877):112–14.

———. "The Tendencies of American Progress." In *The Original Plymouth Pulpit: Sermons of Henry Ward Beecher*. Boston: The Pilgrim Press, 1871.

Beecher, Lyman. *The Memory of Our Fathers: A Sermon Delivered at Plymouth on the Twenty-Second of December, 1827*. Boston: T. R. Marvin, 1828.

———. *A Plea for the West*. Cincinnati: Truman & Smith, 1835.

Bell, Daniel. *The Coming of Post-Industrial Society: A Venture in Social Forecasting*. New York: Basic Books, 1973.

Benedict, Philip. *Christ's Churches Purely Reformed: A Social History of Calvinism*. New Haven: Yale University Press, 2002.

Bentley, Richard. *Eight Sermons Preach'd at the Honourable Robert Boyle's Lecture*. Cambridge: Cornelius Crownfield, 1724.

Bernstein, Peter. *Wedding of the Waters: The Erie Canal and the Making of a Great Nation*. New York: W. W. Norton, 2005.

Berry, Christopher J. "Hume and Superfluous Value (or the Problem with Epictetus' Slippers)." In *David Hume's Political Economy*. Edited by Carl Wennerlind and Margaret Schabas. London: Routledge, 2008.

———. *The Idea of Luxury: A Conceptual and Historical Investigation*. Cambridge: Cambridge University Press, 1994.

Berry, Christopher J., Maria Pia Paganelli, and Craig Smith, eds. *The Oxford Handbook of Adam Smith*. Oxford: Oxford University Press, 2013.

Bicknell, E. J. *A Theological Introduction to the Thirty-Nine Articles of the Church of England*. London: Longmans, Green, 1919.

Bjork, Daniel W. *The Victorian Flight: Russell Conwell and the Crisis of American Individualism.* Washington, DC: University Press of America, 1979.

Blackstone, William E. *Jesus Is Coming.* New York: Fleming H. Revell, 1898.

Blair, Hugh. *Sermons.* 5 vols. London: Printed for W. Strahan; and T. Cadell in the Strand; and W. Creech, Edinburgh, 1777–1801.

Blomert, Reinhard. *Adam Smiths Reise nach Frankreich oder die Entstehung der Nationalökonomie.* Berlin: Die Andere Bibliothek, 2012.

Bodin, Jean. *The Six Bookes of a Commonweale.* Cambridge: Harvard University Press, 1962.

Boettner, Loraine. *The Reformed Doctrine of Predestination.* Grand Rapids: Eerdmans, 1936.

Bogus, Carl T. *Buckley: William F. Buckley Jr. and the Rise of American Conservatism.* New York: Bloomsbury Press, 2011.

Boisguilbert, Pierre Le Pesant de. *Le Detail de la France, la cause de la diminution de ses biens, et la facilité du remede, en fournissant un mois tout l'argent dont le Roi a besoin, et enrichissant tout le monde.* In *Pierre de Boisguilbert, ou la naissance de l'économie politique.* Edited by Jacqueline Hecht, vol. 2, 581–662. Paris: INED, 1966.

———. *Traité de la nature, culture, commerce et interest des grains.* In *Pierre de Boisguilbert, ou la naissance de l'économie politique.* Edited by Jacqueline Hecht, vol. 2, 827–78. Paris: INED, 1966.

The Book of Discipline of the United Methodist Church. Nashville: United Methodist Publishing House, 2012.

Bornkamm, Heinrich. *Luther in Mid-Career, 1521–1530.* London: Darton, Longman & Todd, 1983.

Bowen, Francis. *Gleanings from a Literary Life, 1838–1880.* New York: Charles Scribner's Sons, 1880.

———. *The Principles of Political Economy: Applied to the Condition, the Resources, and the Institutions of the American People.* Boston: Little, Brown, 1856.

Bowler, Peter J. "The Changing Meaning of 'Evolution.'" *Journal of the History of Ideas* 36 (January–March 1975): 95–114.

Bowles, Samuel, and Jung-Kyoo Choi. "The Neolithic Agricultural Revolution and the Origins of Private Property." *Journal of Political Economy* 127 (October 2019): 2186–2228.

Boyd, Richard. "Manners and Morals: David Hume on Civility, Commerce, and the Social Construction of Difference." In *David Hume's Political Economy.* Edited by Carl Wennerlind and Margaret Schabas. London: Routledge, 2008.

Boyer, Paul. *When Time Shall Be No More: Prophecy Belief in Modern American Culture.* Cambridge: Harvard University Press, 1992.

Bratt, James D. *Abraham Kuyper: Modern Calvinist, Christian Democrat.* Grand Rapids: Eerdmans, 2013.

Brewer, Priscilla J. *Shaker Communities, Shaker Lives.* Hanover, NH: University Press of New England, 1986.

Briant, Lemuel. *The Absurdity and Blasphemy of Depretiating Moral Virtue: a Sermon preached at the West-Church in Boston, June 18th. 1749.* Boston: J. Green for D. Gookin, in Marlborough Street, 1749.

Brinkley, Alan. *The End of Reform: New Deal Liberalism in Recession and War.* New York: Alfred A. Knopf, 1995.

Broadie, Alexander. *The Scottish Enlightenment: The Historical Age of the Historical Nation.* Edinburgh: Birlinn, 2001.

Brooke, Christopher. *Philosophic Pride: Stoicism and Political Thought from Lipsius to Rousseau*. Princeton: Princeton University Press, 2012.

Brooke, John Hedley. *Science and Religion: Some Historical Perspectives*. Cambridge: Cambridge University Press, 1991.

Brooks, Phillips. *New Starts in Life, and other Sermons*. New York: E. P. Dutton, 1910.

———. *Twenty Sermons*. New York: E. P. Dutton, 1886.

Brown, Charlotte R., and William Edward Morris. *Starting with Hume*. New York: Continuum, 1988.

Brown, Parker. *He Came from Galilee*. New York: Hawthorn Books, 1974.

Brown, Robert. *The Nature of Social Laws: Machiavelli to Mill*. Cambridge: Cambridge University Press, 1984.

Brown, Vivienne. *Adam Smith's Discourse: Canonicity, Commerce and Conscience*. London: Routledge, 1994.

Brynjolfsson, Erik, and Andrew McAfee. *The Second Machine Age: Work, Progress, and Prosperity in a Time of Brilliant Technologies*. New York: W. W. Norton, 2014.

Buchan, James. *Crowded with Genius: The Scottish Enlightenment: Edinburgh's Moment of the Mind*. New York: HarperCollins, 2003.

Buckley, Theodore Alois, trans. *Canons and Decrees of the Council of Trent*. London: Routledge, 1851.

Buckley, William F., Jr. "Father Fullman's Assault." *Catholic World* 175 (August 1952): 328–333.

———. *God and Man at Yale: The Superstitions of Academic Freedom*. Chicago: Regnery Books, 1951.

———. "The Magazine's Credenda." *National Review* 1, no. 1 (November 19, 1955): 6.

———. "Publisher's Statement." *National Review* 1, no. 1 (November 19, 1955): 5.

———. *Up from Liberalism*. New York: McDowell, Obolensky, 1959.

Buckley, William F., Jr., and Brent Bozell. *McCarthy and His Enemies: The Record and Its Meaning*. Chicago: Henry Regnery, 1954.

Buell, Lawrence. *The Dream of the Great American Novel*. Cambridge: Harvard University Press, 2014.

Burke, Edmund. *Reflections on the Revolution in France*. In *Select Works of Edmund Burke*. Indianapolis: Liberty Fund, 1999.

Burnet, Thomas. *Doctrina Antiqua de Rerum Originibus; or an Inquiry into the Doctrine of the Philosophers of all Nations Concerning the Original of the World*. London: E. Curll, 1736.

———. *The Theory of the Earth*. London: By R. N. for Walter Kettilby at the Bishop's Head in St. Paul's Church Yard, 1697.

Burns, Nancy. "CCES 2014, Team Module of University of Michigan (UMI)." Harvard Dataverse, V1 (2017). Accessed February 7, 2020. https://doi.org/10.7910/DVN/UHVP4U.

Burns, Robert. *Poems, Chiefly in the Scottish Dialect*. Kilmarnock: John Wilson, 1786.

Burr, Aaron. *The Supreme Deity of Our Lord Jesus Christ, Maintained*. Boston: J. Draper, 1757.

Burr, Agnes Rush. *Russell H. Conwell and His Work: One Man's Interpretation of Life*. Philadelphia: John C. Winston, 1926.

Burstyn, Leonardo, et al. "Status Goods: Experimental Evidence from Platinum Credit Cards." *Quarterly Journal of Economics* 133 (August 2018): 1561–95.

Bushnell, Horace. *Nature and the Supernatural, as Together Constituting the One System of God*. New York: Charles Scribner, 1858.

Butler, Joseph. *Fifteen Sermons Preached at the Rolls Chapel*. London: W. Botham, 1726.

———. *Fifteen Sermons*. 2nd ed. London: W. Botham, 1729.

———. *A Sermon Preached before the House of Lords, in the Abbey-Church of Westminster, on Friday, Jan. 30, 1740–41*. London: J. & P. Knapton, 1741.

———. *A Sermon Preached before the Incorporated Society for the Propagation of the Gospel in Foreign Parts*. London: J. & P. Knapton, 1739.

Cady, George Johnson. "The Early American Reaction to the Theory of Malthus." *Journal of Political Economy* 39 (October 1931): 601–32.

"Calls Stock Crash Blow at Gamblers." *New York Times*, October 28, 1929.

Calvin, John. *Commentary on Genesis*. Grand Rapids: Eerdmans, 1948.

———. *Institutes of the Christian Religion*. 2 vols. Louisville: Westminster John Knox Press, 1960.

———. *A Treatise on the Eternal Predestination of God*. London: Wetheim & Macintosh, 1856.

Campbell, John Y., and John H. Cochrane. "By Force of Habit: A Consumption-Based Explanation of Aggregate Stock Market Behavior." *Journal of Political Economy* 107 (April 1999): 205–51.

Cantillon, Richard. *Essay on the Nature of Trade in General*. Indianapolis: Liberty Fund, 2015.

Carey, Henry C. *Principles of Political Economy*. Philadelphia: Carey, Lea & Blanchard, 1837.

Carlyle, Alexander. *The Usefulness and Necessity of a Liberal Education for Clergymen*. Edinburgh: William Creech, 1793.

Carlyle, Thomas. "Occasional Discourse on the Negro Question." *Fraser's Magazine* 40, (December, 1849): 672–73.

Carnegie, Andrew. "Wealth." *North American Review* 148, no. 391 (June 1889): 60–64.

Carroll, James. *Christ Actually: The Son of God for the Secular Age*. New York: Viking, 2014.

Caselli, Francesco, and W. John Coleman II. "Cross-Country Technology Diffusion: The Case of Computers." *American Economic Review* 91 (May 2001): 328–35.

Casserley, J.V. Langmead. *The Retreat from Christianity in the Modern World*. London: Longmans, 1952.

Chandler, Tertius. *Four Thousand Years of Urban Growth: An Historical Census*. Lewiston, NY: Edwin Mellen Press, 1987.

Channing, William Ellery. *Remarks on the Rev. Dr. Worcester's Second Letter to Mr. Channing, on American Unitarianism*. Boston: Wells & Lilly, 1815.

———. *A Sermon Delivered at the Ordination of the Rev. Jared Sparks*. Boston: Hews & Goss, 1819.

———. *Works*. 5 vols. Boston: J. Munroe, 1841.

"Charter of the Province of Massachusetts Bay, 1691." In *Publications of the Colonial Society of Massachusetts*. Vol. 2. Boston: Colonial Society of Massachusetts, 1913.

Chauncy, Charles. *The Benevolence of the Deity, Fairly and Impartially Considered in Three Parts*. Boston: Powars & Willis, 1784.

———. *Seasonable Thoughts on the State of Religion in New-England*. Boston: Rogers & Fowle, 1743.

Chernow, Ron. *Grant*. New York: Penguin, 2017.

Chetty, Raj, et al., "Where Is the Land of Opportunity? The Geography of Intergenerational Mobility in the United States." *Quarterly Journal of Economics* 129 (November 2014): 1553–1623.

Christianson, Paul. *Reformers and Babylon: English Apocalyptic Visions from the Reformation to the Eve of the Civil War*. Toronto: University of Toronto Press, 1978.

Clap, Thomas. *An Essay on the Nature and Foundation of Moral Virtue and Obligation: Being a Short Introduction to the Study of Ethics*. New Haven: B. Meacom, 1765.

Clark, Gregory. *A Farewell to Alms: A Brief Economic History of the World*. Princeton: Princeton University Press, 2007.

Clark, John Bates. *The Distribution of Wealth: A Theory of Wages, Interest and Profits*. London: Macmillan, 1899.

———. *The Philosophy of Wealth: Economic Principles Newly Formulated*. Boston: Ginn & Company, 1894.

———. *Social Justice Without Socialism*. Boston: Houghton Mifflin, 1914.

Clarke, James Freeman. *Vexed Questions in Theology: A Series of Essays*. Boston: Geo. H. Ellis, 1886.

Clarke, Samuel. *A Demonstration of the Being and Attributes of God*. London: Will. Botham, for James Knapton, 1705.

———. *The Scripture-Doctrine of the Trinity*. London: James Knapton, 1712.

———. *Sermons on the Following Subjects, Viz: Of Faith in God. Of the Unity of God. Of the Eternity of God. Of the Spirituality of God. Of the Immutability of God. Of the Omnipresence of God. Of the Omnipotence of God. Of the Omniscience of God. Of the Wisdom of God. Of the Goodness of God. Of the Patience of God. Of the Justice of God*. London: W. Botham, 1730.

———. *Sermons on the Following Subjects, Viz: Of the Glory of God. Of God's being the Father of Mankind. Of being the Children of God. Of Loving God. Of the Wisdom of being Religious. Of Imitating the Holiness of God. Of the Love of God towards Sinners. Of Believing in God. Of the Grace of God. Of the Kingdom of God*. London: W. Botham, 1730.

Cline, Eric H. *Three Stones Make a Wall: The Story of Archaeology*. Princeton: Princeton University Press, 2017.

Coats, A. W. "Alfred Marshall and Richard T. Ely: Some Unpublished Letters." *Economica* 28 (May 1961): 191–94.

———. "The First Two Decades of the American Economic Association." *American Economic Review* 50 (September 1960): 555–74.

Cockburn, Alison. *Letters and Memoir of Her Own Life*. Edinburgh: D. Douglas, 1899.

Cocks, Edmond. "The Malthusian Theory in Pre–Civil War America: An Original Relation to the Universe." *Population Studies* 20 (March 1967): 343–63.

Coffman, Elesha. *The Christian Century and the Rise of the Protestant Mainline*. Oxford: Oxford University Press, 2013.

Cogswell, William. *The Harbinger of the Millennium*. Boston: Pierce & Parker, 1833.

Cohen, Joel E. "Hunger Does Not Pay." Unpublished manuscript, Rockefeller University, 2018.

Collie, Rosalie. *Light and Enlightenment: A Study of the Cambridge Platonists and the Dutch Arminians*. London: Cambridge University Press, 1957.

Collinson, Patrick. *The Birthpangs of Protestant England*. New York: Palgrave Macmillan, 1988.

Comin, Diego, and Bart Hobijn. "Cross-Country Technology Adoption: Making the Theories Face the Facts." *Journal of Monetary Economics* 51 (January 2004): 39–83.

"The Coming Age." *The Independent* 3 (January 16, 1851): 10.

The Committee on the War and the Religious Outlook. *The Church and Industrial Reconstruction*. New York: Association Press, 1921.

Commons, John Rogers. *Institutional Economics: Its Place in Political Economy.* New York: Macmillan, 1934.

Comte, Auguste. *The Positive Philosophy of Auguste Comte.* London: John Chapman, 1853.

Constantinides, George M. "Habit Formation: A Resolution of the Equity Premium Puzzle." *Journal of Political Economy* 98 (June 1990): 519–43.

Conwell, Russell H. *Acres of Diamonds.* New York: Harper, 1915.

Cook, Harold J. "Bernard Mandeville and the Therapy of 'The Clever Politician.'" *Journal of the History of Ideas* 60 (January 1999): 101–24.

Cooper, Martin R. *Progress of Farm Mechanization.* Washington, DC: United States Department of Agriculture, 1947.

Cooper, Samuel. *A Sermon Preached in Boston, New-England, Before the Society for Encouraging Industry and Employing the Poor.* Boston: J. Draper, 1753.

Corak, Miles. "Income Inequality, Equality of Opportunity, and Intergenerational Mobility." *Journal of Economic Perspectives* 27 (July 2013): 79–102.

———. "Inequality from Generation to Generation: The United States in Comparison." In *The Economics of Inequality, Poverty, and Discrimination in the 21st Century.* Edited by Robert S. Rycroft. Santa Barbara: Praeger, 2013.

Cotton, John. *An Exposition upon the Thirteenth Chapter of the Revelation.* London: Tim Smart, 1655.

Crowe, Charles. *George Ripley: Transcendentalist and Utopian Socialist.* Athens: University of Georgia Press, 1967.

Daily Bread for Your Mind and Soul. Bloomington: Xlibris, 2012.

Darby, Michael R. "Three-and-a-half Million U.S. Employees Have Been Mislaid: Or, an Explanation of Unemployment, 1933–1941." *Journal of Political Economy* 84 (February 1976): 1–16.

Darwin, Charles. *The Descent of Man, and Selection in Relation to Sex.* London: John Murray, 1871.

———. *On the Origin of Species by Means of Natural Selection, or the Preservation of Favoured Races in the Struggle for Life.* London: John Murray, 1859.

Davenport, Stewart. *Friends of the Unrighteous Mammon: Northern Christians and Market Capitalism, 1815–1860.* Chicago: University of Chicago Press, 2008.

David, Paul A. "The Growth of Real Product in the United States Before 1840: New Evidence, Controlled Conjectures." *Journal of Economic History* 27 (June 1967): 151–97.

Deaton, Angus. *The Great Escape: Health, Wealth, and the Origins of Inequality.* Princeton: Princeton University Press, 2013.

Defoe, Daniel. *A Review of the State of the English Nation.* Vol. 3, No. 5 (January 10, 1706).

de Hamel, Christopher. *Meetings with Remarkable Manuscripts: Twelve Journeys into the Medieval World.* New York: Penguin, 2017.

Dekker, Rudolf. "'Private Vices, Public Virtues' Revisited: The Dutch Background of Bernard Mandeville." *History of European Ideas* 14 (January 1992): 481–98.

Delano, Sterling F. *Brook Farm: The Dark Side of Utopia.* Cambridge: Harvard University Press, 2004.

Dennett, Daniel Clement. *Consciousness Explained.* Boston: Little, Brown, 1991.

Dias, Elizabeth. "The Apocalypse as an 'Unveiling': What Religion Teaches Us about the End Times." *New York Times,* April 2, 2020.

"Dictatorships." *Moody Monthly* (July 1933): 480.

Dochuk, Darren. *Anointed with Oil: How Christianity and Crude Made Modern America.* New York: Basic Books, 2019.

———. *From Bible Belt to Sunbelt: Plain-Folk Religion, Grassroots Politics, and the Rise of Evangelical Conservatism.* New York: W. W. Norton, 2011.

The Documentary History of the Ratification of the Constitution. Madison: University of Wisconsin Press, 1976.

Doddridge, Philip. *The Rise and Progress of Religion in the Soul.* London: J. Waugh, 1745.

Dolnick, Edward. *The Clockwork Universe: Isaac Newton, the Royal Society and the Birth of the Modern World.* New York: HarperCollins, 2011.

Dorfman, Joseph. *The Economic Mind in American Civilization.* 3 vols. New York: Viking, 1949.

Drutman, Lee. "Political Divisions in 2016 and Beyond: Tensions Between and Within the Two Parties." Democracy Fund Voter Study Group (June 2017).

Duby, Georges. *The Three Orders: Feudal Society Imagined.* Translated by Arthur Goldhammer. Chicago: University of Chicago Press, 1980.

Duffy, Eamon. *The Stripping of the Altars: Traditional Religion in England, 1400–1580.* New Haven: Yale University Press, 2005.

Durkheim, Émile. *The Elementary Forms of the Religious Life.* New York: Macmillan, 1915.

Easterlin, Richard. "Does Economic Growth Improve the Human Lot? Some Empirical Evidence." In *Nations and Households in Economic Growth: Essays in Honor of Moses Abramovitz.* Edited by Paul A. David and Melvin W. Reder. New York: Academic Press, 1974.

———. "Income and Happiness: Towards a Unified Theory." *Economic Journal* 111 (July 2001): 465–84.

Edwards, Jonathan. *Works of Jonathan Edwards.* 26 vols. New Haven: Yale University Press, 1957–2008.

Eichengreen, Barry. *Golden Fetters: The Gold Standard and the Great Depression, 1919–1939.* New York: Oxford University Press, 1992.

Einstein, Albert. "Motive des Forchens" ("Principles of Research"). In *Zu Max Plancks sechzigstem Geburtstag. Ansprachen, gehalten am 26 April 1918 in der deutschen physikalischen Gesellschaft.* Edited by Emil Warburg. Karlsruhe: C. F. Mueller, 1918.

———. "The Problem of Space, Ether, and the Field in Physics." In *Ideas and Opinions,* edited by Cal Seelig. New York: Three Rivers Press, 1954.

Eisenhower, Dwight David. "Letter to Edgar Newton Eisenhower." In *The Presidency: The Middle Way,* in *The Papers of Dwight David Eisenhower.* Vol. 15. Baltimore: Johns Hopkins University Press, 1996.

———. "Remarks at the Opening Session of the Ministerial Meeting of the North Atlantic Council (April 2, 1959)." In *Public Papers of the Presidents of the United States, Dwight D. Eisenhower, 1959.* Washington, DC: U.S. Government Printing Office, 1960.

Ely, Richard T. "The American Economic Association, 1885–1909." *Publications of the American Economic Association,* Third Series, Vol. 11. London: Swan Sonnenschein, 1910.

———. "The Founding and Early History of the American Economic Association." *American Economic Review* 26 (Supplement, 1936): 141–150.

———. *Ground Under Our Feet: An Autobiography.* New York: Macmillan, 1938.

———. *An Introduction to Political Economy.* New York: Chautauqua Press, 1889.

———. *The Labor Movement in America.* New York: Thomas Y. Crowell, 1886.

———. *Outlines of Economics.* New York: Chautauqua Century Press, 1893.

———. *The Past and the Present of Political Economy.* In *Johns Hopkins University Studies in Historical and Political Science.* Second Series. Vol. 3. Baltimore: Johns Hopkins University, 1884: 5–64.

———. "Recent American Socialism." In *Johns Hopkins University Studies in Historical and Political Science*. Third Series, Vol. 4. Baltimore: Johns Hopkins University, 1885.

———. *Social Aspects of Christianity: And Other Essays*. New York: Thomas Y. Crowell, 1889.

———. *The Social Law of Service*. New York: Eaton & Mains, 1896.

Emerson, Joseph. *Lectures on the Millennium*. Boston: Samuel T. Armstron, 1818.

Emerson, Ralph Waldo. *The Conduct of Life*. Boston: Ticknor & Fields, 1860.

———. *The Journals and Miscellaneous Notebooks of Ralph Waldo Emerson*. 16 vols. Cambridge: Harvard University Press, 1960–1982.

———. *Representative Men*. Boston: Phillips, Sampson & Company, 1849.

Emerson, Roger. "The Social Composition of Enlightened Scotland: The Select Society of Edinburgh, 1754–64." *Studies on Voltaire and the Eighteenth Century* 114 (January 1973): 291–329.

Engell, James. "The Other Classic: Hebrew Shapes British and American Literature and Culture." In *The Call of Classical Literature in the Romantic Age*. Edited by K. P. Van Anglen and James Engell. Edinburgh: Edinburgh University Press, 2017.

Engels, Friedrich. "Draft of a Communist Confession of Faith." In *Karl Marx, Friedrich Engels: Collected Works*. Vol. 6, *Marx and Engels: 1845–1848*. New York: International Publishers, 1976.

Erikson, Erik. *Toys and Reasons: Stages in the Ritualization of Experience*. New York: W. W. Norton, 1977.

Evensky, Jerry. "The Two Voices of Adam Smith: Moral Philosopher and Social Critic." *History of Political Economy* 19 (Fall 1987): 447–68.

Everett, John Rutherford. *Religion in Economics: A Study of John Bates Cark, Richard T. Ely, and Simon N. Patten*. New York: King's Crown Press, 1946.

Faccarello, Gilbert. *The Foundations of Laissez-faire*. New York: Routledge, 1999.

———. "A Tale of Two Traditions: Pierre Force's *Self-Interest Before Adam Smith*." *European Journal of the History of Economic Thought* 12 (December 2005): 701–12.

Faccarello, Gilbert, and Philippe Steiner. "Religion and Political Economy in Early-Nineteenth-Century France." *History of Political Economy* 40 (annual supplement, 2008): 26–61.

Fea, John. *The Bible Cause: A History of the American Bible Society*. Oxford: Oxford University Press, 2016.

Ferguson, Adam. *An Essay on the History of Civil Society*. Edinburgh: A. Kincaid & J. Bell, 1767.

Fifield, James. "Religious Ideals and the Government's Program." In Herbert Hoover Presidential Library and Archives. Number 9, series III (July 25, 1937), Box 59.

———. *Spiritual Mobilization* (September 1952).

Finney, Charles G. *Lectures on Revivals of Religion*. New York: Leavitt, Lord, 1835.

Firing Line. Program 153. June 12, 1969.

FitzGerald, Frances. *The Evangelicals: The Struggle to Shape America*. New York: Simon & Schuster, 2017.

Fleischacker, Samuel. *On Adam Smith's Wealth of Nations: A Philosophical Companion*. Princeton: Princeton University Press, 2004.

Fletcher, Andrew. *Two Discourses Concerning the Affairs of Scotland*. Edinburgh, n.p., 1698.

Fogelin, Robert J. "Hume's Scepticism." In *The Cambridge Companion to Hume*. Cambridge: Cambridge University Press, 1993.

Folbre, Nancy. *The Invisible Heart: Economics and Family Values*. New York: New Press, 2001.

Force, James E. *Essays on the Context, Nature, and Influence of Isaac Newton's Theology*. Boston: Kluwer, 1990.

Force, Pierre. *Self-Interest Before Adam Smith: A Genealogy of Economic Science*. Cambridge: Cambridge University Press, 2003.

Fosdick, Harry Emerson. *On Being a Real Person*. New York: Harper & Brothers, 1943.

———. "Shall the Fundamentalists Win?" *The Christian Century* 39 (June 8, 1922): 713–17.

———. "Shall the Fundamentalists Win?" *Christian Work* 102 (June 10, 1922): 716–22.

Fox [Foxe], John. *Acts and Monuments of Matters Most Special and Memorable Happening in the Church* (also known as *Foxe's Book of Martyrs*). 3 vols. London: Company of the Stationers, 1684.

Fox, Richard Wightman. *Trials of Intimacy: Love and Loss in the Beecher-Tilton Scandal*. Chicago: University of Chicago Press, 1999.

France, Anatole. "Sérénus." In *La Vie Littéraire*. Series I. Paris: Calmann-Lévy, 1889.

Frank, Thomas. *What's the Matter with Kansas? How Conservatives Won the Heart of America*. New York: Metropolitan Books, 2004.

Frazer, Michael L. *The Enlightenment of Sympathy: Justice and the Moral Sentiments in the Eighteenth Century and Today*. Oxford: Oxford University Press, 2010.

Freehling, William W. *The Road to Disunion, Volume I: Secessionists at Bay, 1776–1854*. Oxford: Oxford University Press, 1990.

Freeman, Charles. *A.D. 381: Heretics, Pagans, and the Dawn of the Monotheistic State*. New York: Overlook Press, 2009.

———. *The Closing of the Western Mind: The Rise of Faith and the Fall of Reason*. New York: Vintage, 2002.

Frey, Donald E. "The Impact of Liberal Religion on Richard Ely's Economic Methodology." *History of Political Economy* 40 (annual supplement, 2008): 299–314.

Frieden, Jeffrey. *Lessons for the Euro from Early American Monetary and Financial History*. Brussels: Breugel, 2016.

Friedman, Benjamin M. *The Moral Consequences of Economic Growth*. New York: Alfred A. Knopf, 2005.

Friedman, Richard Elliott. *The Exodus: How It Happened and Why It Matters*. New York: HarperCollins, 2017.

———. *Who Wrote the Bible?* New York: Summit Books, 1987.

Friedman, Thomas L. *The Lexus and the Olive Tree*. New York: Farrar, Straus & Giroux, 1999.

Fuhrer, Mary Babson. *A Crisis of Community: The Trials and Transformation of a New England Town, 1815–1848*. Chapel Hill: University of North Carolina Press, 2014.

Fuller, Richard, and Francis Wayland. *Domestic Slavery Considered as a Scriptural Institution: In a Correspondence Between the Rev. Richard Fuller, of Beaufort, S.C., and the Rev. Francis Wayland, of Providence, R.I.* Boston: Gould, Kendall & Lincoln, 1845.

The Fundamentals: A Testimony. 12 vols. Chicago: Testimony Publishing Company, 1910–1915.

Galbraith, John Kenneth. *Economics in Perspective: A Critical History*. Boston: Houghton Mifflin, 1987.

———. *The Great Crash 1929*. Boston: Houghton Mifflin, 1979.

Gallman, Robert E. "Real GNP, Prices of 1860, 1834–1909." Unpublished manuscript, University of North Carolina, undated.

Galperti, Simone. "Persuasion: The Art of Changing Worldviews." *American Economic Review* 109 (March 2019): 996–1031.

Gaunt, Peter. *The English Civil Wars, 1642–1651.* Oxford: Osprey Press, 2003.

Gaustad, Edwin S. *Liberty of Conscience: Roger Williams in America.* Valley Forge: Judson Press, 1999.

Gay, Craig M. *With Liberty and Justice for Whom? Recent Evangelical Debate over Capitalism.* Grand Rapids: Eerdmans, 1991.

Gay, Ebenezer. *Natural Religion as Distinguished from Revealed.* Boston: John Draper, 1759.

Gay, John. "Preliminary Dissertation Concerning the Fundamental Principle of Virtue or Morality." In *An Essay on the Origin of Evil.* London: W. Thurlbourn, 1731.

Gelman, Andrew. *Red State, Blue State, Rich State, Poor State: Why Americans Vote the Way They Do.* Princeton: Princeton University Press, 2008.

George, Henry. *Progress and Poverty: An Inquiry into the Cause of Industrial Depressions, and of Increase of Want with Increase of Wealth: The Remedy.* New York: Sterling Publishing Company, 1879.

Gibbon, Edward. *The Decline and Fall of the Roman Empire.* 12 vols. New York: Fred De Fau, 1906.

Gladden, Washington. *Tools and the Man: Property and Industry under the Christian Law.* Boston: Houghton, Mifflin & Company, 1893.

Gloege, Timothy E.W. *Guaranteed Pure: The Moody Bible Institute, Business, and the Making of Modern Evangelicalism.* Chapel Hill: University of North Carolina Press, 2015.

Goldwater, Barry. "How to Win the Cold War." *New York Times,* September 17, 1961.

Goodspeed, Tyler Beck. *Legislating Instability: Adam Smith, Free Banking, and the Financial Crisis of 1772.* Cambridge: Harvard University Press, 2016.

Goodwin, Gerald. "The Myth of 'Arminian-Calvinism' in Eighteenth-Century New England." *New England Quarterly* 41 (June 1968): 213–37.

Gordon, Robert J. *The Rise and Fall of American Growth: The U.S. Standard of Living Since the Civil War.* Princeton: Princeton University Press, 2016.

Gort, Michael, and Steven Klepper. "Time Paths in the Diffusion of Product Innovations." *Economic Journal* 92 (September 1982): 630–53.

Gottschalk, Peter, and Robert Moffitt. "The Growth of Earnings Instability in the U.S. Labor Market." *Brookings Papers on Economic Activity* No. 2 (1994): 217–72.

Grabiner, Judith V. "Maclaurin and Newton: The Newtonian Style and the Authority of Mathematics." In *Science and Medicine in the Scottish Enlightenment.* Edited by Charles W. J. Withers and Paul Wood. East Linton, UK: Tuckwell Press, 2002.

Graham, Billy. *America's Hour of Decision.* Wheaton, IL: Van Kampen Press, 1951.

———. *Approaching Hoofbeats: The Four Horsemen of the Apocalypse.* Waco: World Books, 1983.

———. "God Before Gold." *Nation's Business,* September 1954.

———. *I Saw Your Sons at War: The Korean Diary of Billy Graham.* Minneapolis: Billy Graham Association, 1953.

———. "Satan's Religion." *The American Mercury,* August 1954: 41–46.

———. *Three Minutes to Twelve.* February 1953. Radio Broadcast. Accessed January 19, 2018. https://billygraham.org/audio/three-minutes-to-twelve/.

———. "We Need Revival." In *Revival in Our Time.* Wheaton, IL: Van Kampen Press, 1950.

———. "Why Don't Our Churches Practice the Brotherhood They Preach?" *Reader's Digest* 77 (August 1960): 52–56.

———. *World Aflame*. New York: Pocket Books, 1966.

Graham, Gordon. "Adam Smith and Religion." In *Adam Smith: His Life, Thought, and Legacy*. Edited by Ryan Patrick Hanley. Princeton: Princeton University Press, 2016.

Grampp, William. "What Did Smith Mean by the Invisible Hand?" *Journal of Political Economy* 108 (June 2000): 441–65.

Great Christian Books. "In His Steps." Accessed May 10, 2019. http://greatchristianbooks.storenvy.com/products/1526181-in-his-steps.

Green, Arthur. *A Guide to the Zohar*. Stanford: Stanford University Press, 2004.

Green, Calvin, and Seth Y. Wells. *A Summary View of the Millennial Church, or United Society of Believers (Commonly Called Shakers)*. Albany: Packard & Van Benthuysen, 1823.

Green, John C. "The American Religious Landscape and Political Attitudes: A Baseline for 2004." Unpublished manuscript, University of Akron, 2004.

———. *The Faith Factor: How Religion Influences American Elections*. Westport: Praeger, 2007.

Greenblatt, Stephen. *The Rise and Fall of Adam and Eve*. New York: W. W. Norton, 2017.

———. *The Swerve: How the World Became Modern*. New York: W. W. Norton, 2011.

Gregory, Daniel S. "Review: *Christian Ethics*, by Newman Smith." In *The Presbyterian and Reformed Review*. Vol. 5. Philadelphia: MacCalla & Co., 1894.

Grewal, David Singh. "The Political Theology of Laissez-Faire: From Philia to Self-Love in Commercial Society." *Political Theology* 17 (September 2016): 417–33.

Gribben, Crawford. *Evangelical Millennialism in the Trans-Atlantic World, 1500–2000*. New York: Palgrave Macmillan, 2011.

Griswold, Charles L., Jr. *Adam Smith and the Virtues of Enlightenment*. Cambridge: Cambridge University Press, 1999.

Groenewegen, P. D. "Turgot and Adam Smith." *Scottish Journal of Political Economy* 16 (November 1969): 271–87.

Grossman, Gene M., and Elhanan Helpman. *Innovation and Growth in the Global Economy*. Cambridge: MIT Press, 1991.

Grune-Yanoff, Till, and Edward F. McClennen. "Hume's Framework for a Natural History of the Passions." In *David Hume's Political Economy*. Edited by Karl Wennerlind and Margaret Schabas. London: Routledge, 2008.

Haakonssen, Knud. *Natural Law and Moral Philosophy: From Grotius to the Scottish Enlightenment*. Cambridge: Cambridge University Press, 1996.

Haakonssen, Knud, ed. *The Cambridge Companion to Adam Smith*. Cambridge: Cambridge University Press, 2006.

Haig, David. *From Darwin to Derrida: Selfish Genes, Social Selves, and the Meanings of Life*. Cambridge: MIT Press, 2020.

———. "Sympathy with Adam Smith and Reflexions on Self." *Journal of Economic Behavior and Organization* 77 (January 2011): 4–13.

Halfin, Igal. *From Darkness to Light: Class, Consciousness, and Salvation in Revolutionary Russia*. Pittsburgh: University of Pittsburgh Press, 2000.

Hallowell, John H. *The Communist Credo and the Christian Creed*. New York: National Council of the Episcopal Church, 1955.

Hamilton, Alexander, James Madison, and John Jay. *The Federalist Papers*. Oxford: Oxford University Press, 2008.

Hampton, Stephen. *Anti-Arminians: The Anglican Reformed Tradition from Charles II to George I*. Oxford: Oxford University Press, 2008.

Handy, Robert T., ed. *The Social Gospel in America, 1870–1920: Gladden, Ely, Rauschenbusch*. New York: Oxford University Press, 1966.

Hankins, Barry. *God's Rascal: J. Frank Norris and the Beginnings of Southern Fundamentalism*. Lexington: University Press of Kentucky, 1996.

Hanson, Paul D. *A Political History of the Bible in America*. Louisville: Westminster John Knox Press, 2015.

Harrison, Peter. "Adam Smith and the Invisible Hand." *Journal of the History of Ideas* 72 (January, 2011): 29–49.

Hartlib, Samuel. *The Reformed Common-wealth of Bees*. London: Giles Calvert, 1655.

Haskell, Thomas L. *The Emergence of Professional Social Science: The American Social Science Association and the Nineteenth-Century Crisis of Authority*. Urbana: University of Illinois Press, 1977.

Hatch, Nathan. *The Democratization of American Christianity*. New Haven: Yale University Press, 1989.

Hayek, F. A. "Dr. Bernard Mandeville." In *New Studies in Philosophy, Politics, Economics and the History of Ideas*. Chicago: University of Chicago Press, 1978.

———. "Lecture on a Master Mind." *Proceedings of the British Academy* 52 (1967): 125–41.

———. *The Road to Serfdom*. Chicago: University of Chicago Press, 2007.

Hazen, Edward. *The Panorama of Professions and Trades; or, Every Man's Book*. Philadelphia: Uriah Hunt & Sons, 1836.

Head, Keith, and Thierry Mayer. "Gravity Equations: Workhorse, Toolkit and Cookbook." In *Handbook of International Economics*. Vol. 4. Edited by Gita Gopinath, Elhanan Helpman, and Kenneth Rogoff. Amsterdam and New York: Elsevier, 2014.

Henry, Carl. "Christianity and the Economic Crisis." *Eternity* 6 (June 1955): 14–15, 43–45.

———. *The Christian Mindset in a Secular Society: Promoting Evangelical Renewal and National Righteousness*. Portland: Multnomah Press, 1984.

———. *Confessions of a Theologian*. Waco: World Books, 1986.

———. *The Uneasy Conscience of Modern Fundamentalism*. Grand Rapids: Wm. B. Eerdmans, 1947.

———. "The Vigor of the New Evangelicalism." *Christian Life and Times*, January 1948.

Henry, John F. *John Bates Clark: The Making of a Neoclassical Economist*. New York: Macmillan, 1995.

Herman, Arthur. *How the Scots Invented the Modern World*. New York: Three Rivers Press, 2001.

Hesselink, I. John. "Calvin's Theology." In *The Cambridge Companion to John Calvin*. Edited by Donald K. McKim. Cambridge: Cambridge University Press, 2004.

Hetherington, Norriss S. "Isaac Newton's Influence on Adam Smith's Natural Laws in Economics." *Journal of the History of Ideas* 44 (July–September, 1983): 497–505.

Heyne, Paul. "Clerical Laissez-Faire: A Case Study in Theological Ethics." In *"Are Economists Basically Immoral?" and Other Essays on Economics, Ethics, and Religion*. Edited by Geoffrey Brennan and A. M. C. Waterman. Indianapolis: Liberty Fund, 2008.

Hill, Lisa. "The Hidden Theology of Adam Smith." *European Journal of the History of Economic Thought* 8 (No. 1, 2001): 1–29.

Hilton, Boyd. *The Age of Atonement: The Influence of Evangelicalism on Social and Economic Thought, 1785–1865*. Oxford: Oxford University Press, 1986.

Hirrel, Leo P. *Children of Wrath: New School Calvinism and Antebellum Reform*. Lexington: University Press of Kentucky, 1998.

Hirschman, Albert. *The Passions and the Interests: Political Arguments for Capitalism Before Its Triumph*. Princeton: Princeton University Press, 1977.

Historical Statistics of the United States, 1789–1945: A Supplement to the Statistical Abstract of the United States. Washington, DC: Bureau of the Census, 1949.

Historical Statistics of the United States: Colonial Times to 1970, Bicentennial Edition. Washington, DC: U.S. Government Printing Office, 1975.

Historical Statistics of the United States: Earliest Times to the Present, Millennial Edition. Cambridge: Cambridge University Press, 2006.

Hobbes, Thomas. *De Cive*. Oxford: Oxford University Press, 1983.

———. *Leviathan*. Oxford: Oxford University Press, 1909.

Hochschild, Arlie Russell. *Strangers in Their Own Land: Anger and Mourning on the American Right*. New York: New Press, 2016.

Hofstadter, Richard. *The Age of Reform: From Bryan to F.D.R.* New York: Alfred A. Knopf, 1955.

Hollander, Samuel. *The Economics of Adam Smith*. Toronto: University of Toronto Press, 1973.

———. "Making the Most of Anomaly in the History of Economic Thought: Smith, Marx-Engels, and Keynes." In *Perspectives on Keynesian Economics*. Edited by A. Arnon et al. Berlin: Springer-Verlag, 2011.

Holton, Gerald. *The Advancement of Science, and Its Burdens: With a New Introduction*. Cambridge: Harvard University Press, 1998.

———. "Einstein and the Cultural Roots of Modern Science." *Daedalus* 127 (Winter 1998): 1–44.

———. "On Einstein's *Weltbild*." Unpublished manuscript, Harvard University [undated].

———. *The Scientific Imagination: Case Studies*. Cambridge: Cambridge University Press, 1978.

Hont, Istvan. *Politics in Commercial Society: Jean Jacques Rousseau and Adam Smith*. Cambridge: Harvard University Press, 2015.

Hooker, Richard. *The Folger Library Edition of the Works of Richard Hooker*. 4 vols. Cambridge: Harvard University Press, 1982.

Hooper, Paul L., et al. "Skills, Division of Labour and Economies of Scale Among Amazonian Hunters and South Indian Honey Collectors." *Philosophical Transactions B* 370 (December 2015): 1–11.

Hoover, Herbert. *The Memoirs of Herbert Hoover: The Great Depression, 1929–1941*. New York: Macmillan, 1952.

Hopkins, Samuel. *A Treatise on the Millennium*. Boston: Isaiah Thomas & Ebenezer Andrews, 1793.

Houghton, John. *A Collection for the Improvement of Husbandry and Trade*. London: Printed for Woodman and Lyon in Russel-street Covent Garden, 1728.

"House of Representatives, Tuesday, June 23, 1840." In *The Congressional Globe*. 26th Congress, 1st Session. Vol. 8. Washington, DC: Globe Office, 1840.

Howe, Daniel Walker. "The Cambridge Platonists of Old England and the Cambridge Platonists of New England." *Church History* 57 (December 1988): 470–85.

———. "The Decline of Calvinism." *Comparative Studies in Society and History* 14 (June 1972): 306–26.

———. *The Unitarian Conscience: Harvard Moral Philosophy, 1805–1861*. Cambridge: Harvard University Press, 1970.

Howe, Julia Ward. "Battle Hymn of the Republic." *Atlantic Monthly* 9, no. 52 (February 1862): 145.

The Humble Advice of the Assembly Of Divines, Now by Authority of Parliament sitting at Westminster, Concerning A Larger Catechism. London: Robert Bostock, 1648.

Hume, David. *Dialogues Concerning Natural Religion and Other Writings.* Cambridge: Cambridge University Press, 2007.

———. *An Enquiry Concerning Human Understanding.* Oxford: Oxford University Press, 2007.

———. *Essays Moral, Political, and Literary.* Indianapolis: Liberty Fund, 1987.

———. *History of England: From the Invasion of Julius Caesar to the Revolution in 1688.* 6 vols. Indianapolis: Liberty Fund, 1983.

———. *A Letter from a Gentleman to His Friend in Edinburgh.* Edited by Ernest C. Mossner and John V. Price. Plaistow: Curwen Press, 1967.

———. *Political Discourses.* Edinburgh: R. Fleming, 1752.

———. *Principal Writings on Religion including Dialogues Concerning Natural Religion and The Natural History of Religion.* Edited by J.C.A. Gaskin. Oxford: Oxford University Press, 2008.

———. *A Treatise of Human Nature.* Vol. 1. Edited by David Fate Norton and Mary J. Norton. Oxford: Oxford University Press, 2007.

Hummel, Daniel. "The New Christian Zionism." *First Things* (June 2017). Accessed March 20, 2020. https://www.firstthings.com/article/2017/06/the-new-christian-zionism.

Hundert, E. J. *The Enlightenment's Fable: Bernard Mandeville and the Discovery of Society.* Cambridge: Cambridge University Press, 1994.

Hunt, Thomas. *The Book of Wealth: in which it is proved from the Bible that it is the duty of every man to become rich.* New York: E. Collier, 1836.

Hutcheson, Francis. *An Inquiry into the Original of Our Ideas of Beauty and Virtue in Two Treatises.* Indianapolis: Liberty Fund, 2004.

———. *A System of Moral Philosophy.* Glasgow: R. & A. Foulis, 1755.

Ingersoll, Julie J. *Building God's Kingdom: Inside the World of Christian Reconstruction.* Oxford: Oxford University Press, 2015.

Inglehart, Ronald. *Culture Shift in Advanced Industrial Society.* Princeton: Princeton University Press, 1990.

Internal Revenue Service, Statistics of Income Division. "Estate Tax Returns Study, October 2017." Accessed August 30, 2018. https://www.irs.gov/statistics/soi-tax-stats-estate-tax-statistics-filing-year-table-1.

International Encyclopedia of the Social Sciences. 19 vols. New York: Crowell Collier & Macmillan, 1968.

Isetti, Ronald. "The Moneychangers of the Temple: FDR, American Civil Religion, and the New Deal." *Presidential Studies Quarterly* 26 (Summer 1996): 678–93.

Isidore of Seville. *Sententiae.* Turnhout, BC: Brepolis Publishers, 2010. Accessed June 9, 2020. http://clt.brepolis.net/llta/pages/Toc.aspx?1239830.

Jackson, Andrew. "Message to Congress, Communicated December 7, 1830." In *Annual Messages, Veto Messages, Protest, &c of Andrew Jackson.* Baltimore: Edwards J. Coale & Co., 1835.

James, Harold. "1929: The New York Stock Market Crash." *Representations* 110 (Spring 2010): 129–44.

James, Henry. *A Small Boy and Others.* New York: Scribner's, 1913.

James, William. *The Varieties of Religious Experience: A Study in Human Nature.* New York: Modern Library, 1902.

Jefferson, Thomas. "Thomas Jefferson, letter to Jean-Baptiste Say (February 1, 1804)." In *The Family Letters of Thomas Jefferson*. Vol. 4. Edited by Edwin Morris Betts and James Adam Bear Jr. Columbia: University of Missouri Press, 1966.

——. *Notes on the State of Virginia*. Chapel Hill: University of North Carolina Press, 1955.

——. "Thomas Jefferson to Doctor Benjamin Waterhouse, June 26, 1822." In *The Works of Thomas Jefferson*. Vol. 12. Edited by Paul Leicester Ford. New York: G. P. Putnam's Sons, 1905.

——. "To the Danbury Baptist Association" (January 1, 1802). In *The Papers of Thomas Jefferson, Volume 36: 1 December 1801 to 3 March 1802*. Edited by Barbara G. Oberg. Princeton: Princeton University Press, 2009.

——. *Works of Thomas Jefferson*. 9 vols. Edited by H. A. Washington. New York: Townsend Mac Coun, 1884.

Jefferson, Thomas, Benjamin Franklin, and John Adams. "American Commissioners to De Thulemeier, March 14, 1785." In *The Papers of Thomas Jefferson, Volume 8: 25 February to 31 October 1785*. Edited by Julian P. Boyd. Princeton: Princeton University Press, 1953.

Jennings, Chris. *Paradise Now: The Story of American Utopianism*. New York: Random House, 2016.

Joffe, Josef. "The Godfather of Post-Truth Politics." *New York Times*, October 22, 2017.

Johnson, Alvin S. "The Fetich of Free Enterprise." *The New Republic* 6 (February 12, 1916): 36–38.

Johnson, Samuel. *A Dictionary of the English Language*. London: W. Strahan, 1755.

——. *A Journey to the Western Islands of Scotland*. London: J. Pope, 1775.

——. *A Letter from Aristocles to Authades Concerning the Sovereignty and the Promises of God*. Boston: Fleet, 1745.

Jones, Robert P., and Daniel Cox. *Attitudes on Child and Family Wellbeing: National and Southeast/Southwest Perspectives*. Washington, DC: Public Religion Research Institute, 2017. Accessed July 16, 2019. https://www.prri.org/research/poll-child-welfare-poverty-race-relations-government-trust-policy/.

Jones, Robert P., et al. *Do Americans Believe Capitalism and Government Are Working? Religious Left, Right and the Future of the Economic Debate*. Washington, DC: Public Religion Research Institute and The Brookings Institution, 2013.

Jordan, Philip. *The Evangelical Alliance for the United States of America: An Evangelical Search for Identity in Ecumenicity in the Nineteenth Century*. PhD diss., University of Iowa, 1971.

Kadane, Matthew. "Original Sin and the Path to the Enlightenment." *Past and Present* (May 2017): 105–40.

Kant, Immanuel. *Toward Perpetual Peace and Other Writings on Politics, Peace, and History*. New Haven: Yale University Press, 2006.

Kelly, Morgan, and Cormac Ó Gráda. "Adam Smith, Watch Prices, and the Industrial Revolution." *Quarterly Journal of Economics* 131 (November 2016): 1727–52.

Keynes, John Maynard. "Am I a Liberal?" In *Essays in Persuasion*. London: Macmillan, 1972.

——. *The End of Laissez-Faire*. London: Hogarth Press, 1926.

——. *The General Theory of Employment, Interest, and Money*. New York: Harcourt, Brace & World, 1936.

Kidd, Thomas S. *Who Is an Evangelical? The History of a Movement in Crisis*. New Haven: Yale University Press, 2019.

Kimmage, Michael. "Buckley Jr., William F." In *American National Biography* (April 2014). Accessed October 26, 2018. http://www.anb.org/view/10.1093/anb/9780198606697 .001.0001/anb-9780198606697-e-1603594.

Kitschelt, Herbert P., and Philipp Rehm. "Secular Partisan Realignment in the United States: The Socioeconomic Reconfiguration of White Partisan Support Since the New Deal Era." *Politics & Society* 47 (September 2019): 425–79.

Klarman, Michael J. *The Framers' Coup: The Making of the United States Constitution.* Oxford: Oxford University Press, 2016.

Krugman, Paul. "The Narrow Moving Band, the Dutch Disease, and the Competitive Consequences of Mrs. Thatcher: Notes on Trade in the Presence of Dynamic Scale Economies." *Journal of Development Economics* 27 (October 1987): 41–55.

Kruse, Kevin M. *One Nation Under God: How Corporate America Invented Christian America.* New York: Basic Books, 2015.

Kugel, James L. *The Great Shift: Encountering God in Biblical Times.* Boston: Houghton Mifflin Harcourt, 2017.

Kuhn, Thomas. "The History of Science." In *The Essential Tension: Selected Studies in Scientific Tradition and Change.* Chicago: University of Chicago Press, 1977.

Kurz, Heinz D. "Technical Progress, Capital Accumulation and Income Distribution in Classical Economics: Adam Smith, David Ricardo and Karl Marx." *European Journal of the History of Economic Thought* 17 (December 2010): 1183–1222.

Kuziemko, Ilyana, et al. "How Elastic Are Preferences for Redistribution? Evidence from Randomized Survey Experiments." *American Economic Review* 105 (April 2015): 1478–1508.

Kuznets, Simon. "Economic Growth and Income Inequality." *American Economic Review* 45 (March 1955): 1–28.

———. "Quantitative Aspects of the Economic Growth of Nations: II. Industrial Distribution of National Product and Labor Force." *Economic Development and Cultural Change* 5 (July 1957, Supplement): 1–111.

Lafitau, Joseph-François. *Customs of the American Indians Compared with the Customs of Previous Times.* Toronto: Champlain Society, 1974.

LaHaye, Tim, and Jerry B. Jenkins. *Left Behind: A Novel of the Earth's Last Days.* Wheaton, IL: Tyndale House, 1995.

Lai, Cheng-chung, ed. *Adam Smith Across Nations: Translations and Receptions of "The Wealth of Nations."* Oxford: Oxford University Press, 2000.

Lake, Peter. *Moderate Puritans and the Elizabethan Church.* Cambridge: Cambridge University Press, 1982.

Landis, Benson, ed. *The Yearbook of American Churches, 1945 Edition.* Lebanon, PA: Sowers, 1945.

Larson, Edward J. *The Return of George Washington: 1783–1789.* New York: William Morrow, 2014.

Laud, William, and Henry Wharton. *The History of the Troubles and Tryal of the Most Reverend Father in God, and Blessed Martyr, William Laud, Lord Arch-Bishop of Canterbury.* London: Rt. Chiswell, 1695.

Lawrence, William. "The Relation of Wealth to Morals." *The World's Work*, Vol. 1 (1901): 286–92.

Lee, Maurice S. *Slavery, Philosophy, and American Literature, 1830–1860.* Cambridge: Cambridge University Press, 2005.

Le Goff, Jacques. *Medieval Civilization, 400–1500.* Oxford: Blackwell, 1988.

———. *Your Money or Your Life: Economy and Religion in the Middle Ages.* New York: Zone Books, 1988.

Leith, John H., ed. *Creeds of the Churches: A Reader in Christian Doctrine from the Bible to the Present.* Louisville: John Knox Press, 1982.

Levinson, Bernard M., and Joshua A. Berman. "The King James Bible at 400: Scripture, Statecraft, and the American Founding." *The History Channel Magazine* (November 2010): 1–11.

Lewis, C. S. *De Descriptione Temporum: An Inaugural Lecture.* Cambridge: Cambridge University Press, 1955.

Lewis, W. A. *The Evolution of the International Economic Order.* Princeton: Princeton University Press, 1978.

Lichtman, Allan J. *White Protestant Nation: The Rise of the American Conservative Movement.* New York: Grove Press, 2008.

Lieberman, David. "Adam Smith on Justice, Rights, and Law." In *The Cambridge Companion to Adam Smith.* Edited by Knud Haakonssen. Cambridge: Cambridge University Press, 2006.

Life in 2050: Amazing Science, Familiar Threats. Washington, DC: Pew Research Center, 2010.

Lincoln, Abraham. "Address to the Wisconsin State Agricultural Society, Milwaukee, Wisconsin." In *Speeches and Writings, 1859–1865.* New York: Library of America, 1989.

Lindsell, Harold. *Free Enterprise: A Judeo-Christian Defense.* Wheaton, IL: Tyndale House, 1982.

Lipset, Seymour Martin, and Earl Raab. *The Politics of Unreason: Right Wing Extremism in America, 1790–1970.* New York: Harper & Row, 1970.

Lipset, Seymour Martin, and Reinhard Bendix. *Social Mobility in Industrial Society.* Berkeley: University of California Press, 1959.

"List of Members." *Publications of the American Economic Association* 1 (March 1886): 43–46.

Locke, John. *The Works of John Locke in Nine Volumes.* 9 vols. London: C. and J. Riving, 1824.

Loconte, Joseph. *God, Locke, and Liberty: The Struggle for Religious Freedom in the West.* Lanham, MD: Lexington Books, 2014.

Lurie, Mark. *The Cowles Catalyst: Why Did Economics Become a Mathematical Science When It Did?* AB Thesis, Harvard University, 2007.

Luther, Martin. "The Freedom of a Christian." In *Luther's Works.* Vol. 31. Philadelphia: Muhlenberg Press, 1957.

———. *Luther's Spirituality.* New York: Paulist Press, 2007.

Lynerd, Benjamin. *Republican Theology: The Civil Religion of American Evangelicals.* Oxford: Oxford University Press, 2014.

Macartney, Clarence. *Shall Unbelief Win? A Reply to Dr. Fosdick.* Philadelphia: Wilbur Hanf, 1922.

Macaulay, Thomas Babington. *The History of England from the Accession of James II.* 5 vols. New York: Harper & Brothers, 1849–1861.

MacCulloch, Diarmaid. *The Later Reformation in England, 1547–1603.* New York: St. Martin's Press, 1990.

———. *The Reformation: A History.* New York: Viking, 2003.

MacGillis, Alec. "Who Turned My Blue State Red? Why Poor Areas Vote for Politicians Who Want to Slash the Safety Net." *New York Times,* November 22, 2015.

Machen, J. Gresham. *Christianity and Liberalism*. Grand Rapids: Eerdmans, 2009.

MacMillan, Margaret. *The War That Ended Peace: The Road to 1914*. New York: Random House, 2014.

Madison, James. "Republican distribution of Citizens." *National Gazette* 1, no. 37 (March 5, 1792): 147.

Maifreda, Germano. *From Oikonomia to Political Economy: Constructing Economic Knowledge from the Renaissance to the Scientific Revolution*. Translated by Loretta Valtz Mannucci. Surrey, UK: Ashgate, 2012.

Mak, James, and Gary M. Walton. "Steamboats and the Great Productivity Surge in River Transportation." *Journal of Economic History* 32 (September 1972): 619–40.

Malkin, Bonnie. "Global Financial Crisis an 'Act of God': An Australian MP Has Raised Eyebrows by Claiming the Global Financial Crisis Is an Act of God." *The Telegraph*, December 5, 2008. Accessed October 4, 2018. https://www.telegraph.co.uk/news/worldnews/australiaandthepacific/australia/3566499/Global-financial-crisis-an-act-of-God.html.

Malthus, T. R. *An Essay on the Principle of Population, as it Affects the Future Improvement of Society. With Remarks on the Speculations of Mr Godwin, M. Condorcet, and Other Writers*. London: J. Johnson in St. Paul's Churchyard, 1798.

———. *An Essay on the Principle of Population, or, A View of its Past and Present Effects on Human Happiness: With an Inquiry into Our Prospects Respecting the Future Removal or Mitigation of the Evils which it Occasions*. 2nd ed. London: J. Johnson, 1803.

———. *An Essay on the Principle of Population, or, A View of its Past and present Effects on Human Happiness: With an Inquiry into Our Prospects Respecting the Future Removal or Mitigation of the Evils which it Occasions*. 5th ed. 3 vols. London: John Murray, 1817.

Mandeville, Bernard. *The Fable of the Bees: Or, Private Vices, Publick Benefits*. 2 vols. Oxford: Clarendon Press, 1924.

[Mandeville, Bernard] Phil-Porney. *A Modest Defense of Publick Stews: or, an Essay upon Whoring, as it is Now Practis'd in these Kingdoms*. London: A. Moore, 1724.

Mansfield, Harvey C., and Delba Winthrop, trans. and eds. Alexis de Tocqueville, *Democracy in America*. Chicago: University of Chicago Press, 2000.

Marsden, George. *Fundamentalism and American Culture*. Oxford: Oxford University Press, 2006.

———. "The Gospel of Wealth, the Social Gospel, and the Salvation of Souls in Nineteenth-Century America." *Fides et Historia* 5 (Fall 1972): 10–21.

———. *Jonathan Edwards: A Life*. New Haven: Yale University Press, 2003.

Marshall, Alfred. *Principles of Economics*. London: Macmillan, 1890.

Martin, David A. "Economics as Ideology: On Making 'The Invisible Hand' Visible." *Review of Social Economy* 48 (Fall 1990): 272–87.

Marx, Karl. *Critique of Hegel's "Philosophy of Right."* Cambridge: Cambridge University Press, 1970.

Massing, Michael. *Fatal Discord: Erasmus, Luther and the Fight for the Western Mind*. New York: HarperCollins, 2018.

Mather, Cotton. *A Christian at his Calling. Two Brief Discourses. One Directing a Christian in his General Calling; Another Directing him in his Personal Calling*. Boston: B. Green and J. Allen, for Samuel Sewall Junior, 1701.

———. *Free-Grace, Maintained & Improved. Or, The General Offer of the Gospel, Managed with Considerations of the Great Things done by Special Grace, in the Election and Redemption and Vocation of those who Embrace that Offer. And the Illustrious*

Doctrines of Divine Predestination and Humane Impotency, Rescued from the Abuses, which they too frequently meet withal; and rendered (as they are) highly Useful to the Designs of Practical Piety.: In two brief Discourses; Published at the Desire of Some, who have been greatly Apprehensive of Growing Occasions for such Treatises. Boston: B. Green, 1706.

———. *Ratio Disciplinae Fratrum Nov-Anglorum: A Faithful Account of the Discipline Professed and Practised; in the Churches of New-England: With Interspersed and Instructive Reflections on the Discipline of the Primitive Churches.* Boston: S. Gerrish, 1726.

———. *Theopolis Americana: An Essay on the Golden Street of the Holy City.* Boston: B. Green, 1710.

Mather, Increase. *Awakening Soul-Saving Truths, Plainly Delivered, in Several Sermons. In which is Shewed, I. That Many are Called, who are not Effectually Called. II. That Men may be of the Visible Church, and yet not be of the Lord's Chosen. III. That the Chosen of God are Comparatively but Few.* Boston: Kneeland for Gray and Edwards, 1720.

Mathews, Shailer. *The Faith of Modernism.* New York: Macmillan, 1924.

Matranga, Andrea. "The Ant and the Grasshopper: Seasonality and the Invention of Agriculture." Unpublished manuscript, New Economic School, 2017.

Mattingly, Garrett. *The Armada.* Boston: Houghton Mifflin, 1959.

May, Henry F. *Protestant Churches and Industrial America.* New York: Octagon, 1963.

Mayhew, Experience. *Grace Defended.* Boston: B. Green, & Company, 1744.

Mayhew, Jonathan. *Seven Sermons.* Boston: Rogers & Fowle, 1749.

———. *Two Sermons on the Nature, Extent and Perfection of the Divine Goodness.* Boston: D. & J. Kneeland, 1763.

Mayhew, Robert. *Malthus: The Life and Legacies of an Untimely Prophet.* Cambridge: Harvard University Press, 2014.

Mayo, A. D. "Liberal Christianity in Western Massachusetts." *Religious Magazine and Monthly Review* 50 (July 1873): 58–69.

Mazumder, Bhashkar. "Fortunate Sons: New Estimates of Intergenerational Mobility in the United States Using Social Security Earnings Data." *Review of Economics and Statistics* 87 (May 2005): 235–55.

McAllister, James L. "Evangelical Faith and Billy Graham." *Social Action* 19 (March 1953): 3–36.

McCollim, Gary B. *Louis XIV's Assault on Privilege: Nicolas Desmaretz and the Tax on Wealth.* Rochester: University of Rochester Press, 2012.

McGee, J. Vernon. "The Millennium." In *On Prophecy: Man's Fascination with the Future.* Nashville: Thomas Nelson, 1993.

McGinn, Bernard. *Visions of the End: Apocalyptic Traditions in the Middle Age*s. New York: Columbia University Press, 1979.

McGrath, Alister E. *Iustitia Dei: A History of the Christian Doctrine of Justification.* Cambridge: Cambridge University Press, 1986.

McLoughlin, William G., Jr. *Billy Graham: Revivalist in a Secular Age.* New York: Ronald Press Company, 1960.

McVickar, John. *First Lessons in Political Economy.* Albany: Common School Depository, 1837.

———. *Introductory Lecture to a Course of Political Economy.* London: John Miller, 1830.

———. *Outlines of Political Economy.* New York: Wilder & Campbell, 1825.

Mede, Joseph. *The Key of the Revelation, Searched and Demonstrated out of the Naturall and Proper Charecters of the Visions.* London: Phil Stephens, 1643.

Meek, Ronald L. "Smith, Turgot, and the 'Four Stages' Theory." *History of Political Economy* 3 (Spring 1971): 9–27.

———. *Social Science and the Ignoble Savage.* Cambridge: Cambridge University Press, 1976.

Melville, Herman. *White-Jacket or the World in a Man-of-War.* Oxford: Oxford University Press, 1990.

Merton, Robert K. *Science, Technology and Society in Seventeenth-Century England.* New York: H. Fertig, 1970.

Mettler, Suzanne. *The Government-Citizen Disconnect.* New York: Russell Sage Foundation, 2018.

Mill, James. "Economists." *Supplement to the Fourth, Fifth, and Sixth Editions of the Encyclopaedia Britannica.* Vol. 3. Edinburgh: Archibald Constable, 1824.

Mill, John Stuart. *Principles of Political Economy.* 2 vols. London: John W. Parker, 1848.

Miller, Perry. *The New England Mind: The Seventeenth Century.* Cambridge: Harvard University Press, 2014.

Miller, Robert Moats. "Harry Emerson Fosdick and John D. Rockefeller, Jr.: The Origins of an Enduring Association." *Foundations* 21 (October–December 1978): 292–310.

———. *Harry Emerson Fosdick: Preacher, Pastor, Prophet.* New York: Oxford University Press, 1985.

Milton, John. *Animadversions upon the Remonstrants Defence, against Smectymnuus.* London: Thomas Underhill, 1641.

Mitchell, B. R. *International Historical Statistics: The Americas 1750–1988.* New York: Stockton Press, 1993.

Mizuta, Hiroshi. *Adam Smith's Library: A Catalogue.* Oxford: Clarendon Press, 2000.

Mohr, Charles. "Goldwater Met Warmly in South." *New York Times,* January 18, 1964.

Montchrestien, Antoine de. *Traicté de l'oeconomie politique: Dedié en 1615 au Roy et à la Reyne Mere du Roy.* Paris: E. Plon, Nourrit et cie, 1889.

Montesquieu, Charles de Secondat, baron de. *De l'Esprit des Loix.* Geneve: Barrillot & fil, 1748.

Moody, D. L. "Regeneration." *Friends' Review,* June 14, 1879.

———. "The Second Coming of Christ." *Northfield Echoes: A Report of the Northfield Conferences for 1896.* Vol. 3. East Northfield: E. S. Rastall, 1896.

Moorhead, James H. "Between Progress and Apocalypse: A Reassessment of Millennialism in American Religious Thought, 1800–1880." *Journal of American History* 71 (December 1984): 524–42.

———. "The Erosion of Postmillennialism in American Religious Thought, 1865–1925." *Church History* 53 (March 1984): 61–77.

———. *World Without End: Mainstream American Protestant Visions of the Last Things, 1880–1925.* Bloomington: Indiana University Press, 1999.

Morgan, Roger. *The United States and West Germany, 1945–1973: A Study in Alliance Politics.* London: Oxford University Press, 1974.

[Morse, Jedidiah]. "Affairs of the University." *Columbian Centinel* 42, no. 26 (November 24, 1804).

———. *True Reasons on which the Election of a Hollis Professor of Divinity in Harvard College, was Opposed at the Board of Overseers, Feb. 14, 1805.* Charlestown: Printed for the Author, 1805.

Morse, Jennifer Roback. *Love and Economics: Why the Laissez-Faire Family Doesn't Work.* Dallas: Spence, 2001.

Mossner, E. C. *The Life of David Hume.* New York: Oxford University Press, 1980.

Mun, Thomas. *England's Treasure by Forraign Trade. Or, The Ballance of our Forraign Trade is The Rule of our Treasure.* London: Printed by J.G. for Thomas Clark, 1664.

Munby, D. L. *God and the Rich Society: A Study of Christians in a World of Abundance.* Oxford: Oxford University Press, 1960.

Murray, Charles Augustus. *Travels in North America during the years 1834, 1835, & 1836. Including a summer residence with the Pawnee tribe of Indians, in the remote prairies of the Missouri, and a visit to Cuba and the Azore islands.* London: R. Bentley, 1839.

Murray, John. *Jerubbaal, Or Tyranny's Grove Destroyed, and the Altar of Liberty Finished.* Newburyport: John Mycall, 1784.

National Bureau of Economic Research. "US Business Cycle Expansions and Contractions." Accessed February 5, 2020. http://www.nber.org/cycles/cyclesmain.html.

Nelson, Eric. "Representation and the Fall." *Modern Intellectual History* (December 19, 2018): 1–30. Accessed March 20, 2020. https://doi.org/10.1017/S1479244318000501.

———. *The Royalist Revolution: Monarchy and the American Founding.* Cambridge: Harvard University Press, 2014.

———. *The Theology of Liberalism: Political Philosophy and the Justice of God.* Cambridge: Harvard University Press, 2019.

———. "What Kind of Book Is 'The Ideological Origins of the American Revolution'?" *New England Quarterly* 91 (March 2018): 147–71.

Newton, Isaac. *Four Letters from Sir Isaac Newton to Doctor Bentley Containing Some Arguments in Proof of a Deity.* London: R. & J. Dodsley, 1756.

Nicole, Pierre. *Moral Essays.* 4 vols. London: Printed for R. Bentley and M. Magnes, 1677–1682.

Noll, Mark A. *America's God: From Jonathan Edwards to Abraham Lincoln.* Oxford: Oxford University Press, 2002.

Noll, Mark A. ed. *God and Mammon: Protestants, Money, and the Market, 1790–1860.* Oxford: Oxford University Press, 2002.

Noll, Mark A. "Jekyll or Hyde? Two Stories about American Evangelicalism." *Books and Culture: A Christian Review* 21 (March–April 2015): 22–25.

Norris, J. Frank. "The New Deal Uncovered." In *New Dealism Exposed.* Fort Worth: Fundamentalist Publishing Co., 1935.

Norris, John. *The Theory and Regulation of Love: A Moral Essay in Two Parts.* Oxford: Printed at the Theatre for Hen. Clements, 1688.

Norton, John. *The Answer to the Whole Set of Questions of the Celebrated Mr. William Apollonius, Pastor of the Church of Middelburg.* With a preface by John Cotton. Cambridge: Harvard University Press, 1958.

Norwich, John Julius. *A History of France.* New York: Atlantic Monthly Press, 2018.

Nunn, Nathan, and Nancy Qian. "The Potato's Contribution to Population and Urbanization: Evidence from a Historical Experiment." *Quarterly Journal of Economics* 126 (May 2011): 593–650.

Oakes, Urian. *New England Pleaded with, And pressed to consider the things which concern her Peace at least in this her Day.* Cambridge: Samuel Green, 1673.

Ockenga, Harold. "Christ for America." *United Evangelical Action* (May 4, 1943): 3–6.

———. *God Save America.* Boston: John W. Schaeffer & Co., 1939.

———. "The Unvoiced Multitudes." In *A New Evangelical Coalition: Early Documents of the National Association of Evangelicals.* Edited by Joel E. Carpenter. New York: Garland, 1988.

"On the Attempt to Deprive Unitarians of the Name of Christians." *The Unitarian Defendant* 1, no. 2 (July 6, 1822): 5–8; no. 3 (July 20, 1822): 9–10; no. 4 (August 3, 1822): 13–15.

Orain, Arnaud. "The Second Jansenism and the Rise of French Eighteenth-Century Political Economy." *History of Political Economy* 46 (Fall 2014): 463–90.

Oslington, Paul. *Political Economy as Natural Religion*. London: Routledge, 2018.

[O'Sullivan, John]. "Annexation." *Democratic Review* 17 (July, 1845).

Otten, Bernard John. *A Manual of the History of Dogmas*. London: B. Herder Book Co., 1918.

Otteson, James R. *Adam Smith's Marketplace of Life*. Cambridge: Cambridge University Press, 2002.

Pagels, Elaine. *Revelations: Visions, Prophecy, and Politics in the Book of Revelation*. New York: Viking, 2012.

Pagnamenta, Peter. *Prairie Fever: British Aristocrats and the American West 1830–1890*. New York: Norton, 2012.

Paine, Thomas. *The Rights of Man, Common Sense, and Other Political Writings*. Oxford: Oxford University Press, 1995.

Paley, William. *The Principles of Moral and Political Philosophy*. London: Faulder, 1785.

Papadopoulos, Kosmos, and Bradley W. Bateman. "Karl Knies and the Prehistory of Neoclassical Economics: Understanding the Importance of 'Die Nationaloekonomische Lehre vom Werth' (1855)." *Journal of the History of Economic Thought* 33 (April 2011): 19–35.

Parente, Stephen L., and Edward C. Prescott. "Barriers to Technology Adoption and Development." *Journal of Political Economy* 102 (April 1994): 298–321.

Parker, Geoffrey. *Emperor: A New Life of Charles V*. New Haven: Yale University Press, 2019.

Parker, Kenneth. *The English Sabbath: A Study of Doctrine and Discipline from the Reformation to the Civil War*. Cambridge: Cambridge University Press, 1988.

Paullin, Charles O. *Atlas of the Historical Geography of the United States*. Washington, DC: Carnegie Institution, 1932.

Peale, Norman Vincent. *You Can If You Think You Can*. New York: Simon & Schuster, 1974.

Peart, Sandra J., and David M. Levy, eds. *The Street Porter and the Philosopher: Conversations on Analytical Egalitarianism*. Ann Arbor: University of Michigan Press, 2008.

Perkins, William. *A Godly and Learned Exposition or Commentarie upon the Three First Chapters of the Revelation*. London: Printed by Adam Islip for Cuthbert Burbie, 1606.

———. *A Golden Chaine: or, The Description of Theologie*. Cambridge: John Legat, 1600.

Perry, Arthur Latham. *Principles of Political Economy*. New York: Scribner, 1891.

Peterson, Mark. *The City-State of Boston: The Rise and Fall of an Atlantic Power, 1630–1865*. Princeton: Princeton University Press, 2019.

Pew Foundation. "The Age Gap in Religion Around the World." June 13, 2018. Accessed June 12, 2019. https://www.pewforum.org/2018/06/13/the-age-gap-in-religion-around -the-world/.

Pew Research Center. "Political Typology 2017." Accessed July 16, 2019. https://www .people-press.org/dataset/political-typology-2017/.

———. "2014 Religious Landscape Study." Accessed July 22, 2019. https://www.pewforum .org/dataset/pew-research-center-2014-u-s-religious-landscape-study/.

Phillips, Kevin. *The Emerging Republican Majority*. New Rochelle: Arlington House, 1969.

Phillips-Fein, Kim. *Invisible Hands: The Businessmen's Crusade Against the New Deal.* New York: W. W. Norton, 2009.

Phillipson, Nicholas. *Adam Smith: An Enlightened Life.* New Haven: Yale University Press, 2010.

Pietsch, B. M. *Dispensational Modernism.* Oxford: Oxford University Press, 2015.

Pocock, J. G. A. *The Machiavellian Moment: Florentine Political Thought and the Atlantic Republican Tradition.* Princeton: Princeton University Press, 1975.

Pope, Alexander. *An Essay on Man.* In *Epistles to a Friend. Epistle IV.* London: J. Wilford, 1734.

Porter, Eduardo. "The Government Check Disconnect." *New York Times,* December 22, 2018.

Porter, Roy, and Mikuláš Teich, eds. *The Enlightenment in National Context.* Cambridge: Cambridge University Press, 1981.

Porterfield, Amanda. *Conceived in Doubt: Religion and Politics in the New American Nation.* Chicago: University of Chicago Press, 2012.

Price, Peter Xavier. "Liberty, Poverty and Charity in the Political Economy of Josiah Tucker and Joseph Butler." *Modern Intellectual History* 16 (November 2019): 741–70.

———. "Sociability and Self-Love in Joseph Butler's *Fifteen Sermons.*" In *Providence and Political Economy: Josiah Tucker's Providential Argument for Free Trade.* PhD diss., University of Sussex, 2016.

Priestley, Joseph. *Lectures on History and General Policy.* Birmingham: Pearson & Rollason, 1788.

Quesnay, François. *Physiocratie, ou Constitution Naturelle du Gouvernement le plus Avantageux au Genre Humain.* Leyde: Merlin, 1767.

Quinnipiac University Poll. "November 15, 2017—Latest Massacre Drives Gun Control Support to New High, Quinnipiac University National Poll Finds; Voters Reject GOP Tax Plan 2-1." November 2017. Accessed June 13, 2019. https://poll.qu.edu/national/release-detail?ReleaseID=2501.

Rabb, Melinda. "Parting Shots: Eighteenth-Century Displacements of the Male Body at War." *ELH* 78 (Spring, 2011): 103–35.

Rader, Benjamin G. "Richard T. Ely: Lay Spokesman for the Social Gospel." *Journal of American History* 53 (June 1966): 61–74.

Rae, John. *The Life of Adam Smith.* London: Macmillan, 1895.

Rauschenbusch, Walter. *Christianity and the Social Crisis.* London: Macmillan, 1920.

———. *Christianizing the Social Order.* New York: Macmillan, 1912.

———. *A Theology for the Social Gospel.* New York: Macmillan, 1917.

Rawls, John. *A Theory of Justice.* Cambridge: Harvard University Press, 1971.

Ray, John. *The Wisdom of God Manifested in the Works of the Creation.* London: Samuel Smith, 1691.

Raymond, Daniel. *The American System.* Baltimore: Lucas & Deaver, 1828.

———. *Elements of Political Economy: In Two Parts.* Baltimore: Fielding Lucas, Jun., & E. J. Coale, 1823.

———. *The Missouri Question.* Baltimore: Schaeffer & Maund, 1819.

———. *Thoughts on Political Economy: In Two Parts.* Baltimore: Fielding Lucas, Jun'r, 1820.

Reagan, Ronald. "Address Accepting the Presidential Nomination at the Republican National Convention in Detroit," July 17, 1980. Accessed June 8, 2020. http://www.presidency.ucsb.edu/documents/address-accepting-the-presidential-nomination-the-republican-national-convention-detroit.

———. "Encroaching Control." Speech Delivered Before the Phoenix Chamber of Commerce, Phoenix, AZ, March 30, 1961. Accessed January 23, 2018. https://archive.org/details/RonaldReagan-EncroachingControl.

———. "Farewell Address to the Nation," January 11, 1989. Accessed June 11, 2020. https://www.reaganlibrary.gov/research/speeches/011189i.

———. "Remarks at the Annual Convention of the National Association of Evangelicals in Orlando, Florida," March 8, 1983. Accessed January 22, 2018. https://www.reaganlibrary.gov/index.php?option=com_content&view=article&id=2177:30883b&catid=31:1983.

"Rebuke to Rolph Is Seen; Roosevelt Scores Our Pagan Ethics." *New York Times,* December 7, 1933.

Redding, Stephen. "Dynamic Comparative Advantage and the Welfare Effects of Trade." *Oxford Economic Papers* 51 (January 1999): 15–39.

"Religion: Riverside Church." *Time,* October 6, 1930.

"Report of the Organization of the American Economic Association." In *Publications of the American Economic Association.* Vol. 1. Baltimore: John Murphy, 1886.

"Republicans Lower Expectations for a 2020 Trump Victory." *Economist*/YouGov Poll, February 1, 2019. Accessed June 13, 2019. https://today.yougov.com/topics/politics/articles-reports/2019/02/01/republicans-2020-trump-victory-tax-reform.

Reynolds, David S. *Beneath the American Renaissance.* New York: Alfred A. Knopf, 1980.

Ribuffo, Leo P. *The Old Christian Right: The Protestant Far Right from the Great Depression to the Cold War.* Philadelphia: Temple University Press, 1983.

Ricardo, David. *On the Principles of Political Economy and Taxation.* In *The Works and Correspondence of David Ricardo.* Indianapolis: Liberty Fund, 2004.

———. *The Principles of Political Economy and Taxation.* With an introduction by Donald Winch. London: Dent, 1973.

Riis, Jacob A. *How the Other Half Lives: Studies Among the Tenements of New York.* New York: Scribner, 1890.

Robertson, William. *The History of America.* 2 vols. London: W. Strahan, 1777.

———. Letter to Margaret Hepburn, February 20, 1759. National Library of Scotland, MS 16711, ff. 234–36.

———. *The Works of William Robertson, DD.* 12 vols. Edinburgh: Peter Hill & Co.; Oliver & Boyd; and Stirling & Slade, 1818.

Rodgers, Daniel T. *As a City on a Hill: The Story of America's Most Famous Lay Sermon.* Princeton: Princeton University Press, 2018.

Rogers, Robert P. *An Economic History of the American Steel Industry.* New York: Routledge, 2009.

Rollin, Charles. *Histoire ancienne des Egyptiens, des Carthaginois, des Assyriens, des Babyloniens, des Mèdes et des Perses, des Macédoniens, des Grecs, par M. Rollin.* Paris: J. Estienne, 1752.

Roosevelt, Franklin D. "Inaugural Address," March 4, 1933. Accessed January 31, 2018. http://www.presidency.ucsb.edu/documents/inaugural-address-8.

———. "Radio Message Accepting 3rd Term Nomination, July 19, 1940 [Acceptance Speech to Democratic National Committee]." In *Franklin D. Roosevelt, Master Speech File, 1898–1945,* Box 52, No. 1291, 15; 19–20. Accessed January 31, 2018. http://www.fdrlibrary.marist.edu/_resources/images/msf/msf01336.

Rosenberg, Nathan. "Mandeville and Laissez-faire." *Journal of the History of Ideas* 24 (April–June 1963): 183-196.

————. "Adam Smith on the Division of Labour: Two Views or One?" *Economica* 32 (May 1965): 127–139.

Ross, Dorothy. *The Origins of American Social Science.* Cambridge: Cambridge University Press, 1991.

Ross, Ian Simpson. "The Emergence of David Hume as a Political Economist: A Biographical Sketch." In *David Hume's Political Economy.* Edited by Carl Wennerlind and Margaret Schabas. London: Routledge, 2008.

————. *The Life of Adam Smith.* Oxford: Oxford University Press, 1995.

————. *Lord Kames and the Scotland of His Day.* Oxford: Oxford University Press, 1972.

Rostow, W. W. *The Stages of Economic Growth: A Non-Communist Manifesto.* London: Cambridge University Press, 1964.

Roth, Alvin E. "Repugnance as a Constraint on Markets." *Journal of Economic Perspectives* 21 (Summer 2007): 37–58.

Rothschild, Emma. *Economic Sentiments: Adam Smith, Condorcet, and the Enlightenment.* Cambridge: Harvard University Press, 2001.

Rousseau, Jean-Jacques. *The Social Contract.* Oxford: Oxford University Press, 1994.

Roy, Ralph Lord. *Apostles of Discord: A Study of Organized Bigotry and Disruption on the Fringes of Protestantism.* Boston: Beacon Press, 1953.

Rush, Benjamin. "Thoughts Upon the Mode of Education Proper in a Republic." In *American Political Writing.* Edited by Charles S. Hyneman and Donald S. Lutz. Indianapolis: Liberty Fund, 1983.

Ryan Patrick Hanley, ed. *Adam Smith: His Life, Thought, and Legacy.* Princeton: Princeton University Press, 2016.

Sacks, Daniel W., Betsey Stevenson, and Justin Wolfers. "The New Stylized Facts About Income and Subjective Well-Being." *Emotion* 12 (December 2012): 1181–87.

Samuelson, Paul. *Economics.* New York: McGraw-Hill, 1948.

————. *Foundations of Economic Analysis.* Cambridge: Harvard University Press, 1947.

————. "Liberalism at Bay." *Social Research* 39 (April 1972): 16–31.

————. "A Modern Theorist's Vindication of Adam Smith." *American Economic Review* 67 (February 1977): 42–49.

Sandeen, Ernest. *The Roots of Fundamentalism: British and American Millenarianism, 1800–1930.* Chicago: University of Chicago Press, 1970.

Sanford, Elias B., ed. *Report of the First Meeting of the Federal Council, Philadelphia. 1908.* New York: The Revell Press, 1909.

Say, Jean-Batiste. *Traité D'économie Politique.* Paris: Chez Deterville, 1803.

Schaeffer, Francis. *The Complete Works of Francis Schaeffer.* 5 vols. Wheaton, IL: Crossway, 1982.

Schaffner, Brian, Stephen Ansolabehere, and Sam Luks. "CCES Common Content, 2018." Accessed September 2, 2019. https://doi.org/10.7910/DVN/ZSBZ7K.

Schiffman, Lawrence. *Reclaiming the Dead Sea Scrolls: The History of Judaism, and the Background of Christianity, the Lost Library of Qumran.* Philadelphia: Jewish Publication Society, 1994.

Schmidt, Georg. *Der Dreissigjahrige Krieg.* 5th ed. Munich: C. H. Beck, 2002.

Schumpeter, Joseph A. *History of Economic Analysis.* New York: Oxford University Press, 1954.

Scofield, C. I. *The Scofield Reference Bible.* London: Oxford University Press, 1909.

Scott, Hal. *Connectedness and Contagion: Protecting the Financial System from Panics.* Cambridge: MIT Press, 2016.

Seaver, Paul. *Wallington's World: A Puritan Artisan in Seventeenth Century London*. Stanford: Stanford University Press, 1985.

Seigle, Mario. "The Growing Economic Crisis: A Biblical Perspective." Accessed October 4, 2018. https://www.ucg.org/the-good-news/the-growing-economic-crisis-a-biblical-perspective.

Sen, Amartya. *Poverty and Famines: An Essay on Entitlement and Deprivation*. Oxford: Oxford University Press, 1983.

Sengupta, Somini. "Carter Sadly Turns Back on National Baptist Body." *New York Times*, October 21, 2000. Accessed October 4, 2018. https://www.nytimes.com/2000/10/21/us/carter-sadly-turns-back-on-national-baptist-body.html.

Sheldon, Charles M. *In His Steps*. New York: George Munroe's Sons, 1896.

Shepard, Thomas. *Eye-Salve or A Watch-Word From our Lord Jesus Christ unto his Churches: Especially those within the Colony of Massachusetts in New-England, To take heed of Apostacy*. Cambridge: Samuel Green, 1673.

———. *The Sincere Convert: Discovering the Paucity of True Believers and the Great Difficulty of Saving Conversion*. London: T. Paine, 1640.

Sher, Richard B. *Church and University in the Scottish Enlightenment: The Moderate Literati of Edinburgh*. Edinburgh: Edinburgh University Press, 1985.

Shleifer, Andrei, and Robert Vishny. "Fire Sales in Finance and Macroeconomics." *Journal of Economic Perspectives* 25 (Winter 2011): 29–48.

Shore, Marci. "The Unbreakable Broken." *New York Times*, August 20, 2017.

Sidney, Algernon. *Discourses Concerning Government*. Indianapolis: Liberty Press, 1990 (1698).

Simpson, James. *Burning to Read: English Fundamentalism and Its Reformation Opponents*. Cambridge: Harvard University Press, 2007.

———. *Permanent Revolution: The Reformation and the Illiberal Roots of Liberalism*. Cambridge: Harvard University Press, 2019.

Sjaastad, Larry A. "The Costs and Returns of Human Migration." *Journal of Political Economy* 70 (October 1962, Part II): 80–93.

Skinner, Andres S. "Adam Smith: The French Connection." University of Glasgow Business School, Working Paper 9703 (1997).

Slack, Paul. *The Invention of Improvement: Information and Material Progress in Seventeenth-Century England*. Oxford: Oxford University Press, 2015.

Smith, Adam. *The Correspondence of Adam Smith*. Edited by E. C. Mossner and I. S. Ross. Oxford: Clarendon Press, 1987.

———. *Essays on Philosophical Subjects*. Oxford: Oxford University Press, 1980.

———. *An Inquiry into the Nature and Causes of the Wealth of Nations*. 2 vols. Oxford: Oxford University Press, 1976.

———. *Lectures on Jurisprudence*. Oxford: Oxford University Press, 1978.

———. *Lectures on Police, Revenue, and Arms*. Edited by Edwin Cannan. Oxford: Clarendon Press, 1896.

———. *Lectures on Rhetoric and Belles Lettres*. Oxford: Oxford University Press, 1983.

———. *The Theory of Moral Sentiments*. Oxford: Oxford University Press, 1976.

———. *The Theory of Moral Sentiments*. With an introduction by Knud Haakonssen. Cambridge: Cambridge University Press, 2002.

Smith, Timothy L. *Revivalism and Social Reform: American Protestantism on the Eve of the Civil War*. Baltimore: Johns Hopkins University Press, 1980.

Smout, T. C. *A History of the Scottish People, 1560–1830*. London: Collins, 1969.

Solon, Gary. "Cross-Country Differences in Intergenerational Earnings Mobility." *Journal of Economic Perspectives* 16 (Summer 2002): 59–66.

———. "Intergenerational Income Mobility in the United States." *American Economic Review* 82 (June 1992): 393–408.

Solow, Robert. "Remembering John Kenneth Galbraith." Accessed July 19, 2017. http://www.epsusa.org/publications/newsletter/2006/nov2006/solow.pdf.

———. "Stories About Economics and Technology." *European Journal of the History of Economic Thought* 17 (December 2010): 1113–26.

Sorkin, David. *The Religious Enlightenment: Protestants, Jews, and Catholics from London to Vienna*. Princeton: Princeton University Press, 2008.

South, Robert. *Discourses on Various Subjects and Occasions*. Boston: Bowles & Dearborn, 1827.

The Spectator. 8 vols. London: Printed for Sam. Buckley and sold by A. Baldwin, 1711–1714.

Spellman, W. M. "Locke and the Latitudinarian Perspective on Original Sin." *Revue Internationale de Philosophie* 42 (January 1988): 215–28.

Spurr, John. *The Restoration Church of England, 1646–1689*. New Haven: Yale University Press, 1991.

Stark, Oded, and David E. Bloom. "The New Economics of Labor Migration." *American Economic Review* 75 (May 1985): 173–78.

Statistical Abstract of the United States, No. 53. Washington, DC: U.S. Government Printing Office, 1933.

Steele, Ian K. *The English Atlantic, 1675–1740: An Exploration of Communication and Community*. New York: Oxford University Press, 1986.

Steil, Benn. *The Marshall Plan: Dawn of the Cold War*. New York: Simon & Schuster, 2018.

Stein, Stephen. "American Millennial Visions: Towards Construction of a New Architectonic of American Apocalypticism." In *Imagining the End: Visions of Apocalypse from the Ancient Middle East to Modern America*. Edited by Abbas Amanat and Magnus Bernhardsson. London: I. B. Tauris, 2002.

Stephen, Leslie. "Mandeville, Bernard." In *Dictionary of National Biography*. London: Smith, Elder, & Co., 1893.

Stern, Fritz. "German History in America, 1884–1984." *Central European History* 19 (June 1986): 131–63.

Steuart, James. *An Inquiry into the Principles of Political Oeconomy*. London: Millar & Cadell, 1767.

Stewart, Dugald. "Account of the Life and Writings of Adam Smith, LL.D." *Transactions of the Royal Society of Edinburgh* 3 (1794): 55–137.

———. *Dissertation First: Exhibiting a General View of the Progress of Metaphysical, Ethical, and Political Philosophy since the Revival of Letters in Europe*. Boston: Wells & Lilly, 1817.

———. "Plan of Lectures on Political Economy for 1800–1801." In *Lectures on Political Economy*. 2 vols. Edinburgh: Thomas Constable, 1855.

———. *Works*. 7 vols. Cambridge: Hilliard & Brown, 1829.

Stratmann, Silke. *Myths of Speculation: The South Sea Bubble and 18th-Century English Literature*. München: Fink, 2000.

Strong, Josiah. *The New Era, or, The Coming Kingdom*. New York: Baker & Taylor, 1893.

———. *Our Country: Its Possible Future and its Present Crisis*. New York: Baker & Taylor, 1885.

Strousma, Guy G. *The End of Sacrifice: Religious Transformation in Late Antiquity*. Chicago: University of Chicago Press, 2012.

"Summary—This Day: American." *The Montreal Gazette,* June 27, 1867.

Sunday, Billy, and William Thomas Ellis. *Billy Sunday: The Man and His Message*. Philadelphia: John C. Winston Company, 1914.

Sunday, William Ashley. William A. Sunday Papers. Billy Graham Center Archives. Wheaton, IL.

Sutton, Matthew Avery. *American Apocalypse: A History of Modern Evangelicalism*. Cambridge: Harvard University Press, 2014.

——. "Was FDR the Antichrist? The Birth of Fundamentalist Antiliberalism in a Global Age." *Journal of American History* 98 (March 2012): 1052–74.

Suzman, James. *Affluence Without Abundance: The Disappearing World of the Bushmen*. New York: Bloomsbury, 2017.

Sweeney, Kevin. "River Gods and Related Minor Deities: The Williams Family and the Connecticut River Valley, 1637–1790." PhD diss., Yale University, 1986.

Swift, Jonathan. *The Bubble: A Poem*. London: Printed for B. Tooke, and sold by J. Roberts, 1721.

——. *Gulliver's Travels*. Oxford: Oxford World Classics, 2005.

Tabb, William. *Reconstructing Political Economy: The Great Divide in Economic Thought*. New York: Routledge, 1999.

Tankersley, Jim, and Ben Casselman. "Many Voters Are in Favor of Taxing the Wealthy." *New York Times*, February 20, 2019.

——. "Voters Back Warren Plan to Tax Rich, Poll Shows." *New York Times*, December 2, 2019.

Tawney, R. H. *Religion and the Rise of Capitalism: A Historical Study (Holland Memorial Lectures, 1922)*. London: J. Murray, 1926.

Tax Policy Center. "Briefing Book." Accessed August 22, 2018. http://www.taxpolicycenter .org/briefing-book/how-many-people-pay-estate-tax.

Taylor, George B. "Society's Future." *The Christian Review* 22 (July 1857): 356–380.

Taylor, John. *The Scripture Doctrine of Original Sin Proposed to Free and Candid Examination*. London: J. Waugh, 1750.

Temin, Peter. *Lessons from the Great Depression*. Cambridge: MIT Press, 1989.

Temple, William. *Christianity and Social Order*. London: Penguin, 1942.

Tennant, Bob. *Conscience, Consciousness and Ethics in Joseph Butler's Philosophy and Ministry*. Woodbridge, UK: Boydell & Brewer, 2011.

Tesler, Michael. *Post-Racial or Most-Racial? Race and Politics in the Obama Era*. Chicago: University of Chicago Press, 2016.

Thernstrom, Stephan. *A History of the American People*. San Diego: Harcourt Brace Jovanovich, 1984.

Thompson, A. C. *Last Hours, or Words and Acts of the Dying*. Boston: Perkins & Whipple, 1851.

Thuesen, Peter J. *Predestination: The American Career of a Contentious Doctrine*. Oxford: Oxford University Press, 2009.

Tillich, Paul. *The Courage to Be*. New Haven: Yale University Press, 2000.

——. *A History of Christian Thought: From Its Judaic and Hellenistic Origins to Existentialism*. Edited by Carl E. Braaten. New York, Simon & Schuster, 1967.

Tillotson, John. *The Works of the Most Reverend Dr John Tillotson*. 10 vols. Edinburgh: Wal. Ruddiman & Company, 1772.

"Time Series Cumulative Data File, 1948–2016." American National Election Survey. University of Michigan and Stanford University. December 8, 2018, update.

Tinbergen, Jan. *Shaping the World Economy: Suggestions for an International Economic Policy.* New York: Twentieth Century Fund, 1962.

Tocqueville, Alexis de. *Democracy in America.* Translated by Henry Reeve. 2 vols. New York: Vintage, 1990.

Todd, Margo. *Christian Humanism and the Puritan Social Order.* Cambridge: Cambridge University Press, 1987.

Toon, Peter. *Puritans, the Millennium and the Future of Israel: Puritan Eschatology, 1600–1660.* Cambridge: James Clarke, 1970.

Treasury of Spiritual Wisdom. Compiled by Andy Zubko. New Delhi: Shri Jainendra Press, 1996.

Truman, Harry S. "Address at Mechanics Hall in Boston. October 27, 1948." In *The Public Papers of the Presidents of the United States: Harry S. Truman, 1948.* Washington, DC: U.S. Government Printing Office, 1964.

———. "The President's Farewell Address to the American People. January 15, 1953." In *The Public Papers of the Presidents of the United States: Harry S. Truman, 1952–1953.* Washington, DC: U.S. Government Printing Office, 1966.

———. "Radio and Television Remarks on Election Eve. November 3, 1952." In *The Public Papers of the Presidents of the United States: Harry S. Truman, 1952–1953.* Washington, DC: U.S. Government Printing Office, 1966.

Tucker, Josiah. *A Brief Essay on the Advantages and Disadvantages, Which Respectively Attend France and Great Britain, With Regard to Trade.* London: Printed for the Author; and sold by T. Tyre, 1749.

———. *The Elements of Commerce and the Theory of Taxes.* Privately published, 1755.

———. *Instructions for Travellers.* Privately published, 1757.

———. *Seventeen Sermons on some of the Most Important Points on Natural and Revealed Religion.* Gloucester: R. Raikes, 1776.

Turgot, Anne-Robert-Jacques. "On Universal History: Plan of the Discourses on Universal History." *Turgot on Progress, Sociology and Economics.* Edited by Ronald L. Meek. Cambridge: Cambridge University Press, 1973.

———. *Reflections on the Formation and Distribution of Riches.* New York: Macmillan, 1914.

Turner, Frederick Jackson. "The Significance of the Frontier in American History." *Annual Report of the American Historical Association for the Year 1893,* 197–228. Washington, DC: U.S. Government Printing Office, 1894.

Tuveson, Ernest. *Millennium and Utopia: A Study in the Background of the Idea of Progress.* New York: Harper & Row, 1964.

Tyacke, Nicholas. *Anti-Calvinists: The Rise of English Arminianism, 1590–1640.* New York: Oxford University Press, 1987.

Tyndale, William. "The Prologue." In *The New Testament.* Cologne: H. Fuchs, 1525.

The Ultimate Book of Quotations. Raleigh: Lulu Enterprises, 2012.

United Nations, Department of Economic and Social Affairs, Population Division. *World Population Prospectus: 2017 Revision, Key Findings and Advance Tables.* Working Paper No. ESA/P/WP/248. Accessed May 30, 2018. https://esa.un.org/unpd/wpp/Publications/Files/WPP2017_KeyFindings.pdf.

Ussher, James. *Annales Veteris Testamenti, prima mundi origine deducti.* London: J. Flesher, 1650.

van den Berg, Richard. "Cantillon on Profit and Interest: New Insights from Other Versions of His Writings." *History of Political Economy* 46 (Winter 2014): 609–40.

Van Kley, Dale. "Pierre Nicole, Jansenism, and the Morality of Enlightened Self-Interest." In *Anticipations of the Enlightenment in England, France, and Germany*. Edited by Alan Charles Kors and Paul J. Korshin. Philadelphia: University of Pennsylvania Press, 1987.

Veblen, Thorstein. *The Theory of the Leisure Class*. Oxford: Oxford University Press, 2007.

Viner, Jacob. "Adam Smith and Laissez Faire." *Journal of Political Economy* 35 (April 1927): 198–232.

———. *The Role of Providence in the Social Order: An Essay in Intellectual History*. Princeton: Princeton University Press, 1976.

Volo, James M., and Dorothy Denneen Volo. *The Antebellum Period*. Westport: Greenwood Press, 2004.

von Mueller, Camillo. "The Invisible Hand and the Case of the Additional Tamquam." Unpublished manuscript, 2020.

Wacker, Grant. *America's Pastor: Billy Graham and the Shaping of a Nation*. Cambridge: Harvard University Press, 2014.

———. *Heaven Below: Early Pentecostals and American Culture*. Cambridge: Harvard University Press, 2001.

Ward, Nathaniel. *The Simple Cobler of Aggawam in North America*. London: J. D. & R. I for Stephen Bowtell, 1647.

Ware, Henry. *Letters Addressed to Trinitarians and Calvinists*. Cambridge: Hillard & Metcalf, 1820.

Washington, George. *The Papers of George Washington: Confederation Series*. 6 vols. Edited by W. W. Abbot. Charlottesville: University of Virginia Press, 1992–1997.

Waterman, A.M.C. "The Changing Theological Context of Economic Analysis since the Eighteenth Century." *History of Political Economy* 40 (annual supplement, 2008): 121–42.

———. "David Hume on Technology and Culture." *History of Economics Review* 28 (Summer 1998): 46–61.

———. "Economics as Theology: Adam Smith's *Wealth of Nations*." *Southern Economic Journal* 68 (April 2002): 907–21.

———. "Is There Another, Quite Different 'Adam Smith Problem.'" *Journal of the History of Economic Thought* 36 (December 2014): 401–20.

———. "Mathematical Modeling as an Exegetical Tool: Rational Reconstruction." In *A Companion to the History of Economic Thought*. Edited by W. J. Samuels, J. E. Biddle, and J. B. Davis. Malden: Blackwell, 2003.

———. *Political Economy and Christian Theology Since the Enlightenment: Essays in Intellectual History*. Basingstoke: Palgrave Macmillan, 2004.

———. "Review of Rudi Verburg's *Greed, Self-Interest and the Shaping of Economics*." *Erasmus Journal for Philosophy and Economics* 12 (Winter 2019): 86–96.

———. "William Paley (1743–1805)." In *The Palgrave Companion to Cambridge Economics*. Edited by Robert A. Cord. London: Palgrave Macmillan, 2017.

Wayland, Francis. *The Elements of Moral Science*. New York: Cooke & Co., 1835.

———. *Elements of Moral Science: Abridged and Adapted to the Use of Schools and Academies by the Author*. Boston: Gould, Kendall & Lincoln, 1835.

———. *The Elements of Political Economy*. New York: Leavitt, Lord & Company, 1837.

———. *Elements of Political Economy: Abridged and Adapted to the Use of Schools and Academies*. Boston: Gould, Kendall, & Lincoln, 1848.

Weber, Max. *Die "Objektivität" sozialwissenschaftlicher und sozialpolitischer Erkenntnis.* Tübingen: J. C. B. Mohr, 1904.

———. *Max Weber: Collected Methodological Writings.* New York: Routledge, 2012.

———. *The Protestant Ethic and the Spirit of Capitalism.* New York: Routledge, 2005.

Weber, Timothy. *Living in the Shadow of the Second Coming: American Premillennialism, 1875–1925.* Chicago: Chicago University Press, 1987.

Webster, Charles. *The Great Instauration: Science, Medicine, and Reform, 1626–1660.* London: Duckworth, 1975.

Weingast, Barry. "Adam Smith's 'Jurisprudence.'" Unpublished manuscript, Stanford University, 2017.

Weir, David R. "A Century of U.S. Unemployment, 1890–1990: Revised Estimates and Evidence for Stabilization." *Research in Economic History* 14 (January 1992): 301–46.

Weisskopf, Walter A. "The Method Is the Ideology: From a Newtonian to a Heisenbergian Paradigm in Economics." *Journal of Economic Issues* 13 (December 1979): 869–84.

Wellhausen, Julius. *Geschichte Israels.* Berlin: Reimer, 1878.

———. *Prolegomena zur Geschichte Israels.* Berlin: Reimer, 1883.

Wesley, John. *Free Grace: A Sermon Preach'd at Bristol.* Bristol: S. & F. Farley, 1739.

The Westminster Collection of Christian Quotations. Compiled by Martin H. Manser. Louisville: Westminster John Knox Press, 2001.

Whatley, George. *Principles of Trade.* London: Brotherton & Sewell, 1774.

Whately, Richard. *Introductory Lectures on Political Economy.* London: J. W. Parker, 1832.

Whatmore, Richard. "Luxury, Commerce, and the Rise of Political Economy." In *The Oxford Handbook of British Philosophy in the Eighteenth Century.* Edited by James A. Harris. Oxford: Oxford University Press, 2013.

Whiston, James. *England's State Distempers Trace'd from their Originals.* London, 1704.

Whiston, William. *A New Theory of the Earth.* London: University-Press, 1708.

Whitby, Daniel. *A Discourse Concerning: I. The True Import of the Words Election and Reprobation II. The Extent of Christ's Redemption III. The Grace of God IV. The Liberty of the Will V. The Perseverance or Defectibility of the Saints.* London: John Wyat, 1710.

Whitefield, George. *George Whitefield's Journals.* Lafayette, IN: Sovereign Grace Publishers, 2000.

Whitehead, Alfred North. *Science and the Modern World.* London: Cambridge University Press: 1925.

William, Stephen. Diary. Storrs Memorial Library, Longmeadow, MA.

Williams, Michael. "Views and Reviews." *Commonweal* 34, no. 13 (July 18, 1941): 303.

Wilson, David B. *Seeking Nature's Logic: Natural Philosophy in the Scottish Enlightenment.* University Park: Pennsylvania State University Press, 2009.

Wilson, James. *Considerations on the Nature and the Extent of the Legislative Authority of the British Parliament.* Philadelphia: William & Thomas Bradford, 1774.

Winch, Donald. *Riches and Poverty: An Intellectual History of Political Economy in Britain, 1750–1834.* Cambridge: Cambridge University Press, 1996.

Winchester, Simon. *The Perfectionists: How Precision Engineers Created the Modern World.* New York: HarperCollins, 2018.

Winthrop, John. "A Model of Christian Charity." In *The Puritans in America: A Narrative Anthology.* Edited by Alan Heimert and Andrew Delbanco. Cambridge: Harvard University Press, 1985.

Wise, John. "Vindication of the Government of the New England Churches." In *The American Puritans: Their Prose and Poetry.* Edited by Perry Miller. New York: Anchor, 1956.

Wood, Gordon S. *Friends Divided: John Adams and Thomas Jefferson.* New York: Penguin, 2017.
———. *The Radicalism of the American Revolution.* New York: Vintage, 1993.
———. "Rhetoric and Reality in the American Revolution." *William and Mary Quarterly* 23 (January 1966): 3–32.
Wood, Paul. "Science in the Scottish Enlightenment." In *Cambridge Companion to the Scottish Enlightenment.* Edited by Alexander Broadie. Cambridge: Cambridge University Press, 2003.
Woolverton, James F. *A Christian and a Democrat: A Religious Biography of Franklin D. Roosevelt.* Grand Rapids: Eerdmans, 2019.
Wootton, Paul. *The Invention of Science: A New History of the Scientific Revolution.* New York: HarperCollins, 2017.
World Bank. *World Development Indicators* (2019).
World Values Survey. Wave 5: 2005–2009. Accessed January 25, 2017. http://www.worldvaluessurvey.org/WVSDocumentationWV5.jsp.
Wright, Conrad. *The Beginnings of Unitarianism in America.* Boston: Beacon Press, 1954.
———. *The Unitarian Controversy: Essays on American Unitarian History.* Boston: Skinner House Books, 1994.
Wright, N. T. *The New Testament and the People of God.* Minneapolis: Fortress, 1992.
Wright, Simon. "Music Publishing, Bibles, and Hymnals." In *History of Oxford University Press: Volume IV: 1970 to 2004.* Oxford: Oxford University Press, 2017.
Wuthnow, Robert. *Red State Religion: Faith and Politics in America's Heartland.* Princeton: Princeton University Press, 2012.
Yolton, Jean S., ed. *Locke as Translator: Three of the Essais of Pierre Nicole in French and English.* Oxford: Voltaire Foundation, 2000.
Young, Michael P. *Bearing Witness Against Sin: The Evangelical Birth of the American Social Movement.* Chicago: University of Chicago Press, 2006.
Zauzmer, Julie. "Christians Are More than Twice as Likely to Blame a Person's Poverty on Lack of Effort." *Washington Post,* August 3, 2017. Accessed January 31, 2018. https://www.washingtonpost.com/news/acts-of-faith/wp/2017/08/03/christians-are-more-than-twice-as-likely-to-blame-a-persons-poverty-on-lack-of-effort/?utm_term=.4e861bbb3205.

Index

Benjamin M. Friedman is the William Joseph Maier Professor of Political Economy, and formerly chairman of the Department of Economics, at Harvard University, where he has now taught for nearly half a century. Much of his research and writing has focused on economic policy, including in particular the role of the financial markets in how monetary and fiscal policies influence economic activity, and he has frequently advised both policymakers and candidates for public office on economic issues. His writings have also addressed broader issues of the connections between economics and society. Mr. Friedman's two previous books for a wide audience were *Day of Reckoning: The Consequences of American Economic Policy Under Reagan and After* and *The Moral Consequences of Economic Growth.* He is also the author or editor of fifteen books aimed primarily at economists and economic policymakers, as well as the author of more than one hundred fifty articles on economics and economic policy published in numerous journals. And he is a frequent contributor to newspaper op-ed pages and to other popular publications, especially *The New York Review of Books.*

Apart from his writing and teaching, Mr. Friedman's current activities include serving as a director of several American companies and nonprofit institutions. He was for many years a director of the Encyclopaedia Britannica. He is currently a member of the American Academy of Arts and Sciences and the Council on Foreign Relations. The various awards he has received include the George S. Eccles Prize for excellence in writing about economics, the John R. Commons Award for achievements in economics and contributions to the economics profession, and the David Horowitz Prize for contributions relating to analysis of monetary policy. He and his wife, Barbara, live in Cambridge, Massachusetts.

A NOTE ON THE TYPE

This book was set in Minion, a typeface produced by the Adobe Corporation
specifically for the Macintosh personal computer, and released in 1990. Designed
by Robert Slimbach, Minion combines the classic characteristics of old-style faces
with the full complement of weights required for modern typesetting.

Composed by North Market Street Graphics, Lancaster, Pennsylvania

Printed and bound by Berryville Graphics, Berryville, Virginia

Designed by Maggie Hinders